A History of England from Edward II to James I

A History of England from Edward II to James I

Anthony Goodman

Longman
London and New York

Longman Group Limited London

Associated companies, branches and representatives throughout the world

Published in the United States of America by Longman Inc., New York

First published 1977

Library of Congress Cataloging in Publication Data

Goodman, Anthony, 1936–
A history of England from Edward II to James I.

Bibliography: p.
Includes index.
1. Great Britain — History — 14th century.
2. Great Britain — History — Lancaster and York, 1399–1485. 3. Great Britain — History — Tudors, 1485–1603. I. Title.
DA225.G66 942.03 76–51405
ISBN 0–582–48281–X
ISBN 0–582–48282–8 pbk.

Set in V.I.P. Times
and printed in Great Britain by
Richard Clay (The Chaucer Press) Ltd,
Bungay, Suffolk

To Jackie

Contents

List of figures

Acknowledgements

We are grateful to Captain M. E. Butler-Bowdon for permission to reproduce extracts from W. Butler-Bowdon's translation of *The Book of Margery Kempe*, published by Jonathan Cape Ltd., 1936

Preface

This book attempts to supply two needs, for the most part separately, but, it is hoped, in complement. One is for a description of English society and institutions spanning parts of the 'later medieval' and 'early modern' periods. The other is for an unashamedly old-fashioned chronicle of 'national events' – other teachers of English history may share the experience of finding that some students with a fairly sophisticated appreciation of general factors have elementary gaps in their knowledge of 'what happened in history'. I have tried to fill such gaps by providing a blow-by-blow account of 'happenings' down to the mid-1580s, and have concluded with a sketch of some of the changes which, I think it is arguable, profoundly affected some traditional political relationships over the next few decades.

The one assured merit which I would claim for the span of time chosen is that it neatly straddles the year 1485, the convenient traditional dividing line between 'later medieval' and 'early modern' in English history. My aim, in contrast, has been to present the period from the early fourteenth century to the early seventeenth as a developing entity. For this purpose, accounts of political and institutional developments can be conveniently commenced at the tensions surrounding Edward II's deposition in 1327, and ended with those between 'court' and 'country' in the reign of James I (d.1625). In the decades after Edward's deposition, relationships between Crown and community were crucially adjusted, creating a lasting, if not entirely stable political order, whose decay in the sixteenth century underlay Jacobean political problems. But that decay was part of a more fundamental process: the ending, in many spheres of activity, of the later Middle Ages.

This book concentrates almost entirely on the history of England. Wales is neglected, Ireland even more so. Their English connections did indeed have important repercussions on England in the period, but a systematic consideration of these would have added considerably to length. On the other hand, a good deal is said about Anglo-French and Anglo-Scottish connections. The emphasis on the former springs from my conviction, as a medievalist, that French politics were of prime importance to English affairs in the period, at least till 1485. The emphasis on the latter reflects my awareness, as a resident of Edinburgh, of the importance of Scottish and Border developments to the

North of England, a world in many respects in our period separate from that south of the Trent, whose political and cultural centres lay in the remote South.

Specialist and general works have been used in this book mostly without specific acknowledgment, though the latter are listed in the general bibliographies. This discourtesy is inevitable in a work intended as a textbook for the senior pupil, university student and general reader: I can only hope that I have not misused authors by misrepresenting their views. I owe a great debt of gratitude to Professor Denys Hay, who suggested that I write a 'later medieval – early modern' history of England, and advised me about the kinds of plan on which it could be written. I have an older debt to my former tutor in later medieval English history, the late K. B. McFarlane. My thanks are also due to those who commented on chapters or sections of chapters, who have saved me from many errors, and made helpful suggestions, which, unfortunately, I have not always been able to follow up, owing to scarcity of time. They are: Dr Christopher Allmand, Mr Derek Baker, Professor A. L. Brown, Dr Gary Dickson, Mr Christopher Dyer, Professor Kenneth Fowler, Mr Alan Harding, Professor D. Hay, Dr Ann Kettle, Mr Andrej Malkiewicz, Mr John A. McGregor, Dr Angus MacKay, Professor Ranald Nicholson, Dr Anthony Tuck and Ms Penelope Winder.

Ms Anna P. Campbell has shown exemplary skill and Job-like patience in typing the MS. Ms Geraldine Hawkes helped to insert corrections. My wife Jacqueline has been my most long-suffering critic.

Chapter 1

The character of an Englishman

Peasants living in pre-industrial societies, such as most of the English people were throughout our period, characteristically focused their perceptions within what we would consider a narrow geographical radius. Their interests, obligations and loyalties blurred at the horizons of villages or regions within whose framework they received sustenance, social regulation and security. Many agriculturalists never needed to go farther to market than a day's journey and back. Indeed, peasants did not lack curiosity about a wider world. But much of this was self-interested curiosity directed at the vertical world of Heaven and Hell, rather than the horizontal world of distant happenings. The latter might have little or no connection in the mind of a subsistence cultivator with the harsh seasonal necessities that ruled his life, the expressions of God's will, and so merged with his fantasy world of tales and ballads.

We must, therefore, always bear in mind the occupational factors in the lives of the common people which tended to narrow and concentrate their fields of vision. We cannot assume that they considered themselves to be English or to live in England, or, when we know certain of them did so, that they attached the same meaning to the concepts as we do. At the Council of Constance (1417), an English academic certainly argued that the inhabitants of England comprised a 'nation', qualifying as such if 'a nation be understood as a people marked off from others by blood relationship and habit of unity or by peculiarities of language, the most sure and positive sign and essence of a nation in divine and human law . . .' But there were over a thousand dialectally differentiated varieties of later Middle English. There were traditional loyalties to the cults of local saints and to 'great families'. There were distinctive local ways of doing as well as saying many things, as diverse as versifying, building and weaving. The countryman's Englishness, if he was conscious of it, may have been a more nebulous and insignificant concept to him than to the scholar at Constance, trying to make a crucial diplomatic point against hostile aliens.

Moreover, we cannot assume that members of the tiny property-owning ruling elites primarily related their interests and loyalties to the scholar's national framework of reference rather than to a regional one. In 1405 the earl of Northumberland and Sir Edmund Mortimer, members of two principal landowning families, apparently intended, if they succeeded in rebellion, to cede some western parts of England to the Welshman Owain Glyn Dŵr, and to partitition the rest, north and south of the Midlands, between themselves [1].* Osbern Bokenham, an Augustinian friar translating saints' lives for East Anglian gentlefolk in the 1440s, noted that 'oftentime . . . mention [is] made of divers parts . . . and countries of this land England, the which, but if they be declared, be full hard to know'. Elites of country landowners (and of the richer urban property-holders and merchants) certainly had wider geographical interests than the mass of inhabitants. Freeholders were suitors of the shire court, which met four times a year. Professor Everitt has emphasised that at the end of our period, and for a long time afterwards, the shire was the chief basis for landowners' obligations: 'The allegiance of the provincial gentry to the community of their native shire is one of the basic facts of English history in the seventeenth and eighteenth centuries'[2]. A sense of shire rivalries is evident in the letter which William Paston wrote to Sir John Paston in 1489, when Henry VII was expected to visit Chelmsford in Essex. The local magnate, the Earl of Oxford, hoped that the gentry would turn out 'well appointed, that the Lancashire men [presumably in the royal retinue] may see that there be gentlemen of as great substance that they be able to buy all Lancashire'.

Yet there were potent factors widely promoting a sense of English unity, of national interests, obligations and identity. A basic stimulus was ease of communications. England is compact relative to its size, with few daunting interior physical barriers, unlike Scotland. No part of it is far from the sea, unlike many provinces of France and Germany. A lively flow of internal traffic over the medieval centuries is attested by the continued use of Roman roads and the development of a supplementary network. Travellers and news did not take many days to reach the remotest parts of the realm. Robert Carey successfully wagered that he could walk from London to Berwick (565 km) in twelve days in 1589[3].

There are, indeed, few contemporary complaints about difficulties of communication, from natives or from foreign visitors sensitive to inconveniences. The author of the fourteenth-century English romance, *Sir Gawain and the Green Knight*, emphasised as exceptional his hero's gruesome journey through 'the wilderness of Wirral'. Two foreigners were impressed by the hazards and bleakness of Pennine dales: Jean le Bel, a knight from Hainault, who campaigned in Weardale in 1327, and Aeneas Sylvius Piccolomini, an Italian diplomat travelling through Northumberland in 1435 (cf. p. 25). Both went off the highways, the former chasing elusive Scots, the latter eluding the vigilance of English officials. A Venetian[4] who had the misfortune to land at Falmouth in 1506 wrote: 'We are in a very wild place which no human being ever visits, in the midst of a most barbarous race, so

* Numerals in [square brackets] indicate notes at the end of the chapter.

different in language and customs from the Londoners and the rest of England that they are as unintelligible to the last as to the Venetians.'

Most travellers were able to bypass wild places. Sixteenth-century politics, economics and scholarship stimulated new interest in them, to some extent breaking down their isolation and lessening their singularity. Protestant royal councillors feared that remote, disordered, ill-instructed corners of the realm would become breeding grounds of papist subversion. Enterprising landlords, keen to keep ahead of inflation, speculated in their mineral exploitation. William Camden, Westminster schoolmaster, toured the country in his vacations, eager, like fellow antiquaries, to note relics of ancient civilisation, regretful at his inability to survey Hadrian's Wall because of 'the rank robbers thereabouts'.

But on main routes banditry was a nuisance, a customary levy, rather than a barrier to communications. William Langland wrote in his immensely popular didactic poem, *Piers the Ploughman* (*c*.1370): 'there are outlaws lurking in the woods and hiding under the banks, who can see every man that passes. They note carefully who goes in front and who follows behind, which men are on horseback and which on foot – for a man on horseback is bolder than one on foot.' A Venetian observed (*c*.1500) that 'there is no country in the world where there are so many thieves and robbers as in England'. The popularity of ballads about the merry deeds of Robin Hood, from the later fifteenth century onwards (and probably at least as early as Langland's time), suggests that such popular mayhem was in some regions regarded as a customary irritant rather than a dire social threat. The anonymous ('Anonimalle') chronicler of St Mary's Abbey, York, shortly after mentioning the Jacquerie, the savage rising against nobles in France, instructively describes an incident in England in 1359 when the Black Prince was escorting his captive, the French king John II, to London. They were ambushed near a forest by more than 500 men clad in green, armed with bows and accoutred like robbers. The prince unperturbedly explained to the amazed king that these were English foresters, outlaws living rough, 'and it was their custom to be arrayed like this'.

The robber might be treated with tolerance by courtly circles in south-east England, but not by the plainsman who raised his eyes apprehensively to the rim of the Pennines or Welsh hills, in fear of more extreme banditry. Such differences in attitude in part reflect long-lasting social contrasts between some regions in the 'highland' and 'lowland' zones, roughly divided by a line from Bristol to York. South of the Humber, Polydore Vergil noted, the country folk were 'very civil'. In the east, Midlands and south were regions whose inhabitants broadly shared similar, highly regulated agrarian systems. Such lowlands were more accessible, more susceptible to governmental control and to cultural influences (such as the Church's disciplining and reconciliatory ethics); and they were wealthier. They formed an easily exploited and unified base from which successive kingly dynasties, starting with the Anglo-Saxon rulers of Wessex, were able to dominate much of Britain and, in some periods, parts of western France and Ireland. These dynasties, West Saxon, Danish, Norman and Angevin, depended heavily for their control of England on their success in forging and maintaining bonds of common interest and loyalty among small groups of great landowners – the magnates. The result, by our period, was that the ruling groups of different provinces were tied by intricate webs of farflung land tenure and kinship, producing common political interests and tastes. In remote parish churches throughout England, the effigies of later medieval knights display identical fashions in armour, their ladies in coiffure. They enjoyed hearing and reading the same chivalrous and courtly romances, such as Sir Thomas Malory's monumental prose redaction into English of the Arthurian cycle. The English peer or wealthy gentleman could often identify with Malory's Sir Ector in being 'a lord of fair livelihood in many parts of England and Wales'.

The medieval Arthur was based on Geoffrey of Monmouth's *History of the Kings of Britain*. Geoffrey (d.1155?), seasoning his vivid imagination with some grains of folklore and written history, had elaborated a line of ancient British kings and dukes stemming from Brutus and his fellow refugees from the sack of Troy, founders of the kingdom of Albion. Generations believed in the literal truth of Geoffrey's history, glorying especially in the defence of post-Roman Britain by Arthur against the Saxons. A popular narrative of English history, up to Edward III's victory over the Scots in 1333, commenced with Brutus and was known as *The Brut*. Continuations were made, some in the original French, some in English and Latin translations; 121 manuscripts of the English *Brut*, 14 of the Latin, have been identified. Geoffrey's history had a tenacious hold over the imaginations of kings and nobles: it gave a heroic shape to their past and, in its prophecies, to their future. While Richard II was being escorted from Flint as Henry of Lancaster's prisoner in 1399, an aged knight of the duke's ruminated on how Merlin had prophesied the capture and ruin of the king. Only a foreigner had the temerity to question the historicity of Arthur in print – Polydore Vergil. He provoked the obloquy of native scholars: the embarrassed silence of their more scientific successors tacitly confirmed his doubts.

Arthurian myths maintained their popularity because they expressed the values of a noble society which believed its interests were maintained and promoted by the cultivation of personal links of dependence and service. At Court, magnates sought royal offices and commissions which would enable them to attract the services of gentlemen. Through the personal links which they formed with ruler and gentry, magnates aspired to act as the hinges of royal authority in the localities. Such chains of mutual obligation and service had been strengthened by the need of later medieval kings for support in their foreign ambitions and against pretenders to the throne, and by the need of landowners to supplement incomes threatened by economic crises.

Service in royal and noble households and military retinues familiarised gentlefolk from different parts of the realm, and produced similarities of outlook, as education at public schools and membership of London clubs were to do among the administrators of the British Empire. Military men dining simultaneously at head tables in the valleys of the Tweed and Dordogne shared a small world in the fourteenth century: their terms of service were drawn up in the same phrases, perhaps engrossed by the same Chancery clerk. The testimony of deponents, in a controversy over the right to bear a particular coat of arms in the 1380s, reveals something of this small gossipy world, as they reminisced over incidents and snatches of conversation on many campaigns[5]. Word soon spread among noble households: the physician John Arderne reflected in 1376 that his successful treatment of a retainer of the duke of Lancaster for an ischiorectal abscess had got him 'much honour and loving through all England'. Here was an elite which could articulate notions of 'common weal' in political as well as medical matters.

It is likely that notions of common interest became diffused widely in the mass of the population during our period. The growing prosperity of lowland regions extended the horizons of some of their inhabitants, giving them incentives to travel further away from home in search of profitable sales and higher wages, and bringing visitors from afar seeking bargains. In the fourteenth century Italian wool-buyers were familiar figures at 'Norleccio' (Northleath), 'Boriforte' (Burford) and 'Sirisestri' (Cirencester), to use the versions of place-names found in the Datini Archives. The dispatch of letters and spread of rumour by a flow of travellers in southern England is suggested by the contents of a letter from Sir John Paston in Hampshire to his brother in Norfolk (1471). Sir John reproached him for not writing: 'Ye might after Bartholomew Fair have had messengers enough to London.' But he had heard about the remarks of a 'Worsted man of Norfolk', who sold worsteds at Winchester, concerning Norfolk affairs, including his brother's. Sir John relayed news items from London, Calais and the North. He was worried about whether there had been plague in Norwich and other Norfolk boroughs, since the gossip of pilgrims and other travellers implied that there was widespread urban infection. Uncertain about some news items, Sir John was categorical on this: 'I assure you it is the most universal death that ever I wist in England.' In the light of this constant, far-reaching diffusion of information, some of it wildly inaccurate and indeed alarmist, it is not surprising that the low-born sometimes reacted strongly to tales of 'national' events, and articulated grievances in 'national' terms. Obscure Yorkshire rioters urged every lord, knight, esquire, gentleman and yeoman from the northern parts of England to assemble armed in 1489, to save king and community of the realm from alleged destruction. Their appeal combined gentlefolk's constitutional concepts with common folk's homely camaraderie. The risers intended 'to gainstand such persons as is about for to destroy our sovereign Lord the King [Henry VII] and the Commons of England, for such unlawful points as St. Thomas of Canterbury died for. . . . And this is in the name of Master Hobbe Hyrste, Robyn Godfelaw's brother he is, as I trow.'

Another factor widely developing a sense of interdependence and of national identity was warfare. By the end of the sixteenth century, when the Royal Navy had proved its worth, Scottish raiding had declined, and Wales had been integrated into English administration, England could be viewed as reasonably secure from hostile incursions behind its defensive moat. But the traditional view had been that the realm was intensely vulnerable to seaborne invasion, as conquests by Romans, Saxons, Danes and Normans bore witness. Later medieval Northumbrians or men of Herefordshire lived in fear of the hillfolk across the Border; those living near England's extremely long coastlines and their estuaries were menaced by pirates as well as the king's enemies.

The Crown's aggressively ambitious foreign policies for much of the later Middle Ages increased these vulnerabilities. But the policies were welcomed for the opportunities which they provided for gain at the expense of foreigners, and sharpened distinctions between English and alien. The nobility's support of Edward I's claims in Scotland and Edward III's in France gave them a sense of the monarchy's imperial mission, which king and community had a duty to promote. Nicholas Upton, writing before 1447, traced the king of England's title to French provinces back to Geoffrey of Monmouth's British kings. The English delegates at the Council of Constance claimed in 1417 that in, under and part of the renowned English nation there had been of old and still were many kingdoms – England, Scotland, and Wales (comprising Britain), the kingdom of the Sea, and four in Ireland.

The destruction wrought abroad by English soldiers and sailors provoked hostile comments on their national characteristics. In 1386 John I of Castile, menaced by their invasion, informed the Cortes how God had marked the English physically, and popes had imposed levies on them, so that their sins would always remain in the memory of men. The English had commonly rebelled against the Church, killing St Thomas of Canterbury and other martyrs, and had abetted and fomented schisms. They had always favoured unjust wars between Christians, not fearing God or caring about anything except to carry things off with pride and haughtiness. The present invader, the duke of Lancaster, was acting true to these ancestral traditions, scheming godlessly and greedily to divide Castile with the Moors of Granada[6].

Foreign visitors to England mixed contempt for the English character with delight at some of the realm's sights and amenities. Gabriel Tetzel of Nuremberg found the natives in 1466 'treacherous and cunning, plotting against the lives of foreigners, and no matter how they bend the knee they are not to be trusted'. Nicolas von Poppelau, a Silesian knight, considered them in 1484 as hotblooded and choleric, and, when in a passion, without mercy. They thought, he said, that the world did not exist outside England. A Venetian noble reported *c*.1500 that 'the English are great lovers of themselves, and of everything belonging to them; they think that there are no other men than themselves, and no other world but England'.

Such firm impressions of a distinctive national character, in which a high degree of identification as members of a nation was manifest, were probably derived from contact with particular categories of Englishmen: invaders, Londoners, and gentlefolk and townsmen from the lowlands of the south and east. Such a degree of national self-consciousness cannot be generally assumed. Nevertheless, these foreign commentators show that members of some influential social groups were exhibiting in the fifteenth century an aggressive awareness of being English. This was no mere bureaucratic imposition or literary artifice: the character of an Englishman was well developed, if not yet generally imprinted.

Notes

1. The Trent was an ancient administrative boundary between north and south. The regions under the jurisdiction of the Kings of Arms, the royal heralds, were also three: Clarenceux had his region south of Trent, Norroy north of Trent, and March in the Marches of Wales and West Country. The distinction between north and south was sharp in contemporary minds. The commission set up by the estates of the realm to carry out the formal deposition of Richard II in 1399 included a northern and a southern knight, to represent from their respective regions the 'bachelors and commons of this land'.
2. A. Everitt, *The Local Community and the Great Rebellion*, London, Historical Association, 1969, 5.
3. In fourteenth-century England people rode 25 km a day on leisurely journeys, up to 50 or even 65 km in emergencies.
4. Polydore Vergil of Urbino, in his *Anglica Historia*, written in the early sixteenth century, categorised the Cornish as the fourth people inhabiting Britain (with the English, Scots and Welsh) and remarked on their distinct British language.
5. See *The Scrope and Grosvenor Controversy,* ed. N. H. Nicolas, 2 vols, London, 1832.
6. I owe thanks for this reference to Dr A. I. MacKay of the University of Edinburgh.

Chapter 2

Rural and urban economy and society

Sources of information about agrarian economy and society

Conclusions about many aspects of these subjects are hampered by the patchiness of precise, statistically malleable evidence. A fundamental fact – the size of total population – cannot yet be confidently ascertained for most of the period. Mr Cornwall, using the military survey of 1522 and the subsidy rolls of 1524–5, arrived at an estimate of 2·3 million, and Dr Hollingsworth calculated one of about 4 million for England and Wales from the 1603 census of communicants and recusants. Yet though satisfactory bases for general census remain elusive, it is often possible to tabulate the tenants of an obscure manor at particular times, and to deduce a considerable amount about aspects of their economy and society. Professor Hallam has calculated from contemporary surveys that population densities in the fenland wapentake of Elloe (Lincs), one of the richest agricultural areas in Europe, were about the same in 1260 and 1951, discounting the bulk of Spalding's population in 1951. 'If all England in 1300 had had the same density of population as Elloe there would have been close on six million people'[1].

There survives a mass of documentation about the administration of the estates of leading landowners, increasing in bulk from the sixteenth and early seventeenth centuries[2]. Accounting methods and categories of records reflect the conservatism of estate management[3]. There was the *valor*, a comprehensive list of sources of income, either in detail or abstract, making plain the 'clear value' of each estate – the lord's expectation of revenue from its bailiff after administrative expenses and standing charges had been deducted[4]. The *compotus* (account) was a financial statement drawn up annually[5] by each bailiff and receiver for audit: such accounts decline in value as sources after 1400 as a result of widespread, long-term leasing. Manorial rolls recorded amercements and fines imposed by the lord's steward on the tenants in the manor court, and the terms of leases he made with them. Chartularies were compilations of the texts of a landed family's title deeds. Estimates of their individual incomes are sometimes found in the verdicts of inquisitions held by escheators on estates seized by the Crown. During the sixteenth century, in the case of wardships, these were to be supplemented by surveys made by feodaries of the Court of Wards (cf. p. 127).

Particularly when conclusions are sought about income, some of this material has to be used with caution. A valor was sometimes based on obsolete ministers' accounts. Escheators' inquisitions, feodaries' surveys, and also assessments for subsidy and recusancy fines, may reflect a family's attempt to conceal or minimise income, or the general unconcern of assessors for accuracy. The survival of occasional rather than consecutive *compoti* may give an inadequate or misleading impression of current income, for a minister's account was not intended as a statement of revenue received for the lord's use, but was a list of the financial liabilities with which the minister was charged, and of his discharges. A bailiff listed under 'Receipts' all the 'rents of assize' (fixed payments from freeholders and copyholders), other rents from villeins or tenants at will, farms from leases, arrears of these, together with the profits from dues, fees and market sales. But he might have actually received only some of the rents and farms owed. It is not always clear from a single account whether failure to pay was temporary or habitual. Lords were congenitally reluctant to write off lost sources of income by allowing them to appear as 'decayed rents' in a bailiff's list of 'Expenses'.

Indeed, it is to be expected that the amount of arrears and domainal profits should fluctuate, in response to climatic and market conditions, and the lord's need for ready cash. The frequency of epidemics was another unsettling factor. The lord needed to be vigilant in case his profits were creamed off by fraudulent ministers. The castigation of reeves by both the courtly Chaucer and the lowly Langland suggests a widespread distrust of their practices. Ministers' accounts may, consequently, sometimes bear only a slight relationship to actual income from estates. In 1433 Lord Talbot's receiver at Whitchurch, John Wenlock, was charged in its court leet with having filched sheaves of corn, grazed his own and his chaplain's sheep in Black Park all winter, and poached the lord's fish. When he supervised the fencing of the little park, 'as one cartful was brought to make the same pale, two or three cartful were brought to his own house to the number of thirty cartful'. In this case, the charges may have been malicious, for Wenlock denied them, and was acquitted by a jury empanelled by the manorial steward.

Generalisations about estate management, agrarian yields and country life are handicapped by dependence on random survivals from the archives of a small elite of lay and ecclesiastical 'great landowners', concerned to record only matters affecting their judicial and financial rights. The tenurial and farming policies pursued by a landowner in one manor might differ radically from a neighbour's in a manor in the same or a nearby village. One might lease all or part of his demesne[6] and commute the labour services owed by his serfs (*villani*, *nativi*, neifs), whilst the other rigidly tried to maintain farming for profit and the exaction of customary obligations. One might preserve stock carefully, whilst his neighbour's estate was run down for quick profits, to satisfy aspirations to cut a figure at Court, or the greed of an unscrupulous guardian. The size of tenements, and their proximity to other parts of the inheritance were factors which might also make crucial differences to methods of exploitation. Before the sixteenth century, there are few records of the estate management of lesser landowners. A gentleman owning a few manors, exercising more personal control over his bailiffs, did not require the magnate's elaborate system of account. Little is known about the economy of estates held by tenants such as 'freeholders' and 'copyholders' (see p. 19). Manorial court rolls and *compoti* provide information about the financial terms of their tenure, but these did not always bear a close relation to their yields.

Regional resources, occupations and tenures

Variations in agrarian organisation and social habits were perpetuated by the diversity of regional resources and the degree of ease in communications, especially with urban and overseas outlets. An underlying determinant was the division between the 'highland zone' to the north and west, and the 'lowland zone' mainly in southern and Midland England, extending northwards along the coasts. Uplands producing meagre crops of oats and barley supported a small, scattered population. Jean le Bel, after campaigning in Weardale in 1327, wrote of the region as 'wild, full of deserts and mountains, and poor in everything except cattle'. Poverty was often increased there by the custom of partible inheritance. Emigration was a means of relief: poor uplanders were familiar in Newcastle, York and the towns of the Welsh Marches. The men of those Marches, the High Peak of Derbyshire and the northern dales were reputed lawless and tough. Henry VIII prized the military worth of Border horsemen, but the Borderers' habits were to irritate several more generations of royal officials; poverty and lack of instruction prolonged thieving, barbarity, and superstition.

Northern society's lack of resources and dynamic for change must not be exaggerated. In the Yorkshire plain and the eastern parts of the bishopric of Durham and Northumberland, wheat and rye were grown in the early fourteenth century by lords with the aid of 'servile works'. Near the frontiers, however, invasions and prolonged insecurity may have caused a contraction in arable farming which, later in the century, plague epidemics like the one in 1379 described by Thomas Walsingham may have intensified. In the years 1336–9 the Cumberland subsidy assessment was reduced by more than a half, and by 1348 ninety-two townships had been altogether exempted. Nevertheless, according to the Scottish chronicler Andrew Wyntoun, in 1385 the earl of Fife's invading army found the shire

a hale cuntre,
And in all gudis abowndand,
For na were [*war*] *was in till that land,*
Syne Robert the Brwys [*Bruce*] *deyd away.*

The goods that delighted their hearts were probably cattle: a surveyor of the Percy estates there in 1570, probably with more productive English shires in mind, was not impressed with Cumberland:

the country consists most in waste ground and is very cold, hard and barren for the winter . . . their greatest gain consisteth in breeding of cattle which are no charge to them in summer by reason they are pastured and fed upon the mountains and waste where they might have sufficient pasture all the year unless great snows chance in the winter to cover the ground . . . because the greatest part of the country consisteth in waste and mountains they have but little tillage.

However, the North's mineral wealth was exploited, with a quickening pace in the sixteenth and seventeenth centuries. Coal-mining, well-established along the Tyne and Wear valleys in the fourteenth century, expanded rapidly to meet growing demand (increased by timber shortage) in London and the South in the sixteenth century. Between 1565 and 1625 coal shipments from Newcastle multiplied twelvefold, and in the early seventeenth century Sunderland developed as a rival port for the newly designed coal transports, 'colliers', which plied down the coast. Readily accessible, cheap coal stimulated the expansion of the salt industry at the mouths of Tyne and Wear by the end of the sixteenth century. In recent decades the Yorkshire coal-mining industry had experienced its first major expansion, with the sinking of hundreds of new pits. Increased southern demand had also spread lead-mining in the uplands of Teesdale, Weardale and Derwentdale.

The enterprise of improving landowners, particularly in the sixteenth century, was a key factor in expansion. They provided the considerable capital needed for mineral exploitation of their estates and those which were rented to them. In 1490 the bishop of Durham (John Shirwood) was showing a sharp eye for enterprise: he sent his gentleman usher of the chamber from Auckland probably to Norfolk, to negotiate a deal with Sir John Paston with a covering letter:

And forasmuch as I have coals and other things in these parts, and also ye have in those parts corns, wine and wax, and as I am informed ye be not evil willed to deal with me, no more than I am to deal with you in uttering and also in receiving of such things, the which might be to the profit of us both, I therefore send unto you at this time this bearer . . .

In the period 1558 to 1642 at least eighty gentle Yorkshire families had coal-mining interests. Industrial and urban growth stimulated agrarian exploitation, and raised their rents. The most general and continuous stimulus was to sheep-rearing, from the rise of a cloth industry in the Pennine dales. Wakefield, for instance, grew as one of its centres in the fifteenth century, becoming wealthy enough to stage its own cycle of miracle plays. The audience would doubtless have appreciated the deprecatory allusion to a rival product in one of Noah's remarks to his wife:

But thou ought to be dressed in stafford blue;
For thou art always depressed, be it false or true.

A much higher percentage of land south of the Trent had experienced three centuries or more of intense agrarian exploitation by the early fourteenth century. Its regions abundant in good soils for mixed farming, its easy communications and greater proximity to principal centres of western European commerce sustained higher population densities. Woods and coverts had been eroded by arable and meadow closes. Schasek, a Bohemian traveller in the south in 1466, noted the effects of timber shortage: the inhabitants, he said, made their fires of bracken rather than wood. The southern English landscape was characterised by a Venetian memorialist (*c*.1500) as containing 'agreeable woods or extensive meadows, or lands in cultivation, and the greatest plenty of water springing everywhere'. Interspersed with isolated farms and hamlets on relatively barren chalk, limestone and sandy uplands were large numbers of populous villages on the clays by valley streams, some of ancient Anglo-Saxon settlement, others founded in post-Conquest clearances. Village tenements were roughly aligned along a street, or convergent on an intersection of ways or a market space. Dwellings had adjacent crofts, which might contain kitchen gardens, orchards and barns. The croft was often enclosed: in Chaucer's *Nun's Priest's Tale*, the yard in which the poor widow's cock strutted was 'enclosed all about with sticks [palings] and a dry ditch without', though the fox burst through the 'hedges' and hid in a bed of herbs.

Crofts frequently abutted on a back lane running along one of the 'great fields', whose configuration shaped the settlement. The tenants sowed, ploughed and harvested their individual crops of grain, peas, beans and related legumes in them, communally determining the basic timing of winter or Lenten sowings and other agrarian tasks. Because of the chronic shortage of fertilisers[7] they had to agree to leave part or whole of one of the great fields fallow each year. They elected wardens to ensure that during the harvest, in which the whole community engaged, traditional regulations preserving everyone's cropping interests should be observed by man and beast.

Fields were divided into strips (selions): tenants occupied a scattering of strips in different fields. Selions were long, narrow sections of arable, of varying width and length, and of a size convenient for ploughing in a day[8]. They were terminated by a headland, the space on which plough teams turned, and their boundaries were often marked by end posts or stones. Harvested strips provided valuable pasturage. The sectioned great fields which they comprised have originated the term 'open-field system' to describe such communally organised agriculture, the pattern in many villages up to the eighteenth century. Meadows, too, were divided into strips; the use of common pastures was regulated by 'stints', and individuals' pigs were herded together in the woodland.

Nevertheless, the use of the term 'open-field' gives misleading impressions. One of the principal aims of communities practising mixed farming was to keep beasts off the crops: open fields and meadows were ditched or hedged. Moreover, there were many enclosed lands which individual tenants occupied and utilised at will – crofts, patches of hemp and flax, strips which the holders had decided to use as pastoral 'leys', and which they sometimes converted permanently to closes. Schasek remarked on the enclosed appearance of the countryside: 'Every wood is surrounded by ditches. In the same manner the peasants dig ditches round their fields and meadows and so fence them in that no one can pass on foot or on horseback except by the main roads.' The open-field system was not uniform nor universal in the mainly southern and Midland regions to whose resources it was well adapted. Woodland areas in almost every county had been enclosed at the time of the widespread clearances in the early Middle Ages.

The countryside was split up into tenurial units of varying size – 'manors', largely owned by gentlefolk. Sometimes more than one settlement comprised a manor, or there were several manors in one village. The division of one manor into two or more separate ones inherited by coheirs did not affect its integral field system, if it had common fields. The community then regulated usage, in default of a co-ordinating lord's court. A high proportion of manorial inhabitants, especially in regions of intense cultivation, were until the early fifteenth century characterised in landlords' estate documents as *villani* or *nativi*. By virtue of their descent they belonged to the manorial lord as certainly as the tenement which they occupied and most of the resources they needed to farm. For the privilege of sustaining his family's life under the lord's protection, the villein owed obligations, varying according to the evolution of manorial custom regarding each tenement. These obligations included a set number of 'work days' for the lord's benefit, when his reeve ordered the villein to herd, cart, cut wood, clear fishponds, set weirs, repair outbuildings, and ditch and hedge. At plough and harvest times, when villeins were anxious to tend their own crops, lords demanded the heaviest amounts of service on demesne strips in the great fields and closes, to supplement their regular paid labourers and cut down the expense of hiring casuals. A large proportion of a villein's gross output, sometimes as high as 50 per cent, was owned by manorial lords, though, according to their current farming and cash requirements, they were prepared on occasion to commute a service for a rent.

There were other customary ways in which lords exploited inhabitants of their manors, and restricted the freedom of some of them. The lord commonly owned mills, woods, fishponds and fowling rights, and exacted fees and fines for their use by all. Villein birth and tenure entailed considerable personal restrictions. These often survived well into the fifteenth century and occasionally into the sixteenth, despite increasing commutations of 'works' for rent, and complete enfranchisements ('manumissions'), especially from the 1350s onwards. A villein might need to pay the lord's reeve for licence to sell land or livestock, send a son to school, or move away from the manor. If his daughter married or, when unmarried, became pregnant, he was fined. When he died, his heir or coheirs had to deliver as 'heriot' his best beast or chattel. At least until the later fourteenth century, a very substantial minority of English folk were legally bound to their landlords.

Nevertheless, even in fertile regions of dense servility, such as the west Midlands, there had long been large numbers of tenants paying dues in rent or kind: free families living next to serfs, free communities next to nests of villeins. Freehold was a characteristic form of tenure in Lincolnshire, East Anglia, parts of the east Midlands, Shropshire, Herefordshire and Kent. The poorest freemen, and the most numerous, were those with tiny holdings. Others were well-to-do, eager to buy parcels of land to increase their sales of crop surpluses and wool clip. Some villeins prospered above their fellows, hiring labourers, leasing and purchasing tenements. There were villagers whose main, and often lucrative, means of livelihood was not tillage: smiths, wheelwrights, carpenters, thatchers, tilers, millers, clothworkers and miners.

Urban and trading developments had important effects on the economy and social structure of many villages. London had uniquely magnetic effects. Its markets required a constant stream of corn, meat, vegetables, fruit, cheese and milk. Villages along the Kent and Essex coasts catered for the Londoners' taste for mussels and oysters. Their fishing fleets, and those of East Anglia, met the huge demand for fish, consumed on holy days, and dried as stockfish to supplement meagre winter meat supplies. By the later fourteenth century some Essex villages had become centres of industry, supplying Londoners with, for example, knives, utensils, furniture.

A more general stimulus to rural change was the rise, from that period onwards, of the cloth industry. Villages with good communications, especially in East Anglia, Essex and the Cotswolds, became production centres. Families sorted, carded and spun, besides tending crops and stock. Some concentrated on the more skilled, specialised processes, such as weaving, dyeing or dressing. These novel rural jobs represent part of the shift in the period away from engagement in subsistence agriculture to other occupations – wool, meat and mineral, as well as cloth, production. This process was neither speedy nor universal. The remarks of Polydore Vergil early in the sixteenth century were intended to pertain particularly to England south of the

Humber, and must be regarded as highly impressionistic: 'The ground is marvellous fruitful, and abundantly replenished with cattle, whereby it cometh to pass that of Englishmen more are graziers and masters of cattle than husbandmen or labourers in tilling of the field.'

Crises and change in rural economy

The start of our period roughly coincides with the tailing-off of two centuries of agrarian growth. Population was outstripping the means of subsistence. Much land taken into cultivation in recent generations was inferior: inefficient agricultural methods failed to maintain its previous yields. In the years 1315–17 disastrous harvest failures produced widespread famines. Perhaps because population was falling, farming for market sales of food became less profitable. In 1348 plague reached England, spreading into a pandemic which declined in intensity from the end of 1349. There were to be general outbreaks in 1361 and 1369: regional outbreaks occurred frequently over the following three hundred years[9]. Plague is a disease afflicting wild rodents. *Pasteurella pestis*, a non-mobile bacillus, multiplies in the rat flea (*Xenopsylla cheopis*), which, when crammed with bacilli to the point of indigestion, kills the host rat by regurgitating them into its blood stream. When the rat dies, the fleas bite humans or other available animals: 'blocked' fleas can remain alive and infectious for up to fifty days without food. Bacilli, discharged into the blood through the flea's bites and faeces, cause a swelling or 'bubo' in the lymphatic glands (in the groin, armpit or neck) which drains the infected limbs. The plague toxins produce high fever, coma, heart failure, inflammation of the spleen or kidneys, sometimes destruction of tissue and consequent internal haemorrhage. The mortality rate in bubonic cases untreated by modern medicine is 60–85 per cent, death occurring on average after five days of illness. Since the bacilli are normally active when the temperature is between 15° and 24° C (60° and 75° F), bubonic epidemics break out in warm weather, though when the rat population is heavily infected plague may persist in winter. There are other forms of plague infection. In a septicaemic attack, the number of bacilli transferred to the host is so high that the victim invariably dies of blood poisoning, often within a day. Pneumonic plague, in which lung congestion is the primary cause of death, is almost always fatal within three days. In contrast to the bubonic and septicaemic varieties, spread only by rat fleas or the infected human flea (*Pulex irritans*), it is spread by human droplet contagion, and is one of the most virulent diseases. Pneumonic plague flourishes in cold weather, when humans, suffering from colds, are particularly likely to be infectious.

During the medieval plague pandemic men were at a loss to explain its causes or to prescribe effective treatment. Some writers expatiated eruditely on a 'corruption of the air' induced by astrological conjunctions, others resorted to a theological explanation, seeing the misery as a manifestation of divine wrath. Isolation of victims and burning of their effects were among measures taken to stop contagion. By the fifteenth century it was recognised that outbreaks tended to be more virulent in towns: kings and gentlefolk hurried thence to rural retreats[10].

Chroniclers imply that over half the English population died of plague in 1348–9. Their general tendency to inflate figures is notorious: random surviving statistics suggest great variations in the incidence of mortality. But it is very likely that, especially in the more densely populated regions, this and the subsequent general outbreaks of the fourteenth century caused a steep population decline. Survivors in heavily stricken villages, lacking nourishment because of a decline in cultivation, may often have succumbed to endemic ailments. Since population growth normally tended to be slow as a result of chronic high levels of infant mortality, it is likely to have taken several generations free from general plague epidemics to replace lost members.

Though landlords received an exceptional number of heriots, they lost work services and other dues through the vacancy of tenements in 1348–9. The rising cost of hired labour was a disincentive to cultivation, but animal husbandry, less labour intensive, continued to be profitable. However, in the following decades many landowners vigorously attempted to maintain or restore demesne cultivation and villein services. They filled tenements and tried to exact customary or even increased dues from the tenants. They tracked down villeins who, in this era of high labour costs, abandoned their holdings without licence, to join the ranks of landless labourers. The lords invoked royal aid to hold down the cost of hired labour. In June 1349 a royal ordinance was aimed 'against the malice of servants, who were idle, and not willing to serve after the pestilence, without excessive wages'. Men and women under the age of sixty were to work when required. Labourers were to accept the wages they had normally been paid in 1346 and the five or six previous years. Employers as well as labourers who contravened the ordinance were liable to fine or imprisonment. A statute of 1351 confirmed the ordinance and elaborated wage maximums. 'Justices of labourers' were commissioned to enforce it. The passage of supplementary statutes, in 1361 and 1388, attempting to regulate the mobility of labourers, implies difficulty in enforcement. In 1361 the savage provision was made that labourers who went from county to county seeking higher wages should be branded on the forehead. Peasants became infuriated by repressive attempts to deny them opportunities which luckier neighbours, dealing with a lord prepared either to commute villeins' work services for rents or to pay high wages to hired labourers, were exploiting. From the 1360s onwards it became common for villeins on a particular manor to league together in refusing services. Many formed leagues during the 1381 revolt and continued to do so in the fifteenth century[11].

From the 1370s onwards, as prices fell, lords increasingly commuted and leased. Leases of parcels of arable demesne or of a whole manor, in return for a share of the crop or a money rent, at first tended to be annual or for a few years, but, as leasing became the norm in the first decades of the fifteenth century, longer periods became common. By the mid-century a very few demesnes of large landowners (mostly the home farms of Benedictine abbeys) functioned under the direct management of the lord. The lessees varied in status; there were gentlefolk, freeholders, and villeins of the manor who valued particular parcels for farming with smaller but more assured profits than under the previous more expensive, impersonal estate management.

Liability for work services generally declined. By the 1430s villein status had been widely transformed. Peasants had purchased 'manumissions', formal releases from the obligations of villeinage. But many landlords maintained 'servile' rights to restrict and fine particular families and the occupiers of particular tenements. Though the economic crisis heavily and permanently reduced the incomes of many peers and ecclesiastical corporations, no more than gentry and well-to-do peasants did they lose the impulse to exploit land for profit. The prudent landlord was concerned that his ministers collected rents efficiently, that his residual feudal, judicial and servile rights were profitably enforced, that tenements were well maintained, and that demesne leases guaranteeing upkeep of the premises were made with well-reputed farmers. T. Cryne, in a letter to John Paston (April 1482), alluded to preoccupations with estate management among Norfolk landowners:

. . . as in long time passed, on Thursday in Easter Week, begin Master Heydons courts and leets, the view of the half year of the household account, the closing up finally of the accounts of all bailiffs, so that the receiver may make his final account, which will extend in all to fourteen days and more . . .
. . . my Lord Rivers in his own person hath been at Hickling, and his counsel learned, and searched his fees for his homages. . . . What it meaneth, my lord is set sore to improvement and husbandry. His counsel hath told him he may set his fines for respite of homage at his pleasure.

Landlords did not always lease. Sometimes they kept in hand flocks and herds, closes for pasture, woods, fishponds, warrens, chaces, mills or mines. But for large-scale estate managers it was not always easy to maintain levels of income, especially from marginally attractive lands. Ministers of the bishops of Worcester were confronted by recalcitrant tenants, who collectively and individually refused to pay rents, amercements and commuted villein services. In a period of opportunities for migratory labour, coercion might have induced abandonment of tenements, resulting in vacancies or new leases on terms unfavourable to the bishopric.

Distraint of cattle, sheep and other chattels was a common expedient of landlords against defaulters. But it was useless when tenants were influential, determined, or maintained by a protector. Agnes Paston was told that her late husband, the judge (d.1444), had never been asked for a certain rent, 'for he was a great man, and a wise man of the law'. In 1451 Wharles, one of her son John's tenants at Gresham, refused to pay a penny till distrained, perhaps emboldened by the intent of Lord Moleyns's bailiff and friends to make good their master's claim to the manor. Paston's agent, the chaplain James Gloys, wrote in despair to his master about his failure with Wharles: 'I have been there divers times for to distrain him, and I could never do it but if I would have distrained him in his mother's house, and there I durst not for her cursing.' Gloys's remarks conjure up a different picture from those in fourteenth-century manuscript illuminations, showing villeins working under the baleful supervision of the lord's ministers. The manor house was no longer the symbol of seigniorial authority. In some places it was occupied by a tenant-farmer working demesne with hired labour; in others, with no resident lord or farmer, and especially where the manorial tenants were renting demesne, it had fallen into decay. The 'country house' was evolving as a noble and gentlemanly residence, often separate from farm buildings, sometimes remote, within its park palings, from the village community.

Though landlords and tenants were sometimes in conflict in the fifteenth century, their relations were often close and harmonious. Demesnes were habitually farmed to familiar servants and kinsfolk. When estate ownership was disputed, the attitude of the tenants could be crucial. There are examples in *The Paston Letters* of attempts to cajole as well as intimidate them. When gentlefolk took up arms to overawe a local rival at a sessions or election, or to support a claimant to the throne, they relied on the armed support of tenants. For the latter it could be important to win their lord's goodwill, not just to promote good tenurial relations, but to get the support of his local influence (e.g. as justice of the peace) in disputes; to gain farms of his land, contracts to supply his household, appointments to ministerial posts in his administration, and places for their children to serve about his person. The rise of many peasants to prosperity as tenant-farmers tended to broaden the scope of the 'political nation', since they abetted the gentry in unruliness, rioting and rebellion. Yet Sir John Fortescue, writing in the 1460s, surprisingly does not condemn the development strongly. To him, 'the commons'' sturdy spirits, martial ability and prosperity were no more horrifying than to his fellow gentry, in contrast to their ancestors' reactions in 1381.

The structure of rural society underwent fundamental changes in the period *c*.1350 to *c*.1430. In its previous form there had been marked variations of status and wealth among peasants, and considerable opportunities for social mobility, affected by the relative buoyancy of local markets, particularly for wool sales. The collapse of demesne farming eroded villeinage. There developed in its place a variety of tenures. Besides freeholds and leases made by indenture there was customary (frequently 'copyhold') tenure. The customary tenant held on terms fixed in the manor court, often recorded on its court roll, for life, for several lives, or in heredity. Then there were the tenants-at-will, whose bargains were not protected by record or custom.

There arose in the fifteenth century a more conspicuous class of well-to-do freeholders, leaseholders and copyholders distinguished by the title 'yeoman'[12]. Some of their families can be traced painstakingly adding over several generations to their holdings by marriage, purchase and lease. They created a pattern of larger peasant tenements, often buying out poorer neighbours, who could make a more assured living labouring for them[13].

Much yeoman prosperity derived from wool sales, stimulated by the expansion of the native woollen textile industry up to the mid-sixteenth century. Gentry and yeomen converted their arable closes to pasture. Village or manorial communities agreed that arable strips might be permanently enclosed and that common pasture and waste should be divided among individuals and hedged, as they wished to increase the facilities for their flocks and herds, and enclosed fields seem to have been recognised as more economical to work. Many villages were so depopulated and lacking in the intensive manpower needed for full arable exploitation that conversion to pasture made the best financial sense. The movement to convert and to enclose reached a crescendo *c*.1450 to *c*.1520: there was a peak in the 1590s, a decade characterised by harvest failures and dearth. Friction and hardship were often caused when landlords or influential tenants unilaterally converted and enclosed, or overbore opposition in the manor court from poorer peasants who depended for their slender livelihood on common grazing rights and a degree of communal cooperation in agriculture.

Tudor statutes, commissions, pamphlets and sermons denounced and attempted to check social ills attributed to the immoral greed of sheepmasters. These reflected fears that the 'decay of husbandry', depriving ploughmen of their livelihood, would intensify social unrest, and debilitate the sinews of the realm's defence. A draft parliamentary Bill of 1514 declared: 'Many merchant venturers, cloth-makers, goldsmiths, butchers, tanners and other artificers and unreasonable covetous persons do encroach more farms than they are able to occupy . . . farms and ploughs are decayed . . . and no more parishioners in many parishes but a neat herd and a shepherd.'

A stimulus to more competitive exploitation by 'unreasonable covetous persons', and a reason why their activities pinched poor villagers sharply, was the price rise. There is some evidence that basic commodity prices, after a long period of relative stability in the fifteenth century, began a sustained upward movement in the second decade of the sixteenth. The basic cause of inflation may have been population expansion, reflecting recovery from the plague pandemic, without an equivalent expansion of food supplies and job opportunities. Accelerating in the 1540s, by the 1550s prices had more than doubled their 1500 level; though the rate of increase slowed in the 1560s, by the late 1570s and 1580s they had trebled. Food prices (which had risen faster than those of manufactures in the early stages of the inflation) rose sharply in the 1590s. By the end of the century prices had at least quadrupled from the 1500 base: they rose at a slower rate till the 1630s.

Since wages lagged behind prices, labourers were particularly at the mercy of inflation. *Rentier* landlords, living not on farming profits but on partially fixed incomes, felt the threat to their life-style. Thomas Cromwell's monastic commissioner Jaspar Fyllole reported to him in September 1535 that the London Charterhouse's rents of assize would not cover the lay brothers' living expenses, according to 'a paper of such proportion of victuals and other needs as the lay brothers here telleth me of necessity must be provided for them. . . . And yet since the making of that proportion, wheat is risen 4*s*. in every quarter, and malt 20*d*. in every quarter, and commonly all other victuals riseth therewith.' In this case the price rise was probably only a contributory cause of the financial problem, but the reluctance to economise which the hostile Fyllole attributed to the brethren may have been a common reaction among landlords. Henry VIII's chaplain, Thomas Starkey, in a treatise presented to the king between 1533 and 1536[14], alluded to one sort of solution: 'Princes and lords seldom look to the good order and wealth of their subjects; only, they look to the receiving of their rents and revenues of their lands, with great study of enhancing thereof, to the further maintaining of their pompous estate.'

There were difficulties in pursuing such courses. The rents of leaseholders were fixed, and some copyholders were able to prove in Chancery or the common law courts that theirs were fixed by manorial custom. Sir William Wentworth wrote in 1604:

Let no tenant whosoever have a lease, unless you be contented to make him your master, or can allow him to join with your enemies. For I have had good and sound experience of such grievous effects. Again your tenants having leases may sue you, or any of your friends, in an action of trespass, if you or they do but come upon the ground to them let. . . . I like much better to have men tenants at will.

The landlord could arbitrarily fix the rents of tenants-at-will: so these, often poorer, villagers bore the brunt of his search for more rent. But he was not without resource in squeezing the better-placed tenants. Copyholders were obliged to pay entry fines, whose amount was 'arbitrable' – subject to his determination. They might be forfeited for trivial offences, or hounded out by harassing lawsuits. When leases or copyholds fell in, the landlord could let at more realistic rents than had been customary in the fifteenth century, or farm for the markets in

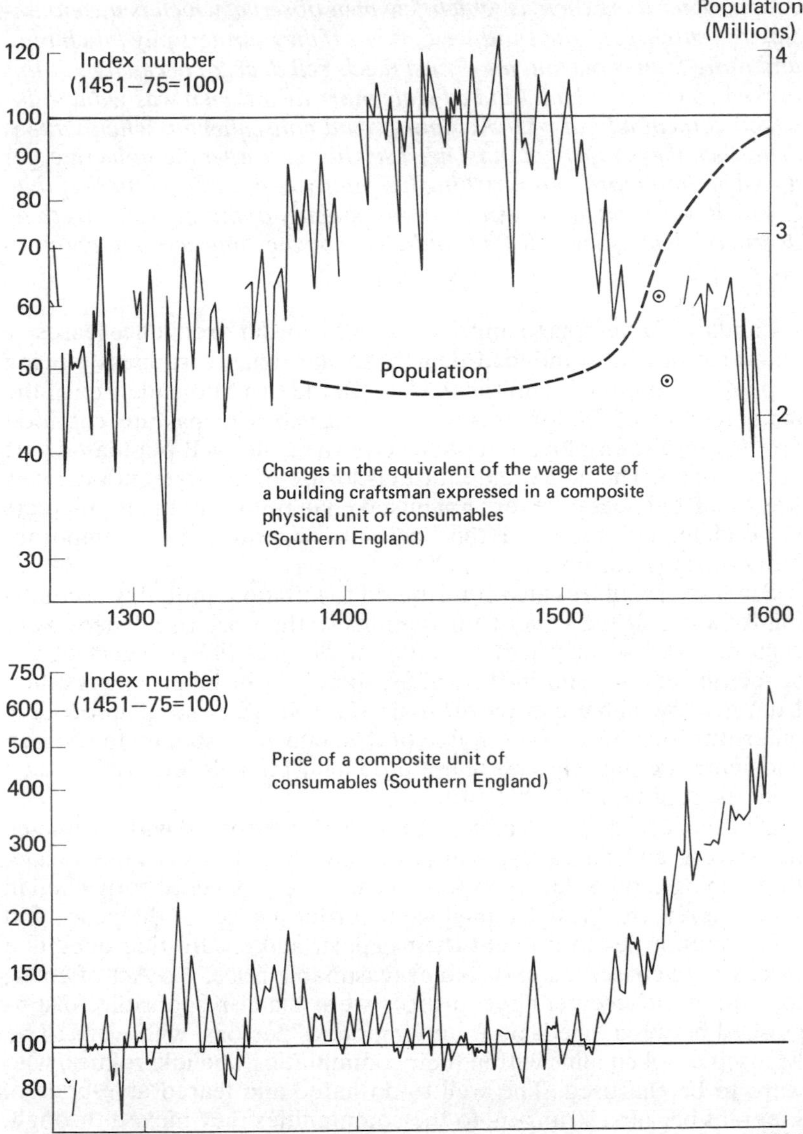

Fig. 1 Population, wages and prices in later medieval and early modern England

wool and foodstuffs himself. Whereas the average rents in Yorkshire early in Elizabeth's reign were 6*d*, 1*s* or 2*s* an acre, by Charles I's they were between 5*s* and 10*s* an acre. There is evidence for a similar movement in other counties. Rent increases were another inflationary pressure, as Starkey believed:

And another thing there is which few men observe, which is the enhancing of rents, of late days induced . . . for if they farmers pay much rent, and more than is reason, they must needs sell dear, of necessity . . . this maketh, without fail, all kind of vittle more dear than it was wont to be, which cometh all out of the country. And consequently, when vittle is dear, then they craftsmen must need sell his ware after the same rate, for it costeth him more in nourishing his family and artificers thereof than before it was wont to do. And so consequently of this root springeth all dearth of all things which we should have by the diligence and labour of the people.

Landlords' attempts to improve estates in order to enhance leases or market profits also induced dearth. In the uplands ruthless fencing deprived peasants of common pasture. In the east Midlands, one of the main regions of Tudor enclosure, conversions to pasture cut food production and employment prospects in a fertile, well-populated part of the realm. The actual extent of enclosure in the sixteenth century was small, but peasants were not mistaken in rioting, nor pamphleteers in condemning greed, for the enclosures aggravated contemporary inflationary hardships.

But harvest failures also contributed to inflation, probably accounting for some of the violent fluctuations in the price rise. There were runs of bad harvests in the 1550s, in the last fifteen years of the sixteenth century, and in the 1620s, some of which perhaps resulted from general climatic deterioration. Many small farmers, depending on profits from 30 acres of arable or less, may have sold up to yeomen and gentry because they were not producing enough corn, rather than as a result of tenurial pressure.

Contemporaries believed that they were confronted with problems of poverty and vagrancy, stimulated by dearth, on a novel scale, threatening good order. In order to guarantee supplies of corn when in short supply, the Privy Council would order justices of the peace and urban authorities to prevent their export, and ensure that adequate stocks were conserved and sold at reasonable price. An Act of 1531, for whose enforcement the justices were made responsible, distinguished between 'aged, poor and impotent' persons, who were to be licensed to solicit alms within their communities, and idle rogues, who were to be chastised. The well-to-do hated and feared able-bodied, itinerant beggars, strangers to the communities they moved through, banded together, it was believed, to intimidate, rob and steal. Intensifications of vagrancy probably stemmed from increases in rural poverty and urban unemployment, especially when depressions in the cloth trade threw large numbers of rural and urban textile workers out of work. Then men, women and children migrated in search of livelihood, reduced to begging and thieving if they could find none.

Legislation on poverty and vagrancy became more elaborate and discriminating in the century. In 1563 parishes were ordered to relieve their poor, justices of the peace being empowered to assess those reluctant to contribute to the costs. An Act of 1576 distinguished between idle and able-bodied poor: the latter were to be provided in their parishes with materials to work on. It was enacted in 1598 that the justices were to fix parish rates for poor relief, richer parishes subsidising poorer ones. The justices were to appoint four overseers in the parish to collect and administer the rate, and were to supervise their maintenance of houses for the impotent poor and apprenticeship of pauper children. But another Act of 1598 continued the policy of treating migrants harshly. Such sturdy rogues were to be whipped and returned to their parishes, and, if deemed dangerous, put in gaols and houses of correction. The effectiveness of this legislation is hard to gauge: it depended on the attitude of the justices. Poor rates were in fact only levied by them in times of dire necessity: urban and private charitable relief seem to have been more efficacious.

The strains placed by inflation on incomes and livelihoods in the sixteenth century sharpened landlords' sense of being a governing class. Many doubtless heeded exhortations by preachers and writers to display a traditional paternalism towards those in their lordship suffering from dearth. Others were impressed by the need to keep the commons in order, if a divinely ordained hierarchy was to be preserved. A depth of fear is revealed by the savagery of the statutory punishments for vagrancy enacted in 1547 (and repealed in 1550): culprits were liable to become the slaves for two years of the informant who had denounced them, or the corporate slaves of the parish. The nightmares shared by gentlefolk, and the responsibility the Crown placed on the magistrates among them for preserving order, may have powerfully enhanced the sense among them that they, the gentry, were the pillars of the commonwealth.

Peasant society

Deficiencies of evidence, and the difficulties of collating much of what survives, have retarded study of peasant society. Since peasants were normally illiterate, they have left few written records. Only from the later sixteenth century onwards is there considerable evidence of some village literacy, especially among yeomen. Manor-court rolls are crucial sources for tenurial obligations, bye-laws, the operations of the village community, inheritance, and land sales. From the later sixteenth century parish registers greatly supplement information. Some medieval landlords' chartularies contain copies of peasants' deeds of sale, showing a brisk market among them in land. Occasionally they were parties to lawsuits concerning their tenurial rights. Their beliefs and intentions seldom appear in their own words before the later sixteenth century, from which a few dictated wills survive. Their words had previously been taken down sometimes as evidence before ecclesiastical and secular courts, or have been handed down through the often distorting medium of oral tradition, in ballads, proverbs and superstitions. In the Middle Ages the educated were not interested in the 'simple' opinions of rustics, except when their testimony was required in lawsuits, especially when they were suspected of transgressions, or when (some of them receiving the grace of spiritual illumination) miracles and visions were bestowed on them. In the sixteenth century the vogue for chorography – comprehensive description of regions on classical models, such as Tacitus's *Germania* – produced a *frisson* of scholarly interest in the habits of natives.

Only haphazard points can be made about such a basic matter as the peasants' standard of living. Langland and Froissart reflect what was probably a widespread belief about many countryfolk in southern England in the last decades of the fourteenth century, that they were enjoying and insisting on a higher standard of living, particularly as regards diet. Mid-fourteenth-century custumals specifying diets which landlords allowed their serfs, when engaged in harvesting the demesne, give an impression of some peasants' occasional fare, probably better than the norm. At noon on one Oxfordshire manor the villeins were to receive wheaten bread, ale and cheese, and at vespers, bread, ale, pottage (a meatless stew with a basis of peas), flesh, or herrings and cheese. But the staples of such peasants were then vegetables and barley, rye or maslin: dairy produce was a typical source of protein. Apart from occasional pork and bacon, meat was probably a rarity, since beasts were kept for sale, milk, manure and clip. The meat preserved in salt and baked in pies after the customary winter slaughter of old and diseased animals may not have been particularly nutritious. Fish, whose consumption the Church attempted to enforce on the numerous fast days (for example, in Lent), was probably eaten more regularly than meat, as were eggs. The poorest cottagers probably had their chicken-runs, like Chaucer's poor widow in *The Nun's Priest's Tale*. A method approved by peasants of supplementing diets of meat and fish was poaching, immortalised on a truly noble scale in the ballads of Robin Hood.

Langland's remarks suggest that by the 1370s labourers were enjoying a more varied diet, insisting on the provision by their employers of fresh cooked meat or fish, rather than being content with bacon and old vegetables. In 1389 justices of the King's Bench, holding sessions at Brentwood in Essex to enquire into breaches of the previous year's statute of labourers, found many offences. Labourers refused to serve on yearly or half-yearly terms, except with large pay rises, because it was more profitable to work by the day. Day labourers were demanding high rates, including the provision of midday and sometimes evening meals, instead of the customary occasional corn allowance. Rural artisans (such as carpenters, tilers, thatchers) were demanding and receiving similar terms.

Population decline in the later fourteenth century may have helped (like the spread of the rural cloth industry) to improve the living standards of many peasants. The incentives to develop stock-rearing provided a more abundant meat supply. By the sixteenth century beef, veal and mutton were tending to displace bacon and pork as staples. Among better-off peasants, life expectancy may have increased. More men may have afforded to marry younger. Such trends would help to account for the signs of population increase evident particularly in the later sixteenth century. A mass of poor cottagers, possessing few or no land rights, probably remained vulnerable to malnutrition, especially during the seasons when there was little agrarian employment, after harvest failures, and during slumps in rural industry. As population pressed increasingly on resources, the lot of the very poor may have deteriorated.

The high mortality rates (especially in infancy) which characterised rural society may be partly ascribed to diet deficiencies afflicting men, women and children who led lives of wearisome physical toil, and partly to their cramped and unhygienic living conditions[15]. Some indications of the form of later medieval peasant buildings are to be found in many surviving structures, though these have usually been altered and enlarged so many times that it is difficult to discern many of the original features[16]. Manorial court rolls provide some evidence, in agreements between lords and tenants about the erection and maintenance of dwellings. Peasant houses were mainly of wood. The rectangular constructional framework was in some regions provided by 'crucks', pairs of massive posts curving inwards and linking to form the elemental rafters. The wall bays (*c*.5 m by 5 m) between crucks were frequently of wattle and daub, their outer surfaces treated with plaster and whitewash. Floors were earthen, or sometimes flagged. The slanted roofs were of thatch, or moss and turves. Smoke from a central hearth escaped through a gable vent, a nearby door, and windows, when they were not blocked by shutters, cloth or skins. One end of the house might be a byre. The family's scantily furnished accommodation provided modest protection against cold, damp, fleas and tics. Such living conditions are likely to have produced chronic rheumatism and skin diseases, frequent pneumonia, and low resistance to epidemics.

An Italian humanist, Aeneas Sylvius Piccolomini (the future Pope Pius II) actually stayed on an English farm. In his *Commentaries* he gave his appalled recollections of a journey (1435) from the Tweed to Newcastle. At a farmhouse he was served with 'many relishes and chickens and geese', but the wine and wheaten bread he brought with him were looked on as rare luxuries. The womenfolk sat up all night round the hearth cleaning hemp, the men having taken refuge far off in case of a Scottish raid. But the honoured traveller was shown to a chamber strewn with straw by two young women 'planning to sleep with him, as was the custom of the country, if they were asked'. The virtuous Aeneas spent an uncomfortable night alone 'among the heifers and nanny goats, which prevented him from sleeping a wink by stealthily pulling the straw out of his pallet'. Not until he reached Newcastle did he find what seemed 'a familiar world and a habitable country'. Aeneas's account graphically sketches characteristic features of peasant life: lack of refined food and drink, hard female labour, absence of beds, proximity of animals. The household seems to have been a large one. His references to the number of pregnant women and to promiscuity are surprising[17]. But this does seem to have been a relatively prosperous community, needing hands for defence as well as farming.

Some fifteenth-century dwellings mentioned in Worcestershire court rolls have up to four bays. Such large houses might have chambers boarded off or in some regions inserted as an upper floor, and be furnished with stools and a trestle table. Winkhurst House, from Bough Beech in Kent, though only of two bays, has an upper room or 'solar'. Bayleaf Farmhouse, also from Bough Beech (both houses are now at Singleton), was built and extended later, in the fifteenth century, on a grander scale. When finished, it had a central hall of two bays open to the rafters, an adjacent parlour with solar above, and, at the other end, pantry and buttery with solar. In the later sixteenth and early seventeenth centuries the hall was divided horizontally to make a complete upper floor, and a chimney-breast with inglenooks was inserted at one end of the hall. These alterations were characteristic of the new standards found in many new and rebuilt farmhouses, as were tiling, glazing, flagging, panelling and interior plasterwork. Inventories and wills of farmers from the later sixteenth century show some of them to have possessed wall hangings, pewter and brass on cupboard shelves, brass pots and pans, and flaxen sheets and towels.

The families living in such improved dwellings were of the yeomanry, whose standard and style of life was distinctive from that of most countryfolk. The owners of Bayleaf were aping gentility: they had a fine public hall, accommodation for domestic service, and private chambers. Their animals were housed separately and they had an indoor privy. The frontage of Bayleaf, with its decorative symmetry and 'jettying', bespeaks social aspiration.

Evidence about most aspects of the peasantry's social behaviour is fragmentary: regional differences in wealth and tradition, and changes in economy and social structure, make generalisation dangerous. Many peasants may have cared as deeply as nobles about handing on inheritances intact to male issue. Primogeniture was the chief system of inheritance: daughters could sometimes inherit. Peasants made settlements to provide an estate for widows, younger sons and unmarried daughters.

Occasional echoes of merry-making, blasphemies, fast-breaking, adulteries and drunkenness are to be found in the records of the ecclesiastical 'bawdy courts' and denunciations of preachers. Joyous customs such as the celebrations of May Day and harvest homes continued, despite the attempts in the seventeenth century of puritanical, improving superiors to inculcate virtuous habits. Ballads give a probably distorted impression of peasants as rollicking, thriftless and licentious. Merry-makers do not sing mournfully about dark aspects of their lives. The lad who waylaid a maid and, after her taunting that his ale ran low, 'tooke her by the middle small, And gave her more of Watkins ale' provided a perennial subject for a lewd song. But her pregnancy made the moral clear:

For surely Watkins ale,
And if it be not stale,
Will turne them to some bale . . .
When you drink ale beware the toast,
For therein lay the danger most.[18]

Marriage was a serious business, a matter which involved the settlement of livelihood and dowry before the public espousals and communal approval of cohabitation. If the lad had no estate he might not be able to sustain the pregnant lass: if she had no tempting dower he might not want to. In those circumstances, unless she had an abortion, she would burden her family with the temporary loss of her labour, an extra mouth to feed, and communal disapprobation.

Pre-Reformation ecclesiastical institutions had a close relationship with communal relaxation as well as social regulation. The liturgical calendar modified seigniorial demands for work services, which could not be exacted for the long holidays at Christmas, Easter and Whitsun or for the many locally observed saints' days. Carousals on holidays and at 'church ales' often took place in churchyards. Villagers were irresistibly drawn there as a social centre, not only because the church provided shelter and a necessary meeting-place, but probably because they were attracted by the magic of the presence of the Host, and of the consecrated ground. It was safer to solemnise contracts there (including marriage contracts) and, perhaps, to get drunk and fornicate there. But Puritan reformers attempted to separate the sacred from the secular. Their need to denounce alehouses and licentiousness may have been sharpened by their success in removing the practices of communal relaxation from an ecclesiastical setting, a separation which made the task of social regulation harder for the Church.

To what extent peasants were aware of a world beyond their own community, except as a subject for tales unrelated to their own experience and perception of reality, is unclear. Remote communities in thinly populated highland regions may have been particularly inward-looking. But the practice of transhumance in the Borders, bringing together at the summer sheilings communities from a wide radius, gave those pastoralists a broad if remote geographical horizon. Hill farmers drove beasts to urban markets. In more densely populated lowland regions economic and social developments were stimulating dissemination of information about the regional or national background, and, to a remarkable extent, the formulation of concepts among villagers about its relevance to their condition. Especially on great roads and near great towns, there were many kinds of wayfarers deliberately or casually spreading information. There were itinerant ballad singers and entertainers, pedlars and quacks, pardoners selling indulgences, friars on preaching circuits, king's messengers and their grooms, soldiers going to and from ports, pilgrims visiting shrines and recluses, wool brokers and clothiers' factors. John Cote, mason of Loose near Maidstone, alleged that local rebels in September 1381 heard that 'pilgrims who had come out of the north country to the town of Canterbury related in the said county of Kent that John, duke of Lancaster, had made all his *nativi* free, in the different counties of England'.

Villagers too were on the move. They were summoned to hundred courts and archdeacons' assemblies, and, as jurors, before justices of assize and of the peace. They went on pilgrimage, enrolled as archers for the king's service, and carried goods to urban markets and fairs, where sheriffs' cryers broadcast royal proclamations. In the changed economic conditions of the later fourteenth century many villagers temporarily migrated as itinerant labourers, especially at plough and harvest times. Those who found permanent work in towns and other villages may have retained links with their birthplaces. Depopulation had stimulated migration to take up vacant tenements – villagers in the later fourteenth and fifteenth centuries were often newcomers.

This quickening of mobility may have been a factor weakening traditional respect for the local authority of landlords and Church. John Cote's confession shows that an extraordinarily bold and cosmopolitan outlook could be attributed to Kentish commons soon after the crushing of the Peasants' Revolt. On hearing pilgrims' information about the duke of Lancaster 'the foresaid malefactors wished to have sent messengers to the foresaid duke, if it were so or not; and if it were so, then the said malefactors consented one and all, to have sent to the said duke, and him, by their own real power to have made their lord and king of England'. It is significant that some contemporaries believed that the 1381 revolt had been produced by a network of travelling agitators who had organised the commons into a 'great society'. Similar beliefs, with more reason, were entertained about the far feebler Lollard revolt of 1414. Village Lollards of the fifteenth century are characteristic of a rural society whose links were not just manorial or parochial. Here were members of village communities whose religious life was determined by their association with an alternative society. Their secret brethren, perhaps in distant villages or towns, might have no other social bond with them.

The conviction displayed by some peasants in 1381 that national as well as manorial issues mattered to them was not readily lost. In January 1400 inhabitants of several Essex villages took up arms and forced local nobles to hand over to them for summary execution the rebel earl of Huntingdon, who had tried to restore his deposed half-brother, Richard II. The royal council was alarmed by this incident and other lynchings of the rebels, 'against all system of order'. The councillors did not share Archbishop Arundel's relief at being saved by 'blessed bumpkins' (*sancta rusticitas*). During the fifteenth century such fears seem to have subsided. Confrontations between landlords and tenants, when they occurred, savoured less of the Peasants' Revolt, more of the mutual chicanery of disputing landowners. When economic tensions increased in the sixteenth century, councillors and landlords once more began to fear popular insurrection.

There are indications that many common folk retained in the fifteenth century an awareness of the realm's political framework which their ancestors had displayed. The use, on behalf of rebel nobles, of appeals in proclamation and ballad to the cause of the 'common weal' reflects the existence of this wider audience. The many 'southern men', 'northern men' and 'western men' who were marched out of their 'countries' during the Wars of the Roses must have gained a better acquaintance with the realm and the aims of its lords. Remote, incomprehensible Cornishmen imitated them by marching on London in 1497. In the sixteenth century lowland communities – principally in the east, Midlands and south – proved remarkably receptive to the new religious ideals sometimes propagated by elites and Crown, whereas those in the highland regions often proved recalcitrant.

Trade

The numerous markets and fairs functioning throughout the period bear witness to exploitation of agrarian and mineral resources, diversity of handicrafts, comparative prosperity of sections of the population, ease of communications and relative political stability. The fifteenth-century correspondence of the Stonors, a knightly family living in southern Oxfordshire, reveals an intricate network of crafts and trade. Their household was supplied with cloth by a Wallingford tailor; shoes, candles and eggs were purchased from Watlington, lime from Nettlebed, bricks from Marlow, ale from Reading Fair, victuals from Wallingford, Abingdon and Oxford. London supplied cloth, red wine, salt, fish, glass and wax. Some goods were transported thence by barge up the Thames to Henley, a journey of four or five days.

The prosperity, not only of London and other ports, but of inland towns and villages, came to depend partly on the buoyancy of overseas as well as internal trade. In an age when transport was easier by water than land, England was well placed to attract international trade. Its southern and eastern coasts were close to main shipping lanes of western Europe, and most parts of it were fairly accessible from the sea or navigable rivers. Parts of East Anglia and the Midlands, for instance, could be reached from the port of Lynn, by the Ouse and its tributaries.

At the start of the fourteenth century, England was mainly an exporter of raw materials (e.g. tin and lead), and its overseas trade was mostly in the hands of aliens, notably Italians, Germans and Flemings. One native product was a magnet to them: wool. The Flemish and Florentine cloth industries relied on the realm's vast quantities of it, prizing especially fine grades from upland flocks.

The Venetians and Genoese had established a dominant position in the international trade of north-west Europe. Their precocious

Fig. 2 The overseas trade of later medieval England

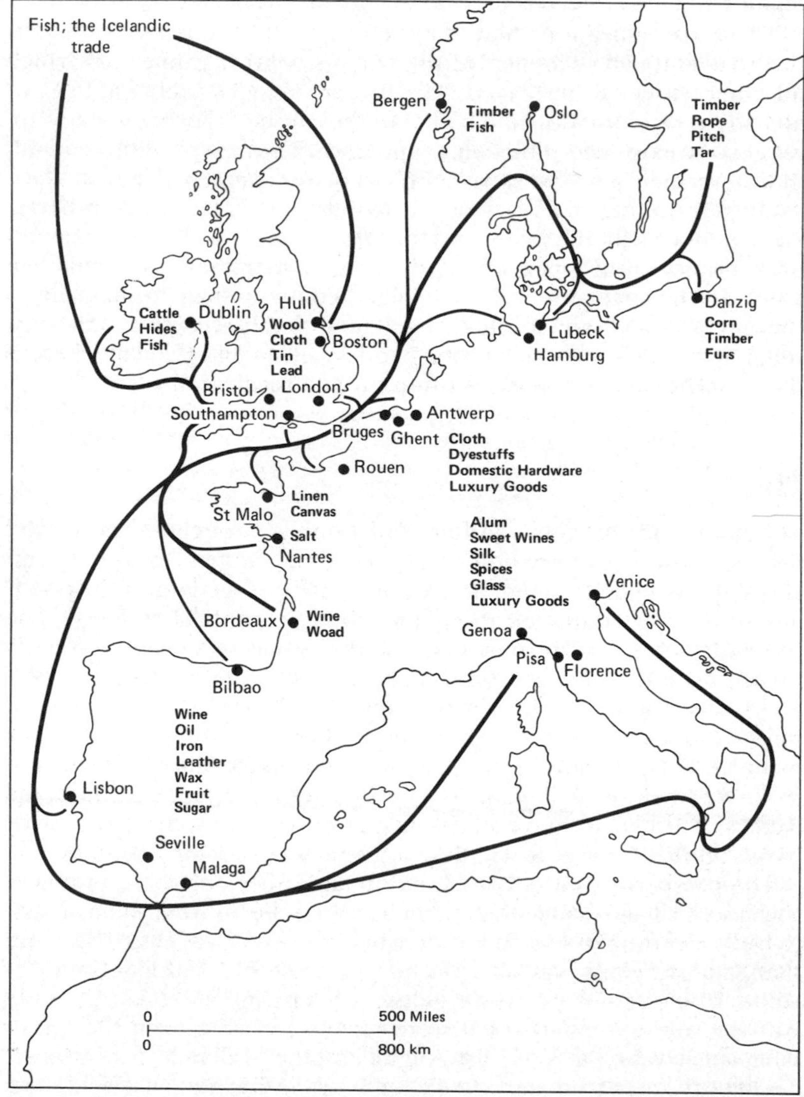

capitalist and commercial techniques enabled them and the Florentines to act as bankers for popes and kings. Their superb maritime expertise enabled them to develop monopolies in the carrying trade between northern seas and the Mediterranean. English kings in the fourteenth and fifteenth centuries often raised loans from Italian companies, and allowed them to export wool direct from London, Southampton or Sandwich, instead of from staple ports designated for the use of native and other merchants. Their expensive imports from the south were prized in rich households: silks and brocades, Mediterranean fruits, wines and oil, Asiatic spices, drugs and perfumes. Their dyestuffs were used in cloth-making.

German traders in Lynn, Boston and Hull were organised (as groups of alien medieval merchants, trading individually, frequently were) in corporate, self-regulating communities, centring their activities on adjacent hostels and warehouses. Their principal residence and trading-depot, the Steelyard, was a prominent feature of London's waterfront[19]. In 1367 over seventy Rhineland, North Sea and Baltic towns, whose merchants combined abroad in fellowships, formed a political alliance, the Hanseatic League. The Hansards shipped fish, corn and raw materials valued in England because native stocks were declining or unavailable, including timber, bow-staves, wax, pitch, tar, furs, hides, iron and steel. The growing English textile industry was to rely on their import of ashes. The Crown exempted Hansards from payment of the customs duty of poundage on imports and exports. On occasion in the fifteenth century kings were prepared to back by diplomatic pressure, or even by force, the demands of native merchants that Hanseatic towns should grant them reciprocal privileges, and that some members of the League should not attempt to exclude them from its German, Scandinavian and Slav trading hinterlands. The English were largely unsuccessful: only in the 1560s did the Hansards lose control of exports of English cloth to parts of the Baltic. The League's privileges in England were drastically curtailed in 1578–9, and the Steelyard was closed in 1598.

English exporters had started to take a larger share of overseas trade in the fourteenth century. The native wholesale merchant 'venturing' cargoes abroad, little concerned with retailing or handicrafts, and sufficiently affluent to lend to king or magnate, becomes a familiar figure. Various factors stimulated enterprise. The recurrent, large-scale, widespread warfare of the fourteenth century, though often disruptive of overseas trade, probably facilitated the accumulation of capital and its investment in trade by an elite of successful merchants (cf. pp. 264 ff). Some profited from Edward III's wool monopolies and borrowings (see p. 266). In 1354 he granted control of the export of wool and woolfells to the Mayor and Company of the Staple. The Company was to remain under the control of rich Londoners, individually carrying on the bulk of native wool exports. The Staplers developed a system of collecting custom and subsidy due from exporters, and paying it to the Crown. They arranged convoys, imposed quality standards and determined conditions of sale to aliens. The Staple was first fixed at Calais in 1363, and finally in 1423. On occasion the Staplers transferred customs revenue or loans direct to the royal treasurer of Calais, for the garrison's wages, and from 1466 assumed responsibility for their pay. The wool staple, so convenient for royal finances, promoted the interests and influence of wealthy wool merchants.

Political factors also promoted the dominance gained early in the fourteenth century by English, particularly London, merchants in Anglo-Gascon trade. Gascony, among other regions of Aquitaine, depended heavily on viticulture. The English Crown's attempts to defend and extend its control there hazarded wine exports to England. But, despite fluctuations in supply and risks of attack at sea, English merchants profited. They could afford to bear the outlay of defence costs. Royal policy assured them of markets by making Bordeaux and its hinterland dependent on England. The wine exports from Bordeaux mostly went there, and in return the English brought the Gascons corn, meat and fish, and commodities purchased in the Low Countries. Early in the fifteenth century it was common for over 200 English ships to dock in the Garonne in the vintage season or early spring, returning home in December or March, laden with wine and other local products.

The customs accounts give the impression that leading merchants in a few ports, such as London, Bristol, Norwich and Lynn, were making most of the profits from overseas trade[20]. It is certainly true that a number of ports were unable to maintain their past prosperity, lacking the accumulations of capital or natural and political advantages necessary to keep their stake in the generally shrinking European markets of the later fourteenth century. But customs accounts give a distorting impression of dependence on overseas trade. Some ports clearly kept a lucrative stake in coastal shipping, smuggling and piracy, for which we lack precise data[21].

Overseas enterprise received its greatest stimulus in the period, and acquired crucial significance in the economy of the realm, as a result of the expansion and diversification of the native textile industry. In the 1330s and 1340s English manufacturers captured the domestic market. Whereas in the decade 1350–60 an average of 5,000 cloths was exported yearly, for the years 1390–99 the total rose to 37,000; 1477–82 to 60,000; 1503–9 to 82,000; 1538–44 to 118,000. By the mid-fifteenth century England was primarily a cloth instead of a wool exporter. The yearly average of woolsacks exported sunk from 32,000 in 1350–60 to 19,000 in 1390–99, and 4,500 in 1538–44.

The rise in the fourteenth century of native textile manufactures was stimulated by the Flemish industry's difficulties. Its prices were pushed up by the huge duties, mounting to about 33 per cent, which Edward III and his successors imposed on wool exports, and it was disrupted by political vicissitudes (see pp. 237 ff). Immigrant Flemish weavers applied and taught their skilled techniques, and in particular helped the development of the industry in Norwich and Coventry. But village production, especially in East Anglia, Essex, the Cotswolds and northern dales, flourished too[22]. Much market production came to be organised and controlled by a new sort of entrepreneur, the clothier, who bought the wool, dispatched it to village artisans for the preliminary processing, paying them at a piece rate, then sold the material to weavers or, as became more common, employed them to finish it for his own sales to cloth merchants. Some sixteenth-century clothiers owned all the plant used in this putting-out system. Some set up their own looms in their tenements and employed journeymen weavers – an embryonic factory system. There was resentment among weavers at the clothiers' increasing dominance over the rural textile industry, giving them control of prices, wages and terms of employment.

The development of rural centres of the industry, undercutting the price of urban weaving gilds' products, may have contributed to the late medieval decay of manufacture in some of its older centres, such as Lincoln, Leicester and Canterbury. Between about 1450 and 1550 textiles shifted out of York and its overseas trade dwindled. The mayor argued in 1561 that

the cause of the decay of the weavers etc. . . . is the lack of clothmaking in the said city as was in old time accustomed, and which is now increased . . . in the town of Halifax, Leeds and Wakefield for that not only the commodity of the watermills is there nigh at hand but also the poor folks as spinners, carders and other necessary work folks . . . have kine, fire and other relief good and cheap which is in this city very dear and wanting.

Much English cloth, produced from coarse lowland wool by inferior weavers, was low-grade: quantities of broadcloths were shipped to Holland and Zealand to be dyed there. Though an English market for high-quality foreign cloth continued in existence, native production posed a further threat to the Flemish industry, absorbing English wool supplies and competing in Low Countries markets.

An incentive to cloth-exporting was the Crown's failure to impose massive duties like those on wool. Italians and Germans were buying up cloth from the later fourteenth century onwards, but an increasing slice of the trade was taken by natives, the value of whose cloth exports was fourteen times greater in 1547 than in 1347. Hull, London, Southampton and Bristol were among the ports booming with cloth. The rise of Bristol in the fifteenth century is particularly notable. The city's excellent land as well as sea communications made it a collecting and distributing centre for inland as well as overseas trade. Bristol merchants bought cloth from Coventry and sold it in London. The city had the advantage of being an inland deep-water port. The diversion of the River Frome through Canons' Marsh enabled ships to dock to the north of Bristol as well as on the Avon to the south[23]. Bristol and Spanish merchants exported cloth woven in the large suburb of Temple Meads, and in Cotswold and Mendip villages, to Castile[24]. They imported large quantities of wine, oil, fruit and salt. Portugal was also a source of southern products: in the later fifteenth century sugar was among the commodities shipped from Lisbon. The trade of southern Irish ports was heavily orientated towards Bristol, and in the mid-fifteenth century Bristol men were predominant in the politically precarious Iceland trade, drawn thither (as to Ireland) by markets for a range of goods and an abundance of fish.

The development of the textile industry stimulated not only the rise of the clothier, specialising in production and domestic marketing, and of the merchant absorbed in 'venturing' goods overseas, but of the large-scale shipowner, profiting mainly from freight hires. William Canynges the younger (d.1474) built up a fleet composing nearly half Bristol's ships. He was a benefactor of the parish church of St Mary Redcliffe, munificently patronised by merchants, a dominating feature

Fig. 3 The rise of the Merchant Adventurers – England's exports of raw wool and cloth 1347–1544.

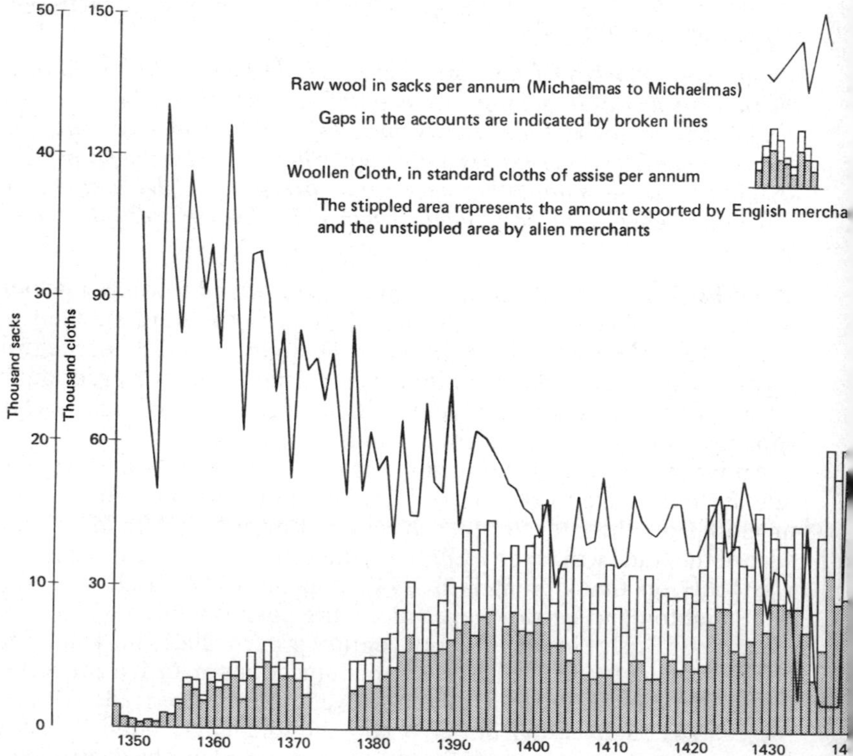

for shipmen arriving on the Avon from abroad[25]. Some of his ships were between 200 and 250 tuns; the *Mary Canynges* was 400 tuns and the *Mary Redcliffe* 500 tuns, considerably more than the 100 tuns, or less, common for English ships in the fourteenth century. Larger and more manoeuvrable craft were built, with two or three instead of one mast, and such additions as a spritsail, topsails and a lateen sail. These developments may have been stimulated by native merchants' need to provide for the transport of bulkier cargoes, often to more distant markets, and to accommodate soldiers and guns for defence.

For, besides the threats from navies of princes in dispute with the Crown and from piracy – which even friendly princes found difficult to suppress – the general contraction of trade in the later fourteenth century and the developing thrust of English merchants in search of 'vents' for native cloth produced friction with foreign mercantile interests. Hansard towns, privileged by the Crown, tried to restrict English access to north German and Scandinavian ports. The Treaty of Utrecht (1474) was an acknowledgement of Edward IV's failure to

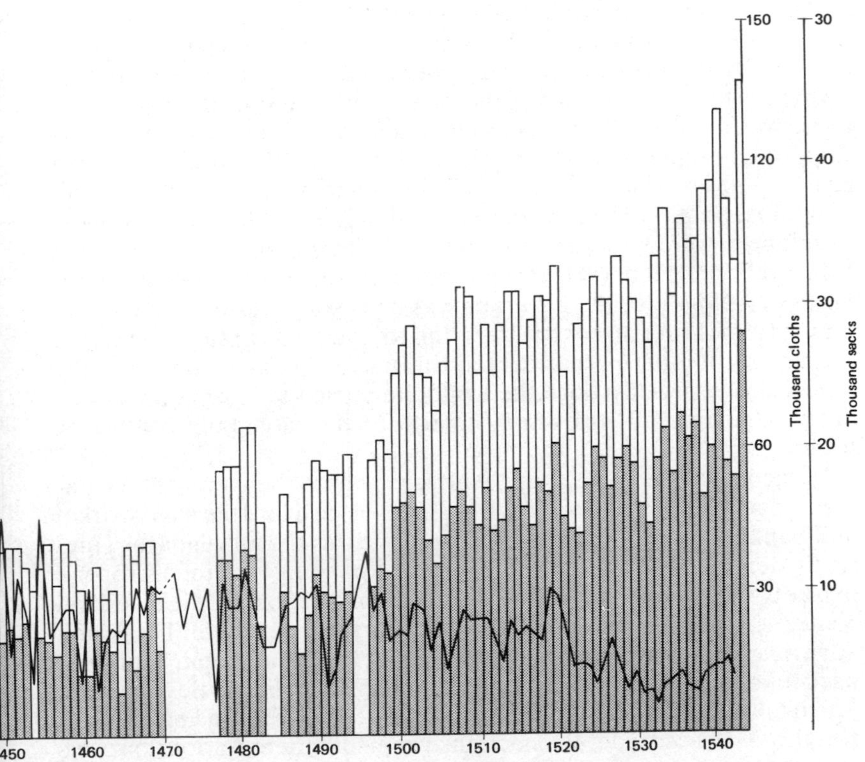

secure reciprocal trading privileges from the League by war. In 1457 Robert Sturmy of Bristol's expedition, venturing in the Mediterranean with cargoes of lead, tin, wool and cloth, had been attacked by the Genoese off Malta. That year, as in 1456 and again in 1463, there were anti-Italian riots in London. Wool exporters to Flanders as well as cloth venturers resented Italian competition. In 1480 Richard Cely's son wrote to him from Calais; 'There is but little Cotswold wool at Calais and I understand Lombards[26] has bought it up in England.' A ban on alien wool exports in 1463 had at least forced Florence to open Pisa to English traders. A wool staple was established there in 1491. Southampton had an important share in the Pisan trade and traded with the Greek island of Chios.

The need of native merchants for mutual support abroad had stimulated the formation of corporate fellowships, such as the 'English Nation' in the Low Countries in the later fourteenth century. By the end of the next century there were groups in London, York, Hull and some other towns, starting to be termed 'merchant venturers', who met as fellowships to concert their trading aims (particularly in cloth exporting) in the Low Countries[27]. By 1483 merchant adventurers in different towns controlled 38 per cent of English exports and more than 66 per cent of imports. In 1486 the common council of London ordained that mayor and aldermen were to elect annually two lieutenants, to act there on behalf of the merchant adventurers' governor in the Low Countries. They were to hold a court on behalf of the fellowship, to determine at which continental marts cloth was to be sold, to charter ships for convoys, fix freight rates and allocate cargo space to individual traders. The governor abroad organised the return convoy. Londoners were predominant in the Netherlands fellowship, and Edward IV and Henry VII recognised their controlling interest over it. Until the mid-1520s the governor was invariably a London mercer; a majority of London adventurers up to the mid-century were too. Merchants of other ports resented this narrowly based control of the fellowship, especially since the Londoners tried to restrict provincial entry. One remedy was simply to ignore the monopoly control by interloping.

In the later fifteenth century Antwerp, where the merchant adventurers had been active since the 1440s, developed into the chief market and banking centre of northern Europe. It was the entrepôt for Hansards dealing with Baltic and rapidly expanding central European markets and, from the 1520s, for Italians preferring the overland routes southwards to sailing the Mediterranean, where Turks and Algerian corsairs menaced. It was a magnet for Spanish merchants too, particularly after the Habsburgs had forged political ties between Spain and the Low Countries. Antwerp became the principal port for English overseas trade. Broadcloths were sold there for local processing, and exported thence to central Europe; best kerseys, finished in Hampshire and Berkshire, were bought there for export to Italy and south-eastern Europe. The phenomenal rise of cloth exporting by native (besides alien) merchants up to the peak years *c.*1550 mainly profited London. Whereas in 1500 less than half English exports were shipped from London, in the 1540s this increased some years to nearly nine-tenths. The international trade of Bristol and Southampton declined. Hull continued to prosper, exporting local cloth in native and Hansard ships to North Sea and Baltic ports. From the 1530s some of the western outports, such as Chester, developed a trade in local cloth with France, Spain and Portugal.

London's domination of overseas trade was to be partially eroded in the second half of the sixteenth century, when established trade routes were dislocated, new ones sought, and the total value of exports rose but modestly. In 1551 the bottom fell out of the Antwerp cloth market, after the preceding year's sales glut[28]. They never picked up to 1540s levels, since Antwerp was entering a phase of general decline. In 1572 it was sacked by the Spaniards, and from 1585 blockaded by Dutch fleets. English merchants perforce sought to establish direct trading links with the more distant buyers and suppliers of products they had previously purchased at Antwerp marts. Extensions of their trading range were facilitated by the commercial decline of old Hanse and Italian rivals, and naval decline of Muslim corsairs in the Mediterranean. In 1579 Londoners, among other merchants, formed the Eastland Company, chartered by the Crown, and modelled on the Merchant Adventurers' Company, to which many of its original members belonged. The aim of the new company was to regulate the Scandinavian and Baltic trade which they had succeeded in establishing at Elbing: in the early seventeenth century Danzig became their staple port. In the 1580s the Adventurers had at last established secure Dutch and German 'vents', respectively at Middelburg and at Stade near Hamburg.

In the 1570s English merchants once more ventured in the Mediterranean on a larger scale, particularly voyaging to the duke of Tuscany's port of Leghorn. In 1581 London merchants founded the Levant Company, shipping from ports of the Turkish Empire mainly Indian and Indonesian nutmegs, indigo, pepper and drugs, in return for kerseys, tin, and silver specie. But after the Dutch started to use the Cape of Good Hope route to the Far East in 1597, the Levanters concentrated on local products: silk, cotton, mohair, yarn and dyestuffs. The East India Company, formed by over a hundred London merchants to challenge the Dutch, received its charter in 1600, and began trading in the Indian Ocean the following year. Excluded by the Dutch from many Far Eastern markets, it imported and sold through Europe great quantities of south Indian and Sumatran pepper[29].

The proliferation of native merchants' overseas markets in the later sixteenth century helped the outports' trade[30]. In the early seventeenth century London never accounted for as much as two-thirds of English exports. The demand in southern markets for fine, finished cloth, and the competition from Dutch textiles, stimulated production changes. The industry was able to meet the challenge more easily because religious refugees from the Low Countries and France, streaming into Kent, Essex and East Anglia in the 1560s and 1570s, established the manufacture of worsteds and semi-worsteds, which contemporaries referred to as the 'New Draperies'. Old weaving centres such as Colchester and Canterbury revived with the introduction of specialised production of cloth, lace and thread. In 1583 more than 4,000 persons were employed in cloth manufacture in Norwich. By the middle of James I's reign broadcloths had ceased to dominate the export market.

The scale of English overseas trade had come by the end of our period to dwarf that in the fourteenth century, but many features emerging then were still recognisable. London had increased its predominance. Despite the new importance of southern markets, the bulk of trade remained with north-west Europe. Textiles had become established as the staple export: by the 1540s cloth manufacture was an important factor in agrarian exploitation in many regions, and rural as well as urban communities were dependent on the buoyancy of overseas markets.

In the second half of the sixteenth century their marketing difficulties and the vicissitudes of alien rivals gave native merchants incentive and opportunities to win their ancient battle for control of English overseas trade, though abroad they now faced formidable Dutch competition. English merchants showed themselves more adept than hitherto in using Italian accounting and capitalist techniques, but theirs still remained predominantly family businesses or small working partnerships within the regulating framework of the late medieval type of fellowship. There was not yet a mass move by landowners to invest in overseas enterprises. One sphere in which some showed a marked interest in the 1570s was transatlantic exploration, in search of mineral wealth or promising areas of settlement, under royal monopoly patents. The attempts to settle Roanoke Island (1585–7), a difficult undertaking, petered out as capital and maritime resources were sucked into privateering against the Spanish Empire. But soon after peace was made in 1607 the *Susan Constant*, *Discovery* and *Godspeed* sailed into Chesapeake Bay under the auspices of the Virginia Company. The Virginian colony was well established by 1611, and in 1614 exported some of its recently planted Trinidad tobacco. Some 19,000 lb reached England in 1617, 50,000 in 1618. Imports direct from Asia and America, nil in 1600, were only 7 per cent of the total in 1621. But they represented the beginnings of a new era in English enterprise and commercial expansion.

Urban government and society

The characteristic English trading centres were small towns probably with a range of about 500 to 1,500 inhabitants, and large villages with a few hundred inhabitants. In the early fourteenth century there may have been nearly as many as 2,000 flourishing markets. In medieval Kent ninety-six places had the right to hold them. New markets were founded there in the late fourteenth and fifteenth centuries, and in Lancashire in the sixteenth, but the numbers functioning had sunk to fewer than 800 by 1640. Many ceased due to the effects of the Black Death, others as a result of changing patterns of economy and settlement in the sixteenth and seventeenth centuries.

The majority of leading towns (sixteen out of twenty-five in 1334, fifteen in 1524) were in eastern England, the rest divided equally in 1334 between the Midlands, South and West. England lacked impressive cities. According to Thomas Starkey:

As touching the goodly building of cities and towns, I trow in the world there is not less regard than here in England. . . . Methought when I came first into Flanders and France that I was translated, as it had been, into another world — the cities and towns appeared so goodly, so well builded, and so clean kept.

Just over half a century later, in 1588, Giovanni Botero wrote: 'in England, London excepted, although the country do abound in plenty of all good things, yet there is not a city in it that deserves to be called great.' In the early fourteenth century London may have had approaching 50,000 inhabitants. According to the 1603 ecclesiastical census, there were 148,747 adults in the diocese of London. York may have been the only other city at the start of our period with over 10,000 inhabitants[31]. In 1524 Norwich was the largest provincial city, with between 12,000 and 12,500 inhabitants: not more than twelve or fourteen others exceeded 5,000. A small proportion of the population (perhaps between 5 and 10 per cent) lived in towns.

In the twelfth and thirteenth centuries there had been a rapid evolution of distinctions in urban organisation and status. The free borough (*liber burgus*) contrasted with the *villa mercatoria*, the village granted merely the right to have market and fair days by its lord and the Crown. Essential to the *liber burgus* was the grant of burgage tenure, freeing its inhabitants from conventional servile and feudal obligations. Holders of burgage tenements could sell or bequeath them at will. As communities of burgesses, they gained the right to appoint bailiffs, who received the lord's precepts, and to have a borough court, replacing the seigniorial jurisdictions of manor, hundred and honor courts. Boroughs sought from lord and Crown (often identical) exemption for their merchants from tolls imposed elsewhere, and, from the Crown, extensions of their own officials' and courts' powers in place of those exercised by sheriff, escheator, royal judges and justices of the peace[32].

Fully-fledged urban governments exercised virtually viceregal powers. Their officers discharged responsibilities towards lord and sovereign, raising rents and levies to pay one or the other the annual fee farm, and subsidies and loans; mustering soldiers when required; supervising militia for defence and policing; imposing murage to repair defensive walls and gates and pontage to maintain bridges. Since outsiders often thought of big towns as rampant with extortions, immoralities and outrages, their governors were anxious to uphold good fame and order by enforcing fair trading as defined in municipal ordinances, suppressing riots and unlawful assemblies and fellowships, punishing violence, theft, drunkenness and prostitution, and composing quarrels. Processions of civic officers and freemen ranged in an order of precedence were public acts to affirm and define authority. hierarchy, community. The governors felt morally obliged to promote the godliness, welfare and good fellowship of those in their lordship by personal example as well as public rule. A Coventry ordinance of 1497 prescribed for civic officers abstention from adultery as well as usury. John Stow described how, in bygone Augusts, in a large tent near Clerkenwell, before the mayor, aldermen and sheriffs of London

were divers days spent in the pastime of wrestling, where the officers of the city, namely, the sheriffs, sergeants, and yeomen, the porters of the king's beam or weigh-house . . . and other of the city, were challengers of all men in the suburbs, to wrestle for games appointed, and on other days, before the said mayor, aldermen and sheriffs, in Finsbury field, to shoot the standard, broad arrow, and flight, for games.

Urban authorities were particularly concerned to control food prices and quality. The mayor of London periodically set prices for grades of ale, wine, meat, poultry and fish. Shops, market and cargoes were inspected, and penalties imposed, such as destruction of goods and loss of citizenship, on those trying to exploit consumers outrageously. During the sixteenth century the authorities became especially concerned about the effects of widespread poverty and unemployment, exacerbated by rising prices, trade recessions and harvest failures. London and some other leading towns (notably Norwich) grappled with the problems by widening the scope of civic control, often in advance of the provisions of statutes and royal ordinances. They combined various measures, such as conserving grain stocks for the poor, punishing and expelling the immigrant unemployed who flocked into towns in times of dearth, licensing resident beggars, and instituting compulsory rates to provide poor relief – most ambitiously, to maintain hospitals where the young might learn a craft, the able-bodied be forced into disciplined work, and the sick and old succoured. Such schemes were sometimes rendered ineffective by lack of finance: the urban poor remained highly dependent on the elite's generous private charity.

Town governments also took responsibility for maintenance of amenities, such as conduits, public conveniences and thoroughfares. The condition of streets was constantly threatened by the rutting of ironshod cartwheels and overladen carts, by the reluctance of residents to fulfil paving obligations, and their propensity to extend tenements into the way. Public nuisances had to be checked, such as the noise of blacksmiths working by night[33], the stench from butchers' offal and from the indiscriminate dumping of rubbish. Edward III wrote to the mayor and sheriffs of London in 1357 that, when rowed past the city

> *we have beheld dung and laystalls and other filth accumulated in divers places and have also perceived the fumes and other abominable stenches arising therefrom, from the corruption of which, if tolerated, great peril as well to the persons dwelling within the city, as to the nobles and others passing along the said river* [the Thames] *will ensue.*

The virulence of urban epidemics may have increased concern with measures of public health.

By the fifteenth century the government of London had been impressively elaborated on a characteristic medley of ancient offices, courts and assemblies. The mayor was elected annually by the existing mayor and aldermen, from two of their number recommended by Common Council. The election was subject to formal royal approval, and the mayor took office on 28 October. There were twenty-four aldermen, one for each ward into which the city was divided[34]. An alderman presided over his wardmote, which met to enquire into breaches of the peace and civic residential ordinances (e.g. concerning fire and health regulations). The alderman presented offenders in the Mayor's Court: he had some powers of arrest. From 1402 onwards aldermen were selected by mayor and aldermen from four candidates chosen by the freemen in the wardmote: they held office in the fifteenth century on average about fifteen years. Two sheriffs – recipients with the mayor of all royal writs, letters, ordinances, proclamations and injunctions concerning civic affairs – were selected annually from among the aldermen, one by the mayor, the other by Common Council. This assembly of citizens' representatives, summoned by the mayor, met occasionally to scrutinise the conduct of some civic officers, and to ratify formally measures affecting the city's constitution[35].

The mayor held the office of escheator: he and the sheriffs and aldermen presided over courts dealing with commercial offences in the markets. The Court of Mayor and Aldermen held in the Outer Chamber of the Guildhall heard common law actions of debt, detinue of goods, breach of covenant, slander, malicious prosecution and assault, as well as actions on city ordinances. On admission to the freedom of London (for which membership of an officially recognised craft gild was a prerequisite), the citizen swore not to bring actions at common law against a fellow citizen outside the city courts, if such suits were within their competence, except by the mayor's licence[36].

London's high degree of gradually acquired jurisdictional self-sufficiency was an important factor working to keep its internal politics disentangled from those of neighbouring 'Court' and 'country'. By a charter of incorporation the Crown granted Bristol in 1373 the right to appoint its own sheriff and justices of the peace: other leading towns were to follow suit[37]. Urban elites may have valued such privileges partly as a weapon in their jurisdictional disputes with neighbouring authorities. Some towns had liberties within their bounds. At Exeter the Bishop's Fee was a cause of friction. The bishop had his own court leet there, his tenants were unwilling to shoulder the common burdens of citizenship, and fugitives from arrest by municipal officers sought refuge within the fee. The York members of parliament sued in vain in 1584 for the city's craft gilds to have the right to 'have search of such artificers as do dwell within the close'. This, the dean and chapter's liberty, included not only the Minster Garth (cathedral close), but parts of the busy trading streets of Petergate and Stonegate.

London authorities disliked the jurisdiction exercised by officers of the Household. They resented the marshal's claims to powers of arrest, and the existence until 1550 of his liberty of Southwark, whither fugitives from civic justice fled. These issues were among the causes of tension between city and Court in 1376: the alleged contempts of the Londoners produced a royal command to depose the mayor and elect another in his place. The citizens' exalted views of their constitution were no protection against royal wrath. In 1392 Richard II removed mayor and sheriffs from office and had them imprisoned. A commission enquiring into defaults in the city's government adjudged its liberties forfeit to the king. He appointed two of his knights successively as wardens to rule the city, as well as new sheriffs and aldermen. Later in the year he restored London's privileges – at a stiff price, including a corporate fine of £100,000.

Royal and noble interventions in urban affairs, with the object of gaining financial pickings, clients and prestige, were facilitated by characteristic kinds of urban tension, as well as frictions over jurisdiction, and common disorders. In London, probably first in the late 1370s, the draper John Northampton led a political movement, in which the smaller masters of non-victualling gilds figured prominently, against the domination of civic government by rich merchants and the privileges of victualling gilds. This movement may have been responsible for the civic ordinance of 1376 which gave gilds instead of wardmotes the right to elect common councillors and the latter the right to participate in mayoral elections. In 1382, when he was mayor, Northampton struck at the London fishmongers' attempt to uphold a sales monopoly, decreeing that all kinds of fish brought by strangers to the city should be sold by them or their servants and no one else. But in 1383 his opponent, the grocer Nicholas Bramber, was elected mayor; plots and disturbances by Northampton's partisans led to his condemnation and imprisonment by the Crown, despite his attempt to enlist the maintenance of his patron, John of Gaunt. The electoral powers of Common Council were swiftly reduced. Anti-oligarchical movements in other towns in our period likewise failed to achieve permanent success. It was difficult to maintain congruity of political aims and a sense of popular unity among producers engaged in a great variety of small-scale handicraft enterprises. Rich merchants, on the other hand, tended to a politic recognition of their common interest in keeping control of civic government. Though magnates and gentlefolk sometimes supported agitation against them, Richard II's backing for oligarchy in London in the 1380s foreshadowed the Tudor conviction that the richest merchants were the best instruments of social control. A Privy Seal letter of Henry VIII (1509) confirmed the recent Exeter ordinance that the council of Twenty-Four should be a self-coopting, not an elected body, and prescribed that the councillors should normally sit for life. The wealthiest and most influential citizens, they selected the mayor and other leading officials from among themselves and appointed and directed all lesser officers.

An ancient form of association which often had close connections with urban government was the gild – an association of neighbours, fellow craftsmen or merchants pledged to mutual amity or support, by endowing chantries for soul masses and intercessions to patron saints. The borough community was sometimes associated in a gild merchant as well as in a religious fraternity, regulating mutual commercial besides spiritual concerns. At High Wycombe the borough community, meeting in the Gild Hall, controlled membership of the Gild Merchant, framed its ordinances and safeguarded its privileges. Larger towns had a variety of craft gilds[38]. The success of a gild depended on its ability to enforce corporate control of manufacturing and trading conditions on 'merchants strangers' who brought their wares to market, and on those whom it insisted should be its members, the producers and shopkeepers in the town. Little is known of the organisation of many craft gilds. The surviving elaborate ordinances of rich merchants may not have always been paralleled among poorer handicraft-men. A highly developed gild regulated such matters as standards of quality, sale prices, the places where gildsmen might sell (for example, over their shop counters rather than in the streets or markets), the terms of training for apprentices and of admission to full gild membership (mastery). The gild's searchers had summary powers of justice: in some gilds, they were the effective rulers during their year of office, in others a governor, master or warden was placed over them. The senior officers held court to judge misdemeanours and compose disputes between masters, sworn not to sue brethren in other courts.

A gild's standing was highly dependent on its relations with urban government. The authorities sometimes suppressed gilds (especially of poor craftsmen), limited their jurisdiction, and, in the case of victuallers, brought down their prices and forbade their masters to hold civic office. On the other hand, admission to the mastery of recognised gilds and to citizenship often came to be closely interlinked. Gilds looked to civic authorities to uphold their monopolies. In 1463 the wardens and many others of the Mistery of Bladesmiths came into the Chamber of the London Guildhall and presented a petition on behalf of their fellowship to the mayor and aldermen, complaining that 'divers Foreign Bladesmiths as well of foreign towns as of places nigh the suburbs of the said City' were selling 'untrue and deceivable' goods at inns and other private places 'to the hurt of the common people'. The fellowship requested that civic ordinance be made obliging these 'foreigners'[39] to sell openly at Leadenhall on market days. In 1495 the London White Bakers complained that Stratford bakers had been breaking the ordinance that foreign bakers should sell bread at assigned places and remove their carts by noon. Instead they had been bringing spare horses, and hawking bread in the streets in every part of the city, 'to the great prejudice of the Fellowship of White Bakers'. The latter also alleged that Stratford bread had been proved underweight and 'unseasonable of paste'.

Craft production was highly domesticated. Each master and his men worked in a shop in his home, and sold goods at its street front over counters which could be raised as shutters. The Shambles, the medieval butchers' row at York, still gives a good impression of the setting. A few specialised industries were carried on in separate premises: tanning in bark houses, horn soaking in horn pits. The work force consisted of journeymen[40] and apprentices. In wealthy trades few of the latter could expect ever to afford the gild fees and expenses, and the capital investment needed to set up as a master. Some artisans lived in the master's household, subject to his paternal authority. As gildsmen, such employees were also treated as servants, owing loyalty, deserving protection, but ineligible to elect to or hold executive office, and consequently unable to share in the fixing of their own wages and other conditions of employment, or in judging their fellows' disputes with masters.

This horizontal division in gilds with a wealthy elite sometimes produced the formation of two fellowships, a controlling one composed of masters, a subordinate one of artisans. The London Mercers Company, a rich and powerful merchants' fellowship, was divided in the fifteenth century. Its chief executives were the master and three wardens, elected for a year. Associated with them from 1463 was the Court of Assistants, which met weekly to discuss current business, and scrutinised wardens' nominations for their successors. Court members were elected from and by the whole body of freemen, who met as a legislative assembly at least four times a year. Those 'outside the livery'[41] (e.g. servants overseeing orders and shipments, and handling goods in warehouse or at counter) were excluded from all this, though a few apprentices might look forward to being liveried one day. The employees had their own fellowship, 'the bachelors', with its eight masters, its own livery, feast days, and barge to make a brave ceremonial show on the Thames. Nevertheless, the lesser members of gilds often showed resentment at their lack of control, and younger masters resented the dominance of older cliques, former senior officers.

In his will of 1407, Robert Appulby of Lincoln bequeathed five marks to its Leathersellers Gild, 'to buy a pipe of wine and drink it at their first banquet after my decease'. Gilds set out to foster the communal spirit of their brethren. The gild year began on its saint's day: the fellowship processed to Mass and held a general assembly. Brethren who absented themselves when feasts and obits were celebrated were liable to fines. Crafts kept up their pride and spirits by vying with one another in turning out magnificently equipped for civic processions and in mounting ingenious and colourful tableaux for the edification and entertainment of royal visitors. A wealthy gild was in some towns responsible for staging one of the 'miracle plays' performed in the streets, often on the feast of Corpus Christi in May or June. The Host would then be solemnly perambulated: the plays, organised and paid for with funds levied on gildsmen by the gild's elected pageant master, were mounted on accompanying carts, or on stationary ones at the Host's traditional stopping-places.

The stately dining-halls of London livery companies are reminders of their medieval predecessors' pomp. The latter delighted in feasting nobles off their fine silverware and entering their names on the fraternity's bede-roll. Nearly all the existing London livery companies' halls are post-medieval, but parts of Merchant Taylors' Hall, including a fine kitchen, are of fifteenth-century construction. The most impressive remainder of a medieval craft's hall is that of the York Mercers Company's Fraternity of the Holy Trinity. The mercers, the wealthiest York company, received a royal charter in 1430, and in 1581 one constituting them as the Society of Merchant Adventurers, with a sales monopoly of overseas goods in the city, except for fish and salt. Their hall, built 1357–68, is 89 feet long, with a firestead added *c.*1420, 'to make the hall more commodious for feasting'. Its undercroft housed the Hospital of the Holy Trinity, an almshouse for impoverished mercers, and the chapel, restored in 1411 (since rebuilt) had as many as five altars.

There were often bitter disputes between craft gilds, over manufacturing and trading demarcations, takeover bids, and precedence in civic ceremonies. But, on the whole, gilds generated remarkably little factiousness. They provided orderly mechanisms for the conduct and resolution of conflicts of interest. Concerned with the minutiae of production and retailing within the town, they did not necessarily represent the principal economic interests of its elite, in notable instances composed of merchants with mutually supportive stakes in far-flung wholesale trading, whose individual membership of various crafts might be nominal, a social chore rather than a vital business interest.

Masters and craftsmen whose livelihood depended on domestic handicrafts frequently identified as the common threat, not another gild, but 'foreign' competitors, such as clandestine producers and retailers within the town, strangers from the suburbs, country towns and abroad, who often thumbed their noses at gild ordinances. During the 1381 revolt Londoners and their rural allies hunted down and massacred Flemings in the city, testing their Englishry by their manner of pronouncing 'bread' and 'cheese'. London chroniclers of the fifteenth century considered anti-alien manifestations there worthy of note. In 1424, for instance, 'the 14 day of February divers bills were cast in London and in the suburbs of the same against merchants strangers'.

Gilds made important contributions to social cohesion, especially in larger towns. The personal relationships and loyalties, and the religious and secular obligations of most medieval townsmen probably focused on their parish rather than on the exalted elite of mayor and aldermen. Parochial living was on a scale familiar to the many who were villagers by origin. But urban living, in streets often housing a dense population, many working premises and an odd, haphazard mixture of ranks, produced special tensions and causes of nuisance. Many inhabitants were not bound in obligations by tenurial and communal ties, characteristics of village life. But the tendency of men of the same craft to live and work in a parish was probably an important element of social cement. Gilds also helped to reconcile the realities of urban parochialism with the needs of urban government. They were instruments of civic control. In 1415 London tailors' servants and journeymen were living in a house in Garlickhithe and using 'a livery or clothing at their unlawful assemblies'. After they had committed assaults, one of whose victims was a master tailor, the mayor and aldermen summoned the craft's Master and Wardens 'to answer for their want of control over their servants and journeymen', and 'ordained that henceforth the servants of the said mistery should be under the rule and governance of the Masters and Wardens, like servants of other misteries'.

The links between civic government and leading gilds had grown close in London by the fifteenth century. In 1467 the masters and wardens of the livery companies, and in 1475 the liverymen, were granted the right to attend elections of mayors and sheriffs[42]. But there were limits to the social and economic effectiveness of gilds. Many inhabitants were outside their jurisdiction: female servants, tapsters, water-carriers, porters, lightermen, scavengers, hawkers, prostitutes. There were about 1,200 gildsmen in York in 1548, less than half the adult male population. In London the freemen were at most a third of that category in the fourteenth century, a quarter in the sixteenth. The growth of urban markets and suburbs then (above all, in London) made it harder for gilds to enforce their economic regulations. Some faced stiffer competition from the rise of rural industries. But though many gilds decayed, amalgamated or disappeared, others kept their vitality. Handicraft-men continued to value protective association: great Elizabethan merchants modelled the organisation of new overseas companies on gilds, and basked in the mastery of ancient prestigious ones, as a traditional means of promoting fellowship, of exercising charity, and of sharing in the control of urban properties and institutions. For gilds chartered by the Crown as perpetual corporations were becoming considerable landowners through their administration of charitable bequests. Their reputation for honest and efficient administration made them popular with founders. On 16 April 1510, John Colet, dean of St Paul's, was mentioned at the Mercers' Court of Assistants; their agents had 'had Communication with him for the foundation of the grammar school which he intendeth to found and make in Paul's Church Yard, and the same Master Dean was very glad that he might have with us Communication thereof in whom he purposeth to put all the Rule and governance of the said school'. Colet amortised land to the company in return for their perpetual obligation to maintain the school according to the articles of foundation.

Mr Cornwall's study of the 1522 musters and 1524–5 subsidy returns for the towns of Buckinghamshire, Rutland and Sussex has demonstrated the general tendency of wealth as well as power to concentrate in the hands of small urban elites[43]. Little is known about the lives and occupations of the large numbers of wage-earning labourers and of the poor who lacked almost any personal possessions, but there has been some social analysis of the elites in leading towns, notably of London's in the later Middle Ages by Professor Sylvia Thrupp[44]. Monopolisation of senior civic office by a few dynasties with outstanding wealth was not characteristic of great towns in the period. Such office could entail burdensome responsibilities. It provided some patronage: there was a growing number of bureaucratic offices, particularly in the administration of city courts and funds (recorderships and chamberlainships). But cities did not possess large revenues which it was worth while to control: they were funded in piecemeal fashion, by *ad hoc* taxes, court fines, fees for the enrolment of documents under the mayor's seal, payments from alien merchants, tolls on carts, landed benefactions for particular purposes.

Election to senior office was a recognition not just of wealth, but of esteem for the gild or company in which the elect had attained eminence. The comparatively wide distribution of wealth in the larger towns' mercantile elites, their mutual interest in regulating handicrafts and retailing, and in maintaining fellowship in sometimes hazardous overseas ventures, sustained traditions of fraternal solidarity, rather than dynastic singularity. John Stow displayed a Londoner's disapproving scorn for a bourgeois architectural folly, too Florentine a pride. Sir John Champneis, alderman and mayor of London 'built in this house a high tower of brick, the first that I ever heard of in any private man's house, to overlook his neighbours in this city. But this delight of his eye was punished with blindness some years before his death.'

There are indications that in some leading towns there was insufficient dynastic continuity for hereditary control of office. Professor Thrupp has calculated that the average number of heirs male surviving London citizens in direct descent between *c*.1300 and *c*.1500 was about one. Barely two-thirds of aldermen's sons followed their fathers into trade. Between 1481 and 1509 the proportion of freemen admitted by London mercers and grocers who were sons of members was only 9 per cent. One reason for this lack of continuity (producing dependence on immigration from lesser towns and the country) may have been high mortality rates caused by urban epidemics. The *Liber Albus*, an official record of London's privileges and customs, was compiled in 1419 by the recorder, John Carpenter, because of the effects of epidemics:

When, as not infrequently happens, all the aged, most experienced and most discreet rulers of the royal city of London have been carried off at the same instant, as it were, by pestilence, younger persons who have succeeded them in the government of the city have been often at a loss from the very want of such written information.

Awareness of the virulence of urban epidemics may have been one reason for the frequent 'rustication' of London merchants – their purchase of country estates, to which they often retired, opting out of gild and civic responsibilities, bringing up their heirs as gentlefolk, and bequeathing urban tenements and rents for chantry and charitable purposes. Some, of immigrant origin, may have rusticated because they had long dreamed, amid the bustle and clamour of counters and wharves, of rural birthplaces. Many London merchants made bequests to their native towns and villages. The fifteenth-century bridge over the Avon at Stratford was built by a local man, Sir Hugh Clopton, who became mercer and mayor of London.

Well-to-do merchants assimilated readily into rural society because, as members of a propertied, hierarchical urban elite, they thought of themselves as a kind of nobility[45]. They were sometimes wealthier than gentlefolk. In the 1379 poll tax ratings, the mayor of London was assessed to pay the same as earls, its aldermen and the mayors of 'great towns' as barons, their officers and 'the great merchants of the Kingdom' the same as knights, and 'sufficient merchants' as landed esquires of lesser estate.

The life-style of leading merchants reflected an awareness of superiority. The Venetian observer of *c*.1500 noted the display by Londoners 'not occasioned by its inhabitants being noblemen or gentlemen; being all, on the contrary, persons of low degree, and artificers who have congregated there from all parts of the island, and from Flanders, and from every other place'. At a civic banquet to celebrate the election of new sheriffs, he says: 'I observed the infinite profusion of victuals, and of plate, which was for the most part gilt; and amongst other things, I noticed how punctiliously they sat in their order, and the extraordinary silence of everyone.' According to Russell, usher to Humphrey of Gloucester (who had political connections with the Londoners in the 1420s) merchants were fit to dine with gentlemen. An usher should seat next to esquires, besides gentlemen 'well nurtured and of good manners', city bailiffs, 'worshipful merchants and rich artificers'. The great hall of Crosby's Place, now removed from Bishopsgate to Chelsea, gives a good impression of the noble style to which the London elite aspired. Built *c*.1466 by Sir John Crosby, draper, warden of the Grocers Company, alderman and sheriff, in plan, size and decorative scheme it is indistinguishable from a baronial hall, and in fact was rented by a prince, Edward IV's brother Gloucester. Merchants also imitated and outshone gentlefolk by enlarging and beautifying parish churches and friaries. The notebooks of William Worcester, a fifteenth-century gentleman who honoured his Bristol and Coventry ancestry, contain his measurements of fine city churches. His romantic feeling for wild, mysterious places and their legends was balanced by the curiosity, excitement and pride which great towns aroused in him. He had new heroes, besides the traditional saints and knights – those towering Bristol entrepreneurs, Robert Sturmy and William Canynges (see pp. 34–6).

Rich burgesses were drawn into sometimes close individual relationships with kings, nobles and gentlemen, not only because of the latter's domestic and financial needs, and the opinions and tastes which they shared with them, but because of merchants' sense of a need for 'national' support in their undertakings, and growing confidence in their significance as an estate of the realm. These mercantile attitudes are reflected in an anonymous poem, *The Libel of English Policy*, a propaganda piece written between 1436 and 1438. The author argues that 'the true process of English policy is to cherish merchandise, keep the admiralty, that we be masters of the narrow sea'. The Crown should attack Flemish trade in the interests of English merchants. The author's aims, and his precise knowledge of overseas trade, make it very likely that he was a Londoner engaged in exporting wool or cloth to the Low Countries. It is interesting that he claims 'gentle' contacts: Lord Hungerford had overseen the poem, and a tale illustrating Edward III's concern for his merchants' overseas interests was derived from a 'scroll' lent him by 'a good squire, in time of parliament'. The tale is part of his ingenious rewriting of English history on the thesis that successful kings' foreign policies had been motivated by the desire to 'cherish merchandise'.

The argument presented in the *Libel* assumes the existence of opinions among gentlefolk that their prosperity was in some measure linked with that of overseas merchants. There is one well-documented case from the fifteenth century (unlikely to have been unique) of a business partnership between a country gentleman and a merchant. In 1475 William Stonor married Elizabeth Riche, daughter and widow of wealthy London merchants. Stonor procured Cotswold wool to be shipped from London by apprentices of the Staple merchant Thomas Betson, a connection of the Riches, who handled the sales from Calais. The partnership was dissolved after Elizabeth's death in 1479. By the mid-sixteenth century gentlefolk were prepared to seize commercial chances: when the Russia Company was founded as a joint-stock venture in 1555, its partners included seven peers, fourteen knights (of whom four were aldermen), eleven esquires and eight gentlemen.

The author of the *Libel*'s fondness for historical interpretation is not surprising in the light of the circulation of the 'chronicles of London'. These anonymous annals in English, intermixing national and urban events, were written for and by London merchants, the first dating from Henry IV's reign. Why Londoners should have made these often random jottings and copyings is not clear – highly prejudiced as they are (e.g. against aliens), they are not polemical works. The chronicles are testimony to the London elite's belief that national history mattered to them; perhaps they felt the need to record events because they were proud of London's role, but sensed (like John Carpenter) that memories of it were threatened by characteristic family discontinuities.

There was published in 1516 the *New Chronicles of England and France*, a skilful redaction of London annals and other sources much used by writers of English national history in the century. The author was Robert Fabyan, draper, alderman and sheriff of London[46]. The London grammar schools may have helped to produce in the second half of the fifteenth century not just literate Londoners, but *literati* whose modish tastes set trends for gentlefolk. William Caxton, London mercer and merchant adventurer, did not hesitate to preface his translations for gentlefolk with his own thoughts. Some of his publications were intended for bourgeois readers as well. Three of his translations were undertaken at the request of London citizens, one an alderman, the other two mercers, and some of his addresses were not made just to gentlefolk, but to 'all men', 'every man living', 'every cristen men'[47]. The merchant venturers at Antwerp in the 1520s, patronising William Tyndale, showed themselves in the van of religious reform. Sixteenth-century Londoners were long justly proud that their city had produced an internationally famous paragon of piety, learning and courtliness – Sir Thomas More[48].

The assimilation of the life-style of the *haute bourgeoisie* to gentility gave added incentives for gentlefolk to visit and reside in leading towns. There they could hear good sermons, buy books, savour the fare and talk of witty citizens[49], and find rich husbands for their daughters[50]. There were, besides, traditional needs and attractions which drew them to towns – to offer at shrines, to shop, to attend assize sessions and episcopal courts. London was assuming the signficance of a capital for business and pleasure. Even a Venetian could be impressed (*c*.1500):

In one single street, named the Strand, leading to St Paul's, there are fifty-two goldsmiths' shops, so rich and full of silver vessels, great and small, that in all the shops in Milan, Rome, Venice and Florence put together, I do not think there would be found so many of the magnificence that are to be seen in London.

Specialised medical treatment could be found in and near London. Two shire knights, up from Berkshire and Wiltshire in 1376, sought out a friar in Fulham skilled in magical healing, pretending they had urinary complaints by exhibiting chamber-pots. Those who had business in law courts or government offices at Westminster went up to town. The Court was often to be found nearby. In the sixteenth century London was the centre of the land market, and London financiers were selling Crown and other estates.

By our standards medieval London was insignificant in size. Its walls enclosed less than a square mile. The country was only a few minutes' walk from any part of the city. Chaucer may have been thinking of twilight sounds and sights at his Aldgate chamber when he wrote of Troy:

The Warden of the Gates began to call
To those outside the city, left and right,
Bidding them drive their cattle, one and all,
Inside, or stay without till morning light.

Down the street from Aldgate, within the walls, was the farm where John Stow (born 1525) had as a boy 'fetched many a halfpenny worth of milk, and . . . always hot from the kine, as the same was milked and strained. One Trolop, and afterwards Goodman, were the farmers there, and had thirty or forty kine to the pail.' Braun and Hogenberg's map of London (1572) appears to show that the Minories was still a rural area, and that, despite the linking of villages to the city by suburban ribbon-developments, it was still engulfed by fields.

Despite London's rural aspects, its wonders and treats were a magnet for countryfolk. There was London Bridge, with its drawbridge, traitors' heads and limbs, shops, and treacherous race. There was the Tower of London, its keep allegedly the work of Julius Caesar, with its royal menagerie and ordnance. Westminster Abbey had the shrine of St Edward the Confessor, relics of King Arthur, royal tombs, and waxwork effigies (later known as 'the ragged regiment') of kings and queens. Strangers were flustered by hawkers crying a multitude of wares; the noisy, roguish street atmosphere is well caught in the fifteenth-century ballad, *London Lickpenny*. At Paul's Cross, crowds heard sermons, sometimes of national importance, sometimes in the

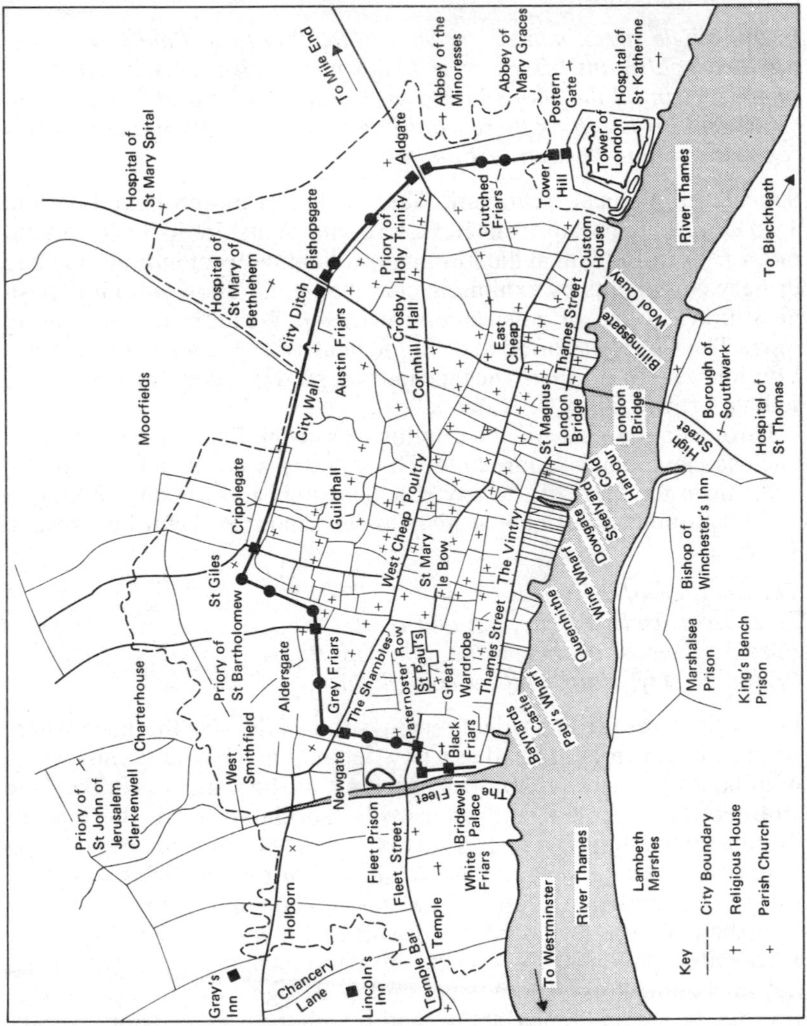

Fig. 4 Later medieval London

presence of princes. More dubious pleasures were to be found in Southwark, in the fields across the river, where, near the bishop of Winchester's house, accomplished girls ministered in the 'stews' (bath-houses)[51].

Many gentlemen acquired a taste for London life in their youth, when an increasing number kept terms in one of the Inns of Court, in the suburbs west of the walls, where attorneys were trained and licensed[52]. Admissions to Gray's Inn rose from 200 in the 1530s to 799 in the 1590s, and 1,265 between 1611 and 1620. Justice Shallow mused: 'I was once of Clement's-inn, where I think they will talk of mad Shallow yet . . . the very same day did I fight with one Sampson Stockfish, a fruiterer, behind Gray's-inn. Jesu, Jesu, the mad days that I have spent'[53]. Gentlemen visiting town stayed either in public hostelries – Sir Richard Waldegrave and Sir William Wingfield, when members of parliament for Suffolk in 1382, were at the 'Swerd of the Hoope' in Fleet Street – or in private inns which they rented or owned. Nobles' residences lined The Strand, between The Temple and Charing Cross, with gardens stretching down to their river gates. Chaucer's Trojan nobles dallied in city gardens and bowers[54], and Schasek remarked in 1466 on London's 'elegant gardens'.

By the early seventeenth century there was a clearly defined London 'season', which began in the autumn, reached its climax at Christmas, and was over by June. It was a commonplace that landowners moved to London to save the charge of country housekeeping: in 1632 about 250 peers, baronets, knights and gentlemen were prosecuted in the Court of Star Chamber for having been found there after a proclamation had ordered them home. They also flocked into provincial towns.

The gentry influx contributed to the enormous expansion of late Elizabethan and early Stuart London. Services increased to cater for their needs, and residential suburbs sprang up where they resided, in the villages of Clerkenwell, Islington, Hampstead and Chelsea. But the main reason for expansion (incidentally increasing the business and amenities which attracted the gentry) was London's overseas trade. The population growth made the governing tasks of corporation and gilds more difficult. The city became overcrowded, life there more anonymous: it underwent a major physical transformation, as the sites and gardens of the former religious houses were built over. Stow's *Survey*, written in the 1590s, records regretfully many of the changes.

The needs of London's increased and more prosperous population, particularly its food needs, had become a major factor in stimulating and determining patterns in the English rural economy by the end of our period[55]. The bulk of its imports necessitated the development of the Queenhythe dock to supplement Billingsgate, and the creation of a common market at Smithfield in 1615, because of the inadequacy of the old ones at Newgate, Cheapside, Leadenhall and Gracechurch Street. Garden plots within and near the city, supplying butter, milk, poultry, eggs, fruit, vegetables, pork and bacon, brought high returns.

Stow wrote of Goodman's son, who inherited his father's Minories farm and 'let out the ground first for grazing of horses, and then for garden-plots, and lived like a gentleman thereby'. Country towns like Hitchin, High Wycombe and Croydon prospered by processing the capital's local grain supplies, their mealmen (who supplied milled grain) and maltmen stocking up the London retailers. But the Port Books show that Kent was the city's great granary. Grain shipments also arrived from Sussex and east-coast ports such as Yarmouth, Wells, Hull and even Berwick. The butter on the Londoner's table might not have come from a Whitechapel or Lambeth farm, but by shipment from Whitby.

Crucial factors in economic and social developments in our period were the two phases of general demographic change – one of sharp decline in population in the later fourteenth century, the other of increase during the sixteenth century, neither of which trends is easy to quantify. The decline triggered off by the plague pandemic resulted in the shrinkage or disappearance of numerous villages. As demesne cultivation became unprofitable, landlords abandoned it in favour of leasing, and commuted villein services for rent. Smallholders benefited from low rents on long leases, and labourers from high wages and relatively stable commodity prices. Landlords and tenants were in some places able to profit from demand for timber, stone, tin, lead, iron and coal, enhanced as a result of increasing national wealth. More generally, they profited from the rising demand for English wool and cloth. The development of a much larger and more broadly based native textile industry not only revived the fortunes of a number of towns and ports, but created many flourishing centres of rural production. Dr Schofield's analyses of the comparative distribution of wealth suggest that its geographical shifts may have been caused partly by the changing emphasis from agrarian to pastoral and textile production[56]. In 1334, according to the assessments for lay subsidy, the twelve richest counties lay in a belt on a south-west to north-east axis stretching from Gloucestershire and Berkshire to Norfolk and the Parts of Holland (Lincolnshire). But in 1515 the wealthiest counties comprised two well-defined blocs, a south-western one (Gloucestershire, Somerset and Wiltshire) linked by Berkshire to an eastern one[57]. These blocs included prime wool- and cloth-producing regions.

Later medieval economic changes promoted the rise of a class of rich peasants holding larger tenements, whose emergence is reflected in the changing usage of the word 'yeoman'. Surges in wool and cloth production were also among the factors stimulating the rise of a greater number and variety of mercantile entrepreneurs. They organised regional production and trade, challenged aliens in markets at home and abroad, and attempted to dominate civic gilds and corporations. The pretentious life-style of such *nouveaux riches* was certainly resented by the inheritors of wealth and power, who tried to curb their political aspirations in shire and town (cf. pp. 132 ff). But the process of acquisition by yeomen and merchants did not generate much conflict, for they were the legatees rather than the precipitators of economic change, cashing in on the ruin of the old agrarian system, and on the rising demand for native wool and cloth, a demand which was probably a principal factor in raising the level of national wealth. Excluding London, the average increase in the wealth of the shires between the early fourteenth century and early sixteenth was almost exactly threefold[58].

Fig. 5 The distribution of wealth, and its rate of growth, in later medieval England

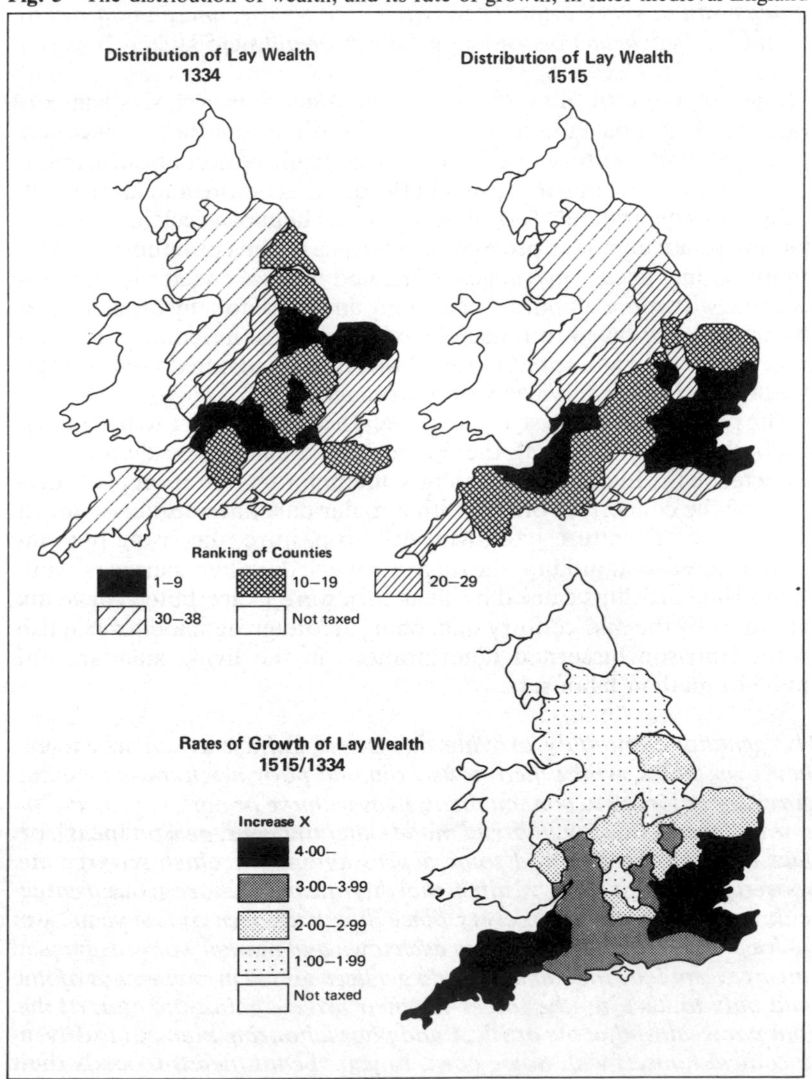

From the later fourteenth century onwards indications of dietary and housing changes suggest that many labourers and smallholders were also benefiting from this increase. The Elizabethan William Harrison was to note old villagers' comments on the remarkable improvements in village housing and furnishings which had taken place in their lifetime, such as

the great (although not general) amendment of lodging, for (they said) our fathers, yea, and we ourselves also, have lien full oft upon straw pallets, on rough mats covered only with a sheet, under coverlets made of dagswain or hap-harlots (I use their own terms), and a good round log under their heads instead of a bolster or pillow[59].

At the other end of the social spectrum, numerous ecclesiastical corporations and noble families were receiving diminished landed incomes in the fifteenth century. Yet, after the difficult period of adjustment from demesne farming to leasing in the decades before and after 1400, there are comparatively few signs of friction between such landowners and the relatively more prosperous sections of the community. Noble political and social privileges remained unchallenged, if perhaps asserted with more elaborate ceremony and more touchy insistence on the precedence owed to rank. Moreover, nobles' hereditary incomes were augmented as a result of the Crown's particular need to buy their military and other services with patronage.

The population increase of the sixteenth century seems to have been the basic factor producing the commons' hardships and discontents, reflected in the indignation of some contemporary writers at profiteering, and the concern of others with popular unruliness. Since so much subsistence agriculture had given way to pasture, the rising population suffered commodity shortages, especially when harvests were poor. The hardships caused by dear corn were exacerbated for many labourers by the mid-century slackening in foreign demand for English cloth. Harrison discerned deteriorations in the living standards of mid-Elizabethan labourers:

The gentility commonly provide themselves sufficiently of wheat for their own tables, whilst their household and poor neighbours in some shires are enforced to content themselves with rye or barley, yea, and in time of dearth, many with bread made either of beans, peason [peas], *or oats, or of all together and some acorns among, of which scourge the poorest do soonest taste . . . albeit that there be much more ground eared* [cultivated] *now almost in every place than hath been of late years, yet such a price of corn continueth in each town and market without any just cause (except it be that landlords do get licences to carry corn out of the land only to keep up the prices for their private gains and ruin of the commonwealth) that the artificer and poor labouring man . . . is driven to content himself with horse corn, I mean, beans, peason, oats, tares, and lentils. . . . If the world last awhile after this rate, wheat and rye will be no grain for poor men to feed on.*

In other ways, according to Harrison, landowners showed an anti-social determination to profiteer:

Men of great port and countenance are so far from suffering their farmers [*tenants*] *to have any gain at all that they themselves become graziers, butchers, tanners, sheepmasters, woodmen . . . thereby to enrich themselves and bring all the wealth of the country into their own hands, leaving the commonalty weak.*

Thomas Wilson made a similar point in 1600:

Gentlemen, which were wont to addict themselves to the wars, are now for the most part grown to become good husbands [*husbandmen*] *and know* [*as*] *well how to improve their lands to the uttermost as the farmer or countryman, so that they take their farms into their hands as the leases expire, and either till themselves, or else let them out to those who will give most; whereby the yeomanry of England is decayed and become servants to gentlemen*[60].

Wilson exaggerated the decay of yeomanry: many of them were prosperous 'graziers, butchers, tanners, sheepmasters, woodmen', whom gentlefolk were keen to emulate or squeeze for larger rents. The determination of the gentry to profit rather than suffer from the effects of dearth was matched by their vigour in ruling the complaining commons, suppressing disturbances, maintaining enclosures against trespass and destruction, regulating conditions of employment and punishing vagrancy. Social tensions united the governing ranks in defence of their wealth, in a period when religious antagonisms threatened to divide them. This was not the only way in which the economic conditions of the sixteenth century had a politically unitary effect. The continued concentration of English overseas trade on north-west Europe, and its expansion in the first half of the century stimulated the remarkable growth of London in size and wealth, as did its development as a capital. The city dominated much of England's domestic as well as overseas trade. The needs of its population and of other growing centres and regions in the lowlands induced fuller exploitation of resources in the more remote and agriculturally ill-endowed highlands. The regions north and west of the Humber and Severn, in 1515 by far the poorest as they had been in 1334, were showing signs of growth by 1625[61]. The coal mines of the north and west, according to Harrison, 'may suffice for all the realm of England, and so must they do hereafter indeed, if wood be not better cherished than it is at this present'. Most cities and towns on the coast were dependent for fuel on the coal trade: he expressed surprise that the iron works of Sussex and Hampshire were using local charcoal: 'I think that far carriage be the only cause'. By his period we can begin to speak plausibly of a 'national economy' in which all parts of the realm were in significant respects integrated.

Notes

1. J. Cornwall, 'English population in the early sixteenth century', *Economic Hist. Rev*. xxiii (1970); T. H. Hollingsworth, *Historical Demography*, Hodder and Stoughton 1969, 79 ff; H. E. Hallam, 'Population density in medieval fenland', *Economic Hist. Rev*. xiv (1961–2).
2. For some comparative estimates of their wealth, see pp. 133, 139–40; and for the general roles of leading lay landowners in society, chapter 4, *passim*.
3. The forms of manorial accounting evolved in the late twelfth and thirteenth centuries. In the sixteenth century account books finally replaced rolls, and English superseded Latin as the language of account.
4. A *valor* sometimes consisted of a complete file of ministers' accounts for all the estates, bound up together.
5. The accounting year ran from the eve (29 September) of Michaelmas.
6. Demesne (from *dominium*, lordship) was that portion of an estate customarily exploited exclusively for the lord by his bailiffs and labourers, distinct from the tenements held of him by peasants. Demesne arable and meadow was sometimes separate from their holdings, sometimes interspersed with them.
7. Stock-rearing was limited by the need to provide crops for human consumption, at the expense of hay for winter feed.
8. In the Midlands one characteristic size of selion was about 10 m by 150 m.
9. Plague disappeared from England by 1671. It was first termed 'the Black Death' in the sixteenth century: the name derived from black-and-blue marks caused by subcutaneous haemorrhaging.
10. London experienced bad outbreaks in 1563, 1593, 1603 and 1625. Between 1579 and 1603 Norwich had one every five years: in that of 1579–80 at least a third of its population is said to have died.
11. Tenants of Waltham Abbey attacked it during the 1381 revolt, and in 1410 and 1423 bondmen in Waltham, Nazeing, Epping and Loughton leagued together to refuse services to it.
12. The term had been applied to freemen of some standing, e.g. to freeholders and superior servants. The Squire and Canon in *The Canterbury Tales* are both accompanied by a 'yeoman', the former's impressively attired as a forester, the latter 'full of courtesy'. There are two impressive incised gravestones of foresters in Blanchland Abbey, displaying some of the foresters' accoutrements described by Chaucer – swords, bows and arrows, and hunting horns.
13. Whereas at the end of the thirteenth century the majority of villeins may not have had more than the ten or so acres necessary (without fen or woodland resources) for subsistence, by the sixteenth century there was a significant minority of tenants with over fifty acres – 8 per cent in Norfolk and Suffolk.
14. *A Dialogue Between Reginald Pole and Thomas Lupset*, ed. K. M. Burton, Chatto and Windus 1948.
15. Peasant households were not consistently large: they apparently averaged 4·75 persons in the later sixteenth century, consisting of the family and servants of one married couple. But living quarters were not normally big, and in villages which experienced a population growth in the sixteenth century, new cottages were probably crowded into the existing streets, so as not to impinge on valuable agricultural land.
16. At the Weald and Downland Open Air Museum in Singleton, Sussex, attempts are being made to restore structures to their original forms.

17. The fact that the women did not hide for fear of rape by the Scots suggests that they were not trying to avoid conception. Perhaps pregnancy by a noble guest who had magical properties (Aeneas's bread and wine were treated as charms by pregnant women) was considered especially lucky.
18. From the broadside ballad *Mother Watkins ale*, printed *c*.1595.
19. Cannon Street station occupies the site.
20. Southampton profited from its use by Italians and Londoners; Yarmouth ships and seamen plied for Norwich merchants, as did those of Hull for York ones; Yarmouth and Grimsby were centres for fish distribution.
21. Numerous small west-country and eastern ports relied on fishing and some piracy (for which Fowey became notorious), and, in the fifteenth century, profited from cloth-exporting.
22. Heavy broadcloths were produced in the west country and East Anglia, lighter kerseys in smaller quantities in Yorkshire. In Oxfordshire and Berkshire finer kerseys were woven: according to John Stow (1598), the late earl of Oxford rode to his house 'by London stone' with a retinue of eighty gentlemen and a hundred yeomen 'in a livery of Reading tawney'.
23. Millerd's map of 1673 shows sailing ships in the heart of the city, at both Avon Bridge and Frome Bridge.
24. The Anglo-Castilian treaty of 1466 boosted trade.
25. Canynges's tomb and realistic effigies are in the church. In continuance of a fifteenth-century benefaction, the mayor and corporation of Bristol attend a commemorative service for Canynges there on Whit-Sunday. Posies are carried, and the floor is strewn with rushes.
26. A name applied generically to Italians in northern Europe.
27. By 1500 a Bristol fellowship of venturers was meeting, concerned with cloth exports to southern Europe, Ireland and Iceland.
28. The number of shortcloths exported from London fell from 132,767 in 1550 to 112,710 in 1551 and to 84,969 in 1552.
29. Unlike the older sort of companies, such as the Staplers and Merchant Adventurers, whose members traded individually under an agreed set of regulations, the East India Company, which had high overheads, remained a joint-stock company, whereas earlier joint-stock companies, the Russia Company (1555) and the Levant Company, had not, once their trade began to flourish.
30. The growth of London's population also helped. In the early Stuart period Kentish, south-coast and East Anglian ports played an important part in shipping the capital's food supplies. Whereas they had provided 17,776 quarters of grain in the famine year 1586, the figures for 1615 and 1624 (not scarce years) were around 60,000.
31. Few English towns found it necessary to increase the area enclosed by their walls in the later Middle Ages. Bristol was an exception. Coventry's grandiose set of walls was completed in the fifteenth century.
32. For notable towns denied borough rights by their lords, see pp. 183–5.
33. In Chaucer's *Miller's Tale* Gerveys, an Oxford smith, is up before first light sharpening share and coulter.
34. Increased to twenty-five in 1394, when Faringdon Ward was divided, but not in 1550, when the city at last acquired jurisdiction over Southwark and made it into the ward of Bridge Without.
35. The number of common councillors was fixed at ninety-six in 1384: there were nearly twice as many by 1549.
36. The ancient city court of Husting acted as a land registry and exercised probate over citizens' wills. Appeals on writs of error from decisions in secular London courts were heard by special royal justices sitting in the church of St Martin's-le-Grand.
37. York (1396), Newcastle (1400), Norwich (1404), Lincoln (1409), Hull (1445), Southampton and Nottingham (1449), Coventry (1459), Canterbury (1463).
38. The terms 'gild', 'craft', 'mistery', 'trade' or 'occupation' were used interchangeably: in the later sixteenth century 'company' became popular. There were eighty-

eight London gilds in 1377, 111 in 1423. There were fifty-seven in York in 1415 and at least sixty-four in 1579.

39. The term was used to describe inhabitants as well as visitors ineligible for membership of a recognised craft gild and for citizenship.
40. Artisans paid by the day (French, *journée*).
41. Leading gilds of great towns, increasingly in the fifteenth century, received royal charters confirming their privileges, sometimes with extensions of control outside their town, and recognising them as perpetual corporations, able to sue and be sued as such throughout the realm. Another frequent privilege was the right to wear a livery.
42. The twelve great merchant companies which monopolised civic office in Tudor London were the mercers, grocers, drapers, fishmongers, goldsmiths, skinners, merchant taylors, haberdashers, salters, ironmongers, vintners and clothmakers.
43. 'English country towns in the fifteen-twenties', *Economic Hist. Rev*., xv (1962–3). The most numerous class everywhere were labourers taxed on wages of £1 a year: in larger towns those earning over £20, forming 5 per cent or less of the population, held two-fifths or more of the property.
44. *The Merchant Class of Mediaeval London* (Univ. of Michigan Press, 1948). Professor Hoskins has suggested that in the early sixteenth century some 35 to 40 per cent of many urban populations may have been employed in three fundamental groups of trades: clothing, victualling and building (*Provincial England*, Macmillan 1963, p. 80).
45. The autobiography of Margery Kempe (cf. pp. 361–7) throws light on bourgeois sense of rank, and on the status of burgess's daughters and wives in Lynn. Many York craft ordinances assumed that some members would be women: in 1529 a civic ordinance gave general sanction to the practice of widows carrying on their husbands' business.
46. Two other known Londoners who wrote chronicles were the skinner William Gregory (d. 1467) and Richard Arnold (*fl*. 1473–1521), apparently a haberdasher.
47. The first datable books printed in England, by Caxton at Westminster, were *The Historie of Jason* and *The Dictes or Sayengis of the Philosophres* (1477).
48. His London reputation is inferred from the play *Sir Thomas More*, written by Munday, Chettle and probably Heywood (*c*.1595–6) and probably revised by a professional scribe, Dekker and Shakespeare (*c*.1600–1). It was never performed, but its emphasis shows a desire for populat appeal among Londoners. I owe thanks to Ms Penelope Winder for discussing the play.
49. According to Sir Thomas More's account of Mrs Shore in *The History of King Richard the Third*, it was not just her physical charms which captivated her lover Edward IV. She was the daughter of John Lambert, mercer and sheriff of London. Her husband, she alleged, was impotent.
50. According to Professor Thrupp, whereas a quarter of the wives of fourteenth-century London aldermen whose parentage is known were daughters of country landowners, the proportion rises to a third for the fifteenth century.
51. Suburbs often became the haunts of rogues because they were outside urban jurisdiction. Chaucer's Canon and his Yeoman dwelt 'In the suburbs of a town . . ./ Lurking in corners and blind lanes, where robbers and thieves naturally [by kinde]/ Hold their secret fearful residence,/As men that dare not show their presence'.
52. The Society of Lincoln's Inn, whose records date from 1422, still preserves much of its Tudor and Stuart plan. The Old Hall, the most ancient part of the buildings, was completed in 1492.
53. *Henry IV*, pt 2, iii, 2.
54. When Chaucer described life in Troy, he probably had London in mind. His contemporaries believed in Geoffrey of Monmouth's fiction that it had originally been called 'Troia Nova'.
55. By 1515 a group of counties not far from London (Kent, Surrey, Middlesex, Hertfordshire, Essex and Suffolk) formed one of the two most prosperous blocs in the realm. By 1515 the assessed lay wealth of London was almost fifteen times

greater than in 1334, accounting for 8·9 per cent of the national total, as compared with 2 per cent in 1334. Middlesex had become by far the wealthiest county by 1515 (R. S. Schofield, 'The geographical distribution of wealth in England, 1334–1649', *Economic Hist. Rev.*, xviii, 1965).

56. Schofield, *op. cit.*, 507 ff; and for further references to distribution of wealth among counties in this chapter.
57. See p. 60 n. 55. The range in the wealth of counties had increased markedly. In 1334 most of them had an average value of between £10 and £30 per 1,000 acres; in 1515 they were spread fairly evenly over the range £10–£100.
58. Average county assessments for lay subsidy rose from £21.50 per 1,000 acres in 1334 to £66 in 1515.
59. From *The Description of England* (1587), ed. G. Edelen (1968). Dagswain and hap-harlots were coverlets of coarse, shaggy material.
60. From *The State of England Anno Dom. 1600*, ed. F. J. Fisher (Camden Miscellany, vol. xvi, Royal Historical Society 1936).
61. In general all counties north of the Wash had failed even to double their lay wealth between 1334 and 1515. Lancashire was the poorest county in 1515, with land worth on average only £3.80 per 1,000 acres.

Chapter 3

The central institutions of government

Crown and commonwealth

By the fourteenth century England was an ancient kingdom. Men thought and argued about its government within a context of tenacious inherited notions and ideals, which helped to regulate and narrow areas of conflict, and to colour and modify thrusts of change. Henry VIII's replacement of papal by royal supremacy over the English Church was to be facilitated by existing views of the exalted nature of English kingship, which he was able to exploit. 'By divers sundry old authentic histories and chronicles', the Act in Restraint of Appeals, 1533, declared,

it is manifestly declared and expressed that this realm of England is an Empire . . . governed by one supreme head and king . . . unto whom a body politic, compact of all sorts and degrees of people, divided in terms and by names of spiritualty and temporalty, be bounden and ought to bear, next to God, a natural and humble obedience.

Such views drew conviction from the sacred nature of kingship, demonstrated in a coronation ritual based on Anglo-Saxon ceremony. The anonymous author of a life of Henry V (reigned 1413–22), addressing Henry VIII in 1513, stressed, as important qualities of kingship, religious as well as secular virtues. Besides justice, these were continence and humility. One of the most significant lessons in royal conduct he drew from Henry V's life was that, between his father's death and his marriage 'he never had knowledge carnally of women'. Yet, like Christ, the king who humbled himself was exalted above men. The Act of Praemunire, 1393 (see p. 337), had declared that 'the crown of England . . . which has been so free that it has had no earthly lord . . . is immediately subject to God in all matters at all times touching the regality of the same crown, and to none other'.

The exalted nature of the Crown had been enhanced not only by its sacredness, but by its supposedly imperial past, described by Geoffrey of Monmouth and popularised in subsequent Arthurian romances, culminating in Sir Thomas Malory's *Le Morte D'Arthur*, published by William Caxton in 1485 and by Wynkyn de Worde in 1498 and 1529. At the battle of Agincourt (1415), Henry V wore a crown 'serclée comme impériale couronne', according to the Seigneur de St Remy's account[1], and in 1529 Henry VIII's embroiderer was paid for decorating sixty-two coats of red cloth for the royal bodyguard with 'the rose and the crowne imperiall'. This background of inherited notions sustained royal authority in Church and State in the sixteenth century against new ideological challenges, from the Roman Catholic Church of the Counter-Reformation and, more basically, from presbyterians who did not accept the mediatory authority of kings between God and mankind, any more than they did that of priests.

The emphasis which Henry V's 1513 biographer placed on the qualities of service appropriate to kingship is linked with another important strand in traditional thinking about it: emphasis on royal obligations to lieges. The concepts of the 'community of the realm' and the 'common wealth' had been able to develop precociously because England was a comparatively small kingdom, in which by the fourteenth century ethnic and juridical unity had been attained, with coincident boundaries, to a remarkable extent, and in which language was following the same trend. Scotland, Wales and Ireland lacked the same conjunction of features promoting political coherence. Englishmen from all parts of the realm shared the conviction that kings had a duty to promote their *common* wealth, not just prized regional and sectional privileges, a conviction which was strengthened by the remarkable development of parliamentary institutions in the fourteenth century. Sir John Fortescue wrote in the 1470s that 'though his [the king's] estate be the highest estate temporal in the earth, yet it is an office, in which he ministereth to his realm defence and justice'. James I (1603–25) told parliament in 1610 that 'every just king in a settled kingdom is bound to observe that paction made to his people by his laws, in framing his government agreeable thereto'.

Kings acknowledged their obligations in the oaths they took at the coronation. Rebels often publicly tried to justify their rising by claiming that the Crown was failing in its duties to the community. Rulers recognised the strength of their subjects' feelings about royal obligation, but what they considered immediately expedient for the Crown's interests sometimes led them to flout public opinion. Accusations of royal tyranny and injustice were not uncommon in the fourteenth and fifteenth centuries, but generally a rough harmony between the Crown's and community's interests was attained with much less difficulty than under the Norman and Angevin kings of the twelfth and thirteenth centuries. Above all, the evolution of parliament, though sometimes the arena for dispute, provided an unrivalled instrument for publicly adjusting the rights of ruler and regional élites.

By the mid-fifteenth century there was a consensus of opinion, accepted by kings, that the Crown ought not to supplement or abrogate laws, or raise subsidies from men's income and chattels, without the advice and consent of the 'community of the realm'. Such views were expounded in the writings of Sir John Fortescue (*c*.1390–*c*.1479), composed in the 1460s and 1470s after a long, distinguished career as Chief Justice of the King's Bench and councillor to Henry VI

(1422–61, 1470–1). A precise expression of his views on the constitution is to be found in the treatise *The Governance of England*. Natural law, he considered, was embodied in the English common law, which had anciently evolved from the form of compact made between rulers and people. This had laid the foundation of a mixed polity, partly monarchical and partly popular (*Jus politicum et regale*). The monarchical element was the king's will, the popular element his consultation, in matters of law-making and taxation, with the 'community of the realm'. It was the king's duty to govern, but his commands vitally affecting the lieges' rights only had legal force when they were registered by due, prescribed process. What makes Fortescue's treatise so significant is the character and standing of the writer: he professed to find no conflict of interest between his roles as royal bureaucrat and country gentleman, but used his expertise gained in the king's service to argue that the English monarchy's traditional power was grounded on the approbation and cooperation of the community.

What Fortescue's treatise conceals is that the consensus of opinion about the constitution which it genuinely reflects was not handed down from time immemorial, but achieved in compromises after sharp conflicts between kings and subjects, particularly from the reign of Edward I (1272–1307) onwards. His grandson Edward III (1327–77) had eventually conceded the necessity of seeking prior consent in parliament to raise subsidies on wool and land, in order to help finance his costly wars. Edward III's grandson Richard II (1377–99), though recognising in principle parliamentary participation in the grant of subsidies and making of statutes, was willing to risk confrontation with elements of the 'community of the realm' because he believed that what Fortescue would have termed the 'politic' component in government was encroaching on the sphere of the 'regal' component's activities. In the replies extracted by Richard from some of the judges in 1387, which he made a parliament endorse ten years later, he tried to establish that recent parliamentary initiatives had restricted the rightful exercise of royal prerogative, and indeed, in their coerciveness towards himself, were treasonable. In 1388 the Crown in parliament (under the pressure of his opponents) condemned these Ricardian views, and again in 1399, after his deposition.

Richard II had rightly perceived, though his reactions may have been maladroit, that the 'politic' tail was on occasion wagging the 'regal' dog. The Crown had become politically weakened because its financial commitments, in a period when incomes from land were tending to decline, outweighed its customary, increasingly inflexible resources. Edward III's decline into indifference in the 1370s, Richard II's minority, the combination of problems converging on Henry IV (1399–1413) impelled peers, royal officials, knights of the shire and parliamentary burgesses to form alliances and take common initiatives in parliament, to reform and supervise the conduct of the king's government. But they did not have revolutionary constitutional aims, even though the measures they took might be interpreted as encroachments on royal prerogative. Their aim was above all to ensure that the king and his officials governed efficiently. If they thought the king was capable of managing his affairs and servants well, they were content that he should appoint his leading councillors and officials, and handle his revenues and patronage how he wanted, without naming his councillors to parliament and agreeing to public undertakings that they should be consulted over some kinds of business and handle them in certain ways. But on a number of occasions subjects felt boldly impelled to resort to such expedients.

Typical of some of the 'reforming' knights of the shire may have been Sir Thomas Hoo, one of the members for Bedfordshire in the 'Good Parliament' of 1376. He gave the chronicler Thomas Walsingham, monk of St Albans Abbey, an account of a speech he made in one of the Commons debates early in that exciting session, urging his colleagues to win the Lords' support for the reform of government. Sir Thomas was an elderly well-to-do landowner, with estates in Bedfordshire, Hertfordshire and Sussex, who had played a worthy part in county administration, and was respected by the monks of St Albans for his devotion and benefactions to their house. His remarks, as reported by Walsingham, suggest that he had a concept of the good of the realm transcending local interests (perhaps to some extent stimulated by the views circulating at St Albans in the household of Abbot Thomas de la Mare), and that he believed it to be within the Commons' sphere of competence to initiate moves for the reform of central government. In the Commons House (on this occasion the chapter-house of Westminster Abbey), Hoo related an allegorical dream to his fellow-members, with the purpose of stiffening their resolve to persist in their controversial purpose, and of persuading them to win over the Lords. In 1376 the Commons were to act with unprecedented daring by their impeachment of a royal minister (see p. 173). It is likely that their striking measure of success, however ephemeral, established a precedent which served to embolden Commons members in subsequent parliaments to express and promote their own views about how the affairs of the realm should be conducted.

Yet the tensions whose eruption into violence this 'mixed polity' facilitated and stimulated sometimes gave English politics an anarchical appearance. Foreign commentators (principally French and Scottish) concluded from the depositions and probable murders of Edward II (1327) and Richard II (1399) that the English were unworthy, faithless, prone to depose and kill their kings. The grave and long-lasting threats to political stability posed by these precedents must not be under-estimated. In the fifteenth century every king faced baronial attempts at a violent overthrow, successful against Henry VI (twice, in 1461 and 1471), Edward IV (1470) and Richard III (1485). Royal policy had tended to enhance the ability of magnates to rebel, by relying heavily on their influence to suppress disorders in shire society, to raise military retinues for service in Scotland and France, and to organise the defence of the king's territories and seas, as Wardens of the Marches towards Scotland, lieutenants in France, and admirals. Competition for such prestigious and lucrative plums of royal patronage (in a period when income from land was static or declining) produced a new baronial motive for rebellion.

Not surprisingly, some Englishmen despaired of their fellow countrymen. Such feelings are expressed by Malory in *Le Morte D'Arthur*, written in the period of the Wars of the Roses (1455–85). Recounting Sir Mordred's rebellion against Arthur, he exclaimed

Lo, ye all Englishmen, see ye not what a mischief here was! for he that was the most king and knight of the world . . . now might not these Englishmen hold them content with him. Lo thus was the old custom and usage of this land; and also men say that we of this land have not yet lost nor forgotten that custom and usage. Alas, this is a great default of us Englishmen, for there may no thing please us no term.

Fortescue, Malory's contemporary, recognised in *The Governance of England* that there was a current danger of baronial rebellion, but propounded as remedies for monarchical weakness administrative reforms of a traditional character. A king rich in private resources, he argued, would be better placed to attract loyalties than any of his lords, and would gladden his subjects' hearts by ignoring their purses. One reason for Fortescue's optimistic stance may have been an underlying fear that an English king, reacting to the dynastic challenges of the Wars of the Roses, would resort to arbitrary government and taxation, as the renascent Valois dynasty had done in France. He had been tutor there to Henry VI's exiled son and heir, Edward, whose upbringing in the midst of soldiers, and then as a French noble, had been somewhat bizarre for a future English king. There had been past fears that Henry VI's government would resort to arbitrary measures characteristic of the French 'new monarchy'. In 1460 the Yorkish lords challenging Henry's government had publicly alleged that

now [*their opponents*] *begin a new charge of imposition and tallages upon the said people which never afore was seen; that is to say, every township to find men for the king's guard, taking example thereof of our enemies and adversaries of France: which imposition and tallage if it be continued to their heirs and successors will be the heaviest charge and worst example that ever grew in England. . .*

Fortescue elaborately contrasted the prosperity and spirit of the English commons with the lack-lustre penury of their French counterparts, attributing these economic and social differences to diverging constitutional developments: the French Crown was free to tax harshly and arbitrarily because it had 'dominium regale', unrestrained by the rights of the community.

As a former common lawyer, royal councillor and knight of the shire in parliament, Fortescue, amid the clash of domestic arms, had a firmer appreciation than literary commentators of basically stable factors in the English polity. In France the greater influence of Roman law had provided the monarchy with a firm basis for autocracy. Likewise in Castile, John II had some justification for his declaration to the Cortes in 1445 that the laws were beneath him[2]. But it was a charge against Richard II in 1399 that he had said that the laws were in his mouth or in his breast 'and that he by himself (*ipse solus*) could change and establish the laws of his realm'. Henry VIII acted more circumspectly than is implied by his remark in 1520, 'of our absolute power we be above the laws'. One of Henry VI's bishops, Reginald Pecock of Chichester, had emphasised the contrary tradition:

If the king of England dwelt in Gascony and would send a noble long letter or epistle into England, both to judges and to other men, that each of them should keep the points of the law of England . . . yet it ought not to be said that that epistle was the ground for any of the laws or ordinances of England; for their ground was provided for them before that epistle of the king, and that by act and decree of the whole parliament of England, which is a true ground for all the laws of England[3].

The convictions about the constitution expressed by Pecock and Fortescue stemmed from the continued vitality in England of feudally based concepts stressing the contractual nature of kingship, enshrined in the famous constitutional document, Magna Carta. If kings had wanted to alter the basis of their relations with the community, they would have had to shift a weight of conservative opinion. On the whole kings had few incentives to fly in the face of their subjects' bent. Rebels were characteristically uncritical of the prescriptive rights and statutory powers exercised by the Crown. They protested, sincerely enough, their desire to uphold royal honour, and concentrated on attacking 'caterpillars of the commonwealth' who had allegedly abused royal favour and oppressed subjects.

The fact that the Crown did not on the whole need to be tyrannical, and was seen not to be, owed a great deal to the political adjustments of Edward III's reign, despite their lasting concomitant problems. The regional elites developed a fuller and more automatic routine of co-operating in the making of royal policy in great councils and parliaments, and of executing it in the localities and abroad. Unlike the Valois, English kings by the mid-fourteenth century had developed routine mechanisms to mobilise the realm's resources for war with assent and without major resort to prerogative levies. The fact that England had large commodity exports – wool and later cloth – was probably helpful, for the Crown could cream off taxes from them without drastically milking their subjects. Consequently there evolved by *c.*1350 a system of government operated by acquiescent gentlefolk rather than grimly coercive royal bureaucrats, a system which was extraordinarily tenacious, surviving the strains of repeated foreign war, social upheavals and domestic conflicts.

This pattern of rule led to an emphasis on particular secular (as well as religious) virtues in later medieval English kingship. Rulers were expected to behave in the warrior pattern of King Arthur. They were expected to uphold imperial claims over neighbouring peoples: their subjects were willing, indeed eager, to govern in their name Irish, Welsh, Scots and French, and urgently looked to their leadership for protection against the oft-displayed malice of such people. Nearly every ruler from Edward III to Henry VIII felt obliged to promise, at least, to ride at the head of an army in France, though a number did so with justifiable reluctance. This Arthurian ethic emphasised anew the contractual relationship of kingship in practice as well as concept. For military and naval service was, literally, organised mainly by a series of contracts between the king and a large number of individual captains.

As Richard II perceived, emphasis on royal secular obligations withered the divinity that should hedge kings. By contrast, French kingship was exalted by numerous holy legends. French writers elaborated theories of how their king symbolically represented their people before God. Such concepts were appropriate to autocracy. Their popular hold is reflected in the approach in 1429 of Joan of Arc to Charles VII of France to resolve his doubts about his sacred descent and right. None of the numerous claimants to the English throne in the fifteenth century is known to have been reassured by a mystically inclined peasant.

The period 1471 to 1547 (from Edward IV's recovery of the throne to Henry VIII's death) has sometimes been considered as one in which a more authoritarian monarchy developed. There are elements of truth in this view. Men who shared Malory's fears, men who had experienced the slaughter of gentlefolk and costs of paying soldiers in the Wars of the Roses, wanted domestic peace to be maintained by a sharp exercise of royal authority. But they wanted it exercised within statutory limits. Fortescue's analysis of the 'mixed constitution' remained popular and influential in the sixteenth century. John Aylmer developed the theme: 'If the Parliament use their privileges, the King can ordain nothing without them'[4]. Kings were still crucially dependent for the enforcement of their will, in parliament and the regions, on the local elites, and these practical limitations were sometimes strikingly revealed. In the 1504 parliament, Henry VII (1485–1509) requested a subsidy for the marriage of his daughter Margaret to James king of Scots. But, according to William Roper's life of Sir Thomas More (then one of the four MPs for London) 'at the last debating whereof he [More] made such arguments and reasons there against, that the King's demands thereby were clean overthrown'. Roper outlines Henry's revenge, a characteristic piece of Tudor tyranny, strictly within the letter of the law, but directed to the unjust punishment of an opponent: 'For as much as he [More] nothing having, nothing could lose, His Grace devised a causeless quarrel against his father, keeping him in the Tower until he had made him pay to him an hundred pounds fine.'

In 1523 More, by then a rising royal official (Under-Treasurer of the Exchequer) was elected Speaker of the House of Commons. In this parliament, which met on 15 April, it was not till 6 June that the Crown was content with the subsidies offered, and these grudging offers were made only after Henry VIII's Chancellor, Cardinal Wolsey, had paid two visits to the Commons. The second time his demand was greeted rudely by 'a marvellous, obstinate silence'. The first grant had been made on 13 May, according to an MP writing to the earl of Surrey, 'after the greatest and sorest hold in the lower House for payment of 2*s*. of the £ that ever was seen, I think, in any parliament'. Henry in fact did not get enough to make any French conquests.

However, in the period of the so-called Yorkist or Tudor 'new monarchy' the Crown was certainly not confronted by those initiatives threatening royal prerogative which had occurred from the 1340s to the 1450s. Though some ministers, such as Edmund Dudley and Richard Empson under Henry VII, and Wolsey under Henry VIII, became as unpopular as their predecessors, no Yorkish or Tudor councillor was dismissed and tried as a result of parliamentary pressure. The next royal ministers to be impeached for alleged misdemeanours in office by the Commons, after the attempt to impeach the Steward Suffolk in 1450, were the Chancellor Bacon in 1621 and the Treasurer Middlesex (Cranfield) in 1624. The conduct of the 'new monarchy's' conciliar and financial administration was never subject to parliamentary scrutiny and direction, though Henry VIII's prodigality could bear comparison with any of his predecessors. In 1523 the Commons' boldness went as far as snubbing the Chancellor, and making cutting remarks about the king's cherished French conquests ('dogholes'). But the Commons' strategy was wholly defensive: they were timid compared to Sir Peter de la Mare, MP for Herefordshire in 1376, who led his colleagues in a comprehensive attack on royal policy. Would any of Henry VIII's shire knights have dared, like Sir Peter, to denounce a royal mistress? In 1523 the Commons did not even request, like some of their predecessors in Henry IV's reign faced with outrageous royal financial demands, the resumption of royal revenues granted out in annuities, or royal commitment to parsimony.

Such contrasts spring partly from the fact that, whereas for much of the period 1373–1471 kings appeared incompetent or insolvent, from 1471 to 1547 they generally inspired confidence. MPs may have been aware that 'public opinion' among their colleagues and neighbours was less tolerant of interference in the king's business. But opinion tolerated royal harshness to recalcitrant individuals, a concomitant of vigorous rule, an antidote to political insecurity. It remained so because the early Tudors, despite all their triumphs, were unable to guarantee that security. The Tudors were unprolific: from his father Henry VII's death in 1509 until the birth of his son Edward in 1537, Henry VIII was the only legitimate male of his family. The slender Tudor dynastic thread was an encouragement to speculation and intrigue about the succession. The religious changes of the 1530s constituted one of those policies, unusual for medieval government, which provoked rumour, uncertainty, confusion and resistance throughout English society. Coincidentally, growing economic tension was producing popular restlessness. When Fortescue had written, in the 1470s, labour relations had been less volatile. Consequently, in *The Governance of England*, despite the knowledge he had of the popular disturbances of 1450 and the commons' turbulent participation in the Wars of the Roses, he felt able to praise their spirit and fighting ability. There is a different emphasis in works of the 1530s, such as Richard Morrison's *A remedy for sedition* (1536), printed by the king's printer Thomas Berthelet:

A common wealth is like a body, and so like, that it can be resembled to nothing so convenient, as unto that. Now, were it not by your faith, a mad hearing, if the foot should say, I will wear a cap with a jewel, as the head doth? If the knee should say, we will carry the eyes, another while. . .

Tudor nobles and their local clients indeed had the same competitive motives for rebellion as their predecessors in the fourteenth and fifteenth centuries, but such a climate of opinion was discouraging. There is a stress in the literature of the 1530s (for example, in the works of the courtier Sir Thomas Elyot and Thomas Starkey, Henry VIII's chaplain) on nobles' duty to serve the king and commonwealth, instead of their old feudal role, in which on behalf of the community they safeguarded royal performance of obligations. The spread of humanist education fostered the change in attitude. Two of the most popular Latin authors were Livy and Sallust. In his *Decades*, Livy reconstructed ancient republican history in order to emphasise the virtue of service to the state; Sallust nobly evoked how honour can be won by it, but described how base passions and selfish ambitions led nobles to be corrupted by foreign bribes, and to indulge in antisocial plotting with the dregs of society.

No wonder, then, that convicted traitors made orations on the scaffold in praise of their sovereign, a habit which would have amazed earlier rebels such as Thomas of Lancaster (d.1322), Thomas of Arundel (d.1397), or the gentlefolk convicted by the law of arms after the battles of the Wars of the Roses, and swiftly shepherded to the block. Henry IV, during an earlier period of dynastic insecurity, lacked the benefit of a climate of opinion hostile to rebellion. His execution of Archbishop Scrope of York in 1405 led to his vilification on a scale which no Tudor had to endure (except from posterity) for the judicial murder of infinitely more pathetic and worthy, less culpable figures than Scrope, such as the youthful earl of Warwick (1499) and his elderly sister Margaret Pole, countess of Salisbury (1541).

Another indication of the growth of a more favourable attitude to a vigorous exercise of royal authority was the decline of popular canonisation of opponents of the Crown. St Thomas of Canterbury had long been regarded as a symbol of opposition to tyranny. Some magnates who had died for their rebellion – Simon de Montfort in the thirteenth century, Thomas of Lancaster in the early fourteenth – had been popularly accounted saints. Archbishop Scrope was the last rebel to produce a cult. Richard duke of York (d.1460) and Warwick 'the Kingmaker' (d.1471), who had posed as champions of the grievances of the commonwealth and died dramatically at the hands of their enemies, did not. But the tradition of St Thomas still lingered: in 1489 the Yorkshire rebels, protesting at the levy of subsidy, cited his example (cf. p. 6). In a proclamation of 1538, an attempt was made to destroy the traditional view of St Thomas: far from being a martyr, he was alleged to have died in a sordid brawl, after resisting 'wholesome laws established against the enormities of the clergy'. The Reformation was to produce new crops of martyrs who, even when executed for treason, such as Sir Thomas More (1534) and Mary queen of Scots (1587), were hallowed for their religious rather than their political significance.

Some of the new attitudes to monarchy are reflected in a treatise written by Edmund Dudley, *The Tree of Commonwealth* (1509–10) (see p. 308). Dudley, a prominent councillor of Henry VII, was expertly acquainted with his methods of government, so harshly extortionate to individuals that Henry VIII had Dudley, as one of their principal instruments, arrested soon after his accession and executed on a fabricated charge of treason. While in the Tower, Dudley penned his remorseful treatise, perhaps in the hope of regaining favour. He saw the Crown as the mainspring of government, in fine working order, not, like the monarchy of Fortescue, in great need of repair. Dudley implied that the king was well placed to follow policies which would alienate 'the loving hearts of his subjects', not by overthrowing the established constitution, but by making stringent financial exactions, by allowing partiality in the administration of justice, and enforcing the many existing penal statutes rigorously against individuals. Their existence helps explain why the powers of the Crown required remarkably few statutory additions. The two most significant ones were those of 1533–4 and 1536, defining the Crown's ecclesiastical authority, and the Treasons Act, 1534. The Act of Supremacy was a recognition of the rights of ecclesiastical headship annexed to the imperial Crown of the realm, to be exercised with statutory force by the king and his successors. The Treasons Act defined a number of rebellious acts as treason, including casting aspersions on the royal dignities and titles of the king, queen or their heirs, and writing or declaring that the king was a 'heretic, schismatic, tyrant, infidel or usurper of the crown'[5]. These extensions and more complex definitions of royal right signal the determination of Tudor government to monitor and control opinion more thoroughly.

For much of the second half of the sixteenth century, government seemed threatened by dynastic challenges, religious discontent and social upheaval. Consequently the Elizabethan political community wanted the Crown to exercise its prerogative and statutory powers vigorously. Nevertheless, political tensions developed anew between Crown and community: influential elements were determined to sway royal policy on sensitive issues. Rulers had handicaps which irritated their subjects' biases: one was a minor (Edward VI, 1547–53), two were women (Mary, 1553–8 and Elizabeth, 1558–1603). The welcome restoration of adult male rule came in the less pleasing shape of a Scot (James I, 1603–25). The Crown displayed a new tendency to insolvency, stimulated by the inflation of the mid-sixteenth century, and exacerbated by prolonged war with Spain. The sheer length of Elizabeth's reign was damaging to the personal authority of English kingship. The queen, surrounded by courtly magnificence, remained remarkably popular until her later years, and never lost her exceptional skill at gauging and controlling noble ambitions and intrigues. But her sex, longevity and obstinacy helped to create, in reaction, a tradition of parliamentary criticism and pressure on policy. For the governing elites were agitated by uncertainty as to whether a woman had the stomach to give effective protection in a period of dire foreign and domestic threats. Her obtuse failure to marry and guarantee the succession exacerbated their insecurity. Her sex weakened her authority to control the Church under God, just when English opinion was being strongly influenced by Calvinist criticisms of the concept of such royal control.

The attempts of the House of Commons under Elizabeth and James I to influence policy, particularly concerning religion and foreign affairs, were treated by these rulers as encroachments on their prerogative more consistently than any previous ruler other than Richard II had treated parliamentary agitation. James I discoursed learnedly on the powers confided to him by God and the constitution. With an emphasis differing from Pecock's or Fortescue's, he declared to parliament in 1610 that laws 'are properly made by the king only, but at the rogation of the people, the king's grant being obtained thereunto'. Commons' presumption in the later Middle Ages had had *ad hoc* aims, by and large – they had wanted to make the Crown more effective, solvent, to protect their purses. The new opposition was more concerned with fundamental policy issues than the individual responsibility of councillors, and it developed more fully into an ongoing opposition, concerned from parliament to parliament with permanently divisive issues.

Besides, critics of the Crown had more contentious concepts of the underlying constitutional issues than their medieval predecessors. The

Reformation had produced new attitudes to institutions: the need to justify the Church of England had stimulated an interest in their historical origins and claims. MPs defended themselves against royal attempts to confine their discussions to the issues laid before them by the Crown, and to punish offensive speeches, by grubbing up their supposed historical rights. The same investigative zeal was to be applied increasingly to other unpopular exercises of royal power. Conflict over the constitution became more insistently a major political issue in itself, as the alarums of Elizabeth's military emergencies subsided. The broad constitutional consensus which had survived tensions for over two centuries had begun to show serious cracks.

The evolution of parliaments: the House of Lords

Parliaments were the physical embodiment of the conjoint will and authority of the king and 'community of the realm'. Their significance was recognised in a statute of Edward II's parliament at York in 1322: this asserted that things established for the estate of the king and his heirs and the estate of the realm and his people were to be considered, agreed and established in parliaments by the king with the assent of prelates, earls and barons, and the community of the realm, as had (allegedly) been customary.

In 1322 it could be plausibly asserted that parliaments had a traditionally established and important role in the making of laws and settlement of policy. But they did not have the rigidly fixed criteria of composition and bicameral division of functions and privileges which were to be crucial features of later parliaments. In the reigns of Edward II and III, parliaments were acquiring some of these features, but lamentably little is known about the early steps in this evolution and why they were taken. A probable general reason for parliamentary experiment and development is that parliaments provided an increasingly important means for kings to develop new bases of support among the politically articulate magnates and gentry. Such royal needs were to remain pressing in a century which was to be characterised by the large scale and long duration of its economic and military crises.

Customarily kings had summoned to parliaments various categories of individuals, according to whether they might be useful in expediting one or more sorts of business with which a parliament might be concerned: judgment of petitions, framing of statutes, commitment to the king's political intent. Kings were likely to summon their leading councillors and officials (for example, the Chief Justices of the King's Bench and Common Pleas, the Chancellor, and the Treasurer of the Exchequer) and the more influential tenants-in-chief (bishops, earls and the wealthier members of a baronage which was, in its upper reaches, showing an acute sense of collective political identity). More occasionally, summonses were sent to procure representatives of the lower beneficed clergy and the freeholders in shires and boroughs.

Numbers of baronial tenants-in-chief were not individually summoned. By the later thirteenth century many such tenants, through the fragmentation of baronies between coheirs and subtenants, were insignificant landowners. Since parliaments were summoned frequently in the 1320s and 1330s, it became customary for Chancery clerks to copy the individual writs of summons from their lists of those enrolled as having been summoned to previous parliaments. The right of summons came to be confined almost entirely to a group whose claim rested on the precedent of the writs. These included the twenty-one bishops (four from Welsh sees) and heads of some wealthier religious houses – twenty-seven were summoned in 1364 (twenty-three of them Benedictine abbots), twenty-nine in 1529. The dissolution of religious orders (1536–40) reduced the number of ecclesiastical lords entitled to writs by over a half[6]. Hereditary secular lords, whose titles all came to be transmissible through females, included the earls and 'barons of parliament'. Their entitlement was creating an exclusive concept of nobility, the parliamentary peerage, whose sense of rights and duties was to be heavily influenced by their well-defined corporative responsibilities. The peerage replaced the feudal baronage, a mass of landowners of varying wealth, each with an individual contractual relationship with the overlord, the king, and habits of associating under the leadership of the greater barons to enforce their view of it.

The king could create new peers by conferring the right to a personal summons. Henry VIII felt that he could not withhold summonses from peers he did not want to attend, but heirs were occasionally denied summons. The Crown refrained from large numbers of creations or denials. It enhanced the dignity of the peerage by introducing new grades: duke in 1337, marquess 1385, viscount 1440. The basic criterion for new creations was not noble descent or possession of estates held in chief (though many new peers had both), but ability and willingness to give loyal and distinguished service to the Crown. Though peers were to pride themselves on their family's long possession of peerage, they never lost the sense of being a nobility of service. As the categories of peerage became rapidly fixed in the fourteenth century, so did their corporate identity as the House of Lords – the Crown's consultative chamber in parliament, whose advice and assent was necessary to the enactment of statutes and grant of subsidies, and who sat with the king and his councillors as the high court of parliament. In 1427 the council was to assert that in certain circumstances, during a royal minority, government was to be exercised by the assembled Lords: it 'belongeth unto the lords spiritual and temporal of his land at such time as they be assembled in parliament or in great council'.

In the early parliaments of Henry VIII's reign, it was to become routine for the Clerk of Parliament to keep a record of the daily attendances of the peers and the business they considered. Later extracts copied from documents no longer existing suggest that the clerks in the later fifteenth century compiled working papers, though these were not yet bound up and kept as official journals. One such fragment recording attendances and notes on Bills considered, known as the *Fane Fragment*, has been identified as a journal of seven complete days of Edward IV's first parliament (1461). It shows how the peers, under the Chancellor's presidency, listened to the reading of Bills: they were accustomed to remitting them to committees, and conferring with the king (who was present on two days and delivered a Bill in person on behalf of London merchants on another) and the Commons.

Magnates were thus obliged to involve themselves in the *minutiae* of the whole range of business which came before parliament. Not surprisingly, they were not always diligent attenders. Eighty-four peers were summoned in 1406: forty-one were present on 7 June to seal an exemplification of the statute entailing the succession to the Crown. Some evidence of attendances in Henry IV's reign (1399–1413) suggests that roughly two out of three secular prelates and perhaps seldom more than half the temporal lords (generally including most of those of the dignity of earl and above) might be expected to attend. The abbots were the most persistent absentees. Lords knew that, if they decided to appear, it would not usually be to dispute excitedly over political grievances and rights, but to assist by tediously debating clauses. There were indeed some occasions when the Lords opposed the Crown on major issues. In 1376 and 1386 some of them encouraged Commons' criticisms of royal ministers. In 1532 the Commons Bill to restrain payment of annates to the papacy, promoted by the Crown, was strongly opposed by the prelates in the Lords. Henry VIII had to get a clause put in delaying the proposed Act's immediate execution, and appear three times himself in the Lords before it was carried against the votes of clerical dissentients. Henry had to resort to management of the Lords by persuading peers unlikely to favour his novel religious policies to stay away and give their proxies to colleagues he could rely on.

But normally the Lords inclined to support royal policy and to suspect magnate cabals. The Lords Appellant in 1388 and Richard duke of York in the 1450s found difficulty in keeping the House in line with their partisan aims. During royal minorities, in 1381 and 1426, the Lords refused to take sides in quarrels between magnates, and imposed settlements on them. The Lords could be useful to the Crown by supporting its Bills before the Commons read them, conferring with the latter over Bills, suggesting amendments to those they sent up, or rejecting them. Elizabeth and James I relied on the Lords to counter the well-organised pressure applied in the Commons against their policies. In 1589, for instance, the Lords refused to read two Bills touching the prerogative which the Commons had sent up.

The fact that the parliamentary peerage's sense of corporate unity as a limb of sovereign authority was stronger than its sense of social unity as an association of barons helped to determine this role. Until the Dissolution, ecclesiastics, conscious of their separate order, outnumbered secular peers (by forty-three to forty summonses in 1406). Among the secular peers there was a contrast in status between the handful of dukes and earls, men often of royal blood and surpassing wealth and local influence, and mere barons, whose fortunes were sometimes no greater than those of some of the rich men in the Commons, and often of recent provenance, through Court favour and royal service. The distinctions of status in the Lords were reflected in their official mode of costume and seating order.

Peerage was prized, not because the Lords developed a great independent political influence, but because they had a close corporate relationship with the Crown, the necessary qualifications for which were wealth and influence: peerage was a formal recognition of one's claims to play a leading role in the local governing hierarchy. Access to the sovereign is reflected in the *Black Book* of Edward IV's Household, which lays down the 'diets' to which different ranks of the peerage were entitled when lodging at Court. A sense of privilege was also maintained by numerical exclusiveness – forty secular peers were summoned in 1406, twenty-nine in 1485. In the sixteenth century the summonses averaged over sixty: it was James I who devalued secular peerage by boosting the numbers summoned from fifty-five in 1603 to ninety-six in 1624.

William Wentworth reported the Lord Chief Justice as saying in 1614 that 'a scandal against a peer was a scandal to the king for that they were by him made his fellows and partners in government and thereupon they are called *comites* [earls]'. The baronial feeling that a peer stood highest in his authority, not when he presided over his retainers and petitioners in his 'country', but when he sat in the high court of parliament, is reflected in fussing over and flaunting privileges associated with membership of the House. In the early fifteenth century there were sometimes virulent disputes about the order of precedence to be observed there. Official costume was lovingly paraded and bequeathed. The earl of Arundel (d.1376) possessed a best coronet and two others[7]. John lord Scrope, in his will of 1451, left his parliament robe to his son. In a society in which modes of costume reflected a shifting distribution of political power and social privilege, based on the possession of wealth, peerage robes symbolised assured legal privileges and, their possessors had more reason to hope, the stability of their governing roles.

The evolution of parliaments: the House of Commons

During Edward II's reign it became customary for the Crown to summon to parliaments two representatives each from thirty-seven shires, two each from a much larger but variable number of boroughs, and representatives of the lower beneficed clergy. The lay representatives were summoned by virtue of writs whose form had evolved under Edward I. Addressed to sheriffs, they ordered them to cause knights and burgesses to be elected by their respective communities, who were to come to the place of parliament on a stipulated date, armed with full and sufficient power to give assent on behalf of the electing community to what might be ordained in parliament by the common counsel of the realm. Edward I had summoned representatives to some but not all of his parliaments, as a means of getting information about public abuses, disseminating it about legislation and royal policies, and procuring binding decisions from the communities to observe and help to implement measures ordained in parliament, notably assent to the grant of subsidies.

Such representation was, therefore, a subordinate feature of parliaments, which were essentially royal consultations to settle the affairs of the realm with magnates and leading royal officials. But the anxiety of contending noble factions in Edward II's reign to win support, by expounding reforms and providing for the hearing of grievances, may have helped to fix this representation as an integral part of parliaments. From at least the mid-fourteenth century onwards, official records and chronicles differentiate between 'great councils' and parliaments. The great council, in which there were no formally elected representatives, was composed of royal officials, magnates, and, occasionally, gentlefolk and merchants, individually summoned according to the royal will. These assemblies considered royal proposals about matters of concern to the community of the realm. They had no power to alter the law or to grant subsidy, but they were useful to the Crown as a means of gaining support for its intentions, for example, by making individual loans or giving prior approval to schemes to raise subsidies. By the end of Edward III's reign (1377), parliament was distinct from all other manner of counsel, a unique institution with a fixed composition, bicameral structure, complex procedure and sole powers to participate in binding the community in certain matters. In contrast to great councils, parliament had become a court of record, a Chancery clerk, the Clerk of Parliaments being assigned as responsible for the compilation and filing of a roll of some of its proceedings and some of the petitions received by the Crown in it. The functions of parliament, its composition and the relations of its constituent parts were setting in a traditional mould, though one not impervious to change and development.

Its representative parts continued to be considered, and to behave, in many respects, as adjuncts to parliaments. But they acquired a fixed form in the fourteenth century. One representative group, the lower clergy, dwindled: the Crown negotiated with them in convocations[8]. Shire knights and burgesses became accustomed to petition and assent as a single chamber, perhaps originally as a matter of royal convenience. This cameral coalescence, and Edward III's demands for war subsidies, stimulated the Commons' habit of making grants in return for royal consideration of their common petitions, concerning general grievances (see p. 171). It is clear that by 1376 members of parliament could display an impressive collective sense of their duty to promote what they considered to be (though such a phrase would have puzzled them) 'the national interest'.

The names of the majority of shire knights and burgesses in our period are known. But the careers and backgrounds of many medieval ones can only be reconstructed in a superficial way, throwing light on the social composition of the Commons, but leaving their individual political motives and roles murky. The comparative scarcity of belted knights hindered fulfilment of the stipulation in election writs that they should be returned for shires. In the twenty-four parliaments of Richard II's reign, Kent was represented by twenty-three men, six of them knights returned only once each. Many shire knights ranked as esquires or gentlemen and, due to their wealth and eminence, were among the 'magisterial' gentry (see pp. 128 ff). Half the gentry in the 1584 parliament held county office: about thirty more, not yet qualified, were also to do so.

There was usually a substantial number of practising lawyers in the Commons – in 1422, as many as between a fifth and a quarter of the members of parliament, but in 1584, only 53 out of 460; in 1614, 48 out of 475. Their technical expertise was essential to the scrutiny, drafting and amendment of Bills, but their tendency to neglect the Commons' public business was a continual source of exasperation to government and, probably, colleagues. They might slip out on private business to the courts in Westerminster Hall, or concentrate, again for financial gain, on drafting and promoting private Bills, and appearing before the Commons or its committees as counsel for such Bills.

The borough representatives always heavily outnumbered the shire knights, by 222 to 74 in the later fifteenth century. Many towns which were ordered to elect two burgesses in the early fourteenth century had persistently failed to do so and were consequently omitted from the urban franchises recognised by Chancery. A deterrent to representation, compounded by widespread urban economic decline, was the expense. In 1327 the daily allowance for attendance and for journeys to and from parliament was fixed at four shillings for shire knights and two shillings for burgesses, raised by purchase of a writ *de expensis* ordering the sheriff to tax the community represented. But the intending borough representative often had to waive his right to a writ, and bargain with the borough community over remuneration, as conditions of election. Even leading towns, which sometimes paid distinguished representatives above the statutory rate, were on occasion keen to economise. In 1533 and 1534 John Brydges, member of parliament for Canterbury, cut his attendances at sessions of the Reformation Parliament: on each occasion the city rewarded him with sums (7*s* and 7*s* 6*d*) to buy a new bonnet. One expedient (which might be useful to promote a Bill in a town's interest as well as to economise) was to engage a resident or neighbouring gentleman as member. John Sackville, esquire, undertook to sit for Weymouth in 1463, in return for a promise to deliver him a barrel of mackerel the following Christmas. Sir John Fogge and Sir George Browne, respectively Canterbury members of parliament in 1467 and 1483, graciously waived their wages. Only a minority of Elizabethan burgesses were paid: small boroughs did not pay, and outsiders were not normally paid in her reign.

A striking increase in the proportion of outsiders sitting for the boroughs occurred in the fifteenth century. In 1422 three-quarters of the 188 burgess members of parliament were resident in their boroughs, though perhaps between eighty and ninety of these were hardly concerned with trade. But in 1442 only 58 per cent of the borough representatives were resident burgesses; in 1478, 43 per cent. The eagerness of gentry to sit for boroughs in the sixteenth century, the enfranchisement of towns (often minuscule 'pocket' boroughs) for their family convenience, and of new county seats, reduced the mercantile element in the Commons[9]. In 1584 only fifty-three members of parliament were primarily merchants or borough officials, but about 240, more than half the total membership, were country gentry running their own estates.

The growing social homogeneity of the Commons in the fifteenth century was not necessarily conducive to political forcefulness. In several parliaments between 1376 and 1406 the tough postures of Commons in which gentry were a minority were to generate excitement of a kind which hardly appears again (except briefly in the mid-fifteenth century) until the period of fully-fledged Elizabethan and Jacobean 'gentry-assemblies'[10]. The gentry influx may have made it more difficult for the Commons to sustain political initiatives. For the eagerness of gentlefolk to get themselves returned for boroughs, if shire seats were unavailable, may in part have reflected a desire to promote or oppose Bills in the interests of local patrons, factions or courtiers. The striking increase in the Commons' size in the sixteenth century (by 56 per cent) may have intensified such particularist pressures. The Tudor Crown's concern with management and discipline of the Commons, and the members' interest in imposing collective control over the House, and forming political caucuses, were probably stimulated by the need to organise what might easily degenerate into an unruly, ineffective assembly. The seventy or so shire knights who dominated the Commons in the later fourteenth and early fifteenth centuries, few in number, linked by mutual ties of kinship, enfeoffments and retaining, could act together effectively with comparative ease, speedily acceding to royal requests, or stubbornly promoting redress of grievances, as the tirades of Richard II and Henry IV testify. But the 400 or so members of the Elizabethan and Jacobean Commons were less easy to set and hold to one tack. The inflation of Commons membership by the gentry (a gradual process, in which the Crown acquiesced) made it a less effective, if more pretentious, limb of parliament. Its comparative unmanageability helped to generate elements of constitutional conflict. Elizabeth and James I, in order to expedite their business, tried to cajole, browbeat, or solemnly define the limits of the Commons' responsibilities. Members articulating the many public grievances of the period worked hard, and often in vain, to link their colleagues together on points of constitutional principle. By the end of our period the Commons, which since the fourteenth century had shown remarkable resilience as a means of connecting and reconciling the needs of the king and his council with those of the local represented communities, was showing serious signs of malfunction.

Up to Elizabeth's reign there is more evidence about the administrative mechanisms of election to the Commons than about the personal and political factors involved. Incorporated boroughs (see p. 42) had election writs sent direct to their own sheriff, instead of the general county's. Elections for lesser boroughs were sometimes held in the county court, rather than at the gild hall. Borough franchise differed according to the varied and variable forms of urban government (see pp. 39 ff). The electors might be just the principal civic officers, or include other burgesses too. The Shrewsbury return of 1478 was attested by as many as 105 electors. There was a tendency in the fifteenth century for boroughs to restrict the franchise, but it remained wide in some larger towns, such as Bristol, Coventry, Gloucester, Worcester. Smaller boroughs were more susceptible to outside electoral pressure. In the second half of the fifteenth century, some borough returns from Surrey, Sussex, Hampshire, Wiltshire, Dorset and Cornwall show signs of having been tampered with, either by sheriffs or Chancery clerks. An earl of Westmorland brusquely ordered even the burgesses of Grimsby to send him their election writ, 'which I shall cause to be substantially returned and appoint two of my Counsel to be Burgesses for your said town'. The intensification of faction in the 1440s may have made peers and courtiers more anxious to get their clients or themselves returned, and spread among them the habit of manipulating boroughs.

It was more prestigious, and gave greater weight in the Commons, to be returned for a shire rather than for some obscure borough. But election for a shire was trickier. It was more competitive: and the desire of Crown and landowners in general to ensure valid representation of the shire community left the elections, at least formally, more 'open' than those in many boroughs. In the fourteenth century, all freeholders who owed suit to the shire court (rather than to the court of a private franchise) were summoned to take part in the elections at the court's next session, by the sheriff's proclamation. To what extent the whole body of freeholders actually determined shire elections is not clear. The only surviving evidence of the process consists of the endorsements of election writs with the names of members of parliament and sureties for their appearance in parliament, sent back to Chancery from the sheriff's office.

In the first half of the fifteenth century, election process, particularly for the shires, became legislatively refined. A 1406 statute laid down the procedure for summoning suitors, and enacted that an indenture should be returned to Chancery by the sheriff, to which the electors had affixed their seals, attesting the validity of the election. Many indentures survive, recording the date and place of election and the names of attesting electors. Since their number varies considerably, from tens to hundreds, fluctuating at different elections for the same shire or borough, the indentures fail to provide a reliable guide to the actual electorate.

A 1413 statute insisted that shire knights and their electors should be resident in the shire at the time of election, and that absentees should have no influence. This was reiterated in 1429, when the county franchise was restricted for the first time by income level. Elections, it was declared, 'have lately been made by a too great and excessive number of people . . . the great part were by people of little substance or of no wealth at all', who claimed an equivalent voice with 'the most valliant knights or esquires dwelling within the same shires'. Only indwellers possessing freehold land there worth at least 40*s* a year clear income were to participate. One aim of the Act may have been to prevent lords from flooding elections with tenants, men lacking 'substance', 'wisdom' and 'sadness', perhaps 'strangers' to the county. The guidelines laid down for contests may have reflected a development of keen competition for the shire seats: the majority principle was now stated.

The statute failed to disenfranchise many who ranked as 'yeomen' rather than gentlefolk. But the 1445 Act apparently sprang from the intention of wealthy, long-established county families to monopolise the shire seats. Choice was confined to notable knights or such notable esquires or gentlemen by birth as could support a knight's estate. The exclusion of yeomen is hardly surprising, but the attempt to exclude too all who had acquired gentility through service, and all gentlefolk lacking a knightly income, carried hereditary elitism to a level which many aspiring gentlemen are likely to have rejected.

The extent to which Lancastrian electoral legislation was adhered to is difficult to judge, though the matter is better illuminated from the second half of the fifteenth century onwards by the survival of election petitions[11] and private correspondence. Though accusations were frequently untruthful, it was not unusual for electors to be overawed, and for the key official, the sheriff (or his deputy) to show undue 'affection'. The particular social structure of a shire, and the current relationships of its peers and magisterial gentry, could make considerable differences in the number and standing of those who took part in choosing the shire knights, and the degree of amicability and decorum with which it was done.

Members of the shire elites were not so much concerned, where elections were concerned, about observing the letter of the law as with having their status, their 'worship' recognised. The Court, magnates, neighbours ought to show due deference to their opinions, their stake in local government. This was the spirit behind the Lancastrian legislation and the occasional angry accusations of 'packing' the Commons. John of Gaunt's opponents accused him of having packed the Bad Parliament of 1377; the charge of having done likewise was made against Richard II in the deposition articles of 1399, and against 'divers estates' in Cade's manifesto of 1450. 'Reformation for the election of knights of the shire and burgesses' was cryptically included in the articles of the Pilgrims of Grace (1536). Nevertheless, there were acceptable ways for Crown and magnates to promote their candidates – by using local territorial influence, negotiating with the locally influential men, and above all, perhaps, putting up as their candidates men who were locally acceptable[12].

The Commons and parliament business

Until the later sixteenth century there are irretrievable gaps in the evidence needed to reconstruct a political history of parliaments. For most later medieval parliaments there survives an official roll: the material which the rolls record is highly selective and occasionally misleading. But some do give indications of trends of debate and clashes of opinion, summarising speeches by royal ministers and Commons Speakers, outlining negotiations over terms of subsidy grants, and giving in full the texts of Commons impeachments and common petitions inspired by discussion of grievances. When excitement about parliamentary proceedings ran high, chroniclers sometimes tried to be informative. But their notices were usually perfunctory, perhaps because they lacked interest, sources of detailed information, or a grasp of parliamentary technicalities. The first Commons journal dates from 1547. The early journals were unofficial *aide-memoires* compiled by the Clerk of the Commons[13] from notes which he and his assistants had made. The first journals are not particularly informative. There is considerably more information about Commons' affairs from the end of Elizabeth's reign onwards; the fuller journals are supplemented by members of parliament's diaries, and printed accounts of individual speeches and proceedings on particular matters.

Writs of summons stipulated the time and place of the opening session, though short postponements were common because of the lateness of peers in arriving. Parliaments were most often held in parts of the 'public' palace at Westminster, with rooms in the Abbey sometimes used as an annexe. Some meetings were held in London, for example in the Blackfriars in 1523. Sessions far from London, which might be personally or politically convenient for the sovereign, were generally unpopular. For some they entailed journeys into 'strange' shires, and the postponement of private business which they had hoped to settle in the capital. There were accommodation problems, too. In October 1378 the monks of St Peter's Abbey, Gloucester, according to their chronicler, had to dine in their orchard, while their refectory was used as 'the place of parliament as a whole', the chamber of their guest house 'for private counsel among the magnates', whereas the Commons deliberated in the chapter-house. In 1447 Alderman Frowick refused to represent London in the parliament to be held at Bury St Edmunds unless he had hearth and lodging.

In the opening session of parliament, a leading royal minister (e.g. the Chancellor) usually expounded the cause of summons to the full parliament, and gave its members their 'charge' – the articles officially selected for their collective consideration and answer. At Westminster, full sessions of parliament were often held in the Painted Chamber of the palace, the peers seated in their ranks, the available Commons who could squeeze in crowded near the door. For their separate sessions, the Lords used the Painted Chamber or another one in the palace, and the Commons were allotted somewhat makeshift quarters, such as the Abbey's chapter-house or refectory. By July 1550 the House (considerably enlarged in recent years) was using what was to be its permanent Westminster home, St Stephen's Chapel, the royal chantry foundation in the palace dissolved in 1547.

The Elizabethan House of Commons normally met every day of the week except Sunday from 8 a.m. till 11 a.m. (the hours kept by the adjacent law courts): committees often met in the afternoon, somewhere in the city or in the Commons committee room in the palace. Before answering to their charge, or presenting petitions, the medieval Commons sometimes requested to consult with a committee of peers. Their eventual answers and requests might be communicated orally or in written form. In the fifteenth century, as a result of the Commons' growing involvement in considering petitions, the Commons Bill was to become the normal basis for statute. One of the traditional functions of parliament was to provide remedies for grievances: receivers and triers of petitions were appointed to sort out and give prior consideration to the flood of requests concerning public and private issues addressed to king and lords in parliament. The practice of addressing the Commons instead, in the hope that they would debate and adopt petitions as their Bills, giving added weight, is found before the end of the fourteenth century, and became common in the Lancastrian period[14].

In the Elizabethan House there was often very little debate on bills, and it was very rare for a debate on any reading to spill over into the next sitting, and seldom that a bill monopolised a morning's session[15]. Voting on motions was by acclamation. Divisions seem to have been rare before Elizabeth's reign: there is no source providing continuous evidence before 1547, but a stray reference reveals a division and scrutiny of votes over election to the Speakership in 1420. In the later sixteenth century the procedure was for the Noes to stay put, and the Ayes to file out into, and back out of, the antechamber normally used by the Clerk of the Commons, his assistants, and suitors to the Commons.

The Commons' business efficiency and political effectiveness seem to have been enhanced by the development of the Speaker's office. In Edward III's reign communications between the Commons and king or Lords had been carried on by outsiders as well as members of parliament. Delegations of the latter represented the Commons in full sessions of parliament. Probably in 1376 the Commons first adopted the expedient of electing a spokesman to head all their deputations and speak for them on all occasions in parliament (see pp. 172 ff). Though his attitudes were highly distasteful to John of Gaunt, the Crown quickly realised the value of having one individual as the recognised, authoritative channel of communication with the Commons. Official recognition of the office of Speaker is reflected in the notices of elections which begin to appear on the Parliament Rolls. In 1384 it was recorded that, at the start of the session, the Commons were ordered to elect a Speaker promptly, and from 1401 the order to elect and the terms of negotiation with the Crown over acceptance were continuously recorded.

The medieval Speakers were in most cases attached to the royal service in some capacity, but, at least in the first half of the fifteenth century, their choice was probably genuinely made by the Commons, not the Crown. From 1435 onwards the Speaker was occasionally rewarded for his services by the Crown; under the Yorkists, fairly regularly. By the sixteenth century the Speakership was normally filled by government nominees: in the Elizabethan Commons they were proposed at the start of the first session by the senior member of parliament, the most eminent privy councillor present. The powers which had accrued to the Speaker made it vital for the Crown to ensure the installation of a trustworthy and efficient member. By the 1480s the Speaker was acting as 'president' of the Commons' proceedings, and had considerable influence over the passage of Bills in the House as well as their presentation to the Crown. The fully-fledged Elizabethan Speaker decided in which order Bills would be heard in the Commons, and read them over, with some explanation, himself[16]. He decided which member should speak, if more than one rose to do so, and controlled the debate from the Speaker's Chair. He licensed absentees and was responsible for keeping attendance records, and the journals of proceedings. He corrected members who misbehaved and had also acquired some powers to punish those who had offended against the liberties of the House, for example by attempted arrests of members during a session for private suits.

It is not always easy to define the rights and privileges of the House, since they were often customary, and only the subject of formal recognition or repudiation when they had become the centre of controversy. In 1404, in response to a Commons Bill, Henry IV recognised that no change should be made to an existing statute without their assent. His attempt to agree terms of subsidy with the Lords before the Commons had been consulted in 1407 provoked their outcry. Henry conceded that financial grants, when agreed by both Lords and Commons, should be announced to the sovereign by the Speaker. In 1414 the Commons petitioned Henry V that no alterations changing the sense of their Bills should be made after the Speaker had submitted them. The king replied that statutes based on their petitions whose sense was contrary to their requests should not be enacted without their assent[17].

These were important formal recognitions of some of the Commons' rights as assentors. But the extent of members' liberty in stirring and speaking to petitions was a delicate matter, not susceptible to neat definitions which would satisfy both Crown and Commons. Sir Peter de la Mare, Commons spokesman in 1376, was subsequently gaoled, presumably because of his leading role in formulating attacks on royal policies and ministers in their assembly, as well as articulating them in parliament. In 1451 Thomas Young[18] was imprisoned after proposing in the Commons that the duke of York be recognised as heir-apparent. He subsequently claimed that this imprisonment infringed the Commons' customary right, 'the old liberty and freedom of the commons of this land, had, enjoyed, and prescribed from the time that no mind is'. Henry VIII, indeed, seems to have been remarkably tolerant of criticisms during the Reformation Parliament. Sir George Throckmorton, member of parliament for Warwickshire, criticised antipapal moves, and lobbied sympathetic fellow members with whom he often dined during sessions at the Queen's Head Tavern.

Sovereigns may have been quite prepared to tolerate the rudeness of individual members and the agitation of caucuses in the Commons, as long as such liberty of speech did not threaten to spark off movements which might thwart or overturn royal policy. Elizabeth, whose first House of Commons had successfully aspired to influence her religious settlement, seems to have been frequently worried that her caucus of privy councillors (seated near the Speaker's ear) and servants in the House would not succeed in deflecting attempts to get the Commons to petition against the trend of her policies, particularly in matters of religion. A pattern of constitutional dispute between Crown and Commons was laid down by her attempts to delimit definitively the House's freedom. Past bold Commons men, such as Sir Peter de la Mare or Sir Thomas Hoo, Sir Arnald Savage (Speaker 1404), Sir John Tiptoft (Speaker 1406), or Thomas Young, might well have stirred in their graves at Sir John Puckering, Lord Keeper of the Great Seal's declaration to the Commons in 1593 that a member's liberty consisted in not being 'restrained or afraid to answer (yea or no to bills) according to his best liking, with some short declaration of his reason therein . . . not, as some suppose, to speak there of all causes as him listeth, and to frame a form of religion or a state of government as to their idle brains shall seem meetest'.

Royal residences and the Household

Since the sovereign's will was normally the executive mainspring of the government of the realm, the Court was a chief centre of political activity. Rulers were more often than not to be found in luxurious palaces or sylvan retreats in the vicinity of London. Among the former were the Tower of London, Westminster Palace and Windsor Castle. The medieval enceintes of the Tower and Windsor Castle have survived, remarkably intact. Westminster Palace has been almost completely obliterated, mainly as a result of the fires of 1512 and 1834. Parts of the palace housed government offices concerned with public affairs; the most prominent survival is Westminster Hall, probably, as rebuilt by Richard II, the most impressive room in medieval England. There was also the 'privy palace', accommodating the ruler's family, companions and guests, and many supporting service departments. An impression of the sort of business offices which it provided is given by the Jewel Tower, built in 1365–6 at the south-west corner of the palace garden to house part of the Privy Wardrobe (the sovereign's personal hoard of jewels, plate and coin) and to provide an office for the Treasurer of the Chamber and his staff, responsible for accounting for receipts and disbursements, and for safeguarding the valuables.

Near London were two frequently visited country houses, Sheen (Surrey) and Eltham (Kent). Henry V spent with uncharacteristic lavishness on rebuilding Sheen. Burnt down in 1499, it was magnificently rebuilt by Henry VII, who renamed it Richmond. The surviving gatehouse does not reflect its former riverside splendour. Edward IV's great hall (*c*.1475–80) remains at Eltham, the least altered remnant of a fifteenth-century royal residence. Under the Yorkists and early Tudors the residences became more numerous and splendid. Fine settings were needed for the revived magnificence of the Household: more accommodation in the capital's immediate vicinity and rural havens from its noisome, unhealthy atmosphere. A particular incentive was provided by the fire at Westminster Palace in 1512, 'since the which time', the Elizabethan antiquary John Stow wrote, 'it hath not been re-edified . . . But the princes have been lodged in other places about the city, as at Baynard's castle, at Bridewell, and White hall . . . and sometime at St James' '[19]. Bridewell was an old royal house in London, and Henry VIII's first major rebuilding. In the early 1530s he was building extensions to Wolsey's two former residences, Hampton Court and York Place; by 1536 the latter, renamed Whitehall, was his chief residence adjacent to the capital (it was burnt down in 1697). Between 1532 and 1540 another palace was built near London, St James's, on the site of a leper hospital. In the late 1530s two imposing country palaces were built not far from Hampton Court, Oatlands and Nonesuch. Nevertheless, the Thames swan whose observations as he paddled down from Oxford were recorded by John Leland in the *Cygnea Cantio* (published 1545) considered Greenwich to be the finest sight of all. Acquired by the Crown in 1447, it remained an abiding royal favourite.

The variety of spectacular palaces which Henry VIII bequeathed to his children dispensed them from the expensive necessity of building anew. Elizabeth was content to be entertained in her nobles' and councillors' palatial new country houses. James I and his family were not: they had a Henrician taste for courtly extravagance. Theobalds (Herts), built by the first Lord Burghley, was acquired by James from his son Robert, and in the late 1610s Inigo Jones was designing works for Oatlands, Newmarket and Whitehall, where his Banqueting House (completed 1622) happily survives. In 1616 work began on his Queen's House at Greenwich, but it stopped when the queen, Anne of Denmark, became ill in 1618, and was not recommenced till the next reign.

There were royal residences in other parts of England at various times, less regularly used. Two old hunting palaces, Woodstock (Oxon) and Clarendon (Wilts) remained popular in the fourteenth century. By the end of Edward III's reign, Clipstone (Northants) was the only royal country house maintained north of the Chilterns. The Lancastrian and Yorkist dynasties brought other, often more distant, residences into the Crown's hands, to which their inclinations, as well as political restlessness in the provinces, often drew them. Henry VI liked Kenilworth (Warwicks), Edward IV spent heavily on the castles at Nottingham and Fotheringhay, Richard III on Warwick Castle. Richard was alone among the sovereigns in our period in being at home in the north: Henry VII progressed there little after 1489, and Henry VIII only in 1541.

The evolution of London by the fourteenth century as the realm's principal food market and business centre provided strong incentives for keeping the Household nearby. Rulers' waning interest in asserting sovereignty over Scotland, and increasing diplomatic entanglement with princes and cities across the Channel, drew them south-eastwards. The Wars of the Roses emphasised that control of London was necessary to secure the Crown. But pleasure as well as convenience attracted sovereigns to the region. They enjoyed the good hunting country, the elaborate palace gardens which soils and climate facilitated[20], the easy riverine communications. They became aquatic monarchs, constantly rowed up and down the Thames, within sight of which (and sometimes on which) many of their personal and political crises were played out. Yet, as they, their courtiers and councillors were wafted from palace to palace, they could not but notice London's wharves, the stately merchants' houses rising beyond them and on London Bridge, the wherries, barges, lighters and laden 'cogs' on the river. An awareness of the city as a background to the Court pervades Chaucer's *Troilus and Criseyde*. This background helped to make kings especially aware of the importance to their policy of the commercial elite. The orientation was reflected in personal habits and tastes: Richard II was familiar with a leading London merchant, Edward IV overfamiliar with the wife of one, and Henry VIII, besides appearing as a chivalrous knight, played at being a shipmaster, with a whistle hung at his neck.

Since royal residences far from London tended to be old-fashioned and ill-kept, sovereigns on progress frequently stayed in monastic guest houses or their servants' country houses. They often travelled with a scaled-down riding household. Such expeditions were congenial times when the king and his chosen companions made merry away from the cares of Court. In 1464, when visiting Northamptonshire with a riding household, Edward IV got married and had a brief honeymoon without his servants' knowledge. Kings possessed their own retreats, such as hunting lodges in Windsor Forest, where they could relax away from Court. The sovereign could behave as a private, elusive person, sometimes to the exasperation of councillors and petitioners.

Household administration can be reconstructed from surviving financial accounts of chief officials filed in the Exchequer, and from royal ordinances which aimed to control peculation and waste at Court. *The Black Book of the King of England's Household*, compiled *c*.1471–2 after deliberation by Edward IV's councillors, was intended to guide officials as to the 'diets' allowable to sojourners of various status, and as to the duties and entitlements of their own offices. For instance, a duke in attendance, 'sitting in the king's chamber' was allowed to have 'eating in the hall' one of his knights, a chaplain, three esquires and four yeomen. He was assigned a 'chamber' (suite of apartments), where he breakfasted, and on occasion dined or supped 'out from the high presence'. His chamber was allocated a daily livery of ten loaves, four messes of 'great meat and roast', four pitchers of wine, six gallons of ale, candles, wax and fuel according to seasonal needs, and litter and rushes. When present a duke was to have only twelve resident attendants, the rest of his liveried company lodging in the country within seven miles of the court. He was to pay for his own carriage, harness and other expenses.

The *Black Book* divides the Household into two parts: the 'Domus Magnificencie' and the 'Domus Providencie'. The latter comprised the service departments[21]. They were staffed by about half the Household's personnel of 550[22]. The Domus was then presided over by the steward, and its heads of department had no independent funds assigned direct by the Exchequer or local receivers, financial control being the responsibility of a board including the Treasurer, Controller, Cofferer and various clerks of the countinghouse. This office was the principal financial and accounting centre for the daily running of the Household. The Cofferer deputised there for the Treasurer, receiving his Exchequer or other assignments. Departmental clerks crowded in to have their accounts examined and validated by the Clerks of the Green Cloth. The Cofferer issued authorised payments: prests (advances) for purveyance of commodities, the price of necessities already purchased, due wages, annuities and rewards owed to Household officers.

The board of the Domus Providencie was composed of ranking officials either high in royal service or expecting to rise high. But there were in the service departments only about thirty officials – clerks, sergeants and master cooks – whose appointments carried the rank of esquire. Sir John Elryngton, Cofferer of the Household in 1471 and Treasurer in 1474, had been clerk of the kitchen. Some others could hope for big financial rewards and advancement to squirearchy. In September 1386 John Worship was described simply as king's servitor, when with three colleagues he was granted a wardship, worth 40 marks a year, and a marriage, by Signet letter. Though he had served the king since 1377, he was only yeoman of the cuphouse when granted an annual rent of 10 marks (apparently his first royal annuity) in May 1387, by advice of the Council. By by March 1390 Worship was a 'king's esquire' and in June he could afford to set himself up as a Bedfordshire landowner, by purchasing for 800 francs from Fontevrault Abbey a joint life tenancy with his wife in Leighton Buzzard. He sat as knight for the shire in parliament in 1393, 1394, twice in 1397 and in 1407. By September 1395 he had made the transition to the Domus Magnificencie: he was described as usher of the Chamber. He became justice of the peace in Bedfordshire in 1397, and there is no doubt that his abilities had come to the attention of Richard II or of one of the councillors, for he was appointed sheriff of Bedfordshire and Buckinghamshire in November 1397, and was one of the sheriffs illegally prolonged in office by reappointment in November 1398. But most denizens of the Domus Providencie had no hope of such advancement – servants such as the scullions serving under the master cooks in the king's kitchen, who were forbidden by the Eltham Ordinance (1526) to 'go naked or in garments of such vileness as they now do and have been accustomed to do, nor lie in the nights and days in the kitchen or ground by the fireside'.

The Domus Magnificencie provided the setting for the sovereign's public and private life, amidst close kinsmen, noble companions and guests. There were the hall and chamber, the latter a series of state apartments (great chamber, privy chamber, bedchamber) where public receptions were held. There were sets of private apartments to which the sovereign, royal kinsmen and guests retired. The staff of the

Domus (later known as the Chamber) was headed by the Chamberlain and Vice-Chamberlain, and directed in its duties by gentlemen ushers. There were in the 1470s knights and esquires of the king's body, and gentlemen, yeomen, grooms and pages of the chamber, some of whom were described in the *Black Book* as carvers, cupbearers, sewers, ushers, physicians and surgeons. There was the chapel royal, subject to its dean, which *c.*1449 had an establishment of forty-nine, including choirboys[23]. The financial organisation of the Chamber was in some periods less unified in structure than that of the lower, service departments: the Keeper of the Privy Purse and the senior officers of the Robes, Revels, Tents and Toils, and Works accounted in the early seventeenth century not to the Treasurer of the Chamber, but to the Exchequer[24]. But all denizens of the Court were subject to the jurisdiction of the Marshal and Steward, whose Court of Verge dealt with trespasses, disputes and contracts within the Household and its environs.

The group of 250–300 office-holders in the *Black Book*'s Domus Magnificencie performed 'honourable', albeit sometimes menial services. They were companions and attendants frequently present when the king or members of his family prayed, hunted, diced, danced, sung. Some of them were allowed glimpses of royal emotions concealed from great nobles and officers of state, and were sometimes entrusted with commissions into the regions or abroad involving the ruler's particular wishes, secrets of the royal bosom. Officers of the Chamber whose company was enjoyed or whose talents were valued by the sovereign were well placed to promote policies, and to beg for favours and offices. Robert Beale advised the prospective councillor and Secretary of State in 1592 to 'Learn before your access her Majesty's disposition by some of the privy chamber, with whom you must keep credit, for that will stand you in much stead'. George Cavendish, a former member of Wolsey's household, gives an instructive account of his master's rise in favour. Appointed a royal chaplain through the influence of his patron (Sir Richard Nanfan, treasurer of Calais), Wolsey having

then a just occasion to be in present sight of the king [*Henry VII*] *daily, by reason he attended, and said mass before his grace in his privy closet, and that done he spent not the day forth in vain idleness, but gave his attendance upon those he thought to bear most rule in the council, and to be most in favour with the king.*

Two eminent councillors, Bishop Fox and Sir Thomas Lovell, impressed by the chaplain's 'fine wit', considered him worth entrusting with matters of state, and Henry VII was pleased with his conduct of missions.

A hothouse for ambitions, the Court was for many the most exciting, absorbing, teasing, oppressive place in England. Courtiers vied with one another, or allied in factious coteries, in order to secure the royal favour on which their credit in the public glare depended. Order and decorum were preserved by the stately ceremonial which the German Tetzel noted at Edward IV's Court in 1466. The tensions beneath the surface sometimes snapped when ceremonial was breached. Buckingham publicly raged at Wolsey for washing his hands in a basin of water which Henry VIII had used, and Norfolk flared out at Dudley for wiping his hands on Queen Elizabeth's napkin. In this bizarre setting men and women behaved extravagantly, eccentrically, sometimes dangerously. Some of Richard II's Chamber knights became obsessively devout, violently despising their 'carrion' flesh[25]. Henry VI peered through spyholes to catch his courtiers making love. The youthful Henry VIII and his knights tried to astonish by athletic feats and disguisings. Two of his queens failed to discourage sufficiently the cult of courtly love with which some courtiers too ardently surrounded them.

The Household frequently provoked public discontent. An issue which smouldered, and occasionally flared up in the period was purveyance. Household officers were entitled to pre-empt commodities for Household consumption, at prices which they fixed – a system open to abuse, especially at times of rapid price inflation. In the later fourteenth century and first half of the fifteenth, there were criticisms of waste and extravagance at Court, and of the greed of courtiers. Household expenditure, and the tendency of kings to please their friends and attract talented administrators into their service by lavish rewards, easily got out of control. This caused acute political crises when the Crown was unable to meet its commitments from customary revenues, resorting to loans and taxes. Gentlefolk acknowledged that the king ought to have an imposing Household and that the way he had it run was none of their business, for they too strove to maintain households appropriate to their rank. But cardinal precepts in their education were that they should live within their means, and not maintain wasters and idlers. So the spectacle of insolvent kings and grasping courtiers struck them as outrageous, and as conscientious members of parliament they felt bound to voice criticisms and promote schemes of reform[26].

Yet nobles and gentry were to acquiesce in lavish royal expenditure on Court and courtiers by the Yorkist and early Tudor sovereigns. Their complacence was due to serious attempts by kings to control Household expenditure (to which the *Black Book* and ordinances bear witness), and to their success, by extending Household officers' governmental responsibilities, in providing funds to pay for the Court (see pp. 107 ff). The latter now played with *éclat* its role as the nursery of chivalry and courtesy, without provoking any political crises. Chamber funds were spent – rightly, in contemporary eyes – on extravagant toys and trifles, banquets, masques and apparel. When William Makefyrr sent friends a description of Henry VII's meeting with Philip I of Castile near Windsor in 1506, he concentrated on the apparel of the courtiers and the furnishings of the castle's state apartments: 'and so went to the King of Castile chamber, which is the richestly hanged that ever I saw; vii chambers together hanged with cloth of arras wrought with gold as thick as could be; and as for iii beds of estate, no king Christianed can show such iii'. The credit of kings, and the credit which they accorded to their guests, was judged by the thickness of gold thread. Sir Thomas Malory's Roman senators reported apprehensively to their emperor about King Arthur, since he held 'the most noble court of the world, all others kings nor princes may not compare unto his noble maintenance'. Roger Machado, Henry VII's envoy to the Catholic Kings of Spain in 1489, reported minutely on the circumstances of his embassy's public receptions, concluding, 'I believe that no ambassadors ever went who had more honour done to them than was done to the said ambassadors in everything'.

Thus the Household did much more than provide a luxurious standard of living and magnificent surroundings for king and queen. The Court was a sensitive refractor of the impulses of personal monarchy. In its public aspects, it was a stage where the king, for the benefit of an amorphous audience of bystanders and of gossips spreading rumour throughout the kingdom, ceremonially or symbolically displayed his authority, his favours, his alleged intentions. The Court was a medium of communication, more awe-inspiring, more convincing, more psychologically satisfying than proclamations by sheriffs' cryers and admonitions by sessions judges. The Court also provided secret, private springs to facilitate the sovereign's executive action and political control. It brought key governing personnel, present and future chief ministers, into a close personal relationship with the ruler, through domestic duties or companionship. It was the customary meeting-place of kings and the local rulers of society – the nobles. Many were brought up as children there in the company of future kings, and visited regularly as adults, for old acquaintance' sake, for recreation, as well as for business discussions. At Court they donned their ceremonial robes to process at the solemn 'crown-wearings' held on great feast days[27] and, more lightheartedly, arrayed in appropriate finery to exchange New Year's gifts and revel, and to ride to hounds or after the French in the summer. The relationships formed by these habits help to account for the hesitancy of kings and rebels to proceed to extremes, and their mutual savagery when they had decided to do so. Indeed, the beginnings of tensions were sometimes signalled by unwillingness to participate in Court rituals, to affirm one's membership of the *familia* (cf. p. 145), as reflected in Gloucester's baleful mien and swift withdrawal from Eltham in 1395, and Norfolk's unwillingness to return when summoned in 1569. The articulation of nobles' rivalries and resentments at Court was a means for rulers to influence the balance of political forces at large in the realm.

At the end of our period James I and his queen enthusiastically maintained the magnificence of Court culture. But the costs were once more straining royal resources and provoking adverse comments, some reminiscent of those heard at times before Edward IV's Household reforms. Inflated in personnel, the Jacobean Court was becoming a major cause of tension between Crown and community. The need and expectation of courtiers for reward above their often meagre official salaries, depleted by inflation, helped to inspire the drive to seek sources of revenue (such as customs impositions and monopoly patents) exasperating to subjects. Moreover, though the Court still provided the sovereign with useful points of executive and political contact, some of its historic functions may have been declining. Majesty was grasped by a more literate public from books and pamphlets, from theories of right and analyses of conduct, rather than from the ancient forms of visual symbolism. Royal power was exercised, less through the informal relationships of kings and nobles, more through those between Secretaries of State and Privy Council, on the one hand, and lords lieutenant and justices of the peace, on the other.

The Council

The mutual feudal obligations between kings and leading tenants-in-chief, and the virulent disputes in the early Middle Ages over their interpretation, had deeply and widely imprinted the ideal that kings should consult magnates about the realm's affairs. They were not generally viewed as the Crown's exploiters at the community's expense, but as the protectors of both against the greed and ambition of upstart counsellors. Frequent blood affinity between kings and nobles in the later Middle Ages enhanced the conviction that this was the latter's natural role. Within such an indulgent conceptual context, barefacedly greedy and ambitious rebel magnates like Warwick, Clarence and Archbishop Neville could represent themselves in 1469 as acting in the honourable tradition of great lords of the blood royal whose counsel had been neglected to the misfortune of Edward II, Richard II and Henry VI. They had trusted counsellors lacking 'respect or consideration to the welfare of the said princes, nor to the commonwealth of this land, but only to their singular honour and enriching of themselves and their blood'.

Noble counsel had been seen as a panacea for Crown and commonwealth by anonymous pamphleteers in the two decades or so before 1469. The Cornish rebels of 1549 were to hark back to arguments about 'natural' counsellors: 'We think it very meet, because the lord Cardinal Pole is of the king's blood, should not only have his free pardon, but also sent for to Rome and promoted to be first or second of the king's counsel.' The Cornishmen's political concept was behind the times. The Privy Council of 1549 was indeed exceptionally rich in eminent and noble blood – arising from the special circumstances of Edward VI's minority – but the traditional ideal of 'natural' counselling by nobles had declined. The bloodletting and expense caused in the Wars of the Roses by self-styled noble saviours of society may have lessened general enthusiasm for the ideal. The rise in power and status under the Tudors of expert, dedicated professional councillors weakened the prestige and effectiveness of a noble conciliar presence. When the Pilgrims of Grace complained in 1536 about the 'villein blood' of Henry VIII's councillors, they were echoing an anachronistic distrust of humbly born professionals. In many medieval eyes, they lacked the desired 'virtue' inherent in noble blood, and the 'substance' necessary to give their counsel weight. But by the time of the Pilgrimage, councillors were exercising more vigorous investigative and judicial authority. Their standing had been raised too by the spread of an ethic upholding the virtue of enlightened service to the state by the well-educated citizen, a standard by which some Henrician writers professed to find the nobility sadly wanting (see p. 135).

Sovereigns were free to seek the advice on matters of state of anyone they wished. They frequently turned to their chief ministers (e.g. the Chancellor, Treasurer of the Exchequer, Keeper of the Privy Seal), and to members of the Household, sojourning noble kinsfolk and officers of the Chamber with access to the presence. The latter often held the key to decisions, as they waited at the royal bedcurtains, closet door or saddlebow. Those whom rulers chose to hear sometimes belonged to categories considered by contemporary opinion as lacking the requisite virtue or substance: aliens, women, persons who were youthful, humbly born or of low status. During periods when the ruler was for one reason or another incapacitated, the community of the realm represented in parliaments was particularly anxious that the reality of royal power should not accrue to such people. Therefore it was publicly delegated to a group of councillors considered as reliable in character, pledged before the community to carry out their charge conscientiously. There was pressure in parliaments about conciliar personnel and responsibility in 1376, when Edward III was ill, and in the early 1400s, when Henry IV and his ministers seemed incapable of dealing with the Crown's financial problems. For much of Richard II's minority (1377–89) and during Henry VI's minority (1422–37) and periods of real and alleged adult incapacity (1454–5, 1455–6), parliaments formally accorded the exercise of royal powers to a Council.

The coincidence of recurring royal incapacity probably stimulated the evolution of a duly constituted Council, with defined responsibilities and powers. Contemporary awareness of the importance of the emergent institution is reflected in distinguishing references to the king's 'continual', 'privy' or 'secret' council, distinct from the individual counsel of nobles and ministers, and the collective counsel of great councils (see p. 77) and parliaments. The councillors appointed in October 1377, during Richard II's first parliament, were to receive wages for their attendances *per diem*. Rules for the Council were drawn up early in Henry VI's minority. Membership was fixed and restricted (rarely exceeding twenty-four): there had to be a quorum for business, and agreement for decisions. In 1424 annual salaries were granted to thirteen councillors (the Chancellor, Treasurer, one earl, four bishops, four barons and knights and two esquires) in recognition that they were bearing the daily burden of business. There was a strong recurring tendency for regular Council work to be carried on by small groups with a high content of professional royal servants – sometimes smaller and higher than this[28].

The Council sometimes met in a chamber of a royal palace or of a member's house, but in the fifteenth century it had its own offices in Westminster Palace, known from the paintings on the roof of the chamber where it convened as the Star Chamber (*camera stellata*). Moreover, it already had its own secretariat. There is evidence that a Clerk of the Council was appointed in October 1377, the first of a succession, normally Privy Seal clerks. The Clerk endorsed petitions considered by the Council with notes of its decisions, the witnesses to them, and sometimes other memoranda. These, and draft letters embodying Council decisions, were dispatched as warrants to the Privy Seal Office. For their private convenience some Clerks compiled registers. John Prophete kept attendance lists and notes of decisions which he wrote up as a Council 'journal' covering some of the meetings in 1392–3. In a similar manner Richard Caudray, Clerk 1421–35, had rolls stitched up (known from their present form as the 'Book of the Council') bearing his notes on select meetings.

Reconstruction of conciliar history from 1461 is inhibited by the disappearance of many of its warrants, which perished in the fire at the Banqueting House in Whitehall in 1619. The Council under the Yorkists and Henry VII seems to have had many familiar features. Though the title of councillor was conferred widely by Edward IV, the working Council probably averaged between nine and twelve. Leading ministers, high ecclesiastics and knights and barons who had risen in royal service were frequent attenders. Magnates, as so often during our period, except at times of emergency and tension, were generally not. Henry VII's councillors included large numbers of bishops and lay peers, but few of the latter attended regularly. The working core consisted mainly of professional bureaucrats, at most twenty-four. The commonest attendance was seven: Henry himself was often present.

The functions of the Council were remarkably stable, but its responsibilities, priorities and industriousness varied according to the predilections of the ruler and chief ministers, and the particular pressures on government. Conciliar work was advisory, administrative, investigative and judicial. Little is known about the tenor of many conciliar debates and of much advice tendered to the sovereign, not just as the result of record losses, but because so much of the process of decision-making was deliberately kept verbal and confidential. Fifteenth-century conciliar records show that the Council made recommendations for appointments to offices and embassies, drafted terms of tenure and diplomatic instructions, assigned revenues for payments, and bargained with the Crown's creditors and debtors.

Traditionally the Council considered petitions for redress of grievances, investigating, arbitrating or remitting complaints to a court or commission of oyer and terminer. By the end of the fifteenth century the Council was acquiring a settled jurisdiction in cases of riot, hearing suits which alleged breaches of statute or ordinance, many of them fundamentally aimed to score in disputes between landowners. In Henry VIII's reign the regular judicial sessions of councillors dealing with such suits began to be referred to as the 'Court of Star Chamber'. John Stow, writing in the 1590s, described

the Star Chamber where in the term time every week once at the least . . . and on the next day after the term endeth the lord chancellor and the lords and other of the Privy Council and the chief justices of England, from 9 of the clock till it be 11 do sit. . . . There be plaints heard of riots, routs and other misdemeanours which, if they be found by the King's Council, the party offender shall be censured by these persons . . . and he shall be both fined and commanded to prison.

The court attracted litigants because of its effective process. Witnesses as well as parties were efficiently summoned and examined. Star Chamber often extracted bonds for good behaviour, but, not being statutorily constituted, it could not sentence to loss of life, limb or freehold.

The pressure of private Bills and the Crown's drive in the later fifteenth century to develop financial administration had led to greater specialisation by councillors as judges and revenue officers, as well as contributing to the increase of councillors. There were more than sixty-two in 1526–7. In 1483 a second Clerk of the Council had been appointed to receive petitions, which particular councillors were delegated to hear. The earliest recorded proceedings of this tribunal, known from 1529 as 'the Court of Requests' date from 1493. The court, which appears to have dealt mainly with civil suits, observed similar process as Star Chamber and Chancery, and was popular with litigants because of its speed and cheapness. It acquired offices in the White Hall at Westminster in 1516.

Such developments produced a Council largely composed of highly trained lay bureaucrats, many of them too absorbed in their special departmental responsibilities to take part in the Council's general advisory and administrative tasks. Henry VII and Wolsey, both prepared to shoulder exceptional burdens of government, were content to consult with or delegate to the councillors available. But in the 1530s, there reappeared a Council with a restricted membership, whose prime duty was to meet regularly and exercise collectively the principal responsibility for advising and co-ordinating affairs of state. This 'Privy Council', as it was termed, had its own registers, described by Sir Julius Caesar in 1625 as 'great fair . . . books . . . where all the acts of that counsel should be written, and copies of letters, and whatsoever that table [the Council board] should ordain'[29]. In 1555 the Privy Council received its own seal: warrants under it were to be regarded as sufficient to authorise payments by the Elizabethan Exchequer.

Political supporters, in addition to the core of bureaucrats, had added conspicuously to the Privy Council's size in Edward VI's and Mary's reigns. But Elizabeth had twenty-one councillors in 1558, fifteen in 1568, eighteen in 1578 and thirteen at the time of her death. In 1603 James I hastily added thirteen more (including six Scots who never sat). Elizabeth's choice was determined by her need for a select, chiefly ministerial group to give advice on problems of state, coordinate the central institutions of government, and supervise the regions. The effectiveness of the Elizabethan Privy Council depended in no small measure on the co-ordinating role of her Principal Secretaries (see pp. 99–100). The Secretary was the principal means of communication between sovereign and Privy Council, drawing up agenda and memoranda for its sessions based on a personal appreciation of her requirements and problems, receiving the opinions of absent privy councillors, and sometimes conveying and interpreting the Council's collective views to the queen.

The Principal Secretaries usually attended Council sessions. Surviving registers for the period 24 May 1570 to 29 June 1575 show that eight councillors consistently bore the burden of its administrative duties: the Treasurer and Comptroller of the Household, the two Principal Secretaries, the Lord Chamberlain, the Lord Admiral, the earl of Leicester and the Lord Treasurer (Burghley). In this period the average recorded number of meetings was 6·6 times a month and 1·5 times a week, with considerable variations, according to the amount of business on hand. Apart from its term-time meetings as a court in Star Chamber, the Council met most frequently near the royal presence, at Greenwich or Hampton Court.

Julius Caesar, a councillor of James I, described the Council's meeting-places with its secretariat:

The Privy Counsel have had always, and so now, a fair chamber in every standing house, where the king's majesty's abode is, where they keep the counsel table, with a little room thereto adjoining, where the clerks of the said counsel and their servants sit and write. The Privy Counsel is attended on by three or more ordinary clerks to enact their orders, and write such letters, or answers as their Lordships shall command them.

The Clerks, who received quarterly salaries augmented by fees, paid their assistant subclerks themselves. A Clerk sometimes wrote only the date, place and attendance details of a session, leaving the rest to be filled in by his assistant. Council letters were often written by subclerks, who also wrote up the registers from their master's and their own notes.

Privy Seal, Signet and Chancery

Under Edward III the process was completed whereby the king's personal seal, the 'Privy Seal', ceased to be his private seal kept by its keeper in the Household, and became an instrument of public administration, validating documents from a writing-office which authenticated and formally drafted them in the king's name. Orders were addressed to the keeper for Privy Seal validation from a variety of sources. He received direct expressions of the royal will, by letters from the king, by report of his word of mouth, and by receipt of petitions endorsed with the decisions which he approved. The Council and individual royal officials also sent drafts and instructions. On their receipt, the keeper authorised his clerks to draft a warrant[30]. Among the sorts of letters issued by the office were instructions to officials, communications to foreign princes, pardons, licences and safe-conducts, requests for loans and benevolences, summonses to appear before the king[31]. Privy Seal warrants (e.g. for royal grants and remissions) were dispatched to Chancery, where their tenor formed the basis for letters issued under the Great Seal and for Chancery enrolments, and where the warrants were filed. Privy Seal warrants addressed to the Treasurer and Exchequer officials authorised payments.

The traditional establishment in the Privy Seal Office, under its keeper, was four clerks, but there were often more in the fourteenth century, and the establishment seems to have been larger in the fifteenth. In 1400 there were six clerks, in 1422, twelve; in 1444 there were five clerks and seven under-clerks. An under-clerk (quite likely to be of humble origins) would commence writing for an established clerk, in the hope of eventual promotion to a clerkship, with its royal rewards and fees for engrossment[32]. The ultimate promotion was to the secondary clerkship, with its superior rewards, but the keepership was out of reach in the fifteenth century – a great office of state whose holders came from outside the office. The clerks were responsible but not potentially high-flying clerical officers, their office (apart from occasional travels with the king) perhaps accommodated in a corner of Westminster Hall or rooms in the palace, their private quarters in a hostel in the London suburbs rented by the keeper.

Under the Yorkist and early Tudor kings the Privy Seal Office lost a great deal of its business. The number of its warrants communicating financial orders to the Exchequer declined, since Chamber financial administration was conducted largely without formal reference to Exchequer or Council, being warranted by the king's Signet letters, sign manual or verbal orders, and the letters of Chamber officials. The sixteenth-century revenue courts warranted with their own seals. Wolsey as Chancellor authorised the issue of Chancery missives which would normally have had Privy Seal authentication, and dispatched administrative orders direct from his private secretariat. Tudor royal missives often went straight from one of the secretariats controlled by the Secretary. In the later sixteenth century Privy Seal warrants were still used as the principal, though not exclusive, means of moving Chancery and Exchequer to administrative action, and the Court of Requests still summoned by them. 'Lord Privy Seal' remained a minister of first rank, an *ex officio* privy councillor.

In the fourteenth century, since the offices of the Great and later the Privy Seal were normally 'out of Court', kings often used whatever signet rings they had to hand to seal letters which they wished to be sent promptly. In 1377, after Richard II's accession, the office of King's Secretary is first mentioned. The holder, the cleric Robert Braybrooke, is the first known Secretary in a continuous series (with a gap during Henry VI's minority), who resided in the Household and were custodians of Signet seals, using them to authenticate the king's personal correspondence (for example, with kinsmen, the Council, officials and other princes). Signet letters were also dispatched to the Keeper of the Privy Seal, instructing him to issue letters to move the Great Seal: the main surviving body of texts of Signet letters are Privy Seal and Chancery warrants. The letters were written in French till the second decade of the fifteenth century, when English superseded it. There is evidence in Richard's reign of clerical assistance for the Secretary: under the Lancastrians he had an establishment of at least four or five clerks. The Secretary and his office continued to attend on the sovereign. The *Black Book* prescribed that when resident in the Household, on account of his office the Secretary was entitled to have eating in the hall four clerks, 'sufficient writers of the king's signet'. He was to receive parchment, paper and red wax from Household officials, and 'when he hath need of much writing', tallow and wax candles. The warrant of appointment for Sir Thomas Wriothesley and Sir Ralph Sadler as Principal Secretaries in 1540 entitled them to 'an ordinary chamber or lodging within the gates of his Grace's house, in all places where the same may be, conveniently furnished; and every of them to have like bouche of court[33] in all things as is appointed to the secretary'.

Secretary and Signet office gained greater importance under the Yorkists and early Tudors. The Secretary became an *ex officio* councillor, and Signet letters increasingly replaced Privy Seal letters as warrants for payments and as missives conveying administrative orders to officials and local authorities[34]. Henry VIII's Secretaries were concerned in drafting his vast correspondence, diplomatic and mandatory. Thomas Cromwell (Secretary 1534–40) made the office for the first time the *de facto* principal ministry. Subsequent appointments of two Secretaries (one of whom was regarded as senior) reflected how pivotal and onerous the office had become. The Elizabethan Secretary's letters were sufficient warrant to activate all government departments and officials. To deal with business as instructed by sovereign and Privy Council, he had 'to use the help of such her Majesty's servants as serve underneath him, as the clerks of the Council, the clerks of the signet, the secretary of the Latin and French tongues, and of his own servants'[35]. Especially during the Secretaryships of the future Lord Burghley (1558–72) and his son Sir Robert Cecil (1596–1600), the office tended again to be a prime ministerial one – a logical development, in view of the Secretary's continued attendance on the sovereign, personal control of the central secretariats, and supervision of Privy Council business.

Privy Seal, Signet, Council and Secretaryship secretariats were offices with small establishments which at various times in our period were central agencies producing drafts to validate royal administrative action, quick to react to the will of sovereign, principal ministers and Council. But the most ancient, authoritative and largest writing-office was Chancery. Its head, the Chancellor, was formally considered as the Crown's first minister, and was custodian of the Great Seal, which he ceremonially received on taking office, and kept sealed in a velvet bag. The Chancellor presided in Chancery, in Westminster Hall, attended by some of his clerks, examining a stream of private requests to king and Council for justice to be expedited, and of complaints about abuses, particularly those allegedly committed by royal and franchisal officers. In Chancery the Crown's acts and commands were publicly authenticated. Charters, letters patent and close[36], and original writs (see p. 103) were passed to the spigurnel, for sealing, assisted by the chafewax, who tempered the wax. The seal impression was threaded or stamped, in green wax (a symbol of perpetuity) for charters, in white for letters close and writs.

Chancery had two departments, Rolls and Hanaper. The Clerk of the Rolls was the working head of the writing-office, the most eminent of the twelve 'greater clerks', clerks 'of the first form'. They were responsible for formalising drafts of the more important letters, each having one or two under-clerks writing in their name. Then there were twelve clerks 'of the second form', and the cursitors whose duty was to write the conventional writs 'of course' (*de cursu*), as 'commanded', that is to say, directed and supervised, by the greater clerks. The Clerk of the Rolls was responsible for the maintenance, filing and storing by his staff of the largest body of records in the realm: warrants, memoranda, records of suits in Chancery, inquisitions, and the great rolls of Chancery, records of categories of letters issued, as well as of some other royal and private business[37].

The Hanaper was the accounting department of Chancery. Suitors for letters and writs received them there on payment of the fixed official fees. The Clerk of the Hanaper accounted, at the Exchequer or in the Chamber, for all Chancery receipts and expenditure. The Chancery acquired a staff of well over 100; though much smaller than the Household, it was the second largest department of state. As in other central administrative departments, clerks, often of humble background, entered the office young as writing assistants employed by the established clerks. If the under-clerks were lucky enough to be appointed to a Crown clerkship, they could look forward to eventual promotion in order of seniority, sometimes accelerated by exceptional ability or fortune. Many had lengthy careers solely devoted to the practice of the special drafting skills required in Chancery. The need for this expertise led to the development of the Inns of Chancery as teaching institutions. In the fourteenth century these hostels, where established Chancery clerks lived, began to admit students to learn the arts of drafting 'writs of course'.

The lucrative status of the medieval greater clerkships, and their potential as stepping-stones to higher royal office, is indicated by the frequency with which cursitors, hoping that the Chancellor would promote them to vacancies, had to endure the royal nomination of outsiders. The greater clerks received allowances out of the Chancellor's annuity, and expected the Crown to bestow fine benefices and other rewards on them for particular services. The increase of married clerks from the end of the fourteenth century suggests that suitors' fees for favours and the engrossment of letters, paid to the clerks in addition to the official fees, were enabling Chancery officials to set up their own households. In 1593 the twenty-four cursitors and their under-clerks made out more than 35,000 writs – a great deal of profitable business.

Since Chancery's principal offices attracted talented administrators, the Crown was able to use it as a pool of expertise in various governmental spheres. For instance, some clerks became specialists in the drafting of diplomatic documents: ministers and envoys found it indispensable to consult some over proposals for truce and peace between the English and French Crowns in the fourteenth and fifteenth centuries. But expertise was to be most strikingly developed in judicial administration, leading to the emergence of the Court of Chancery. In the early fourteenth century, the Chancellor, assisted by his clerks, had sifted through and examined petitions, prompted royal officials and courts to provide remedies, and helped to enforce judgments. By Richard II's reign, petitioners were addressing the Chancellor in person, praying for his remedy in such cases as alleged maintenance and false imprisonment. The Chancellor summoned defendants and witnesses to appear before him by a writ which stated a financial penalty for default (subpoena), a more effective method of summons than the 'original writs' used in other courts (see pp. 103 ff). Not being circumscribed by the rigid form of common law suits, the Chancellor had the ability to provide redress supplementary to actions in Common Pleas or King's Bench. For instance, he might take recognisances to give protection to possession whilst an action over property was in progress, stay a trial in order to allow time for evidences to be produced, or appoint a special commission of oyer and terminer to enquire into and determine a dispute. He might order a party to fulfil a contract, in cases in which the common law only awarded damages for non-fulfilment, or in which it for long did not recognise the intention of the contract (enfeoffment to uses; see pp. 125 ff).

In the Lancastrian period, Chancellors' judicial powers were enhanced by the statutory authority which they received to oversee justices of the peace and sheriffs: Acts of 1487 and 1495 supplemented their statutory authority to deal with offences against public order. The number of written petitions to the Chancellor increased markedly under the Lancastrians, and enormously under the Yorkists and early Tudors[38]. The Court of Chancery was being used by litigants in the sixteenth century not only as a means of redress for grievances which were genuine as stated, but as an arena in which to win advantages in property disputes which were essentially covered by common law actions in other courts. For instance, a complaint in Chancery alleging wrongful detention of title-deeds might result, after their examination, in a decree effectively pronouncing on title, enjoining the loser to allow his opponent peaceful possession.

The rise of the Chancellor as judge had far-reaching effects on Chancery administration. From the 1470s onwards, greater clerkships were conferred on law graduates, rather than by the promotion of cursitors, who continued to fulfil the historic clerical routines of Chancery, under the supervision of the Clerk of the Rolls and greater clerks – or, as they came to be termed, Master of the Rolls and Masters in Chancery. In the sixteenth century the Chancellorship and Masterships were practically taken over by the common lawyers. The masters, concentrating on judicial work, claimed to be judicial officers of Chancery in their own right. The Master of the Rolls supervised the Clerks of the Petty Bag, responsible for drafting and storing records concerned with the Chancellor's statutory jurisdiction; the Six Clerks, who as the Court's attorneys had many duties connected with its judicial administration; and the Examiners, who copied the answers of witnesses.

Procedure in the Court of Chancery was akin to that in conciliar, not common law courts, though justices of the King's Bench and Common Pleas were often invited to sit in the Elizabethan Chancery (as they did in Star Chamber). There was no jury, and proceedings were conducted by what had become a highly formalised pattern of written depositions, sometimes supplemented by *viva voce* examinations of parties and witnesses. Many cases were settled by commissions to Master and other officials, rather than by formal decree in Chancery. The elaboration of procedural rules provided parties with opportunities to manoeuvre tactically (as they had long been able to do in King's Bench or Common Pleas). Nevertheless, William Lambarde (d.1601), a Master in Chancery, could refer to the popularity of the court's procedures, to the impatience of 'the *Common Man* . . . to have his Causes determined either at the *Councell-board* without open hearing, or by absolute authoritie, without prescribed rule of ordinary proceeding'[39].

Though its case-load was much smaller than that of Common Pleas or even King's Bench, by the sixteenth century Chancery had become one of the principal central courts, supplementing the work of the others with its equitable jurisdiction, as well as exercising a statutory jurisdiction in certain spheres. But it had ceased to be such an important writing-office and pool of general expertise as it had once been.

King's Bench and Common Pleas

Much of the routine enforcement of common law, as well as the drafting and interpretation of statute, depended on a select band of royal servants and councillors, the professional judges. In vacation they might be found presiding in the shires as justices of assize, oyer and terminer or gaol delivery; in term time in the courts which, like Chancery, usually met in Westminster Hall. There were four legal terms, commencing in the autumn after Michaelmas, in January after the feast of St Hilary, after Easter, and in summer after Trinity. Each lasted about three weeks, apart from the longer Michaelmas term. King's Bench and Common Pleas each had a Chief Justice (the former's being head of the judiciary) and, at most, five other judges each.

King's Bench dealt particularly, though not exclusively, with cases in which the Crown had an interest, and in which criminal charges were preferred. Its justices accepted suits brought by private Bills and criminal appeals. The Crown retained an attorney in the court responsible for promoting and recording criminal prosecutions. Convictions were obtained through cross-examination and confession, and resort, if necessary, to the verdict of a jury from the county where the offence was alleged to have occurred. Like some other central courts in the sixteenth century, King's Bench was to be frequently occupied with the civil pleas of private litigants (e.g. debt, detinue, covenant, account): modifications in its procedure for bringing in bills of trespass in the 1540s favoured the suitor and increased court business.

Common Pleas, whose staple was civil disputes concerning property, was the busiest court[40]. The suitor initiated 'mesne process' (the machinery for bringing the defendant into court) by purchasing an 'original' writ in Chancery, specifying the 'form of action' and ordering the defendant's appearance[41]. Sheriffs' endorsements of returned writs often indicate a failure to execute them, because the defendant was out of the jurisdiction of the sheriff, or bailiff of a liberty with return of writs. There were other possible obstacles to getting a case started or concluded. A defendant might procure postponements of hearings by legitimate excuses (essoins), royal letters protecting from prosecution as on the king's service, or the transfer of the case to another court. Cases were often delayed by the non-appearance of defendants or jurors. Sir John Fortescue's remarks show a lawyer's tendency to feel justified complacence when faced with the exasperation of long-suffering clients: 'It is most necessary for delays to be made in the process of all actions. . . . For by such delays the parties, especially the defendants, can often provide themselves with useful defence and counsel, which they would otherwise lack'[42].

When the case came to court, a professional pleader engaged for the plaintiff argued that it fitted within the terms of the form of action, and his opponent tried to demolish his argument. Judgment was pronounced if one of the parties failed under cross-examination, or if the issue to which the case had been reduced in court turned on a point of law. If the issue depended on a point of fact, the case was almost invariably dismissed for conclusion at local assizes by verdict of the county. Once jurors were brought into play, the parties became even more dependent on the local 'affection' they could command, particularly in the hearts of the sheriff and his deputy.

The defects of the central common law courts in the later Middle Ages have often been remarked on. Their control of summons and jury was inadequate: their forms of action were adhered to with undue rigidity. As a consequence, by Henry VIII's reign they seem to have been losing a lot of business to the Court of Chancery and the conciliar courts. But there are signs of recovery in the 1540s: one reason was their reception of litigation on the device of property by will, consequent on the Statute of Wills, 1540 (see p. 126).

By the fifteenth century the profession of common lawyer was becoming large and well defined, as the strictures of polemicists on lawyers as a group bear uncomplimentary witness. The last appointments of clergymen as judges occurred in the fourteenth century. The office was highly lucrative, a means to found a landed fortune. In addition to their fixed annuities, judges could look forward to supplementary royal rewards, a shower of suitors' presents, and a great deal of well-paid private business, such as counselling over family settlements. But their offical responsibilities remained arduous. Besides fulfilling the routine work of office, judges were summoned to give the Crown legal advice in councils and parliaments, and, on occasion, assembled with their colleagues the Barons of the Exchequer to settle important legal points at issue. As royal servants, they found it hard to resist occasional royal pressure to promote legislation, and make decisions on cases, which they may well have considered unduly partial to the sovereign's will. But the harsh punishments experienced by the judges who advised Richard II in 1387 (cf. p. 193) may have helped to induce in their successors a desire to be considered as professional men safeguarding the laws, and eschewing high and dangerous controversies.

The judges came to share a professional outlook with lawyers who held offices in and practised in their courts, derived from a background of shared training.[43]. The organisation of the Inns of Court as teaching institutions for apprentices at law probably took place in the reigns of Henry IV and V. About 200 to 300 apprentices currently took courses which normally lasted for three years. But it needed many more years of residence to master the great body of precedents required for graduation as a pleader. The majority of apprentices, after gaining basic knowledge from attendance at lectures, readings and mock trials in their Inn, and at court sessions, left to build up urban and country practices, conveyancing, counselling, acting as attorneys, and holding offices in local courts. Others practised in one of the Westminster courts, assuming responsibility for procedural moves in their clients' suits, and sometimes retained by the rich as an attorney-general, ready to engage counsel for the patron in various suits and courts.

A small number of pre-eminent senior apprentices were appointed by the Crown as serjeants-at-law. In the fourteenth century, the serjeants, an elite of professional pleaders, had obtained a monopoly of examining witnesses, and presenting evidence in the Common Pleas, where they mainly worked. Their appointments singled them out as potential judges. Some were retained by the Crown: the king's serjeants were reminded in parliament by the Chancellor in 1460, when they showed a prudent reluctance to advise about York's claim to the throne, that they were 'the King's particular counsellors, and therefore they had their fees and wages'. Other senior apprentices granted admission as pleaders were termed 'barristers'[44]. After 1400 they gained a monopoly of pleading in King's Bench, and some were retained as 'king's counsel learned in the law', with the duty of working with the Attorney-General and Solicitor-General[45].

Financial departments, sources of income, and revenue problems

Precociously established in the twelfth century, the Exchequer had become the principal department of state customarily accounting for royal revenues, validating their receipt and issue from a variety of sources, according to routines which reached a full evolution in Edward II's last years[46]. The Exchequer was housed in Westminster Palace, and acquired treasuries in the Chapel of the Pyx in Westminster Abbey, and in a chamber off its cloister, near the chapter-house. Henry VI provided it with an additional repository, under the Council's Star Chamber in the palace. The medieval Exchequer worked according to rigidly observed methods, many hallowed by age. They were to prove inadequate to fulfil the Crown's need for more comprehensive and flexible revenue administration in the later fifteenth century. The antiquity of some Exchequer offices was reflected by Henry lord Stafford's reaction when appointed to one of the two Chamberlainships of the Receipt in 1554: he consulted the twelfth-century treatise on the Exchequer, *Dialogus de Scaccario*, to establish the precedence of his office.

Twice yearly, at the start of the Exchequer terms (after Easter and at Michaelmas), sheriffs, customs officers, subsidy collectors and guardians of Crown lands answered their summons to Westminster, accounting for sums due at the Exchequer. In the Exchequer of Receipt the specie they handed over was counted and 'assayed' (checked for purity). They were each presented with a 'tally', the spliced half of a stick marked with notches, the number, size and position of which indicated the sum. The debtor handed in the tally as evidence of payment at the Exchequer of Account and Pleas, where his liabilities were finally examined, enrolled, and acquitted.

But if he failed to give satisfaction, he was liable to prosecution in the Exchequer of Pleas. This most specialised of old central courts administering common law was concerned with suits to protect royal financial rights, and with prosecutions involving financial officials. Actions were brought on information, Bill, original writ and inquisition. Four or five Barons of the Exchequer sat in judgment, and Exchequer clerks acted as attorneys. By the late fifteenth century the Exchequer Court was handling comparatively few suits (see p. 119 n. 40), mainly private prosecutions of officers accounting at the Exchequer. A decline in business may have been induced by the shrinkage of the Exchequer's fiscal responsibilities, and the expansion of business in the conciliar courts, in the later fifteenth century.

The cash paid into the Exchequer by 'farmers' who satisfied its auditors and were acquitted, often did not correspond to the full amount of the debt, because they had already handed over some to royal creditors. The common practice of assigning revenues at source to the latter meant that less than half the sums accounted for at the Exchequer actually passed through its treasuries. A royal creditor (such as an annuitant) would present a writ of *Liberate*, or mandate under the Privy Seal, directing the Treasurer and Chamberlains of the Exchequer to pay an instalment of his annuity out of the king's treasury. If he was lucky, cash would be produced, the payment being recorded on the Issue Rolls. But it was more than likely that he would instead receive one half of a tally marked with the amount owed, which a debtor (such as a customs or subsidy collector) would be ordered to pay, and credited with on the sets of Receipt Rolls. The annuitant handed over his half of the tally to the debtor on receiving the money from him, and the latter took it to the Exchequer when presenting his account, for comparison with the other half. What often happened, however, was that because of previous assignments, and casual falls in revenue, the debtor could not pay the creditor, who then hastened back to the Exchequer, agitating for a cash payment there, or a reliable assignment, that is, one on which the Exchequer ordered him to be given preference.

The virtue of the Exchequer was that, through the rigid maintenance of precise traditional routines, it upheld an exemplary system of audit of royal officials' accounts. The Exchequer was not designed to exploit royal revenues or to determine financial priorities. The leases which it made of estates in the king's hand had their terms based on valuations made by local royal officials, not Exchequer clerks. Its warrants for payments were automatic responses to authentic authorisations from whatever government source. The Exchequer has sometimes been blamed by historians for not doing what no contemporaries expected it to do. Budgeting, exploitation and other matters of financial policy were properly matters to be determined by king and Council. The narrowness of Exchequer responsibilities facilitated devolution of financial work to other offices, in accordance with royal priorities. In the period 1333–56, for instance, there was an accumulation of estates not leased under Exchequer control, but administered independently by officials of the Chamber of the Household as a central office of land revenue. During Edward III's campaigns, some revenues assigned for their costs, and paid directly into his Household treasuries, were not accounted for at the Exchequer by Chamber and Wardrobe officers.

The financial strains imposed on the community's as well as the Crown's customary resources by frequently concurrent needs to maintain the Court, provide for the king's family, bestow patronage, and pay for defences and campaigns, produced manifestations of concern about royal financial administration, particularly budgetary priorities, among taxpayers as well as councillors. The Lancastrian Commons interfered over such priorities, considering that Henry IV's and Henry VI's poverty, and reliance on aid for ordinary as well as extraordinary expenses, fundamentally stemmed from too lavish grants of fees, annuities and rewards. They promoted Acts of Resumption as a remedy, abrogating grants, and so freeing funds for application to Household and other standing charges. The Crown used resumptions in the second half of the fifteenth century, as a means of redistributing revenue, as well as impressing public opinion.

Edward IV, who experienced the problems of usurpation in the first decade of his reign, was anxious to have adequate supplies of cash available to pay expenses, wages and rewards, and to refrain from alienating his subjects by frequent levies (cf. p. 288). When Clarence's share of the Warwick, Despenser and Salisbury estates came in the Crown's hands as a result of his forfeiture in 1478, they were not placed under Exchequer control, but in the charge of salaried receivers, who accounted to specially appointed auditors (Household officers), and paid the clear incomes to the Treasurer of the Chamber. The king also ordered direct payments into the Chamber, bypassing Exchequer assignment, from a variety of sources, such as profits from the temporalities of vacant sees and from the exercise of royal prerogative rights (e.g. from wardship and livery), the annual pension from the French Crown acquired in 1475, benevolences, and some of the proceeds of parliamentary taxation. The Treasurer of the Chamber and his clerical staff disbursed at the king's command: surviving accounts from Richard III's reign show that the Treasurer accounted to the king in person, compiling books of receipt and issue, which listed cash dealings in order.

In the first year or two of his reign Henry VII reverted to the traditional system of Exchequer financing. But eventually he recognised the advantage of Yorkist methods, which provided a surer and fuller cash supply. Though during the first ten years of his reign land receipts in the Chamber remained small, and less than the total attained under the Yorkists, in the second ten years the sums markedly increased, due to the diligence and expertise of the king and his financial officers. By Henry's last years, the Treasurer of the Chamber had become the receiver-general of all Crown lands and of most other revenues, four-fifths of whose total were received, stored and disbursed in the Chamber. The Exchequer had sunk to a minor revenue department, whose assignments now sufficed to cover little more than the salaries of its own officers and rewards due to sheriffs and customs officers. Though receivers and auditors of Chamber revenue remained technically liable to Exchequer audit, in practice this had become a dead letter. Books of summaries of accounts of some forty receivers appearing for audit before Henry and groups of his councillors survive for several years of his reign. These auditors or 'general surveyors' also heard a number of other accounts, and acted as a supreme board of management for almost all the landed revenues of the king. Henry himself audited Treasurers' accounts, as his initialling of pages of their books with the royal sign manual shows. Early in Henry VIII's reign, in reaction against his father's methods of government, the General Surveyors' arbitrary powers were curtailed and controlled, but were gradually and partially restored on the basis of successive Acts of parliament, permanently from 1536.

Thomas Cromwell, stimulated by the need to devise methods of controlling the Crown's new ecclesiastical revenues in the 1530s, instigated the creation of new revenue agencies, as well as reforming existing ones. These departments of state, like the financial administration of the Yorkist and early Tudor Chamber, were modelled on late medieval methods of administering magnates' estates, with local receivers accounting to and being controlled by a central board of officers. Like the duchy of Lancaster (organised in this way), the new departments were granted the powers of a court, capable of adjudicating disputes and enforcing punishments on defaulters. The first new court was 'of the Augmentations of the revenue of the Crown' (1536), which was to administer all lands coming to the king by surrender, escheat or purchase (primarily the former monastic lands). The Court of Wards, and of First Fruits and Tenths (for clerical dues) were statutorily constituted in 1540, and in 1542 the Court of General Surveyors took complete control of lands administered by the Treasurer of the Chamber.

This complex reorganisation of revenue administration, whose early working was hampered, not surprisingly, by overlapping claims to responsibility, never had the chance to display its potential in entirety. Cromwell's fall and the Privy Council's increasing absorption in the 1540s in political manoeuvring deprived the system of firm direction. The revenue courts became hunting-grounds for peculating officials. In 1554 they were abolished, except for the duchy of Lancaster, and Wards and Liveries, whose incomes were relatively small. Exchequer control was restored over other revenues – but the control of a reformed Exchequer. In the 1560s it had auditors accounting according to modern methods, with particular responsibilities for handling the accounts of receivers of different branches of revenue; the leasing system was not revived. As a result of the rise of Chamber financial administration, the ancient 'course' of the Exchequer had long since atrophied. The keeping of Issue Rolls and two of the three sets of Receipt Rolls had ceased. Already, early in Henry VIII's reign, there had been a revival of the Exchequer's auditing responsibilities.

Despite the efficiency and ingenuity with which financial administration was adapted in the sixteenth century to maximise the yield from customary revenues, the Crown lurched into financial crises, even resorting to coinage debasements late in Henry VIII's reign and in Edward VI's. The revitalised customary revenues could not sustain the huge costs of Henry VIII's and his children's wars, above all the war with Spain (1585–1604). Concurrently, inflation gnawed at the value of what had recently seemed to be assured sources of income, and intensified discontents at various expedients to milk more from the community. Subjects had long accepted that the Crown could not sustain war without levying their wealth. But James I was to seek large levies to finance his peacetime expenses, an expedient resented by the community in the fourteenth and fifteenth centuries, which Yorkists and Tudors had largely succeeded in avoiding.

There were many customary revenues, some casual and fluctuating, to which the Crown was entitled. These included the annual 'farms' of counties and boroughs, payments for grants of privileges and for dispensations from the operation of statutes and ordinances, fees for the issue of sealed letters and mandates by the Hanaper of Chancery and the Privy Seal Office, fines and amercements, and feudal dues, particularly the profits of wardships and liveries (for the latter, see pp. 124–7). These revenues in aggregate could make substantial contributions[47]. Their exploitation by Yorkist and early Tudor Chamber administration contributed to the conspicuous wealth of the new dynasties. But the biggest contribution came from exploitation of the Crown lands which fortuitous circumstances enabled Edward IV and Henry VII to accumulate and retain. In 1483 the cash receipts from Crown lands may have approached between £22,000 and £25,000[48]. In 1502–5 Henry VII's Chamber was receiving about £40,000 p.a. from them – a higher amount than the Crown's total annual cash receipts from non-parliamentary sources in Henry VI's later years. Revenue received in the Chamber from all sources in

1502–5 averaged about £105,000. The Reformation increased royal revenue in the 1530s to about £222,000 p.a. (excluding taxation) (see p. 374). The value of this magnificent estate was badly depleted by mid-century inflation, and the need to sell Crown lands to meet military and ordinary expenses. Elizabeth, by dint of careful management, kept an adequate customary revenue of between £200,000 and £300,000.

Customs duties were an important prop of Yorkist and early Tudor finances, though in some earlier periods they had been a mainstay. In the first decade of Edward III's reign (1327–37), they had averaged about £13,000 p.a. Henry VI's average of £25,000 was his principal assured source. In 1275 Edward I had been granted regular dues on the export of wool, woolfells and untanned leather (later known as the 'ancient custom'), by the community of merchants, with the assent of the great men of the realm. The 'petty custom' originated in the dues imposed in 1303 on merchandise not subject to the ancient custom, including two shillings on every tun (252 gallons) of wine, and an *ad valorem* levy of threepence in the £ on general merchandise ('tunnage and poundage')[49]. Wool subsidies were levied in the first half of the fourteenth century, on pleas of royal necessity for the common profit, often by agreement with groups of merchants. Edward III eventually recognised the right of parliaments to give assent to subsidies, but kings continued to exercise some prerogative to tax on their own initiative. Edward IV levied wool custom and tunnage and poundage before being granted them for life in 1465[50]. Tudor rulers issued revised Books of Rates, such as that of 1558 raising valuations and specific duties, and adding some 300 commodities. This revision and others up to 1590 raised rates on average by 75 per cent. Jacobean impositions of additional duties were bringing in £70,000 p.a. in 1614, when the Commons attacked them (as they had done in 1610) as unconstitutional.

When customs were not farmed out for collection by the deputies of private individuals receiving them as assignments for loans or as rewards, royal collectors were appointed in each port (often local merchants). There were usually two to collect the wool custom and subsidy, and two for the ancient custom and subsidy[51]. The collector was obliged to account for his levies at the Exchequer, appointing deputy collectors when unable to attend to the business in person. He kept one half of the cocket seal, which was used to authenticate indented acquittances for payments, one copy of which was retained by the merchant or shipmaster, the other at the wharf for exhibition by the collector at the Exchequer. One half of the cocket seal was in the custody of the controller, whose duty was to write rolls as a check on collectors' business. There was also a troner and peser, who weighed wool and bulky commodities on a trone, and lighter articles on scales: searchers were employed to detect evasions. Port books were first introduced in 1428. The collectors were to produce books of accounts as well as particular accounts; tide-waiters, who checked cargoes on arrival or departure, made up certificate books with their particulars. Yorkist and early Tudor financial officials were keen to augment Chamber resources by a more thorough exploitation of the rising volume of trade. In 1471 there were the first appointments of powerful new controlling officials, the surveyors of customs[52].

Apart from customs, the most enduring and widely accepted form of parliamentary taxation was the aid assessed on the capital value of movable wealth, last granted in 1623. Its mechanisms embodied the principle, long dear to English taxpayers, but not always advantageous to the Crown, that assessment and collection should be in the hands of *ad hoc* commissions appointed by the Crown, composed of local gentlefolk or burgesses. From 1332 the levy was always fixed at a fifteenth in the shires, a tenth in the boroughs[53]. In fact, assessments of liability, made by juries before district deputies selected by the collectors to gather the money, came to be of only local relevance, for from 1334 the sums due from shires and boroughs remained fixed, with a total gross yield of £37,430. In 1433 a cut of £4,000 in the yields from a fifteenth was conceded, and a further cut of £2,000 was made in 1446. In the later fifteenth century the net worth of an aid was about £29,000, reduced by collectors' expenses, exemptions on grounds of poverty, and bad debts. The Crown tried to increase the yield by bargaining in parliament for the grant of more than one-fifteenth and one-tenth. There was a long period of occasional, uneasy experiment with other forms of aid. The Commons displayed recurring reluctance to countenance the development of new taxes. The 1371 tax on parishes, whose yield was disappointing, was not repeated in that form, nor were the capitation taxes tried from 1377, after the 1381 Peasants' Revolt (see p. 178). In 1404 the Commons granted an aid of twenty shillings on every knight's fee, and one shilling on every £1 of land, goods and other sources of income. But they insisted that its records should be destroyed, lest it be used as a precedent. Nevertheless, experiments in granting aids based on assessments of various income-related elements continued into the early sixteenth century, though some were never collected and others had a disappointing yield[54]. From early in Henry VIII's reign a form of subsidy became regularised, in which contributions were related to prescribed criteria of wealth, being individually assessed by local commissioners. The 'Tudor subsidy' for long produced a satisfactory yield, sometimes over £100,000.

Subjects were traditionally obliged to aid sovereigns in emergencies in other ways besides granting subsidies (cf. pp. 170 ff). Short-term, interest-free loans were requested under the obligation. Subjects could excuse themselves on grounds of poverty, and need not lend more than was appropriate to their degree. Characteristic figures requested were £100, 100 marks and £40 from lesser prelates and from gentlefolk, descending to £5 or 5 marks from yeomen and parsons and from the combined men of a township. Sergeants-at-arms delivered requests in

Signet or Privy Seal letters to well-to-do individuals, listed in loan books by Elizabethan Secretaries of State. Shire commissioners (often including royal servants) bargained with the men of township or locality over the sum and date of payment, drawing up an indenture of terms including a promise of repayment. Recipients of royal wages, annuities and rewards were considered as under a special obligation to lend. In 1464 all who had received grants and pensions worth at least 10 marks p.a. since Edward IV's accession were to contribute a quarter of their annual value. General loans sometimes produced disappointing returns. Many exemptions were claimed, and some of the evasion rife was beyond commissioners' ability (and sometimes will) to control[55].

More resented was the imposition of arbitrary forced levies. So-called 'benevolences' were raised nominally in lieu of the obligation to defend the realm incumbent on adult males. There was no question of repayment and no limit set on benevolence – a prescription for extortions. Royal servants often took a leading part in collection. The 1475 benevolence, whose returns are incomplete, brought in at least £21,656; that of 1544–5, £129,551. Such arbitrary levies were resorted to occasionally, for they were considered a hateful abuse of prerogative.

Under James I the problem of finding sufficient revenues was to be complicated by criticisms of a whole range of fiscal expedients as unconstitutional breaches of prerogative. At his accession the Crown's financial position did not appear bad. The prudent Elizabeth had managed to maintain a surplus of non-parliamentary revenues over non-military expenses. Though the gross debt at her death was £400,000, £300,000 in war subsidies granted in 1601 was still due, and the French Crown and the Dutch were heavily indebted to her for military aid. But there were underlying weaknesses. Her sales of Crown lands to help pay for war, particularly in the 1590s, had depleted the base for customary revenues: at the end of the reign, lands in hand were producing only £60,000 in cash. Her income, though raised considerably, does not seem to have kept pace with inflation. Subjects' experience of inflation increased their pressure on her for reward, and discontent at royal fiscal exploitation, particularly in the 1590s.

The problem of maintaining an adequate peacetime revenue in these circumstances was magnified by James's lavishness. An unknown alien king with a sharp sense of majesty, he had a political need to buy the services and loyalties of bureaucrats, magnates and gentlefolk, and to maintain an impressive Court. But he did not show a sustained appreciation of the need to reconcile these requirements with the availability of income. He failed to restrain spectacular rises in the costs of Household expenses, annuities and rewards. By 1608, when Salisbury (Robert Cecil) became Lord Treasurer, there was an accumulated debt of £597,337, and the annual deficit was running not far short of £100,000.

Jacobean financial administrators were fertile in expedients to meet king's, courtiers' and bureaucrats' voracious demands: in some later years of the reign, even economies were effected. In 1604 there was the Great Farm of the Customs, a contract with London financiers for them to collect many duties for seven years, in return for a farm of £112,400 p.a. As in Elizabeth's later years, patents of monopoly to manufacture or trade in commodities were sold, or granted as rewards. The collection of particular dues, such as the alehouse tax, and fines imposed in courts, was farmed. In 1608 Salisbury issued a Book of Rates with new impositions on 1,400 items, calculated to raise an extra £60,000 p.a. He sold Crown lands, and attempted to improve the administration of those remaining. After his death in 1612, such expedients were continued and others tried. Wardships and liveries were heavily milked, sinecures in central government offices created and sold, and titles of honour put on the market.

This heavy and, in some respects, unprecedented exploitation of prerogative rights provoked widespread fury among gentlefolk and others who were mulcted, especially since many of the pickings were ostentatiously swooped on by Court cormorants. The achievements of royal administrators (for example the economies which Cranfield effected from 1617 onwards) consequently failed to receive public credit. The unresponsiveness of taxpayers was one reason for the tendency of the yield from subsidies to fall off. Whereas an Elizabethan grant brought in as much as £130,000, in 1621 only £70,000 was raised; in 1628, £55,000.

One instructive attempt had been made by Crown and parliament to cooperate in putting royal revenues on a sounder, mutually agreeable basis. In 1610 preliminary agreement was reached over Salisbury's proposal, the 'Great Contract'. Wardship and purveyance were to be abolished, and old debts owed to the Crown cancelled, in return for a guaranteed annual levy of £200,000. But in the next parliamentary session, when details were to be concerted, the project foundered on extreme royal stipulations and unfavourable Commons reactions. There were doubts in Court and Council about the prospective loss of customary sources of patronage, and the possible inadequacy of the new tax. There was apprehensiveness in the Commons about novel forms of taxation, and suspicion of the way in which they might be exploited for private gain at Court. The episode demonstrated widespread awareness that royal finances had, once again, become a major problem for Crown and community. But there was a conspicuous absence of constructive agitation for a solution in the community, or of a consensus of opinion among leading royal officials that priority must be given to finding one that was generally acceptable. Early seventeenth-century reactions to royal revenue problems provide in these respects instructive contrasts with fifteenth-century ones. But in the fifteenth century, it had required the incentive of a civil war to make solvency the royal priority.

In 1592 Robert Beale wrote that a prospective Secretary of State should 'avoid opinion of being newfangled and a bringer-in of new customs'. More than a century before, Sir John Fortescue had written appreciatively of the English constitution and common law, and of their antiquity. Such attitudes attest lasting attachment to settled precedents in judicial and administrative relations between Crown and community. Officers of central royal administration, from at least the mid-fourteenth century onwards, predominantly envisaged themselves as operating in harmony and co-operaton, not in competition and conflict, with the generality of property-owning authorities.

The implementation of the royal will, of statute and common law, depended, in the first instance, on the skill and reliability of the Westminster workhorses. The current concepts of 'public office', in our eyes, seem to have been in many respects inadequate, producing what we would condemn as corruption and inefficiency. Patronage as well as ability played a large part in appointment and promotion. Salaries were often erratic and inadequate, necessitating supplementary extraction by officers of fees and gifts from suitors, and inducing a preoccupation with the hunt for additional royal rewards through the intercession of patrons. Offices tended to be regarded as fiefs, for the tenants to exploit, showing loyal eagerness to serve the Crown in lucrative ways, and employing their private staffs to do the donkey-work of official business.

Nevertheless, Westminster offices inherited, especially from the Angevin period, some valuable administrative traditions and routines. The specialist expertise required in accounting, engrossing, pleading and in the technicalities of courtly and domestic service produced professional standards which militated against the possibly deleterious effects of promotion by patronage, and of 'fief-holding' attitudes. Many officers spent their whole careers as specialists in a particular department. Departmental heads whose appointments were 'political' were expected to exercise a working knowledge, monitoring deputies whom they had appointed, if they were licensed not to hold office in person. The Exchequer system of account spread the practice and concept of public accountability through much of central administration.

The secularisation of personnel, creation of new departments, multiplication and duplication of offices and depreciation of salaries in the sixteenth century did have some adverse effects on the functioning of central administration, though not fundamentally undermining its traditional virtues or destroying its ability to translate the royal will into action. Office-holders had additional incentives to chase profits: their general success was reflected by the eagerness of gentlefolk to get places. Some succeeded in creating a hereditary interest. Peter Osborne, Lord Treasurer's Remembrancer in the Exchequer, thanked Burghley for securing him the reversion of his office, 'which will be the stay of his house, his wife, and children after him'. The Crown acquiesced in a brisk traffic in the sale of reversions by office-holders. Profiting at the community's expense was a respectable occupation for officials: it was, after all, a principal means of paying for the 'civil service', if a somewhat arbitrary one. Excessive peculation at the Crown's expense was less acceptable. John Beaumont, receiver-general of the new Court of Wards (1545–50), confessed that he had robbed the Crown of £11,823, by omitting from his receipts various sums paid into the Court. The Star Chamber judges were shocked at 'so many foul matters as we think have seldom appeared in one man'. Beaumont's crimes were exceptional – principally, perhaps, in scale. Others had certainly taken advantage of Henrician administrative reorganisation, dipping into the coffers of the newly erected courts.

The search for profit and patrons made officials sensitive to political currents at Court, but there were in some departments traditions of keeping aloof from great national controversies – an aid to efficiency and continuity. Certainly Household officers of standing, particularly those of the Chamber, had in many notable instances not shared their colleagues' studiously neutral sentiments. Some of Henry VI's Household men (and one of his judges, Fortescue) went into exile with him; some of Richard III's died with him. But apart from Chamber officers, and heads of Household and other central departments, Westminster men suffered little from political purges. They were too useful. Their offices continued to function in periods of civil commotion (e.g. in 1381), and their expertise was welcomed by usurpers (1399, 1461, 1485), and by Tudors determined to reverse predecessors' religious policies (1553, 1558).

Had 'public opinion' regarded central officers' activities as generally oppressive, they might not have been so free to eschew partisanship. The assassinations of a Chancellor and Treasurer in 1381, and of a Keeper of the Privy Seal (Moleyns) in 1449 were motivated by animus against them as councillors, not against their departments. Public opinion was satisfied in 1510 with the execution of two over-zealous ministers, rather than a wholesale purge of those who, spurred on by Henry VII, had been acting oppressively. The community had acquired a customary tolerance of central administration. By the fourteenth century many of its officers (and by the sixteenth century, a greater number) were concerned with the operations of judicial process dealing with individuals' and communities' bills of complaint, including plaints for redress against royal officers. As was strikingly demonstrated in 1376, parliament in certain circumstances might be used as a court of appeal for the indictment of leading ministers.

Moreover, central administration was concerned with the routine enforcement of laws and royal privileges, rather than with arbitrary impositions. The administrative extensions of state authority in the sixteenth century were, in important respects, biased along traditional guidelines. Central officers (apart from the customary assize judges) remained rare birds outside Westminster. In the localities, the Crown's more extensive statutory jurisdiction and supervision was largely upheld under royal commission by the leaders of shire and urban society. But from the later sixteenth century onwards there was growing hostility to the activities of central officers', and Court monopolists' local deputies (see p. 127).

The ability which central departments displayed for most of our period to adapt to the changing needs of Crown and community was probably facilitated by the small total of their personnel (apart from the Household staff), and the interlocking and overlapping nature of their responsibilities[56]. Despite the sixteenth-century numerical increases, central administration remained an intimate, familiar business. In term time, the visitor to Elizabethan Westminster might have found Chancery, King's Bench and Common Pleas in session in Westminster Hall. A few minutes' walk by adjacent passages, stairs and alleys would have brought him to the Exchequer or the Courts of Wards and Liveries, of the Duchy of Lancaster or of Requests. Household, Signet Office and Secretaries were often nearby at Whitehall, or at a palace less than a day's ride away. A judge of the King's Bench or Common Pleas might be found variously consulting or presiding in Council, Star Chamber, Chancery and Exchequer. There was a constant flow of documents moving between departments – as the modern researcher perceives when chasing the records of a suit in the Public Record Office, perhaps through the archives of half-a-dozen departments.

In the later fifteenth and sixteenth centuries, some departments were absorbing new sorts of personnel, the common lawyers and university-trained lay administrators; some were adapting to new judicial and administrative requirements; some were hiving off new departments. Since many councillors shared experiences and sympathies with leading officers, remained in close physical proximity to them, and were sometimes responsible as heads of departments for their work, the Council was well equipped to use the expertise of central administration knowledgeably. Kings could easily learn what practical steps might be taken to adapt administrative devices to policy needs. The central administration's particular combination of traditionalism and adaptability facilitated its development in the sixteenth century as the engine of the embryonic state. But by James I's reign it may have been less responsive to pressures for change from councillors and community, as its officials became more entrenched in their determination to hang on to and enlarge perquisites, more divided by personal and departmental rivalries, more closely linked to Court factions.

Notes

1. I owe this reference to Professor K. A. Fowler.
2. I owe this reference to Dr A. I. K. MacKay.
3. The passage occurs in a tract Pecock wrote *c.*1450 against the Lollards, *The Repressor of Overmuch Blaming of the Clergy.*
4. *An Harborowe for Faithfull and Trewe Subjectes, agaynst the late blowne Blaste, concerning the Government of Women* (Strasbourg, 1559) – Aylmer's reply to John Knox's diatribe against female rule.
5. Treason had previously been somewhat narrowly defined as a number of overt acts by the 1352 statute, intended to safeguard nobles against a variety of royal accusations. Kings had normally respected the letter of the Act, though manipulating trial process to ensure that they got their man convicted.
6. Henry VIII created six new sees: Westminster, Oxford, Peterborough, Gloucester, Bristol and Chester. Westminster was abolished in 1550.
7. There is a representation of a comital circlet on the fine brass of Thomas Boleyn, earl of Wiltshire and Ormonde (d.1538) in Hever church, Kent.
8. Writs of summons to bishops continued to contain mandates ordering them to cause proctors to appear in parliament on behalf of the lower clergy.
9. Sixty-nine boroughs received representation or had it restored in the sixteenth century. Calais was also transiently represented, and thirty-one new shire and borough seats were created when Henry VIII brought Wales, Monmouthshire and Cheshire into the representative system.
10. There were fewer parliaments to be excited about: whereas there had been twenty-four in the twenty-three years of Richard II's reign, twenty-two in the twenty-three years of Henry IV's and Henry V's, there were only twenty-six between 1439 and 1509, one during Wolsey's ascendancy (1515–29), and ten in Elizabeth's reign. Edward IV set precedents for repeatedly convening the same parliament: that of 1472–5 had seven sessions, covering forty-four weeks, the longest before the Reformation Parliament. Elizabeth, averse to parliaments, tried to keep sessions short and infrequent: hers averaged ten weeks (which, in 1376, had been an unprecedently long session).
11. Disputed elections were usually adjudicated in Chancery, until in 1604 James I recognised the Commons as the judge of election returns.
12. In the 1478 parliament, out of 291 members, no fewer than fifty-seven had close connections with central government: at least forty-three of them were active members of the Household, and twenty-four of these sat for shires.
13. The Commons had their own clerk, a deputy of the Clerk of Parliaments, from 1363.
14. Government measures came to be introduced into parliament in the fifteenth century in the form of Commons Bills, which makes it difficult to be certain whether measures originated with the Commons.
15. Debates may have been lengthier before the development of an efficient committal procedure.
16. In Elizabeth's reign the practice of three readings was established as normal, with no debate on the first reading (but occasional rejections), and committal and report stage after the second. The majority of Bills had not been committed under Edward VI and Mary, but under Elizabeth committal became usual. The number and size of committees tended to grow: the committee of the whole House was a Jacobean development.
17. For privileges which the Commons had gained under Edward III, see pp. 171 ff.
18. A lawyer sitting for Bristol: this is an early example of an important initiative by a burgess in parliament.
19. *The Survey of London*, first edition 1598.
20. Inigo Jones designed a 'Vienyard Gate' for Oatlands.
21. Such as bakehouse, cellar, buttery, cuphouse, great spicery and confectionary, chandlery, ewery and napery, laundry, kitchen, larder, poultry, pastry, scullery, woodyard.

22. In 1450–1 the Household staff was over 800, but the conciliar ordinance of 1454 tried to reduce it to 582. In 1509 it was *c.*647, plus a royal guard of 300. Professor G. E. Aylmer has calculated the size of Charles I's Household as being a minimum of *c.*1,840–1,860, plus an unknown number of officers' servants (400 minimum, but possibly 700–800). Probably a third to a half of his staff were on duty at any one time (*The King's Servants: the Civil Service of Charles I 1625–1642*, Routledge 1961, 26ff).
23. When there was a queen or resident royal children they were given additional servants of their own. The 1454 ordinance prescribed that, in a Household establishment of 582, 120 were to be of the queen's household and thirty-eight of the infant prince's. Catherine of Aragon's household in 1509 was 147, and Henrietta Maria's was 172.
24. The Office of Works was then responsible for the construction and maintenance of buildings, Robes partly for royal clothing and officers' liveries and uniforms. Robes share this responsibility with the Great Wardrobe, a supply department which stored bulky commodities.
25. An associate of this group was Sir Philip la Vache, to whom Chaucer addressed his *Ballad of Good Counsel*, an early example of the genre of Court poetry reflecting on courtiers' obsessive competitiveness.
26. See pp. 172 ff. Individuals were expelled from the Household against the king's will in 1376, 1381, 1388 and 1404. Courtiers were attacked in verse, and sometimes physically, in the 1390s and 1440s. The Steward (Suffolk) was impeached in 1450.
27. In the mid-fifteenth century the king usually wore his crown ceremonially in the chapel royal at Christmas, Epiphany, Easter, Whitsun, All Saints and the feast of St Edward the Confessor. In April, on the feast of St George, nobles congregated at Windsor for a chapter of the Order of the Garter.
28. John Prophete's record of thirty-four of the Council meetings between January and May 1392 shows an average attendance of 6·4, there being only seven regular attenders (the Chancellor, Treasurer, three bishops and two knights of the Chamber), who contributed three-quarters of the attendances.
29. From August 1540 Privy Council and Star Chamber had their own distinct clerical organisations and sets of records. The Court's books registered its acts, orders and decrees.
30. In the 1430s many Privy Seal letters came to be written in English instead of French, and by the 1440s the use of English was common.
31. Parties purchased Privy Seal writs to further their private suits, for example, to summon an adversary to appear before the Chancellor.
32. In the mid-fourteenth century the clerks were paid daily wages, but this practice gradually died out and ceased by Henry IV's reign, when they were granted annuities. After his reign few new annuities were granted: clerks probably relied on income from fees, favours and miscellaneous royal grants.
33. Stipulated allowances of Household food, fuel and candles.
34. The survival of a Signet Office docket book for Richard III's reign (British Library, MS Harley 433) reveals the important role which the office played as secretariat in Yorkist land administration.
35. Robert Beale, *Treatise of the Office of a Councillor and Secretary to Her Majesty* (1592).
36. The broad distinction (less rigid in practice) was that letters patent were addressed 'to all whom it may concern', with seal appended, and letters close to named individuals, closed by the seal. The number of letters close declined in the sixteenth century, when financial courts and central secretariats tended to send administrative orders direct under their own seals.
37. Individuals often considered it worth while to pay the clerks to enrol private recognisances of debt and land grants. Among the Chancery rolls were patent, close, fine, charter, statute and parliament rolls, and, for parts of the period, French, Gascon and Norman rolls. Chancery had a record repository in the Tower of London, and acquired offices in Chancery Lane.

38. The Chancellor also had particular jurisdictional rights in mercantile affairs (e.g. in cases involving aliens). Petitions to the Chancellor began to be calendared and perhaps filed separately in 1387. Between then and 1426 surviving petitions average only twenty a year; 1432–43 (during Stafford's tenure), 136 a year; 1475–85, 553; 1500–15, 605; 1515–29 (Wolsey's tenure), 770.
39. From *Archeion*, a compilation about the law courts first published in 1635.
40. In two terms in 1466, Common Pleas was engaged (approximate figures) on 13,452 cases, King's Bench on 1,601, the Exchequer of Pleas (for which, see p. 106) on 77. In Henry VII's reign the annual number of actions in the Common Pleas was over 10,000, in King's Bench over 2,500; in the year 1506–7 there were 212 actions in the Exchequer of Pleas.
41. Subsequent 'judicial' writs initiated further stages of the case.
42. *De Laudibus Legum Anglie*, ed. S. B. Chrimes (Cambridge U.P., 1942).
43. In the sixteenth century, lawyers practising in Chancery and the conciliar courts had common-law training, as did some of the judges. The background which they shared with those of the common law courts helps to explain why the two systems of jurisdiction, often in rivalry for the same sorts of business, for long managed to coexist with so little mutual abrasiveness.
44. The name derives from the fact that they sat on the form or 'bar' reserved for senior students called upon to argue at moots or mock courts in the inns of court. According to Dr E. W. Ives, there were probably about 400 Westminster lawyers in the early Tudor period: eleven judges and barons, fewer than ten serjeants, about fifty barristers and a similar number on the clerical staffs of the courts, and in the region of 240 attorneys and miscellaneous clerks ('The common lawyers in pre-Reformation England', *Trans. Roy. Historical Society*, fifth series, **18**, 1967, 146n). There were 313 attorneys of the Common Pleas in 1578, 1,383 in 1633 (A. Harding, *A Social History of English Law*, Penguin Books 1966, 171).
45. These offices, intended to 'advance royal aims by litigation' in the Westminster courts, were in existence in the fifteenth century (Harding, *op. cit.*, 181–2).
46. In 1333 the duchy of Cornwall and the county palatine and earldom of Chester (to which Flintshire was annexed) were declared to be inalienably settled on the king's eldest son. When in the king's hands, their principal officials accounted to 'foreign' auditors in the Exchequer, who compiled 'foreign' account rolls. The royal duchy of Lancaster had its own financial organisation.
47. In 1345–6 the Exchequer received £15,721 from hereditary revenues other than customs, of an order sufficient to meet the normal costs of Household and administration with which it was charged.
48. In the early fourteenth century the yield of the ancient demesne of Crown lands and fee farms was probably not less than £10,000–£12,000, and possibly as much as £15,000. Cromwell's 1433 estimate suggests that total cash revenues were then about £36,000, and cash revenues from land a maximum of about £8,250. In the 1460s the normal annual charges on royal revenue may have been about £50,000.
49. Alien merchants were charged an additional rate on wool and leather.
50. Richard II had been granted the wool custom for life in 1398, Henry V that and tunnage and poundage in 1415, and Henry VI in 1454. From 1484 it became customary to grant these customs in the first parliament of a reign.
51. Deputies of the King's Butler collected an ancient levy, and sometimes custom, on wine.
52. Between 1471 and 1483 customs revenue averaged £34,000, an improvement on the £25,000 average of the 1460s.
53. Unenfranchised palatinates were exempt. So were ecclesiastical goods, except those acquired corporately since 1291. The clergy's personal goods were not. Convocations granted clerical tenths. Estimates of their yield are, for the 1330s, about £18,900; in the fifteenth century, about £15,500; from 1486 to 1534, possibly about £9,000. From 1534 the Crown was statutorily entitled to receive taxes on ecclesias tical preferments – First Fruits and Tenths (which Mary relinquished). Under

Henry VIII the income from them was about £40,000, under Elizabeth between £15,000 and £25,000.

54. There were such grants in 1411, 1427–8, 1431 (withdrawn), 1435, 1450, 1472 (withdrawn), 1489 and 1497 (provoking revolts) and 1504.
55. Throughout our period the Crown needed to anticipate revenues by raising interest-bearing as well as obligatory loans on their strength, particularly from foreign bankers and from London merchants, individuals and syndicates (cf. pp. 173, 266). At her death in 1558 Mary owed foreign bankers £106,649. They were currently charging her 12–14 per cent interest rates.
56. In the later Middle Ages the central offices probably employed 200–250 clerical officers, 30–35 of whom in the fifteenth century were Household officers (N. Orme, *English Schools in the Middle Ages*, Methuen 1973, 36ff). Dr D. A. L. Morgan's estimate of the total staffs of Common Pleas, King's Bench, Exchequer, Chancery and Privy Seal in the fifteenth century as not much more than 200 seems rather low ('The king's affinity in the polity of Yorkist England', *Trans. Roy. Historical Society*, 5th ser., **23**, 1973, 2).

Chapter 4

Shire government and society

The sheriff and the local enforcement of royal rights

England largely lacked the sort of professional bureaucrats who enforced royal and princely authority in the localities in France. There were, indeed, English royal officials charged with the custody of the ruler's local properties (castles, palaces, parks, hunting-lodges, manors, studs). They were concerned with the enforcement of his rights as a private landowner, rather than of his public ones as a sovereign. There were also in most shires at any time individuals and groups commissioned by the Crown to carry out specific or general judicial, financial, administrative or military tasks: for example, to hear and determine (oyer and terminer) a complaint of assault and riot; to apportion and collect parliamentary subsidies; to survey the estates of minors in royal wardship; to muster and review those selected for defence[1].

Most commissioners were not professional servants of the Crown, but influential local landowners – peers, knights, esquires and gentlemen normally sensitive in the discharge of public duties to their own interests and those of their neighbours. Assertions of royal authority by 'strangers' – magnates, judges, or officials of the Household lacking property and acquaintance in the shire – were tolerated as temporary intrusions, perhaps deemed necessary by elements in the shire community because the region was disordered by faction or rebellion.

The sheriff was the most ancient and one of the most important shire officials. Commons' petitions in the fourteenth century reflect the shire communities' anxiety to influence the terms of a key office. They secured that sheriffs should hold office for only a year at a time, and that they should be residential property-holders. The Crown kept control of appointments, in which chief royal ministers were usually concerned. In the sixteenth century the Chancellor, Treasurer, councillors and judges compiled short lists of candidates, three for each shrievalty, and in November the sovereign came into the Exchequer and signified the royal choices by pricking the parchment against their names. Eighteen of the thirty-seven shires had joint shrievalties, but these were separated in 1567 and 1575. Those appointed were usually well-to-do local landowners, probably chosen because of their ability to promote their fellows' co-operation in royal administration, and perhaps on occasion because they had lobbied for the job through friends at Court. Exceptionally, during periods of national political tension, sheriffs may have been selected on partisan grounds[2].

The sheriff's concentration of administrative and judicial powers, which had often made him a controversial and hated local figure, had declined considerably by the 1340s. But the office was still a very busy one. The sheriff presided over regular meetings of the county court, held in most shires once every four weeks. Its suitors gave judgment in minor civil suits and pleas of trespass. The sheriff acted on the writs he had received ordering either proclamations to be made in the court and elsewhere, or a trial or inquest on the court's verdict, or its election of a coroner, verderer[3] or parliamentary knights of the shire. Twice a year the sheriff or his deputy presided over the courts of those hundreds or 'wapentakes' (a northern term) which were not private franchises. Hundreds were administrative and judicial divisions of the shire, whose juries made presentments of petty offences in their courts.

All writs dispatched to the shire from Chancery, Exchequer and the Westminster justices were delivered to the sheriff's office. He was responsible for acting on them (e.g. by arresting, distraining, or empanelling a jury) through his subordinates, or ensuring that the officers of private franchises acted on them, and for returning the writs to Westminster with an appropriate endorsement. As custodian of the county gaol[4], he was responsible for the safeguard of prisoners, their production for trial, and for execution of sentences on the convicted: hanging, burning, branding, whipping, fining.

The sheriff's right to appoint to vacancies in some of his subordinate offices gave him patronage. In hundreds which were not private franchises he could often appoint a steward of the court and a bailiff. The latter executed many of the sheriff's administrative orders in the hundred, on receipt from him of the original writ or his mandate based on it. Among the bailiff's assistants were two high constables, and, elected by the inhabitants, two or three constables in each village, who were responsible for helping to suppress crime. The bailiff and the steward of the hundred court (which met every three weeks) levied fees for wages and might profit from bribery and extortion. According to a draft petition from John Paston to Henry VI and the lords of parliament (1450), complaining of the occupation of his manor of Gresham by Lord Moleyns and his adherents

they compel poor tenants of the said manor, now within their danger, against their will, to take feigned plaints in the courts of the hundred there against the said friends, tenants and servants of your said beseecher, which dare not appear to answer for fear of bodily harm, nor can get no copies of the said plaints to remedy them by the law, because he that keepeth the said courts is of covin with the said misdoers, and was one of the said risers which by colour of the said plaints grievously amerce the said friends.

The sheriff also employed clerks, a receiver (for sums owing), an itinerant bailiff, a gaoler, and messengers to return writs to the central courts. His most important official was the deputy whom he appointed, the under-sheriff, who could act in his place in receiving and returning writs, and in other capacities. Sir William Wentworth advised his son (1604) that if he was pricked sheriff of Yorkshire, he should 'take heed of a foolish or knavish under-sheriff'. If his son was involved in a suit, 'the under-sheriff must in time have a brace of angels[5] to return an indifferent [impartial] jury'.

A sheriff who was complaisant towards his deputy's negligence might frustrate royal aims. Encouragement of or connivance in an under-sheriff's partiality might stimulate faction and peace-breaking. A letter from John Osbern to his master John Paston (May 1451) illustrates local pressures on sheriffs and their deputies, and how they might react. Osbern had vainly tried to persuade the sheriff of Norfolk to collect a Paston present left with his under-sheriff. Despite his past oaths to protect Paston's interests, the sheriff declared his intention not to favour Paston in a suit against Moleyns's men

in so much as the King [Henry VI] *hath writ to him for to show favour to the Lord Moleyns and his men, and as he saith the indictment belongeth to the King, and not to you, and the Lord Moleyns a great lord. Also, as he saith, now late the Lord Moleyns hath sent him a letter, and my Lord of Norfolk another, for to show favour in these indictments, he dare not abide the jeopardy of that, that he should offend the King's commandment. He knows not how the King may be informed of him, and what shall be said to him.*

Osbern concluded that the sheriff had promised an acquittal, but pressed him hotly about showing favour to Moleyns in a suit over the ownership of Gresham: 'Then I said, by that means, in default of a Sheriff, every man may be put from his livelihood'. The sheriff swore to resist Court pressure on that issue: 'He will no longer abide the jeopardy of the King's writing, but he trusteth to God to empanell such men as should to his knowledge be indifferent, and not common jurors.' Despite Osbern's cynical surmise that 'he looketh after a great bribe', his exchange with the sheriff about the property suit suggests that the concept of shrieval office was influenced by the shire community's desire to have its tenurial rights protected.

The sheriff's patronage of local office, and opportunities for illicit gain and for favour with powerful interests help to explain some gentlemen's willingness to be appointed. John Shynner wrote two letters to his patron Sir William Stonor (?1481) urging him 'to get acquaintance, love and dread within this shire' by suing for appointment[6]:

And in the reverence of God labour ye to be sheriff: for it is a presentable office, the worshipfulest in the shire have been sheriffs and yet they hope to be: and William Fowell . . . said it will be worth to you a hundred nobles[7] *above all costs and avail many other men under you: and if ye be sheriff I beseech you that John Tollocke may be cryer of the shire, and he shall please you also largely as any other shall, the which John Tollocke is my sister's son.*

Shynner's remarks help to explain why, after the fourteenth-century legislation about the tenure of the sheriff's office, there was no general agitation over shrieval conduct – one object of holding office was to gain local respect. Pressure of opinion weighed heavily on the sheriff. He needed the approval of his neighbours to gain obedience.

The attempts by Moleyns and Paston to win over the sheriff of Norfolk in 1451 show how wariness was needed in office. A sheriff might easily make local enemies. If he disobeyed the royal will, or was unable to make himself obeyed, he stood to lose favour and face. Sheriffs received only small fees: they had to pay the wages of their deputies and clerical staff, and the costs of lodging and entertaining visiting justices of assize. In some counties ancient, uncollectable rents and dues debited to the sheriff were not written off by the Exchequer. He was financially liable for uncollected debts. Wentworth had no doubt about whether it was worth becoming sheriff of Yorkshire. He advised his son to avoid being chosen by all means, as the consequence was 'great loss and danger'.

Another important local official for much of our period was the escheator. His office was succinctly described by Francis Bacon:

Every shire hath an officer called an escheator, which is an office to attend the king's revenue, and to seize into his majesty's hands all lands escheated, and goods or lands forfeited, and therefore is called escheator; and he is to inquire by good inquest of the death of the king's tenant, and to whom the lands are descended, and to seize their bodies and lands for ward if they be within age, and is accountable for the same; he is named by the lord treasurer of England.

The office as Bacon described it evolved in the later fourteenth century, particularly in the 1340s, after a long period of experiment. In 1340 appointments were vested by statute in the Chancellor, Treasurer and Chief Barons of the Exchequer. Office was not to be held for more than a year. In 1341 escheatries were regrouped to coincide with the shires, and their respective sheriffs were chosen as escheators. But within a few years the two offices were separated. Escheators too accounted for their issues at the Exchequer. Resident esquires and gentlemen held office.

Like the sheriff, the escheator was subject to strong pressure from local landowners. The rule of royal 'prerogative wardship' was that all the estates of a feudal tenant-in-chief of the king, even if nearly all of them were not held in chief, were liable to remain in royal custody until an heir who had inherited as a minor was of age (twenty-one for a boy, sixteen for an unbetrothed girl). The king also had the right to dispose of the heir's marriage. Grants of custody and marriage of a ward, and of particular estates or a whole inheritance until the ward was of age, were often bestowed by sovereigns as favours or rewards to nobles, courtiers and servants. The Crown also profited from the sale of wardships and marriages, the rents paid by custodians, and fines by heirs, when of age, for livery of estates. A minor's kinsmen were often anxious in case wardship and marriage should fall into the clutches of a stranger, perhaps a courtier eager to make a quick financial killing by selling off assets, or prepared to marry the ward into a family of which his kin disapproved. Consequently the latter often took the prior precaution of concealing a minor's lands. Numerous commissions were appointed to search out escheats, sometimes on the initiative of informers hopeful of receiving part or whole of the concealed estate in custody as a reward. In September 1395 John Worship, usher of the Chamber, was granted custody of Bernard Missenden's inheritance in Buckinghamshire without farm 'in consideration of his great expense in recovering the king's right to the premises'. In the previous months a commission of his associates, fellow Bedfordshire landowners, had been appointed to enquire into concealments of the property, and the escheator (a near neighbour of Worship's) had reversed his predecessor's verdict.

Concealments are likely to have had the connivance of escheators, jurors or the sheriffs who empanelled them. They sometimes treated inquisitions perfunctorily. When William Paston died in 1444, the escheator of Norfolk and Suffolk, Robert Clere, had a servant send the verdict of his inquest on the inheritance to the deceased's son and heir John, who was of age, for his personal correction. Clere's servant conveyed his obliging master's wishes to the latter:

Seal it [*the inquisition*] *with your seal, or what seal else ye will, in his* [*Clere's*] *name, and seal it also with as many of other seals as there be jurors, and deliver it to William Bondes, his deputy, to deliver into the Chancery . . . and what so ever ye do, or say, or write, or seal, or avouch in this matter in my master Clere's name, he shall avow it, and* [*i.e. if*] *it should cost him great part of his goods.*

Pressures from the landowning community tended to depress royal profits from wardships. Moreover, in the fourteenth century, particularly from the 1340s onwards, the Crown granted licences to tenants-in-chief to employ a conveyancing device circumventing wardship: 'enfeoffment to uses'. A landowner granted his property by charter to a group of trustees – kinsfolk, neighbours, estate officials and lawyers – to hold to his use. In the eyes of the common law, they became the joint owners. But the trustees (or 'feoffees') would convey the property back to him or to another, in accordance with his instructions as to the form of tenure. The device had spread in the early fourteenth century, facilitated by Edward I's statute, *Quia Emptores* (1290), which enabled tenants not holding directly of the Crown to alienate their fiefs by substitution. The purposes to which it was put proliferated in the second half of the fourteenth century, by when, with Edward III's acquiescence, it had become popular among magnates.

Enfeoffment to uses gave landowners a new flexibility in settling their estates. Trustees received grants to fulfil the terms of sales and mortgages, and to dispose of properties in ways which evaded the rules of feudal tenure. They might be instructed by the grantor to convey estates to himself and his wife jointly in survivorship; to hold them until his heir was of age, or grant them after his death not to the heir but to younger sons or to a chantry foundation. These instructions often came to be scheduled in a 'last will' annexed to the testament disposing of chattels. On his deathbed at Heversham in 1384, Sir William Windsor willed before witnesses that his estates (enfeoffed) be inherited by his nephew John Windsor, who was to bear his coat of arms. This cut out the rights of Sir William's legal heirs, his three sisters, and his wife's right to dower[8]. But some of his trustees ignored his instructions and granted property to his infuriated widow. A danger in enfeoffing to uses was that untrustworthy feoffees would ignore the grantor's instructions, keeping the estate for themselves, or selling it. In many cases there was no remedy at common law, which recognised only their possession, and therefore the necessity arose of petitioning king and Council, or Chancellor. Moreover, deep grievances were aroused by disinheritances. Some of the local violence and factiousness of the fifteenth century stemmed from the claims of the disinherited. But landowners' ability to will land as they wished, especially to the detriment of heirs male, was limited by the growing practice of turning fee simple into fee tail, guaranteeing the latter's rights.

Until the later fifteenth century, general attempts to tighten up the enforcement of depleted royal rights of wardship were spasmodic. The Crown's acquisition by forfeiture and inheritance of noble estates under the Yorkists and Henry VII may have made wardship potentially more lucrative, bringing former magnates' tenants more consistently within its scope. In the 1490s the Treasurer and officials of the Chamber of the Household initiated searches for evasions. In 1503 Sir John Hussey was appointed Master of the Wards, and a statute of 1540 constituted the Court of Wards, with five senior officers: master, attorney, receiver-general (responsible for revenue) and two auditors[9]. They had a corporate responsibility for the grant of wardships, which were formally made by letters patent issued by Chancery, on receipt of a bill signed by the master. The latter, aided by the attorney, sat in the court as judge, dealing with cases of evasion, collusion and concealment. Judicial as well as administrative efforts were made to increase the Crown's revenues from wardship, by curtailing device by uses (statutes of 1490 and 1536). But the Statute of Wills (1540) conceded that tenants-in-chief might devise by will two-thirds of their tenures, the Crown receiving the rest in wardship. The grants under Henry VIII of former monastic properties to be held in chief increased the estates liable to wardship. Whereas the earliest account of the receiver-general of wardships (for 1523–4) shows a net profit of £3,134, in 1542–3 wardships (with the addition of liveries) brought in £5,452, and in 1545–6, £10,550. Though substantially higher profits were to be made under Elizabeth, the payments fixed by the court remained moderate, so that wardships continued to be a good investment, and heirs were not unduly mulcted.

The Court of Wards was heavily dependent on its local officials, the feodaries appointed by the master. From 1513 onwards there was a continuous series of feodaries responsible for two shires each: by Elizabeth's reign, one shire had become the norm. The feodary was eclipsing the escheator, normally being present at the latter's inquests, sometimes as one of a group of commissioners sharing responsibility for the inquest. The feodary made his own survey of the value of a minor's estate, which was used as a basis by the court for fixing the purchase price and farm of the wardship. He received rents for the lands in wardship within his shire. The office of feodary, and of the deputies employed from the later sixteenth century onwards, were occupied by men of modest standing. Feodaryships were eagerly importuned, presumably for the opportunities to profit from gentlefolk anxious not to have the worth of minors' estates valued high. The Court of Wards under Elizabeth and James I relied heavily on contracts with professional informers to share with them the profits of concealed wardships, for which they were authorised to search under letters patent.

Though the court, especially under Burghley's long mastership (1561–98) was not lacking in paternalist regard for the welfare of wards, the Tudor revival of fiscal wardship was widely unpopular. The court's local activities, especially through the agency of feodaries and informers, introduced a new, unwelcome bureaucratic element into shire society. There were complaints in Elizabethan and Stuart parliaments about their activities, and in 1606 vociferous demands in the Commons for the abolition of wardship. The concession was made in 1611 that a minor's mother or next of kin had, within the first month of wardship, prior claim to a grant. But this may have been balanced by hardships arising from Stuart government's greater concern with the fiscal exploitation of wardship. The system, and the court which had administered it, were abolished by the Long Parliament in 1646.

Justices of the peace

By the early fifteenth century the habitual bearers of the widest variety of judicial powers in the shires, through most of the realm, were the justices of the peace. The keepers of the peace, local men receiving royal commissions, had been frequently ordered to enforce Edward I's policing regulations in the Statute of Westminster (1285), by organising their shire's able-bodied men in readiness to suppress riot and disorder, and by keeping records of breaches of statute, to be used in evidence at assizes. During Edward II's reign and the early decades of Edward III's, keepers of the peace were sometimes commissioned to hold sessions, receiving presentments of felony and trespass, and to arrest those indicted, and others they suspected of crime. In 1361 powers to act as justices were statutorily conferred on them. The standardisation of the terms of their commissions as justices of the peace by *c*.1410 shows how their position had consolidated. In addition, they were to be frequently empowered to enforce many new statutes, especially in the sixteenth century, reflecting the Crown's widening competence in social regulation. The Crown also looked to them increasingly to enforce its administrative orders in the localities. Sir Thomas Smith gives a good impression of some of the justices' duties in 1565:

The justices of the peace be those in whom at this time for the repressing of robbers, thieves and vagabonds, of privy complots and conspiracies, of riots and violences, and all other misdemeanours in the commonwealth the prince putteth his special trust. Each of them hath authority upon complaint to him made of any theft, robbery, manslaughter, murder, violence, complots, riots, unlawful games, or any such disturbance of the peace and quiet of the realm, to commit the persons whom he supposeth offenders to the prison . . . till he and his fellows do meet.

. . . The justices of the peace do meet also at other times by commandment of the prince upon suspicion of war, to take order for the safety of the shire, sometimes to take musters of harness and able men, and sometime to take order for the excessive wages of servants and labourers, for excess of apparel, for unlawful games, for conventicles and evil orders in ale houses and taverns.

The grants of judicial powers to the keepers in the early fourteenth century were prompted by outbreaks of local disorder, and the inability of the existing machinery to cope. General eyres of itinerant justices were unable to deal with the volume of complaint. The sheriffs' judicial competence was more regularly exercised, but less impressive in scope, and they were preoccupied with expediting a mass of royal business. The commissions of the peace sent to small groups of landowners enhanced their regional influence. It was perhaps in recognition of this that, soon after their statutory grant of judicial powers, the Crown developed the habit of conferring more powers on them in response to widespread crises. In 1368 justices of the peace were commissioned to hear and determine cases under the statutes made for labourers and artificers, and to award damages according to the extent of trespass. In 1388 they were to enquire of mayors, bailiffs, stewards, constables and gaolers whether they had executed the ordinances and statutes concerning servants and labourers, beggars and vagabonds – a foretaste of the justices' extension of supervision and control over the more ancient rural offices of government, which was to be most marked in the sixteenth century.

The art of ruling, for Crown and magnates, became to some extent that of influencing and managing the magisterial gentry. Some early fourteenth-century judges and royal councillors doubted whether landowners would use their powers as intended. Justices of the peace did indeed, under cover of office, perpetrate crimes and protect the interests of patrons and servants. The Commons complained to Edward III in 1377 that the justices were appointed through the influence of 'the maintainers of the country who commit great outrages by maintenance [see pp. 146–50] to the poor people of the country'. Margaret Paston wrote to her husband John in 1465: 'If it pleased you, I would right fain that John Jenny were put out of the Commission of the Peace, and that my brother Wyll. Lumner were set in his stead, for me thinketh it were right necessary that there were such a man in that county [Norfolk]that owed you goodwill.' The Elizabethan councillor Sir Nicholas Bacon wrote that many became justices 'more to serve the private affection of themselves and friends as in overthrowing an enemy or maintaining a friend, a servant or tenant, than to maintain the common good of their country, respecting more the persons than the matters'.

However, justices of the peace did not fully engross local royal jurisdiction. Some of the suits heard by them were transferred to King's Bench: twice a year professional judges on their circuits held county assizes. Outbreaks of exceptionally bad crime or factious disorder might be dealt with by specially commissioned magnates, judges and knights. In the sixteenth century the assize judge became the trier of serious crimes, the JP their investigating prosecutor – a division of function mandated by the statutes of 1554–5.

Appointment of JPs remained in the Crown's hands, though attempts were made in some later fourteenth-century parliaments to secure their nomination by the Commons or knights of the shire, perhaps as a means of preventing magnates and 'maintainers' from using Court influence to get nominees appointed. Letters appointing justices were issued out of Chancery, at irregular intervals. New ones were made out to supplement numbers, and, on occasion, to aid a faction. Justices sometimes held office for years or for life, but Dr Hassell Smith, in a study of Elizabethan Norfolk[10], has shown that seventy-five of its 149 justices were put out of the commission at least once, and that membership was by no means stable or free of political pressures. By the later sixteenth century (and probably much earlier) commissions of the peace named justices in order according to their rank and putative standing. It was a matter of overriding concern to justices to have their own valuation of status recognised and reflected in the precedence accorded to them at sessions. From 1368 a 'keeper of the records' (*custos rotulorum*) was named in the commission. He supervised and organised the work of his colleagues, with the assistance of the clerk of the peace, appointed by him, who compiled and filed the Bench's records. The commission also named the *quorum*, a group of trusted or expert members, the presence of one or more of whom was stipulated as necessary at full sessions.

Commissions were normally headed by peers owning estates in the county, followed by some local knights. Shire communities were biased in favour of the appointment of wealthy landowners, though it may have often been expedient for the efficient discharge of business to appoint well-known local lawyers or stewards of estates. Early in Richard II's reign the Commons petitioned that 'insufficient men' should be excluded, and only resident knights and esquires appointed. In 1430 justices of the peace were statutorily required to have lands or tenements to the value of at least £20 p.a. In 1582 the earl of Leicester expressed satisfaction that 'numbers of base men should be left out'. Elizabethan councillors feared that the inclusion of large numbers of lesser men had caused a decline in peace-keeping, since, according to Sir William Cecil 'the better sort of the justices being of gravity and credit have forborne to intermeddle in exercise of these offices as thinking themselves associated with a number of unmeet [persons] either for wisdom, virtue, learning or other quality of credit'. He looked back regretfully to an age when six or seven, or few more, had been appointed. In 1390 the number had been statutorily fixed as six for each shire. In Norfolk there was an average for the period 1389–99 of 10 justices of the peace; 1422–61, 15.6; 1461–83, 24. In 1577 there were 34; in 1602, 61. There were 25 local men in the Wiltshire commission in 1562, 46 in 1600, and 48 in 1638. The Elizabethan Privy Council's attempts to reduce the numbers of JPs were ultimately unavailing. They were countered by pressure from gentry through Court contacts to gain appointments, as a means of asserting a position in their shire's magisterial elite.

Justices of the peace were unpaid[11]. For the conscientious justice, office could be arduous. There is abundant evidence from the later sixteenth century of the Privy Council trying to prod justices into action with a stream of orders and admonitions, supplemented by those of visiting justices of assize. Besides investigating allegations of felonies, JPs tried a mass of petty rural offences, the mayhem and trespass which were the staple of mutual recrimination between disputing landowners, and of peasant criminality. Later fourteenth-century statutes obliged them to hold plenary sessions four times a year at fixed times, lasting up to three days if necessary. These 'quarter sessions', attended by sheriff, coroner, high constables and hundred bailiffs, usually met in the chief town[12]. But quarter sessions, even when additional ones were held, could not cope with all the business. It became customary for one, two or three justices to hold intermediate sessions dealing with minor offences in one part of the shire. A statute of 1530 (repealed in 1540) attempted to formalise these arrangements, laying down that each shire should be divided into four, six or eight areas, in which the local justices should meet every six weeks. Shires did in fact become partitioned into 'divisions', where the divisional justices met regularly for what were termed in the seventeenth century 'petty sessions'.

It would be rash to attempt definitive judgments about the extent to which JPs observed the letter and spirit of their commissions. The fact that the Crown tended to add to their responsibilities does not necessarily imply that they were predominantly efficient and public-spirited. Except perhaps in some noble appointments, the office certainly did not degenerate into an ornamental, semi-hereditary one. Cecil believed in its traditions of honourable service. But his strictures and those of his conciliar colleagues on present conduct were not novel: there had been no 'golden age' of justices of the peace. Nor had there been the opposite. During periods of ineffective rule and dynastic strife in the fifteenth century, factious and criminal violence did not generally reach the stage of threatening the fabric of local society. This may have been due in part to the JPs' responsiveness to shire communities' wish to maintain peace. Exceptions can confidently be made of Westmorland, Northumberland, Cumberland and parts of Yorkshire. There, for much of our period, JPs on their own could not rely on a local consensus of obedience, and could not individually be relied on by the Crown. They had to be prodded, backed up or bypassed by more authoritarian royal institutions: Wardenships of the Marches, lieutenancies and the Council of the North[13].

Elizabethan councillors, reliant on justices' vigilance to suppress or arm against the threats of economic disruption and popular disorder, Catholic dissidence and foreign invasion, were nervous lest their measures proved inadequate. They were required to come together in their sessions as a sort of shire government, concerting how they should implement Privy Council priorities, giving orders to and supervising the work of sheriffs, high and parish constables, and new officials, such as surveyors of roads and overseers of the poor. They were empowered *to tax* – fixing, apportioning and compelling payment of rates for public works, poor relief, purveyance, and, above all, for the maintenance of shire defences, and the equipment and training of the reformed militia, which might have to withstand deadly Spanish infantry. Councillors feared that justices might not enforce measures unpopular among fellow gentry. Consequently royal reliance was placed in lord-lieutenants. These had been appointed occasionally before Elizabeth's reign to control the military measures of one or more shires, particularly in emergencies. At the start of the war with Spain, in the years 1585–7, commissions of lieutenancy were issued for nearly all shires. Those appointed, who held office effectively for life, were peers, often privy councillors. They were responsible for maintaining defences, and holding summer musters, when able-bodied men were selected for military training. They relied on the deputies whom they appointed for different regions, assisted by military officials (such as the muster master and provost marshal).

As local landowners, lieutenants and their deputies were not unsusceptible to opinion in the shire. But the Privy Council regarded lord-lieutenants as its most authoritative and reliable local agents. They collected royal loans; arbitrarily fixed rates for local military expenditure; ordered justices to carry out urgent tasks, and carried them out without consulting justices. There is evidence, particularly in the case of Norfolk, that some gentry resented the activities of late Elizabethan lieutenants, and viewed some of these as unconstitutional intrusions into matters which the sessions had the statutory right to regulate[14]. In Yorkshire, the Council of the North's often vigorous exercise of superior criminal jurisdiction was resented by magistrates.

Elizabethan administration has sometimes been characterised as conservative, in contrast to Henrician innovation. In local affairs, Henry VIII certainly innovated by bringing peripheral parts of the realm under much closer institutional control. Elizabethan use of the local conciliar courts – and, more generally in the realm – of justices of the peace and lord-lieutenants followed precedents. But there were differences in scale and emphasis. Elizabeth's ministers had a sophisticated awareness of dynastic, religious and social threats, based on anxieties not fully shared by their Henrician predecessors. In response, they loaded the magisterial class with more complex responsibilities and closer supervision, enhancing their sense of constitutional identity, yet attempting to impose a more strict tutelage. The stresses of the Spanish war increased these tendencies, stimulating the activities of lord-lieutenants, high-powered, Court-orientated. The traditional roles of Crown and gentry were being significantly modified by the pressure of the Crown's necessities, and in ways which produced unresolved incompatibilities.

Blood and rank

In the seventeenth century the term 'the gentry' started to be a common usage to describe the elites of rich landowners from whose upper echelons the holders of magisterial office were principally drawn. A study of the 1524–5 subsidy returns, supplemented by the 1522 musters, suggests that in some counties the gentry comprised a very small proportion of the population – between less than 1 per cent and a little more than 2 per cent of the totals[15]. Moreover, whereas the population of Yorkshire *c.*1600 may have been over 300,000, only 679 gentry families have been found resident in the shire in 1642[16]. It seems likely that the gentry of a shire were not too numerous to be unknown to each other: their tenurial and governmental obligations provided opportunities for them to become better acquainted. John Paston, wishing in 1461 to have a new deed of enfeoffment and letter of attorney made, assumed that his trustees would attend the shire court: 'that the deed bear date now, and that it be sealed at the next shire; for then I suppose the said feofees will be there if it may not be done ere that time'.

In some shires the gentry owned a preponderant proportion of the land. In Buckinghamshire, in the early 1520s, they held about 57·6 per cent of lay-owned land, and 35·7 per cent of all land. Peers held only 6·3 per cent of lay-owned land. Numerous freeholders owned in aggregate a fraction of the gentry's holdings[17]. The use of the term 'the gentry' in the seventeenth century reflected the continued domination of property and office in the shires by a relatively small and distinct group; and, probably, a consciousness of their recently increased power at the expense of other groups.

In the fourteenth century two terms had been used, with Latin, Norman French and English variants, to distinguish and characterise the tiny landowning elites whose seventeenth-century successors called themselves peers or gentlemen: 'gentle' and 'noble'. 'Gentle' stemmed from the Latin *gens* = kin, and retained the connotation that gentility was in the blood, an inherited physical characteristic. In Malory's *Morte D'Arthur*, the innate gentility of Tor, a king's son, shows despite his upbringing by a cowherd, who declares 'this child will not labour for me . . . but always he will be shooting or casting darts, and glad for to see battles and behold knights, and always day and night he desireth of me to be made a knight'. Tor did not resemble the cowherd and his twelve other sons 'in shape nor countenance, for he was much more than any of them'. The physical and behavioural contrasts between governing ranks and peasants were so extreme that they could be related to supposed divinely ordained racial types: 'gentility' and 'villainy'. Gentlefolk, because of their distinctive dietary, housing, hygienic, occupational and cultural standards, tended to be taller, less prone to deformity and rheumatism, cleaner, better clad, and less inclined to physical and verbal crudity. Skin white as palest parchment or whale's bone was extolled by poets as a characteristic of feminine attractiveness, for it implied gentility. The honour, rank and noble qualities of Chaucer's Criseyde could be deduced from her deportment. The ignoble nature of Langland's peasants was equally reflected in their appearance – his serf's beard was typically bespattered with bacon fat and his ploughman wore 'working clothes, all darned and patched'. Malory's Arthur failed to recognise Merlin disguised as a churl, 'all befurred in black sheepskins, and a great pair of boots, and a bow and arrow, in a russet gown, and brought wild geese in his hand'.

Malory's contemporary William Worcester, in a kindly reference to the commons, characterised them as 'of bestial countenance'. Their 'uncouth' speech and mannerisms had been the butts of Chaucer's humour, and continued to amuse (especially in the persons of the Shepherds of the Nativity) in miracle plays produced by urban gilds.

By contrast, Griselda in Chaucer's *Clerk's Tale*, though a poor cottager's daughter, showed innate gentility. This was the wondrous point of the tale for its courtly audience:

God had such favour sent her of his grace
That it ne seemed not by likelihood
That she was born and fed in rudeness,
As in a cottage or an oxen-stall,
But nourished in an emperor's hall.

Griselda illustrated the exceptions which God made. Belief in such operations of divine power enabled firm upholders of hereditary principles to accept that gentility (or enhancement of it by a grant of peerage) could be conferred by God's deputies, kings and magnates, on their familiar servants. But, without such sanction, presumptuous aspiration to an unnatural role was to be condemned. In the person of Beaumains, Malory bemused his readers with an outrageous hero, a flouter of rank. Arthur's steward, infuriated by a youth with the appearance of good breeding who merely requests a place in the household, exclaims: 'I dare undertake he is a villain born, and never will make man, for if he had come of gentlemen he would have asked of you [Arthur] horse and armour.' Beaumains's behaviour and the implied degradation have social parallels. It was not unknown for those of gentle birth to seek craft apprenticeship, forfeiting their gentility. There were too other ways of losing the quality of noble blood. Langland sees the Jews as having forfeited it by treating Christ unchivalrously on the Cross. Those who betrayed their lords, those who were convicted of treason, jeopardised the hereditary grace bestowed by God. The duke of York, fearing that his rival Somerset might procure his condemnation for treason in 1452, complained that he 'works to corrupt my blood, and to disinherit me and my heirs, and such persons as are about me'.

Loss or usurpation of hereditary privileges could be seen as cracks in the social order. The vehemence of the damsel's complaints against the supposed menial Beaumains's knightly aspirations springs from her belief that he is affronting that order, as well as insulting her gentility: 'Away, kitchen knave, out of the wind, for the smell of thy bawdy clothes grieveth me. Alas, she said, that ever such a knave should by mishap slay so good a knight as thou hast done.' Christ on the Cross, according to Langland, had His blood shed not by a common officer, but by a knight, 'for since He was a true knight and the Son of a king, Nature, for once, saw to it that no common fellow should touch Him'. Contemporaries were shocked when baseborn men spilled the blood of undeserving lords – the earl of Huntingdon in 1400 and the duke of Suffolk in 1450. Those who acquired wealth were anxious to observe hierarchical proprieties by grubbing up pedigrees. Acceptance by gentle neighbours of the right to display an armorial coat affirmed gentility. A rudimentary check on armigerous pretensions was provided by the Kings of Arms, the chief royal heraldic officers[18], who by the fifteenth century had the duty of registering arms in their regions, and before the mid-century were issuing letters patent conferring the right to bear them. After then their visitation records indicate greater vigour, and from 1530 onwards Clarenceux and Norroy received royal commissions to carry out visitations, obliging the armigerous to produce their evidences, and forbidding those found wanting to use the style of gentility. The survival from the sixteenth century of forged blazons and ancestral tombs may reflect attempts to deceive heralds. Such ingenuity shows the continued liveliness of medieval concepts – racial concepts – of blood.

In contrast to 'gentle', the stem-word of noble (Latin, *nobilis*), had, besides its application to hereditary aristocracies both in the Roman and medieval worlds, the sense of generally ideal attributes. Highly literate *parvenus* who flourished in Henry VIII's service used the New Testament concept of nobility of soul, and the Roman concept of nobility as service to the *res publica*, to criticise undue emphasis on nobility of blood. Cranmer asserted that God 'giveth his gifts both of learning and other perfections in all sciences, unto all kinds and states of people indifferently'. Sir Thomas Elyot and Richard Morrison wrote respectively:

Nobility is not only in dignity, ancient lineage, nor great revenues, lands, or possessions. . . . I conclude that nobility is not after the vulgar opinion of men, but is only the praise and surname of virtue.

True and perfect nobility, springeth of virtue, wherefore it is great madness for any man, to crack of his parents, being naught himself, dishonouring their noble acts, with his lewd doings.

Such elitists of virtue, heady with their humanist education in semantics and history, swung their axes at hereditary pretensions. Their confidence, not their concept of nobility, was new. The commoner Langland had long before opined that 'on Calvary the whole of Christendom sprang from Christ's Blood . . . and "as newborn babes" we all acquired noble birth'. But for him that remained a pious sentiment, not a basis for social arguments, all the more so, perhaps, because his contemporary John Ball (see p. 179) turned egalitarian sentiments into a plea for revolution. Chaucer the vintner's son forcefully attacked the pretensions of hereditary gentility. But he was careful not to offend his courtly audience. His fine peroration on gentility is put into the mouth of a highly mythical female character, in *The Wife of Bath's Tale*, after he has thoroughly established the wife as a churlishly sensual personality:

Gentilesse is only the renown
For bounty that your fathers handed down
Quite foreign to your person, not your own;

Gentilesse must come from God alone.
That we are gentle comes to us by grace
And by no means is it bequeathed with place.

Opposing views of the relationship between heredity and nobility were sharpened by the possibilities for social mobility within, and in and out of, a gentle society where status and office were heavily influenced by the possession of landed income, a highly variable factor. The feudal rule of primogeniture made an eldest son, or an only son, the heir to a whole estate at the expense of rendering brothers and sisters landless. In fact younger sons in particular were often cushioned by a wealthy father's settlement on them and their heirs male of part of the estate. But most gentlemen, whose incomes were relatively small, are unlikely to have been able to prop up several sons' aspirations to gentility. Sir William Wentworth advised (1604) that younger sons 'be kept to the study of the laws and if there be many of them, let one be apprentice to a merchant'. Entailed lands, and annuities settled on younger children, could seriously deplete the heir's estate, as could a long minority under dishonest guardians, and (before the dissolution of chantries) injudicious alienations in mortmain by repentant parents. Langland exclaimed: 'Alas! you lords and ladies, how ill-advised you are to deprive your heirs of their ancestral heritage, and hand it over, for the sake of their prayers, to men who are rich already.' Temporary, though sometimes lengthy, deprivation was often caused by grants of jointure. An heir might spend years waiting for a widow to disgorge not only dower, but a large part or all of the inheritance. In 1392 the sheriff of Buckinghamshire was ordered to procure the election of a coroner in place of Sir Edmund Missenden, 'who has no lands in the county whereupon he may dwell according to his estate' (the state appropriate to a knight). His properties in the shire had long been in the hands of his widowed mother Isabella.

In order to maintain an appropriate life-style, many gentlemen worked for fees, wages and livelihood: certain kinds of service (but not apprenticeship to a merchant) were regarded as honourable. Another expedient which was not (according to Sir John Ferne's *The Blazon of Gentrie*, 1586) was marriage to a commoner: 'It is the unequal coupling in yoke of the clean Ox, and unclean Ass, an injury not only done to the person of the young Gentleman, but eek a dishonour to the whole house from which he is descended.' In our period a growing number of families probably established their gentility, outnumbering those who lost it. Agrarian, trading, political and social developments gave enterprising commoners opportunities to buy their way up the social scale. Nicholas Upton wrote: 'In these days we openly see how many poor men, labouring in the French wars, are become noble . . . of whom many on their own authority have assumed arms to be borne by themselves and their heirs'[19].

The law was another avenue of advancement (cf. p. 104). Landowners needed lawyers to draft entails and administer enfeoffments, to act as councillors and attorneys in suits to which such devices often gave rise, and as stewards to safeguard their rights against the recalcitrance of tenants. They needed receivers and auditors skilled in estate administration and accounting, to maintain their rents. Moreover, the development of a peerage intensified magnates' needs to display status by maintaining great households, whose principal offices were 'gently' staffed. For, as a Venetian observed (*c*.1500), the higher nobility lacked some of the attributes of rank distinguishing continental nobles: '[They] are nothing more than rich gentlemen . . . the jurisdiction, both civil and criminal, and the fortresses remain in the hands of the Crown.' Opportunities for advancement in princely households appear in a manual written by John Russell, usher of the hall to Humphrey duke of Gloucester. Whereas according to Malory 'the customs of noble gentlemen' were appropriate to those 'that bear old arms', Russell set out to teach their rudiments to a person of 'simple conditions', training him to be a 'gentle officer': 'Do not claw your head or your back as if you were a flea . . . Retch not, nor spit too far, nor laugh or speak too loud . . . do not lick a dish with your tongue to get out the dust.' His advice to an usher on seating order in the great hall shows that, in the house of one of the most sophisticated royal dukes of the fifteenth century (see p. 220), rank in service and courteous demeanour were criteria of status as well as blood and wealth. The knight who possessed the latter attributes ranked higher than the 'poor and simple knight'. But a king's groom could be set to dine with a knight, and gentlemen 'well nurtured and of good manners' with esquires.

The peerage's and gentry's need to be honourably served in various capacities led to the creation of new 'gentle' families. The gentry's need to supplement landed income also encouraged them to consider certain kinds of service as honourable. But movement upward in rank provoked counterpressures, reflected in the attitudes of Malory and Ferne, and articulated in the heralds' visitations. In the second half of the sixteenth century, many established families were troubled by the effects of inflation on their incomes and the resistance of tenants to their attempts to raise them. Threats to the social order, from destroyers of closes, alleged bands of impudent vagabonds, and insinuating Jesuits, inflated the magisterial gentry's sense of responsibility. They may have tended self-consciously to close rank, trying to pre-empt for their orders the rewards of honourable service, and more narrowly examining the credentials of those who rose by the profits of trade and manufacture. Moreover, some of the honourable highways to gentility may have been narrowing. Warfare does not seem to have offered the opportunities it had in Upton's day. The princely housekeeping known to Russell was declining.

Yet the gentry did not become a closed *noblesse*. Heedless of Ferne's anthropological warnings, they remained eager to replenish their wealth by marriage alliances into other prosperous sections of the community, especially when, under the Stuarts, commercial wealth grew so conspicuously. The gentry had no compelling motive for exclusiveness. Since landholding in England did not (as the Venetian observer noted) confer automatic magisterial rights, the tiny, familiar shire elites were well placed to regulate who should be admitted to places of local influence. They might not have been if a large, pushing royal bureaucracy, staffed by irreverent humanist *parvenus*, had developed. But it did not markedly: the well-to-do gentry, having imbibed the new educational standards, and swamping out the grammar schools, universities, and Inns of Court, were well placed themselves to fill many of the offices of central government.

Comparative social mobility and lack of hereditary territorial privileges produced a relative lack of fixity of rank. The English reaction was extreme punctiliousness about the external marks of respect which should be observed in a divinely ordained hierarchy. Russell wrote: 'Each estate shall sit at meat by itself, not seeing the others, at meal-time or in the field or in the town; and each must sit alone in the chamber or in the pavilion.' The first statute laying down that knights, esquires and other *gentils* should alone wear, according to their estate, luxurious apparel, was passed in 1363. Strength of feeling about correct attire is reflected in a London chronicler's disgust that the rebel Jack Cade paraded in 1450 in knightly guise 'though but a knave', and in Sir Thomas Pope's alleged advice to Sir Thomas More to change out of the best apparel he had donned for execution, 'saying that he that should have it [the headsman] was but a javel [low fellow]'. It was inappropriate and deceiving for low fellows, lacking gentle qualities, to don apparel whose fineness was pure and honourable. But don them they did, and the other marks of gentility. The English comedy of manners, and a characteristic literary preoccupation with appearance, gesture and inflection (for example, in Anthony Powell's novels) echo ancient obsessions about contrasts of blood and rank.

Partly perhaps in response to an increased upward thrust of social mobility, the nomenclature as well as social privileges of gentility became more categorical from the later fourteenth century onwards. The evolution of the House of Lords (see pp. 73–6) exalted magnates as a graded, hereditary but not exclusive peerage, endowed with political and social privileges in parliaments and at Court, and with claims on royal patronage. The development of the Lords produced a curious terminological distinction. The term 'nobility' came to be applied almost exclusively to peers, 'gentility' to other *nobiles*. The latter's gradings were already fixed partially by non-hereditary military rankings – knighthood and its apprenticeship, squirearchy. Their prestige sprang from the chivalrous qualifications and incomes required to fulfil their function and appropriate life-style.

Comparatively few of those qualified to sustain knighthood took it up. In 1434 there may have been only about 250 knights in the realm.

John Paston did not take up an offer of knighthood at Edward IV's coronation (1461), despite Thomas Playter's urging that it would be 'for the gladness and pleasure of all your well willers, and to the pain and discomfort of all your ill willers'. Paston may have considered that knighthood entailed expensive and perhaps arduous service to a king needing to defend his Crown. The rank retained a residual connotation of professional soldiering. Chaucer's Knight starts his pilgrimage fresh from campaign, his clothes stained by armour. Knights received special rates of military pay, contracted to lead military retinues (sometimes with the superior military rank of knight banneret) and were commissioned to array shire levies. By 1611, when James I created hereditary baronetcies, knighthood, though still possessing military associations, was largely regarded as a title of honour, reflecting pre-eminence as a courtier, royal official, landowner or, simply, as a man of wealth. Merchants were disqualified by profession from the career of arms. Yet William Walworth, mayor of London, vainly protested his ineligibility to Richard II in 1381. Up to 1439 eleven London citizens were knighted: Edward IV made the practice more common by knighting eighteen between 1461 and 1471.

The title 'esquire' had lost its distinctively military connotations and acquired hereditary ones earlier. Chaucer's Squire, though not without military experience, is a predominantly civil figure, whose accomplishments are appropriate to a lord's household companion. The title was being assumed in the fourteenth century by landowners sustaining a life-style comparable to that of household esquires. Chaucer's country landowner is not styled esquire, but simply Franklin – freeholder[20]. Unlike the Squire, he is not said to be a knight's son or to have courtly accomplishments, though he thinks it would be valuable if his son bothered to 'learn gentilesse aright'. When Chaucer used the term 'franklin' in the 1380s, it may have been giving way to 'gentleman'. Standardisation of the terminology of rank in the fifteenth century was promoted by the development of English as the one 'gentle' language, and by a 1413 statute, according to which a defendant's 'estate, degree or mystery [craft]' was to be stated in all original writs and appeals concerning personal actions at law, and in all indictments involving process of outlawry. The entitlements 'esquire', 'gentleman', 'citizen', 'yeoman', 'husbandman'[21] became stereotyped in documents. Sometimes individuals were named as having more than one rank. As Russell made plain to his pupils, there were several criteria for rank: income (not always reflected in appearance or behaviour) was one of them. Mr Cornwall's survey of subsidy assessments for five counties in 1524–5 [see n.15] shows that knights had a median income of £204, esquires of £80 and gentlemen of £16. 11*s* 4*d*. This was near the start of the period of rapid Tudor inflation: the median incomes given by Dr Cliffe for Yorkshire landowners in 1642 [see n. 16] are much larger. He uses a contemporary distinction between upper, middling, and lesser or inferior gentry. The seventy-three families in the first category, whose heads were mainly baronets, knights or sons of knights, had incomes of £1,000 and upwards. The 244 in the second category, whose heads included a few baronets and some knights but were mostly esquires, had between £250 and £1,000. The 362 who mostly styled themselves 'gentlemen' had incomes of less than £250 a year. These figures suggest a continuing correlation between rank and wealth, and also considerable differences in income between the majority of the various ranks of gentility. The 'gentry' may have been a small elite, but it comprehended, in a bond of shared gentility, families with vastly different incomes, concerns and aspirations.

Social bonds

The tribe, the kindred, was a basis for social bonds in the ancient communities of Britain. The kin was a large and intricately linked group, extended by marriage. Through the traditional authority embodied in its hierarchy, internal disputes were regulated. The kin provided mutual protection, above all through the common obligation to wage blood feud in revenge for manslaughter. But in the centuries when Germanic barbarians settled within the former provinces of the Roman Empire, other social bonds among them took over some of the functions of kindred. In the larger Anglo-Saxon settlements, men co-operating in intricate seasonal farming routines looked to the community, in the village court, to protect and adjudicate their interlocking, narrowly defined, agrarian rights. Neighbouring territorial lords, dependent on villagers' labour, produce, and rents for their income, found it less expensive to compose the communities' disputes through the public award of money compensations for injuries, rather than the disruptive pursuit of feud. Kings were the most powerful of protectors. Before the Norman Conquest English kings had extended their 'peace' to cover not only kinsfolk and servants, wherever they might be in the realm, but all their subjects, whose assailants would be pursued for the blood-price by royal agents

The effectiveness of lords' armed power rested on another sort of bond, that between the lord as confident leader of a host and his skilled, well-armed retainers, who kept their swords burnished in his hall, where they ate and slept. Such retainers, for example those in King Hrothgar's hall, figure prominently in the Anglo-Saxon poem *Beowulf*. An ethic developed which was highly charged with mutual obligations, even endearments. The retainer had to protect the lord's life at the hazard of his own, as the Anglo-Saxon historian Bede describes King Edwin of Northumbria's man Lilla doing, by throwing himself in the path of an assassin's dagger. The lord had to respect his retainer's interests, and avenge his death: the audience of *The Song of Roland* (c.1100) would have been as concerned about the correctness of Charlemagne's methods in obtaining vengeance for Roland's death as about his manner of dying for his lord.

In one part of England the extension of links characteristic of kinship seems to have had particular vigour as a component of social regulation in the sixteenth century: the Borders with Scotland. 'Over all these wastes', wrote the Elizabethan antiquary William Camden, 'you would think you see the ancient nomads . . . a martial sort of people, that from April to August lie in little huts . . . among their several flocks'. These 'shielings' were each occupied in the summer by groups from villages as many as twenty or more miles apart, sharing a common 'surname'. On long winter nights, as long as the weather held,

Fig. 6 The Anglo-Scottish Borders

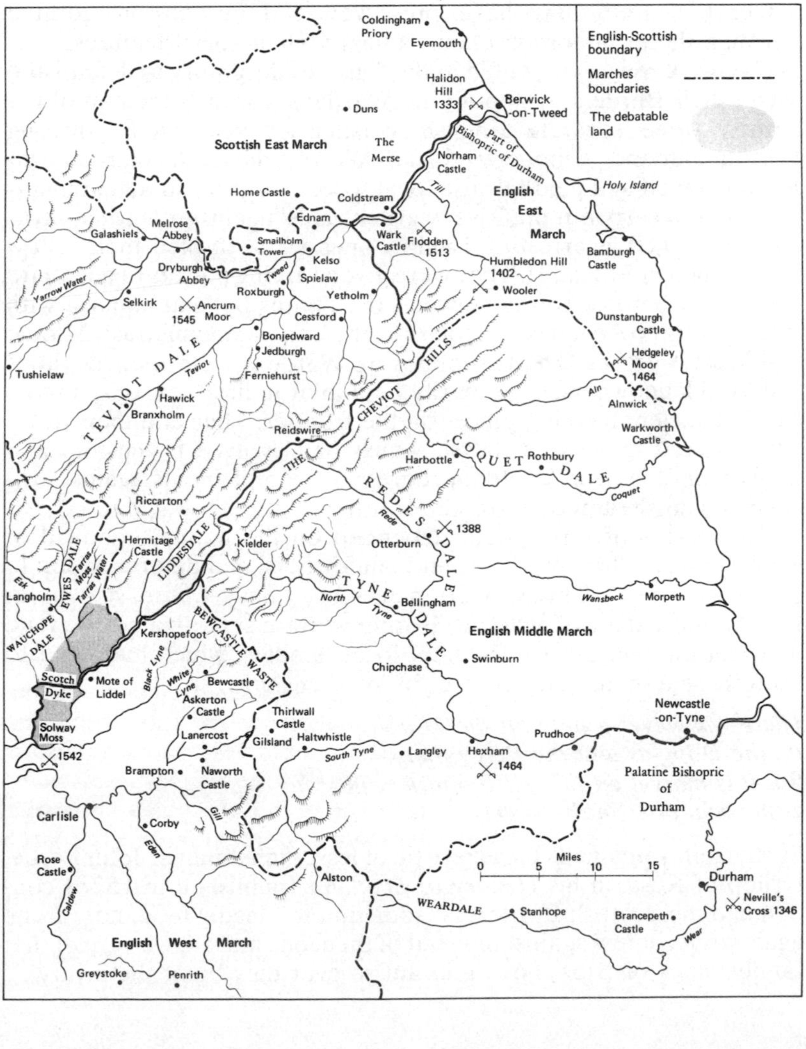

little bands of kinsmen, often allied with neighbours of the same or another 'surname', supplemented their seasonally meagre livelihood by the theft of cattle and sheep ('reiving'). Sir Robert Bowes made some interesting comments on the Borderers (1550): 'There be more inhabitants . . . than the said countries may sustain . . . the people of the country, especially the men, be loath to depart from the same but had rather live poorly there as thieves than more wealthy in another country.' Scottish Borderers were identical in their habits. Pressure of population in the sixteenth century may have been one factor producing the banding into surname groups, for better protection and larger-scale reiving. The remoteness of parts of the region from royal authority, its proximity to a disordered frontier, and perhaps the tendency of great families such as the Percies to reside elsewhere in the sixteenth century may have preserved and perhaps invigorated (through the proliferation of surnames) archaic social features.

The two Crowns attempted in the fourteenth century to defend and pacify their Borders by appointing Wardens: towards the end of the century three separate English Wardenries developed, covering Northumberland, Cumberland and Westmorland. A Warden was commissioned and paid to raise local forces, in order to defeat incursions and to carry out punitive 'warden raids' against offending Scots reivers, as well as arresting English ones who attacked their fellow countrymen or Scots[22]. They were given varying powers to negotiate and jointly enforce truces between the realms by land and sea with their Scottish colleagues, Wardens of the corresponding East, Middle and West Marches. The two opposing Wardens, with their deputies and local landowners, customarily held joint judicial sessions, 'march days' at ancient meeting-places on the frontier. They and their juries administered the 'march laws', which had evolved by custom and treaty from the need to obtain redress for complainants against miscreants who sheltered across the frontier.

The success of this system depended on the mutual goodwill of English and Scottish Wardens and landowners, and determination to enforce the laws. This was often lacking. *Chevy Chase*, a popular Elizabethan ballad, depicts past Border warfare as motivated by a feud between the two most influential local families, which had tried to exercise semi-hereditary control of Wardenships:

There was never a time on the March parts
sin the Douglas and the Percy met
But it is marvel an the red blood run not
as the rain does in the street.

Such habits remained characteristic of lesser inhabitants: John Leslie, bishop of Ross, in his *History of Scotland* (published in 1578) condemned the Scottish Borderers' addiction to 'deadly feud, not of one against one, or few against few, but of them one and all, who are of that family, stock or tribe, how ignorant so ever they be of the injury'.

But in the later sixteenth century, changing political and social conditions were eroding ancient custom. After the 1540s, English royal forces only once conducted a major disruptive campaign in the Borders, in 1570[23]. The English Crown, fearful that papistry might flourish in a superstitious society, whose poverty handicapped the endowment of a reformed ministry, became sensitive about the obedient conduct of the gentry. Elizabethan Wardens and their deputies, often southern magnates or lesser local ones, dared not flout royal authority by outrageously condoning or participating in feuding or reiving (though Scottish ones sometimes still did). Robert Carey, Deputy Warden of the West March in the 1590s, proudly recounts how, when his local levies came to him 'crying with full mouths' to carry on feuds against Scottish surnames, he forbade them: they 'durst not disobey'. A newcomer to the office zealous to uphold the queen's authority, when later Deputy of the East March he took stern measures against the Scottish Warden and surname chief, Robert Ker of Cessford. The Northumbrian gentry showed themselves so unlike their warlike predecessors as to beg Carey to desist – otherwise, they said, 'they must be forced to quit their houses and fly the country'.

The gentry, affected by new standards in education and religion, were probably inclined to condemn the old *mores* as 'barbarity'. Matthew Hutton, archbishop of York (1595–1605) wanted to teach a 'gentle' Scottish hostage, requesting

whether he may sometimes be brought to sitting to the common-hall, where he may see how careful her majesty is that the poorest subject in her kingdom may have their right, and that her people seek remedy by law and not by avenging themselves. Perhaps it may do him good as long as he liveth.

Carey's report of the confession of a notable Scottish reiver, Geordie Bourne, depicts the new morality triumphing over the old:

He voluntarily of himself said, that he had lived long enough to do so many villainies as he had done, and withal told us that he had lain with above forty men's wives, what in England, what in Scotland; and that he had killed seven Englishmen with his own hands, cruelly murdering them; that he had spent his whole time in whoring, drinking, stealing, and taking deep revenge for slight offences. He seemed to be very penitent, and much desired a minister for the comfort of his soul.

Some of the best-known 'Border ballads' are about sixteenth-century events, perhaps reflecting the urge of unregenerate chiefs and surnames to preserve and extol their traditional habits and values, especially when James VI set out to crush them as 'barbarous' – a policy facilitated by the union of Crowns in 1603, which within a few years was followed by the abolition of the Wardenships, and harsh measures against criminals, such as hangings and deportations.

But generally in later medieval England, the kin had lost its pre-eminence as a basis for social regulation. The residual sense of cousinhood was still useful as a means of strengthening other bonds of loyalty and of assuaging conflicts. A Buckinghamshire landowner, Thomas Gate, uses emotional terms about kinship in a letter to Thomas Stonor (d.1474), appealing for his reconciliation of a dispute with their mutual kinsman, Thomas Ramsey. The latter, Gate complained, was making 'great strangeness' towards him: 'I marvel why: our fathers . . . did not so, for their mothers were cousins german. . . . Also I marvel of this unkindness of your said kinsman to me ward and my friends in saying, writing and doing . . . it pleased him to take part with strangers as to his blood, both against me and my ally'. Gate wanted Stonor to acknowledge the ancient reconciliatory obligation of kinship. Sir William Strickland, in a letter to Lord Wentworth (1639) alluded to its patronal obligations. The latter had been 'pleased to acknowledge me as a partaker of your blood': by his bestowal of patronage he had ensured that the blood be 'reserved to be employed in your service'.

Likewise, obligations to give special protection and honour to those who shared blood were pressed on the sovereign. The rebel Cade declared (1450) that Henry VI 'should take about his noble person men of his true blood'. In 1469 Clarence and Warwick compared Edward IV to the deposed Edward II, Richard II and Henry VI, who had 'estranged the great lords of their blood from their secret council and were not advised by them'. That year Lord Scales wrote to the duke of Norfolk's council that 'I doubt not that your reason well conceiveth that nature must compel me the rather to show goodwill, assistance and favour' to Sir John Paston, since a marriage contract had been concluded between the latter and 'one of my nearest kinswoman'. In 1492 the duchess of Norfolk wrote round Norfolk gentlemen requesting them to move Sir Harry Grey 'of conscience and kindness to his blood' not to disinherit his nephew Thomas Martyn, reminding Sir Harry that Thomas 'is to divers of you of kin and alliance, and to many other gentlemen in the shire in like case'. The duchess considered that since Thomas was 'of my lord's [the late duke's] near blood', it would be a great pity if 'he fell to penury and poverty' by disinheritance and 'for that blood's sake' it would be 'a singular pleasure' to her if they dissuaded Sir Harry.

Many instances could be given of kinsmen maltreating one another in the period, the most prolonged and spectacular being the internecine slaughter of 'the royal race' in the Wars of the Roses. The mutual fury of kinsfolk was not new. But in this period there was a readiness to put other ties first, which society condoned. The disinheritance of their heirs by the earl of Pembroke in 1372 and the earl of Northumberland in 1535 (on the excuse that the heirs had behaved unnaturally towards them) shows how the development of the land law facilitated repudiations of kinship obligations. Kinsmen could often plausibly lay claim to property. Sir William Wentworth advised his son to treat them with caution (1604): 'If any of all these have lands or goods joining with you in no case trust them too much, for such occasions breed suits and future enmities.' Thus the frequent appeals to cousinhood, to the traditional extended ties of blood, may have arisen from the fact that they were a weakening, if not yet moribund, force in society. One reason for gentlefolk's concern with their blazons and pedigrees (a progenitor of the rise of antiquarianism) was their need to find out who was distantly related to them, in case they needed to appeal to a dormant connection, or forearm against a suit it had bred. As Thomas Gate remarked in his letter to Stonor: 'It is reasonable a gentleman to know his pedigree and his possibility: saint Paul forgot not to write to the Romans of what lineage he was descended, Ad Romanos xi'[24].

Moreover, by our period there was a variety of social bonds infused with familial kinds of loyalty – bonds which often proved tougher, more durable, than the kinship ties on which they were modelled. Lords who lived in large communities, the households of gentlefolk, were considered to have a paternal responsibility for the right behaviour, for the welfare of souls as well as bodies, of all who attended them, whether kinsfolk or not. The esquire, the apprentice, the ward, the lad striving to learn how to serve at table, or dress or bath his lord, were supposed to show filial loyalty to him. They were to treat other members of the household with due reverence or fellowship. Significantly, the Latin word used for 'household' was *familia*. The godly household (no Puritan invention) was a microcosm, albeit an imperfect one, of the divine, into which the priest prayed that the congregation might be received: 'To us, also, Your sinful servants (*peccatoribus famulis tuis*), who hope in the multitude of Your mercies, be pleased to grant some place and fellowship (*partem aliquam et societatem*) with Your holy apostles and martyrs' (Canon of the Mass).

Medieval society had long been adept at forming varieties of familial societies. Fellow parishioners and fellow craftsmen joined in religious fraternities, seeking the patronage of a saint to help them get a place in God's household, and assuming fraternal obligations, as befitted sinning servants, towards each other and each other's kin, often elaborately codified. The Hundred Years War stimulated the formation of bonds between 'gentle' soldiers. As 'brothers-in-arms', pairs of them swore to give mutual protection and contracted to share spoils and losses in war. In Chaucer's *Troilus and Criseyde*, Pandarus's conduct, which amounts to pimping for the lovesick Troilus, in breach of the bond of kinship, has a justification if he is regarded as the latter's 'brother-in-arms', whose bed, and whose sorrows and joys, he shares. If the poem can be read this way, the relationship between Troilus and Pandarus instructively reveals the highly charged emotional content of some brotherhoods' bonds[25].

The survival of rules enforcing the mutual obligations of members of households, gilds, confraternities and chivalrous Orders, and of contracts between brothers-in-arms, and lords and retainers, should not lead to underestimation of other bonds so universally assumed that they were not matters of contract. Noble as well as peasant society was held together by obligations resulting from forms of tenure, methods of agrarian exploitation, and mechanisms of shire government. Any late medieval family archive of title deeds shows surnames recurring in the lists of feoffees and witnesses, sometimes over several generations. The security of sales and of often complex transmissions of property depended, when threatened by frauds, suits and disseisins, on the fidelity of neighbours, friends and servants. The great men of Westmorland rallied to certify what, to the best of their knowledge, Sir William Windsor's deathbed intentions about his estate had been (cf. p. 126). Especially when landowners were under age or absent from the shire (perhaps during term time at the law courts or in a great household), good neighbours were needed to discourage poaching, trespassing, the negligence of tenants and fraudulence of reeves. Sir William Sandes wrote *c*.1481 denouncing to Sir William Stonor the latter's tenant farmer at Penton Mewsey, far from Stonor's residence: 'As I walk in my recreation I may see that in your woods he hath made great waste and destruction, the which should cause a great displeasure to me if it were done in my woods as it is in yours.'

These and other needs of landowners for good service generated a variety of forms of clientage, devoted or casual, general or minutely particularised, ephemeral or lasting. Besides the need for technical services, administrative, legal, military, religious, there was the requirement for a host of 'well-willers', for all seasons. Gentlefolk were anxious for the patronage of local magnates, and were ready to give their own favours for friendly ears in lords' chambers, quick to detect intended malice. Gentlefolk sought the 'interest' of lesser neighbours as jurors, electors of MPs, stewards of noble estates and franchises, royal commissioners, and armed risers to intimidate a hostile sessions or guard against a riotous assembly. In return, according to the nature of the bond and of the service performed or hoped for, various sorts of benefit were dispensed: liveries of fees, wages, food, accommodation and clothing, offices of profit, presents, bribes, and, ubiquitous and wide-embracing, 'good lordship'. Securing protection against suits for a petitioner, Sir William Stonor was assured in 1482, 'should cause other men to be glad to do you service in that country, if ye keep this man harmless', and the same year another correspondent wrote to Stonor begging assistance in quarrels for one of the latter's old servants, 'so that he by the means of your mastership may live in quiet and rest: and I am sure he will do you service to the uttermost of his power to put his poor life in jeopardy'.

Those who sought most services, and whose patronage was the most sought, were the magnates: dukes, earls and other wealthy and influential peers. They often held court in shires where they had concentrations of property, to attract not only a host of small men, but the leading local gentry. Nobles could dispense not only favour in the form of offices and rewards pertaining to their own properties, but could often, through their standing at Court, influence appointments to royal offices and the disposition of royal wards and patronage. Rulers hoped to use the local influence of magnates as a means of making their will obeyed: magnates with impressive local followings were well placed to enhance their wealth and increase their powers of patronage, for example, by gaining prestigious military and naval commands. Ideally, then, the dominance of magnates rested on the secure maintenance of influence at Court and in the country. Eclipse in one sphere might be quickly reflected in the other. Under Henry VII (as during Henry VI's brief Readeption, 1470–1) the Norfolk gentry paid court to the rising sun of the Lancastrian earl of Oxford. The former influential local families, the De la Poles and Howards, came under a cloud after 1485 because of their Yorkist associations. In either Court or country, magnate dominance was often insecure, or, at least, could not be taken for granted. An ambitious gentleman might win favour at Court, setting up – perhaps with the added prestige of a peerage – as an intermediary and patron rivalling the local 'great family'. In some shires (e.g. Yorkshire and Norfolk), several magnates had territorial interests, which they might decide to use as a base from which to challenge an existing predominance. Some families had a traditional primacy, and traditional links with the local magisterial families, but there were no guarantees of stability. The proclamation by John Mowbray, duke of Norfolk (1452), concerning his commission to enquire into wrongdoings in Norfolk, fulminates against the affinity defying his power, including Lord Scales, whose servants

put men in fear and dread to complain to us at this time of the said hurts and griefs, saying that we would abide but a short time here, and after our departing he would have the rule and governance as he hath had afore time. We let you know that next the King our sovereign Lord, by his good grace and licence, we will have the principal rule and governance through all this shire, of which we bear our name, whilst that we be living, as far as reason and law requireth, whosoever will grudge or say [*the contrary*]

It suited the Crown to deal with a peerage which, as a Venetian wrote *c.*1500, had 'no fortresses nor judiciary powers'. But noble instability sometimes produced faction, dividing local communities and even threatening kings. Documentary evidence from royal and noble archives of the fourteenth century reveals a characteristic pattern of client relationships and, in the later decades, a volume of complaint about the effects of some of them. One such sort of relationship was life retainership. There survive, principally from this century, a number of contracts made by kings and peers with knights and esquires, laying down terms of service according to standard formulae. For instance, in March 1366 Sir Hugh Hastings contracted in London to serve John of Gaunt, duke of Lancaster, for life. When summoned by the duke in peace, he was to have board in the duke's household with a retinue of two esquires, a chamberlain and three boys. When summoned to serve in war, he was to appear with a specified retinue and receive wages of war for himself and them. Various conditions were agreed about war service. Hastings was to receive a fee of £20 p.a. (increased in wartime), in peace from the issues of the duke's manor of Gimingham[26].

The Hastings contract reflects Gaunt's need to impress embassies and fellow magnates with his prestigious retinue, and to have a company ready quickly if an expedition against the king's 'adversary of France' or his allies was planned. Such contracts were not always adhered to for life, nor did they preclude life-retainers from receiving fees from other lords, except in so far as the stipulated duties were mutually exclusive. It is likely that most retainers did not have a fee settled on them for life by contract – only high and lasting expectation merited such a considerable investment. Servants, lawyers and 'well-willers' might for years receive a retaining fee and a livery of cloth to make up a New Year's array in their lord's armorial colours. But they had to be treated as potentially dispensable.

In the second half of the fourteenth century it was fashionable to distribute tokens, in the form of distinctive collars and badges, to be worn by life-retainers, fee-holders and well-willers as a mark of their relationship with the lord. The narrator asks Pearl in the poem of that name (*c*.1350):

Tell me, bright one, what great degree
Bears as badge so spotless a pearl?

It is the badge of the Lamb of God. In the Wilton Diptych, painted *c*.1395 for Richard II, the angels wear his badge of the white hart, and Charles VI of France's collar of broom cods. The popularity of token-giving seems to coincide with a swell of complaint that the expectation of 'good lordship' was being abused by the wearers. In the Salisbury parliament of 1384 and the Cambridge parliament of 1388, the Commons complained bitterly about extortions committed in the shires by men who believed that lords' badges gave them immunity. The Lords refused to agree to the abolition of such tokens. In 1390 a royal ordinance denounced oppressions 'by various maintainers . . . procurers and embracers of quarrels and inquests in the countryside, of whom many are the more emboldened and encouraged in their maintenance and evil deeds because they are of the retinue of lords and others . . . with fees, robes and other liveries called "liveries of company"'. All except dukes, earls, barons and bannerets were forbidden to give 'liveries of company' – and their gift was restricted to life retainers and domestic servants. Lords were enjoined to eject maintainers of quarrels from their service. The problem was tackled more fundamentally in Henry IV's first parliament (1399) by a statute enacting that no lord 'shall use or give any livery or sign of company'. Only the king was to do so, but recipients were not to wear his livery out of Court.

The Commons' agitation, the 1390 ordinance and 1399 statute were not intended to destroy retaining bonds and the associated mutual favouring – lawful maintenance – which had helped to cement gentle society throughout the fourteenth century. 'Good lordship', it was felt, should be used only in favour of social peace, and lords should not wink at the broadcast flaunting of their colours by those they could not control.

Fears of the consequences of such lack of control increased in the later fourteenth century because political and economic tendencies were encouraging common folk to form fellowships, which might be used to challenge or pillage gentlefolk. In 1381 some of the latter attributed the Revolt to the organisation of a 'great company' of conspiring commoners. There was familiarity with the companies of English and other professional soldiers who banded together to fight for gain, often usurping lordships, in France; and in 1379 the earl of Northumberland co-operated with Scottish nobles to suppress a group with similar aspiration in the Marches. Groups of men-at-arms and archers banded together to negotiate terms of military service in the retinues of knightly captains going abroad (cf. p. 259). Journeymen of a craft formed gilds sometimes frowned on by their masters. Groups of labourers united to sell their services, like the six or eight whom Robert Archer led out of Forncett each autumn in the early 1370s in search of illegally high wages. In 1379 the abbot of Dieulacres, allegedly 'desiring to perpetrate maintenance in his marches' was said to have retained twenty-one miscreants who had been ambushing and levying fines on Staffordshire folk. In 1381 outrages were said to have been committed in Scarborough by 'the rebels having made livery of a suit of white hoods with red tippets, that each should maintain what the other had done therein'.

Animus against livery-holders may have also been high in 1399 because, despite Richard II's show of care about abuses ten or so years before, he had failed to check those of his livery and of his lords' in recent years[27]. The earl of Huntingdon, for instance, had maintained his steward of the household, the *parvenu* Sir Thomas Shelley, in extortions: when the earl rebelled against Henry IV in 1400, there were widespread attacks on his retainers.

There are many instances of unlawful maintenance by lords and gentlefolk in the fifteenth century. The deterioration of Lancastrian rule in the 1440s, and the following periods of dynastic conflict, facilitated abuses, and concomitant giving of fees and liveries contrary to statute. Chronicle accounts of the Wars of the Roses make it clear that the wearing of lords' badges and colours by their military retinues was normal. A series of statutes (e.g. in 1468, 1487, 1504) attempted to curb retaining. But throughout the century many peers and gentlemen at least formally acknowledged the livery prohibitions. The only livery collars displayed on their tomb effigies and brasses are royal ones. When Henry VI's retainer Edward Grimston had his portrait done by Petrus Christus, it may be significant that, being out of Court at the time, he is depicted holding his livery chain of SS, not illegally wearing it.

The abuses condemned by the statutes were characteristic of an aristocracy highly dependent (especially during periods when the Crown was not providing 'good governance') on mutual goodwill and on obtaining loyal service for the maintenance of individual wealth and standing. Such abuses had a long vitality. The local elites of Elizabethan England were honeycombed with clientage, and privy councillors were occasionally concerned about the operations of the networks. In 1572 proclamation was made enjoining rigid compliance with the laws restricting the wearing of liveries to household servants. The Yorkshire landowner Sir Thomas Reresby (1557–1619) enjoyed 'great attendance, seldom going to church or from home without a great many followers in blue coats and badges, and beyond the usual number for men of his quality and fortune'. Landowners considered it permissible to breach the statutes in defence of their interests, especially when involved in a contest to control property. But from their inception those statutes expressed their opposition to the development of local alliances using clientage to extort, threaten men's freeholds, and monopolise shire offices, impervious to the community's sense of justice.

Social ideals

Gentlefolk derived income and local power from the possession of land and rent, purchased or supplemented by the profits of service. Their main concern was to protect and improve their estates, and transmit them intact to their heirs. The inventory of chattels made after Sir William Stonor's death in 1474 records: 'Also these be the standards of Stonor that shall abide in the Manor of Stonor from Heir unto Heir'. Heirlooms symbolised strong dynastic feelings. The complexities of the land law, and their susceptibility to manipulation often threatened property titles. This situation provided a justification for resort to chicanery and violence, with the aid of unlawful maintenance, both directly in defence of title, and to increase one's influence generally in local affairs. John Colyngrygge, having failed in a suit (1467–72) to establish a claim to the Berkshire manor of Makney, seems to have occupied it. Henry Makney wrote to his 'especial good Master' William Stonor: 'Colyngrygge and I be at open war: I purpose to enter in the Manor of Makney with God's grace on Monday or Wednesday; and if I have need, I pray you send me a good lad or two that I be not beat out again.' When the law was expensive and often ineffective, violence was seen as a legitimate appeal to divine judgment. Noble rebels often sought the sympathy of gentlefolk by claiming that kings had wrongfully deprived them and others of their inheritances, similarly distinguishing between law and justice.

The consequences of such attitudes are reflected in the monotonously virulent accusations of violence and corruption running through later medieval petitions, legal proceedings and private correspondence. But petitioners to the Crown needed to exaggerate the scale and brutality of attacks in order to maximise the breach of the king's peace. Moreover, the violence of gentlefolk was neither indiscriminate nor professional – the bands of gentle robbers which plagued several districts in the 1320s and 1330s never became a normal social feature. In the fifteenth century the building of heavily castellated manor-houses declined. According to the Italian Polydore Vergil, writing in the first decade of the sixteenth century, 'they [the English] neither build forts and castles, neither do they repair them, which, being builded long since, through time are become old and ruinous'. Only in the Border country were tower-houses and fortified farmhouses called 'bastles' commonly built in the sixteenth and early seventeenth centuries. The typical country-house in most parts of England in the fifteenth century had strong walls and a stout front door, park palings and sometimes a moat – defences against poaching, trespass and the occasional disseisin, such as that at Makney, not against chronic forces of disorder. Even in the Yorkshire of 1604, Sir William Wentworth thought some defence necessary: 'Let the doors at night be surely shut up by some trusty ancient servant and your men so lodged as they may defend your house.' But regular private warfare was unusual. The Pastons' oft-cited defence of Caister Castle against the siege of the duke of Norfolk's adherents in 1469, involving the expensive use of cannon and professional soldiers, took place during a crisis over Edward IV's rule (cf. pp. 285–6).

The force which was sometimes able to regulate the mayhem of gentlefolk, without the necessity of royal intervention, was the opinion of the neighbourhood. The preference was for disputes to be settled by arbitration rather than resort to violence or trial at law. A letter from Oliver Wittonstall (before 1470) to Thomas Stonor sketches the model for amicable settlement:

And foras[*much*] *as ye desire to know how I will be disposed, as touching your land for title thereof, for certain my wife and I will be with you upon Easter to see if ye and we can agree within ourself: and we, if we cannot agree, desire your friends and ours to see a direction between you and us: if they cannot find the means therein, then ye and we in Pach.* [*Easter*] *term to take our evidence with us to London, and by the advice of a judge take a learned man or two indifferently, and to abide the rule of them in all such things as we show and declare . . . if it be your right ye shall be truly content.*

But John Paston failed to show an accommodating spirit to his opponents. John Russe, in May 1465, for his heart's ease felt moved to write boldly to Paston in criticism of his proceedings:

This I know for certain and it had pleased you to have ended by the means of treaty, ye had ma[de] . . . peace . . . with the fourth part of the money that hath been spent, and as men say only of very wilful[ness of your] own person. For the mercy of God remember the unstableness of this world . . . leave wilfulness which men say ye occupy too excessively . . . I would well God help me so it grieveth me to hear that ye stand in no favour with gentlemen nor in no great awe with the commons.

Later in life Paston's son John (knighted in 1487) emerged as a pillar of magisterial respectability, a trusted councillor of the earl of Oxford, whom Henry VII relied on to rule Norfolk. The duchess of Norfolk wrote to him concerning a dependent's case (1493?), hoping that

by your help and wisdom, a friendly communication may be had, so as the matter may be had in examination by such gentlemen as shall be named by the assent of both parties, such as tender and love the weal of both parties, and also the peace and tranquility of the country and love to eschew variance and parties in the country.

Her sentiments cannot be dismissed as singular, or conventional, or simply the reflection of a new, Tudor revulsion against disorder. The *Paston Letters* show that they were a commonplace of public opinion in Norfolk earlier in the fifteenth century, even though that opinion was often ineffective by itself as an influence on individual conduct. In 1465, for instance, Suffolk's men brutally sacked Paston's manor of Hellesdon. The reaction of the latter's wife Margaret, in a letter to her husband, was that this had raised the victim's reputation (so lowly rated by Russe earlier in the year), and depressed the duke's:

There cometh much people daily to wonder thereupon [the sacked manor], both of Norwich and of other places, and they speak shamefully thereof. The Duke had been better than a £1,000 that it had never been done; and ye have the more goodwill of the people that it is so foully done.

When two knights connected with the duke of Norfolk, Sir John Paston and Sir Gilbert Debenham, raised 'fellowships' in 1465, whilst disputing control of the tenants of a manor, a yeoman of the duke's chamber, according to Paston

said unto my Lord and my Lady, and to their counsel, that without that my Lord took a direction in the matter, that there were like to be done great harm on both our parties, which were a great disworship to my Lord, considering how that he taketh us both for his men, and so we be known well enough. Upon which information and disworship to my Lord, that twain of his men should debate so near him, contrary to the King's peace, considered of my Lord and my Lady and their counsel, my Lord sent for me and Sir Gilbert Debenham to come to him to Framlingham both.

Such reactions, however ineffective on occasion, show that nobles were expected to play a reconciliatory role, especially (in accordance with the 1399 statute on retaining) as regards their dependents.

The most eloquent exponent of gentle ideals of conduct in the fifteenth century was Sir Thomas Malory, in the *Morte D'Arthur*: the bond holding society together is that 'he that gentle is will draw unto him gentle tatches [habits], and to follow the custom of noble gentlemen'. Roger Ascham, the sixteenth-century humanist, in *The Schoolmaster* condemned Malory's work: 'The whole pleasure of which book standeth in two special points – in open manslaughter and bold bawdry; in which book those be counted the noblest knights that do kill men without any quarrel and commit foulest adulteries by subtlest shifts.' But, in his asides, Malory shows an elementary sense of anachronism, making plain that some of the habits he describes are characteristic of a bygone, heroic but rude age. Like some modern purveyors of historical fiction, he used popular concepts of a colourful epoch to inculcate certain virtues, whilst at the same time indulging fantasies. The Arthurian reader could be uplifted and at the same time indulge in day-dreaming about marvels, heroic fights, terrible injuries, seductions, for the most part far removed from his 'gentle' way of life, circumscribed by prim, decorous and devious conventions[28].

The principles of order in Malory's world, secular rather than religious, are maintained by the Arthurian household. The king and his retainers (like the duke of Norfolk and his entourage in 1465) must set and inculcate a pattern of faithful, familial dealings among gentlefolk, whether their bond was kinship, service, casual hospitality, or, indeed, quarrelling or spilling each other's blood. 'Amongst your neighbours deserve to be counted a man of a sincere conscience and let your word be as good as an obligation', advised Sir William Wentworth. Secure landowning depended on the mutual trust of neighbours. Traditional feudal and chivalrous values had a contemporary relevance. Fief-holders still sometimes maintained special ties with their feudal lords. In the fourteenth century three successive heads of the knightly family of Hastings of Elsing, vassals of the house of Lancaster, were retained by its earls and dukes, and fought for them. Retaining links might be infused with feudal and chivalrous sentiment. 'And, next to the King, I answered plainly I was bound to do him [the earl of Oxford?] service, and to fulfil his commandment, to the uttermost of my power', wrote Sir Edmund Bedingfield in 1487'[29].

An ancient custom maintained by nobles and gentry for much of the period was 'open house' for their fellows in the great halls of their mansions, as well as for dependents, especially on principal feast days. Chaucer's description of the Franklin is mainly a succulent paean on his customary bill of fare. According to a poetical effusion on the departure abroad of an Oxfordshire esquire, Chaucer's son Thomas, he fulfilled the ideal of 'householding and fulsome abundance'. His greatest joy was to entertain gentlemen of every degree:

Ye gentlemen dwelling environ
His absence eke ye ought to complain
For farewell now as in conclusion
Your play, your Joy . . .
farewell hunting and hawking . . .
Come home again like as we desire
To suppowaylen [*succour*] *all the whole shire.*

Thomas Chaucer was a well-educated royal servant, whose talents were appreciated by Henry IV and V. A century later another such, Richard Pace, advocating humanist education, poured scorn on the landowners who thought that 'it becomes the sons of gentlemen to blow the horn nicely, to hunt skilfully, and elegantly to carry and train a hawk'. Pace was right in emphasising the need of the polity for a well-educated nobility, responsive to the weal of the *res publica*, but his bureaucratic zeal must not be allowed to obscure the fact that, out in the shires, bucolic sports and entertainment were vital in promoting harmony and solidarity among their governing groups.

At the principal Christian festivals, particularly at Christmas, noble households were centres of entertainment. Lady Morley said that after her husband's death in 1476, she did not permit Christmas 'disguisings, nor harping, nor luting, nor singing, nor no loud disports, but playing at the tables, and chess, and cards'. Father Bokenham described how at Epiphany 1445 he walked the chamber with the countess of Eu, talking over legends of holy women, while her four young sons revelled and danced 'and others more, in their most fresh array disguised'. The exchange of New Year's gifts, and the 'liveries' of fresh array by masters to dependents, were ritualised affirmations of the bonds of family (*familia*) and fellowship, as were the joyful games, and the disguisings, in which men and women ritually met again for the first time and renewed their relationships. It was perhaps particularly shocking to contemporaries that the plotters against Henry IV in 1399 planned to trap him during these festivities after Christmas, and to gain access to his rejoicing household at Windsor disguised as 'mummers'.

A sparkling picture of Christmas games and country hospitality is given in the descriptions of King Arthur's court and Sir Bertilak's household in *Sir Gawayn and the Green Knight*. This anonymous poem, surviving in a single late fourteenth-century manuscript, is written in a dialect of Cheshire and south Lancashire. The poet dwells lovingly on the impressive architectural features and furnishings of the knight's castle, on the formalities and courtesies of life in its great hall and in the lord's and lady's private chambers, and on the arts of hunting which Malory was to consider attributes of gentility. Chaucer and his courtly audience might have found the poem quaintly provincial in its dialect, its alliterative verse form, its primitively awesome, rather than politely marvellous, magical happenings, its self-conscious preoccupation with fashionable behaviour and luxuries. *Sir Gawayn* provides insights into the mentality of a provincial elite. They may have been strongly influenced by Edward III's Court. Gawain is breathlessly watched and heard by Sir Bertilak's retainers as a model of conduct from Arthur's court. After the poem is written the motto of the Order of the Garter, founded by Edward *c*.1347. It points up the analogy with the fellowship founded by Arthur and his knights at the end of the poem. They adopted the wearing of a green baldric, an act which had shamed Gawain, so symbolically adopting the burden of his guilt. Cheshire and Lancashire gentlefolk had played a prominent part in Edward III's wars, and it is not surprising to find ideals of chivalrous fellowship which he promoted at Court circulating among them.

A Venetian observer commented *c*.1500 on the characteristically magnificent estate which English nobles had kept:'The titled nobility . . . were extremely profuse in their expenditure, and kept a very great retinue in their houses (which is a thing the English delight in beyond measure).' Moralists perennially castigated the luxury of gentlefolk. But there was a strong current of opinion that display was not self-indulgence, but served important social functions. Pearls, for instance, were reminders of obligations, for the pearl was a symbol of perfection, and hence, in the poem *Pearl*, of Christ.

Whereas there were French, Scottish and Castilian writers in the fifteenth century who blamed ills in their realms on the nobility, this was not a common English theme. The peerage of English nobles, with its strong connotations of obligation to serve as well as right to inherit, and their need of 'well-willers' at Court and in country to maintain influence, may have made them especially susceptible to the moulding forces of both secular and religious ideals. The magnate's adornments – blood, wealth, display – ought to be used, it was widely felt, to provide 'indifferent' government. Appropriate behaviour for a flashily bejewelled noble was not dashing bravura, but a demeanour suggesting that his desires and emotions were controlled by a sense of obligation. The heroine of *Pearl* is described as having an air as grave 'as duke's or earl's'. Chaucer's Knight was 'of his port as meek as is a maid'. 'Sadness' was another prized quality: Margaret Paston thought that Norfolk needed a 'sad' rule in 1462.

According to William Worcester, Thomas Beaufort, duke of Exeter (d.1426) kept a splendid household – he 'had 140 horsemen in his house' – yet discharged his lordship with a keen awareness of his paternalist and religious duties. He had thirteen paupers fed and given 3*d* every day; he distributed stew and wine daily to between 100 and 300 of the needy; on the eve of St Mary, he gave almswomen 40*d* each and, if they were poor, sets of bedclothes; he had women lying in childbirth given food and wine daily. 'Also he wished to make the children Christians and gave to each little one 40*d*.' The last of the poor whose feet he washed on Maundy Thursday received his cloak, doublet, belt and purse. He would have no swearers, liars or talebearers in his household; he accepted no gifts or rewards; he succoured veterans from his French campaigns who had fallen on evil days; refreshed and rewarded every wayfarer who came to his house, and offered Mass every day. According to John Rous, Edward IV's magnificent brother-in-law, Anthony Earl Rivers, 'was found to be wearing, at the time of his death, the hair-shirt which he had long been in the habit of wearing against his bare flesh' (cf. p. 359).

English knights were not used to having chivalrous biographies written about their deeds. From the mid-fourteenth century onwards they preferred a conformist style of representation on their funeral effigies and brasses, lacking in flamboyance. An illumination in the 'Bedford Book of Hours' (1423) shows the duke of Bedford kneeling before St George. The duke, in Garter robes, is magnificently attired in cloth of gold, the chamber embellished with his motto and badge. But he is not the centre of attention: he is subordinate to the saint and the rays of heavenly light streaming down through the window. The Lancastrian prince's symbolism of rank is placed within a divinely ordained hierarchy: the magnate is seen as the natural lynchpin of society.

The settings within which Elizabethan nobles were portrayed contrast with Bedford's. The religious symbolism has been replaced by a secular world: arms and military scenes emphasise a commanding role, heraldry a dynastic and landowning one. But some of the figures have a highly individual appearance, an ephemeral, even fanciful context. Nicholas Hilliard's miniature of a noble attired as a champion is a Spenserian fantasy of knight-errantry. Isaac Oliver's miniature of the earl of Dorset (1616) has his gorgeously attired figure in a surprisingly blank setting, appearing between flickering curtains as if on stage, drawing attention to the extravagant plumage on his helmet. These are less secure, less elemental images than Bedford's. In them, wealth, lineage, sensibilities, and qualities of mind and body are hectically paraded as evidence of Court sophistication and worthiness for royal office.

Perhaps it is not too fanciful to see, in the relative emphasis of these paintings, a reflection of some changes in the roles of nobility. The territorial influence of many leading families declined in the Yorkist and Tudor periods, due to drastic dislocations of succession and tenure, particularly during the Wars of the Roses and the uncertainties of the 1530s. The concurrent development of conciliar courts, central and regional, made noble arbitration of local disputes, and intermediacy between suitors and the Crown, less needful and vital. The nobles' initiatives as informal governors of local society were superceded by the closer supervision of the Elizabethan Privy Council over magistrates. The 'great house' ceased to be such an important focus of activities, as gentlefolk increasingly preferred to send their sons to universities and Inns of Court for polite as well as technical education, and as the noble family abandoned 'country hospitality' for the select company of the long gallery. The nerve-centre of shire government was less likely to be at the high table of a great hall, but rather at the magisterial board in quarter sessions. Sir William Wentworth considered it dangerous (1604) for gentlemen to be 'familiar' with noblemen 'or to depend upon them, or deal with or trust them too much': 'For their thoughts are bestowed upon their own weighty causes . . . albeit they be most courtly in words, yet they could be contented that rich gentlemen were less able to live without depending on them.'

But the decline of magnatial authority must not be exaggerated. Noble birth, especially when allied to wealth and talent, gave prior consideration for appointment to lord lieutenancies, admiralties, presidencies of local councils, wardenships and the command of armies. Wentworth himself, in listing the ways in which he had served the earl of Shrewsbury between 1597 and 1612, shows how a leading gentleman might still consider it worthwhile to put his local influence at a magnate's disposal:

Item *at his lordship's earnest request the said Sir William went to York with all the free holders he could possibly procure for the choosing of Sir John Savill one of the knights of Yorkshire.*
Item *at the request of the said Earl Sir William made Wormall his undersheriff, 44 Eliz. . . .*

Notes

1. County Durham, Cheshire and (from 1377) Lancashire were palatinates, whose public officials were appointed respectively by the bishops of Durham, the earls of Chester (kings' eldest sons) and the dukes of Lancaster (from 1399, the sovereigns).
2. There is some evidence that sheriffs appointed in November and December 1397 were chosen by Richard II or his Council on the basis of political reliability. Fifteen of them were reappointed, contrary to statute, in November 1398.
3. Coroners, resident property-holders nominally elected for life, kept Crown pleas in their jurisdictional region. They recorded, on rolls to be used in evidence at assizes, investigations and indictments in cases of serious crime, including the findings of inquests they held on dead bodies, when foul play was suspected. Verderers kept records for use in forest courts.
4. The survival of early medieval keeps of royal castles in county towns (e.g. at Exeter, Norwich, York and Newcastle), is partly due to their use by sheriffs, often appointed as their constables, as gaols and offices.
5. An 'angel' noble was a gold coin worth 10*s* in 1553.
6. Shynner was incumbent of Stonor's living at Penton Mewsey in Hampshire, for which county he apparently wanted Stonor to seek appointment, despite it not being, as he says, Stonor's 'country'.
7. The worth of a noble was then 6*s* 8*d*.
8. His wife was the notorious Alice Perrers, formerly Edward III's mistress, with whom he had quarrelled.
9. In 1542 the separate office of Master of Liveries was abolished, and his duties were annexed to the Court of Wards, in the hands of a surveyor of liveries.

10. A. Hassell Smith, *County and Court: government and politics in Norfolk, 1558–1603*, Oxford U.P. 1974.
11. In 1388 JPs were statutorily granted four shillings expenses for daily attendances, their clerk two shillings, deducted from the fines and amercements which they imposed, and from the judicial profits of private franchises.
12. In the sixteenth century, as the investigative role of JPs became more important, that of the grand jury declined. Trial juries developed, from being groups of witnesses, into assessors of the evidence presented, as guided by the assize judges.
13. The Council originated with the public uses to which Gloucester put his private council, when lieutenant of the north for Edward IV. After the 1537 commission, it had a continuous role as the principal agent of royal justice mainly in Yorkshire. In many respects the Council became the northern equivalent of the Privy Council, issuing mandates under its own seal and enforcing its orders partly through its own officers. The Council, under its President, consisted of nobles, gentlemen and lawyers, and met in four annual sessions, from 1582 invariably at York. As well as having powers of criminal jurisdiction, it was commissioned to settle a wide variety of civil disputes, including suits involving ejection from tenements, tenant right, leasehold and debt. The Council in the Marches of Wales, which exercised jurisdiction in some adjacent English shires, had a parallel, often similar evolution (cf. p. 306). The Council of the West (see p. 323) was shortlived.
14. Towards the end of the reign the financially straitened Crown was lavish in the grant, often to courtiers and their local connections, of licences exempting from export prohibitions, customs farms, and monopolies in the distribution (and sometimes manufacture) of a commodity. The activities of grantees, their deputies and sub-licencees, often aroused local resentment.
15. J. Cornwall, 'The early Tudor gentry', *Economic Hist. Rev.*, xvii (1964–5); the counties are Rutland, Suffolk, Buckinghamshire, Sussex and Cornwall.
16. J. T. Cliffe, *The Yorkshire Gentry from the Reformation to the Civil War* (Athlone Press, 1969).
17. Buckinghamshire had no dominant magnate family in the later Middle Ages: there were other shires in which nobles were much greater landowners. For some comparable calculations, using different bases, see J. P. Cooper, 'The social distribution of land and men in England, 1436–1700', *Economic Hist. Rev.*, xx (1967).
18. Clarenceux, Norroy and March; the last disappeared before 1500. Garter King of Arms, with an ill-defined superior authority, was instituted in 1415.
19. In *De Studio Militari*, dedicated to Humphrey Duke of Gloucester (d.1447).
20. Medieval Latin *francus*, Old French *franc*.
21. Husbandmen were those engaged in field labour; for yeomen, see p. 19.
22. The Wardens also often paid and commanded frontier garrisons in their Wardenries, e.g. at Carlisle, Wark, Roxburgh and Berwick.
23. An aftermath of the northern rebellions of 1569–70; cf. p. 331.
24. 'For I also am an Israelite of the seed of Abraham, of the tribe of Benjamin.'
25. At this time such male intimacy does not imply homosexuality. In *Sir Gawayn and the Green Knight*, the agreement between Sir Gawayn and Sir Bertilak to share their daily winnings reflects the solemn convention of 'brotherhood-in-arms' – a context which heightens Gawayn's betrayal of principle by concealing the green baldric the lady gives him.
26. Norfolk and Norwich Record Office, MR 314 242 × 5.
27. Richard II retained many with the livery of the white hart in the 1390s.
28. The likely identification of the author Malory with a Warwickshire knight frequently accused of violent proceedings, which seem at odds with the ideals of the book, has puzzled literary scholars. If we could fit the controversial references into the context of Midlands politics, they might appear less damning.
29. Builder of Oxburgh Hall in Norfolk.

Chapter 5

The royal will and its opponents, 1325–1449

The fall of Edward II (1325–27)

The starting-point of this narrative of domestic politics has been chosen as shortly preceding the deposition of Edward II; its conclusion as marking the start of a period in which Henry VI's rule was increasingly troubled, culminating in his deposition in 1461. In between these two depositions, Richard II was deposed in 1399. Such recurrent royal abasements suggest the continued strength in the period of elements in the community with urges to oppose the royal will. Yet there was no continuous opposition 'interest', or continuous programme to lessen or control the authority exercised by kings. The evolution of parliamentary assemblies in the fourteenth century, particularly in Edward III's reign, provided customary mechanisms for the mutual adjustment of the Crown's and property-holding communities' interests. On the whole, they displayed appreciation of each other's rights, aims, and usefulness: some kings (notably Edward III) were prepared to make considerable constitutional concessions.

Paradoxically, then, in a period when kings were threatened or treated with degradation, elements of underlying political harmony developed between them and a broad political community. Consequently, there were no lasting breakdowns of royal government or general destructions of royal prerogative. But the intensity of quarrels between kings and subjects over the latter's communal demands must not be minimised. In the fourteenth century the politically articulate on occasion raged against royal taxation and wastefulness, and against royal failure to defend them from the incursions of Scots, French, and Castilians. Kings were to be infuriated by the successful flexing of political muscles in parliaments against their policies and ministers, and alarmed by the implied threats to the privileges of the royal 'estate'. Such discontents sometimes helped to facilitate rebellions by magnates.

A common element in the risings which led to all three depositions was the discontent of a few magnates, aggrieved that the king was undermining their local interests and aspirations for royal rewards by blatant preference and neglect. Instructive comparisons can be made between royal favourites and their political repercussions – Edward II's Gaveston (before our period) and Despensers, Richard II's Oxford and *duketti*, Henry VI's Suffolk and Beauforts. Since the monarchy was heavily dependent for the enforcement of its authority in the shires and abroad on the good will of a handful of magnates, who conceived of themselves as privileged royal kinsfolk, the king who neglected them was at risk. Moreover, gentry and townsmen often seem to have been tolerant of a magnate's rebellion, some slow to support the king, others joining in against him. They may have thought sometimes that it was not their quarrel, but one amongst the king's family; or that the rebels were sympathetic to their current grievances. The great weakness of the Crown, as Richard II perceived, was that there was as yet no general consensus of interest on principle condemning and opposing magnate revolts.

By the end of Henry VI's long minority, in 1437, many of the causes of tension which had rendered his predecessors more vulnerable may have seemed things of the past. There were now traditional guidelines for relations between king and parliaments. The problems of the Anglo-Scottish Borders had not dangerously impinged on English politics since the 1400s. As a result of Henry V's French conquests, the Lancastrian dynasty was firmly accepted, and the frontier with hostile Frenchmen was, in the main, still deep in France. The situation stimulated royal complacence about the arts of government. Henry VI's impolitic behaviour led to the crises of the 1450s, precipitating prolonged dynastic insecurities and significant changes in governmental aims and methods.

In 1325 there had been reason why those well informed about the affairs of the realm might have felt optimistic about future developments. A truce intended to last for thirteen years had been made with the Scots in 1323, ending most of the misery in the North caused for years by continual Scottish incursions. The mediation of Edward II's queen, Isabella of France, helped to produce a formula for ending the war which had broken out in 1324 with her brother Charles IV. Within the realm, there had been greater tranquillity since the suppression of the rebellion in 1322 of the king's cousin, Thomas, earl of Lancaster, for years his principal and most powerful critic: the troublesome earl had been executed before a jeering crowd outside his castle at Pontefract. The king himself, Edward II, was in the prime of life in 1325, a vigorous and athletic man of forty-three. The succession to the throne was assured, two of his four children being boys: Edward, prince of Wales (the future Edward III) and John of Eltham. The king was in control of royal government. Among his leading officials running central institutions were some of the most conscientious and hard-working royal servants appointed by English kings in the later Middle Ages. Particularly notable were Walter Stapledon, bishop of Exeter (Treasurer of the Exchequer, 1320–1 and 1322–5), and Robert Baldock (Chancellor, 1323–6). With the service of such officials and the aid of bankers' loans, and without the necessity of financing campaigns, the Crown was able to meet the expenses of the Household, of patronage and government. In the York parliament of 1322, after the suppression of Lancaster's rising, the king had taken pains to reassure the 'community of the realm' that its 'liberties' would not be infringed by the Crown. Magna Carta and more recent ordinances restricting the powers of royal officials were publicly reaffirmed.

But the men who formulated and largely articulated whatever 'public opinion' existed about the affairs of the realm – magnates and important gentry, citizens of London and other leading towns – were seemingly not reassured. The basic reason was that they lacked confidence in Edward II. He was certainly no nonentity. He had striven consistently, and at last with some success, to retain his freedom to govern and appoint his servants. But Edward was not a skilful politician: apparently he was lazy, emotional and rather stupid. By 1325, after a reign of nearly twenty years, in which his conduct had inflated problems into tense political crises, few trusted him or believed that his rule was likely to remain stable and peaceful. The 1322 rebellions had finally undermined the credit of a group of politically moderate magnates who had arbitrated between Edward and his opponents, striving to make him and his favourites conform to the reforming 'Ordinances' of 1311. The harsh and somewhat arbitrary punishments meted out to leading rebels in 1322 made landowners fear that their lives and inheritances might be similarly jeopardised by judgments of treason.

One of the causes of revolt in 1322 had been the determination of a group of well-established magnates to destroy the power and influence accumulated by a *parvenu* landowner endowed by royal favour. In the later Middle Ages such endowment, especially when rapid, sometimes disturbed provincial balances of power, provoking local tensions and outbreaks of violence which might escalate into revolt, if the king did not move quickly to arbitrate and appease local discontents. Before and after the troubles of 1322 Edward showed no inclination to placate the powerful neighbouring rivals of a lord of lesser rank, Hugh Despenser, who was accumulating properties in the southern Marches of Wales. By a royal judgment he was awarded the lordship of Glamorgan and other estates in right of his wife Eleanor, coheiress to the Clare earldom of Gloucester: by royal grant he received the prized lordship of Gower.

Edward II, despite his success in overriding Marcher opposition to the rise of Despenser, was dangerously placed in 1325. He had alienated 'public opinion'. He seems to have lost the sympathy even of his close relations. His half-brothers, Thomas of Brotherton, earl of Norfolk, and Edmund of Woodstock, earl of Kent, felt that he had neglected their counsel. His wife Isabella, supported by influential exiles, refused to return from France or to allow her son Edward to return until Despenser and his father Hugh earl of Winchester had left Edward II's Household. Then in September 1326 Queen Isabella landed in Suffolk with some of the lords who had been in France with her (including the earl of Kent) and a force of soldiers commanded by John, brother of the count of Hainault. According to a London chronicler, 'the English sailors did not wish to prevent the arrival of the queen and her son and their company by reason of the great hate they had towards Sir Hugh Despenser'. This may be an example of that occasional but significant involvement of the 'commons' in high politics which is characteristic of the fourteenth and fifteenth centuries. Conflict among the great led to the involvement of the lesser, and encouraged the latter to articulate their own grievances against the Crown. The queen was soon joined by her brother-in-law, Norfolk, influential in East Anglia, and by local gentry. The hostility of the Londoners forced Edward II to abandon his attempt to defend the city, where some of his servants were viciously lynched by the 'commons', including Bishop Stapledon. The citizens opened their gates to the queen. Support swelled for an army which served a mere foreign woman and her illicit lover, the Marcher exile Roger Mortimer of Wigmore, whose relationship with her had scandalised the French king's household. This discreditable pair believed that their only hope of safety lay in the deposition of Edward. They seem to have had little difficulty in persuading others to support their aim, though some were to have doubts and scruples over the method of procedure. A parliament summoned in the king's name met at Westminster in January 1327. The king, who had been captured, was not present, being held at Kenilworth Castle, residence of the late Thomas of Lancaster's brother Henry. The king's absence cast doubt on whether the assembly of estates could be regarded as a legally constituted parliament. But Londoners threatened to intimidate anyone who spoke in favour of the king, and at the Guildhall the mayor and aldermen of the city repudiated their allegiance. Articles were read to the estates accusing Edward of crimes, as a justification for a similar withdrawal of allegiances, and without being given the chance he wished to answer the charges, he was declared deposed by the estates. His son and heir was proclaimed as Edward III and the former king was imprisoned in Berkeley Castle. His death was proclaimed in September 1327. Presumably he had been murdered on the orders of Roger Mortimer, fearful of projected rescue attempts.

Edward's pitiful demise did more for his good reputation than any of his acts when living. His memory was cherished in some noble families and his tomb in Gloucester Abbey (now the cathedral) became a centre of pilgrimage. The fine effigy which the monks ordered still adorns it. But in the fourteenth century pilgrims also visited the tomb in Pontefract Priory of the leader of baronial opposition, Thomas of Lancaster. The St Albans monk Thomas Walsingham noted that in 1359 blood flowed from the tomb of 'Saint Thomas, formerly earl of Lancaster'. Edward's great-grandson Richard II was to foster the king's cult, attempting to procure formal canonisation. The slain earl and king remained significant figures in the minds of the following generations.

The manner in which Edward's authority collapsed in 1326 demonstrates basic aspects of the defences and political structure of the realm. Until the navigational advances of the sixteenth century (and even after then), naval interception of incursions and invasions from the continent was a hazardous expedient. Reliance was placed mainly on land defences, but in the absence until the mid-seventeenth century of a standing army, these depended on the will and efficiency of the local communities, particularly in the coastal shires. If the provincial leaders of society to whom kings looked for leadership were tardy and reluctant, or the captains of royal garrisons were disloyal, defence was liable to be sporadic and badly co-ordinated. In 1326 the shire communities and their natural leaders were at best indifferent to Edward's fate. His reliance on urban fortifications was useless in face of the hostility of citizens, first in London, then Bristol. A king who offended the susceptibilities or damaged the prestige of influential men in these oligarchies was in danger of becoming politically isolated, supported by a narrowly based 'Court interest', by groups themselves fragmented by competition for royal patronage and torn by 'country' ties. If a ruler wished to offend influential landowners with impunity, he had to isolate them, to build up enmities and widen fissures within local oligarchies. There were plenty of opportunities for a king to divide and act arbitrarily, but Edward II was not the man to utilise them successfully. The Northumberland landowner Sir Thomas Grey (d.1369?), in his *Scalacronica*, reflected on the deposition of Edward II. The 'commons', he said, were delighted by the change of ruler, 'because of the misdoing of the father [Edward II], and because of their fickle habit, so characteristic of a medley of races'. Some, he continued, thought that this diversity of spirit in the English was the cause of the great changes which occurred amongst them. Even after twenty-five or so years of Edward III's reign, he regarded the English polity as an unstable one.

The reign of Edward III (1327–77)

Sir Thomas Grey's reflections on the fall of Edward II indicate how his successor needed to restore the confidence of property-holders in the Crown. Fifty years after his accession in 1327, Edward III, sick and weak, was taken from his house at Havering and rowed up the Thames to another royal residence, Sheen. As the king was passing London, lords flocked out in barges to greet him and crowds waved and cheered on the banks 'to his great comfort and content'. This touching demonstration of esteem and affection shows how well Edward III had succeeded in winning the confidence of his subjects. It is even more striking that this demonstration occurred less than a year after the end of the 'Good Parliament' of 1376, in which there had been the most telling assault on royal authority for decades.

Edward III throughout his reign strove to enhance the dignity and security of magnates, and to keep the loyalty and goodwill of property-holders. In return they allowed him freedom to rule in pursuit of his ambitions and love of luxury. But events in the Good Parliament were to show that when the king's patronage and his financial and military affairs had been badly handled, this 'community of the realm' whose self-confidence he had done much to foster would be quick to interfere once more in order to condemn and reform royal government. Moreover, by saddling his successors with burdensome foreign claims and problems, Edward unwittingly ensured that they would be especially dependent on the goodwill and co-operation of the community, whose financial and military support was necessary to defend the realm and raise expeditions for service out of it. Edward III, in order to restore loyalty to the Crown within the realm and its prestige abroad (in both of which aims he largely succeeded) created conditions for the further evolution of that 'limited monarchy' analysed nearly a century after his death, in the treatise *The Governance of England* by the royal councillor and lawyer Sir John Fortescue (cf. pp. 63 ff). His enthusiasm for this firm 'mixed' constitution contrasts with Sir Thomas Grey's cry of despair at English instability. Nevertheless, all was not plain sailing between the times of Grey and Fortescue. The events of Richard II's and Henry IV's reigns were to show that the shift in the balance of power between king and community which had occurred in the fourteenth century produced situations of political crisis, kings worrying that their 'prerogative' was vitally threatened.

In 1325 Edward, when prince of Wales, aged thirteen, performed homage to his uncle Charles IV of France for the duchy of Aquitaine, as a means of recovering parts of the duchy which his uncle the earl of Kent had ingloriously lost the previous year. Edward may not have considered this a humiliating expedient. But he may have resented his betrothal the following year to Philippa, daughter of William count of Hainault, Holland and Zealand, if he understood that his father's permission had not been obtained, and indeed that the betrothal was the price of military support to overthrow his father.

Edward III's accession took place in the most disgraceful and shameful circumstances within memory, and real power remained in the hands of his mother and Roger Mortimer. In the spring of 1327 Edward's spirits probably lifted briefly when he rode to York to lead an army against the Scots, who had launched new attacks since his accession. In July Edward and his men took the road to Durham and thence plunged inland into trackless moorland in an attempt to catch up with an inferior Scots force. Even when the English, hungry and sodden, confronted the Scots at Stanhope in Weardale, they hesitated to attack their skilfully positioned camp, and the Scots, in a night foray, penetrated to Edward's tent. The Scottish forces extricated themselves from Stanhope without opposition. Sir Thomas Grey says that 'the king, a mere boy, burst into tears; he broke up and retired towards York, engaging no more in this war so long as he was under the governance of his mother and of . . . Roger de Mortimer, Earl of

March'. Further blows to the young man's esteem were the peace of Northampton (1328), which the pair made with the Scots as a corollary to the failure of the campaign, and the subsequent unchallenged siege of Norham by Robert I (Robert Bruce). By the treaty Edward's claim to the overlordship of Scotland was abandoned and Robert's kingship was recognised – concessions which Edward II, no matter how many times chased by the Scots, had never made.

Mortified by what was in fact a sensible and realistic policy towards Scotland, and aware that some magnates, such as Henry earl of Lancaster, chafed at March's influence over royal policy and patronage, Edward III countenanced plotting in his household against the favourite. In October 1330 some of his servants seized the earl of March in his mother's bedchamber at Nottingham Castle. March was condemned by his peers as a traitor, firstly for having 'usurped to himself the royal power and the government of the realm over the estate of the king, and dismissed and caused to be dismissed officials in the king's household and elsewhere throughout the realm and others set in their place at his will'. March was not allowed to defend himself, since recently 'nobles were not allowed to defend themselves, but perished without defence and lawful conviction'. Henceforward Edward was determined to be his own master, and to appease the magnates over such grievances.

Edward III had a good physical constitution. His handsome and dignified features were remarked on by contemporaries, and are reflected in maturity on the bronze effigy over his tomb in Westminster Abbey. He was an impetuous and imperious man, given to unreasoning outbursts of temper, and capable of acting harshly and unfairly to his servants. The famous story of his treatment of the submissive burgesses of Calais, immortalised by Rodin's sculpture, illustrates his savagery, and the manner in which he shrewdly paused and modulated it, when the effects this would have on his 'public image' occurred or were pointed out to him. Near the end of his life, after a number of lethargic and self-indulgent years, he could be passionately assertive, overturning a measure agreed on by the Council with the remark 'I alone am the sovereign judge', and threatening to withhold his blessing from his sons if they did not obey his will. His impetuosity is seen at its best in warfare. In 1336, when the English military position in Scotland was doubtful, he arrived in the Marches, according to Sir Thomas Grey, with scarcely more than fifty men-at-arms. Having recruited some Marchmen, he set out for Perth with not more than 100 soldiers. 'He arrived at the said town so unexpectedly that all his people marvelled at his coming, and that he should have dared to act in such a manner.' With a mere raiding party Edward toiled across the Highlands to rescue Catherine Beaumont, countess of Atholl, besieged in Lochindorb Castle by Sir Andrew Moray. In 1350, Froissart recounts, he was acting with the same disregard for personal danger when attacking a superior Castilian fleet off Winchelsea. The king ordered his helmsman: 'Steer at that ship straight ahead of us. I want to have a joust at it.' The hapless seaman, aware that the Spaniard had the weather gauge, had to obey. 'The king's ship was so shattered by the collision that its seams cracked and water began to pour in.' Fortunately Edward's knights managed to board and capture another Spaniard.

Such exploits delighted nobles. For them Edward was in many ways an ideal king, a steadfast friend who shared their love of sports, military pastimes and banquets, and was lavish in his rewards. He can still be seen feasting with his nobles on the brass of Robert Braunche (d.1364), a leading merchant of Lynn who entertained him. In 1337 he had created six earldoms: William Montague, William Clinton, Robert Ufford, William Bohun, Hugh Audley and Henry of Grosmont became respectively earls of Salisbury, Huntingdon, Suffolk, Northampton, Gloucester and Derby. Most of these were 'new men' who had risen in his personal service. Yet their elevation does not seem to have provoked protests from the 'old nobility'. For he did not exclude them from his luxurious favour and intimate pleasures. His foundation, the Order of the Garter, survives as a memorial to his concept that chivalry should bind together as companions men of gentle but differing status. Traces of his impressive reconstruction of Windsor Castle, as a fit setting for a court to rival King Arthur's, survive too.

Characteristically, one of Edward's boon companions was a distinguished soldier, a conventionally devout knight with a taste for sensual pleasures. This was Henry of Grosmont, earl of Derby and duke of Lancaster, the greatest secular landowner in the realm, whose family Edward's father could not abide. Henry was Thomas of Lancaster's nephew. In middle age he composed a devotional treatise, *Le Livre de Seyntz Medecines*, in which he admitted that he had often drunk so much with his companions that his legs could not carry him to bed, and that he preferred to kiss common women rather than noblewomen, because they responded more frankly. Perhaps there are echoes here of the tone of Edward's Court. It may be significant that the motto of his chivalrous order is an injunction to avoid scandalous thoughts, and that a story current about its foundation concerned an item of feminine underwear. Edward certainly behaved towards the end of his life in ways of which righteous treatises on noble conduct disapproved, becoming slothful and inseparably attached to a mistress, Alice Perrers, denigrated for her lack of gentle birth and qualities. But Edward's indulgences, unlike some of his father's, were the kind that nobles winked at.

Edward's spell-binding ability to transfix the potentially troublesome secular magnates was demonstrated even more dazzlingly than in his friendship with Lancaster in his extraordinarily harmonious relations with his eldest son. Edward, duke of Cornwall and prince of Wales, who came of age in 1351, was a restlessly active, ambitious man, an outstanding soldier. Heirs to the throne have been notorious for caballing against their fathers. Prince Edward ('the Black Prince') was an adult heir for a quarter of a century, yet he remained content to share his father's chivalrous Arthurian pastimes at Court, and execute his imperial Arthurian policies in France.

In the fifteenth century Edward III's reputation was to stand higher than that of any king before Henry V. This may have been because of his victories, because congenial memories of him were preserved in noble households, and because so many nobles were descended from him. There was a tendency to attribute, often quite unhistorically, an approved line of conduct to him. The reputation of his Household for good internal administration combined with magnificence was so great that when, about a century after his death, Edward IV's officials drafted a scheme for the organisation of that king's Household (see pp. 88 ff), they took the supposed precedents of Edward III's as their model.

But during his reign, some sections of the community felt that the means employed by Edward to restore the prestige and promote the claims of the Crown abroad were oppressive. Chroniclers occasionally echo their grievances. Under the year 1343 the Anonimalle Chronicler noted that 'the king of England with 300 knights and the same number of ladies held at Windsor the round table [a mock-Arthurian gathering] at outrageous cost and great expense'. Sir Thomas Grey was concerned about the implications of Edward's extravagance: 'The king bestowed so liberally of his possessions that he retained for himself scarcely any of his lands appertaining to the Crown, but was obliged to subsist upon levies and subsidies, which were a heavy burden on the people.' As yet not much is known about domestic history during Edward III's long reign, apart from events in fairly brief periods of political crisis. This is partly because the comparatively few monastic chroniclers who conceived their task as one of writing the history of the realm, rather than of their house, found that their secular informants' news tended to be about campaigns in Scotland and later in France. The absence of magnates and their retainers abroad and the enlistment of outlaws for service there in order to gain pardons may have helped to tranquillise provincial society, after the rebellions and outrages of criminal bands characteristic of the 1320s and early 1330s. It may be significant that from the 1380s onwards there was to be an increase of complaints in parliaments about local oppressions committed by evil-doers under cover of the protection and favour shown to them by patrons, for this was to be a period in which fewer magnates, knights and wrongdoers campaigned outside the realm for long periods than had done so in several decades of Edward's reign.

Edward's first sphere of military involvement was Scotland, whose king and nobles had humiliated him in 1327–8. Robert I had died in 1329, leaving a son and heir David, aged five, married in 1328 under the terms of the Treaty of Northampton to Edward's sister Joan of the Tower. Edward continued to adhere to the treaty, but did not prevent a group of northern English lords from sailing to Scotland with a small private expedition (July 1332) to claim lands seized from their families by Robert I. The unexpected victory of the 'disinherited' at Dupplin Moor, their capture of Perth, and the coronation at Scone of their leader Edward Balliol, as king of Scots rapidly ensued. But by the end of 1332 it had become clear that they were too few to hold the land against the adherents of David II. Balliol, according to an English chronicler, the canon of Bridlington, 'sought fidelity in the Scots as vainly as seeking strength in a knot tied in rushes'. Only Edward III's intervention in 1333 salvaged the cause of Balliol, who had recognised the English Crown's overlordship over Scotland before undertaking his expedition. In return for English aid, Balliol ceded parts of his realm to Edward: the sheriffdoms of Berwick, Roxburgh, Selkirk, Peebles, Edinburgh and Dumfries, and the forests of Selkirk, Ettrick and Jedworth. This was entitlement to English domination of the southern Lowlands. In 1333 Edward III besieged Berwick, which surrendered after he had decisively beaten a relieving force at Halidon Hill. By Christmas 1334 the English had overrun the Lowlands. Though in the York parliament of 1332 the lords had shown a realistic lack of enthusiasm for war in Scotland, Edward may have hoped that this settlement would restore the prestige of his Crown, so often humiliated by the despised Scots, provide better security for the northern shires of England and a Scottish sphere of influence for their gentry.

But Edward III failed to detach allegiances permanently from David II, who in 1334 was given refuge in France by Philip VI. Edward had saddled himself with an expensive and incomplete occupation of hostile country, a situation he seems to have later tried to avoid in his French wars. In 1337 the Scots, raiding again south of the Border, even attacked Carlisle. Edward's determination to resist Philip VI of France, who declared war against him that year, necessitated a painful and prolonged withdrawal from Scotland, leaving the north of England once more, as in his father's reign, exposed to retaliation. Sir Thomas Grey hinted at the exasperation of the lords who in 1338 had to abandon the siege of Dunbar Castle, when Edward was absorbed in his German alliance against Philip VI: 'The king, on the advice of those who had set their heart upon this alliance, crossed the sea and arrived at Antwerp, where he lay for fifteen months without making any war, only jousting and leading a jolly life.' Grey was piqued that his fellow northerners were left to fend for themselves.

David II, a young firebrand, returned to Scotland in 1341 determined to emulate his father's successes. After the fall of Stirling (April 1342), the English held in Scotland only the fortresses of Berwick and of Lochmaben in Annandale. In that year David raided Northumberland as far south as the Tyne. During Edward's absence in France in 1346, there were further raids. David with a large force penetrated the West March and ransomed Cumberland and Westmorland. His army passed through Hexham to invade the bishopric of Durham, camping in Bear Park. But the northern levies rallied under their gentry at Richmond. Encouraged by the presence of their spiritual leader, William la Zouche, archbishop of York, they decisively defeated the Scots at Neville's Cross (October 1346). The victory was a triumph for Henry Percy, Ralph Neville, Thomas Rokeby and other soldiers who during the past few decades had invested profits made in the Scottish wars in local estates, and had built up 'affinities' among the gentry. Neville's Cross proved their claims to dominate Border society and its defences. One esquire, John Coupland, even captured David II in the battle. The consequent Scottish weakness enabled the northern lords to overrun much of southern Scotland. But it was an insecure hold. Though until 1355 the regent, Robert the Steward, concluded almost continuous truces, the English managed to keep control only of the areas dominated by their strongholds of Lochmaben, Roxburgh and Berwick. In 1356 the Scots even took Berwick: Edward hastened northwards to recover it. Both parties were prepared to make terms rather than go on inflicting mutual damages without the power to strike decisively. In October 1357 the Scots at last accepted Edward's terms for David II's ransom, which was fixed at 100,000 marks to be paid over ten years. Edward recognised David as king of Scots. The latter remained on fairly amicable terms with the English Court until his death in 1371, being more concerned to restore royal authority in his kingdom than to recover the English-held Border fortresses.

Edward III's aggressive and ambitious policies towards Scotland in the 1330s did not lead to irreparable disasters. But his rejection of the 1328 settlement, his annexations of burghs and sheriffdoms and imposition of a hard ransom treaty involved him and his successors in bad relations with Scotland. There was to be haggling over the fulfilment of ransom payments. In 1383 it was asserted in parliament that Richard II intended to claim sovereignty over Scotland: Henry IV claimed it at the head of an invading army in 1400. The chronicler John Hardyng produced for Henry VI's Council a series of forged documents supporting the English Crown's supposed rights. The revival of such pretensions helped to stimulate Franco-Scottish amity, increasing the misery of inhabitants both sides of the Border and hampering English aims in France. The attempt to alter the Anglo-Scottish frontiers implicit in the annexations of the 1330s and 1340s in southern Scotland, though helping to provide needed protection to the northern English shires, created a 'Border problem' with complex international and domestic repercussions (see pp. 141 ff).

Edward's French wars produced for his successors a legacy of extravagant claims, bad foreign relations and the need to garrison permanently expensive bases. His dispute with the Valois over the right to the French Crown and his peace of 1360 (see pp. 227 ff) based on the attempt to absorb much of south-western France in full sovereignty, saddled later kings of England with claims which they lacked the power to enforce or prestige to abandon. But the financial and political consequences of Edward's ambitious French policies were much more significant in the development of relations between Crown and community than were those of his earlier Scottish wars. Whereas under Edward II the principal political problems had concerned relations between Crown and magnates, in the period of the French wars these were to be subsumed within the tensions caused by an altered pattern of relations between the Crown and the whole political community as represented in parliament.

In the first years of the French war, Edward attempted to win a quick victory, based financially on his subjects' co-operation in an exhaustive effort. Prerogative rights to raise money, materials and soldiers at the community's expense without specific prior assent – by purveyance, judicial fines, feudal aids and array – were stretched to extortionate limits. In September 1336 an assembly including knights and burgesses assented to a wool subsidy, and a year later a parliament did likewise to an aid, unprecedented in size, for the defence of the realm in the king's absence and the costs of his expedition. He had already agreed terms with a group of leading merchants for their purchase and export of part of the wool crop: they were to make the Crown an immediate loan and pay it half the eventual sale profits. These proved disappointing: in 1338 parliament authorised the Crown's pre-emption and priority sale in Flanders of half the wool crop. Resistance by growers to the merchants licensed to operate the royal monopoly, and a market glut, reduced the expected profits. The royal attempts to manipulate wool markets caused mounting domestic annoyance, without covering Edward's rising military debts and obligations.

By the summer of 1339 there was tension between the king and the ministers in England to whom he dictated policy, with such disappointing results. In September he tried to appease discontent there by allowing the ministers, headed by John Stratford, archbishop of Canterbury, real authority. When parliament met in October, Lords and Commons presented separate petitions complaining about the ways in which the Crown had recently exploited feudal and prerogative revenues, and asserting that all unaccustomed royal demands should receive common consent. King and councillors showed anxiety to remedy grievances. But the measures petitioned for in the parliament which met in March 1340 savoured of constitutional constraints clamped on royal prerogative by Edward II's critics. The community sought the withdrawal of royal administration of the realm, and notably of financial dispositions, from the king into the hands of a magnate council, answerable to parliament. However, such a scheme was intended to ensure the efficient and just conduct of government during Edward III's absence abroad, not to deprive him of his rights.

The council certainly did exercise extensive powers in 1340, but failed to provide for the king's financial needs: the sorely tried communities were sluggish and evasive in meeting the commitments of parliamentary subsidies. In September Edward, heavily indebted, agreed to the truce of Espléchin. He arrived stealthily at the Tower of London, from Antwerp, furious at what he considered to be treacherous misconduct of his officials and lieges. Punitive commissions were appointed. Officials were deprived of office, some arbitrarily imprisoned. Stratford, prime object of royal wrath, was summoned for trial. But the archbishop was a skilful and determined politician. His eloquent denunciations of the king, in which he drew pointed, ominous comparisons between Edward's conduct and his father's, evoked widespread sympathy. His assertion of the right to trial by peers struck the right note with nobles whose families had suffered from executions without its benefit in recent generations. In the parliament which met in April 1341, Lords and Commons jointly presented petitions in effect requesting statutory embodiment of the 1340 constitutional scheme. Magnates pressed baronial claims, resurrected from the conflicts of Edward II's reign, to control the choice and appointment of royal ministers. Edward III assented to the enactment of notable concessions. Barons against whom the king alleged trespasses were to answer them only before their peers in parliament. Opportunities were to be given in parliament for accusations to be made against leading royal officers, and those found guilty were to be punished by their peers. New appointments to such offices were to be made by the advice of the Lords and other councillors around the king.

In other reigns this royal abasement might have led to civil war. But Edward and his magnates, beneath their frayed tempers, had an underlying mutual respect. In October, with their assent, he revoked his statutory consent to the 1341 concessions: later in the month, he and Stratford were publicly reconciled. The Commons vainly expressed dismay at the revocation in 1343. But the king's responses to their petitions showed that he had not lost the willingness displayed in 1340 to consider complaints about abuses of royal justice, and make redress in parliaments for the malpractices of his officials.

There was continued discontent at the exploitation of prerogative levies to help pay for the war, which were to be particularly heavy during the strenuous military efforts of 1346–8. But such levies were not producing enough to sustain warfare. By 1352 the last of the English mercantile syndicates, with whom Edward had bargained to exploit the wool trade and supply him with loans, had collapsed. He had become heavily dependent on the regular grant of parliamentary subsidies, not only in time of war, but to help pay defence and other costs in time of truce or peace, when there was not such a clearcut obligation on the community to supply aid. The Commons showed their political maturity by making stipulations, in the indentures formally granting subsidies, about how they were to be collected or spent, about provision for answer to their petitions, and for guarantees of the cessation of various forms of prerogative taxation[1]. In 1352 Edward gave assent to a Commons petition that no one be compelled to find soldiers unless by common assent and grant in parliament. Though he guarded his rights to levy purveyance and feudal aids, and to institute judicial enquiries at will, by affirming statutory limitations to their operation he surrendered the prerogative of exploiting them (and extra-parliamentary levies of wool) as major sources of taxation.

The exhaustive financial demands of warfare had eventually produced regular, reliable sources of taxation for the Crown, but ones which required parliamentary assent, promoted the Commons' awareness of their bargaining power, and the concept that the king's ministers were accountable to the community for their disposal of all the resources that came into his hands. After 1341 the old baronial resource of mobilising popular support against the Court, by championing local grievances about abuses of prerogative rights, declined. But the new fiscal relationship of Crown and community could also be exploited by discontented magnates. On occasion they were to argue that the greed of ministers and favourites, not the malice of foreigners, primarily threatened the impoverishment and destruction of the community. Accusations of treason, which the Crown had used to dissuade the community from aiding baronial rebellion, could now be used by the king's opponents to arouse feeling against his principal officers, and to justify parliamentary restraints on government. Growing disquiet with its conduct in the 1370s and 1380s, during Edward's last years and the early part of Richard II's reign, found expression particularly in parliamentary agitation, exploiting the institutional framework developed in the mid-century.

In 1371 agitation by the secular peers resulted in the replacement of two bishops (Wykeham of Winchester and Brantingham of Exeter) as Chancellor and Treasurer by laymen. In 1373 the Commons would not grant subsidy until they were permitted to consult a committee of peers. In the parliament which met in April 1376 they took a similar line. The Anonimalle Chronicle has what appears to be an eyewitness account of the parliament, giving the fullest and most vivid glimpse of the medieval Commons at work. The Chancellor, Sir John Knyvet, outlined the business before the assembled estates, requesting grants to defend the realm, imperilled by French, Spanish, Gascon, Flemish, Scottish and other enemies. Next day the Commons met to consider their 'charge'. A succession of shire knights came to the lectern to denounce defaults of government. The first speaker set the tone by lamenting the impoverishment of the community and waste of grants. The king, he said, should be counselled as to how he could live, govern and maintain war with his own goods. He had heard that the king had been cheated. The Commons made no move towards granting a subsidy, to the government's exasperation. The king's son John of Gaunt acceded with a bad grace before the assembled estates to the request of the forceful Commons' spokesman, Sir Peter de la Mare, that his colleagues should consult a committee of twelve peers. Sir Peter continued to act as Commons spokesman throughout parliament, and was to justify amply the Commons' confidence. An eloquent critic of misgovernment in the opening session, he was a knight of the shire for Herefordshire, and steward to young Edmund Mortimer, earl of March, husband of the king's granddaughter, Philippa of Clarence. March was one of the committee of peers consulted by the Commons, which presumably encouraged their attempts to reform. Gaunt's inability to protect his ailing father's government from Commons' interference was probably enhanced by his failure to secure the solid backing of the young generation of magnates and royal kinsmen such as March.

After the consultation of peers and Commons, Sir Peter in the presence of Gaunt and the estates asserted that if the king had been well advised and his resources well spent, the subsidy demand would have been unnecessary. He specifically accused William lord Latimer, Chamberlain of the Household, and the London merchant Richard Lyons of having subverted the wool customs to their profit, made a loan to the Crown at excessive interest, and profitably redeemed royal debts they had bought up cheaply. Sir Peter also bitterly denounced Alice Perrers as a woman of uncertain status in the king's company, a useless consumer of royal grants. Gaunt was unable to deflect the Lords' determination to probe the charges against Latimer and Lyons. Edward III acceded to their clamorous requests that former ministers should testify. The evidence of the former Treasurer Richard lord Scrope tended to confirm the charges. The Commons used their whiphand with confidence. Sir Peter persuaded the Lords to agree in requesting the removal of false councillors, the dismissal of the Chancellor and Treasurer, the expulsion of Alice Perrers from Court, and the appointment of bishops, earls and barons as councillors in whose presence all important business should be terminated, and all wardships granted, and who should redress grievances. Edward graciously allowed the Lords to name the councillors, who were sworn in before parliament. Sir Peter produced further accusations against Latimer and Lyons, and publicly requested the new councillors to fulfil their commission by having the accused arrested and brought to justice. Gaunt and the Lords determined the appeals brought by the Commons against these two and other offenders, bringing in convictions. In July, to mark the end of a memorable and unprecedently long session, Sir Peter and his fellow shire knights held a feast for magnates, knights, and citizens of London and other towns. Gifts of money and wine helped them to provide a fine spread. The king genially sent two tuns of red wine and eight deer. Except for a wool subsidy, he had received no grant. Gaunt was not present at the banquet though his younger brothers were.

It is arguable that the Commons won the political initiative in 1376. Even if, as some might argue, they were acting to an extent as the Lords' mouthpiece, it is surely remarkable and of constitutional import that they *appeared* to have won the initiative. They received the encouragement of men with every reason for loyalty to the Crown, including Wykeham, a typical clerical careerist in royal service, and, it was widely believed, the prince of Wales, who, as he lay dying in his house at Kennington, spurned a bribe disguised as a barrel of sturgeons sent across the river to him by Lyons. The prince's incapacity, at the same time as his father's, helps to explain noble attitudes to the Commons. The grasp of these two men over policy had at last become unsure in the 1370s. The nobles, at a loss, utilised the newly displayed political maturity of the Commons to help resolve the crisis.

But after the session Gaunt – perhaps enduring parental wrath at his maladroit handling of parliament – determinedly set out to reverse its achievements. Councillors were dismissed: Latimer was pardoned in October. Alice Perrers returned to Court. At a great council meeting in October at Westminster, Wykeham, who may have been regarded as a Judas in some Court circles, was found guilty of technical defaults committed when Chancellor and deprived of his temporalities. In November Sir Peter de la Mare was imprisoned in Nottingham Castle. In the parliament which met in January 1377, a docilely inclined Commons elected as Speaker Sir Thomas Hungerford, knight of the shire for Wiltshire, and a leading official of Gaunt[2]. Those condemned in the Good Parliament were pardoned. But soon after the session, the policy of reaction crumbled as it became clear that Edward III's death was imminent: he died on 21 June, possibly of a stroke. Just beforehand he had restored Wykeham's temporalities. He also probably arranged for the export of Alice Perrers's money and jewels to the value of £5,000. Her wealth is an illustration of how royal rewards and influence could be combined with shrewd dabbling in the provincial land markets to make a fortune. The St Albans monk Walsingham, whose hostility was probably sharpened by his abbot's failure to make any headway in recovering property in Watford which she occupied, alleged that she was a thatcher's daughter (possibly from Hanney in Berkshire) and that she had been employed as a domestic servant with the lowly task of fetching water from the conduit. He said spitefully that she lacked beauty of face or figure, but had a persuasive tongue. After Edward's death part of her fortune was seized, possibly as it was being spirited out of the country[3]. Sir Peter de la Mare was released. Gaunt realised that, with the accession of a minor as a king and the renewal of the war, government would have to seek the community's approval.

The new reign: the Peasants' Revolt (1377–81)

Richard of Bordeaux succeeded to the Crown in June 1377, at the age of ten. The rule of minors was usually anticipated with foreboding in the Middle Ages. Willian Langland, author of *Piers the Ploughman*, was probably one of many Englishmen filled with apprehension at Richard's accession. They had taken more or less for granted that

Edward III would be succeeded by the chivalrous hero, the prince of Wales, sometimes prematurely referred to as Edward IV. His death in 1376 had left his next surviving brother, John of Gaunt, duke of Lancaster, as the natural protector of Richard, once the ailing Edward III died. The unpopular manner in which Gaunt exercised influence over royal government in 1376–7, his riches as the greatest lay landowner in the realm after the king, his ambition, ability and impressiveness, made many fear that he would be dominant in Richard's minority, and there were even fears that he had designs on the succession.

Royal government during Richard's minority certainly seems to have turned out to be unpopular. This impression is in part derived from the powerful, vituperative accounts in the chronicles of a contemporary writer, Thomas Walsingham, monk of St Albans Abbey, who was commencing those literary labours which were to make him the most prolific English historian of his generation. Walsingham appears from his writings to have been a man of sweeping and extravagant emotions, who avidly and uncritically recorded rumours and gossip about high politics which circulated in his abbot's household, and with which he and his *confrères* were regaled by pilgrims – magnates, gentry and London merchants – paying their devotions at the fashionable shrine of St Alban, protomartyr of Britain. Walsingham blamed the troubles of the realm in the years 1376–80 chiefly on Gaunt, in his delineation a haughty and intemperate man, contemptuous of the clergy, country knights and London citizens, who openly cohabited with Catherine Swynford, to the shame of his chaste Duchess Constance of Castile. Crown and duchy records, and Walsingham's own attitude to Gaunt from 1381 onwards, show that this picture is in many respects distorted and exaggerated. Nevertheless, during the minority there does seem to have been a widespread and persistent lack of confidence in Richard's close kinsmen and leading ministers. Other chroniclers of the period, such as the Anonimalle Chronicler, and Henry Knighton, canon of Leicester, confirm this impression, which even the officially compiled *Rolls* of the frequent parliaments do not always hide. The latter show that knights of the shire and burgesses, displaying the confidence which emerged in the 1376 parliament, were eager to assert a high degree of parliamentary control over the appointment and dismissal of councillors and principal ministers, and to ensure that they did not abuse their office or misspend subsidies: the Lords proved willing to acquiesce and co-operate in these aims.

There certainly were setbacks for both Crown and property-holders during the minority. Expensive expeditions against the French and their Castilian allies proved indecisive. The attempts of gentry and burgesses to shift more of the heavy burden of war taxation directly on to peasants and artisans culminated in disaster, when efforts to collect the ungraded poll tax granted in the Northampton parliament of 1380 precipitated the Peasants' Revolt of June 1381. After its suppression the remarks of the Speaker of the Commons, Sir Richard Waldegrave, show the tendency of the shire knights and burgesses to blame royal ministers for what had gone wrong. This was characteristic of the sour and hostile mood with which government had to contend, especially from the 1370s onwards.

Despite the costly (but hardly disastrous) military setbacks from 1377 onwards, and the long-remembered terrors of the Peasants' Revolt, it is difficult to understand why property-owners were so dissatisfied with the conscientious and parsimonious councillors of Richard's youth. Perhaps economic difficulties lay at the root of the malaise: more research is necessary to confirm or refute the surmise. Many landowners may have been experiencing falling or static incomes, for a variety of causes: continuing low cereal prices, high costs of labour, difficulty in exacting unpaid villein services and reduced opportunities to make gains in war overseas (see pp. 16–17, 236–7). The profits of native merchants trading abroad may have dropped due to depredations at sea, about which the Londoners complained, and the heavy impressment of ships by the admirals to transport the frequent expeditions. The revolt of Ghent against Louis de Mâle, count of Flanders in 1379 (a revolt which persisted until 1385) disrupted principal English markets: revenue from the wool customs fell, inducing the Crown to lean more heavily on hard-hit producers and exporters for tenths and fifteenths.

Besides economic troubles there were other contemporary developments which caused distress and depression. To the devout and reflective, the papal schism which broke out in 1378 was a monstrous occurrence, a punishment for mankind's sins, and perhaps a portent of more dreadful things to come. In 1379 there was another severe outbreak of plague, especially distressing because the young were particularly vulnerable. The heathen still raged furiously in the eastern Mediterranean and along the Baltic coast, but there was no remedy in sight, as the princes of the west – and now the rival popes – continued to ally against each other, neglecting their prime duty of freeing Jerusalem. Two talented theologians, John Wycliffe, the leading Oxford pundit of the day, and Thomas Brinton, bishop of Rochester, were among the most notable of those preachers and writers who heightened men's and women's awareness of contemporary sinfulness by denouncing the faults of society with reckless and pitiless abandon. Their audiences were prepared to believe the worst about those in high places, because the manner in which courtiers had shamelessly exploited their access to royal patronage in Edward III's last years had been well publicised. During Richard's first parliament, which met in October 1377, and in which the Commons elected Sir Peter de la Mare as their spokesman, members of the late king's Household, anxious to dissociate themselves from Alice Perrers (especially since some of them had been involved in her business affairs) gave scandalous, intimate testimony in her trial about the last days of their master. She had sat at the head of his bed, prompting and relaying his commands from within the curtains, to her own and her friends' advantage.

Ever since the Good Parliament, great men had had to contend with more than the usual London abusiveness. John of Gaunt, dining one day there in the house of his official John of Ypres had to flee the mob with Henry lord Percy, abandoning his half-eaten oysters, and barking his shins in his haste. He took boat and found refuge at the Kennington house of his sister-in-law, Princess Joan of Wales. His youngest brother Thomas of Woodstock had a similarly humiliating experience. Lying abed in his London house, he was disturbed by shouts and blows at the front door: a mob had pursued his servants from Cornhill. The widespread suspicion and hatred of magnates and ministers evinced during the minority was not without beneficial effects on government. It was remarkably free from corruption and factional strife. The Commons were determined to prevent magnates, councillors, officers of the Household, and royal companions in the Chamber from misappropriating revenue or dictating policy. Parliamentary attempts at control and scrutiny, though not always manifestly effective, helped to keep down expenditure. Frequent changes of ministers and councillors, resulting from consultations in great councils and parliaments, prevented the development of monopolies over patronage. No magnate made or improved his fortunes in the way that numbers were to do in the minorities of Henry VI and Edward VI, nor did tensions between magnates fissure and polarise politics as they were to do in these later minorities. The traditions of good fellowship characteristic of relations between magnates at Edward III's Court and on his campaigns calmed disputes in the years immediately after his death. The more than occasional obtuseness of the Commons, especially in haggling over the grant of war subsidies, may have also produced a common front among the lay peers.

This comparative noble homogeneity was to be shattered by the intrigues of Richard and some of his youthful companions in the 1380s. Not until Henry V had drawn the higher nobility together in the mud of siege and battlefield was the Crown able to rely once again on a peerage generally self-confident in their mutual relations, and consequently stable in their loyalty to the Crown. But in the late 1370s and early 1380s, before Richard's brash assertiveness had stirred up bad blood and caused general unease among nobles, their quarrels were muted. There had probably been considerable tension between Gaunt and another leading landowner, Edmund Mortimer, earl of March, in the years 1376–7, complicated by the fact that both of them had arguable claims to be recognised as Richard's heir. But young March chose in 1378 to go to Ireland as royal lieutenant, rather than jockey for power with Lancaster. It was left to their respective descendants, the dukes of York and Somerset, to throw the realm into turmoil by their rivalry for influence, and possibly for the succession, in the early 1450s. John of Gaunt, though determined to play a leading part in

Council and on campaign in Richard's minority, prudently failed to press for a formal regency or protectorship, and publicly bowed to the wishes of his fellow magnates for collective leadership under a king nominally in control of government. He clashed openly with only one of them in the next few years – his former political ally Henry Percy, created earl of Northumberland in 1377. In 1381, when Gaunt was in the North acting as king's lieutenant, disturbing rumours about the Peasants' Revolt and the attacks on Gaunt's interests in the South spread. Northumberland cancelled his invitation to the duke to dine at Alnwick Castle: his lieutenant in the royal castle of Bamburgh refused the duke admission. Gaunt took refuge among the Scots: returning after the rebellion, he formally complained to the king about the earl's conduct. Both lords brought armed retinues to London for the 1381 parliament, but fellow nobles who were mutual friends helped to keep the peace. The force of their moderating opinion probably induced Northumberland to make a qualified apology before the assembled Lords. Aristocratic quarrels were not to be so easily appeased during Richard's later years.

The occasion of the sudden outbreak of the Peasants' Revolt at the end of May 1381 was the recent series of attempts to levy a new kind of tax at a high rate on the general populace. The 'poll tax' granted in the parliament which met in November 1380 differed from the grant of one in 1379 in that the average individual contribution was fixed at the high rate of a shilling a head, with a partially ineffective stipulation grading contributions according to wealth. The tax commissioners encountered widespread resentment and evasion. Since there was a large shortfall in the estimated receipts, commissions of enquiry were appointed in January and March 1381. The March commissioners were to examine collectors' records, estimate the numbers liable for payment and arrest contrariants in fifteen counties. On 1 June 1381 one of them, John Bampton, when holding a session of enquiry at Brentwood (Essex), became involved in angry exchanges with the men of Fobbing. In response to his threats they banded together with the men of neighbouring fishing villages, Corringham and Stanford-le-Hope: Bampton fled. The Chief Justice of the Common Pleas, Sir Robert Bealknap, was promptly dispatched to hear and determine indictments in Essex. His arrival was so alarming that it intensified opposition. According to the Anonimalle Chronicle (the most reliable literary source), the commons 'proposed to kill all the lawyers, jurors and royal servants they could find'. Such were to be the frequent scapegoats of the rebels, particularly in the south-east. The compulsion which, according to Walsingham, the Essex men used to spread their revolt, was to be common too. They also asked for help from nearby Kent, where there was a ready response.

The Kentish revolt broke out at Gravesend, after a knight of the Household had arrested an inhabitant, his escaped villein, spurning the pleas of neighbours, and throwing him into the royal gaol at Rochester

Castle. Bands from the neighbourhood looted at Maidstone, by 7 June captured the castle and (as became usual during the Revolt) released its prisoners from gaol. At Maidstone, the commons made a local man, Walter Tyler (possibly a former soldier in France), their captain. They acquired as a leading counsellor John Ball, an unbeneficed priest with an inveterate grudge against wealthy 'possessioner' clergy. His eloquent, egalitarian sermons gave him the reputation among the commons of a prophet. Ball had been languishing in Archbishop Sudbury's gaol at Maidstone.

The rebels forced men to join them, compelling even pilgrims travelling to and from the shrine of St Thomas at Canterbury to take oaths of adherence. Pilgrims and other wayfarers may have played an important role in disseminating the Revolt. By 10 June the rebels were in control of Canterbury, whose bailiffs were co-operative. The rebels carried out some executions, entered the cathedral, urged the monks to elect a new archbishop, and sacked the latter's palace. This pattern of activity was to be repeated in London. There was no indiscriminate slaughter or general pillage of the rich. St Thomas's shrine, fabulously encrusted with jewels, was left intact. The rebels, in the spirit of the simple Christian rhymed couplets which had become popular, and of Ball's sermons, conceived themselves as agents of God's will, righting wrongs, not despoiling His saints and their fellow Christians. Another reason why the rebel army of Essex and Kent was quite well disciplined, and paralysingly successful, may have been that the French wars had accustomed its leaders and many in its ranks to a system of military organisation. Strategic thinking and confidence in a chain of command are reflected in the Kentish captains' orders to coastal inhabitants to stay put and guard against foreign invasion. Two captains, John Rakestraw and Tyler, commissioned a group to proclaim and compel a military levy in the church of St John in Thanet, imitating a royal commission of array. The display by the Kentish commons at Blackheath of two banners of St George and sixty pennons implies complex subdivision, perhaps on a regional basis. The influence of English military practice among the rebels appears in their use of a device current on expeditions and in garrisons abroad, the 'wache word', consisting in this case of the challenge 'With whom haldes yow?' and the response 'Wyth Kynge Richarde and wyth the trew communes'.

The content of the watchword indicates another reason for the degree of unity and singlemindedness displayed by the south-eastern rebels. Their leaders expressed some well-defined aims. Chroniclers were indeed confused as to what their priorities were (partially, perhaps, reflecting differences of opinion among the rebels), but the watchword embraces a broad if vague measure of agreement. The south-eastern rebels asserted their loyalty to the Crown and their determination to purge the realm of those considered disloyal to king and community: royal servants, lawyers, jurors, aliens. Their political phraseology, with its Christian and feudal undertones, derived from the traditions of baronial protest on behalf of the *communitas*. But their grievances were not slanted, like traditional ones, completely against the agents of royal tyranny. They were determined to destroy the agents and the infrastructure of the tyranny of the rich. Indeed, notions circulated among them of almost entirely abolishing the hierarchy of noble and rich clerics and laymen.

From Canterbury the rebels moved swiftly with their enlarged force to Blackheath, which they probably reached by 12 June. The Essex men assembled east of London at Mile End. The king hastened towards the rebels, from Windsor Castle to the Tower of London, where he stayed with magnates and leading officials. The Mayor of London, William Walworth, and the aldermen saw to the closure of the city gates. Some notable magnates were absent. John of Gaunt was negotiating with the Scots in the Marches, luckily for him, as he was specially hateful to the rebels. The reason for this animus is not clear; perhaps it was an echo of his intense unpopularity at various levels of society in London in 1376–7. His brother Edmund of Langley, earl of Cambridge, was at Plymouth, supervising the assembly of an army to embark for Portugal and promote Gaunt's claim to the Castilian throne. Cambridge, with a force reaching 3,000 in strength, failed to go to Richard's rescue. It may be that the royal councillors, once they had realised the extent of the rebellion, feared that if Cambridge's army was ordered to London its approach would provoke the rebels to further excesses. Froissart says that, when news of the rebellion reached Plymouth, the expedition cast off, worked its way out of the haven and weighed anchor at sea, waiting for a favourable wind there in order to avoid involvement in domestic affairs. Whether deliberately or not, it seems that Lancastrian affairs were promoted at the expense of the king's.

The councillors with Richard in the Tower appear to have been divided about how the rebels should be treated. The king was rowed to Greenwich for a parley, but the menacing aspect of the commons lining the bank led the royal party to retreat hastily up-river without receiving petitions. The rebels swarmed into the suburb of Southwark, at one end of London Bridge, and sacked Archbishop Sudbury's hostel nearby at Lambeth. The circumstances in which the Kentishmen were allowed across the bridge into the city, and the Essex men through the gates (13 June) are obscure. Walworth and his councillors, menaced by growing excitement among apprentices and artisans who sympathised with the rebels, apparently chose appeasement in hopes of avoiding a full-scale urban rising. The jubilant rebels and their London allies proceeded to hunt down and kill those they hated. Prisons were emptied. The dwellings of apprentices at law in the Temple were ransacked and their books, rolls and remembrances torn from cupboards and flung into Fleet Street for burning. The worst destruction of property owned by a 'traitor' was outside the city, at The Savoy, Gaunt's magnificent hostel fronting the Thames and the Strand, which they set ablaze, adding to the destruction by throwing in three barrels of ducal gunpowder. They also congregated at the other end of London below the walls of the Tower, intending to intimidate king and councillors, protected there by a sizeable garrison.

Richard and his supporters desperately tried to find a way to disperse the crowds. He appeared on a turret and had it cried that they should go home, and would be pardoned for their offences. But the commons were not moved by this, nor by the king's written promise to consider their grievances. The next day (14 June) Richard rode out of the Tower to meet the commons outside the city at Mile End, at seven o'clock in the morning. He may have planned to draw them away from the Tower, so that the 'traitors' taking refuge there could escape. At Mile End Richard conceded to Tyler and his companions that they could seize all traitors, to be dealt with by law, that serfdom should be abolished and land rented at four pence per acre, and that no man should be compelled to serve another, but that employment should be voluntary upon agreed terms. The demands illustrate the varied interests, of the poor, serfs, rent-paying tenants, labourers, involved in the rebellion, and the comparative success of its captains in welding together a common programme.

But rebel actions displayed either an ominous disregard for covenants by the leaders or their inability to control exultant followers. The commons invaded the Tower: the garrison, now that they no longer protected the king, apparently had orders not to provoke by resistance. The 'traitors' were dragged out and lynched, not brought unharmed to the king for judgment. The Chancellor, Archbishop Sudbury, the Treasurer, Robert Hales and three others were executed on Tower Hill. These executions may have been to Richard's immediate political advantage – next day there was certainly a reaction in the city in his favour. They spared him the embarrassment of being forced to condemn his own ministers, and they demonstrated the rebels' bad faith. The beheading of an archbishop of Canterbury, however personally unpopular, may have provoked mixed reactions at a popular as well as at elite levels of society.

After the Mile End conference, Richard and his retinue entered the city and took refuge with his mother, Princess Joan, in the King's Wardrobe near Blackfriars. Proclamation was made of a further meeting between king and commons, to be held next day (15 June) in Smithfield – much nearer the city than Mile End, dominated by its north-western walls and easily accessible from Newgate, Aldersgate and Cripplegate. Tyler, Ball and other captains may have pressed for another conference in order to maintain the cohesion of the commons and the authority of their leadership. Rebels were streaming homewards, trusting in the charters confirming the Mile End terms which Chancery clerks were busily engrossing. Others may have inclined to disperse with city cronies, carousing, stealing or finding employment.

Tyler's conduct at Smithfield, which precipitated the crisis of the

Revolt, and was the subject of shocked comment by chroniclers, may have been intended to inspire his followers and reaffirm his leadership. He treated the king with studied disrespect, not behaving as a base person and petitioner ought, but as the king's kinsman and equal. Advancing into the royal presence on horseback, and holding a naked weapon, after dismounting Tyler did not fall to his knees but grasped Richard's hand and addressed him as 'brother'. Tyler's demands went much further than those agreed at Mile End, reflecting the revolutionary rather than the reforming strands in the commons' agitation. Besides abolition of serfdom and other legal modifications, he requested drastic ecclesiastical changes, on terms perhaps framed by Ball. The lands and goods of the clergy were to be divided among laymen, leaving clerics 'sufficient sustenance'. There was to be only one bishop. Richard made a conciliatory reply. Stifled by the June heat, Tyler called for a jug of water and 'rinsed out his mouth in a very rude and villainous manner before the King'. In the increasing heat of the day some of the royal retinue may have been growing impatient and irritable. Many, like the mayor, may have been sweltering in armour under their civilian robes. Such conditions may have driven some royal companions to react to Tyler's behaviour with unprecedented recklessness. A Kentish valet loudly accused him of being a notorious local thief. Tyler tried to kill him. Stung by such *lèse-majesté*, Walworth attempted Tyler's arrest. While resisting, Tyler was mortally wounded by the mayor and a royal valet. The commons, seeing him fall, bent their bows and started to shoot. Richard seized the initiative, riding out towards the menacing ranks. Responding to discipline, they followed him and were arrayed by him further away from the city, in the more salubrious standing corn of St John's Fields. According to the Anonimalle Chronicle, at the moment of crisis Richard was deserted by almost all the knights and esquires of the Household. If Walworth took a firm line at Smithfield in the knowledge that a stroke against the rebels was planned, he precipitately bungled affairs. Nevertheless, it was mainly the Londoners who saved the king. Walworth did not lose his nerve, but sent to have the men of the twenty-four wards arrayed by their aldermen. They promptly came to the king's aid, supported by gentlemen who had armed their servants in their hostels, notably the military veteran Sir Robert Knolles. The commons, their morale shattered by the bewildering sequence of events, were easily enveloped in the open fields 'like sheep within a pen'. They were allowed to disperse homewards.

As news of the rebel successes in Kent and London had spread, there were disturbances elsewhere, mainly, the patchy narrative sources (perhaps distortingly) suggest, sporadic and less co-ordinated. These were mostly confined to southern, Midland and eastern parts of the realm. Within the affected regions (even in Essex and Kent) it is unlikely that the majority of inhabitants were involved in agitation outside their villages. Even in Hertfordshire, where there was a well-organised rising against St Albans Abbey, besides risings against monastic houses near its borders (Dunstable Priory and Waltham Abbey), a number of townships were seemingly unaffected. There appear to have been only tenuous ideological and organisational connections between most of the major risings. The main common factor was the determination of aggrieved individuals and communities, when astounding rumours of doings in London arrived, to seize the opportunity to settle scores and intimidate opponents. On many manors in the Midlands and south-east where villeinage was enforced, serfs tried to extort manumission, banding together to withdraw their services, as had become common in recent decades. Inhabitants of some towns rose to restrict the authority of an unpopular lord or monopolistic patriciate. Sometimes such movements coagulated into a rising of more than local significance. But the sophistication of the Essex–Kent attempts to unite a variety of grievances into one programme was apparently not matched elsewhere.

In the soke of Peterborough, neighbours and tenants of the abbot proposed to kill him. In Cambridgeshire men took to arms on account of the poll tax. On 15 June the bailiffs and commonalty of Cambridge rode south to Shingay to concert plans with the country rebels. The townsmen elected Jakes of Grantchester as their captain and governor and, with the aid of the countryfolk, compelled the masters and scholars of the university to renounce their royal privileges and acknowledge the townsmen's full control of urban affairs. The university had to issue a general acquittance for all current suits against burgesses, and to surrender corporate charters and letters patent as material for a bonfire in the market-place.

At Liston in Suffolk, not far from the Essex border, an armed company congregated on 12 June, captained by a cleric, John Wrawe from Sudbury, nearby. For a week they intimidated individuals and communities in Suffolk, exacting fines in the manner that English 'free companies' were accustomed to do in France. At Lakenheath, in the north of the county, this band, some of whom were well-to-do, killed John Cavendish, Chief Justice of the King's Bench (14 June). Then they moved into the prosperous, clothworking town of Bury, championing the cause of the townsmen, who wished to extort a charter of self-government from the abbot and convent of St Edmunds. With characteristic brutality Wrawe's company slew the prior, John Cambridge and another monk, John Lakenheath, keeper of the abbot's barony. On 23 June William Ufford, earl of Suffolk, who had fled from the shire on the outbreak of revolt, arrived at Bury to suppress the rebellion. West Norfolk was plagued by several companies, but in the east rebels acted under the notable leadership of Geoffrey Litster, a dyer of Felmingham. Litster's band encamped on Mousehold Heath outside Norwich, where they lynched a defiant Norfolk knight, Robert Salle, who despite his servile origins refused to join them. They captured Norwich on 17 June. Next day Yarmouth fell to an allied company led by a local knight, Roger Bacon of Baconsthorpe.

A leading part in the suppression of bands in the east Midlands and East Anglia was taken by a cleric, Henry Despenser, bishop of Norwich. This daring young nobleman on his own initiative led a small company of knights which rescued the monks of Peterborough, occupied Cambridge (19 June), Norwich (24 June), slaughtered Litster's band at North Walsham (26 June), and hunted down and executed other Norfolk rebels.

These provincial risings seem to have differed markedly in aims and character from the Essex–Kent rising. The south-eastern rebels aimed to reform government and radically change the social order by negotiation with the Crown. This explains their comparative restraint in London. They saw themselves as petitioners and reformers, engaged in a portentous dialogue with the king. Richard and most lords, clerics and merchants seem to have gone around London on their avocations without molestation. The rebels made no concerted attempt to take over the machinery, the personnel and offices of government – their invasions of the Tower and Westminster were mainly in pursuit of fugitives. They thought they could destroy the tyranny of the literate by killing the experts and burning their parchments, and by procuring their own charismatic charters from the king.

In London's social and economic hinterlands, the rebellion was seen not as a prelude to a refashioning of society, but as an opportunity to settle claims and scores, and to make a profit. The civic dignitaries of Cambridge, the wealthy townsmen of Bury and St Albans are unlikely to have sympathised fully with the extremer egalitarian sentiments voiced by some rebels in London. This lack of ideological unity between the rebel army and the provincial bands, together with the mainly negative evidence for organisational contact, goes far to invalidate the view of some chroniclers that the revolt sprang from a widespread conspiracy. One group whose conduct was influenced by events in London was the Hertfordshire band who revolted against St Albans Abbey, whose deeds are especially well documented by a scandalised Thomal Walsingham. Their leadership was drawn from the urban elite of St Albans: their captain, William Grindecobbe had been educated in the abbey. They aimed to procure the communal liberties persistently denied them by abbot and convent. A delegation went to London and conferred in the church of St Mary Arches. There was a division of opinion as to how their liberties might best be secured. Some thought that 'they should receive power from Walter Tyler . . . for they believed that there would in future be no more important man than Tyler within the kingdom and that the laws of the land would be henceforth invalid – because most of the lawyers had already been destroyed and they expected the remainder to perish soon'. Others more cautiously wished to procure a Privy Seal letter from the king ordering the abbot to restore their alleged liberties. In the event both policies were followed. Grindecobbe 'obtained the said letters after he had knelt to the king six times in presence of the mob'. In contrast to Tyler at Smithfield, he behaved as a subject ought. But he and his fellows also took oaths of obedience to Tyler, and received a bloodthirsty promise of his military assistance. Returning to St Albans, they assembled the abbey's villeins from its Hertfordshire manors, copying the military methods they had observed among the rebels in London. A leading townsman of St Albans, Richard Wallingford, had a banner displayed before him with the arms of St George, as if he were a knight. He had it set up in the square outside the abbey: the villeins were made to wait congregated around it whilst the townsmen negotiated with the abbot, Thomas de la Mare. He had intrepidly stayed at his post, though well informed about the gravity of developments in London. He matched the moderation of the St Albans rebels with a politic willingness to compromise for the time being[4].

The Smithfield confrontation broke the rebellion in London, though it was to be several weeks before the provincial rebels were fully dispersed. Indeed, there were yet to be some fresh, though isolated disturbances, including risings in Yorkshire against unpopular urban regimes at York, Scarborough and Beverley. Meanwhile, in London the king and his councillors concerted measures to pursue the rebels. By 23 June a royal army had assembled on Blackheath. Defiant Kentishmen were intimidated. Some of the Essex men continued to show spirit. At Waltham Abbey their delegates vainly petitioned an angry Richard for confirmation of their charters. The king's uncle Thomas of Woodstock, earl of Buckingham, and the experienced soldier Sir Thomas Percy attacked rebel bands on 28 June near Billericay, defeating them and pursuing the remnant to the death. On 2 July the royal revocation of the charters conceded at Mile End was proclaimed at Chelmsford. On 12 July Richard arrived at St Albans, whose townsmen had been cowed by the threat that the royal army, rampaging in Essex, would be turned against them. In the royal presence Robert Tresilian, Chief Justice of the King's Bench, condemned to death fifteen local ringleaders, including Grindecobbe. Hundreds of the 1381 rebels are known to have been killed in the field or executed, including many of the ringleaders: Tyler, Litster, Grindecobbe, Wrawe, Ball and Jack Straw. But the great majority escaped with their lives, and were to be covered by the general pardon confirmed (as was the revocation of liberties) in the parliament which met in November 1381.

The demands which, according to chroniclers, the Kent and Essex rebels had put to Richard, reflect major social and political tensions of the period (see pp. 16–17). There were tenurial conflicts between landlord and peasant. There were wage disputes between master and labourer. The renewal of war with France had led to high taxation and, in southern coastal regions, insecurity. The highly taxed, the insecure, the lowly paid, the poor resented the wealth of ecclesiastical corporations and the exactions of rich clerical incumbents: their indignation was buttressed by the righteous denunciations of moralists. In London alien commercial rivals and flourishing overseas traders, especially Flemings and Italians, were popularly hated.

There were factors in the social structure of south-east England which probably helped to fuse these elements into a formidable revolt. In some areas abundant agrarian, pastoral and fishing resources, their productivity increased by the voracious demands of London markets, had helped to create communities of well-to-do free peasants and craftsmen. Landlords who tried to insist on servile obligations and low wage levels were likely to encounter resentment and defiance. The proximity of London and the comparative ease of communications with it made sections of the populace more aware of 'national affairs' than remote communities. Chroniclers of the revolt recognised in the demands made by south-eastern rebels a reflection – albeit one which appeared to them hideously distorted – of their own conceptual framework, the 'community of the realm'. Walsingham conveys convincingly the rebels' fleeting confidence that they could reform and revitalise a whole society: 'At that time they gloried in such a name and believed no name was more honourable than the name of 'community'; according to their foolish minds there would be no lords thereafter but only king and commons.'

Walsingham, who perhaps took too seriously snatches of wild talk among rebels, was one of the commentators emphasising their commitment to what we would call 'class warfare'. The conservative mould clinging to their bursting aspirations is illustrated by another writer's account of crowd reactions to the assault on Tyler in Smithfield: 'Now the company of rebels cried, "What is the king doing with our spokesman?" Others said, "He is making him a knight." And all shouted, "Let us cross to St John's Field and let our new knight come to us." ' Here there is elation that their captain has supposedly received the 'class' privilege of knighthood, requiring for its maintenance a substantial land grant (with concomitant services of labourers), and possessing the right to wear more luxurious apparel, to sit among more distinguished guests in hall, receive higher wages for services in peace and war, and to be eligible for appointment among the first-named on county commissions and for election as knight of the shire.

The rebels lacked reverence for lords and ladies whom they encountered, but showed little hostility except to those who opposed them or who were 'traitors'. Their hatred was vented on officials – the men who made a business of literacy and expertise with quill and parchment, the *legisperiti* (legal experts), who through their cursed knowledge and their portmanteaux of documents baggaged on packhorses, regulated the work, the wages, the misdemeanours of the 'true commons'. Since in recent decades landowners and employers had been stimulated by economic and other crises to intensify exploitation of their resources (see p. 16), the activities of their agents – stewards, justices, tax collectors – had helped to create a fragile sense of unity among the exploited. Preaching and political scandals probably added to the conviction of commons that they were the truly faithful Christians and lieges. It was the force of the resulting ideological convictions that enabled base men to strike down Simon Sudbury, successor of St Thomas of Canterbury, primate of all England, Chancellor of the realm. With Jacobinical purity of soul they struck off the consecrated head, replying to his spiritual warnings, according to Walsingham 'with the horrible shout that they feared neither an interdict nor the Pope'. Within such a context it is credible that the executioner would subsequently break down: he 'soon experienced divine vengeance and was driven mad and struck blind'.

Why were the reactions of the rulers in society to the outbreak of revolt generally so timorous? At Huntingdon the 'good men' of the town and neighbourhood demonstrated the effectiveness of resolute defence. They defended the bridge over the Ouse: the commons retreated after losing only two or three men. Elsewhere the rulers may have been stunned by the ideological as well as physical threat: rumour, as reflected in chronicle accounts, may have magnified both. Since alleged revolutionaries were said to control London and speak with royal approval, old certainties hung in the balance: men must act prudently. John of Gaunt did not stir from exile in Scotland until he was sure that the king no longer favoured the commons. Lesser men also bowed to the times: they were familiar with the Wheel of Fortune, and probably felt confident that this malign twist of it would soon be righted. Walter at Lee and William Hoo, knights connected with St Albans Abbey, saw their immediate task as one of ensuring a composition between the abbot and rebels. Other landowners and burgesses may not have recognised in the revolt a dire challenge to their status, but an opportunity to further their local interests. The Norfolk knight Roger Bacon (subsequently pardoned) saw it as a chance to humiliate the men of Yarmouth. One militarily distinguished royal retainer, Sir William Windsor, took advantage of the confusion to seize land in Watford which he claimed from the abbot of St Albans.

The changing situation in London was crucial to the fortunes of provincial revolt. By appearing to countenance rebel actions in London, Richard boosted local disturbances. But as long as he did not flee, remaining to appease the commons, they refrained from indiscriminate plunder and from the destruction of royal and civic government. Lords and burgesses presided in their hostels for the price of a few barrels of wine and a gracious demeanour. Chancery, Exchequer and Household continued to function with little dislocation. Royal, noble and burgess appeasement of the rebels wrongly helped to convince them that they were accepted as the 'true commons': the governors of society were enabled to plot their overthrow.

The young king (1381–89)

After 1381 quarrels between magnates were not to be so successfully scotched as the Gaunt–Percy dispute had been, due principally to Richard II's attitude. In 1381 he had acted as formal mediator: it is not clear whether his sympathies lay with the earl of Northumberland, though in the next few years he was to emerge as chief opponent of his uncle's influence. Little is known about Richard's upbringing and education. He seems to have been more obsessively articulate in his opinions about the government of the realm than was usual among later medieval English kings. He possessed a well-stocked library of pious and romantic works in Latin and French, and was certainly capable of reading French: in 1395 he took the finely bound volume of love poems which the ageing Froissart presented to him into his bedchamber at Eltham, and read from them aloud in the poet's presence. The king's interest in literature is attested in John Gower's original preface to his romance in verse, *Confessio Amantis*. Gower tells how when sailing on the Thames in 1390 he met and was invited into the king's barge. Richard there charged him to write something new.

Richard's perhaps gloomy interest in English history is reflected in his preoccupation with Edward II and in the melancholy discourse on the fall of kings (the genesis of Shakespeare's fine soliloquy) which Adam Usk heard him utter when a prisoner in the Tower in 1399. In his youth Richard may have been continuously irked by parliamentary attacks on the Crown's policies and servants, and attempts to regulate the conduct of affairs, promoted by bumptious country knights of the shire and despised burgesses. He may have resented the failure of his uncles and other near kinsmen among the magnates to oppose these developments. He was educated by knights and clerics of his parents' households. Among his tutors were the chivalrous Poitevin noble Guichard Dangle, earl of Huntingdon (d.1380), Sir Simon Burley, who carried the tired boy on his shoulders to the coronation banquet, and another veteran of Edward prince of Wales's campaigns, Sir Richard Adderbury.

Some of the former princely and royal servants whose services in the Household were retained after Richard's accession may have resented parliamentary parsimony which prevented the boy from rewarding them handsomely, or maintaining a Household as magnificent and lavish as their previous masters' had been. Richard in 1383 granted Adderbury two manors as compensation for having lent money to the king during his youth at a time of great necessity, a grant which may reflect royal penury at some stage of the minority. The king's mother Princess Joan (whom he greatly revered) and some members of the Household may have instilled into Richard the determination to assert the kind of mastery, especially in the control of patronage, which his grandfather had exercised. He may have been bred upon tales of the princely generosity, extravagance and haughtiness of his father (whom he resembled physically) – certainly he was to revel in these politically ambiguous paternal traits. The shocks he endured in the Peasants' Revolt may have made him contemptuous about the behaviour of some eminent men, self-reliant, and convinced that God intended him to assert his regality triumphantly by his own efforts.

In 1389, when Richard was aged twenty-two, his minority was formally declared at an end. But this declaration arose from special political circumstances. Kings were expected to exercise control when younger than male heirs to feudal inheritances, who came of age at twenty-one. In 1374 a French ordinance laid down that heirs to the Crown should reach their majority in their fourteenth year. In 1380 the Commons successfully petitioned that Richard should have no more ministers and councillors appointed in parliament. Richard was allowed to assert himself when only a boy – this is worth bearing in mind when his behaviour in the 1380s is considered. In the early 1380s a substantial income was provided to staff the Chamber of his Household, whose clerks and knights he came to trust and reward above most. He dispatched personal orders – notably in the distribution of royal patronage – under his Signet seal, kept by his Secretary. In 1382 he gave orders for the custody of Roger Mortimer's estates, in royal wardship as a result of his father the earl of March's death in 1381, to be granted to his own Household servants. According to Walsingham, the Chancellor Richard lord Scrope hesitated to authorise his Chancery clerks to engross and seal letters patent warranting the grants. Members of the Household insinuated to Richard that Scrope was defying royal authority. The boy became enraged and dismissed him from office (July 1382), an action which Walsingham considered to be unconstitutional, as Scrope had received office with parliamentary authority.

The reason the chronicler gives for condemning the royal initiative shows how some expedients of the minority threatened to be a continuing challenge to royal freedom. His version of Scrope's dismissal may indeed have been derived from Scrope, for the latter probably visited St Albans Abbey sometime in 1382, the year in which he was received as a lay brother of the confraternity of St Alban. It was several months before another Chancellor was appointed: the Great Seal was put into commission. Richard's determination to master his servants is apparent in an angry letter he addressed to the commissioners from Devizes Castle in 1382, castigating them for making grants without his approval. Further probable marks of the king's assertiveness are the appointments as Chancellor of his Secretary, Robert Braybrooke and, in 1383, of Sir Michael de la Pole, a retainer of Gaunt and former servant of Richard's father, who had been given Household responsibilities by the 1381 parliament. Richard became attached to Pole, who proved amenable to his use of the Signet.

Richard's handling of the Scrope affair in 1382 was perhaps the first step in his alienation of many responsible members of the political community: magnates, royal officials, influential property-holders, some of whom had been his friends or had served him well in his youth, such as his youngest uncle, Thomas of Woodstock, earl of Buckingham, Thomas Arundel, bishop of Ely, for whom he publicly expressed affection, William Courtenay, archbishop of Canterbury, whose family had close Household links, and Robert Braybrooke. It was not so much Richard's determination to control his own patronage that they resented, rather his inclination to use it inordinately to reward and elevate his coterie of friends with titles, offices, profits and lands.

Another development which stimulated noble resentments against Richard in the early 1380s was the manner in which he and some of his friends – notably his young companions, Robert de Vere, earl of Oxford, and Thomas Mowbray, earl of Nottingham – opposed John of Gaunt, duke of Lancaster. Unfortunately we lack contemporary informants who tell us in convincing detail the reasons for the growth of enmities in Court and Council during this period, particularly why Richard hated John of Gaunt as much as chroniclers suggest. Gaunt's influence over royal policy received a humiliating check in 1383, when the Commons refused to grant a subsidy for a scheme to invade Castile, which he had already touted without gaining much support for it in the two previous parliaments. Instead they favoured what they considered to be a cheaper and more useful expedition to uphold the control of Ghent over Flanders, and to prevent French influence from dominating English merchants' principal market for wool. The invasion of Flanders was proposed in the novel form of a crusade against schismatics (as was Gaunt's), its advocate being Henry Despenser, bishop of Norwich, a courtly, persuasive prelate whose firmness had rallied the gentry of East Anglia against the rebels in 1381. Prominently encouraging Commons' support of the Flemish crusade were two well-reputed soldiers, Sir Philip and Sir Peter Courtenay. They may have done so at the instigation of their brother William, the archbishop of Canterbury (an old opponent of Gaunt). But since they were Household knights of the king, well liked by him, their lobbying may have been motivated too by his determination to lessen Gaunt's influence. However, Bishop Despenser's farcical failure in Flanders underlined the realm's dependence on Lancaster. He was appointed in August 1383 to supersede the bishop as lieutenant in France, for he was the magnate best able to muster promptly a sufficient military retinue to guard against a French attack on the March of Calais, and best equipped with the prestige and expertise necessary to salvage a truce from defeat and surrender.

The new ascendancy over the conduct of foreign affairs which the duke gained in 1383 may be one reason for the hostility which the evidence indicates that Richard displayed towards him in 1384–5. The deference men paid to the duke may have infuriated his nephew: his other uncles, Cambridge and Buckingham, seem habitually to have followed Gaunt's lead, despite differences of opinion and conflicts of interest. In the autumn of 1384 they withdrew with the duke from a meeting of the Council, after he had ominously threatened not to co-operate, if the royal undertaking in the recent parliament to invade France was not adhered to. Royal ministers were worried by his attitude, and the king and his young friends were enraged by what they regarded as treasonable presumption.

It is hard for us to understand the reasons why men reacted to Lancaster in the ways that they did at various stages of his career, for, despite the wealth of information about it, his personality does not stand out clearly and his motives are often obscure. By contrast, his brother Thomas of Woodstock and Richard himself, despite contrasting interpretations of historians, do appear (perhaps deceptively) as recognisable human types. It is not clear why Lancaster inspired extravagant reactions. During the Salisbury parliament (April 1384) he alone dared to break the horrified silence among the peers, when Richard, crimson with rage, publicly insulted Richard earl of Arundel, who had abrasively criticised the recent conduct of the affairs of the realm. When the Commons complained about oppressions commited in the shires by the livery-holders of magnates, it was Lancaster who replied on behalf of his fellow peers, decisively opposing the Commons' request for a statutory curb on the freedom of lords to distribute their liveries (see p. 148). The duke's unsympathetic attitude cannot have won him friends among the lesser property-holders, any more than the firm control he was exercising over Anglo-Scottish relations can have pleased the Percies. Considering the potential anti-Lancastrian feeling in the air, it is a measure of the ineptitude of Richard and his juvenile friends that they managed in this and the following year to increase general sympathies for the duke.

During the Salisbury parliament, according to one usually reliable chronicler, Richard shocked lords by ordering his uncle to be summarily executed on a specious charge of treason, a measure recalling uncomfortably some of the arbitrary judgments against nobles of the early fourteenth century. Later that year, after the duke's withdrawal from Council, courtiers plotted his assassination. Peers do not seem to have rallied to support the king when Lancaster took the ominous measure of riding to visit his nephew at Sheen accompanied to the verge of Court by an armed retinue. A public reconciliation between Richard and Lancaster did not entirely alleviate the tension. Richard listened politely to his uncle's strictures on his servants and their conduct of policy, but did not dismiss any of them. At a great council Archbishop Courtenay spelled out to the king the ominous and intolerable implications for magnates of the manner in which the duke had been treated. Richard lost his temper and threatened the archbishop: the meeting broke up in some disorder. Later that day the king encountered the archbishop on the Thames, when he was coming to see him under a royal safe-conduct procured by Buckingham. Richard actually drew his sword in Courtenay's presence. Hard as it is to believe, it seems that the king had to be physically restrained by Buckingham and the Household knight Thomas Trivet from surpassing the most notorious royal crime in English history, the murder of St Thomas, by personally cutting down an archbishop of Canterbury. The archbishop fled from the king's presence. It is perhaps symptomatic of Courtenay's moderation that he did not follow precedent and court martyrdom by going to Canterbury and denouncing the tyrant, but sought obscurity in the West Country, under the protection of his nephew the earl of Devon.

The parliament which met in September 1385 was a turning-point in the reign, for as a consequence of developments in it Richard added the hostility of property-holders at large to the distrust he had provoked in the circle of his kinsmen and peers. The coalescence of these two strands of opposition facilitated the restraints placed on his prerogative in the period 1386–9. The 1385 parliament took place just after the king had led his first campaign, an impressive and expensive invasion of the eastern lowlands of Scotland. The need for another royal campaign, in France, especially after the recent French invasion attempts from Scotland and Flanders, was widely anticipated. Faced after several relatively quiescent years with pressing royal demands for a high rate of war subsidies, the Commons reverted to precedents of the early years of Richard's reign, laying down conditions of expenditure and procuring the appointment of a commission to survey and control royal finances. The king and his Chancellor, Michael de la Pole, earl of Suffolk, after the dissolution of parliament ignored or flouted these restraints. The subsidy was spent, partly on paying for Lancaster's dispatch with an expedition to claim the Crown of Castile (July 1386), partly on naval and other measures against the growing threat of invasion from Flanders and Brittany.

By late summer it was evident that the summons of another parliament was necessary to help pay for the expensive and inconveniencing defence measures in hand (see p. 238). At the start of the session in September, Suffolk assured parliament that, contrary to scandalous rumour, the king intended to lead an expedition across the Channel, especially now that he was more his own master than hitherto. The estates were unimpressed. The Commons, with the approval of peers, vehemently petitioned for Suffolk's dismissal from the Chancery, so that they could impeach him. The king's uncle, Thomas of Woodstock, and the earl of Arundel's brother, the bishop of Ely, were delegated by parliament to speak to the king at Eltham. According to the circumstantial account of their conference by Henry Knighton, canon of Leicester, Richard was so cowed by the brutal threats of deposition made to him that he agreed to Suffolk's dismissal. The earl was impeached, found guilty by his peers of not exceptionally heinous offences, and punished by imprisonment. The king was forced by further public and private threats to assent to the appointment of a commission empowered to investigate royal income and expenditure, and to supervise and reform Household administration. The commissioners' tenure was to be for a year. Gloucester and the Arundel brothers were among those appointed: the bishop received the Chancery.

Richard, badly shaken, attempted in 1387 to undermine his critics' achievements, by rallying loyalties in the localities, by evading the commission's scrutiny of his Household, and demonstrating the illegality of proceedings in the 1386 parliament. The Justices of the King's Bench and Common Pleas who answered his summons in August 1387 endorsed the principle that certain specific sorts of attempts to coerce and control the royal will, such as those made in parliaments, were either treasonable in intent or acts of treason. Whatever the theoretical merits of Richard's case, his threatening methods of promoting it, especially by definitive, unilateral extensions of the law of treason, proved blunders. The judgments leaked out, and tended to unite against him and his partisans those who had been active in opposition and criticism. Richard seems to have been again taken aback with horror and surprise by his subjects' resort to violence. In November 1387 Thomas of Woodstock, duke of Gloucester, Arundel and Thomas Beauchamp, earl of Warwick (a middle-aged, moderate noble), assembled with an armed force at Hornsey, just north of London. They received safe-conducts to appear before the king in Westminster Hall, where they launched an appeal of treason against five prominent courtiers and councillors (Alexander Neville, archbishop of York, Robert de Vere, duke of Ireland, Suffolk, Sir Robert Tresilian, Chief Justice of the King's Bench and Sir Nicholas Bramber, citizen of London). Since his subjects appeared disinclined to oppose the 'lords appellant', the king had to promise them that a parliament would be summoned in which their appeal would be considered.

It seems that Richard hoped to gain a few months in which he could raise forces against the appellants, perhaps among the Londoners (who had rallied to him in 1381), more certainly through the agency of the duke of Ireland. He was commissioned to raise retinues in the western royal appanages, especially in the earldom of Chester, of which he was justiciar. However, the appellants remained prudently on their guard, managing to attract more military support through the adherence to the appeal of two young, influential and warlike nobles. These were the king's former companion Thomas Mowbray, earl of Nottingham and earl marshal, and Henry of Bolingbroke, earl of Derby, the absent John of Gaunt's son and heir. Derby was custodian of the Lancastrian inheritance, far greater than that of any other magnate, including the county palatine of Lancaster and the earldoms of Leicester and Lincoln. Though Gaunt was not involved, his son's adherence gave the rising the ominous dimension of Lancastrian support, which, as Richard doubtless knew, had so menaced Edward II, whom he venerated. The appellants were influential landowners, some in regions not far removed from London. Arundel was the principal landowner in Sussex, Gloucester commanded the loyalties owed to his wife's family (the Bohuns) in Essex, Warwick was the most powerful subject in Warwickshire and Worcestershire, and Nottingham had influence in Lincolnshire. Like several other appellants he may have commanded some East Anglian services, for he was heir apparent to Margaret countess of Norfolk.

The appellants speedily intercepted Ireland's Welsh and Cheshire army advancing towards London, in Oxfordshire, and routed it at the battle of Radcot Bridge (December 1387). Soon afterwards the victors were admitted to London and to Richard's refuge, the Tower. Cowed by clamorous threats of deposition (arousing a fear which by now must have been familiar to Richard), he meekly acquiesced in the appellants' domination of government, their dismissals and appointments, and their prosecution of the appeal in the parliament which met in February 1388. Those appealed were condemned as traitors by their peers: only two of the four laymen among them condemned to death, Tresilian and Bramber, were available for execution. An intensely partisan Commons impeached four members of the Household. They were found guilty of treason and, despite Richard's brave efforts to save their lives, were executed too. These judicial murders were the first judgments of blood in what were essentially political disputes for over fifty years. Noble sympathies with Richard had been alienated in the 1380s by his threats to bring in such judgments, but it was his opponents who first resorted to the expedient, and reaped the resentment of their fellow peers. The two younger and more recent appellants, Nottingham and Derby, seem to have cooled in their enthusiasm for extreme measures, once the royal favourites had been scotched. They do not seem to have shared the personal animus against Richard and his courtiers that Gloucester and Arundel displayed, and they may not have relished the determination of these older men to profit most from their influence over government.

The decline of noble support for their measures undermined one of the bases of the appellants' influence. Medieval government and challenges to it ultimately depended for success on the goodwill of lords, secular and ecclesiastic. The appellants rebelled successfully because by and large they were treated by their fellow peers with sympathetic neutrality. Why then did Gloucester and Arundel insist during the first 1388 parliament on flying in the face of this mainly moderate body of opinion – by, for instance, spurning the king's entreaties and the queen's tears for the life of his former tutor, Sir Simon Burley? Gloucester and Arundel may have been sufficiently politic to realise that support for them among their fellows would in any case ebb soon after the fulness of their success had undermined their opponents. Knowing Richard well enough not to rely on his future goodwill, they may have calculated that they must utterly destroy his recent supporters, and by such acts of extremity bind themselves together with a body of associates in parliament, who would have a common interest in defending them and their judgments. Perhaps there is a measure of political justification for their violent proceedings in Richard's slowness to overturn the acts of their parliament, and the widespread fear and hostility he provoked by eventually doing so.

The appellants' supporters among the lesser property-owners soon showed that they considered continued appellant influence over royal government irksome rather than necessary. The gentry of the Midlands, East Anglia and the south-east, many of whom probably provided the mainstay of engaged support, proved fickle, despite the appellants' territorial influence. In the parliament which met at Cambridge in September 1388 the Commons showed their main source of discontent to be no longer the Crown, but the private 'governments' of magnates and the local abuses of power they produced (see p. 148). The Commons petitioned for a statute which would entirely prevent the grant of liveries. The peers strenuously opposed this attempt to restrict their prerogative. Gloucester showed none of his wonted ability to influence the Commons: it was Richard who appeared in the uncharacteristic (but not unprecedented) role of their sympathiser. Moreover, the appellants may have attracted the same sort of parliamentary unpopularity as had previous Ricardian councillors. They had attempted to keep down the expenses of the Household; they had not acted outrageously by monopolising royal patronage; nor had they been vindictive in the treatment of the families of convicted noble traitors. But they had little to show for the large subsidy granted in the previous parliament, which had probably been swallowed up by wage bills for rebellion and Arundel's futile French expedition.

The growing political isolation of Gloucester, Arundel and Warwick had its sequel on 3 May 1389: Richard then declared to his councillors that he was of an age to rule his affairs. He dismissed the three original appellants from the Council, and the ministers they had appointed from their offices. The proclamation announcing Richard's majority stressed his intention to govern with good counsel and to punish those who oppressed neighbours by colour of liveries. He promised not to overturn the statutes of the first 1388 parliament. Richard had demonstrated his good faith by appointing 'neutral' ministers, such as the respected Wykeham as Chancellor.

The rule and deposition of Richard II (1389–99)

The early years of this period were the most tranquil, politically, in the later fourteenth century. But there were certainly tensions, especially over the terms on which peace might be negotiated with the French Crown (see pp. 240 ff). However, throughout the period truces with France and Scotland were regularly renewed and not drastically infringed. Parliaments, no longer burdened by the financial needs of warfare, showed less inclination to meddle with the royal will. The Court attained a magnificence, inspiring a desire to serve, not seen since the 1360s. Lords turned their energies, finances and retainers towards making a brave show at tournaments and on chivalrous journeys abroad. Some planned crusades, becoming more interested in Mediterranean or Baltic politics than English affairs.

But there was one continuing source of political instability, which occasionally erupted and eventually swept all into turmoil. This was Richard himself. He probably believed – not altogether unreasonably, since as a youth he had faced the threat of losing his Crown in 1381, 1386 and 1387 – that many lieges, especially in the south-east and Midlands, were incorrigibly rebellious at heart, and that the parliamentary measures imposed with their approval in 1386 and 1388 threatened the integral powers of divinely ordained kingship. He probably feared Gloucester and Arundel as the still flourishing architects of what he regarded as treason. In the 1390s the tensions inherent in his view of the situation may have grown less bearable. Personal griefs added to his bitterness. He found it less easy to conceal his true feelings. In 1392 his dear friend Robert de Vere, who had vanished abroad after the débâcle at Radcot Bridge in 1387, died in exile. In 1395 he had the corpse brought back for a sumptuous burial among Robert's ancestors at Earls Colne Priory and displayed great emotion at the sight of it. In 1394 he had become distraught at the funeral in Westminster Abbey of his beloved queen, Anne of Bohemia. Giving vent for a change to the temper displayed in his youth, he created a political crisis by hitting the earl of Arundel so hard that he drew blood, because the earl had arrived late for the service. Arundel went to the Tower and had to produce sureties for future good behaviour. There may have been fears that he would revolt. Kings were not supposed to hit earls in later medieval England. Richard was consumed by the desolation of a lover's grief. He ordered the demolition of his house at Sheen, where he and his queen had passed happy hours.

But it was several years before Richard gained the confidence to strike deliberately at his former opponents, Gloucester, Warwick, the Arundel brothers, and their leading former political adherents. In May 1389 his assertion of will had appeared a daring gesture, one which might in the months following have provoked Gloucester to renewed rebellion. It was the return of John of Gaunt from his lieutenancy in Aquitaine in December 1389, which Richard had tried to hasten, that gave the settlement a chance of stability. Gaunt alone could overawe his brother Gloucester. Richard, who had so resented Gaunt's influence in his youth, made the significant gesture on once again meeting his uncle of taking the duke's livery collar from his neck and putting it on himself. This was a token that he would henceforth faithfully promote Gaunt's interests, just as any liveried servant was obliged to promote his lord's. Gaunt hastened to reconcile Gloucester formally with the king. Until Gaunt returned to Gascony in 1394, he firmly upheld his nephew's personal authority, taking the leading part in his attempt to make peace with Charles VI, and managing to reconcile Gloucester to the *détente.* But by then Richard was showing signs of renewed impatience with Gaunt's predominance.

Once more the king was surrounded by a congenial set of ambitious young nobles, who restored his confidence – men such as his half-brother John Holand, earl of Huntingdon, his cousin Edward earl of Rutland, the former appellant Nottingham and John lord Beaumont. The success of Richard's expedition to Ireland in their company (1394–5), and the growing trust between him and Charles VI made him less concerned to maintain the political compromises of the last few years: the favouring of Lancastrian interests, the respect accorded to Gloucester, the show of concern about the abuses of maintenance, and the failure to rake up the controversies of 1386–8. The increasingly inflammatory atmosphere at Court was sensed by the chronicler Jean Froissart, who in 1395 visited the Household for the first time for thirty years, taking a finely bound volume of his love poems to present to the king. Froissart encountered the Court at Canterbury, and accompanied its progress through Kent, first to Leeds Castle near Maidstone, then to Eltham Palace. Though Froissart recognised few familiar faces, he soon grasped facets of the political situation. He says that the young nobles and knights who enjoyed Richard's favour were not concerned to support the interests of Gaunt, absent in Aquitaine, bitterly resenting Gloucester's determination to uphold them and maintain his own enjoyment of large royal annuities, the amount of which they seem to have greatly exaggerated. Some courtiers shuddered when Gloucester, on his rare visits, eyed them balefully, for his expression reminded them of the fate Richard's revered friend Sir Simon Burley had experienced at the duke's behest. Tattlers distorted imprudent remarks Gloucester made about politics to his guests at Pleshey Castle, arousing the susceptible king's suspicions.

Froissart's vivid reflection of ominous undercurrents at Court in 1395 provides a valuable background to the extraordinary and puzzling events of July 1397. Then Richard dramatically ordered the arrests of Warwick, Gloucester and Arundel. The precipitate manner in which they were carried out suggests that he may have become suddenly convinced that they were plotting against him. In September the three were found guilty of treason by their peers in parliament, on an appeal (modelled on that of 1387–8) made by a group of young nobles, including Rutland and Huntingdon. The charges all related to the events of 1386–8, which were raked up in embittered detail, some of it probably supplied to these new lords appellant by Richard himself. But it seems that before the appeal was heard in parliament Gloucester had been suffocated on royal orders, in the Princes Inn at Calais. Richard may have feared the effects of his uncle's public appearance to answer charges. Arundel was produced, to be verbally attacked by Lancaster and Derby, and after speedy condemnation was hustled the same day to his execution on Tower Hill. Warwick proved a trump card for the king. He tearfully acknowledged his treason to parliament, and was rewarded by a sentence of forfeiture and life imprisonment. The new appellants received dukedoms, earldoms and blocs of the forfeited Arundel and Beauchamp inheritances. Arundel lordships in the northern Marches of Wales were annexed to the favoured royal county palatine of Chester, to form a potentially impressive new principality in the north-west.

In the 1397–8 parliament, the offensive programme of 1386 and 1388 was attacked. The measures which Richard considered as infringements of royal prerogative were reversed and condemned, as were the judgments made on 'traitors' in 1388. The judicial definitions of treasonable encroachments on the king's will pronounced in 1387 were reaffirmed. But the acts of the 1397–8 parliament failed to provide a stable basis for Richard's assertion of the Crown's rights. They made too many people feel insecure about their past actions, and others alarmed at the full revelation of Richard's vindictiveness and willingness to coerce the hesitant. Communities and individuals who had aided or sympathised with the opponents of royal policy in 1386–8 were obliged to seek pardons. Property-owners were disquieted by the confiscation and partition of ancient noble inheritances. Exactions of royal loans and fervently partial favouring of royal retainers, and of the king's particular noble friends and their retainers, added to the discontent.

The nobles who had aided Richard in his 1397 coup, elevated as dukes (*duketti*, 'mini-dukes' to some unimpressed contemporaries) bristled with mutual suspicion. Nottingham (duke of Norfolk) may have been mortified because, as captain of Calais, he had probably been ordered to organise Gloucester's murder, hardly the way in which a Marshal of the Realm was expected to treat his colleague the Constable. When the inviolability of the royal will seemed to be at stake, Richard was as disinclined to tolerate chivalrous susceptibilities as any other kind: his *idée fixe* was obedience. As Norfolk rode down Savoy Street, just outside London, in October 1397, he is alleged to have confided to his knight William Bagot that the murderous deed had been performed against his will. Norfolk seems to have been a garrulous rider. In December he apparently told Derby (now duke of Hereford), a chance fellow traveller, that the king intended to punish both of them for their part in the 1387 rising, and that noble courtiers were plotting their downfall and the dismemberment of the Lancastrian inheritance. Hereford, understandably but perhaps mistakenly, did not trust Norfolk: he repeated this dangerous conversation to his father Gaunt, then to Richard, and with royal consent accused Norfolk of treason. At Coventry in September 1398 Richard dramatically prevented a spectacular judicial duel between the dukes. At last he punished the two junior lords appellant of 1387–8, whom he may have suspected with good reason of being unenthusiastic about his recent triumphs. Norfolk was sentenced to exile for life, Hereford for six years.

At the end of May 1399 Richard embarked with an army to crush the Irish rebels who had undermined his cherished settlement of 1395 and in 1398 killed his lieutenant and kinsman, Roger Mortimer, earl of March. With hindsight, historians have condemned Richard's departure from England at this juncture as foolhardy. He may have been prepared to take the risk, and to accept the hazards and discomfort of Irish campaigning, because he wanted to demonstrate that no one could rebel against his authority with impunity. Moreover, possibly in part as a measure to ensure security in England, he took many nobles with him, including Hereford's son (the future Henry V) and Gloucester's son Humphrey. He left some of his most able councillors (notably William Scrope, earl of Wiltshire, Sir William Bagot, Sir Henry Grene and Sir John Bussy) to govern the realm under the regency of his loyal if uninspiring uncle Edmund of Langley (since 1385, duke of York). No foreign power threatened the realm. Former adherents of the rebels of 1387 may have seemed too cowed by the recent fines imposed to cause trouble. But Richard made fatal miscalculations about the behaviour of Hereford and of the northern lords – the latter had in the 1380s tended to keep out of Court controversies. Hereford seems at first to have intended, as probably anticipated, to spend his exile in princely revels and chivalrous expeditions. But when John of Gaunt died in February 1399, Richard made Henry's banishment perpetual and, in effect, disinherited him.

Probably with some encouragement and material assistance to return from the duke of Orleans, Henry sailed from France at the end of June, making his final landfall at Ravenspur, in Holderness (Yorks). He was accompanied by a few exiles, the most distinguished being Thomas Arundel, the able archbishop of Canterbury deprived of his see and banished in 1397 as punishment for supporting the lords appellant. Henry successfully rallied the military support of Lancastrian officials and retainers in Yorkshire and elsewhere. At Doncaster he was joined by northern lords, including the earls of Northumberland and Westmorland. His ostensible intention was to claim his inheritance, an aim with which landowners could readily sympathise, especially if (as was to be reported) he swore so on the relics of John Thweng in Bridlington Priory, much revered in northern society.

Henry moved through the Midlands and their Lancastrian lordships with his northern army, then westwards to secure Bristol, an important base for Anglo-Irish communications, which Richard's supporters tried to defend (28 July). But the regent York and his fellow councillors, despite energetic efforts, were unable to muster sufficient shire levies to secure London and Westminster, or firmly challenge Henry's advance. From Bristol he moved through the Welsh Marches in order to occupy the principality of Chester before it could be consolidated as a Ricardian bastion. His successes posed a more formidable challenge than Richard, in Ireland, may have been able to respond to or even comprehend. His army there was recuperating after a gruelling, demoralising march through barren, hostile terrain with supplies running low. Richard had soldiered valiantly but without success. Perhaps because of the effects of this campaign, perhaps because he trusted foolishly or treacherously optimistic advice, he failed to take the measures needed to secure a base in his realm. Edward III would have sailed immediately to confuse and confront rebels. But Richard dispatched John Montague, earl of Salisbury, as governor of north Wales and Chester. The earl failed to maintain a force large enough to challenge the advance of Henry's army, which captured Chester on 9 August. Cheshiremen and Welshmen may have been deterred from supporting Salisbury by the size of Henry's army, the fact that he had licensed them to ravage by having 'havoc' cried (an unusual licence in later medieval domestic conflict in England)[5] and by the king's absence.

Richard seems to have been misinformed about Salisbury's increasingly desperate situation at Conway, for on or about 27 July he had embarked with the rest of his forces at Waterford to land at Milford Haven in *south* Wales. Thence he rode to Conway, abandoning his disintegrating army. He could probably have escaped from Conway by boat, but, as he had shown in 1381 and 1387, he was not the man to flee danger. He intended once more to deceive his opponents. Again Northumberland acted as a mediator, but failed to display the good faith which Richard had come to expect of him. His assurance of the king's regality on Henry's behalf, sworn on the sacrament, induced Richard to abandon his strong defensive position in Conway Castle and ride to Flint to receive Henry's petitions. The testimony of a French esquire in the royal retinue suggests Richard's duplicity. In the privacy of his household he said 'There are some of them who I will flay alive. I would not take all the gold in the land for them; please God, I continue alive and well.' But Richard was himself duped. On the road Northumberland and the Lancastrian knight Thomas Erpingham[6] ambushed his small retinue. It was as a prisoner that Richard listened to Henry's fair promises in Flint Castle and was escorted to London.

Several years later the Percies were to claim that when they had joined Henry in arms at Doncaster he had solemnly sworn that he had come to claim only his inheritance and that of his wife. Oaths seem to have come readily to determined men in the summer of 1399, engaged in the desperate business of disarming a treacherous king. Henry's principal supporters, with their knowledge of Richard's character and of the difficulty of shackling lasting restraints on the royal will, surely realised that they were committing themselves to deposition. There was nothing new about the idea of deposing Richard. The problem was to manage it in a manner which would provide divinely sanctioned, stable rule. One possible candidate for the throne was Edward III's next surviving heir (after Richard): Edmund Mortimer, son of the earl of March killed in 1398. Edmund, aged eight, was unlikely to provide the stability which would have enabled Richard's opponents to protect themselves from his sympathisers. Henry's candidacy was the only expedient one.

On 30 September 1399 members of a parliament summoned in Richard's name assembled at Westminster to grapple with the problems of changing kings. One difficulty for Henry's partisans had been Richard's obduracy. Despite his understandable depression, the royal prisoner in the Tower remained convinced of his God-given authority. According to his apologists, he refused to abdicate, demanding a public hearing, and was coerced into acquiescence only by threats of death. But the estates were told in their first session by Sir William Thirning, Chief Justice of the King's Bench, that Richard had voluntarily confirmed his resignation before prominent witnesses in the Tower, and designated Henry as his successor. Thirty-two charges against Richard, amounting to a comprehensive accusation of tyranny, were recited to the estates, who withdrew their allegiances. Henry appeared before them, claiming his hereditary right to the throne in a studiously vague manner, and pointing out that God had shown favour to his claim to rule the realm when it was about to be undone by bad government. His claim was recognised, and new writs in his name were issued summoning parliament for 6 October. He was crowned on 13 October, being anointed with holy oil which, Lancastrian propaganda suggested, especially indicated divine approval. The oil came from a phial given by the Virgin Mary to St Thomas of Canterbury, recovered in France during Edward III's reign by Henry of Grosmont, duke of Lancaster, and given by him to Prince Edward for his coronation, but never used by Richard. Thus Henry's accession was linked with the names of sacred and chivalrous persons hallowed by fourteenth-century Englishmen. The fact that Henry was the first English king to be anointed with this oil made many believe, according to Walsingham, that he had been 'elected by God'. 'Sir Richard of Bordeaux', divested of the royal robes in which he appears magnificently before us in painting and effigy, was escorted from the Tower in the lowly, unknightly guise of a forester. He was taken to Leeds Castle in Kent, where Froissart had observed him surrounded by his Court in 1395. Subsequently he was removed to the remoter Lancastrian fortress at Pontefract in Yorkshire, where Thomas of Lancaster, arch-enemy of the ancestor he had wished to canonise, Edward II, had been executed. There Richard was soon to die.

The reign of Henry IV (1399–1413)

Henry of Lancaster, if his effigy on the tomb in Canterbury Cathedral can be relied on, was in middle age a short, round-faced, regular-featured, stocky man. There is no hint in the effigy of his youthful hardiness and athletic ability, possibly because he deteriorated physically as king because of the increasingly sedentary life forced on him by the collapse of his health. The regal plumpness is accentuated by the effigy of his second wife, Joan of Navarre, widow of the duke of Brittany, whom Henry married in 1403: she is portrayed with slender neck and slim, rounded figure. Henry, unlike his predecessor, was much travelled, well known and liked in the courts of Europe. He may have been the first king of England to pride himself on his Scots ancestry: according to a Scottish chronicler he said, 'I am half a Scot by blood and in heart, as being of the stock of the noble Comyns, earls of Buchan.' He was a cultivated and well-educated noble, a distinguished jouster, a patron of musicians, perhaps himself a composer, and a bibliophile. He had a study built at Eltham, furnished with two desks, a small one and a large one of two stages to keep his books in. There perhaps, beneath the angels and archangels flying on the roof bosses, and gazing at the figures of the Trinity, the Salutation of the Virgin and of saints glazing the seven windows, he dwelt on youthful memories of his journeys as an applauded crusader in Prussia and as a pilgrim to Jerusalem, before the fateful encounter with Norfolk in 1397 which was to turn his world upside down.

Henry was by preference an easy-going man, whose charm in his pampered youth masked a latent energy, keen political intelligence, tenacity of purpose, and a savage temper. As king he was easier to deal with than Richard II, more prepared to endure criticism with a show of patience and to forgive his opponents. Walsingham thought that he went to humiliating lengths before the battle of Shrewsbury (1403) to reconcile the rebels. Having matured when a magnate, he appreciated that royal prerogative could not ride roughshod over the will of nobles, gentry and burgesses. Kingship drew out his qualities and defects. He did not reign happily. His subjects never gave him the respect shown to his predecessors. A rumour spread that the coronation oil had produced a swarm of lice in his hair, a sign of divine disapproval. Henry himself probably had qualms of conscience about the deposition and death of Richard. Like many Englishmen, he may have thought that the collapse of his health in 1405 was a punishment for the execution of Archbishop Scrope as well as for earlier misdeeds. There is some warrant in contemporary evidence for Shakespeare's unquiet king.

Within months of the usurpation troubles multiplied. Before Christmas 1399 some of Richard's favourites, deprived of their recent titles and territorial gains in Henry's first parliament, plotted his overthrow, holding some meetings practically a stone's throw from the precincts of his palace, in Abbot Colchester's house at Westminster. Richard II's half-brother, John Holand, earl of Huntingdon (formerly duke of Exeter), the latter's nephew Thomas Holand, earl of Kent (formerly duke of Surrey), John Montague, earl of Salisbury, and Thomas lord Despenser (formerly earl of Gloucester) determined to seize Henry and his family as they celebrated Twelfth Night in Windsor Castle. But rumours of a plot reached Henry from several sources. The rebels seized the castle only to find that the Household had decamped hastily for London. Henry arrayed his retinue, called out the armed support of the London gilds, and advanced to secure the bridge at Kingston-upon-Thames. The rebels, finding that their proclamations elicited negligible support in the south-east, retreated, the main body westwards. The fleeing leaders were seized and lynched by the townsmen of Bristol and Cirencester, and by countryfolk in Essex. The commons once more intervened violently in the affairs of the realm. The chronicler Adam Usk commented that 'seeing that all these things were done by the savage fury of the people I fear that they will make this a plea to wield still more in future against their lords possession of the sword, which has now been allowed to them against all system of order.'

The conspiracy was the death-warrant of the former king. In March 1400 his body was exhibited in St Paul's Cathedral. Henry vindictively forbade burial in accordance with Richard's intentions, in Westminster Abbey, perhaps because he feared that a cult might develop there, centring on the tomb. Instead Richard was laid to rest in the friary at Langley (Herts), near one of his favourite residences. Rumours were to persist that King Richard was alive in Scotland, and would come again to claim the Crown. In 1404 Thomas abbot of Byleigh confessed that one William Blithe had talked treasonably to him and a local squire, John Prittlewell. In the abbey garden Blithe alleged that 'King Richard was coming out of Scotland and Queen Isabel and the Duke of Orleans were in the sea purposing to arm at Orwell and Glyn Dŵr out of Wales with a strong power and all this people should meet together at Northampton'. The abbot thought it would be imprudent to refuse all favour to this supposed emissary of the former king: 'I supposed he was a perilous man and if it happened other than well he might have dis-eased me and our place. And I sent him two marks. . .'

The 1400 attempt had been premature. The conspirators may have felt compelled to move with such fatal haste in order to forestall Richard's probable demise. Henry's rule was then popular at all levels of society, but within a year Richard's friends might have gained solid support. Henry's troubles were partly fortuitous, partly consequent on his relationship with his subjects, inherent in the events of 1399.

At first it seemed that his main preoccupations would be with the Scots and Welsh. In October 1399 the Scottish Borderers had sacked Wark Castle on the Tweed. But the balance of forces among the Border lords was dramatically altered when, in 1400, George Dunbar, Scottish earl of March entered Henry's allegiance, after the lieutenant of Robert III, his son Rothesay, had repudiated a betrothal to March's daughter. In the 1370s and 1380s March had done as much as anyone to undermine the remains of the hegemony English Borderers had been trying to maintain since 1346 in the Scottish frontier shires (cf. pp. 169, 237). His defection opened the way to Edinburgh: in August 1400 Henry was at the cross between there and Leith, surrounded by his army, vainly claiming the overlordship of his Scots fellow countrymen. Subsequent truce negotiations did not prevent large-scale Border raiding. The earl of Douglas, whose daughter had married Rothesay and who had been granted March's forfeited lordship of Dunbar, may have feared that the Percies, in alliance with March, would attempt to wrest it from him. In February 1401 he wrote to Henry accusing the earl of Northumberland bitterly of bad faith in truce-breaking, and he kept up the pressure against Percy country. In September 1402 March and Sir Henry Percy defeated a returning Scots raiding party at Humbledon Hill near Wooler. Among the captives were Douglas and Murdoch Stewart, earl of Fife, son of Robert III's ambitious brother Albany.

The presence in England of the two principal Scots Border lords, March and Douglas, was to complicate domestic affairs for Henry: the political tensions of this remote region, not usually of much concern in Court politics, probably became a crucial factor. But relations with the Scots Crown were not to trouble Henry greatly. In March 1406 Robert III's son and heir James, a minor being taken by sea to France, was captured off Flamborough Head in time of truce by Hugh Fen and men of Yarmouth. King Robert died within weeks. Albany as governor of the realm for his nephew, the captive James I, was generally inclined to renew truces with Henry, anxious for him to release his own son Fife, but not his nephew.

In the autumn of 1400 there had been disturbances in the northern Marches of Wales, which were unexpectedly to assume the proportions of a major revolt. Their principal instigator was Owain Glyn Dŵr, a highly reputable Welsh landowner. A descendant of the princes of Powis and Deheubarth, he was lord of Glyndyfrdwy and Cynllaith Owain, and married to the daughter of a royal justice, Sir David Hanmer. In 1384 he served in the garrison at Berwick and, according to bardic verse, distinguished himself on Richard II's 1385 Scottish expedition. With a scarlet flamingo feather waving on his helmet, he drove off the Scots 'howling with fear like wild goats'. In 1387, maintaining family links with the leading noble family of the northern Marches, he served at sea in the earl of Arundel's retinue. In 1399 Owain had a territorial dispute with another neighbouring marcher, Reginald Grey, lord of Ruthin. Owain seems to have sought vainly for royal redress against Grey. The political situation after the usurpation may have dashed his hopes of gaining 'good lordship'. The administration of the newly created prince of Wales, the king's eldest son Henry of Monmouth, was controlled by royal servants who may have considered Grey more useful than Glyn Dŵr. The latter may have been denied the comital patronage his family were accustomed to hope for. Thomas Arundel, restored to the earldom of Arundel when under age in the 1399 parliament, received seisin of his inheritance only in October 1400. Unlike his father Earl Richard (executed 1397), whom Grey and Glyn Dŵr had both served, the young and perhaps callow earl as yet lacked the authority which lords were supposed to exercise in arbitrating and resolving the disputes of their neighbours and dependants.

In September 1400 Owain raided Ruthin shortly before fair day with about 270 adherents, including three wives, two widows and a concubine. Subsequently other towns in the northern Marches and parts of the principality were attacked. In 1401 Owain's kinsmen Gwilym and Rhys ap Tudur ap Gronw of Penmyndd in Anglesey seized the royal castle at Conway. In 1402–3 Owain extended his assaults into south Wales. Marcher lords and loyal Welsh landowners were unable to oppose effectively a movement which Owain came to colour with more than familial and local aspirations. Bards spread his fame at various levels of society into parts of Wales where he could not rely strongly on appeals to kinship and connection. There was a widespread response to the ideal of reviving a native principality from clerics and gentlefolk, some of whom perhaps saw it as a means of extending their hold on local administrative offices. Excitement spread to the Welsh abroad: Welsh students at Oxford held meetings, even in the public convenience, and numbers left for home. By 1404 Owain's claim to be Prince of Wales was regarded as plausible in foreign lands as well as among his fellow-countrymen. Henry IV's several Welsh campaigns (1400–3) by their failure to crush the rebellion had raised Owain's prestige. For several years the rebels got control of some of the Principality's formidable castles, raided and levied ill-protected Marcher lordships and evaded punitive expeditions. But Lancastrian efforts were relentless. Owain may have had difficulty in maintaining well-disciplined forces willingly sustained by the civil population, since he was dependent on the wasting resources of a poor province. English domination of sea communications restricted effective external aid, and helped the maturing Prince Henry and his able lieutenants to victual and recapture key fortresses. Aberystwyth was recovered in 1408, Harlech in 1409. The following year Owain sustained heavy losses in a raid on Shropshire, his last major effort. He had died by 1417, still defiant, protected and honoured by his people, who had accepted the inevitabilty of Lancastrian rule.

At its height Glyn Dŵr's revolt had posed a dire threat to that rule in England as well as Wales. In June 1402 he had captured Sir Edmund Mortimer, whose young nephew of the same name was heir to the earldom of March, and, in the eyes of some Englishmen, Richard's rightful successor. Sir Edmund was to ally with his captor and probably helped to bring him into contact with English dissidents. The Welsh embarrassment may have seemed to the Percies to provide an opportunity for revolt. Their motives for turning against Henry are obscure.

They and other northern lords, notably the earl of Westmorland, may have rebelled against Richard in 1399 principally because they considered that he had neglected their regional interests. By 1396 the aim to recover the *terra irridenta* in southern Scotland had apparently been dropped from English diplomacy. Richard was to appoint favoured kinsmen, Huntingdon and Albemarle, to Border commands. But Henry rewarded the Percies well. Northumberland was granted the Constableship of the Realm for life, the Wardenship of the West March for ten years, and two-thirds of the Mortimer inheritance in wardship. His brother Thomas earl of Worcester was appointed Steward of the Household in 1401 and, instead, in 1402 lieutenant in south Wales and chief councillor to Prince Henry. Northumberland's son Sir Henry Percy had been granted in 1399 the Wardenship of the East March, the constableships of Chester, Flint, Conway and Caernavon, and the justiciary of Chester for life: in 1402 he was appointed lieutenant in north Wales. In these circumstances the Percies may have accepted Henry's failure to support a 'forward' policy in Scotland: his ambassadors had been instructed in September 1401 to negotiate the possession solely of Berwick, Roxburgh and Jedburgh and the allegiance of their inhabitants.

The Percies' attitude may have been changed by their capture of Douglas in 1402, for as a consequence they stood a good chance of dominating the Anglo-Scottish Borders. Henry, however, showed little inclination to let them exploit the situation. He insisted that he, and not they, should negotiate the terms of Douglas's ransom. On the other hand, he inclined to allow the Scotsman March to benefit from Douglas's capture. In the parliament of October 1402 the king assented to his petition that if any conquest were made in the realm of Scotland, he might have restoration of his castles and lands (in Douglas hands). March might have any of his lordships conquered by Henry or any of his soldiers, to hold of the king as of his Crown. This undertaking perhaps implied royal approval for an extension of the English Crown's lordship into Scotland at the expense of Douglas interests, not for the benefit of English lords but a Scottish one. Henry showed no similar sympathy for Percy claims in Scotland. The family needed royal financial help to continue their advance into Roxburghshire in 1403, but there was little likelihood that arrears owed them by the Crown would be forthcoming speedily. Fears that Henry might refashion the frontier in favour of the Dunbars may have been the reason why Percies and Douglas, whose families had been in dispute for decades over the ramifications of the 1333 settlement, allied against Henry in 1403. The consequences of their failure were to be blamed in Percy country on the Dunbars. The countess of March was to write to Henry: 'We suffer great enmity for the death of Sir Henry Percy, in so much that it is often so heavy to my baron and his men, that they wish to be dead, if they may not retire from the land.'

Northumberland's son Sir Henry, a middle-aged Border raider

renowned as 'Hotspur', had raised the standard of revolt at Chester, proclaiming that Richard II was alive. Supporting him in arms were his uncle the earl of Worcester, and Douglas. But the king was a match for this formidable array of military veterans. Moving with the alacrity he had displayed in 1399, and against Richard's friends and the Scots in 1400, and relying heavily on March's advice, he confronted the rebels near Shrewsbury, before Welsh or northern support could come in. A grim battle was fought. Walsingham says that the king's men fell 'as fast as the leaves fall in autumn after the hoar-frost'. Prince Henry was wounded and the earl of Stafford killed. But the rebel army collapsed when Hotspur was slain. Worcester and Douglas were captured, the former to be summarily executed. The battle of Shrewsbury is commemorated by Battlefield Church, founded as a college by Henry in 1408 for the sake of the souls of those killed there.

The fight did not appear as decisive at the time as it turned out to be. Glyn Dŵr still dominated Wales and the earl of Northumberland, though deprived of his offices and castles, still retained his title, estates and influence. The rules of politics were not as cynically hardheaded as they were to be after the Wars of the Roses. Under a Tudor monarch charges of treason would have been manufactured against the earl: under a Yorkist the Mortimer boys would have quietly faded from view in royal custody. Because Henry was compassionate and untyrannical he had to face the malice and presumption of more rebels, leading him to imperil his soul and ruin his health. In 1405 Yorkshiremen were rallied in revolt by manifestoes in the name of their archbishop, Richard Scrope, member of a leading local family. Also participating were Scrope's nephew Sir William Plumpton, a Percy retainer, and young Thomas Mowbray, earl marshal, son of Henry's adversary Norfolk (d.1399). One chronicler says that Mowbray resented the earl of Westmorland's possession of lands and of the office of Marshal – Henry had granted it to him in 1399, and made him a great man in Yorkshire by a grant of the honor of Richmond for life. Before either Northumberland and his Marchmen could arrive to support the revolt, or Henry to suppress it, Westmorland had by skilful diplomacy persuaded the assembly to disperse. Henry soon arrived in York, and, with a sacrilegiousness which appalled many of his followers, had Scrope executed. So were Mowbray and Plumpton: clerics and burgesses of York who had supported the rising were harshly punished. It was said that Scrope had declared he was about to die for laws and good rule in England, and that after he fell the king appeared like a leper. But he cowed the North. Northumberland and his supporter Lord Bardolf fled to Scotland, abandoning Berwick to assault by the king's bombards. They were unable to raise support when they returned in February 1408. Passing through wintry Tynedale into the bishopric of Durham, they proclaimed at the former Mowbray town of Thirsk (Yorks) that they had come to relieve the English people from oppression. But the local sheriff, Sir Thomas Rokeby, barred their progress at Knaresborough, reacted quickly to their flanking movement through Wetherby, and caught up with them at Tadcaster. The opponents agreed to fight on Bramham Moor. Northumberland was killed and Bardolf died of his wounds.

Northumberland's untimely and ill-supported last fling may have been precipitated by information that Henry had come to terms with Douglas. By an agreement subscribed with his own hand in March 1407 the earl promised to work for a truce of sixteen years between the two kingdoms: his lordships and men were to observe a truce until Easter 1408. He pledged himself and his men to support Henry and his sons against its breakers. The release of Douglas implied a return to the *status quo* in royal Border policy: the status which Henry accorded to Douglas undermined his 1402 pledge to March, who, not suprisingly, returned to Scottish allegiance in 1409. Though March's son George had managed to establish himself in the family's lordship at Cockburnspath, lacking the co-operation of English Border families he had not been able to recover the earldom.

Henry's acquiescence in 1408–9 in the re-establishment of the two leading Scots Border magnates, when he had no Percies to counterbalance them, appears rash. But he probably believed that an understanding with them was the key to an enforcement of truces. Minor chiefs were less likely to subordinate raiding profits to high policy. The earl's brother James Douglas had boldly admitted to Henry in 1405 his responsibility for burning Berwick in reprisal, and in 1409 the men of Teviotdale captured the former Percy castle at Jedburgh, which Henry had turned into a hereditary lordship for his son John. Douglas and March, after several years' absence, probably found it difficult to reassert their influence over the lairds: though not well placed to restrain truce-breaking, neither were they yet to escalate it. Fighting remained concentrated around the English enclaves in Scotland, without spilling disastrously over the frontier. Luckily for Henry, the situation in the North after the fall of the Percies cooled down the enmities which had boiled over into national politics.

Despite Henry's successes, his subjects remained doubtful about the legitimacy and stability of his rule. A sure sign of this was the continued circulation of rumours and prophecies inimical to it. Some Franciscans denounced Henry up and down the realm as a traitor to his lord, usurper and tyrant. At Huntingdon assizes in 1405, two cattle thieves confessed with a wealth of detail how they had acted as collectors in England of contributions to support Glyn Dŵr's rebellion, accusing abbots, priors and gentlemen of having subscribed. In fact their confessions did not save them from hanging, but the fact that men conjuring their wits to save their lives regarded such charges as plausible shows how uncertain loyalties to Henry seemed, even in parts of the realm and among individuals where one would have expected them to be firm. There were occasions when Henry suspected some of his closest kinsmen and supporters of treason. In the parliament which met in

January 1404, Archbishop Arundel asked that he, the duke of York and others accused of sympathy with rebels should be declared loyal. In 1405 York's sister Constance Despenser tried to spirit Edmund Mortimer and his brother from royal custody to Wales. York was temporarily imprisoned and Archbishop Arundel exculpated himself.

One reason for the consistent failure of the numerous movements of opposition in England to Henry IV's rule was that no convincing leaders emerged to rally the diverse incoherent elements. There were, as a result of accidents of birth and forfeiture, few adult, well-established lay magnates who might have fitted the roles. The Percies were northerners, whose centres of influence mainly lay far from the capital and most of the prosperous parts of the realm. They had compromised themselves as Henry's supporters in 1399 – an involvement from which they went to considerable lengths to excuse themselves in their propaganda. Mowbray was young and generally unknown. Given more time, Archbishop Scrope might have become a formidable opponent of the dynasty; he had managed to incite support from the middling ranks of society.

Another handicap to rebels was that, whether formally allied with Glyn Dŵr or not, they were aiding his cause, hateful to many Englishmen, as savage anti-Welsh petitions by the Commons show, and inimical to the interests of Marcher lords such as Thomas earl of Arundel, Edmund earl of Stafford (d.1403), and Reginald Grey lord of Ruthin. Henry could hope to rely on the loyalty of some magnates because of kinship, his revival of their fortunes in 1399, and possibly because they feared that his overthrow in favour of the 'Ricardian' heir Edmund Mortimer, might lead to their condemnation for conniving at the usurpation. The Arundels and Staffords proved reliable, as did the young Richard Beauchamp, who succeeded to the earldom of Warwick in 1403. Henry's most valuable noble supporter was Ralph Neville, earl of Westmorland, the husband of his half-sister Joan Beaufort. The earl, a middle-aged, seasoned warrior, sensible and levelheaded, constantly checked the volatile Percies and, particularly after the confiscation of Northumberland's castles in 1403, represented royal interests in the North. But there were few available magnates on whom Henry could rely to use local influence in his favour. Royal resources were too fully committed for him to endow new earldoms. In the parliaments of October 1404, 1407 and 1410 the Commons petitioned that the king should endow his younger sons, Thomas, John and Humphrey, with titles and appropriate estates. The only one who did eventually benefit was Thomas, created duke of Clarence in 1412. Henry made only two other new peers: his son Henry received the heir to the throne's customary appanages (1399), and the king's half-brother Sir Thomas Beaufort became earl of Dorset (1412).

Since Henry could not rely so implicitly as his predecessors on magnates to raise military retinues for the Crown, to prompt the speedy proclamation and observance of ordinances and statutes, ensure the efficient fulfilment of judicial commissions, and arbitrate disputes, he depended particularly on the co-operation of lesser peers and of leading gentlemen whose representatives sat in his frequent parliaments. Special reliance by the Crown on the 'middling ranks' for the local enforcement of justice and order had been a brief expedient of Richard II's uncertain government in the years 1388–90. But the Crown was perhaps not to develop such a conjunction fully and wholeheartedly until the political and religious upheavals of the 1530s: thenceforward it became a permanent basis of the polity. Henry IV's enforced reliance on the co-operation of the gentry was, in the long run, to provide a solid basis of loyalties to his dynasty. But in the first years of his reign, when his government appeared incompetent to manage royal resources and ensure the security of the realm, it exposed him to a barrage of carping criticisms and parliamentary restrictions. Earnest knights of the shire rode up to parliament fully realising the Crown's need for their support, indignant at the failure of royal councillors to provide for the expenses of the Household and to check Welsh insolence, and determined to agitate for reform of government, as their predecessors had done in the Good Parliament of 1376.

The middling ranks who had greeted Henry of Lancaster's appearance so rapturously in 1399 soon showed bitter disillusionment with aspects of his rule. In 1401 his friend and confessor, Philip Repingdon, abbot of St Mary's Abbey, Leicester, wrote stiffly upbraiding him for not dispensing justice evenly, contrary to the promises he had made. Repingdon predicted that discontent would become more vociferous 'until the law and the lawful justice of your realm shall be kept . . . and, by the upright ruling of justice, every man shall have his own'. It had been widely expected, in accordance with the rash pledges that Henry had initially made, doubtless magnified by rumour, that he would not demand a high rate of taxation: the manifestoes of the Percies and Archbishop Scrope exploited feeling about the cost of his rule. The accumulating emergencies necessitated parliamentary grants on a scale comparable to those made during the warfare of the early years of Richard's reign. The Commons were irritated and baffled by the penury of a king whose customary endowments and sources of income were augmented by the duchy of Lancaster, substantial parts of the Bohun earldoms of Hereford, Northampton and Essex and of the duchy of Norfolk, the escheated Holand, Montague and Despenser inheritances, besides later forfeitures. But the duchy of Lancaster was heavily burdened with annuities granted by John of Gaunt, which Henry, who relied notably on the service of Lancastrian retainers, had to confirm. It was necessary for him to keep the loyalty of most of Richard's servants by confirming many of the grants and annuities charged on Crown revenue which the latter had granted with increasing lavishness in the 1390s, and expedient to reserve the services of Ricardian magnates' former retainers by confirming their fees and rewards. Such a loyal servant of Richard as the Gascon esquire Janico Dartasso, who refused to discard the badge of the white hart after his master's capture near Flint in 1399, once he had given his allegiance to Henry, was confirmed in all his annuities, and became a devoted Lancastrian.

The financial handicaps arising from the circumstances of Henry's usurpation were to be compounded by subsequent developments, partly outwith his control. The Glyn Dŵr revolt transformed the principality of Wales from a source of revenue to a heavy financial liability, in addition to which the Crown had to shoulder part of the burden of the defence of Marcher lordships. At the same time there was a marked drop from the customary level of wool exports, the custom and subsidy on which were normally one of the most reliable sources of royal revenue. If this fall reflected a decline in wool production as well as diversion to the needs of the growing domestic cloth industry, sheep-owners and native exporters may have been more than usually reluctant to contribute to any sort of taxation. If, as is likely, many landowners were in the process of making often painful financial adjustments from a demesne to a *rentier* economy (see p. 17), this too helps to explain their sensitivity about taxation. There are indications that in the 1401 parliament the Commons expressed dissatisfaction with the conduct of government. They probably petitioned that Henry should charge great officers and councillors with their responsibilities publicly in parliament, with some of the Commons present. In the parliament of January 1404, at the Commons' petition, the king communicated the names of the lords appointed as councillors. The grant was to be partly administered by specially appointed war treasurers accountable to parliament, and the king undertook measures to provide a sure revenue for his Household expenses, a problem with which the Commons were to concern themselves more fully in the October parliament at Coventry. In the 'Long Parliament' of 1406 the Commons were most recalcitrant. Assembling in March, parliament met for three sessions totalling twenty-three weeks, not making the needed grant till December. Henry was eventually drawn to submit to humiliating restrictions on his initiative. He agreed to expel aliens from the Household, and nominated councillors who were to assume considerable responsibilty for the conduct of his business. In December, at his command, they subscribed before the estates to a series of ordinances aimed to guarantee their provision of justice, regular dispatch of business, close personal contact with the king, control of the disposition of patronage and supervision of the conduct of Household and other officials.

But in the 1407 parliament the councillors were discharged from their oaths. In 1410, at the Commons' request, councillors were once again nominated and charged in parliament, in their presence, but in 1411 Henry informed their Speaker Thomas Chaucer 'that he did not want to have any kind of novelty in this parliament, but that he wished to retain his prerogatives (*ses libertee et fraunchise*) as fully as any of his said progenitors or ancestors had previously'. He got his way. Though irked by the past outrages concocted on his liberty in the Commons, the mildness of his reactions (compared to Richard's) may indicate that he realised their motive was to shore up his rule. By 1411 the fruits of his and the Commons' tenacity had begun to appear. The menace of the Percies had been broken, the Welsh rebellion was in decline, and the French princes were preoccupied with their domestic quarrels. The easing of such pressures improved the Crown's position: criticism in the middling ranks quietened.

The last years of the reign did not lack political tensions, but of a kind basically less threatening to the dynasty's rule and the Crown's rights. There was friction between factions led by magnates for favour at Court and dominance in Council, a characteristic jockeying in a normally flourishing medieval monarchy. Controversy and intrigue polarised, on occasion almost to the point of violence, around the enigmatic figure of Henry prince of Wales, who, after his return from campaigning in the principality in 1409, attempted to dominate government, with the support of his uncles Henry Beaufort, bishop of Winchester, and Sir Thomas Beaufort, and of youthful fighting lords, the earls of Arundel and Warwick. In 1409 Archbishop Arundel, Chancellor since 1407, gave up the office and the next month Sir Thomas Beaufort received it. But towards the end of 1411 the ailing king, supported by his second son, Clarence, and by Archbishop Arundel, dismissed the prince and his adherents from offices and Council. In the summer of 1412 tension was high, with the prince and other magnates bringing armed retinues to London. But in the autumn Prince Henry sought out his father for a reconciliation, and remained in favour till Henry IV's death in March 1413. These obscure, family-centred crises may be an indication that the dynasty had gained a higher level of acceptance. Henry of Lancaster's loyal kinsmen and supporters, reassured by the vigour and youthful promise of his four sons, could now indulge in the luxury of promoting their enmities and ambitions, without endangering Lancastrian rule.

For much of Henry IV's reign his rule was regarded ambivalently by many of his subjects. Its lack of gracious inception, spotless legitimacy and divine blessing were not compensated in the early years by cheapness or stability. By the end of the reign most subjects mustered a tepid loyalty. Henry had shown an appreciation of the need, after the events of Richard's reign, for property-owners to be reassured that the Crown respected their liberties, and tolerated attempts to remedy grievances. In this sense he was a 'constitutional' king. He laid firm foundations for the Lancastrian polity. Some of his statutes were to have lasting significance as expressions of the aspirations of large sections of propertied society, for example, the 1399 Act concerning liveries and maintenance, the 1401 Act laying down royal co-operation in process against heretics, and the 1406 Act to safeguard the rights of parliamentary electors. The conservatism of aims was characteristic of his rule. Henry was no innovator, despite the Crown's temporarily altered relationship with magnates and gentry. Unlike a later usurper, Henry VII, he did not develop a stringent and profitable exploitation of royal rights. Henry IV's lack of administrative ability was, in his financial circumstances, a particular handicap. But he did have a gift for friendship. Archbishop Arundel, with whom his relations had sometimes been bad, came to cherish him in adversity, and he willed, exceptionally for an English king, to be buried in the archbishop's cathedral. Henry was a loyal, fair master. The toilworn king declared in his will of 1408: 'I thank all my Lords and true people for the true service that they have done to me, and I ask them forgiveness if I have mistreated them in any way. And also I devise, that of my goods restitution be made to all them that I have wrongfully grieved, or any goods had of theirs without just title.' The families of many gentlefolk whom he retained were to remain staunchly faithful to his troubled dynasty.

Henry's rule was the victim of several concurrent, unusual crises. The unprecedented usurpation inspired other magnates to covet the Crown. The decline of wool exports temporarily undermined a crucial source of royal revenues. Tensions in Wales and on the borders with Scotland, usually of only local interest, assumed the proportion of major crises. But Henry did not flinch. He was prepared to defend what he had won with the sword, to array and ride against rebels, saving his state at the expense of his spiritual and physical health. The impolitic recklessness of his opponents played into his hands. Those who spread rumours that Richard was alive and would soon come again to claim his own were using, considering Richard's vindictiveness, double-edged arguments. Supporters of the Mortimer claim discredited their cause when they abetted and allied with the malignant, rebellious Welsh, who had menacing links with the French and Castilians, hardened adversaries of the English people.

The reign of Henry V (1413–22)

Henry V began his reign in more auspicious circumstances than any of his predecessors since Edward I. In the last Exchequer term of his father's reign receipts had exceeded expenditure. Since France was riven by a violent civil war, the chances of favourably settling the English Crown's claims there seemed brighter than they had done for over fifty years. In a manner reminiscent of his famous great-uncle Edward prince of Wales (d.1376), Henry had started to gain the confidence and admiration of the chivalry by his display of military ability, when heir to the throne. His awe-inspiring character is revealed by the ease with which he dominated English government during his absences in France, and easily handled the more mettlesome members of his family. His brother Thomas of Clarence, his recent opponent in his father's reign, despite the fear the latter had expressed to Henry about future dissension between the two, served him with distinction. His able and arrogant uncle, Bishop Henry Beaufort, succeeded in securing the promise of a cardinalate from Martin V in 1418 without Henry's permission, but apologetically withdrew in face of his dire threats. The king's youngest brother Humphrey, whose later career amply revealed his obstinate, mercurial temperament, strove to please Henry by diligent military service, so impressing the king that he nominated him regent of the realm in his will.

Henry's long face and stern mien beneath fashionably cropped hair are familiar from the portrait in stained glass in a window of the chapel of All Souls' College, Oxford. This may be a fairly accurate likeness, since it was made in 1442 by John Glasier, commissioned by Henry Chichele, archbishop of Canterbury, who owed his eminence primarily to the king, and had founded the college partly for the purpose of providing prayers for the soul of his master of 'glorious memory'. Henry of Monmouth, born in 1387, had probably received the best education available to a young English nobleman of his generation. As a boy he had stayed in the households of his cultivated grandfather, John of Gaunt and of Richard II. Rumours persisted of his youthful wildness and immorality, but as king he was to display in exceptional measure the virtues and skills currently prescribed as the pattern of princely conduct. In conversation he was serious, courteous and inclined to be taciturn; he was punctilious in religious observance, a stern but appreciative master, an able and chivalrous fighter, a connoisseur of edifying literature. Henry as king impressed contemporaries as much by his self-control as by his remarkable military and diplomatic successes. Posterity has been concerned above all with the assessment of his aims and achievements. As far as medieval appreciation was concerned, Shakespeare went to the heart of the matter by recreating, not just the outline of his victories, but the traditional lineaments and inflections of the man. By the later sixteenth century there had been other English kings – Edward IV, Henry VII, Henry VIII – who were as successful as Henry, but none of them reputedly approximated so closely, in their gestures, words and deeds, to ideals of kingship.

Though Henry IV may have had some doubts about the justice of his claim to the Crown, and Henry V may have had reservations about his father's treatment of Richard and other opponents, the new king seems to have convinced himself that in God's eyes he was the rightful king of England and France, and set himself the task of confounding those who doubted. Whereas at Shrewsbury his father had had doubles clothed in his arms to deceive his enemies, at the battle of Agincourt Henry was to flaunt his crown over his helmet. But early in his reign he had to deal with threats of rebellion which may have seemed to presage a recurrence of the instability of the first years of Lancastrian rule. In the autumn of 1413 the heretical Lollards (see pp. 368 ff) plotted revolt. The chief instigator was Sir John Oldcastle, in Walsingham's chronicles a sinister, lurking figure, as elusive, ubiquitous and subversive of true religion as notable Jesuits were to be in the eyes of Elizabethan Puritans. Oldcastle, a Herefordshire landowner, experienced soldier and formerly trusted retainer of Henry as prince, had promoted the spread of heretical preaching on his estates, including those of his wife Joan de la Pole, granddaughter and heiress of the baronial Cobhams of Kent, whom he married in 1408. In 1413 Oldcastle was condemned for heresy, but escaped from the Tower and hid in London. A desperate plot was evolved for bands of his sympathisers to rally on the night of 9–10 January 1414 outside London in St Giles' Fields, while one group disguised as mummers gained access to the Court at Eltham, and seized the king and his brothers. But the plot was betrayed: Henry moved to secure London and easily rounded up the provincial bands as they arrived at their rendezvous. They were not numerous or formidable: few gentlefolk had taken up arms, and groups like the forty or so craftsmen up from Bristol, mostly weavers – the largest single party – were no match for hard military men used to fighting the Welsh. Oldcastle, however, escaped, and eluded capture and execution till 1417. The Lollard rising evoked no general sympathy. Its firm suppression enhanced the new king's reputation. His father had belonged to a generation which received daring religious criticism and speculation with a measure of tolerant approval. But by the time Henry was growing up, the new heresies had been clearly defined and absolutely condemned, and as prince he had displayed an uncomprehending horror of heresy.

But in July 1415, while magnates and their military retinues moved into and around Southampton in preparation for the king's expedition to France, the young Edmund Mortimer, earl of March, whose claim to the throne had been canvassed against Henry IV, and whom the new king had granted livery of his estates, confessed that Richard of Conisborough, whom Henry V had created earl of Cambridge in 1414, was plotting to put March on the throne. Cambridge, York's younger brother, whose first wife had been March's sister, was condemned for treason by a commission of his peers: also executed were Henry lord Scrope of Masham, a trusted friend of the king, and Sir Thomas Grey. Why the hitherto insignificant Cambridge intended to betray his royal benefactor is a mystery. But he may have been influenced by a north-country coterie who hoped to revive in some form the old alliances of Mortimer, Percy, Glyn Dŵr and Douglas.

Hotspur's son Henry Percy, in Scottish exile, was now of age to receive the forfeited earldom of Northumberland. In November 1414, he had petitioned parliament to be restored to his estates: the most powerful family in the North, the Nevilles, may have shown an interest in patronising the young man. But Cambridge does not seem to have wanted Percy's reconciliation with Lancaster and Neville. He was pleased when, in the summer of 1415, the Scottish regent Albany's son Murdoch, whom Henry V had agreed to ransom, was mysteriously abducted in Yorkshire, while on his way to Scotland. Cambridge wished to patronise young Percy by effecting his exchange. Northerners may have incited this aim. Cambridge was related by marriage to the Percies and Cliffords. Scrope, nephew of the archbishop executed in 1405, was the husband of Cambridge's stepmother. Grey's son had married Cambridge's daughter. As lord of the exposed castle of Wark on the Tweed, Grey would have doubtless welcomed a revival of Percy influence. It was hoped that other leading Northumbrian gentry would share such feelings: there were attempts to draw John Widdrington and the captain of Roxburgh, Sir Robert Umfraville, into the plot. But it was to be Henry V who effected Percy's restoration in the 1416 parliament. The new earl completely rejected the tradition of treason: he was to die fighting in defence of Henry's son in 1455. Henry showed his trust in March, too, despite his treasonable involvement. March (d. 1425) repaid this by behaving impeccably during the minority of Henry's son. The heads of other magnate families who had opposed Henry V's father – Montagues, Holands, Mowbrays – were converted by him into steadfast Lancastrians.

The personal impact Henry made is reflected in the assertion by several lords present around his deathbed that, overcome with grief, they were unable to remember all of his instructions. His brother Humphrey of Gloucester years after his death harped on his political aims. He commissioned the poet and orator Tito Livio Frulovisi to write the king's biography (1438)[7], the first account of an Englishman fit to be compared in style with classical panegyrics of Roman emperors. By then Gloucester and other gentlefolk who had served their military apprenticeship in Henry's wars may have wistfully recalled, through the tarnish of disillusion, their gilded youth, when the king of Scots had been in their master's train, the duke of Orleans, now a middle-aged romancer in their midst, had been a prize of Agincourt, when they had cut a swathe through the demoralised Norman garrisons, and when the fickle and magnificent 'great duke of the west', Philip of Burgundy, had been an uncertain, tearful youth looking to Henry's guidance (see pp. 246–7).

Henry dominated the community of the realm with almost as much ease as he did his magnates. In the period 1413–17 the Commons granted six subsidies, apparently with little demur, whereas his father had received only eight, with much grudging, during the whole of his reign. When parliament met in November 1415, a week after news arrived of the astonishing victory at Agincourt, in the briefest session since Edward III's reign, the Commons agreed to the grant of generous subsidies and (for the king's life, from Michaelmas 1416) the wool subsidy and tunnage and poundage. There was only one precedent for the life grant – the wool subsidy extracted by Richard II in 1398 from a cowed parliament (cf. p. 119 n. 50). Henry's innate sense of majesty and his masterfulness might have been admired by Richard, who had cherished and knighted him. But Henry was more politic than his mentor – he had been a sad witness of the débâcle of kingship in 1399, and was careful not to infringe subjects' susceptibilities by the manner of his exactions.

Despite Henry's absorption in French affairs, he was not seriously troubled (as English medieval kings often were in such circumstances) by Scots threats to northern England. His absences certainly helped to magnify breaches of truce, but the vigorous leadership of Umfraville and the Percy restoration sufficed to cope. In 1415 the earl of Douglas burnt Penrith, but the English retaliated on Dumfries. In 1417 there was a major Scots effort: Douglas besieged Roxburgh and Albany besieged Berwick, but this 'Foul Raid' was a dismal failure. The English then raided Liddesdale and Teviotdale, and burnt Hawick, Selkirk and Jedburgh. In 1419 William Haliburton failed to consolidate his capture of Wark. Douglas, most likely to rally the Borderers in aggressive raids, may have found his authority weakened as a result of his past absorption in English affairs, and disputes with the Dunbars. It is perhaps significant that Scottish attentions were now directed to the pickings of soldiering in France rather than northern England. The earl of Douglas's son Archibald took part in the expedition which sailed to support the dauphin against Henry V in 1419, and in 1421 the earl himself contracted to aid Henry and his prisoner James I of Scotland.

There were limits to the community's willingness to finance Henry's overseas campaigns: now more than ever before they had reason to hope for a speedy final victory. In the parliament which met in October 1419 it was stipulated that subsidy was granted for defence purposes alone. The Commons insisted that they were not committing themselves to support future wars in France and Normandy. Partly to meet the emergency caused by the Scots victory at Baugé, Henry toured England from March to May 1421 raising £38,000, mainly from the gentry. But this expedient could not be repeated without loss of dignity and popularity. Henry may have hoped that future French campaigns could be financed from his resources in France. His policies of alliance, raid, conquest, and marriage treaty there may have been phases of a bold but calculated gamble to vindicate the rights of his family, to win the loyalty of magnates, and to end the need for high expenditure on defence of the realm and its overseas appendages, which had been a principal cause of friction between Crown and community.

It is arguable that Henry recklessly staked the future of his dynasty in England on intervention in the dangerous whirlpools of French politics. In the humanist view, great men were those who, invoking God's aid, and using to the full their exceptional abilities, plunged into the flood and braved hazards for worthy aims. By such criteria Henry was a great king. However specious, even reprehensible, some of his aims may now be judged, marks of that greatness survive, in the imprint of his personality, in his ability to create politically, rather than just reacting to situations, and in the speed with which he resolved some major problems, notably the widespread lack of loyal feeling towards his family. It was his tragedy that neither he nor some of his ablest lieutenants in France lived long enough to deal with all the challenges thrown up by his successes there. His conquests reaffirmed, for better or worse, the secular, military, imperialist ethos which had moulded English kingship in the previous century. As an inscription on his tomb at Westminster proclaimed, *Dux Normannorum verus conquestor eorum – heres Francorum decessit et Hector eorum* ('He died the rightful duke and conqueror of the Normans – the heir to the kingdom of the French and their Hector').

Henry VI's minority and first decade of rule (1422–49)

Henry V died near Paris in August 1422, leaving a son of nine months, Henry of Windsor, as his heir. In the parliament which met in November 1422, the infant's younger uncle, Humphrey duke of Gloucester, desired, as the Lords recalled to him in 1428, 'the governance of this land, affirming that it belonged unto you of right, as well by the means of your birth, as by the last will of the king that was'. But his fellow peers rejected the claim. Gloucester was appointed chief councillor, during the anticipated absences of his elder brother John duke of Bedford in France. The Lords reminded Gloucester in 1428 that in 1422 they had devised him 'a name different from other councillors, not the name of tutor, lieutenant, governor, nor of regent, nor no name that should import authority of governance of the land, but the name of protector and defensor, the which importeth a personal duty of attendance to the actual defence of the land'.

In 1427 the Council defined the execution of royal authority during the minority as belonging to the lords spiritual and temporal, when assembled in parliaments and great councils, and at other times 'unto the lords chosen and named to be of his continual Council'. The councillors, chiefly bishops and earls, had laid down their conditions of service in the 1422 parliament, which were assented by the Lords and inspected by the Commons. These provisions and the supplementary ones approved in the 1423 parliament show the concern of councillors to ensure the efficient and impartial dispatch of business, and the maintenance of collective responsibility in dealing with petitions and the distribution of patronage. Special deference was to be paid to the advice of Bedford or Gloucester as chief councillor, but the powers the protector could exercise on his own authority were severely limited. The protectorship was formally terminated by Henry's coronation in 1429, but his minority continued till 1437.

Knowledge of politics in the minority and early years of his personal rule is handicapped by the paucity of literary evidence, though conciliar and other kinds of record evidence are plentiful. Cultural developments were hastening the decline of monastic chronicle-writing. Thomas Walsingham, the last monk to write up national events in detail throughout his career, died *c.* 1422. Monks were less inclined to practise assiduously an old-fashioned, Latin *genre* when literate laymen were turning to the composition as well as collection of vernacular chronicles more attuned to secular interests (cf. p. 50). London chronicles of this period are rarely more than vaguely informative about high politics. They circulated in the middling ranks of society, who were not generally well informed about doings at Court, nor always interested. Moreover, the writers had not yet evolved a sophisticated, analytical method of composition.

The conciliar system of government laid down in 1422–3 was remarkably durable in the minority. Lay and clerical councillors had proved their ability to work in a mutual enterprise through their military and administrative services in Henry V's wars. They now showed concern to preserve collective responsibility, and awareness of the need to administer justice and placate landed interests. Some magnates, preoccupied with consolidating offices and titles in France, may have been halfhearted in backing factiousness either in Council or their regional spheres of influence. Bedford's successes in France staved off the need for a high level of war subsidies, so not provoking the Commons to agitate about conciliar personnel and powers. A crucial role in financing government was played by the king's great-uncle, Henry Beaufort, bishop of Winchester (created cardinal in 1426). The first of his great loans to Henry VI was contracted with the Council in 1424: he lent 14,000 marks, with repayment partly assigned on the customs, one of the surest sources of royal revenue, with an option, if repayments flagged, on the king's jewels. Beaufort's royal blood and shrewd management and investment of the resources of his richly endowed see were not the only bases of the influence on royal policy he tried to maintain till his death in 1447. He was respected for his long political experience. After the death of his elder brother, John earl of Somerset in 1410, he was the senior member of the Beaufort family, extremely well connected in the peerage by kinship and marriage. But the cardinal did not have a brood of close relations whose promotion might have created factious tensions in the 1420s. His nephew John earl of Somerset, captured at Baugé in 1421, was not released till 1438. Edmund, John's brother, had his main early territorial interest in France, where he received the *comté* of Mortain in 1427.

For twenty or so years, Gloucester was to attack Beaufort's influence. The duke resented Beaufort's opposition to the enlargement of his powers as protector and, later, the deference paid to him by the young Henry. Gloucester repeatedly elaborated and refined the theme that his uncle had been a disloyal and grasping force in politics since Henry IV's time, always prepared to put first personal gain and ecclesiastical allegiance, and to flout the guidelines of national policy laid down by Henry V. The duke's views had a certain popular appeal. The cardinal was thought to be unsympathetic to merchants' grievances against their Flemish rivals. His involvement from the mid-1430s in attempts to make a peaceful settlement with Charles of Valois may have disquieted the militant. But in governing circles the duke's accusations cut remarkably little ice. His agitation over his constitutional powers, his liking for popular acclaim and his self-interested foreign adventures may have swelled Beaufort's support. Nevertheless, the latter's acceptance of the cardinalate gave him a useful issue for attack. Councillors were worried that Beaufort, who aspired to a role in the ecclesiastical politics of Christendom, might use his legatine authority in derogation of the statutory rights claimed by the Crown over the administration of the English Church.

Humphrey of Gloucester, born in 1390, was the youngest of Henry IV's sons. In May 1414 he was created earl of Pembroke and duke of Gloucester. Having fought gallantly in France, he was appointed regent of England during Henry V's absence in May 1422. Duke Humphrey is perhaps, in modern eyes, a more appealing figure than his self-righteous, competent brothers. He was a well-intentioned man whose human frailty was transparent, but whose intellectual interests were sublime. His literary patronage ranged far beyond his brothers'. He was the first English prince to patronise humanism, commissioning Italian *literati* to translate Greek texts into Latin and giving the university of Oxford in 1437 and 1444 a total of 263 books, including some classical texts. A few books from the ducal library still exist, such as a translation of Books 1 to 5 of Plato's *Republic* by Piercandido Decembrio, sent to the duke, written in his own hand, in 1438[8]. Decembrio wrote marginal notes, two specifically calling his patron's attention to passages. Humphrey's classical enthusiasms are reflected in the name he gave to his illegitimate daughter – Antigone – and in the classical *memento mori*, 'gardens of Adonis' carved on his otherwise conventional chantry chapel in St Albans Abbey.

Duke Humphrey's political career suggests that he was far from being an exponent of what has been termed 'Renaissance statecraft'. His forcefulness and verve sometimes made him a formidable opponent, but shrewder, cooler men eventually outmatched him. Whereas Beaufort was a financial asset to the Crown, he was a liability. He made damaging marriages to unprofitable, pretty, dangerous women. To aid his first wife, Jacqueline of Hainault, he led an expedition in 1424 which brought him into conflict with Burgundy, consequently infuriating Bedford, and necessitated a royal loan of 20,000 marks to him in 1425 for its expenses (cf. p. 250). In 1428, to the indignation of London market women (doubtless amusing to his 'gentle' opponents), he deserted Jacqueline for her lady, Eleanor Cobham. She was to bring shame on her husband by her condemnation for witchcraft in 1441.

Luckily for the realm, the duke's words were invariably more violent than his deeds: he was intensely loyal to his eventually unappreciative nephew, and unwilling to challenge political reverses by trial of arms. His basic self-control accounts for the muted character of the minority crises he provoked. Such restraint (his one political virtue) goes some way to justifying the inflated popular reputation he gained as 'Good Duke Humphrey'.

The first Gloucester-Beaufort crisis flared in 1424. There was unrest in London over the issue of alien merchants. The protector felt affronted when the Council, advised by Beaufort, ordered Bedford's chamberlain Richard Wydeville to occupy the Tower. The bishop remained nervous that Gloucester, backed by the Londoners, would try to seize control of government. In 1425 he brought to his episcopal inn at Southwark a force of armed retainers who, according to a London chronicler, 'made ready for battle and barricaded windows and set up casks as if it had been in a land of war, as though they would have fought against the king's people and breaking of the peace'. Gloucester insinuated to leading citizens that his uncle intended to invade the city and seize the infant king, then at Eltham. On news of the bishop's men's warlike proceedings, mayor and aldermen called out the Londoners to man the bridge; 'all the shops in London were shut in one hour'. But violence was averted by the strenuous mediation of Archbishop Chichele and of a visiting Portuguese kinsman of the king, the duke of Coimbra. The fact that peace was preserved on this occasion (and in the following months) makes it one of the most remarkable incidents in fifteenth-century English history.

In February 1426 a parliament met far removed from London, at the Lancastrian town of Leicester. One of its purposes was to hear the charges, amounting to treason, which the protector had now made against his uncle. Bedford had come from France to deal with the grave family crisis. A commission of peers refused to convict Beaufort and instead insisted that Gloucester should publicly clasp his hand. Beaufort, as a man of peace with more universal interests, consented to a diminution of his English standing by resigning the Chancellorship and going abroad. After his return in 1428 he endured attacks by Gloucester for several years. The latter tried to get him excluded from the Council, ousted from his bishopric and condemned for alleged offences. He had a very limited success. In 1440 he outlined the cardinal's misdeeds over thirty or so years to the young king, pleading 'Please it to your highness . . . to estrange them [the cardinal and Archbishop Kemp of York] of your counsel, to that intent that men may be at their freedom to say what they think; for though I dare speak of my truth, the poor do not dare so.' Henry was unimpressed: he reverenced both ecclesiastics. The duke was no longer faced by fellow-peers who tolerated his diatribes, but by royal servants suspicious of his criticisms, and a royal master who may have been implacably hostile.

In Yorkist historiography Henry VI was to be projected as a misled simpleton: the Tudor defence of his reputation relied on his posthumous reputation as a saint. Modern historians have sometimes written him down as mentally unstable: the principal contemporary evidence for this concerns some sort of breakdown he experienced for some months in 1453–4. But despite the disasters which were to overwhelm Henry there is reason to believe he was still capable of lucidity. In 1458 and 1460–1 he was concerned with the difficult problem of finding a suitable site for his tomb in Westminster Abbey. Many years later witnesses testified about his visits to the abbey, relating behaviour characteristic of regal state and determination. On one occasion he prayed for over an hour at St Edward's shrine, consulted with the abbot, leant on his companion Sir Richard Tunstall's shoulder, and measured out the length of seven feet with his own feet. When a prisoner in the Tower (1465–70) he discoursed with visitors rationally.

Henry had had a carefully supervised upbringing. In 1428, when he was six, the Council appointed the chivalrous Richard Beauchamp, earl of Warwick (d.1439)[9], as his governor, to replace the deceased duke of Exeter. The earl was charged to teach Henry to worship and fear God, to tell him about past instances of grace and prosperity befalling virtuous kings and their subjects, and of calamities experienced by the unrighteous. He was to have the boy instructed in letters, languages, good manners and other things 'it fitteth so great a prince to be learned of', and to chastise him when he misbehaved. At that age, according to Archbishop Kemp, Henry could already recite liturgies. But in 1432, when he was eleven, Warwick was worried about his waywardness. He informed the Council that Henry had grown in stature and in 'conceit and knowledge of his high and royal authority and estate'; he was coming to resent the earl's chastisement of his faults and to mix with companions who distracted him from his lessons and conversed on unsuitable topics.

He was not unsusceptible to feminine attractions. When a bride was being sought for him in 1442, the painter Hans was instructed to portray the count of Armagnac's daughters for the king to make his choice, 'in their kirtles simple, and their faces, like as you see their stature and their beauty and colour of skin and their countenances, with all manner of features'. When his eventual bride Margaret of Anjou landed in England in 1445, he is alleged to have greeted her in disguise – a gallant fancy. Well-authenticated stories of Henry's reactions to nudity and femininity suggest that he may have been fearful of not mastering his desires. When a lord presented him with a Christmas entertainment in which ladies were to dance with bare bosoms, 'perhaps to prove him, or entice his youthful mind', Henry stormed out of the chamber, and he persecuted his servants by spying on them through peepholes, 'lest any foolish importunity of women coming into his house should grow to a head, and cause the fall of any of his household'. Such concern stemmed from a discipline nourished by moralising and contemplative literature, which enhanced in other sensitive fifteenth-century layfolk a desire to free themselves from the weight of sin, and achieve a sense of rapt union with Christ. The requisite schooling of feeling and desire might be hindered by marital obligations. In the *Incendium Amoris* (cf. p. 357), the fourteenth-century hermit Richard Rolle[10] had written 'he who looks at a woman with natural affection yet not with lustful desire finds he is unable to keep free from illicit urges or unclean thoughts. Often enough he feels in himself the stain of filth and even may take pleasure in the thought of developing it.' It is curious that Henry's wife, in a period when married women normally conceived annually, is only once known to have been pregnant in over twenty years of marriage, though she was a robust and attractive woman. Henry had his breakdown during the pregnancy, looked without emotion at the baby and, several years later, concurred in its disinheritance. Perhaps the conflicting attractions of spiritual fulfilment and marriage placed strains on Henry's temperament: he may have been, like Rolle, a man of strong physical desires happier away from female company. But Henry was obliged by his office to lead an active as well as a contemplative life. He may have been aware of Rolle's challenging, hard words on the subject: 'If any man could achieve both lives at once, the contemplative and the active, and sustain and fulfil them, he would be great indeed. . . . I do not know if anybody has ever done this: it seems to me impossible to do both at once.'

Henry's biographer Blacman relates how the king, disturbed in their mutal study of holy books at Eltham, exclaimed against the interruptions of business. Sir Thomas More's biographers were to attribute to him a similar exasperation with the duties of office. In fact More seems to have reconciled the active and contemplative lives more happily than Henry. But then he had better-controlled emotions, he was schooled by the need to earn a living and make a career, and he was infinitely better equipped intellectually to resolve emotional dilemmas. Sir Thomas, until reconciled to martyrdom, exercised a highly developed political sense. Henry, with regal disdain, never attempted to acquire any – and may have been happiest as a prisoner, free to concentrate on his soul's wellbeing.

Henry's simplistic, almost nonchalant, attitude towards ruling was exceptional. Even the youthful Henry VIII, equally absorbed in private pleasures (albeit of a different sort), showed an awareness that he could not automatically expect to be obeyed. Henry VI's attitude may have been influenced by his regal upbringing and the political circumstances of his minority. Warwick informed the Council in 1432 (soon after the king's French visit) that the boy had gained a good conceit of his authority. When, in 1437, he was declared of age, he started to use that authority wilfully. He alarmed his councillors by his prodigality with gifts. From about 1440 he alienated Crown lands to principal members of his Household at an unprecedented rate. Impatient with business, he tended to delegate to an inner group of councillors, a coterie of Household officials. These youthful ruling habits set into inflexible routines. The hallmarks of Henry's adult rule were excessive generosity, and tenacious partiality to trusted familiars. This produced more general, sustained resentment against particular courtiers than was usual, and a deterioration in the Crown's will and ability to arbitrate and resolve local landowning tensions, which became exceptionally tangled with Court faction.

During the lengthy minority, royal authority and the realm's tranquillity were unusually secure. The Border counties, for instance, no longer endured Scottish raiding on the scale of the 1380s. Lords of opposing allegiance (often now more preoccupied with French or domestic affairs) inclined to respect each other's *de facto* sphere of influence. So did the two Crowns, collaborating in setting up complex truce mechanisms. Charles VII was more successful in attracting Scots to attack the English in France than on the Borders, though his Scottish diplomacy gave English councillors anxious moments. James I, who had been released from English captivity in 1423, and married Bishop Beaufort's niece Joan in 1424, reversed his policy of truces by attacking Roxburgh in 1436. His murder and the succession of the minor James II in 1437 led to renewed truces. In 1448–9 an old-fashioned war of Border lords briefly flared, possibly forced on them by lesser men's depredations and encroachments, especially where, as in parts of the West March, the frontier was ill-defined.

The events of Henry's minority do not seem to have imbued him with any sense of a need to uphold and assert royal authority by confounding domestic critics and foreign adversaries. Though he revered the memory of his bellicose father, and was encouraged by Warwick to learn swordplay, he showed no interest in fighting in France or in encouraging Gloucester's proffers to do so for him. More congenial were the pacific policies advocated by Beaufort. Henry pinned his hopes on making peace with his uncle Charles VII. He did not (except in the treatment of Gloucester) attempt to forestall opposition. Probably he failed to anticipate difficulties, either with the French adversaries or his own magnates and other lieges. He expected the latter to behave in the same obedient fashion as they had in the minority. Yet the older generations of lords, companions and servants of Henry V, were passing away. Salisbury died in 1428, Bedford in 1435, Warwick in 1439, Chichele in 1443, Gloucester and Beaufort in 1447, Kemp in 1452.

The circumstances of Gloucester's death revealed the ruthlessness of some councillors whom Henry and his French bride trusted. During the 1447 parliament, at Bury St Edmunds, Gloucester and members of his household were unexpectedly arrested and charged with treason. A few days later, in that bleak February, 'Good Duke Humphrey' died in his lodgings. So the evidence probably intended to demonstrate that he was plotting to usurp the Crown remains a mystery.

It is not clear who was primarily responsible for devising the duke's ruin. A likely candidate is William de la Pole, marquess of Suffolk (grandson of Richard II's unfortunate Chancellor), in whose local sphere of influence parliament met. Suffolk had made a career and lost a fortune in France. He had, he said, 'continually abode in the war seventeen years without coming home or seeing of this land'. He had been captured in 1429, and paid £20,000 in ransom. After 1430 he concentrated on being earl of Suffolk rather than count of Dreux. His personality helped him to win friends. He was courtly, literary-minded, ostentatiously devout. The churches he rebuilt grandly at Wingfield and Ewelme, and the almshouse and schoolhouse he founded at Ewelme, testify to his piety and success. His notably grasping, imperious exploitation of the influence he quickly built up at Court and in East Anglia may have reflected an outlook induced by his French background, an awareness that his English interests had been neglected, a remembrance of bereavements, privations and losses endured in the king's service, an admiration for the more rigid authority enjoyed by French Crown and *noblesse*.

Suffolk entered the inner circle of Lancastrian kin by marriage to the recently widowed niece of Cardinal Beaufort, Alice countess of Salisbury (Thomas Chaucer's daughter). Suffolk's political standing at Court may have been enhanced by his friendships with pro-Valois French nobles, as well as his general knowledge of French affairs. In 1431 he was appointed councillor, in 1433 Steward of the Household. Royal rewards were lavished on him after Henry came of age, especially when, in the 1440s, he played a key role in Anglo-French negotiations and the king's marriage[11]. The grant to him in reversion (1443) of the childless Gloucester's earldom of Pembroke may have fuelled enmity between them.

Some gentlefolk and townspeople in Norfolk seem to have resented Suffolk's maintenance of his clients' interests and evasion of customs duties on wool and other exports. But magnates do not seem to have been generally opposed to his role in royal policy and the exceptional scale of his rewards. He had taken on the thankless task of putting Anglo-French relations on a new basis. He seemed admirably suited to influence a young king and receive commensurate rewards. Richard II's favourite, Oxford, had been young, unproven, feckless, heir to a relatively undistinguished comital family. Suffolk was a mature, gallant knight, who had enhanced his family's notable record of service to the Lancastrians. Moreover, other nobles were profiting from Henry's generosity; Suffolk was not attempting to monopolise royal favour, and apparently enjoyed good relations with most of the king's close kinsmen. For instance, John Beaufort (d.1444) and his brother Edmund, the cardinal's nephews, advanced in royal favour at the same time as Suffolk: they were respectively created earls of Kendal and Dorset in 1438, and John was created duke of Somerset in 1443.

Suffolk may have enjoyed intimate relations with Henry and the bride he escorted to him in 1445. The king gave the duke's little son John the armour inlaid with gold which he had worn as a boy in France in 1430. Anne Beauchamp, who died aged five at Ewelme in 1449, had been transferred from the queen's to the duke's custody, and he had intended to marry her to John. Anne was the only daughter of the king's namesake and near-contemporary Henry Beauchamp, created duke of Warwick in 1445, a little over a year before dying. Henry may have intended Suffolk's son to hold the lands of two duchies, one the inheritance of the Beauchamps, a family which meant much to him in his youth. If Suffolk's relationship with the royal couple was paternal, he was well placed to moderate Henry's prodigality and to teach him how royal justice should be enforced. Such courses would not have suited Suffolk's predilection for gain and for genial relationships at Court. Maybe the sailors who lynched him in 1450 had a true instinct. Better placed than anyone to make Henry a respected king (as Wolsey was to make Henry VIII), he had shown neither the will nor the ability.

Notes

1. Though the community had no right to refuse assent to aid on a royal plea of necessity in defence of king and realm, in February 1340 the Commons took a novel initiative by making a large grant of woolsacks conditional on royal adherence to conditions stipulated in the indenture (in addition to an immediate, unconditional levy).
2. The ruins of the fine castle Sir Thomas built at Farleigh Hungerford (Somerset) contain his chantry chapel and tomb, with effigies of himself and his wife.
3. A reminder of Alice Perrers's jewel collection may exist in the church of Kingston-upon-Thames (Surrey), on the brass of one of her daughters, Joan Skerne (possibly Edward's daughter). The cord of Joan's mantle is secured by two highly ornamented brooches and round her neck is a chain with a similar brooch pendant.
4. Thomas de la Mare's brass is in St Albans Cathedral, one of the largest and finest ecclesiastical brasses in England.
5. According to Richard II's 1385 ordinances of war, the penalty for those who raised or joined in the cry of havoc was execution.
6. His effigy can be seen over the fine Erpingham Gate (1420) in the precinct wall of Norwich Cathedral.
7. The dedication copy, probably in Frulovisi's hand, is in the possession of Corpus Christi College, Cambridge.
8. British Library, MS. Harley 1705.
9. His posthumously made bronze effigy, the finest surviving English medieval attempt at portrait sculpture, is in his impressive chantry chapel in Warwick Church.
10. Henry is likely to have been familiar with the works of Rolle and other contemplatives. His chaplain and biographer, the Carthusian John Blacman (whose anecdotes about Henry are used above), had the finest library of contemplative literature in England.
11. Suffolk's earldom was advanced to a marquessate in 1444, a duchy in 1448. These were some of his offices: steward of the north parts of the duchy of Lancaster (1437), Chief Justice of south Wales (1438–40), Chamberlain of the Realm for life, Constable of Dover Castle and Warden of the Cinque Ports, joint steward of the south parts of the duchy of Lancaster, Admiral of England during the duke of Exeter's minority (1447), governor and protector of the Staple at Calais (1448).

Chapter 5

The Hundred Years War, 1337–1453

The origins of the war

The Hundred Years War was in origin a conflict between the conflicting claims which the kings of England and France put forward in support of their competitive and overlapping attempts at state-building. During the course of the war some of their respective subjects came to think of it as a struggle between Englishmen and Frenchmen for mastery, independence or wealth. But the principal issues publicly at stake concerned the jurisdiction and authority of the two Crowns. The issues were in some respects seen and presented by kings as personal ones. Edward III proposed that Philip VI should test his right to the French Crown by walking into a cage of lions and by attempting to heal scrofula; Richard II proposed to Charles VI of France that they should settle their claims by a duel. These expedients, not surprisingly rejected by the Valois kings, were intended as appeals to the judgment of God, which would not lead to breaches in the fragile peace of Christendom and to the lavish effusion of Christian blood. Instead, the kings of England had to pursue their aims by warfare: it became necessary for them to present the quarrel as one involving the interests of their subjects: the adversary of France, they publicly proclaimed, threatened the lives, goods and language of their English lieges.

From the last two decades of the thirteenth century onwards, during the reigns of Philip IV of France (1285–1314) and Edward I of England (1272–1307), a number of connected problems exacerbated relations between the two Crowns. Some of these concerned the great duchy of Aquitaine, whose provinces covered south-west France. The kings of England claimed the duchy by virtue of their descent from Henry II's queen, Eleanor of Aquitaine (d.1204). By the treaty of Paris (1259) her grandson Henry III had abandoned most of his other territorial claims in France – to the duchy of Normandy and the counties of Anjou, Maine, Touraine and Poitou. In return Louis IX of France (St Louis) recognised Henry's existing lordship in Aquitaine, though he in fact held only a few coastal fragments of the duchy (principally Gascony). Louis conditionally granted Henry some other parts of Aquitaine. The latter agreed that he and his successors would hold this truncated duchy and other lordships which he possessed in France by performance of 'liege homage' to the kings of France. This form of feudal investiture implied that the vassal, once he had performed the ceremony, owed unswerving loyalty and obedience to his overlord, being prepared to submit to his jurisdiction and to bring aid against his enemies, never behaving in ways which the overlord considered damaging to his interests.

The treaty of Paris created a delicate relationship between the two Crowns, increasingly fraught with difficulties, as both by the later thirteenth century were attempting to rule in accordance with a concept of total 'sovereignty'. Since the time when twelfth-century kings of England had performed less binding 'simple homage' to kings of France for their French possessions, Crown lawyers in western Christendom had been defining more stringently the obligations owed by vassals to their royal tenants-in-chief. Philip IV's lawyers received his sanction to summon the English Crown's lieges and officials from

Fig. 7 France and its neighbouring principalities in the later Middle Ages.

Gascony to answer plaintiffs who had appealed against them to his council or to the *parlement* of Paris[1]. In a series of Anglo-French 'processes' (conferences), the French kings' representatives argued that, since the king of England, in his capacity as duke of Aquitaine, was their sovereign's vassal, on their master's behalf they alone should be empowered to adjudicate all outstanding disputes, for example, the conditions on which certain territorial concessions made to Henry III in 1259 should be fulfilled; English complaints of the French Crown's interventions in the affairs of Gascony, and even matters unconnected with the English kings' possessions in France, such as claims arising from piracy in the Channel. English representatives could not agree to remit the decision on their masters' affairs to their French colleagues. The king of England was a sovereign too, attempting to tighten his administrative control over Gascony as an appurtenance of his Crown.

Breakdowns in negotiation led French kings to treat Edward I and II as disobedient vassals. In 1294 Philip IV confiscated the duchy of Aquitaine, restoring it to Edward I only when peace was made in 1303. In 1324 Philip's son Charles IV once more confiscated the duchy, never restoring it in entirety to Edward II or his son, though peace was concluded in 1327. The French Crown was tending to use its feudal superiority over the kings of England as a means of controlling their policies. Such pressure was bound to rankle with rulers who were proud and wilful descendants of the domineering Angevin dynasty. The kings of England regarded themselves, and were regarded by their nobles, as sovereign heirs of an 'imperial' power which had dominated Gaul and Rome, the doughty Britons under the leadership of King Arthur. Why then did English kings prefer diplomacy to war as a means, albeit unsuccessful, of countering French pressure? A determining factor in Anglo-French relations in the late thirteenth and early fourteenth centuries was probably the notorious trouble which Angevin kings had in ruling their English subjects, to which Edward I added the difficult tasks of subduing the Welsh and Scots. Edward III was eventually to alter the direction of many threads in English royal policy, by diverting his resources to the primary aim of solving the Anglo-French problem by war.

Edward III (1327–77) was involved from his youth in Anglo-French diplomacy. In 1325, when prince of Wales, he performed homage to Charles IV for the duchy of Aquitaine. Charles died childless in 1328: his cousin Philip of Valois was recognised as his heir and crowned as Philip VI. A claim to the French throne put forward on behalf of Edward III, the son of Philip IV's daughter Isabella, was rejected, and in 1329 Edward performed 'simple homage' to Philip VI. In 1331 he visited the French royal household for the third time, promising that he would perform 'liege homage' for Aquitaine. A conference was arranged to settle outstanding issues. But the 'process of Agen' (1331–4) was a failure, and Anglo-French relations became more tense when Philip VI opposed Edward's Scottish ambitions, extending his protection to the infant David II of Scotland. Hostile gestures culminated in May 1337, when Philip notified his *baillis* and *sénéchaux* that he had confiscated Edward's French possessions, on the grounds that this vassal had received and given aid to Robert of Artois, a 'capital enemy' of Philip, banished from the realm 'for many crimes'.

The early stages of the war: the campaigns of Edward III's reign (1339–75)

Philip VI seems to have based his estimate of Edward's reactions in 1337 on those of his recent predecessors. If so, he proved disastrously wrong. Edward was prepared to jeopardise the success of his current attempt to dominate Scotland, and to risk the security of northern England in his determination to keep Gascony, whose great financial worth to the Crown he probably appreciated. Its principal town, Bordeaux, comparable in size to London, controlled the export of wine from the valleys of the Garonne and Dordogne, and produced vast sums in customs revenue levied on the cargoes of tuns at the mouth of the Gironde. Edward sent reinforcements to Gascony and allied with the king of the Romans, Ludwig duke of Bavaria, who was incensed at the encroachments of French royal jurisdiction within the Holy Roman Empire. Ludwig granted Edward an imperial vicariate in Lower Germany, by virtue of which he summoned and subsidised the military services of princely Rhenish allies. But they were to prove sluggish and lukewarm: more promising was the Anglo-Flemish alliance of 1339. A royal prohibition of the wool export to Flanders (August 1336) had deprived its cloth-working towns (principally Ypres, Ghent and Bruges) of an essential raw material, the finer grades of English wool. This induced them, led by the burgesses of Ghent, to revolt against their pro-French count, Louis of Nevers. In September 1339 Edward advanced from Flanders with his Anglo-German army. The invaders burnt the villages of the Thiérache and Cambrésis, but were unable to take any towns or bring Philip VI to battle. In January 1340 Edward added a new dimension to the war by having himself proclaimed king of France, unilaterally taking his claim a bold step further and legitimising the adherence to his cause of the French Crown's Flemish (and other) lieges.

Count Louis of Nevers and his king challenged Edward's control of Flanders by concentrating a fleet of French, Genoese and Castilian ships within the Zwin estuary off the port of Sluis. Sailing from England, Edward and his noble companions bore down on this fleet and decisively defeated its soldiers (June 1340). One contemporary English chronicler, Geoffrey le Baker, casting his mind back to the absorbing Arthurian past, considered this victory to be a fulfilment of one of the elusive prophecies made by the magician Merlin. In July Edward, with the support of his Flemish and English subjects, invested the city of Tournai. But his financial resources dried up before he could capture it. Papal mediators at last had the limited satisfaction of concluding a short truce between the adversaries in the nearby village of Espléchin (September 1340).

It may seem that Edward had achieved little at great expense. At least he had dangerously threatened the north-east borders of France and had undermined the policy which kings of France had successfully pursued in Flanders over recent decades. Though the seriousness of his assumption of rule over the French realm is open to debate, to him and to contemporaries it may have appeared that his new title gravely threatened 'Philip of Valois's' authority. Provincial nobles and communities, often upset (like the dukes of Aquitaine) by the juridical presumption of the royal council and the *parlement*, now had a justification for ignoring them and the sovereignty they claimed to represent. There existed a rival king of France, who wooed them by talk of his respect for their 'liberties'.

In the 1340s Edward showed resourcefulness in exploiting his title and probing for the weaknesses in his rival's position. On the death of Duke John III of Brittany in 1341, inheritance of the duchy was disputed between Charles of Blois (in right of his wife Joan of Penthièvre) and John count of Montfort (d.1345). John's wife, fearing an adverse decision by the suzerain Philip VI, accepted Edward's aid to secure the duchy for her captive husband, in return for a recognition of his title to the French Crown and suzerainty over the duchy. In 1342 Edward sailed to Brittany with one of the expeditions which helped to establish English garrisons, who received the right to sustain themselves by collecting ducal revenues. Control of such a port as Brest and its hinterland safeguarded sea communications between England and Gascony, threatened French shipping and facilitated the launching of raids into France. During the next three decades, various Breton castles, especially in the south and west of the duchy, were in the hands of English captains, who in the name of John de Montfort's son and heir John (Edward's ward) levied neighbouring villages. Many of the garrisons of the interior, not receiving pay by the hands of the king's or duke's officials, were under the full control of neither. Their presence was resented by Breton lords, and the harsh exactions of some made them unpopular with all sections of the community. The English occupation was to be an important factor in ensuring the Montfort succession. Duke John was to make use of the English connection to counter the Blois claimants and the French Crown, but what he ultimately aimed for (and achieved in the 1380s) was the latter's recognition. The last English garrison in Brittany, at Brest, was withdrawn in 1397, and from then on until the 1460s the Montfort dukes tried, not always successfully, to maintain neutrality in Anglo-French conflicts.

The Breton allegiance added weight to Edward's claim to the French Crown and strengthened his strategic position in France in the 1340s and 1350s, but it did not produce a general collapse of Valois allegiances or intolerable pressure on Philip VI's resources. Further military efforts were needed. Edward failed in 1345 to renew the truce of Malestroit (1343). In a series of brilliant campaigns his lieutenant in Aquitaine, Henry of Grosmont, earl of Derby, rallied the loyalties of lords and towns which had fallen away under strong French pressure. In July 1346 Edward himself landed at Saint Vaast-la-Hougue, in the Cotentin peninsula of Normandy, captured Caen and advanced into the Seine valley, moving from Normandy into 'douce France', where lay principal domains and towns of the French Crown. Before reaching Paris he turned northwards to cross the Seine and the Somme, and was intercepted at Crécy by a much larger army under Philip VI, comprising, besides the French feudal levy, a Genoese mercenary force and one commanded by the blind John of Luxembourg, king of Bohemia, an opponent of Edward's ally Ludwig of Bavaria. The well co-ordinated English defensive tactics, in which dismounted knights and men-at-arms combined with archers to form an infantry force, won the day against cavalry attacks. The outcome was a grave blow to the prestige of French kingship, which since the days of St Louis had been eclipsing popes and emperors. According to Froissart, King Philip rode from the field accompanied by only five lords, lamenting and mourning for his men, until he came to the castle of La Broye:

He found the gate shut and the drawbridge up, for it was now fully night and pitch-black. He called for the captain of the castle, who came to the look-out turret and shouted down: 'Who comes knocking at this hour?' 'Open you gate, captain', King Philip answered. 'It is the unfortunate King of France.'

His defeat had been due above all to the mutual trust and confidence between Edward and his noble commanders, reflected in his decision during the battle to leave the safety of his hard-pressed heir, the prince of Wales, to the latter's companions. Many of the English leaders had been soldiering together under Edward's standard, in Scotland and France, for over ten years. Edward exploited his victory by mounting, with reinforcements from England and Germany, a lengthy siege by land and sea of the Channel port of Calais, in the county of Boulogne. The garrison capitulated, after Philip's failure to relieve it, in August 1347. Valuable as Calais was to prove to the English until its loss in 1558, Edward might more profitably have occupied greater parts of the rich duchy of Normandy, whose defence (as Henry V was to show) did not have to be almost entirely subsidised from English resources, as did that of Calais.

In 1347 the adversaries, financially exhausted, once more made a truce. They were to remain for nearly ten years in a state of diplomatic and military deadlock. The advent of the Black Death (see pp. 15–16) slowed down military activity for a few years. English diplomacy shifted between attempts to make peace, and to consolidate alliances which might gain better terms. In 1346 Louis de Mâle succeeded as count of Flanders. The attempt to ally with him (1348) failed, as did subsequent searches for an anti-French alliance in the Low Countries. In the early 1350s Edward negotiated with the young, personable and ambitious Charles II, king of Navarre, a leading Norman landowner who, like himself, was a grandson of Philip IV. The Valois Philip VI had died in 1350, being succeeded by his energetic and courtly son, John II, whose Scottish and Castilian allies helped to divert further English military efforts. It was vital for John to bring the struggle to a successful end. His was a new dynasty failing to give the French the protection which the Capetians had provided since the tenth century. Mounted forces in Edward's allegiance carried out raids (*chevauchées*) from their castles in Gascony, Brittany, Normandy and Picardy, levying or burning the possessions of the faithful communities, who suffered too from hindrances to trade and from heavy royal war taxation.

These discontents coagulated into an internal crisis of authority for the French Crown, as a result of the capture of John II by the English and Gascons at the battle of Poitiers (September 1356). A raiding force commanded by Edward's lieutenant in Aquitaine, his son the prince of Wales, had been skilfully intercepted by a much larger army under John's command. The prince was prepared to make quite abject conditions in return for passage to Gascony. But the king of France and his kinsmen scented victory in battle. Once again, as at Crécy, the initial advantages enjoyed by the French (supported this time by a Scottish contingent) were lost as a result of tactical clumsiness in face of a desperate, well co-ordinated defence. The prince's army trailed back to Bordeaux, replete with royal prisoners and spoils.

During King John's captivity in England his youthful, untried son, Charles duke of Normandy (the future Charles V) acted as lieutenant, then regent of the realm. He concluded a truce with the triumphant Edward III in 1357. His rule was all but submerged by the crisis of authority. The Crown was violently criticised in meetings of the Estates of Languedoil (northern France) in Paris (1356–8). Charles of Navarre patronised the Estates and the Parisian rebels who restricted the regent's authority. In 1358 the Jacquerie broke out, a series of abominably savage assaults on the *noblesse* by peasant bands: from Normandy to Champagne, regions of northern France were affected. The regent and his political opponents united in pitiless efforts to suppress a rebellion which seemed to contemporaries an alarming threat to social order.

However, none of those disillusioned with Valois rule turned to Edward III for succour. His habitual military methods, with their emphasis on destructive raids and reliance partially on garrisons whose pay he did not control, probably alienated inclinations to succumb to his propaganda and accept him as king. Edward now pinned his hopes of an advantageous peace on negotiations for the release of King John. The second of the 'ransom treaties' which he made with John in 1358–9 was unacceptable to the Estates, because he had demanded so much territory in full sovereignty and such a monstrously large sum of money. Edward prepared to lead an army once more to France, in an attempt to impose his terms on the divided and leaderless realm. In October 1359 he crossed to Calais with a large force. Marching south-east towards Champagne, he fruitlessly besieged Reims, ransomed Burgundy and reconnoitred Paris from the south. Searching for fresh supplies, the English retreated south-west to the plains of Beauce. Edward's army was reduced to dire straits by its inability to capture towns, to which the regent had victuals rigorously removed. In May 1360 the opponents ratified a truce and preliminary agreements for a peace conference, at the village of Brétigny near Chartres. The parties agreed by the treaty of Calais (October 1360) that by October 1362 John II and his son the regent would transfer to Edward, his heirs and successors, all the Crown's sovereign rights in perpetuity in a large part of Aquitaine, in Ponthieu, Calais and neighbouring lordships, and Guines. In return for the long-sought prize of sovereign jurisdiction, Edward and his son Prince Edward were to renounce 'the claim to the name and right of the crown and kingdom of France', and the sovereign rule which Edward had been exercising in parts of Brittany, Normandy and Flanders. He was to receive a ransom of three million crowns for the release of King John, with whom a firm alliance and friendship was to be established.

The treaty proved only a temporary and unstable basis for peace. The mutual renunciations of sovereignty were never made. The treaty did not reflect a permanent balance of power between the two Crowns, but a temporary imbalance caused by the recent difficulties which the French Crown had experienced in exploiting the resources of its customarily faithful vassals. Moreover, Edward conceded some of his gains in northern France (where Henry V, a better strategist, was to concentrate his efforts), for chimerical cessions in more distant regions south of the Loire. In the early 1360s the prince of Wales, as lieutenant in Aquitaine, largely failed to cement allegiances in newly acquired lordships, whose communities had in the past trembled at his vicious raids, and did not wish to sever their ancient connection with the prince of the lilies, the line of St Louis. For a number of years the prince was unable to rid them from the burden of levies raised by garrisons which had been upholding English allegiance before the treaty, and were reluctant to give up their castles. When he did take many of them into his pay, in order to protect Aquitaine from Franco-Aragonese menaces by intervening in the Castilian civil war (1367)[2], it was only at the cost of heavy taxation. Moreover, the prince failed to reconcile the *noblesse* to his rule. He was familiar with Gascon and English veterans, but acquired the general reputation of being a haughty and distant ruler.

While the prince embroiled himself in the expensive Castilian fiasco, ruining his health in the process, Charles duke of Normandy, who had succeeded his father as Charles V in 1364, avoided rash commitments, and concentrated on restoring royal prestige and strengthening the Crown's judicial, financial and military resources. In 1368 he allowed the *parlement* of Paris to accept an appeal by two Gascon lords against the prince's imposition of a hearth tax, thus implying a denial of Edward's sovereignty in Aquitaine. The prince angrily refused a summons to appear before the *parlement*. In June 1369, with the agreement of the prelates, magnates and commons of the shires of England assembled in parliament, Edward resumed the name of king of England and France. In November Charles formally confiscated his French lands as a contumacious vassal. Small English garrisons, lacking local support, speedily capitulated to advancing armies. The dispatch of forces to Calais in 1369, 1370 and 1373 kept the French on the defensive in the north, and may have slowed up their southern operations. One small force, sent by sea in June 1372, was completely defeated off La Rochelle in an action with Castilian galleys. One of the prisoners was the lieutenant in Aquitaine, John Hastings, earl of Pembroke, who, it had been hoped, might rally resistance in Poitou.

By 1375 Edward's French possessions had shrunk to a minute proportion of what he had been ceded by the treaty of Calais. In Aquitaine he controlled only the ports of Bordeaux and Bayonne and their adjacent coastal regions. Inland many scattered castles continued to fly the red cross down to the early 1390s, but these were held by 'free companies', bands of professional soldiers of various nationalities who ruled districts, levied taxes and raided for their own profit, and were only sporadically in touch with agents of the English Crown. The March of Calais, including Guines, remained more or less intact. The one serious threat to it, by Philip duke of Burgundy, Charles V's brother, in 1369, had been promptly checked by reinforcements under John of Gaunt, duke of Lancaster. In 1373 the remnants of the English interest in Brittany were threatened when Duke John fled to England, after his failure to rally Breton support to his alliance with Edward III against the French Crown. He returned with a powerful English force in 1375. But by then financial exhaustion had made both Edward and Charles willing to undertake serious negotiations. In June 1375, at a conference held at Bruges under the mediation of delegates of Pope Gregory IX and the count of Flanders, a truce of one year was agreed. In 1376 this was renewed for a further year.

Whatever glory and gains Edward III's French wars had brought him, he failed to substantiate fully his claim to the French Crown or to consolidate a sizeable duchy in Aquitaine held in full sovereignty. He succeeded in defending parts of Gascony from confiscation and, *de facto*, kept them in his sole jurisdiction. He secured political influence and strategic footholds in several French provinces. He shook off the subservience to which the French Crown had tried to subject his predecessors and undermined its widening hegemony in western Christendom. His wars caused great misery in France, precipitating social upheaval and political change. He succeeded remarkably well in imposing unity of aim on foreign policy. It was perhaps a sign of his failing grasp that divergent policies seem to have clashed in 1375. The manner in which John of Gaunt concluded the Bruges truce appears to have taken no account of the interests of his fellow peers campaigning in Brittany. Such conflicts over foreign policy were to characterise the two decades after Edward's death. They were not due solely to the absence of his magnetism and forcefulness. He and his son Prince Edward had widened the conflict into a European one. They had engaged their subjects' interests in it by playing on their fears for security and love for gains of war. They had saddled the English Crown with aspirations, entanglements, obligations and cessions. Their successors were burdened by a high level of expectation. Future English kings were now supposed to be, like Edward and his prototype King Arthur, invincible, imperialistic leaders in war.

In foreign affairs Edward III was a wilful and astute gambler. Englishmen were to remember his successes rather than his failures. Down to 1420 Anglo-French relations largely revolved around his claims, his diplomatic and military achievements, his expedients. It was still Edward III's war, a heavy harness for some of his blood.

War and truce under Richard II and Henry IV (1377–1413)

The outbreak of war once more with France and its ally Castile on the expiry of the truce in 1377 coincided almost exactly with the accession of the minor Richard II – an unhappy conjunction for the English. Until 1380, when Charles V died and was also succeeded by a minor, his son Charles VI, the French resumed attacks on remaining English enclaves in France. More offensively, thanks to the support of a formidable fleet of Castilian galleys based on the royal dockyard (*clos des gallées*) at Rouen, under the French admiral Jean de Vienne, there were wide-ranging attacks against English ports along the Channel coast. The English Crown at great expense held on to its remaining French possessions. In 1378 the Border magnate John lord Neville was dispatched to Bordeaux as lieutenant in Aquitaine, taking reinforcements in an attempt to reverse the situation in Gascony after the defeat and capture of his predecessor in office, Sir Thomas Felton, at Eymet. The lease of two ports safeguarding lines of sea communication with Bordeaux was acquired: the duke of Brittany handed over Brest to an English garrison in 1377, and Charles II of Navarre allowed one into the Norman port of Cherbourg in 1378. But the English armies which landed in Brittany in 1378 (commanded by John of Gaunt) and France in 1380 (commanded by his brother Buckingham), confronted by determined and skilful defences, failed to capture further bases though they caused considerable devastation.

In the early 1380s English councillors and parliaments, discredited or exasperated by this tale of costly failures to win a decisive success, became too divided over strategy, over the raising and allocation of finance and over personalities to take military advantage of Charles VI's minority. By contrast, the growing dominance in the French royal council of one of the king's uncles, Philip the Bold, duke of Burgundy, ensured its pursuit of increasingly clear-cut war aims, though not necessarily the aims of his late brother Charles V. The regency council, by recognising John de Montfort's claim to Brittany (April 1381), deprived the English expedition then in the duchy under Buckingham of its base. The council was able to promote French influence in Flanders, whose count, Louis de Mâle, had tried in recent years to maintain neutrality. The revolt of Ghent against his rule in 1379 eventually forced him into reliance on the military aid of Burgundy, his son-in-law. English influence was not only threatened in Brittany and Flanders, where Edward III had tried to maintain it; in Scotland it had practically evaporated. Robert II, the first Stewart king, on succeeding his anglophile uncle David II in 1371, had promptly made a defensive alliance with Charles V. By 1384, when French soldiers arrived in Scotland to concert attacks on northern England, Border lairds, led by the Douglas and Dunbar families, had swept the English Borderers from much of the land they had acquired across the frontier since 1346, and the English Border counties had become accustomed to more intense raids.

The threats to English interests in different quarters which the French regency council and its foreign allies skilfully maintained in the 1380s accentuated English indecision about strategic priorities. Remaining enclaves in France appeared vulnerable. To the northerners the revival of the Scottish threat loomed larger. Inhabitants of the southern coastal counties were incensed by Franco-Castilian raids. John of Gaunt, who since 1372 had assumed the style of king of Castile in right of his wife, Pedro the Cruel's daughter Constance, advocated intervention in the Iberian peninsula. Wool producers and exporters wanted Flemish markets kept open. In 1381 an expedition under Gaunt's brother Cambridge sailed to Portugal, but accomplished nothing against the Castilians. Gaunt's 1384 expedition to Scotland secured a year's truce. Forces sent to the aid of Ghent against Philip of Burgundy (1382–5) were too small or ill-led to prevent the duke's subjection of Flanders, to which he succeeded as count in right of his wife Margaret in 1384. Buonaccorso Pitti, a Florentine serving in the army which the young Charles VI took to Flanders to support his uncle Burgundy, was moved to an uncharacteristic display of emotion when recounting the shambles left by the retreat of an English expedition in 1383:

In the middle of the night, the English tried to escape and, as the townspeople wanted to prevent them, skirmishes broke out in which many were killed. In the end all the English and townsfolk who could fled the city before daybreak. When it was light we closed in on the town, cut off all means of retreat, and entered unopposed. Inside we found most of the houses on fire and heaps of dead English and townsfolk. I saw one cruelly horrifying sight: a woman, who appeared from her clothing to be of good class, was sitting with a two-year-old child in her arms, a three-year-old clinging to her shoulders and a five-year-old holding her hand, by the door of a furiously burning house. She was pulled up and moved some distance away to prevent herself and the children coming to harm but, as soon as she was let go, rushed back in the door of the house, despite the great flames which were billowing from it, and was finally burnt inside with her three children. In the end, the whole town was burnt and destroyed.

With the allegiances of Brittany and Flanders uneasily secured and susceptible to English pressure, Philip of Burgundy and his fellow royal councillors had the incentive to plan an invasion of England for 1385. As count of Flanders, Philip was aware that he would not fully win the loyalties of the dissident towns until exports of English wool were restored and English depredations on their commerce reduced. The main French army under Charles VI was to sail to southern England from Sluis, whilst a Franco-Scots force invaded across the northern Border. But the continued opposition of Ghent forced a postponement of the main expedition, whilst the French commander in Scotland, Jean de Vienne, admiral of France, soon fell out with his allies among the Scots lords, who refused to support his plans for set-piece battles and sieges. Richard II led a fine army unopposed from Newcastle into the Lothians and Robert II sought a truce. The French and Scots knights parted on bad terms, the French because their chivalrous instincts had been thwarted and because they had been charged high prices for supplies and insolently addressed by Scots peasants, the Scots not least because Jean de Vienne had imprudently seduced a kinswoman of the king.

But in 1386 Charles VI and many of his kinsmen and nobles assembled at Sluis a large army and fleet for the invasion of southern England. At the port of Tréguier in Brittany the Breton lord Olivier de Clisson, constable of France, collected a subsidiary force. Richard II's councillors feared a French landing on the south-east coast or in East Anglia. A large army was arrayed for the defence of London, contingents of archers from as far afield as Cheshire and Yorkshire billeting in neighbouring villages. Towns were ordered to repair their defences and to send contributions of men or money towards the defence of London. Household knights were dispatched to their country domiciles and to the ports to ensure that unpopular orders were complied with. The Vice-Chamberlain of the Household, Sir Simon Burley, who was also Constable of Dover Castle and Warden of the Cinque Ports, evacuated the vulnerable Isle of Thanet, and further exacerbated Kentish susceptibilities by removing the precious shrine of St Thomas from Canterbury Cathedral to the more secure but profane precincts of Dover Castle. The monks of Westminster Abbey debated in chapter whether it was lawful for them to fight in defence of the realm. Concluding that it was, they despatched Abbot Litlington and two of their brethren in full armour to the coast. One of those chosen was John Canterbury, selected doubtless because he was reputed to be one of the tallest men in England.

It seems likely, in view of these energetic defence measures and the well-tried tactical ability of the fourteenth-century English soldier, that had Charles VI and his kinsmen effected a landing, they would have suffered defeat or that, at best, they would have succeeded in seizing and garrisoning an English port. The reasons why they never came are obscure. In the autumn of 1386 delays caused by the difficulties in concentrating such a large army in the hostile county of Flanders may have produced the dangers of mounting costs, dwindling supplies, insecure lines of communication and bad weather. English naval activity in the summer had probably worsened the position of the army in Flanders. The English no longer had to contend with thc threat of Castilian galleys: in July 1386 John of Gaunt had at last mounted a formidable threat to Castile, sailing from Plymouth to land with an army in Galicia. The admirals Thomas lord Darcy and Sir Thomas Trivet blockaded the supply routes to Flanders: sections of a prefabricated wooden castle the French intended to erect after landing in England were captured at sea. In October Clisson embarked his fleet from Tréguier and sailed up the Channel, but his formations were broken up by bad weather before he disembarked at Sluis. Buonaccorso Pitti, who was serving in Charles VI's army there, says that the invasion was postponed to the following year on the advice of shipowners and experienced sea-captains: 'In their opinion it was impossible to cross with such a large number of boats. It was already late November. "And," said they, "if we were to meet with rough weather and bad winds while at sea, the ships would collide with each other and many would perish." '

The group of English magnates who asserted control over royal policy in the period 1386–9, whose ringleaders were the king's uncle Thomas of Woodstock, duke of Gloucester[3] and Richard earl of Arundel, wished to retaliate against the French Crown, but they were hampered by lack of diplomatic opportunities and by the reluctance of parliaments to grant large subsidies for the purpose. Early in 1387 a fleet was collected, whose objective was to encourage a new Flemish revolt: in March Arundel put to sea, and intercepted off Margate a fleet commanded by the admiral of Flanders, Sire Jean de Bucq, sailing home laden with wine from La Rochelle. In a running fight the Flemings and their French and Castilian allies tried to reach the haven of Sluis, but found English ships blocking access and were compelled to fight or beach their ships on the Cadzand sands. Arundel then blockaded Sluis and devastated its hinterland, but soon re-embarked and returned with his prizes. In June 1388 Arundel went to sea with a new expedition, intending to invade France in alliance with the duke of Brittany, once more toying with the English allegiance, and with John of Gaunt, who had abandoned his claim to Castile and was installed as lieutenant in Aquitaine. But the two dukes failed to help Arundel, who was merely able to plunder shipping lanes and raid inland in Poitou and Normandy.

The French were now inclined to negotiate seriously for peace, to further the interests of the princes of the blood, important factors in determining the course of Anglo-French relations during royal minorities. The failure of French invasion attempts and renewed English vigour at sea may have inclined Philip of Burgundy, anxious to secure the Flemish trade routes, to seek a conference. His brother John duke of Berry wanted to establish good relations with his new neighbour in Aquitaine, John of Gaunt. The enthusiasm of the latter's brother, Gloucester, for war in France may have been temporarily damped by his need to win Gaunt's support in domestic politics and his anxiety not to alienate the community by more heavy war taxation. Moreover, Border defences were wavering in face of renewed Scottish vigour. In the summer of 1388 Robert Stewart, earl of Fife, invaded Cumberland. The young James earl of Douglas, with his fellow Border magnates George Dunbar earl of March and March's brother John earl of Moray, separated from the main force to levy Percy lands in Northumberland. Sir Henry Percy, recently appointed Warden of the East March, failed to halt Douglas's withdrawal from Newcastle, but caught up with him at Otterburn in Redesdale. Sir Henry ('Hotspur') impetuously attacked the Scottish camp by night: the steady nerve and discipline of the Scots leaders staved off defeat. Douglas was mortally wounded, but Hotspur and the spoils of victory were triumphantly carried off by Moray to Dunbar Castle (August 1388). Tensions among the English Border magnates left the Marches vulnerable to further attacks. But in June 1389 a truce of three years was concluded between the French and English Crowns, which was to be continuously extended (though not always well kept) until 1414. Lacking French support, the Scots Crown adhered to the truce in September 1389, though some of its lieges and the English they encountered took little notice of it.

In May 1389 Richard II had imitated the recent action of Charles VI by dismissing the councillors who governed against his will. Neither king was to show himself enthusiastic about the military aims of his predecessor. The youthful Richard had in the 1380s been inclined to seek peace with the French Crown at the price of some of his claims. In 1393 he relinquished Cherbourg to Charles III of Navarre and in 1397 Brest to John of Brittany. These withdrawals from bases useful in securing the sea route to Gascony were related to the negotiations for peace and alliance between the parties which developed apace when the dukes of Burgundy and Lancaster met in conference at Amiens in 1392. Richard seems to have been prepared to abate his claim to the

French Crown. The principal problems concerned the extent and status of territories claimed by him in Aquitaine. Burgundy and his brothers were well versed in the difficulties of resolving the English Crown's claims honourably to both parties. Key proposals – variations on a scheme first apparently mooted at the Bruges conference in 1375 – survive in a draft of 1393. Its terms imply the grant to Gaunt and his heirs of a duchy of Aquitaine larger than that granted to him as duke by Richard in 1390, to be held of the French Crown. In the circumstances this was probably the best offer the English Crown could expect. It solved the longstanding problem of the sovereignty of Aquitaine by detaching the duchy from the English Crown, but for the benefit of a branch of the English king's family. But to many Englishmen such a scheme savoured of a sell-out. Gloucester and Arundel publicly voiced the misgivings particularly of those who had expectations of the fortunes of war and those who inveterately distrusted French offers. Gaunt seems to have brought his troublesome brother round. But in 1393 there was a movement of protest in the king's county palatine of Chester (many of whose knights, esquires and archers had fought in France). In Gascony there was strong opposition in 1394 to a scheme which would have deprived the Gascons of their traditional lord and protector of liberties, the king of England. Richard may himself have lost enthusiasm for a scheme which enhanced Lancastrian interests.

These ultimately abortive negotiations had a highly significant result. They enhanced rather than undermined the growing personal trust between Charles VI and Richard II, two young men imbued with belief in the holiness of their authority, and contemptuous of rebellion and disobedience. That marvellous painting, the Wilton Diptych (National Gallery, London) shows the closeness of feeling between the two courts. The kneeling figure of Richard II wears Charles VI's livery collar of broom cods. The symbolism of the painting stresses the sacred nature of kingship, a theme which had been given intense literary expression at the court of Charles VI's father, but had no such counterpart at Edward III's, with its stress on worldly, imperialistic chivalry. In the right panel of the diptych the infant Christ blesses the banner of St George, held by an angel. In the left Richard kneels before Him and His Mother, sponsored by his patrons, St Edmund, St Edward the Confessor and St John the Baptist.

The two young kings were alike fired with the current zeal to unify the Christian people, divided by the Great Schism, and to destroy the spreading tyranny of the Ottoman Turks, so grievous to Christ and the Christians of the Orient. When Richard's queen Anne of Bohemia died in 1394, he seized the opportunity to cement friendly relations with Charles by seeking in 1395 to marry into his family. In March 1396 the king's cousin Edward earl of Rutland and Thomas Mowbray, Earl Marshal, ratified in Paris the terms of a truce to be prolonged for twenty-eight years, and of the proposed marriage between Richard and Charles VI's daughter Isabella, then aged six. In August Richard crossed to Calais to consult the French royal uncles, visiting his realm of France for the first time since his infancy. In October 1396 he went there again for the wedding. A Valois king entered the church of St Nicholas at Calais, welcomed by his rival for the Crown, whose family had unjustly occupied the town since 1347. This extraordinary congregation reveals the inner meaning of the 1396 truce. Formal peace had proved impossible, for it would have involved too much loss of legal face by one or both parties. This was an informal peace, in which both sides implicitly relinquished their ambitions, Richard to recover lands claimed by the English Crown, or the French Crown itself, Charles to exercise sovereignty in those lands the English still held in France. During the remaining years of Richard's reign the trust on which the agreement was precariously built waned, due partly to increasing internal tension in both kingdoms. Anglo-French relations did not deteriorate through a revival of the old matters of conflict. They were no longer the vital issues to the men in charge of policy in the 1390s. But the ghost of Edward III was not to be easily laid.

Had Richard not been deposed in 1399, it is no more likely that the truce would have lasted for its full length than it did under his Lancastrian successors. Though Richard had recognised the importance of being able to ignore the crippling burden of pretensions in France, he was a man of restless foreign as well as domestic ambitions, which might have led to hostility with Charles VI and the French princes. He was receiving homages from German princes, perhaps at one point with the intention of trying to gain the kingship of the Romans, replacing his former brother-in-law, the absentee alcoholic Wenzel. Such an extension of influence is unlikely to have been welcomed by Philip duke of Burgundy, busy extending his rule over imperial principalities in the Low Countries. In the last year of his reign Richard showed an awareness of and interest in the struggle developing for control of the French Crown (as Charles VI lapsed into further bouts of insanity) between the king's brother, Louis duke of Orleans and Philip of Burgundy. If Richard had been reigning in 1410, like Henry IV he might not have resisted the temptation to intervene in the civil war between the French princes which broke out then, reviving some or other of the old territorial ambitions.

It was from France that Henry of Bolingbroke set sail with a small company in 1399 to claim his father's duchy of Lancaster, confiscated by Richard after John of Gaunt's death the previous year. In Henry's reign deteriorating political stability in both England and France encouraged renewals of hostilities, but ensured that they were on a small scale. The truce with France was confirmed in 1400. Henry hoped for good relations with the French court, where he had been an admired and pitied guest in 1398, but his usurpation poisoned the atmosphere of Anglo-French trust which had already deteriorated in Richard's last years. French princes who had regarded sympathetically Henry's desire to gain his Lancastrian inheritance were, or affected to be, horrified at his treatment of his liege lord, the king. Waleran of Luxembourg, count of St Pol, who had been married to Richard's half-sister Maud Courtenay (*née* Holand) waged a personal war against Henry, promoting minor but irritating attacks on English ports and shipping. In 1403 Plymouth was sacked by the Bretons and French, and in that year and the following there were French landings on the Isle of Wight. Also in 1403 the duke of Orleans invaded Gascony, after failing to evoke a favourable response to his challenge to Henry, his former ally, to personal combat. The persistence of disaffection in England and of revolt in Wales encouraged French hostility. In 1404 Charles VI recognised Owain Glyn Dŵr as prince of Wales, and a French force went to the aid of his siege of Caernarvon Castle. An attack on Dartmouth was repulsed with heavy losses, but in 1405 the French, with some assistance from Castilian galleys, were more successful.

Gutierre Diaz de Gamez, esquire of the Castilian Don Pero Niño, count of Buelna, in his panegyrical biography of his master, *El Vitorial*, graphically described the *mêlées* which occurred when a Franco-Castilian force raided along the Channel coast from St Ives to the Isle of Wight. On the whole, the local inhabitants offered a plucky and skilful defence, particularly in the piratical port of Poole, where the Castilian standard-bearer was so assaulted with arrows that he appeared like 'a bull in the ring'. In August 1405 a French force landed at Milford Haven to support Glyn Dŵr. They helped to capture Carmarthen and advanced towards Worcester, which Henry came to defend. The French retreated into Wales and re-embarked. Like their compatriots in Scotland in 1385, they soon discovered that they had chosen a base which could not sustain them adequately and an ally whose fighting methods differed from their own. English vigilance at sea in 1405–6 hampered further French raids and attempts to support Glyn Dŵr: attacks on Gascony, whose garrisons had been reinforced, petered out by 1407.

The contradictions in French policy towards England in Henry's early years and the ineffectiveness of the attacks inspired by princes were symptomatic of the increasing chaos in French politics, especially after the grim and determinedly ambitious John the Fearless succeeded his father Philip as duke of Burgundy in 1404. After Duke John had contrived the assassination of Orleans in 1407 he was at last able to gain control of royal policy: as the ruler of Flanders he was anxious that the truces should be observed with England. But his ascendancy at court was threatened by an alliance of ousted nobles and former dependents of the murdered Orleans, headed by a Gascon lord, Bernard count of Armagnac, whose daughter married Orleans's young son and heir, Charles, in 1410. The resulting civil conflicts aroused English ambitions. In 1411 John the Fearless offered to hand over Flemish towns to Henry IV and to marry his daughter Anne to Henry prince of Wales in return for military aid. Thomas earl of Arundel led a retinue from Calais which assisted Duke John in regaining control of Paris. But the dismissal of Prince Henry and his political allies from his father's Council led to a switch of alliances. In May 1412, in return for subsidies and the promise of assistance in the recovery of the rights he claimed in Aquitaine, Henry IV agreed to send retinues commanded by his forceful third son, Thomas duke of Clarence, to support Charles duke of Orleans and his anti-Burgundian allies. But the campaign was soon halted by a reconciliation between the warring French princes: the following March Henry died.

The invasions of Henry V and Lancastrian rule in France (1415–35)

The resumption of civil war in France spurred on courtship of the new king of England. The French princes may not have realised the formidable calibre of the man whose ambitions they assiduously stirred. John the Fearless broke off negotiations in 1414. He would not accede to English claims for either the fulfilment of the 1360 treaty or for the French Crown. The proposal by his opponents that Henry V should marry Charles VI's daughter Catherine stalled because of Henry's intransigence. His final 1414 demand, in return for renouncing the French Crown, claimed the ancient Angevin empire, including Normandy, in full sovereignty – a revival of claims abandoned in 1259, to which even Edward III had hardly aspired. Thwarted in diplomacy, Henry resorted to the hazardous expedient of war. In August 1415 he landed with a small force in Normandy, at the mouth of the Seine, and established the siege of the port of Harfleur, which Richard earl of Arundel, whose son was one of his retinue leaders, had attempted to seize in 1378. When hope of relief faded, the garrison surrendered. Their force depleted by an epidemic, and the detachment of a garrison for Harfleur, the English trailed north-east towards the protective walls and shipping of Calais. But near Agincourt in Artois (not far from the site of Edward III's victory at Crécy in 1346) Henry was intercepted by a numerically superior army in which some Burgundians and Armagnacs had tardily managed to combine. Among its leaders were two of John the Fearless's brothers, besides Orleans and his brother John count of Vendôme. The French military leadership, as had appeared as early as the 1380s, no longer had reservations about attacking substantial English field forces. In an engagement which bore tactical similarities to Crécy (especially in the French cavalry attacks and the English defensive use of dismounted knights and men-at-arms combining with archers), the French were bloodily defeated (25 October 1415). Henry's army was able to escape intact to Calais, bearing spoils of war and a few surviving noble prisoners, including Orleans and Vendôme.

Agincourt brought no territorial gains, but it made clear, not least to

Henry's subjects, that in the eyes of God and of men the austerely pious king's French claims had to be taken seriously. On several occasions parliaments had heard Richard II's and Henry IV's representatives proclaim the seriousness of their masters' intent to ride in France at the head of an army. But only Henry V, whose right to the English throne some wondered at, showed a firmness of purpose reminiscent of Edward III. He made the fading reminiscences of old men about the exhilaration of riding victoriously through France suddenly and startlingly into reality for another generation. It is perhaps not too fanciful to see their emotional response reflected in the Agincourt Carol: the English people have not often sung joyously about a foreign battlefield.

Our king went forth to Normandy,
With grace and might of chivalry;
There God for him wrought marvellously,
Wherefore England may call and cry,
Deo gracias!

After Agincourt, in the period 1415–17, both sides jockeyed for military, naval and diplomatic advantages. The English garrison at Harfleur, threatening communications between Rouen and the Channel along the Seine, was besieged. French ships, aided by hired Genoese carracks, attempted blockade. But in two naval engagements (1416–17) first Henry's second brother John duke of Bedford, then his cousin John Holand, earl of Huntingdon, defeated the Franco-Italian fleets. Their successes owed much to the navy of specially large ships which Henry had built. On the diplomatic front too Henry scored a success which added considerably to his prestige if not his material resources. Sigismund of Luxembourg, king of the Romans, was anxious to reconcile the disputes dividing western Christendom. His diplomacy had already helped to secure considerable princely unanimity in endorsing the deposition and resignation of rival popes achieved by the Council of Constance. He wished to ensure an undisputed resolution of the Great Schism and united efforts to suppress heretics, especially the adherents of Hus infesting Bohemia. In 1416 Sigismund attempted to mediate between Charles VI and Henry V. After visiting the French court, he was impressively entertained by Henry and his nobles, going so far in compromising his neutrality as to become a Knight of the Garter. But he worked to secure a truce. Blaming his failure on French unco-operativeness, in August 1416, at Canterbury, he allied with Henry to promote his claims.

More significant for their fulfilment was the secret promise which John the Fearless made to Henry in October, to become his vassal as soon as Henry had acquired a notable part of France. The duke, in control of Paris and the royal court, was in effect abandoning his Norman adherents, in order to have English support in his attacks on the Armagnacs. In August 1417 Henry landed at Touques with an impressive army and siege-train. By July 1418 he had conquered lower Normandy and the Cotentin peninsula. Reasonably secure from Burgundian attacks, the English were able to invest Rouen through the autumn and harsh winter of 1418. In January 1419, after the poorer inhabitants had endured appalling hardships as a result of their superiors' deluded hopes of relief, the city capitulated to the alien king, who sternly proclaimed himself its rightful lord. Henry and his noble lieutenants then proceeded to conquer the rest of Normandy[4], and to threaten Maine, Anjou, Touraine and the Île-de-France.

In his early negotiations and first French campaigns Henry had shown a particular interest in Normandy, his right to which, with that obsessive antiquarianism often displayed by fifteenth-century property claimants, he traced back to the Angevin King John and his forbears. This preoccupation radically altered the nature of Anglo-French conflict. After his conquest of Normandy, the patterns of competing interests, of diplomacy and strategy were differently set. Already by the 1390s the French and English Crowns had deflated the Aquitainian problems: Henry revived them only as diplomatic counters. Though the city of Bordeaux, its vine-raising hinterlands and the shipbuilding port of Bayonne were worth defending, their revenue value to the English Crown had declined, and experience had shown how difficult and expensive it was to maintain any extension of English lordships in south-west France. In 1417 Normandy's proximity to England, its importance for domination of the Channel trade routes, and the access it provided to the Île-de-France and princely appanages stretching down to the Loire may have been incentives for Henry's conquest. Moreover, he had an unprecedented opportunity to pick up the duchy on the cheap: John the Fearless was prepared, albeit reluctantly, to sell the keys of Rouen. Henry's military success in Normandy, brilliant though it was in execution, rested on Burgundian acquiescence rather than on the strength of his resources. Edward III had never enjoyed so much diplomatic good fortune – he perforce had to make himself congenial to a motley and sometimes unsavoury collection of Norman exiles, German barons, Flemish burgesses and Breton lords.

Duke John soon reacted against Henry's success. In September 1419 negotiations on his behalf with his principal opponent, Charles VI's son and heir the Dauphin Charles (the future Charles VII) culminated in a personal meeting between the two at Montereau on the bridge over the River Yonne. There, in the dauphin's presence, John was mercilessly butchered by prominent members of the former's retinue. Georges Chastellain, a ducal court chronicler, drew a memorable picture of the horrified reactions of the duke's son and heir, Philip, and the latter's wife Michelle, the dauphin's sister. Both collapsed, stunned and prostrate with grief, surrounded by their agitated attendants. Charles VI, prompted by his Burgundian councillors, now proposed a settlement to Henry V, amounting to a capitulation to the English invader, more binding than Duke John's secret promises. In May 1420 at Troyes in Champagne, a peace was ratified between the kings of France and England which was to be a basis for war and diplomacy as much as the 1360 peace had been, though not for so long. Henry was to marry Charles's daughter Catherine. He and his heirs were to succeed Charles as kings of France. During the infirm Charles's lifetime Henry was to be regent and to conquer on his behalf the lands held by the *soi-disant* dauphin. Charles, Henry and Burgundy were pledged not to make a separate peace with the dauphin. Henry undertook to uphold the laws and customs of the realm and the 'authority and superiority' of the *parlement* 'in all that is due to it, in all manner of places that now, or in time to come, are, or shall be, subject to our said father [Charles VI]', and, on his own accession, to place Normandy and all his conquests in France in obedience to the French Crown.

The dauphin's public rejoinder was that the treaty was against 'the honour of the fleurs-de-lys'. The lilies were a symbol of the sanctity of French kingship: they were supposed to have appeared miraculously on the shield of Clovis, founder of Frankish hegemony in Roman Gaul. Parties to the treaty had soiled and damaged the lilies: 'the right of the crown of France neither can nor ought to be conveyed to strangers, especially those who are ancient enemies'. The treaty, he declared, 'under pretext of peace and marriage . . . tends to innumerable and perpetual divisions'. This judgment, furiously partisan, was none the less prescient. Moreover, Lancastrian government was in notable aspects to derogate the sovereignty of the *parlement*. Gascony and the March of Calais continued to be in Westminster's sole jurisdiction and a semi-autonomous centre for local administration was set up at Rouen. The termination of regional pleas by the *grand conseil* in Rouen and its denial of the *parlement* of Paris's appellate jurisdiction was a continuous source of grievance to the latter.

Such lapses were basically expedients springing from the Lancastrian inability to implement the treaty fully, rather than from a lack of respect for the honour and interests of the French Crown. The parties may have fashioned the peace in the expectation that they could speedily fulfil it in entirety. In territorial terms Henry certainly made considerable immediate gains as a result of the treaty, notably Paris, parts of the Île-de-France not yet conquered, and much of Champagne. Philip of Burgundy withdrew his household from Paris and the pro-Burgundian officials controlling central administration obeyed Henry. But there were still isolated Armagnac garrisons in the northern frontier regions of France, some not far from Paris. South of the Loire, bordering Burgundy, the dauphin's supporters were solidly entrenched.

The Treaty of Troyes certainly brought peace to some regions. By helping to consolidate Lancastrian authority in northern France it produced for much of three decades unwontedly peaceful relations between England and the adjacent parts of France. The north-western waters and shores of Europe ceased to be the arena for violent Anglo-French conflict. The ports of Flanders and Brittany were in the hands of rulers who desired friendship. The menacing naval base at Rouen was destroyed. Throughout the fourteenth-century conflicts with France, English shores and shipping had been menaced. The struggle had now shifted to the more remote French interior: it was an internal matter of suppressing rebels. As far as the English in their own country were concerned, a peace had been made with France, ratified in parliament in 1421.

But the dauphin and his supporters would not play their allotted supine role. In March 1421 Henry's brother Clarence was defeated and killed at Baugé in the frontier region of Anjou by a larger Franco-Scottish force commanded by John Stewart, earl of Buchan. Formally banished from the realm by the *parlement* the dauphin may have been, but soon after this victory his army was investing Chartres, uncomfortably near Paris. To reassert control over the Île-de-France, Henry hurried back from England with a small force, all he could afford to muster (July 1421). His death, aged thirty-five, at Bois de Vincennes near Paris (31 August 1422), from illness contracted at the siege of Meaux, had little immediate effect on the strategic and political situation. Burgundy, though reluctant to aid expeditions undertaken solely in the English interest, and prepared to make truces to protect his vulnerable duchy and the adjacent county of Nevers from dauphinist attack, could not contemplate giving his allegiance to the man who had presided over his father's murder. Though Duke Philip refused to act as regent for Henry V's infant son Henry VI, who succeeded after Charles VI's death (21 October 1422), he did not dispute his title as king of France. Government continued to function in Lancastrian France due to the soundness of Henry V's military and administrative arrangements and the profound appreciation of them shown by his brother Bedford, who acted as regent for Henry VI.

Henry V had given his protection to the lives, inheritances and privileges of those French people who were prepared to enter his allegiance. Because he was careful to provide regular pay for his soldiers, he could ensure protection by enforcing discipline. Hostile as well as friendly chroniclers relate anecdotes illustrating his pitiless harshness in punishing plunderers, especially those who had laid violent hands on priests and ecclesiastical property. Nevertheless, many landowners in Lancastrian France spurned his peace, and forfeited their inheritances. Henry encouraged English nobles and gentlemen to take up estates and residence in Normandy. He conferred castles and lordships in return for specific obligations of military service for the safeguard of the locality and the frontiers. He started the creation of an 'English interest' of great and small landowners in French society, especially in Normandy and Maine, an interest which had an important stake in upholding his conquests. There had been nothing of the kind on the same scale in the fourteenth century.

John of Bedford, the most remarkable of Henry V's brothers, spend most of his life from 1422 as regent in France, trying to implement the peace of Troyes. In 1423 he married Burgundy's sister Anne. An austere, serious man of pronounced literary and artistic tastes, the regent evoked the same sort of trust and loyalty as his eldest brother had done, but perhaps possessed more human warmth. A big, strong man and a fine soldier, in 1424 he ensured control of Normandy, on the verge of revolt, and weakened Charles VII's military potential by annihilating a formidable Franco-Scottish army at Verneuil. He attempted to enforce discipline as strictly as the king had done. According to his 1423 ordinance, pillage was made a criminal offence. Captains of garrisons contracted to deduct from their soldiers' pay the value of any goods wrongfully seized. Before receiving assignment of wages, captains had to certify that their provisions were paid for.

To protect the inhabitants, military and civil administration were, as far as possible, kept apart. The principal regional royal officials, the *baillis* (mainly English), who received orders from the regent and his council, had among their supervisory tasks to ensure that soldiers in their *bailliages* were under discipline, and that frequent musters and reviews of garrisons were held to inspect their numbers and preparedness. They summoned contingents on expedition. Their regional deputies, *vicomtes* (often French), supervised judicial and financial administration in the *vicomtés*. In striking contrast to administration by captains of English garrisons in Brittany in the fourteenth century, rule under Bedford was well reputed. Charles VII's later partisan Thomas Basin, bishop of Lisieux (a Norman by birth) acknowledged that Bedford 'was courageous, humane and just; he was very fond of the French lords who obeyed him and he took care to reward them according to their merits. As long as he lived Normans and Frenchmen in this part of the kingdom had a great affection for him.'

Though such developments were looked at askance by royal officials and lawyers in Paris, the erection of a chancery and council at Rouen dealing with the affairs of Normandy and adjacent regions was probably convenient for the inhabitants as well as facilitating tighter English control over their most important conquest. Bedford's benevolence to the Normans and intent to foster their own institutions is strikingly shown by his foundation of the university of Caen, at first (in 1432) solely as a centre for the study of canon and civil law. The peace of Troyes facilitated Norman trade with England and Burgundy, as well as Norman provisioning of English armies in France. Basin commented: 'The Bessin and the Cotentin and Lower Normandy which, under the sway of the English were far enough away from the enemy's defence line, less easily and less often exposed to the robber raids, remained a little better cultivated and populated, though often borne down by great poverty.'

The province's relative prosperity (and a cause of impoverishment) is shown by the large sums for defence purposes which Bedford wrung from the frequently summoned Norman estates. Perhaps the clearest indication that in the 1420s Henry VI's rule over his father's acquisitions in France (including some of its biggest towns and finest corn-growing regions) had achieved a degree of stability is that the war against Charles VII was then financed almost entirely from its own resources, hardly at all from English ones (used principally in France for the defence of Calais and Gascony). But the resources at the regent's disposal (especially in view of Burgundy's limited military commitment) were, despite his striking conquests, insufficient to subdue Languedoc. In the long run Henry V's death did weaken the prospects for Lancastrian rule in France, not so much because his personal qualities were missed, but because he alone might have got further substantial commitments of English resources. In the last two years of his reign there had been signs of increasing English reluctance to pay for a distant war – Henry had relied more on raising loans than subsidies. Henry VI's minority Council entirely lacked the authority to reverse this trend of disengagement, and to support Bedford's emergencies relied too on loans and, on one occasion, the misappropriation of crusading funds. Englishmen may have felt that it was up to the king's loyal French subjects to pay for the suppression of his remaining rebels.

In London in the 1420s tidings from France were rivalled in interest by the attempts of Henry V's youngest brother, Humphrey duke of Gloucester, to establish control of Hainault, Holland, Friesland and Zealand, in right of his wife Countess Jacqueline, whom he married in 1423. His unsuccessful efforts were strenuously opposed by her uncle Philip of Burgundy. Had Duke Humphrey succeeded he might have been able to provide English cloth exporters with the assured markets which their Flemish rivals, intermittently supported by Philip, tried to deny them. Gloucester's attempts complicated Bedford's policy; as regent of France the latter was determined, despite pressure from English interests, to maintain good relations with Burgundy.

The continued vigour of English rule in France was demonstrated in 1428 by the offensive directed by Thomas Montague, earl of Salisbury, on the Loire. The siege of Orleans which he began in October threatened appanages of princes loyal to Charles VII. His court had a strong incentive to reinforce Orleans. Inspired by Joan of Arc, the mysterious virgin from a well-to-do peasant family living in Domrémy, on the borders of Lorraine, the royal forces relieved Orleans (May 1429). The English military leadership fell into unprecedented disarray. The expert Salisbury had been killed during the siege by debris thrown up by a cannon shot. His successor, the earl of Suffolk, fell prisoner at Jargeau a short while later. After the English had abandoned the siege, one of their best soldiers, John lord Talbot, was captured in the rearguard action at Patay, and another, Sir John Fastolf, was discredited by his conduct on this occasion.

The fragility of the English hold on the Île-de-France was revealed when Joan of Arc rode with an army to Reims, where Charles VII received the sacred unction of kingship in the tradition of his ancestors (July 1429). The Council in England intervened to aid Bedford. Henry VI appeared in person at Rouen (June 1430) and Paris, where he was crowned at Nôtre Dame in an unhistoric and unimpressive ceremony, which his greatest vassal, the duke of Burgundy, failed to attend (December 1431). The *parlement* may have been exasperated when its sovereign, an intelligent and well-educated boy, addressed it in English. But the sudden cracks in his rule had been plugged. Joan of Arc's balefully numinous influence had been destroyed by her capture in May 1430. Charles VII could not afford to keep his recent acquisitions; reinforcements from England displayed the usual skill and morale. But the need of Lancastrian France to rely on English resources revealed its vulnerability, after having long been burdened with the cost of its own defence. In 1434 Bedford asked the English Council to divert duchy of Lancaster and other royal revenues to maintain a force in France, and to authorise his use there of the garrisons in the March of Calais.

The greatest blow was yet to fall. Faction shifts at Charles VII's intrigue-ridden court at last facilitated the long mooted reconciliation with Philip of Burgundy, whose French possessions had been made more vulnerable by the resurgence of Valois military activity. In July 1435 an international conference met in Duke Philip's town of Arras, presided over by cardinal mediators authorised by Pope Eugenius IV and the general council of the Church convened at Basel. The conference was a strained occasion, lacking in cordiality, except between the French and Burgundians. The Valois and Lancastrian delegations, not recognising each other's authority in France, avoided direct negotiation. The duke of Burgundy and his councillors intensified English suspicion by stressing their separate interest. The Lancastrian government did not favour the making of peace or substantial concessions during their king's minority. Their offers harked back to the 1396 solution: a marriage alliance between Henry and the adversary of France's daughter, and a lengthy truce. Peace was to be deferred until Henry was of age, and Charles's tenure in the lands he held was to be recognised. The English claimed that Christ's authority lay behind the marriage solution, as expressed in a vision of St Bridget of Sweden. The French delegates were unimpressed. The Valois experience of marriage alliances with English kings had not been fortunate. The English territorial offers were derisory. The French insisted that Henry should renounce his claim to the French Crown and hold any conceded French possessions as a vassal of Charles VII. Both sides probably had little expectation of a diplomatic deal. The English were preparing to fight, the French to conciliate Burgundy. The English withdrew after

Cardinal Beaufort's failure to dissuade Duke Philip from repudiating his allegiance. This was Charles VII's triumph, despite his display of public humility in the treaty made at Arras with the duke. The king expressed his regret for the murder of John the Fearless, promised to hunt down his murderers and found chantries for the repose of his soul, exempted Philip (though not his heirs) from the performance of homage, and confirmed most of the territorial concessions made to him by the Lancastrians, allowing him to retain the 'towns of the Somme' until the Crown paid an indemnity which in 1435 seemed beyond its capacity.

The decline of English rule in France (1435–53)

Henry VI, a boy not yet fourteen, wept publicly at Burgundy's repudiation of allegiance. Feeling about this desertion was so intense in English ruling circles that an alliance with Duke Philip was never again concluded, a steadfastness to be paralleled by that of the ageing duke, who held with remarkable firmness to his reconciliation with the Valois, despite the political disappointments and provocations involved. The failure of the English and Burgundian courts to reconcile and pursue their mutual interests after 1435 created favourable conditions for Charles's conquest of nearly all the English possessions in France, and, ultimately, for Louis XI's conquest of Burgundy in 1477–8. Bedford died a few days after the English delegation withdrew from Arras. French and Burgundian forces assaulted Lancastrian possessions. Philip's attack on Calais in 1436 was a failure, due to inability to maintain a naval blockade. This attempt on the centre for English merchants' wool exports by the 'perfidious' duke seems to have evoked an outburst of popular feeling in London. Rhymsters and London chroniclers enthusiastically related the Flemings' humiliation and the subsequent ravaging of the Flemish coast by a force under the duke's old enemy Gloucester. Meanwhile the French drove the Lancastrians back on the defences of Normandy and Maine: Paris fell in 1436.

Henry's lieutenants in France, such as his young cousin Richard duke of York, shored up the shaky military position, but were less successful than Bedford in reconciling its needs with stable civil rule. The dwindling resources of Lancastrian France failed to meet military costs, garrison pay tended to fall more heavily into arrears and discipline cracked. The extortions and depredations of the soldiery, in addition to heavy taxation, burdened and provoked the peasants. They were also forced to sustain bands of 'brigands' and partisans of Charles VII, and punished for doing so. There were peasant insurrections, bloodily suppressed. English rule was no longer guaranteeing the protection and relative prosperity which had made it tolerable. Sir John Fortescue was to recall the bleak situation:

there were never people in that land [*France*] *more poor, than were in our time the commons of the country of Caux* [*in Normandy*], *which was then almost desert for lack of tillers. . . . And yet the said commons of Caux made a marvellous great rising, and took our towns, castles, and fortresses, and slew our captains and soldiers, at such a time as we had but few men of war lying in that country.*

This deterioration, the dislocation of English trade due to hostilities with the Burgundian Low Countries, and the ending of Henry VI's minority, inclined his councillors in the 1440s to seek a new Anglo-French settlement more determinedly and accomodatingly. In June 1439 this new mood, prompted particularly by Cardinal Beaufort, appeared in the English embassy which met at Oye near Calais to confer with Isabella duchess of Burgundy and a French delegation. The negotiations broke down: the English would not agree to Henry's relinquishing his title to the French Crown, holding the extensive lands he claimed in France of the Valois, or compensating dispossessed French landowners. But Beaufort showed a genuine desire to seek peace by exploring these and other problems. However, English belief in the rectitude of their cause and optimism that they would recover the military initiative worked against compromise, especially since Gloucester's crude but powerful invective was directed against it in Council. The duke, over whom his beloved brother Henry V had stood as he lay wounded in the *mêlée* at Agincourt, rigidly advocated adherence to his brother's policies.

In the 1440s William de la Pole, earl of Suffolk, promoted *rapprochement* between Henry VI and the French court, so continuing the policy pursued by Cardinal Beaufort (d.1447), the most senior member of the Lancastrian house and the one most revered by the king. Suffolk was mistakenly convinced that he had the personal weight and influence to negotiate a settlement, as some of Richard II's trusted kinsmen had done in the 1390s. After his capture in 1429 he had made contacts at the French court and, returning to England on his release, he befriended Orleans, a prisoner since 1415. In 1440 Orleans was released, despite Gloucester's opposition, in the hope that he would help to bring the French and English courts to a better understanding. In 1444 Suffolk assisted in making a brief truce at Tours and an agreement that Henry should marry Margaret, daughter of Charles VII's faithful kinsman René, duke of Anjou, titular king of Sicily. In 1445, in order to secure a new truce and facilitate peace negotiations, Henry agreed to cede Maine to its claimant King René. But it proved difficult to get the English captains there to implement the agreement. In 1448 a French force compelled their surrender of Le Mans. Some of the dispossessed captains took up Gloucester's cry of a Court 'sell-out': it was fortunate for the Court that he had died in 1447. In March 1449 an English force seized the Breton town of Fougères, a move which the lieutenant in France, Somerset, seems not to have discouraged, perhaps because it was connected with attempts involving dispossessed veterans to revive English influence in Brittany. Charles VII's demands for reparations fell on deaf ears, as the English would not admit that Brittany was in his jurisdiction.

To Charles it must have appeared that English activities in France were contrary to the alleged reconciliatory aims of Suffolk's diplomacy. He mounted an invasion of Normandy, whose undermanned and demoralised garrisons fell with a speed shameful in comparison with the resistance to Henry V's conquest of the province. Gascony was also invaded: Bordeaux fell in 1451, but its citizens rose in revolt and admitted a weak English expedition, commanded by the ancient veteran John Talbot, earl of Shrewsbury. In July 1453 he led an Anglo-Gascon army to relieve Castillon in Perigord, besieged by Charles VII. Hoping to take the French by surprise, he attacked their entrenched encampment with his advance-guard. The attack was repulsed: Shrewsbury was badly wounded in the shin by a gunshot from the excellent French artillery. His demoralised force was then routed, he being killed in the *mêlée.* Bordeaux surrendered in October.

The English attempts to come to an accommodation with the Valois were too inflexible and consequently maladroit to be realistic. Charles VII perforce offered old-fashioned proposals designed to allow the English Crown to keep some French lands. But the English failed to lower their pretensions, trapped in the scheme of claims laid down by Henry V at Troyes. The French Crown consequently adopted crude, intransigent concepts so often advocated by its literary propagandists, articulated by Joan of Arc: 'good Frenchmen' were those who gave their prime allegiance to the Valois; Englishmen had no business to rule in France.

This policy need not have triumphed so strikingly in the early 1450s if the English had been more adaptable and determined. In the decade or so after Troyes, warfare in France had become relaxingly dissociated from urgent need to guard English shores and borders. But in the 1440s, with the losses in the Île-de-France and the French capture of Harfleur, English councillors came to realise that rule in France could only be maintained by large injections of men and money. The need to revive the involvement of the 'community of the realm' to provide these might have produced unpleasant political consequences. Such considerations may have encouraged Henry's councillors to seek a compromise. Though the future of Lancastrian France was rendered critical by Philip the Good's change of allegiance in 1435, and by Charles VII's growing financial and military power about ten years later, dissolution was not inevitable. Lancastrian France required more English aid: a new balance needed to be struck between the two parts of the 'dual monarchy' in the 1430s. Had Bedford lived longer, he might have been able to revive English will to rule in France. No other kinsman of Henry VI had the prestige to do so: the English lost the initiative and resorted to disastrously *ad hoc* diplomatic and military measures.

The root of their difficulty was that they were bound within the construction of Henry V's powerful creative intelligence. Before his conquests, English claims had been more protean, capable of identification with the aspirations of Flemish burgesses, Breton dukes, Gascon counts. Disaster in one part of France was counterbalanced by success elsewhere: networks of European alliances helped to provide further insurance cover for the contenders. But Henry V focused English interests intently on the domination of the principal organs of French government, and of certain regions of France by English landowners. This was more ambitious and contentious. Before his time the English in France had a mentality more akin to early colonial entrepreneurs. They were eager to seize opportunities and more prepared to cut losses. But he gave them 'empire', as King Arthur had to the Britons. In the twentieth century we have seen how imperialists, faced with the need to adapt to a diminished role, have veered from intransigence to a failure of will.

Historians have sometimes considered 1453 as the year in which what was first labelled in the nineteenth century 'the Hundred Years War' ended. Contemporaries were not so prescient. The English Crown continued to claim the French one and to hold intact the March of Calais. Gascon sentiment remained pro-English. Former holders of titles, estates and commands in France did not forget their losses. Natives of France who had adhered to the English allegiance were not unfamiliar figures in the England of the 1450s. Invasion of France was not impracticable: the new power of the French monarchy was not so firmly established. Nor had traditional English methods of warfare become ineffective. In 1459 and 1461 English kings led armies which contemporaries considered formidable in size and discipline. Writing in the 1470s, despite his knowledge of the débâcles in France, Fortescue displayed complete faith in the traditional qualities of the English soldier. What ended the war in 1453 was a decade or so of domestic conflict: the Wars of the Roses. English kings of the later fifteenth century showed themselves alive to the possibilities of pursuing their French claims, but time had freed them from the incubus of defending the 1420 settlement and they intervened more in the spirit of Edward III in the 1340s and 1350s, being flexibly prepared to exploit the internal and diplomatic difficulties of a 'tyrannical' and expansionary Valois monarchy.

Military organisation and the consequences of the war

A state of war with the French Crown was a situation to which fourteenth-century Englishmen became accustomed from the 1340s, apart from a comparatively brief period of peace (1360–9), though a general truce was in operation in more years than hostilities – continuously from 1389 till the end of the century. Nevertheless, at some time during almost every decade from 1337 onwards the inhabitants of southern England, especially in coastal counties, lived in fear of attack. In 1377 sixteen townships in the Isle of Wight were said to have been 'utterly burnt and destroyed by the enemy' and in 1378 the inhabitants of Thanet had 'recently withdrawn through fear of invasion'. The tendency to flee and the spread of rumours of war inland is reflected in the confession of Robert Benet of Barford St John (Oxon) in 1381 that he had received part of a bribe from an esquire of the Admiral of France, John de Vienne, at Portsmouth, and, when the admiral landed at Rye, was to have received more with his accomplices 'on condition that they withdrew themselves and as many others from England as they could, permitting the enemies of France to lay terror to parts of England . . . and there to burn, kill and destroy'.

Defence relied partly on militarily experienced gentlemen, bearers of royal commissions of array, who by their authority summoned able-bodied men between the ages of sixteen and sixty to appear armed, and inspected and organised them for action. On the coasts the arrayers for the shire supervised watches and ensured that beacons were maintained to signal alarms. The quality of the defence depended on the presence and zeal of local magnates and leading gentry, first-named in the commissions of array, whose life-retainers provided a professional fighting nucleus, and on the determination of urban elites to spend on defence works and man them. The chronicler Thomas Walsingham was convinced that the absence of the earl of Arundel and his lances from Sussex, when the French and Castilians landed in 1377 and 1380, sapped the local will to resist.

But among coastal dwellers, who could not afford to endure local devastation as easily as magnates, there was a movement to invest in fortifications. A surviving section (*c.*1345) of the town wall at Southampton, which was unwalled when it was sacked and burnt in 1338, and the impressive West Gate at Canterbury (*c.*1380) provide evidence of high municipal expenditure. In the 1380s Bishop Rede of Chichester fortified his manor-house at Amberley, and Sir Edward Dallingridge built Bodiam Castle. In the same period John lord Cobham built Cooling Castle (Kent) near the Thames estuary, specifying his purpose in terms of local patriotism on an engraved plaque affixed to the gatehouse:

Knoweth that beth and schal be
That I am mad in help of the cuntre
In knowyng of whyche thyng
This is chartre and wytnessyng.

It may not be entirely coincidental that both Dallingridge and Cobham, who built defences at a time when Richard II's government seemed unable to prevent invasion threats to their exposed estates, supported his critics in the period 1386–88. But there were comparatively few Englishmen who suffered by the devastation of their estates or were burdened by the need to erect costly defences. The only regions which suffered general and repeated rural devastation, radically affecting prosperity and social structure, were those northern parts most exposed to Scottish raids (see pp. 141 ff).

Even though England suffered few attacks, these (and the fear that they might escalate) contributed to an intensification of national feeling. Hatred of foreigners was also deliberately stirred up by the Crown as a means of extracting war subsidies. Speeches by royal representatives in parliament and proclamations cried in shire courts and market places harped on the malignant intentions of the French and other adversaries, sometimes crediting them with the aim of wishing to subvert utterly the use of the English language. Such an argument could only have been fully effective among property-holders in a period when English was becoming their common tongue. In the second half of the fourteenth century it gradually supplanted Norman-French as the polite, literary language of the educated laity. In 1363 a Chancellor addressed parliament in English and in 1404 two English envoys to France confessed themselves to be 'as ignorant of French as of Hebrew'. By the 1450s a standard written English was becoming established, displacing the literary use of dialects. This development was probably facilitated by the comparative homogeneity of the realm's ruling elites, and stimulated by a more general social and geographical mobility, resulting from the demographic crisis of the later fourteenth century.

The length of the Crown's confrontations with Scots, French, Spaniards and, more briefly, Welsh, helped to promote this sense of common 'Englishness' reflected in the new pride in a common tongue. Men from Devon, Kent and Northumberland became aware of their interdependence for the sinews of defence. Deeply inherent feelings for kin, neighbourhood and province were now contained within a wider sense of community, which identified as aliens those who spoke a foreign tongue. Henry V's 1419 ordinances of war decreed that 'no manner man give no reproach to none other, because of the country that he is of, that is to say be he French, English, Welsh or Irish, or of any other country'. Men who spoke English with an unfamiliar accent were frequently denounced as Scots in the fifteenth century. The retired professional soldiers who had spent long hours peering up the Tweed estuary from Berwick, Wark and Norham, or foraging the farmhouses around St Omer and Boulogne, may have promoted the concept that Englishmen should stand together against 'them'. Some foreign commentators – Froissart, Pitti, Diaz de Gamez – remarked on the mutual savageries of Anglo-French warfare. The way in which hatred of foreigners spread among those not directly affected by warfare is shown by the St Albans monk Walsingham's account of the activities of a Scots raiding force in Northumberland in 1379. He condemned them as barbaric and depraved enemies of humanity, who did not spare the inhabitants despite the plague raging there. He resorts to linguistic ridicule, reproducing in an approximation to Lowlands dialect the invocations which the Scots with misplaced confidence in their saintly cults used to ward off the plague. Walsingham almost certainly derived his highly charged account of distant events from a *confrère* of Tynemouth Priory, cell of St Albans Abbey.

Despite the fact that members of the chivalrous elite acquired French estates and titles, had courteous dealings with foreign allies and adversaries and illicit affairs with French girls, the war seems to have made them more aware of their 'Englishness'. Some foreign writers complained of the way in which the English nobility tried to belittle chivalrous visitors. Fortescue, whose sophistication derived from his travels as well as his learning, argued that the commons surpassed Scots or Frenchmen in 'heart'. The former Justice of the King's Bench claimed that superior English courage was shown by the larger numbers of Englishmen convicted of robbery and manslaughter. English robbers, he alleged, attacked in spite of unfavourable odds, whereas French ones hardly did so when they outnumbered the potential victims. Scots preferred to commit larceny in the absence of owners. His sentiments, hardly in the spirit of international chivalry, would doubtless have been approved by Charles Brandon, duke of Suffolk, who, to Henry VIII's embarrassment, declared during an Anglo-French conference in 1520 that, if he thought he had any French blood, he would rather lose all his blood.

Threats of foreign incursions did not loom so large for most of the fifteenth-century phase of the war. To the author of *The Libel of English Policy* (see p. 49), the threats that mattered were those from Breton pirates (especially from St Malo) and the Flemish pirate Hannekin Lyon. Through the dissemination of chronicles produced for the London mercantile elite, their anti-alien attitudes, partly inspired by the likes of Lyon, not the Valois treatment of their sovereign, were spread through the realm. In the 1420s, the Crown had promoted Anglo-French amity. The theme appears in Henry VI's English coronation banquet (1429), part of the first course of which was 'Custard royal with a leopard of gold sitting therein. Fritter like a sun with a fleur de lis therein. A subtlety, St Edward and St Louis, clad in coat armour bringing in between the king in his coat armour' (bearing a celebratory verse). The Crown's war aims did not always promote anti-alien and national feeling, and there were other social and economic factors in the period which did.

Without more detailed statistical information than is at present available it is difficult to be certain whether the English on the whole gained or lost financially through participation in the war, or whether individual gains or losses significantly affected the social structure. A complicating factor is that part of the period during which the war was fought (especially the second half of the fourteenth century) was one in which the recurrence of virulent epidemics (whose level was not notably increased in England by warfare) undoubtedly produced important social changes.

The fourteenth-century reduction of population aggravated the shortage of English manpower. Naval and overseas military service, customarily paid for by the Crown, was remunerated at generous rates, graded according to social rank and military function. Able-bodied men could take advantage, provided they could equip themselves adequately, the lowly receiving pay whose differential from that of their social superiors was much smaller than in civilian life[5]. Recruitment was partly carried out by commissions of array, the arrayed men travelling from their county boundary at the county's expense and receiving the king's wages from their arrival at the embarkation port. Also individual captains made contracts with the Crown to raise retinues. They bargained and then indented to serve for a specific period on an expedition or for the safeguard of a castle with an agreed number of knights, men-at-arms and archers. The captain was to receive royal rates of pay for himself and his retinue, first instalments being paid to his clerks when he mustered his retinue at the embarkation port or the castle, in the presence of Exchequer clerks. In the meantime the captain had drawn up similar contracts for service in his retinue with knights and men-at-arms, individually or in pairs, specifying service by themselves or accompanied by an agreed number of other men-at-arms and archers.

Though large numbers of contracts between Crown and captains survive in the Exchequer records, comparatively few subcontracts do. There is a batch of twenty-four which Sir Hugh Hastings of Elsing (Norfolk) made to constitute partially the retinue he contracted to take on Buckingham's French expedition of 1380[6]. These show that Sir Hugh did not conclude uniform bargains: some of his retainers agreed to receive royal rates of pay, but others settled for lower and considerably varied ones. The variations may reflect degrees of military skill and experience. Negotiability of pay was probably an accepted principle, enabling the captain to recoup from differentials on his own heavy incidental expenses. But one governing factor in this flexible bargaining was the need to recruit well, possibly attempting to attract the service of experienced companies, such as may have been the four men-at-arms and five archers whom Jankyn Nowell contracted to bring as a company into Hastings's retinue in 1380. In 1492 Roger L'Estrange, recruiting archers, advertised that 'as for their wages, they shall have the King's wages and some what else, so that I trust that they shall be pleased'.

Control of pay was a vital element in the success of English forces: on it hinged the maintenance of discipline. The mutual obligations of Crown and captain, laid down in standard formulae, were cemented by the payment of the whole retinue's wages to the latter. The Crown could withhold pay from the recalcitrant captain: his subcontracting knights and men-at-arms were beholden to him, and the segments of the retinue receiving pay from a particular subcontractor had a motive for obedience to him. A consequence was that English soldiers were rarely disobedient: mutinies only occurred, as in Spain in 1382 or at Calais several times in the fifteenth century, when pay was in arrears. An expedition in which the normal pay structure was not adhered to illustrated the wisdom of the system. In 1370 Sir Robert Knolles and other distinguished knights led an expedition to France intended to support itself by levying land not in the king's allegiance. It was a complete failure, partly due to the fact that the captains lacked the authority which control of pay normally gave them.

The maintenance of this authority frequently left the captain out of pocket, especially as he had already had the expense of equipping himself and his servants for an expedition and, possibly, of anticipating Crown payments in order to attract good soldiers into his retinue. For, once the expedition was under way, to maintain authority, the captain sometimes had to pay out of his own pocket later instalments promised by the Crown, especially when the original period of service on campaign was extended. There are numerous petitions from former captains claiming that the Crown owed them wages, allegedly to their impoverishment, some made years after performance of the services claimed for.

Men did not contract to supply or join retinues necessarily because they considered it would be a profitable venture. Many probably did so because it was part of their obligation to a patron to serve him in peace or war. Sir Hugh Hastings's service on his feudal lord John of Gaunt's expedition to Castile in 1386 was in the tradition of his family's Lancastrian service. His father Sir Hugh (d.1369) had been retained by the duke in 1366 to serve in war and peace, and had previously served Henry of Grosmont, duke of Lancaster, on military expeditions. There were other motives for service: the promise of a pardon for outlawry, the opportunity to sue out a writ of protection which suspended legal processes against the soldier in royal service. Young men may have been eager for a chivalrous, exciting life, free from the constrictions of school or apprenticeship, seeking male companionship in what must have often been the emotionally tight-knit circles of well run retinues. By the end of the fourteenth century the English professional soldier was a familiar figure, in times of truce serving in garrisons, going on crusade, fighting as a mercenary in the Low Countries, Spain and Italy, or joining 'free companies' of *routiers* in the south of France, ruling regions under the nominal allegiance of the English Crown. Chaucer's Knight is one example of a professional soldier newly arrived from abroad.

For those going on a single expedition, or adopting the life of the professional, there was more than the chance of making a sometimes tenuous, sometimes well-paid living, and of winning honour and patronage. War was a lottery in which the lucky few made fortunes through ransoms. Others suffered disasters, such as Bleddyn ap Dafydd ap Madoc, who was said in 1384 to have deserted to the French side, after being captured by them for the third time. According to the formula in indentures for service which became standard by the end of Edward III's reign, captors of prisoners were obliged to pay one-third of the value of ransoms, captured horses, armour, etc, to their retinue captain, who in turn was obliged to hand over one third of his receipts to the Crown. Indentures between Crown and captains specified that if a 'capital enemy' was captured (such as David II at Neville's Cross, 1346; John II at Poitiers, 1356; Charles of Orleans at Agincourt, 1415), he became the king's prisoner, the other parties being compensated. Similar laws, with a different basis of division, governed the allocation of naval prizes.

In practice the man-at-arms or archer who captured a soldier of higher status probably sold his prisoner to his captain. A ransom was a gentlemanly investment, which required the capital outlay necessary to maintain the prisoner according to his rank, sometimes for years. Prisoners were traded in England like other pieces of property, often with the assistance of mercantile capital and sometimes as a joint or syndicated investment. The capture of prisoners was a preoccupation of all ranks. When the English were encumbered with prisoners at Agincourt, the soldiers would not obey Henry V's orders to kill them. He sent members of his retinue to do the job, depriving many at a stroke of the fortune of a lifetime.

There were other opportunities to profit from the English mode of warfare. In the fourteenth century a prominent feature of strategy was the attempt to undermine Valois resources by pillaging communities in the enemy's obedience. Henry V, more consistently intent on getting these communities to accept his allegiance, strove to limit military destructiveness. But this probably ran counter to his soldiers' instincts. Nicholas Upton, who served the earl of Salisbury (d.1428), remarked that the 'canonical truce', intended to give churchmen and their goods, pilgrims, hermits and cultivators of the soil carrying on their work, complete immunity from warfare, was not observed in France in his time. English forces in the last decade or so of rule in France may have tended to plunder. William Worcester, informed perhaps by his master Sir John Fastolf, remarked how many soldiers, in default of payment of wages, took victuals without compensation from the king's subjects in France 'by ten or twelve years daily continuously before the said lands were lost, neither corrected nor punished, as turned to the great undoing of your said lieges, and one other of the great causes that they have turned their hearts from us, breaking their allegiance by manner of coercion from such rapine, oppressions and extortions'.

One lucrative source of profit was the occupation of French estates. In the fourteenth century the English garrisoned castles in many parts of France, particularly in Brittany. There in the 1350s and early 1360s garrisons evolved and applied a system of taxing castellanies. They levied agricultural produce, raw materials for the maintenance of their castles and labour services. Their collectors, making circuits, accounted to the receiver at the castle at Easter and Michaelmas. Fortunes were made in Brittany: the best known profiteer was Sir Robert Knolles. After Henry V's conquest of Normandy (1417–19), Englishmen were recipients of his grants of castles and estates there whose dauphinist owners had forfeited. Similar grants were made in other provinces where English control was consolidated under Bedford: Anjou, Maine and Touraine. As late as the 1440s, when the English hold on Normandy was weakened, Fastolf was remitting through his bankers to England substantial profits from his Norman estates. Fastolf is the classic example of a gentleman of originally moderate means who had a distinguished military career and made a fortune. He was appointed councillor to Bedford, and to Richard duke of York, when he was first lieutenant in France, and was elected Knight of the Garter. With his war profits he purchased in the 1420s and 1430s estates in East Anglia and elsewhere, and constructed, at Caister near Yarmouth, a castle on a scale of magnificence envied in Norfolk. Retiring from active commands in France in the 1440s, he moved into Caister in the 1450s, a sick, querulous old man, like others disgruntled by the loss of his French estates, and scheming to recover huge debts which he claimed the Crown owed him for military services.

Considerable information survives about Fastolf's finances because his secretary Worcester filed his papers for an intended biography. Many documents were subsequently preserved by those who acquired parts of Fastolf's disputed inheritance – the Paston family and Magdalen College, Oxford. No other 'war profiteer' is so well documented. There are some literary indications that contemporaries believed that fortunes or at least livelihoods were made on a significant scale in the war. Chroniclers of the 1340s and 1350s speak of great quantities of plunder brought back from France by commons as well as nobles. According to Froissart, a cause of opposition to Richard II's peace diplomacy in the 1390s was the dependence of many knights and esquires on the war for their livelihood. Others had doubtless risen along the paths described by Adam Usk in the case of Sir Roger Acton (a Lollard knight):

This knight, the son of a tiler, sprung from a lowly family of Shropshire, being enriched with the plunder and spoils of the Welsh war [*against Owain Glyn Dŵr*]*, and being puffed up beyond measure, got himself honoured with the privilege of the military order and with the belt of knighthood by King Henry IV.*

In Henry VIII's reign, the antiquary John Leland noted traditions that a number of castles and country-houses were paid for by war profits. This is certainly likely to have been true in the case of houses built by careerist soldiers, such as Sir William Oldhall (d.1460). One of the most experienced Lancastrian knights in France – seneschal of Normandy (1425) and recipient in the 1420s and later of captaincies in the *pays de conquête* and of Norman estates – he built Hunsdon House in Hertfordshire.

Despite hints of great individual profits, it is unlikely that the incomes of any rank in society became more than locally dependent on war profits, or that the gains and losses of soldiers had generally significant effects on the economy. Rich veterans such as Fastolf and Oldhall were probably as unique as West Indian planters and East Indian 'nabobs' were to be in eighteenth-century English society. There is almost no information available as to whether the profits of common soldiers improved the lot of peasant and artisan families. Population decline (see pp. 16 ff) gave the commons opportunities for betterment besides those arising from military service. Landowners experiencing a fall in revenue did not need to turn to it: there were other respectable ways of recouping 'gentle' fortunes (see pp. 136 ff). Norfolk may have produced the best-known veteran profiteer, Fastolf, and the best-documented example of a soldier who rose from the ranks, Sir Robert Salle of Salle (d.1381), son of a villein and mason. But in 1492 Roger L'Estrange and William Paston despairingly scoured the county, one of the most populous, to recruit for the retinues which they had contracted to take on the royal expedition to France. In such agriculturally rich and industrially burgeoning regions, men did not need to take up the fighting profession.

The same may not have been so true of less well endowed regions. In parts of the West Country some communities lived on the profits of warfare, robbing Channel shipping. In Henry IV's reign some of their naval commanders, such as Henry Pay of Poole, and Robert Hawley of Dartmouth, grew rich on prizes, and achieved international ill-repute equal to that of Elizabethan privateers. Such men tended to be indiscriminate in their choice of victims, who often found redress was not forthcoming, on appeal to sometimes collusive conservators of truces in the local admiralty courts. In barren parts of the highland zone, there may have been especial dependence on military service in France. There Scottish raids made the gentry more military in their habits. Northern magnates and knights figured prominently in French campaigns. This is reflected in the wealth of detail the anonymous chronicler of St Mary's Abbey, York, was able to procure about them in Edward III's reign. But the war did not produce a general 'militarisation' of English society. Chaucer's Franklin remained a more characteristic figure in most parts than his Knight, and there was no great increase in the small proportion of landowners able to bear the costs of knighthood who took it up. Worcester, in his *Book of Noblesse*, presented to Edward IV in the 1470s in anticipation of his invasion of France, lamented that gentlemen neglected the military arts: he who was influential in the shire as a justice of the peace or sheriff was 'as the world goes now, more esteemed among all estates than he who has spent thirty or forty years of his days in great jeopardy in your ancestors' conquests and wars'.

A bourgeois, William Caxton, harangued Richard III in an epilogue (*c*.1484) in remarkably similar vein:

Oh, ye knights of England, where is the custom and usage of noble chivalry that was used in those days [of the ancient British kings]? What do ye now but go to the baths[7] *and play at dice? . . . how many knights be there now in England that have the use and the exercise of a knight, that is to say, that he knoweth his horse, and his horse him . . . his armours and harness meet and fitting.*

The effects of the war on industry, commerce and capitalist enterprise have yet to be fully researched. The manufacture of armour and iron-based weapons and implements (arrow-heads, rings, nails, etc), must have been stimulated, though production of larger and more complex armaments such as guns and armours may have been limited by competition from the established, large-scale centres of production in Flanders and Brabent. William Paston decided to buy his military harness in Calais rather than London in 1492, probably because cheap imported products might be more available there. Swords and armours of high quality were imported from Lombardy and Westphalia.

Significant profits were probably made by native farmers, artisans, craftsmen and merchants supplying commodities, facilities for lodging and transport, and capital. This may have been especially the case in the usual base ports and their hinterlands, mostly in the more prosperous regions. Expeditions to the Low Countries and northern France customarily assembled at Yarmouth, Ipswich, London, Dover or Sandwich; at Portsmouth or Southampton for western Normandy, Brittany and Aquitaine; at Plymouth for Aquitaine and the Iberian peninsula. Newcastle and Berwick were the principal bases for invasions of Scotland.

English cloth manufacturers were well placed to compete with Flanders in the supply of banners, tents, bags, horse-blankets, bedding, warm clothing, bandages and the red crosses of St George which, it was ordained on a royal expedition of 1385, every soldier was to wear. Before 1350 soldiers from Flintshire, Cheshire and north Wales were supplied with hats and jackets of green and white. Worcester tells us how Fastolf clothed his retinues: 'For the space of twenty-two years or more Sir John bought every year to the value of more than £100 of red and white cloth of his tenants in Castle Combe.'

Timber was much in demand, being needed for storage tuns, provision and gun carts, gangplanks for horses, partitions to stable them on shipboard, 'castles' to be fitted stem and stern to improve the defensibility of merchant ships, the construction of the king's navy, scaling ladders, ridgepoles, pikeshafts, arrows and bowstaves. In 1356 the chamberlain of Chester was unable to obtain arrows from England, 'because the king has . . . taken for his use all the arrows that can be found anywhere there'. Perhaps because of the high price of timber in York, John Swerd, bowyer there, considered it economic in 1373 to procure licence to send his employees 'to Prussia to stay there for four years to fashion bows there and send them to York'. Warfare probably made horse-breeding as well as emparking more profitable, especially since mobile expeditions in France were normally mounted from the 1340s onwards.

Farmers, victuallers, ale-keepers and prostitutes profited from an army's assembly. Its ships needed provisioning, often for a voyage of several weeks' duration. Bad weather, logistic difficulties and political uncertainties often detained armies at assembly ports for long periods. John of Gaunt's Castilian expedition remained encamped around Plymouth for several months in 1386. Admirals and sheriffs had responsibility for ensuring sufficient supplies. Ports sometimes equipped and victualled their own ships for royal service. In 1340 Yarmouth supplied thirty ships for forty days' service between England and Flanders, fully victualled. Three contractors undertook to supply a gallon of ale a day for each of the 1,510 seamen aboard. Such demands must have driven up local commodity prices. In 1492 William Paston, writing from London about his preparations for taking part in Henry VII's expedition to France, complained that 'I am as yet no better horsed than I was when I was with you, nor I know not where to have none, for horse flesh is of such a price here that my purse is scarce able to buy one horse; wherefore I beseech you to hearken for some in your country'.

Once expeditions landed, they were often dependent for supplies on English shipments, since they were operating in country scoured to the bone. According to a letter written home during the siege of Calais in 1346

the king hath sent to you for victuals and that too as quickly as you can send; for from the time that we departed from Caen, we have lived on the country to the great travail and harm of our people, but thanks be to God, we have no loss. But now we are in such plight that we must in part be refreshed by victuals.

Henry V's armies before Harfleur in 1415 and Rouen in 1418–19 likewise relied heavily on home supplies, dispatched through Southampton. The garrisons permanently established near and outside the borders of the realm required victualling too. Among the principal royal garrisons within the king's ancient possessions were those at Carlisle, Yarmouth, the Tower of London, Dover, Sandwich, Southampton and in the Channel Islands and Gascony. The nature of the Gascon economy made it necessary to dispatch English corn and meat for the soldiers there. But in time of truce local supplies were brought into the English garrisons at Calais, Cherbourg, Brest, Lochmaben, Roxburgh, Berwick etc. by men not in the king's allegiance, as well as neighbouring inhabitants who had accepted it. On a notorious occasion in 1379, during time of truce, the Scottish earl of March attacked Roxburgh when its fair was being attended by a large number of Scotsmen. Many English were killed, and goods burnt and plundered. However, frontier garrisons still depended heavily on English merchants. The large establishment in the March of Calais (1,000 in time of truce) was supplied by their contracts with wheat, malt, oats, beans, peas, beef and bacon carcasses, and English garrisons in the Marches towards Scotland, whose hinterlands were not highly productive, were supplied from Newcastle and the North Sea ports with corn, dried fish, beer and wine.

The Crown, in order to get expeditions speedily off the ground, needed to anticipate subsidies granted for the purpose by raising loans. In the first decades of the war Italian companies were Edward III's principal creditors. But in 1343 he failed to fulfil terms of repayment to the Florentine houses, Bardi and Peruzzi, precipitating their collapse. Afterwards Italian companies were more cautious in financing the English Crown. English merchants figured increasingly prominently as Edward's backers, notably Sir William de la Pole of Hull (d.1366), the one bourgeois war profiteer who founded a magnate inheritance. He proved more astute than some London creditors in getting good security for his loans to the Crown. Overestimation of the yield of taxes was the ruin of native and alien merchants. In the early 1370s syndicates of London merchants, using good government contacts, carefully secured their profit margins (see pp. 172–3). In the fifteenth century kings relied heavily on magnates to supplement loans, above all in the reigns of Henry V and his son on their kinsman Bishop Beaufort of Winchester, better placed than most to procure excellent security for prompt repayment from the Crown.

The transport, supply and financing of expeditions may have tended to concentrate capital in the hands of wealthy merchants of the leading ports. It is probably not coincidental that native capitalist entrepreneurs are prominent in the period, though other factors, such as the cloth industry, help account for their rise. The adverse conditions for overseas trade caused by the war probably drove the weaker to the wall. There was the heavy war taxation on wool exports. All cargoes were vulnerable, since much of the war was fought in the sea-lanes of north-west Europe. English shipping, sailing seasonally along well-defined coastal lanes, was funnelled along the North Sea shores of England and through the 'Narrow Seas' to the Low Countries, Gascony and Castile. Truces were hard to enforce at sea, as the Crown issued licences to take reprisals and there were hostile piratical communities who lived by plundering commerce. It was advisable to invest in the addition to ships of defensive superstructures, the purchase of guns, hiring of soldiers and adherence to a convoy system. Freight rates consequently rose. Royal records are full of merchants' and shipowners' complaints. In 1377 John Philpot and other London merchants complained that during the previous year's truce the French had plundered their goods, in ships sailing from Flanders and Calais, to the value of £1,340, taking them in to St Valery and Harfleur. In 1384 London vintner John Clopton, 'formerly a man of honour', unable to support his wife and five children, was in hiding from his creditors, as a result of his losses at sea, particularly of one consignment the previous year.

Another subject of complaint was the impressment of ships and mariners by the admirals into the royal service: until the evolution of the warship with its gun-decks in the sixteenth century, the Crown relied mainly on merchant shipping for its fleets, especially the two- and three-masted ones built increasingly in the fifteenth century to export cloth. Owners were entitled to payment rated according to the tunnage of their vessels, and compensation for damage to fittings and loss of stores: crews received royal pay, simple sailors at the rate of threepence a day. But the Commons complained in 1378 of failures and delays in payment.

Periods of hostility exposed English ships and cargoes to seizure in neutral ports in reprisal, and closed some lucrative markets. The Crown placed embargoes on trade with Flanders, whose rulers at times endeavoured, not always successfully, to exclude English traders from the Netherlands, in part for strictly commercial reasons. The Franco-Scottish alliance tended to deprive the English of Scottish markets, a 'natural' hinterland. The depressions of the Gascon economy as a result of war and the conquest of the region by the French Crown finally in 1453 deprived overseas traders of a mainstay. The hostilities with Castile, mainly in the fourteenth century, were against Bristol interests. But warfare itself provided another means of compensation. There were prizes to be gained, in which the humblest mariner received a share. In 1378 John Philpot fitted out a private naval expedition, struck a telling blow at the Scots privateer John Mercer, and captured fifteen Spanish ships. In 1380 the men of Hull and Newcastle captured a Spanish ship whose cargo was said to be worth 7,000 marks. The owners of the *James* of Bristol found a means to recoup themselves for the cost of transporting the duke of York and his retinue to Normandy in 1436: they procured a licence to make war at sea.

The effects of the war can at present be more clearly seen in the spheres of national politics and royal finances than in the economy. A fundamentally important point is that before the outbreak of the war it had been established that military service to the Crown outside the realm should be paid for. Though wage scales remained remarkably stable, technical advances increased the costs of warfare. By the 1370s artillery was becoming effective against fixed defences. The Crown developed an ordnance department (the Tower of London being its chief depot) and improved fortifications to resist as well as mount guns. Moreover, the interminable war, becoming in a sense institutionalised, necessitated permanent defences in times of truce as well as war. Royal castles protected the northern borders at Carlisle, Roxburgh (lost in 1460) and Berwick (lost 1461–82). The castles founded in Wales by Edward I (e.g. Conway, Aberystwyth) had to be garrisoned, the royal defences of vulnerable south-eastern England to be maintained and strengthened. In the 1360s Edward III built an entirely new castle at Queenborough (Kent) to guard the confluence of the Thames and Medway. In the 1380s Southampton Castle was extensively reconstructed. In the years 1416–22 Henry V spent more than £1,000 providing defences for his expanding royal navy by the construction at Portsmouth of a round tower with attached chain-boom.

Garrisons outwith the realm, in Scotland, Picardy, Normandy, Brittany and Gascony, were at various times financed by English revenues. The March of Calais was the most expensive base. The town's flat hinterland and partly alien population necessitated the maintenance of large garrisons in its castle and at Guines, Oye and Sangatte. The defences at Calais were threatened by erosion. In 1439 breaches in the sea wall led to flooding in the north-west corner of the town: the castle defences started to crumble. Between then and 1451 about £11,000 was spent on works at Calais.

Some impression of the financial burden placed on the Crown by the cost of only some garrisons (and apart from the cost of expeditions) can be gained from the estimate of royal liabilities and revenues compiled by the Treasurer, Ralph lord Cromwell in 1433. At that time the English Crown did not have to provide for Breton or Norman garrisons, urgently maintain English and Welsh coastal defences or fight the Scottish Crown. The estimate of total current expenditure for the year was £56,878. £19,487 of this was accounted for by the expenses of the East and West Marches, Roxburgh, Aquitaine and the March of Calais. The last item alone cost £11,930. These figures are to be contrasted with his estimate of the Crown's current cash revenue (about £36,000). In addition to his statement of current liabilities, Cromwell tabulated ancient royal debts for expenses in Calais, the Marches towards Scotland, Aquitaine and Ireland totalling £110,584.

Such figures indicate why the Crown found difficulty in financing the defence burden without the aid of subjects. It was more dependent for the launching of offensives on the grant of subsidies. Before the end of Edward III's reign the Commons had shown a realisation of the bargaining power that his resort to a high and regular level of parliamentary taxation had given them. Soon after his death, when a youthful king was unable to give a decisive lead, and magnates were bitterly divided over war strategy, there is evidence that the Commons attempted to influence the conduct of the war.

But they apparently used their power mainly to gain redress of domestic grievances and to ensure that their grants were spent for the intended purposes. Their impressively co-ordinated agitation swung the balance of power between Crown and community, provoking political tensions, especially in Richard II's reign. This was one symptom of a partial atrophying of royal power in England characteristic of a period in which kings sought to retain or gain glittering prizes abroad. Dependent on the co-operation of local elites to wage war overseas, the Crown was tender of their domestic susceptibilities. In Edward III's reign the abuses of arbitrary royal levying and purveyance declined, tenants-in-chief were frequently licensed to evade 'prerogative wardship' for their heirs, the grip of royal bureaucrats on the local administration of justice further weakened, and government showed itself sensitive to issues agitating the landowning milch-cow, such as the competition for benefices of alien provisors and the rise in labourers' wages. One individual's sense of his ability to bargain for favours with the Crown is reflected in Richard lord Scrope's will, made at Rouen in 1420 after his participation in its capture. He was willing to waive half the wages the king owed him if his executors received royal favour in fulfilling his intent, for example over the grant of a royal licence to alienate land to a college of chantry priests. The rebels of the later fourteenth century, even the commons of 1381, professed themselves ardent royalists, defenders of royal prerogative, because men had the expectation of royal power being used in the interests of the community. The Crown was the prism through which local elites conceived authority and rights should be refracted to them. The king's role as their arbiter rather than their more arbitrary exploiter was a diminution to which the needs of his war probably contributed. Yet his involvement of the community in the war enhanced his martial authority and splendour: kings were looked on as the necessary defenders of the realm, more actively than their predecessors.

The Crown was remarkably successful in the Hundred Years War in developing and regularising means of repeatedly and automatically concentrating the community's resources to provide effective forces for service abroad or at sea. This caused hardships: taxation was sometimes heavy, regions of labour intensive agriculture had their manpower shortage exacerbated, patterns of overseas trade were disrupted. The community had the motive and opportunity to extend and fix its parliamentary rights. There were other adjustments within the polity. The influence of magnates in the localities was boosted. War taxation from the community at large was funnelled through their hands – mainly back to the community, but especially to the benefit of poorer regions and of entrepreneurs, members of powerful urban elites whose expansionist dynamism it enhanced. Though the Crown's need to appease local circles of landowners may have accentuated their semi-autonomy, the war helped to promote a sense of common English interests. Edward III and his successors had involved the fears, ambitions and antagonisms of many of their lieges in their French claims, and the concepts of the English polity which this fostered remained strongly imprinted in the English consciousness. Shakespeare's history plays reveal the large extent to which the sixteenth-century Englishman was a product of the Hundred Years War.

Notes

1. The *parlement*, whose organisation was evolving markedly in the later thirteenth century, was the sovereign court of France, whose tribunals, consisting of lay and ecclesiastical judges, heard appeals from the judgments of lesser courts, noble as well as royal, from throughout the realm.
2. A possible relic of this episode is the so-called Black Prince's Ruby in the Imperial State Crown, which may well have been among the jewels Prince Edward acquired from his Castilian ally, King Pedro 'the Cruel'.
3. Earl of Buckingham; created duke of Gloucester 1385.
4. A garrison in the island-abbey of Mont St Michel resisted all English attempts to dislodge them. Two fifteenth-century cannon reputedly used by the besieging English can be seen there.
5. In 1355 the customary daily rates for service were: earls, 6*s* 8*d*, bannerets, 4*s*, knights, 2*s*, men-at-arms, 1*s*, mounted archers, 6*d*, foot archers, 3*d*, Welsh lancemen, 2*d*. A peasant could therefore earn as a mounted archer as much as a quarter of the knight's pay.
6. Formerly in the possession of Lord Hastings's family, they are deposited in the Norfolk and Norwich County Record Office (MR 514 242×5). I owe thanks to the Archivist, Miss J. M. Kennedy for her advice about the documents, and to Mr J. W. Sherborne, of the University of Bristol, for his comments on them.
7. Bathhouses in the fifteenth century had the same sort of reputation as the dubious sort of massage parlours in the 1970s.

Chapter 7

Dynastic instabilities, 1450–1587

The last phase of Lancastrian rule (1450–61)

From 1450 onwards the Lancastrian dynasty, whose rulers had entrenched themselves so successfully after the difficult early years, encountered a series of crises which culminated in the deposition of Henry VI in 1461. In the early 1460s Henry became the first English king to endure the ignominy of seeking refuge among the despised Scots (once, reportedly, 'at Kirkcudbright with four men and a child'), and of hiding as a poor fugitive in the remote northern parts of his own realm. In 1465 he was handed over as a prisoner to the man who had seized his throne, Edward of Rouen, eldest surviving son of his cousin, Richard duke of York (d.1460). In 1470 Henry was briefly restored, a pitiful figure, apparently lacking a change of regal clothes, according to a London chronicler. The disastrous failure of his restoration, known to contemporaries as the 'Readeption', ended the hopes of his dynasty. Henry's probably violent death in the Tower of London in 1471, not long after his only child, Edward prince of Wales, had died in battle at Tewkesbury, terminated the main Lancastrian line, which had become unprolific in the generation of Henry IV's children.

In 1471 Edward might have plausibly claimed to be the next heir of Henry VI (as his father may have wished to claim in 1450), as well as having a hereditary right arguably superior to Henry's. Nevertheless, Lancastrian sentiments lingered on. The Castilian and Portuguese royal houses and the Burgundian ducal house honoured their descents from John of Gaunt. In England Henry V's martial exploits were blithely recalled by writers of London chronicles favourable to the house of York. The pious cult of Henry VI started to flourish soon after his death. In 1479 Laurence Booth, archbishop of York, forbade veneration of an image of Henry VI. Nevertheless, miracles were attributed to the king and intercessory verses were composed. Early in June 1484 Thomas Everingham, knight of the Household, fought a naval action off Scarborough with French privateers. One of his men, injured by a cannon-ball, was laid in an open boat and there had a vision which he recognised as King Henry, come to his aid: 'One appeared to him in visible form, elegantly built, and a pilgrim by his dress – he seemed to have a gown of blue velvet, and had a yellow cap on his head, and a pilgrim's scrip slung at his side.' Having survived eleven days in the boat and confounded subsequent medical predictions, he sent his sister to the king's tomb with an image of himself in wax. This was soon after Richard III had transferred the body from Chertsey Abbey (Surrey) to St George's Chapel in Windsor Castle, 'at which time especially he [Henry] began to be famous for his miracles'. Eventually the man recovered completely and himself came to Windsor to give thanks.

Henry VII was to try to exploit lingering pro-Lancastrian feeling by stressing, in his badges and official life by the French humanist Bernard André, his links with the dynasty: his mother Margaret countess of Richmond (d.1509) was the daughter of John Beaufort, duke of Somerset (d.1444), and great-granddaughter of John of Gaunt. Henry VII and his son both promoted the cause of the canonisation of Henry VI: the former planned to translate his body to Westminster Abbey, where Henry VII's Chapel was first intended to house this second royal saint, proclaiming the hallowed traditions of the English Crown (recently besmirched by the strife of royal kinsfolk) near the tomb of Edward the Confessor. Nevertheless, at Henry VII's Court there may have been ambivalent feelings about the Lancastrians. Apart from a few ageing diehards such as his uncle Jasper Tudor, duke of Bedford (d.1495) and John de Vere, earl of Oxford (d.1513), most of the leading early Tudor nobles, courtiers and royal officials had either completely reconciled themselves to the House of York or made their fortunes in its service. It is curious that Henry VII kept a fool nicknamed 'the foolish duke of Lancaster'. Henry VIII had less reason than his father to stress his Lancastrian blood: as the son of Edward IV's eldest daughter Elizabeth he had the best claim to represent the House of York. In complexion and physique Henry VIII probably resembled his grandfather Edward rather than his own father. Moreover, Henry's presence as a young man powerfully impressed those who met him. He was so dazzling that it was difficult to doubt that here stood the rightful heir of famous and great kings of England.

The fortunes of Henry VI had started to deteriorate alarmingly in the years 1449–52, when Charles VII's lieutenants speedily conquered Normandy and Gascony (see pp. 253–4). To Englishmen these reverses seemed extraordinary and shattering. Famous towns which had been 'English' for decades, and in some cases for centuries, fell in months and even weeks. 'Treason' was the only explanation which readily occurred to most who reflected on the matter. Somerset surrendered Rouen in October 1449. In less than a year all the other undermanned Norman garrisons surrendered too. French invasion of Gascony also produced swift success. The March of Calais, the one remaining English possession in France, was not attacked – a successful assault required Burgundian co-operation. Moreover, the port defences had recently been strengthened. This was one sphere in which the Lancastrian government was not negligent. Somerset was appointed captain of Calais in September 1451 and took vigorous measures against a siege, reinforcing the garrison and ensuring that it was paid and well equipped. Nevertheless, Charles VII's conquests increased the insecurity of Calais and of southern England. Norman sailors threatened English coasts and commerce, as they had done before Henry V's victories, and English merchants no longer had their ancient havens in the Bay of Biscay. An ominous foretaste of what might follow was the attack on Winchelsea in 1457 by Pierre de Brézé, the victor over the English army under Sir Thomas Kyriel which had landed in Normandy in 1450.

The outbreak of war with France and the reverses produced swift political repercussions in England. In February 1450, during the second session of the parliament which had first met in November 1449, the Commons commenced impeachment of the duke of Suffolk, accusing him, among other offences, of being an adherent of Charles VII:

Upon which adherence, counsel and comfort of the said Duke of Suffolk, the said Charles calling himself king hath made open war against you in your said realm of France, and hath it beguiled unto him, and the most party of your duchy of Normandy, and taken prisoners the full noble Lords and courageous Knights, the Earl of Shrewsbury and the Lord Fauconberg, with many other nobles and people of your true lieges, to their likely final undoing, your greatest disinheritance, and our great lamentable loss that ever has come afore this to you, or any of your full noble progenitors, or to your true subjects.

Suffolk spiritedly repudiated the charges and successfully evaded judgment by submitting himself to the king's 'rule and governance'. In the presence of Henry and of peers, in the king's 'innest chambre with a gabill wyndowe over a cloyster' in Westminster Palace, the Chancellor ordered Suffolk to remove to the king's lordships in France, or elsewhere outside England. In May the duke was intercepted off Dover by a ship, the *Nicholas of the Tower*, whose master hailed him aboard with the ominous words 'Welcome, Traitor'. Deserted by his own sailors,

in the sight of all his men he was drawn out of the great ship into the boat; and there was an axe, and a stock, and one of the lewdest of the ship bade him lay down his head, and he should be fairly treated, and die on a sword; and took a rusty sword, and smote off his head within half a dozen strokes, and took away his gown of russet, and his doublet of mailed velvet, and laid his body on the sands of Dover.

The indignation of the master and crew of the *Nicholas* was probably shared by many gentlemen and commons in southern England, in regions where the failures in France were well known and menacing. There, too, courtiers since the king's majority had used their access to royal favour and patronage narrowly and blatantly in their friends' interests. In one of the articles of impeachment Suffolk was accused of having used his Court favour malignantly:

Many of your true lieges by his might and the help of his adherents disinherited, impoverished and destroyed, and thereby he hath purchased many great possessions by maintenance [see pp. 148 ff], and done great outrageous extortions and murders: manslayers, rioters in every part of this your realm have drawn to him and for great goods to him given, have been maintained and supported in suppressing of justice.

The intensity of feeling which some expressed against those trying to monopolise the Crown's influence and wealth is reflected in satirical verses which survive, denigrating and abusing leading councillors and courtiers such as Suffolk, Somerset and men of their 'affinities'. Riots and breaches of the peace culminated in June 1450 in a rebellion of the commons of Kent, Essex, Surrey and Sussex, headed by the mysterious Jack Cade, joined by a number of gentry and echoed by disturbances elsewhere in southern England. When the royal force sent into Kent was defeated, Henry and his Court retired to a Midlands residence, Kenilworth Castle. The rebels denounced the 'insatiable covetous malicious pomps' of those who deceived Henry, who were 'daily and nightly . . . about his person and daily inform him that good is evil and evil is good'. Their manifesto went on to argue that a dangerous distinction had arisen between 'law' and 'right'. By resorting to force they were in fact doing on a grander scale what many of those who rioted, assaulted, trespassed and maintained, claimed they were doing in the localities in the period – taking extra-legal remedy when resort to the courts had failed:

Also the law serves for nought else in these days but to do wrong, for nothing is sped almost but false matters by colour of the law for bribery, dread, and favour, and so no remedy is obtainable in the court of conscience in any way. Also we say our sovereign lord may understand that his false council has lost his law, his merchandise is lost, his common people is destroyed, the sea is lost, France is lost, the king himself is so beset that he may not pay for his meat and drink, and he owes more than ever any King of England ought, for daily his traitors about him, when any thing should come to him by his laws, at once ask it from him.

Some of these complaints echo (reflecting the diffusion of political notions) protests and petitions in recent parliaments about treason in high places and the need for an Act of Resumption (see p. 107) to increase the royal revenue available for the expenses of the Household. Cade feared, rightly, that Suffolk's death had not altered the political situation at Court. Like the writers of some contemporary popular verses, he wanted the magnates to be more assertive in government. The king should dismiss and punish 'all the false progeny and affinity of the duke of Suffolk' and retain about his person the true lords of the blood royal – the dukes of York, Exeter, Buckingham and

Norfolk and all the true earls and barons of this land: 'Then shall he be the richest King Christian.'

The rebels swarmed into Southwark and were soon admitted across London Bridge by the city governors. The lieutenant of the Tower, Thomas lord Scales, handed over to Cade two men sheltering under his protection; James Fiennes, lord Saye and Sele, a former Treasurer, and Saye's son-in-law William Crowmer, late sheriff of Kent. The pair were executed. But Cade was unable to keep discipline over his men, who were driven back to Southwark: the failure of their fierce assault on London Bridge may have finally undermined the coherence of his force. Cade, the 'captain of mischief' as one chronicler termed him, was soon reduced to flight into Kent, but was trapped and mortally wounded near Lewes (Sussex).

A graphic recollection of capture by Cade's adherents was written in 1465 by J. Payn, former servant of the veteran commander in France, Sir John Fastolf. Payn was sent by his master to the rebel encampment at Blackheath to get a copy of the articles of complaint. Brought before Cade, 'the captain of Kent', Payn was identified as Fastolf's servant and denounced by the captain as a spy, whose master was a traitor because he had 'diminished all the garrisons of Normandy and Mans and Maine, the which was the cause of the losing of all the King's title and right of inheritance that he had beyond sea'. Cade furthermore maintained that Fastolf had furnished his place in Southwark with the old soldiers of Normandy and habiliments of war, in order to destroy the commons of Kent. 'And so forthwith I was taken, and led to the captain's tent, and i axe and i block was brought forth to have smitten off my head.' Payn was saved by the intervention of Robert Poynings, a Kentish gentleman related to Fastolf who acted as Cade's sword-bearer and carver. Payn claimed that he was forced to join the rebels and fight for them for six hours at London Bridge; meanwhile Fastolf on his advice dismissed his soldiers and took refuge in the Tower.

The behaviour of Henry VI towards Cade's rebellion provides a contrast with Richard II's during the Peasants' Revolt of 1381. Henry soon abandoned the capital and took no part in driving out the rebels. One reason for his flight may have been that men remembered the dire peril in which the king had stood in 1381: a reason for his continued passivity was perhaps that the rebel aims, much more than in 1381, evoked the sympathy of the gentry. Henry's caution proved justified, in the sense that the rebellion disintegrated without royal pressure, but it was a dangerous demonstration of his inability to provide resolute leadership. Moreover, he did not allay the fears of the wealthiest lay magnate in the realm, his cousin Richard of York, who had resided as lieutenant in Ireland since 1449. Rumours reached York that he was slandered at Court as a fomenter of treason. In September 1450 he landed in Wales, raised an armed retinue from his Mortimer lordships in the Marches and rode towards London, alarming the Court but securing Henry's word that he was not regarded as disloyal. Summonses went out for a parliament: opponents of courtiers looked eagerly to the duke's influence to gain them legal redress and royal offices.

In fact, though York's chamberlain Sir William Oldhall was elected Commons Speaker when parliament met in November, the king continued to place all his trust in his wife Margaret of Anjou and his old councillors and servants, notably Edmund Beaufort, duke of Somerset. In some ways the favourites were becoming less easy to assail. Lynchings had removed some of Henry's most hated officials – Adam Moleyns, bishop of Chichester, Suffolk, Saye and Sele, Crowmer. Such assaults on governors of society may have outraged peers and inclined them to oppose criticisms of the Court. The Crown's financial needs were becoming less pressing. The loss of France left only Calais to be subsidised. The Act of Resumption, which the Commons promoted in the 1450–1 parliament, was to give the Crown a more assured income for Household and other expenses. York's criticisms did not effect a palace revolution, though he doggedly sought the alliance of aggrieved nobles, encouraged Commons' criticisms and tried to popularise his concern to procure justice in manifestos. Some historians have criticised him for ineptitude, but he had a genuine grievance – his lack of Court influence – and was to some extent the victim, in trying to remedy it, of circumstances which had nullified the opposition of previous magnates. In the 1376 and 1386 parliaments, lords had patronised Commons' demands for 'reform'. But once the Crown's political position had improved, once its exploitation of the community had been modified by exemplary punishments, widespread support for continued checks had dwindled. Government was commonly regarded as the king's business, and as long as it was not being blatantly misconducted, men were content to leave it as such. York found plenty of fuel, especially in the localities, with which to rekindle opposition, but he was too late: feeling had been white-hot in 1449–50, when he was absent in Ireland. In February 1452 York once more raised an armed force in the Marches: requesting assistance from the men of Shrewsbury, he protested that

with the help and supportation of Almighty God, and of Our Lady, and of all the Company of Heaven, I, after long sufferance and delays, [*though it is*] *not my will and intent to displease my sovereign lord, seeing that the said Duke* [*of Somerset*] *ever prevaileth and ruleth about the King's person,* [*and*] *that by this means the land is likely to be destroyed, am fully persuaded to proceed in all haste against him with the help of my kinsmen and friends. . .*

But the only peers who joined him in his march on London were two who were not highly reputed – Thomas Courtenay, earl of Devon, and Edward Brooke, lord Cobham. York's wealthy kinsmen Richard Neville, earl of Salisbury, his son Richard Neville, earl of Warwick, and the highly respected Humphrey Stafford, duke of Buckingham, hastened to bring military retinues to support the king, who moved with his army to menace the volatile Kentishmen: they failed to stir in York's behalf. The duke had to submit, swearing publicly in St Paul's, touching the Gospels with one hand and the altar cross with the other, that he would never be disloyal to Henry or raise assemblies without royal licence, except in his lawful defence, as approved by the king and by his peers: 'But whensoever I find myself wronged or aggrieved, I shall sue humbly for remedy to your Highness, and proceed after the course of your laws, and in none other wise, saving in mine own lawful defence in manner above said. . .'

The magnates thus showed their suspicion of one of their number who had tried to impose his will on Crown and community, but their determination that he and his family should not be alienated by harsh punishment. The magnates of the mid-fifteenth century were a small group, intensely aware of their corporate and individual privileges, eager to secure royal favour, sensitive about rights of inheritance, and traditionally hostile to 'overmighty' individuals and families who tried to dictate to the king. Moreover, York's abundant royal blood may have made men reluctant to support his menacing and equivocal armed demonstrations. By virtue of his mother Anne Mortimer's descent from Edward III's son Lionel of Clarence, he had a hereditary claim to the throne arguably better than Henry VI's, which he was to put forward in 1460. Moreover, in the period between the death of Humphrey of Gloucester (1447) and the birth of Henry's son Edward (October 1453), the rivals York and Somerset could both have claimed to be Henry's heir, leaving aside the Mortimer claim. York's nearness to the throne may have encouraged Court insinuations that his agitation concealed treasonable designs, and may also have been a cause of tension with Somerset. The succession was certainly in some men's minds. According to an article in Suffolk's impeachment, he had planned to marry his son John to Somerset's niece Margaret Beaufort (the future mother of Henry VII), with a view to gaining the Crown for him (cf. p. 85).

The political situation, which might have been improved by Edward's birth, was ultimately to be worsened by the repercussions of the breakdown which Henry suffered by August 1453. This illness may have been induced by recent political shocks, or by horror at his wife's pregnancy after five years of barren and perhaps practically celibate marriage. Royal authority needed to be exercised by a protector and Council of regency, as in Henry's minority. There was tension in the households of nobles and their retainers, as it became clear that the queen and York would both claim the protectorship. The lack of royal governance further encouraged those struggling for local influence and control of office to resort to violence. Conflicts in the West Country and Yorkshire were exacerbated. In the west the Courtenays, holders of the earldom of Devon, had long smarted at the rise to local influence of William lord Bonville. A member of a wealthy gentle family from

Shute (Devon) which had made marriage alliances with noble families (including the Courtenays), Bonville had been active on military service in France under Henry V. From about 1430 he was appointed on commissions in the western shires; in 1437, in succession to Devon's brother, he was appointed steward of the duchy of Cornwall estates in Cornwall. In 1440 he was removed from office and so was his successor, the earl. Tension ran high between him and the Courtenays. Uncertainty about Court favour probably led Devon to support York's rising in 1452. Its failure was followed by the grant of the stewardship and other local offices to Bonville. In April 1454 this situation produced rioting in Exeter.

The tension in Yorkshire was connected with the rising influence of Richard Neville, earl of Salisbury, the eldest son of Ralph earl of Westmorland's second marriage to John of Gaunt's daughter Joan Beaufort. During the reign of Henry V and the minority of Henry VI, Richard benefited from his Beaufort kinship by receiving grants of land and offices in the northern counties. When Warden of the West March (1420–35, 1443–60), he built up an inheritance and an affinity in Cumberland, Westmorland and Yorkshire. He married Alice, daughter and heir of the earl of Salisbury, and was himself recognised as earl after his father-in-law's death at the siege of Orleans. The spread of Richard Neville's influence in the Borders and Yorkshire seems to have displeased the leading comital families in the North, the Percies and his Neville kinsmen. In the 1430s and early 1440s there were local disturbances involving his servants and those of his nephew, Ralph Neville, second earl of Westmorland, who entered on his inheritance in 1425. The earl was aggrieved that his grandfather had settled substantial parts of the Neville inheritance on Salisbury. In 1443 royal arbitration between the parties produced a settlement on the whole favourable to the latter. But then in the early 1450s some of the Percies started to jockey with him. Thomas lord Egremont, a feckless younger son of the earl of Northumberland, led the challenge to Salisbury and his family, attacking them in 1453 with a large force of York citizens and Yorkshiremen: the region was plagued by Percy–Neville reprisals and confrontations.

In March 1454 the Lords in parliament resolved the crisis caused by the king's incapacity by procuring the appointment of York as protector and defender of the realm, titles by which Humphrey of Gloucester had exercised a restricted authority in Henry's minority. Somerset's influence was eclipsed by his imprisonment. York laid the foundations of what was to be, to the misfortune of the Lancastrian dynasty, a crucial alliance, by visiting Yorkshire in 1454 to support the interests of Salisbury and promote the punishment of Percy supporters who had broken the peace.

By Christmas the king was recovering his faculties. In February 1455 Somerset was released and the protectorship terminated. In May the king rode towards Leicester for a great council. York set out to intercept him, fearful that the assembly far from London was intended for his harm. The duke's force was more formidable than in 1452, for it now included Salisbury and his son Warwick. The Nevilles may have taken York's part so fully because they feared that Court influence had become firmly ranged against their various local interests. The Yorkist army blocked the king's highway north of St Albans. Henry refused petitions to give up Somerset. The lords attacked the king's men in the town. The young Warwick's forceful leadership won through: Somerset was allowed no quarter. Heads of northern families opposed to the Nevilles, the earl of Northumberland and Lord Clifford, also fell in the fight: Buckingham was injured, as was a hated courtier, the dandified James Butler, earl of Wiltshire. The king, wounded in the neck by an arrow, was greeted by York on bended knees in the abbey and honourably escorted to Westminster.

In the session of parliament which met in November 1455, York was again appointed protector, on the same circumscribed terms as before, ostensibly to compose the western troubles instigated by Devon and Bonville and disturbances elsewhere. He was able to use royal patronage to reward his Neville allies. Salisbury and Warwick received a grant of the Wardenship of the West March to last till 1475, at higher rates of pay. Neville influence was extended to the Channel by Warwick's appointment to Somerset's former captaincy of Calais. It was the Nevilles rather than York who derived permanent benefits from the battle of St Albans: that vicious little fight with the king and his companions seems to have discredited him in the eyes of many landowners. Though York had the firm support of his Neville kinsmen, and had rid himself of his enemy Somerset, he had no mandate from 'public opinion' to take permanent control of government. No more than during his first protectorate could he produce better order in the localities, since those who feared his intervention looked to maintenance by his opponents. The battle had increased their ranks. The Percy family now identified him with the interests of Salisbury. He had a blood feud on his hands with the Cumberland landowner Clifford, whose father had died at St Albans. Neither Lords nor Commons protested when Henry dismissed York from the protectorship during a parliamentary session (February 1456).

The period 1456–9 was one of uneasy political tension between magnates. Margaret and her noble allies on the whole successfully excluded York and the Nevilles from further patronage. Henry lacked the forcefulness and genuine impartiality necessary to impose the general reconciliation which he so ardently desired. From the time of Suffolk's hated ascendancy he had shown himself tenaciously loyal in supporting those he honoured. Henry attempted to use the sacramental power of Christianity as a means to reconcile feuds. In March 1458, at his behest, lords who had fought on opposite sides at St Albans processed hand-in-hand to the high altar of St Paul's, to receive the Host together. Nevertheless, at Court particular animosity continued to be shown against Warwick, and attempts were made to oust him from the captaincy of Calais.

In the autumn of 1459, fearing Court moves against them, York and the Nevilles devised a military assembly at the duke's castle of Ludlow (Salop). This time the Court was well prepared. Peers rallied to the Crown, determined perhaps to prevent York from outraging Henry as in 1455, and encouraged to hope for wages and rewards by the Crown's good financial position. Henry, riding for once like his father, in arms at the head of an impressive army, furnished with artillery, moved swiftly, confronting the Yorkists at Ludford Bridge (October 1459). Some of their retinues showed the reluctance to fight which occasionally characterised English soldiers in the coming struggles. Retainers, tenants, burgesses, often answered summonses to arm from the king or their lord unwillingly, appearing only because they feared to lose 'good lordship'. York's army disintegrated without a blow struck, after Sir Andrew Trollope, master porter of Calais, and a substantial number of the soldiers Warwick had brought from Calais, deserted to the king. York fled to the Irish lieutenancy which he had recovered when protector in 1454. Warwick, with Salisbury and the duke's son Edward earl of March made a perilous journey through the West Country, hired a fishing boat at Exmouth and sailed via Guernsey to Calais. There and in Ireland Yorkists held out in defiance of the Crown. But within two years these precariously placed fugitives were to return in triumph. What caused the reversal in fortunes?

One reason may have been that in 1459 the queen and her adherents alienated opinion by behaving for the first time in an extremely harsh fashion towards York and some of his sympathisers. At the intensely partisan Coventry parliament (November 1459), Acts of Attainder were passed against the duke, the Nevilles and others. Many adherents were pardoned on payment of fines. Proscriptions were on a scale to become familiar in the later fifteenth century, but with no recent precedents. Special judicial commissions, operating particularly in Kent and other parts of southern England where opposition to the Court had been vociferous, condemned many for offences committed as far back as 1450. Such punishments, the Court's revenge for a decade of popular abuse, revived alienation in local communities.

The arrogant folly of the Lancastrian vengeance in 1459 was compounded by a persistent failure to appreciate the difficulty of recovering Calais from York's adherents. Warwick was able to raise money from the wool staple at Calais. He raided alien shipping in the Straits of Dover, helping to strengthen his naval power, to keep the loyalty of the Calais garrisons, and to win popularity among the seafaring folk of the Cinque Ports. They were disinclined to aid the captain of Calais who had been appointed to supersede Warwick: Henry Beaufort, duke of Somerset. His base, Sandwich, was twice raided by Warwick's forces: in June 1460 the Yorkist lords landed there to challenge Court rule. The manifesto they circulated quickly won support in Kent. The Yorkists advanced on London before Henry, in the Midlands, could have reached it: the Tower alone was vigorously defended. Lords with estates in the Midlands and Marches of Wales brought armed retinues to support the king, including Buckingham, John Talbot, earl of Shrewsbury, and Edmund Grey, lord of Ruthin. The northern lords sent what soldiers they could muster. The royal army encamped outside Northampton (July 1460), entrenched in the water meadows near Delapré Abbey. Henry's councillors repudiated Warwick's histrionic attempts to negotiate favourable terms. But the impressive royal artillery train failed to disorganise the rebels' assault, 'for that day was so great rain, that the guns lay deep in the water, and so were quenched and might not be shot'. Grey of Ruthin, commanding the vanguard, had come to an understanding with Warwick: his retinue helped to pull the earl's men out of the trenches. Grey was apparently discontented with the Court because he had failed to round off his influence in neighbouring Bedfordshire, when the Crown had awarded the estates of John Cornewall, lord Fanhope (d.1444) to the duke of Exeter. Buckingham and Shrewsbury, like Arthurian heroes, died fighting before the king's tent. Henry was greeted courteously by his captors, and once more escorted to Westminster by men who had just slaughtered his faithful lords.

The Yorkist success owed much to the energy and popularity of Warwick. He had capitalised on the Court's failure (as in 1397–9) to keep the loyalty of south-eastern communities. Henceforth the Yorkists were able to rely on substantial support in some of the wealthiest parts of the realm, where money was more readily available to pay the costs of armies. But Yorkist control of the realm was limited: the queen had forged strong provincial links. In the West Country the Courtenays' sympathies were now firmly Lancastrian. Royal lordships gave the Crown influence in parts of the Midlands: the Court had rallied loyalties there as well as in the earldom of Chester and principality of Wales. The Welsh landowner Jasper Tudor, earl of Pembroke, the king's half-brother, was now firmly committed to the Court, as were influential northern lords. The difficulty inherent in royal reliance on remoter provincial circles was that they were not so well placed for influencing events in London, the main political and economic centre of the realm. Border lords were not always willing to divert attention to southern affairs. The introduction of provincial armies into the south-east was often counterproductive. Northerners and Welshmen were despised in London, and feared when in arms. Moreover, support for the Lancastrians in the provinces was not absolute: there too there were families eager to oust the regional supremacy awarded by the Court to its principal supporters.

The limited control the Yorkists had gained in 1460, and the irritation some peers may have felt at their killing of Buckingham and Shrewsbury, made it expedient for York to behave circumspectly when he returned from his Irish refuge. But his actions in the parliament which met in October at Westminster caused controversy among his leading supporters. A decade of political rebuffs had at last driven him to aim at the Crown – much more slowly than some rebels of previous generations. He entered the parliament chamber in great state, walked under the cloth of state above the throne, and laid his hand on its cushion. He then broke into the unoccupied royal apartments in the 'privy palace' and lodged there. In justification of his behaviour he claimed that his right to the Crowns of England and France and the Lordship of Ireland was superior to Henry's, by virtue of his descent from Edward III's son Clarence. The peers and justices were unwilling to pronounce on his claim in parliament, but the former eventually concluded that his title could not be defeated. Parliament enacted that Henry was to retain the throne for life, to devolve on the duke and his heirs. York and his sons March and Rutland swore not to plot Henry's death, and to withstand any who did. It was declared treason to plot York's death: he became protector and, with his sons, was promised large grants to sustain the family's new royal status.

The Act was a prescription for civil war. Realists may have concluded that this newly raised succession issue could not be settled in the council chamber (as there had been hopes that the faction struggles of the 1450s might be), but only by an appeal to divine judgment in battle. The Act shamefully disinherited Henry's son, besides excluding the claims of Somerset, his cousin Margaret Beaufort, countess of Richmond, and her son Henry Tudor.

York soon went to Yorkshire, to rally old allies there, and to disrupt the concentration of a Lancastrian army at Hull. At Wakefield (December 1460) his outnumbered and outmanoeuvred army was decisively beaten by a combination of western lords (Devon and Somerset) and northerners (Northumberland, Ros, Clifford, Greystoke and Westmorland's brother Lord Neville). York and his son Rutland were killed in the fight; Salisbury was executed next day. York's head, wearing a paper crown, was placed on Micklegate Bar, York. The victory gave the queen and her allies the chance to win control of East Anglia, London and the south-east. On 23 January 1461 Clement Paston wrote to his brother John in Norfolk, advising him to ensure that the country was ready to send foot and horse for defence against 'the further Lords' (the victors of Wakefield): 'In this country every man is well willing to go with my Lords here, and I hope God shall help them, for the people in the north rob and steal, and be appointed to pillage all this country, and give away men's goods and livelihoods in all the south country, and that will ask a mischief.'

Less than a month later Warwick, with an army drawn from Kent, Essex and East Anglia, was defeated when attacked by the northerners at St Albans. His foreign mercenaries failed to co-ordinate their tactics with traditional English ones. A Kentish captain deserted with his retinue. Warwick escaped, but Henry was restored to his stout-hearted queen and bellicose little boy. The intense hatreds which had embittered magnates since 1455 were reflected (and intensified) by the summary execution of captured Yorkist nobles and gentlemen, reinforcing the baleful precedent set at Wakefield. But at this point the cause of York, twice defeated, was saved by the queen's failure to secure London. Feeling there rapidly hardened against admitting her unruly soldiers. The city government's morale was sufficiently boosted for it to prevaricate over submission and provision of finance. Many northerners had already deserted before the battle. The reduction of the queen's army, its difficulties in procuring victuals, and its lengthy communications through country grown hostile as a result of plundering, may have influenced the momentous decision to retreat northwards.

Once more there was stalemate. York's son and heir March (born 1442) seized the opportunity. Having secured much of Wales by defeating Pembroke, he joined Warwick in the south Midlands and moved on London. The city governors admitted the Yorkists. March's claim to the throne was expounded to and acclaimed by a crowd of soldiers and Londoners 'in the big field at Clerkenwell'. This was reported to a group of magnates meeting in his city house, Baynard's Castle, who advised Edward to accept the Crown, which he did. A few days later he was acclaimed by the Londoners, swore to keep the laws before the archbishop of Canterbury in Westminster Hall, and received St Edward's sceptre at the door of Westminster Abbey from the abbot (4 March 1461). Within a month he marched north with a well financed and equipped army. In a hard-fought engagement south of York, at Towton, the Lancastrian magnates were decisively defeated. Northumberland and Lord Neville were killed, Devon and Wiltshire caught and executed; Henry, his queen and son, Somerset, Exeter and Ros escaped to Scotland. Victor in trial by combat, Edward returned for his coronation in June at Westminster, then set out for Canterbury to pay his respects to the Church's defender, St Thomas.

The rule of Edward IV (1461–83) and the Readeption of Henry VI (1470–71)

The battles of 1461 sealed Edward's control of East Anglia and of southern and Midland England, and gained for him the city of York and the West Country. The Borders and parts of west Wales remained to be subdued, but many men were prepared to support the new dynasty, especially after the savage Court reprisals of the past two years. Yorkist supporters hoped that the king would increase their local influence at the expense of Lancastrian 'affinities'. But there were fears, in some cases well founded, that he would come to terms with former Lancastrians. In July 1461 John Berney wrote a letter to John Paston and his own cousin William Rokewode, esquire, the latter of whom was in Thomas Bourchier, archbishop of Canterbury's household. He asked them to procure a letter from the king expressing thanks for the 'goodwill and service' he had displayed against the king's enemies in the north and Norfolk:

And in that the King should please the Commons in this country; for they grudge and say, how that the King receiveth such of this country, etc., as have be his great enemies, and oppressors of the Commons; and such as have assisted his Highness, be not rewarded . . . And in aid of this changeable rule, it were necessary to move the good Lords Spiritual and Temporal, by the which that might be reformed, etc. And in case that any of mine old enemies, Tudynham, Stapylton, and Heydon, with their affinity labour the King and Lords unto my hurt, I am and will be ready to come to my sovereign Lord for my excuse, so that I may come safe from unlawful hurt, purveyed by my said enemies.

Berney added a postscript asking his correspondents to 'move this unto' the archbishop of Canterbury and the bishops of Ely and Norwich (William Grey and Walter Lyhert) and others. Sir Thomas Tuddenham of Oxborough, Sir Miles Stapledon, and John Heydon of Baconsthorpe were Norfolk gentlemen who, with the aid of their influence at Court in the 1440s, particularly through Suffolk's favour, had manipulated local office and judicial administration. There were good reasons for Berney's fears, for the principal local opponent of their influence, John Mowbray, duke of Norfolk, died in November 1461, whereas Suffolk's son, John de la Pole, was a young man enjoying royal favour, married to the king's sister Elizabeth. Edward IV's need to please his most influential supporters, and his anxiety to win over Lancastrian noble families which had only accepted his rule because of force, conflicted with his genuine desire to provide the 'indifferent' justice necessary since the political uncertainties of the past few years had encouraged resort to violence. Margaret Paston wrote despairingly to her husband John in January 1462:

People of this country beginneth to wax wild, and it is said here that my Lord of Clarence and the Duke of Suffolk and certain judges with them should come down and sit on such people as be noised riotous in this country. . . . The people saith here that they had rather go up whole to the King and complain of such false shrews as they have been wronged by afore, than they should be complained of without cause and be hanged at their own doors. In good faith men fear sore here of a common rising but if a better remedy may be had to appease the people in haste, and that there be sent such down to take a rule as the people hath a fancy in, that will be indifferent. They love not in no wise the Duke of Suffolk nor his mother[1]*. They say that all the traitors and extortioners of this country be maintained by them and by such as they get to them with their goods, to that intent to maintain such extortion still as hath been done by such as hath had the rule under them before time. Men believe, and the Duke of Suffolk come there shall be a shrewd rule but if* [*unless*] *there come other that be better beloved than he is here . . . God for His holy mercy give grace that there may be set a good rule and a sad in this country in haste, for I heard never say of so much robbery and manslaughter in this country as is now within a little time.*

Edward was to prove unwilling to arbitrate disputes in which the Paston family had become involved over the inheritance of Sir John Fastolf (d.1459). By a last testament whose validity was disputed by the majority of his trustees, Fastolf was alleged to have given sole executive power to one of them, John Paston (d.1466), and to have willed his estates to Paston on condition that he converted Caister Castle into a college of priests to say masses for his soul. Paston had entered on most of the knight's East Anglian properties after his death, but others who had claims or designs on Fastolf's estates sought grants of them from the trustees who denied Paston's right. The dispute was one which provoked maintenance and violence. In 1465 a group of Suffolk's servants and tenants sacked the Paston manor of Hellesdon, just outside Norwich (cf. p. 152). When the king visited Norfolk in 1469, John Paston the younger tried to arrange for his attention to be drawn to the event as he rode out of the city on pilgrimage to Our Lady of Walsingham. He described what happened in a letter to his brother Sir John:

The king rode through Hellesdon Warren towards Walsingham, and Thomas Wingfield promised me that he would find the means that my Lord of Gloucester [*the future Richard III*] *and himself both should show the King the lodge that was break down, and also that they would tell him of the breaking down of the place. Contrary to this matter, and all the comfort that I had of my Lord Scales, Sir John Wydeville, and Thomas Wingfield, my uncle William says that the King told him his own mouth, when he had ridden close by the lodge in Hellesdon Warren, that he supposed as well that it might fall down by the self as be plucked down, for if it had been plucked down, he said that we might have put in our bills of it, when his judges sat on the* oyer determiner *in Norwich, he being there. And then my uncle says how that he answered the King, that you trusted to his good grace that he should set you through with both the Dukes* [*of Suffolk and Norfolk*] *by means of treaty; and he says that the King answered him that he would neither treat nor speak for you, but for to let the law proceed, and so he says that they departed.*

This was cold comfort for the Pastons, since they believed that without royal favour they would not succeed at common law against such powerful opposition. But Edward's irritation with the Pastons is understandable: their tenacity, greed and refusal to compromise had alienated the two most powerful local families, one of which, the Mowbrays, had been their own lords. The king could not at that juncture afford to alienate Yorkist magnates: in the politically tense year 1469, the youthful duke of Norfolk actually so far defied the king's peace as to besiege John Paston the younger in Caister Castle. The siege was directed by members of his council, locally eminent gentlemen who clearly had no time for the *parvenu* Pastons, and it was prosecuted to a successful conclusion, despite the frantic Paston attempts to enlist the patronage of other nobles. Not surprisingly, the Pastons were supporters of the Lancastrian Readeption in 1470: they fought against Edward at Barnet in 1471.

The Pastons were connected in the 1460s with Warwick, a link which helps explain Edward's reluctance to favour them against the ducal assaults, and their conversion to the Lancastrian cause in 1470-1. Edward's rule wavered and eventually collapsed in the years 1469–70 as a result of Warwick's opposition. In the early years of his reign Edward had relied on the Neville brothers in the North: until 1464 the outcome of the struggle with the Lancastrians in the Borders remained in doubt. Warwick's brother John lord Montague was granted the earldom of Northumberland and almost all the forfeited Percy estates in Yorkshire (1464). His brother George (Chancellor 1460–7) was promoted to the see of York (1465). The Neville hegemony was further propped up by generous royal grants of land and offices to Warwick. But it is unlikely that the concentration of such power in the hands of one family entirely pleased the king, especially after the recession of Lancastrian threats in the North.

Warwick's discontent over Edward's foreign policy (see pp. 392–3) was compounded by the diminution of his influence at Court consequent on Edward's politic determination to broaden the basis of his support, by restoring defeated opponents, and rewarding Yorkists with the estates of irreconcilables. Henry Beaufort was pardoned and granted the duchy of Somerset in 1463. He resided in the Household and even shared the king's bed, but by the end of the year had reverted to Lancastrian allegiance. Even the attainted Henry VI was gently treated. Captured in a Lancashire wood in 1465, he was lodged in the Tower, waited on honourably, and allowed to receive visitors. If insufficient care was taken to see that he was washed and cleanly dressed, that is unlikely to have troubled Henry. Meanwhile Edward had married in 1464, at first secretly, into a former Lancastrian family which had once seemed highly offensive to him and his fellow Yorkist lords. Elizabeth Wydeville, widow of Sir John Grey, was the daughter of Richard lord Rivers, who had fought against the king and Warwick in 1460. He was created Earl Rivers in 1466 and appointed Constable of the Realm for life in 1467. The inclusion of the numerous Wydevilles and Greys within the inner circle of royal kinsfolk, a necessary consequence of the marriage, was unwelcome to its eminently descended scions. Warwick, probably annoyed like other lords by what they considered was a self-willed and demeaning marriage on Edward's part, became increasingly alienated by the influence wielded by the queen's kinsfolk, by failures to consult his opinion over royal policy and distribution of patronage, and by the dismissal of his brother

George from the Chancellorship in 1467. Besides, some stauch Yorkists not allied to Warwick were increasing in favour at Court, such as Sir William Herbert of Raglan, granted many Welsh estates and offices, and created earl of Pembroke in 1468.

In 1469 there were outbreaks of popular discontent in Yorkshire, which Warwick's adherent Sir John Conyers converted into rebellion on the earl's behalf. Warwick crossed to his command at Calais with his intended son-in-law, the king's brother George duke of Clarence. Thence he returned, attempting, as in 1460, to stir opinion against a Court clique. Edward had been vainly trying to raise a force in East Anglia and the Midlands to lead against the northerners. The sizeable army raised in his interest in Wales and the West Country was worsted in July at Edgcote (Warwicks.) by the Neville adherents. Clarence and Warwick had the captured Pembroke summarily executed. Soon afterwards the dispirited, deserted king was ignominiously roused from bed by Archbishop Neville, who escorted him to the rebel lords. Edward, though courteously treated, was a prisoner, and could not prevent the summary execution of Rivers.

It was a tribute to the degree of Yorkist success in imposing the dynasty's rule that there was no general Lancastrian reaction. Peers seem to have disapproved of Warwick's ambition, violence and overt manipulation of the Crown. By October 1469, with impressive magnate support, Edward had extricated himself from a dishonourable tutelage. His cautiously benign treatment of Clarence and Warwick failed to reconcile them to their manifest loss of influence. In March 1470 there was a Lincolnshire rising in which Warwick's agents were probably concerned. Edward promptly suppressed it, rallying magnate support and moving north to confront Neville rebels in Yorkshire. Warwick, his complicity now clear, fled with Clarence to Calais, where his deputy, John lord Wenlock, refused him admittance, and thence to Normandy, where he was allowed refuge by Louis XI. In September 1470, Warwick and Clarence were to land in the Lancastrian West Country, proclaiming King Henry (see p. 393). Edward, who had concentrated his energies on suppressing northern disturbances, was unable to rally sufficient noble retinues. He had to flee abroad after Warwick's brother Marquess Montague deserted him, publicly blaming Edward for depriving him of the Percy title and inheritance, and making him marquess with only 'a magpie's nest to maintain his estate'.

Thus within two years, Edward twice lost control of the realm. This is one reason why he has sometimes been judged a 'weak king'. But he was handicapped by usurping the throne in less auspicious circumstances than any other later medieval king. The usurpations of 1399 and 1485 were not preceded by periods of what contemporaries considered to be exceptional local factiousness and violence. On those occasions royal councillors and retainers had smoothed the transition by rallying to the new king. 1461 was different. Politics had become unusually polarised in the previous decade. Some influential councillors and Household officials of the 1450s became exiles and plotters in the 1460s. Edward was surrounded by servants whose standing, whose faces, were generally unfamiliar: until their authority was clear, the tasks of reconciling local elites to the new dynasty and calming their disputes could not be completed.

Between 1461 and 1470 Edward worked hard to defeat his opponents, to reconcile men to his rule, and raise its prestige by enhancing the splendour of his Court. The servants of a Bohemian noble, Leo of Rozmital, were awed in 1466 by its good order, stately ceremony and display of opulence. Edward was anxious to cover Household and other expenses without continuing to alienate his dubiously loyal subjects by resort to subsidies and loans. He told the Commons in 1467: 'I purpose to live upon mine own, and not to charge my subjects but in great and urgent causes concerning more the weal of themselves, and also the defence of them and of this my realm, rather than my own pleasure.'

Yet it is clear from the ease with which Warwick overturned his rule in 1469 and 1470 that it evoked no general enthusiasm. Both these magnate rebellions were preceded by regional disturbances. Edward to some extent failed to give 'good government'. Men continued to complain of local oppressions and lack of royal redress, and to look to noble factions for remedy, as they had become especially accustomed to do in the 1440s and 1450s. But Edward's rule was not without lasting achievement. His recovery of the Crown in 1471, due in part to Franco-Burgundian conflict, in part to his own energy and icy nerves, demonstrated that he had created a Yorkist 'interest' among landowners who saw advantage in his rule.

As a result of the long delay in the arrival from France of Margaret of Anjou, her son and leading supporters, Warwick once more had to rule in 1470–1 without strong support. Nobles who had prospered under Edward resented their eclipse. John de la Pole, duke of Suffolk, and influential lesser landowners in East Anglia who had served the Mowbrays, such as Sir John Howard, had now to accept the Essex landowner John de Vere, earl of Oxford, as the Crown's chief representative in their region. Henry Percy, recently restored as earl of Northumberland by Edward, might expect a Neville resurgence in the North. Percy remained neutral when in March 1471 Edward landed in Yorkshire with a small but well-equipped company, though feeling among the commons, the burgesses of York and the gentry seems to have been hostile, or at best indifferent, to a king whose soldiers had often killed Yorkshiremen. Edward prudently proclaimed that he had returned only to claim his duchy of York. With bland duplicity he donned an ostrich feather, the livery of Henry VI's son. Avoiding confrontations, Edward rode into the Midlands, collecting his retainers and their bands. The Lancastrians showed the hesitancy and inability to co-ordinate characteristic of those facing foreign-financed dynastic invasion in this politically unstable period. The failure of the Lancastrian lords to hold Newark lost Warwick any hope of rallying northern support. He tried to buy time by garrisoning Coventry and relying on his brother, Archbishop Neville, to keep London. But the prestige of his cause was badly shattered by Clarence's desertion, Edward's easy admittance to London and the failure of principal Lancastrians in France and England to come to his aid. Perhaps fearing political isolation, Warwick set off after Edward, who barred his progress towards London at Barnet. In a hard-fought engagement confused by fog, Lancastrian resistance foundered in mutual fears of treachery. Montague was killed and so was Warwick, attempting to flee and fight another day, as he had often done before. His body and his brother's were exposed in St Paul's, so that men would not believe they might come again.

Warwick's character remains an enigma. If he had been interested in literature, the writers he patronised and books he collected might have revealed more of his character and tastes. If he had had a son, filial piety might have produced a eulogistic account of the subject who bestrode English politics more firmly than any other between Thomas of Lancaster and Wolsey. We have no portrait, effigy, or detailed description of his appearance. His random surviving letters are conventional and businesslike; occasional allusions by chroniclers and correspondents hint at an ability to catch men's imagination by a vivid and well-publicised gesture or turn of phrase. He does not seem to have been a great builder or religious founder. His large revenues may have been absorbed by his exceptional, continuous need to cultivate a large network of dependants and 'well-willers', and to pay soldiers. From early on in his comital career, his father's recently planted northern influence was under attack. Their decision to back York did not immediately procure its consolidation. To uphold the northern predominance which the Nevilles won in the 1460s, Warwick may have felt that he required an unusual degree of royal favour, together with diplomatic guarantees.

His dilemma was unique only in scale. Other nobles, inheriting challenged interests or overturning regional rivals, became obsessed with the need for a sure anchor in the shifting sands of Court favour, and were eventually impelled by the lack of it into revolt. The Percies provide examples in the period 1399–1405: later ones include a Stafford, De la Poles, a Howard, a Devereux. Such were prey to restless smarting, grandiose brooding. They were closely connected by kinship or favour to the Crown and exalted in the peerage. But their status did not guarantee their influence, dependent on the barometers of Court favour and local repute. Shakespeare well understood the temperament and fixed its vexations and temptations in the characters of Hotspur and Gloster; uninspiring literary sources probably deterred him from portraying Warwick with the same perceptiveness. Moreover, Warwick's popular fame may have proved ephemeral because he failed to maintain an identity with causes of grievance. In the 1450s and 1460s there were antagonisms between the Court and southern communities: Warwick attracted support as the champion of the 'common weal'. But by the late 1460s these dislocations may have been lessening. Warwick was primarily interested in promoting a northern hegemony, an interest which did not concern southerners, by a means (alliance with France) which they distrusted. He was not to be remembered as 'the good earl' like Simon de Montfort or Thomas of Lancaster, flourishing in periods when the communities had more deeply engrained grievances against the Crown.

In April 1471, days after Barnet, Queen Margaret and her son the prince, long delayed by contrary winds, landed at Weymouth. With the aid of local lords, Devon and Somerset, they raised the West Country. The Lancastrians decided not to move precipitately against Edward, but to turn northwards, recruiting their well-willers in Wales, Cheshire and Lancashire. This gave him an opportunity to recruit new levies and strike westwards to intercept the Lancastrians, who entered Bristol but failed to secure Gloucester. Edward caught up with them in a strong defensive position at Tewkesbury, which his artillery (possibly with the addition of Warwick's) and archers harassed. Somerset bungled a diversionary attack and exposed the Lancastrian defences. In the rout Henry VI's son was killed. Somerset and other Lancastrian lords and knights were speedily executed. Margaret was captured[2]. Lancastrian stirrings in the North died down. But a force of Calais soldiers, sailors and Kentishmen assaulted London, commanded by Warwick's kinsman and naval lieutenant, Thomas Neville, the 'bastard of Fauconberg'. The citizens, fearing plunder, held firm. Edward returned to London: Henry VI immediately expired in the Tower. The embers of rebellion were stamped out in Kent. From 1471 until his death Edward was never again seriously threatened. In 1473 Oxford landed near his ancestral estates in Essex, cruised the Channel and eventually tried to raise rebellion in the West Country by seizing St Michael's Mount, off the Cornish coast. Isolated, he surrendered on terms. More dangerously, Clarence appeared discontented. In 1472 he was aggrieved by his brother Gloucester's marriage to his sister-in-law Anne Neville, co-heiress to Warwick's inheritance. After the death of his own wife in 1476, he was annoyed by Edward's failure to support his schemes to marry into the Burgundian and Stewart dynasties. His behaviour was indiscreet and disrespectful to Edward's authority. In 1478, without apparently causing much adverse comment, Edward personally accused his brother in parliament of treason, procuring his condemnation. Clarence, like Henry VI, was probably assassinated in the Tower. Such sinister blood-lettings, so alien to English politics – characteristic rather of Italian *signori* whose authority lacked the deep-rooted stability of the successors of St Edward the Confessor – were to provide precedents for shedding the blood of Edward's sons.

Edward's comparative security after 1471 was displayed by the way in which, for the first time in that generation, formidable English armies and navies threatened neighbouring powers. In 1475 the king rode on French soil with one of the largest English armies ever seen there. In 1482 the English menaced Edinburgh and Lothian, for the first time since 1400. Berwick was recovered. Foreign rulers, notably Charles of Burgundy, Louis XI, Francis of Brittany and Henry IV of Castile courted Edward. His comparative wealth attracted well-to-do gentry from different localities into his service as well as foreigners, who were impressed by a splendid Court which in its lavish banquets and tournaments emulated the marvels of the Burgundian court. Some signs of Edward's wealth and magnificence survive. There is the great hall which he built at Eltham Palace, St George's Chapel which he rebuilt at Windsor Castle, and the chapel at King's College, Cambridge, a religious and educational foundation of Henry VI whose works had languished until he spurred them on towards completion. In the north transept of Canterbury Cathedral there is a fine set of windows portraying Edward, Elizabeth and their children, kneeling at *prie-dieux*, wearing crowns and robes of state, cloth of gold beneath ermine and purple cloaks. Here in the principal shrine of England, Edward's family blazons forth the majesty they had attained and hoped to keep, but which was to be so dramatically eclipsed.

A conjunction of factors facilitated the success of his rule after 1471. The Lancastrian line was almost completely extinguished. Edward himself could have claimed to be the nearest in descent to Henry VI, as well as having a superior claim to the throne. His only possible rivals were Margaret Beaufort, countess of Richmond, married by 1473 to Thomas lord Stanley, a peer unlikely to stir unless Yorkist rule was *in extremis*, and her son Henry Tudor, who after Tewkesbury was taken to Brittany by his uncle Jasper earl of Pembroke. Edward vainly tried to persuade his ally Duke Francis of Brittany to give the fugitives up. However, the duke kept Henry under strict surveillance and did not allow him to claim the Crown until after Edward's death. When James III of Scotland went to war with Edward in 1480, he had no claimant to the English throne to promote, though Edward had his candidate as king of Scots.

The destruction of the dominating Neville influence in the North enabled leading Lancastrian families there – the Percies, the Neville earls of Westmorland, the Cliffords and Dacres – to reconcile themselves more wholeheartedly to Yorkist rule. The extinction of the Beaufort and junior Neville families drained away the feuds which had engulfed the nobility since the 1450s. Edward showed a ruthless determination to enforce obedience. The deaths of Warwick and Montague were a deterrent to rebellion. It is likely that there were continued resentments at the Wydeville ascendancy: the prudent kept them muted. Clarence was harshly disposed of, Gloucester sensibly retired to his northern estates. Hastings allowed the full venom of his feelings about the queen and her kin to emerge only after Edward's death. Lord Howard endured the royal failure to allow him his due as co-heir of the Mowbrays, since the king wanted to keep duchy of Norfolk estates as an endowment for his second son Richard. Northumberland and other northern lords acquiesced in the growth of Gloucester's local influence.

As long as Edward lived, rivalries and resentments which under Henry VI might have produced rebellion failed to do so. Edward's personality made a great deal of difference. So did his power of patronage. His part as a youth in stirring up popular grievances had taught him the wisdom of showing determination to control as well as reward his servants, and to remedy complaints. His administrative achievements in the 1470s were to provide a sound basis for early Tudor rule (cf. pp. 107 ff). Edward's misfortune was that he could not guarantee the rule of his family: they spectacularly lacked underlying solidarity. He died unexpectedly when his son and heir Edward, a promising boy of twelve, was a few years too young to control the pent-up rivalries between his father's kinsfolk, friends and servants.

Edward V and Richard III (April 1483–August 1485)

Edward IV had foreseen the need of a trustworthy and able magnate, near in blood to the Crown, to act as his son's protector during what should have been a brief minority – Henry VI had been sixteen when he came of age. The obvious choice was Edward V's only surviving paternal uncle, Richard of Gloucester, Edward IV's much younger brother (born in 1452). He had emerged in recent years as an able soldier and prudent ruler of the northern parts, where he attracted strong loyalties, particularly in Yorkshire. He seems to have deliberately cut himself off from the rivalries and intrigues of the Court: his lack of involvement may have facilitated the trust which influential men were prepared to show him in the troubled months of Edward V's reign.

In fifteenth-century England the nature of the protectorship was an object of controversy. The powers and rights which Humphrey of Gloucester and Richard of York had exercised as protectors had been conferred and rigidly circumscribed in parliament. Duke Humphrey had persistently claimed that he was being denied the royal prerogative, as guardian of the infant Henry VI, which his brother Henry V had intended him to have. York had been in some doubt as to whether he or the queen would get the guardianship of the realm during Henry VI's incapacity in 1454, and his second protectorate had been abruptly terminated by parliament in 1456. When Edward IV died memories of these precedents may have been among the preoccupations of his queen, Elizabeth Wydeville, of Gloucester and other nobles.

The queen was at Westminster, in control of the Household (where her husband's treasure was stored), of her younger son Richard duke of York and her daughters. Her cultivated brother Anthony Wydeville, earl Rivers, the new king's tutor, was with him at Ludlow Castle in the Marches of Wales: he promptly prepared the prince's household for a journey to London. It is probable that the queen, her son Thomas Grey, marquess of Dorset, and Rivers either might have tried to deny Gloucester's right to the protectorship, or to insist that he should hold it on severely restricted terms. Since the intentions of the queen's party were forestalled and denigrated, we cannot be clear as to what they were.

Gloucester and other leading nobles, suspecting that the Wydevilles and Greys were making some kind of bid to ensure their continued predominance, took swift and efficient preventive action. Urged on by a message from Lord Hastings, Gloucester rode south from Yorkshire with his retinue, meeting Henry Stafford, duke of Buckingham, at Northampton. The dukes encountered the king at Stony Stratford. Despite Edward's protests they detained Rivers and other members of his company, including the king's half-brother Sir Richard Grey. The queen, unable to raise support in London, fled with her other children into sanctuary within the precincts of Westminster Abbey. Edward IV's former councillors acted more coolly and complacently. They recognised Gloucester as protector, but rejected his accusations of treason against the queen's relatives. During May, Gloucester seems to have been the determining force in Council. In June there were the bewildering events culminating in the usurpation. To what extent they represented a premeditated scheme by the protector, and to what extent his febrile reactions to imagined or actual threats to his authority from opponents or conciliar colleagues, is not clear. At a Council meeting in the Tower on 13 June, when men's minds were focused on preparations for Edward V's coronation, the protector dramatically arrested some fellow councillors: Thomas Rotherham, archbishop of York, John Morton, bishop of Ely, Lord Stanley, and the unfortunate Hastings, who was hustled out to be summarily executed. Nevertheless, bishops and lay peers backed a visit by Thomas Bourchier, archbishop of Canterbury, to the queen, at which he at last successfully persuaded her to allow her son Richard to be united with his brother under Gloucester's protection.

Despite the political tension there may have been a strong current of noble opinion that it would be dishonourable to the Crown if Edward was crowned whilst his brother sheltered round the corner in a refuge for fugitives from justice. But days later the drift of affairs, about which men were confused by rumours of plots, became starkly clear. In the protector's presence Dr Ralph Shaw discoursed from the pulpit at Paul's Cross on Edward IV's illegitimacy and Gloucester's right to the Crown. In the Guildhall, Buckingham eloquently explained to the mayor, aldermen and liveried citizens that Edward IV's marriage had been null on account of a precontract of marriage. On behalf of the peers, Buckingham petitioned the protector to assume the Crown, which with a becoming show of modesty he accepted. He began his reign on 26 June, ceremonially occupying the king's seat in Westminster Hall and processing to receive St Edward's sceptre from the abbot of Westminster. Meanwhile, according to an Italian then in England, Dominic Mancini, the deposed king had been deprived of his customary attendants:

He and his brother were withdrawn into the inner apartments of the Tower proper, and day by day began to be seen more rarely behind the bars and windows, till at length they ceased to appear altogether. The physician Argentine, the last of his attendants whose services the king enjoyed, reported that the young king, like a victim prepared for sacrifice, sought remission of his sins by daily confession and penance, because he believed that death was facing him.

On 6 July Richard III was crowned, his wife Anne Neville, the Kingmaker's daughter and widow of Henry VI's son, being crowned queen.

The events of April–June 1483 fascinated some of those historians modelling their works on classical Roman authors who were starting to flourish in northern Europe in the last decades of the fifteenth century. The report written by Mancini for a French royal councillor, Angelo Cato, archbishop of Vienne, is the earliest 'humanist' account of the usurpation. Two later ones relied heavily on the testimony of men well placed in 1483: Polydore Vergil composed his *English History* in the first two Tudor reigns. Sir Thomas More, Henry VIII's future Chancellor, was writing his analysis in the early years of that king's reign. The humanists were interested in reconstructing political sequences in such a way as to show how events flowed from the qualities and defects in the souls of men. They agreed in creating a 'character' for Richard III illustrating him as the archetype of guilty tyrants: in More's detailed study the theme is most fully worked out, presenting a figure in depth possessed of extraordinary talents, which are harnessed to the deep-laid, frenzied schemes of a flawed, inhuman, despairing *psyche*. Thus the fascination of Richard's usurpation to men of his and the succeeding generation has resulted in the survival of fuller accounts of events in 1483 than of any comparable span of English political history in the fifteenth century.

But the powerful historiographical concepts of the principal writers (rather than their supposed political bias) led them to impose interpretations which have dazzlingly overlaid the image of the historic Richard. The impression that we try to reconstruct from their portraits and from documentary evidence is too uncertain for assured conclusions to be made about his character and motives. It is an unrewarding task to speculate on why the protector claimed the Crown, or at what precise point he formulated the ambition. To cast light on the events of 1483 it would be necessary to know more about the enmities at Edward's Court: what is clear is that his kinsfolk and friends were too distrustful and envious to settle peacefully the form of minority government. Despite tensions, Edward III's and Henry V's circles had managed to co-operate in running government during minorities. The disintegration of the House of York and its adherents from 1483 onwards may in part be a reflection of the decline of political morality during a long period of dynastic strife, in which magnates had to resort to treacheries against kinsfolk and patrons in order to protect their propertied interests. Edward IV, himself the victim of such treacheries, gave in kind: he was steeped in the blood of companions, kinsfolk, even his own brother. During his last years, according to later English chroniclers, he was renowned for sloth and indulgence in sensual pleasures.

Modern historians have appreciated his political will and revealed his fine and lasting administrative achievements. To an age which is repelled by elitist images, Edward's 'common touch' is attractive: we sympathise with Commynes's report that he killed nobles but spared the commons after battles, with Burgundian surprise at his affability to the man in the street, when in exile in 1470–1, and with merry tales of his familiarity with London merchants and seduction of their wives. 'He was so genial in his greeting', wrote Mancini, 'that if he saw a newcomer bewildered at his appearance and royal magnificence, he would give him courage to speak by laying a kindly hand upon his shoulder.' But to fifteenth-century men the king's image was an earthly reflection of God's. The king was a sacred person, anointed with Heavenly power, and able to work miracles. Henry VI, so completely lacking in the ability to rule, was accorded long-suffering respect precisely because he exemplified so purely the sacerdotal qualities of kingship. Edward's immorality may have been gravely impolitic, discouraging respect for his House, and the mutual *gravitas* that his companions ought to show to one another.

Richard certainly seized on the weaknesses of Edward and his Court in order to help destroy his own nephews. The obscure circumstances of the notoriously lecherous king's marriage (a marriage of passion), and the rumours of precontracts enabled the legitimacy of his heirs to be queried. The laxity of his companions' morality was used by Richard to discredit them in the eyes of 'public opinion'. He made much play with Hastings's association with the notorious whore, Jane Shore, previously Edward's mistress. Dorset's unbridled lechery was to be denounced in a proclamation of October 1483. Richard's propaganda may have had some effect, for the near-contemporary sources give no indication that there was public indignation at the denigration of Edward IV or of his wife's relatives. Fears and rumours about the fate of Edward V show that there was deep regret for this young man, stories about whose kingly qualities had led people to have great hopes of his future.

In his attainment of the protectorship and the Crown, Richard relied above all on the support of Buckingham, who was rewarded by him generously with royal grants. Others similarly paid for their active support or acquiescence were Stanley, John lord Dinham, the earl of

Northumberland and the Howards. Lord Howard was created duke of Norfolk in place of the 'bastard' Richard of York, and his son Thomas was created earl of Surrey. However, in the autumn of 1483 a movement of revolt against Richard's rule among the gentry of the south-east and south-west suddenly gathered force, stimulated by noble intrigues and the spread of rumours that the former Edward V and duke of York, prisoners in the Tower of London, had been or soon might be put to death. The Wydevilles and Greys had retained widely in south-east England. Some of their former servants, such as the Kentish landowner Sir Richard Guildford and Sir William Stonor of Stonor Park (Oxon) were prepared to arm when Edward IV's widow (still in sanctuary with her daughters at Westminster) and her son Dorset gave the signal. But the plot had wider and more ominous ramifications. Elizabeth Wydeville had allied with Stanley's wife Margaret Beaufort, mother of Henry Tudor. The latter had been joined in exile in Brittany by Sir Edward Wydeville, brother of Earl Rivers, executed at Richard's behest in July. The involvement of Henry's interest in the rebellion strongly suggests that the Wydevilles believed that the 'princes in the Tower' were dead.

The most dangerous feature of the rebellion for Richard was the participation of his principal fellow-plotter Buckingham, ostensibly as a supporter of Henry's claim, but perhaps with the undeclared ambition of gaining the Crown for himself as a descendant of the Beauforts and of Edward III's youngest son Gloucester. But the alliance of Yorkist and Lancastrian in 1483 worked no better than in 1471. Buckingham's recent aggrandisement in the Marches of Wales, as well as his part in Richard's elevation, may have deterred Lancastrian and Tudor partisans there from joining him. Magnates whom the king had rewarded, such as Norfolk, came to his support. With a large force Richard moved on Salisbury, threatening rebel communications. Buckingham was brought from hiding in the Marches to be executed there. The Kentishmen and other south-eastern rebels, who had assembled at Guildford, fled. Richard advanced from Salisbury on Exeter, which its bishop, Peter Courtenay, and the marquess of Dorset, did not stay to defend.

Richard's impressive victory over all his opponents, with the formidable show of support from lords who did not want Buckingham and the Wydevilles to challenge their recent acquisitions, ought to have consolidated his rule. In 1484–5 there were indeed some indications that it was becoming acceptable and firm. Richard tried hard to win his subjects' affection. Apart from the ringleaders, large numbers of the 1483 rebels were pardoned. From his considerable landed and financial resources, administered with the same care as under his brother, lords and royal servants were handsomely rewarded. In the parliament which met in January 1484 the king requested no direct subsidies, forbade royal extortion of 'benevolences' and showed concern that royal justice should be uncorrupt. He made more progresses through the provinces than had been customary under his recent predecessors, and in a crown-wearing ceremony of great magnificence in York Minster demonstrated how successfully since 1479 he had attached and kept the Neville interest and goodwill in the city and Yorkshire. Like Richard II or Margaret of Anjou, he could call on loyalties in remoter provinces, rather than in the capital and its region. As often during the dynastic conflicts of the fifteenth century, opinions in the 'northern parts' diverged from those in the South and Midlands and were determined by different factors.

In August 1485 Henry Tudor landed with a small force at Milford Haven in Pembrokeshire (see p. 400). He attracted a considerable amount of Welsh support, though probably not as much as he had hoped for, and marched unopposed into the Midlands, threatening communications between Richard and London. The king barred the way to Henry, whom no English magnate had joined, near Leicester. This was an opportunity for Richard to solve one of his few remaining problems – the threat from Henry, who since the 1483 rebellion had provided a rallying-point for fugitives.

It was bad luck for Richard that he had failed to capture Henry as a result of the Anglo-Breton alliance of 1484 (see p. 399), and that he had not been able to reconcile two of Henry's most dangerous companions, Dorset and Sir Edward Wydeville, as a result of his *rapprochement* with Elizabeth Wydeville. An ominous and unexpected blow had been the defection of the Hammes garrison in the March of Calais, due to the success of Oxford, imprisoned there, in suborning its captain, Sir James Blount. The veteran intriguer Oxford's ability to win over Blount, like Bishop Morton of Ely's persuasion of his gaoler Buckingham in 1483, may have sprung partly from the general weakness of dynastic loyalties. Another weakening factor may have been Richard's inability to consolidate loyalties in the close family circles of magnates or among those who had observed his usurpation at close quarters.

The reminiscences of contemporaries used by Polydore Vergil and Sir Thomas More reinforce the impression of earlier sources that the events of April–June 1483 were stamped on the minds and hearts of magnates, central royal officials and bystanding Londoners. The anti-Ricardian propaganda of the rebels of October 1483 may have intensified horrified feelings. In noble circles there were probably some who could not bear Richard's rule, however mild, and others who favoured it only for what they could make out of it. We do not really know what Richard's personality was like, but there may have been aspects of it, expressed in nervous physical mannerisms, which jarred on and disturbed fellow nobles. According to Polydore Vergil:

Whilst he was thinking of any matter, he did continually bite his nether lip, as though that cruel nature of his did so rage against itself in that little carcass. Also he was wont to be ever with his right hand pulling out of the sheath to the middle, and putting in again, the dagger which he did always wear.

Buckingham's son is alleged to have said that his father, before his execution, wanted an opportunity to stab Richard, an attitude implying a surprising degree of personal revulsion. But a Silesian noble, Nicolas von Poppelau, who paid court to Richard probably at his castle of Middleham in 1484, was much impressed by this courteous, gangling, mettlesome prince who declared his determination to destroy his enemies, in a fierce line of conversation which, if customary, may have rather repelled and shocked English gentlemen. Even during his reign Richard's opponents considered him a man who could be plausibly represented as capable of any evil. It was scarcely dignified for a king of England to feel compelled by rumour to deny before peers, and the Mayor and Aldermen of London, as Richard did in 1485, that he regarded the queen's death as an opportunity to marry his niece (Edward's daughter Elizabeth of York):

he shewed his grief and displeasure, and said it never came into his thought or mind to marry in such manner, nor was he pleased or glad at the death of his queen but as sorry and heavy in heart as a man would be.

A few peers joined the king to oppose Henry Tudor in 1485: Norfolk, Surrey, Northumberland and Lovell. An account of the battle of Bosworth written in March 1486 by the Castilian Valera reinforces the impression in some other sources that Northumberland was pledged to Henry before the battle. The earl may have been anxious to re-establish Percy influence in Yorkshire, by destroying a king who had established a 'Neville' primacy there – a motive similar to the one the earl had displayed in 1471, when he had not hindered Edward's invasion. Valera says that Henry discovered, after he had won the throne, that Northumberland really wanted to have as king Clarence's young son, Edward earl of Warwick, married to one of his own daughters.

Nevertheless, despite noble absenteeism and reservations at Bosworth, Richard had in his company a strong contingent of Household knights and their retainers. The accounts of the battle by Valera and by the continuator of the Crowland Abbey chronicles stress treachery as the cause of the king's defeat and death. The only long account of the battle, by Polydore Vergil, emphasises the fears of treachery within the king's army: Richard staked the issue on a bold and risky tactical manoeuvre. While the royal vanguard was indecisively and somewhat timidly engaged with Oxford's men, the king led the Household men round Oxford's flank, personally leading a charge against Henry and his retainers, who were not yet engaged. The fighting between the rivals' retainers was intense[3]. The issue was decided when Sir William Stanley led his retinue to the support of Henry, but Northumberland and Lord Stanley failed to come to the king's rescue. Thus in Polydore's account the real treacheries occurred when the king, who had tried to settle the issue by a rash move, got into difficulties. Richard was killed, and so was Norfolk, still leading the royal vanguard in combat with Oxford (22 August 1485).

The insistence in the other sources that treason in the royal host made Henry's victory a foregone conclusion may have sprung from the anxiety of royal supporters, after the event, to emphasise that their real commitment from the start had been to Henry. It is likely that a number had answered the king's summons, pledged to both sides; such conduct had not been uncommon in the Wars of the Roses: memories of its past occurrence, as well as justified suspicions that his rule was not popular in many quarters, may have been the reasons for Richard's and his adherents' fear of treachery, spurring him on to rash tactics. Richard, angry and upset at the ease with which Henry had penetrated to the Midlands, and at the tardiness and hesitations of some nobles in coming to his support, threw away his fortunes in a gamble on the battlefield, sacrificing the lives and fortunes of many loyal supporters. In conversation during the battle with his Spanish mercenary captain Salaçar, who urged him to flee, as in his remarks the previous year to Von Poppelau, he showed himself to be a man of extremes – perhaps displaying some of the qualities extolled in Sir Thomas Malory's protagonists of chivalry, but not in the ruler of the complex and settled polity admired by Fortescue. According to Valera, Salaçar went up to the king and said:

'Sire, take care to put your own person in safety, for you cannot hope for victory in this day's battle because of the manifest treason which has come to light among your supporters.' And the king answered: 'Salaçar, please God that I do not take one step backwards, for I want to die like a king or win victory in this battle.' And then he placed the royal crown over the armour on his head — they say that it was worth 120,000 crowns — put on his coat of mail, and began to fight with such great strength and courage that those who remained loyal to him fought long in the battle by means of his example[4].

It may be, then, that Richard failed to win sufficient loyalties not so much because of the specific crimes attributed to him, but because there was something about his temperament which worried and disturbed men: he may have been what contemporaries described as a 'dangerous man', whom the prudent took care to appease but treated with a secret reserve.

Richard's stripped body was exposed to public view in a hermitage near the battlefield, draped only by black cloth of rather poor quality. It was trussed naked on a horse's back and conveyed for further exposure and burial without honour in the insignificant Franciscan friary at Leicester.

The end of the Wars of the Roses

The term 'Wars of the Roses' has been frequently applied by twentieth-century historians to those domestic conflicts which occurred in the 1450s and 1460s, seemingly ended in 1471 and flared up again in the mid-1480s. Though the precise term appears to have been first used only in 1829 by Sir Walter Scott in *Anna of Geierstein*, it embodies earlier beliefs that the partisans of Lancaster and York respectively wore badges of the red and white rose and that these symbolised the dynastic basis of the conflicts. This theory of their cause is enunciated in the papal dispensation (1486) for the marriage of Henry VII and Elizabeth of York: the theme of reconciliation by the marriage was symbolised in frequent Tudor iconographical use of the mixed red and white rose. In the sixteenth century the expression 'white rose' was applied, often with treasonable implications, to Yorkist descendants. Edward IV's great-grandson Edward Courtenay, earl of Devon, was described in a list of Paduan students in 1556–7 as 'Courtenay an English noble from the royal family of the White Rose of the Britons'[5].

But there is no firm contemporary evidence that supporters of Lancaster and York habitually wore these badges, whereas there is some that on occasion they used others, some of which implied the importance of loyalties to the interests of particular magnates. Henry VI's son distributed a livery of swans in 1459 to Cheshiremen and others. Edward of York, falsely trying to insinuate his allegiance to the prince, sported his ostrich feather in 1471. At Barnet the suns worn by Edward's men were confused with the personal stars of the Lancastrian Oxford[6]. To combat Henry Tudor in 1485, Norfolk wrote to John Paston bidding him array a company in the ducal livery. A Nottingham contingent of 1463–4 was provided by the town with jackets of red cloth sown with letters in white cotton twill.

Modern scholarship has tended to see the dynastic issue as a cloak for factional motives, and to emphasise the readiness of partisans to change sides according to their family interests and alignments in Court and country. The origin of the wars is to be sought in the factious tensions of the early 1450s. The recurrence of dynastic rebellion, often supported by foreign subsidies, stemmed from attempts to recover lost or slipping noble influence. Yet concern about rightful inheritance was fundamental to society. In 1469 northern rebels sought to restore Henry Percy as 'legitimate heir' to the earldom of Northumberland. In 1471 West-Country men joined the dispossessed earl of Devon and duke of Somerset in arms 'for that they reputed them old inheritors of that country'. Men were especially concerned that the rightful king should rule: the usurper, illegal in the eyes of God, could not be expected to bring His blessing on the realm or respect its laws. The Yorkists were anxious to demonstrate publicly the legitimacy of their claim, and Fortescue attempted in his earlier writings to revive the respectability of the Lancastrian one after Henry VI's extraordinary abandonment of it in 1460. The survival of a number of rolls setting forth royal genealogies demonstrates concern over the matter.

A study of the peerage's allegiances suggests that they tended to be prudently concerned to preserve their inheritances by an often reluctant acceptance of dynastic change, and slowness in coming to the aid of threatened kings. But, though there were some agile trimmers and notorious turncoats, the number of peers who fought on both sides was only about half the total of those who fought on one side. With few exceptions the peerage was prepared to settle down under Yorkist rule in 1461–2 and under a Tudor in 1485–6. The spread of the saintly cult of Henry VI in the Yorkist period may have been partly due to hankerings for an allegiance which some men had had to reject abruptly and reluctantly as impracticable. The family of the Cornishman John Trevelyan, who had prospered in Henry's service, possessed a roll of prayers invoking him, among other saints, and in 1526, in their house at Nettlecombe (Somerset), there was 'A clothe of Kyng Henry', possibly his portrait. Henry VII may not have been entirely insincere when he professed himself in a proclamation to northerners (1485) 'moved as well of pity as for the great dangers, perils, losses of goods and lives, that the ancestors of the inhabitants of that country have borne and suffered for the quarrel and title of the most famous prince, and of blessed memory, King Henry VI, our uncle'.

There is contemporary warrant for the view, much canvassed by sixteenth-century writers, that the wars caused widespread misery and hardship. For instance, the continuator of the Crowland chronicles wrote: 'The slaughter of men was immense: for besides the dukes, earls, barons and distinguished soldiers who were slain, multitudes almost innumerable of the common people died of their wounds. Such was the state of the kingdom for nearly ten years.' Modern research has deflated this and later rhetoric. In many campaigns a handful of peers and small armies were involved in a few weeks' fighting. The defeated common soldiers were often allowed to escape. Participants were frequently pardoned. In the period 1453–1509 about 64 per cent of the 397 attainted traitors or their heirs (exclusive of members of the Houses of Lancaster and York) had the sentence reversed. There was little plundering. Northerners had a bad reputation. John Whitele of Nottingham was alleged to have said in 1459 that 'there rode many strong thieves with my lord of Northumberland and my lord of Westmorland through the town'. They may have taken part a few days later in the sack of York's town of Ludlow. In 1461 the arrival of the northerners was much feared in eastern and southern regions.

Nevertheless, there were other reasons why the wars may have been balefully remembered. Since opponents often made a point of killing gentlefolk in and after battles, their losses were probably disproportionately high. At least thirty-one peers were killed, a very large number whose slaughter must have generated much bad feeling in the closely related circles of nobility. In every year between 1459 and 1464 there were major military efforts: contemporaries considered that the forces which struggled for the possession of York in 1461 were exceptionally large. In the following years Edward's government had to make strenuous efforts to impose its rule in the remote and vulnerable northern parts of the realm, at first involving much of the peerage in the attempt.

Recruitment for the armies probably relied heavily on intimidation. Elite bodies of paid foreign professionals and lords' retainers were supplemented by a mass of soldiers, mainly footmen, if they could be arrayed quickly enough. A hostile account of the bastard of Fauconberg's recruitment in 1471 may reflect, if exaggeratedly, typical methods. Some Kentishmen

that would right fain have sat still at home, and not to have run into the danger of such rebellion, by force and violence of such riotous people . . . for fear of death and other great menaces, and threatenings, were compelled, some to go with the bastard, in their persons . . . and such as were unharnessed, aged and unable, and of honour, they were compelled to send men waged, or to give money wherewith to wage men to go to the said bastard's company.

Reluctance may have been normally increased by the lack of opportunities to plunder or ransom, the expense of equipping, and the chances of loss. Thomas Denyes, hoping to solicit Warwick's patronage, wrote that he had fought for him at St Albans (1461) and 'there lost I £20 worth horse, harness and money, and was hurt in divers places'. John Williams claimed in a Chancery petition that he had to bear part of the costs of his own and his company's wages in the Towton campaign (1461), as the sums provided by Richard Browne of Norwich had been insufficient, and he had been unable to recover the debt from Browne's executors.

There are frequent references to the provision of wages to soldiers: the expense tended to limit the scope and duration of campaigns. If soldiers were not waged, it was difficult to maintain discipline and prevent plundering – to be avoided by lords trying to win support and appear sympathetic to popular grievances. A London chronicler may have been repeating Yorkist lords' propaganda when he alleged that, before the battle of Northampton (1460), their opponents had it proclaimed that, if their soldiers won, they could make havoc in London, Coventry, Bristol and Salisbury. The Londoners showed strongest disinclination to admit armies, in 1461, 1471 and 1497, when they were reputed ill-disciplined. Henry VII seems to have been appealing to popular memories of the northerners' ill-repute in 1461 when he proclaimed in 1489 that the Yorkshire rebels intended 'to rob, despoil and destroy all the south parts of this his realm, and to subdue and bring to captivity all the people of the same'.

The main burden of the wars was their cost. Communities could not be certain that they would not be plundered and had to take safeguards, by defence or provision of help. In 1461 William Grey, bishop of Ely 'for fear of the Northernmen' hired professional Burgundian soldiers, and sent for men from all his manors in Essex, Norfolk, Suffolk and Cambridgeshire to defend the Isle of Ely and Wisbech Castle. Armies, though occasionally subsidised by foreign princes, were usually paid for partly by lords and their dependants, and by levies on communities. Near-contemporary chronicles suggest that there were widespread complaints, especially in the period 1459–63, about the large sums raised by authority of Privy Seal letters. It is probably not just an illusion produced by the survival of urban records that both sides relied heavily on raising finance, contingents and supplies from the principal towns: there, resources were concentrated and more readily available. Control of the towns was as much a financial and logistic necessity as a strategic one: much of the campaigning centred round attempts to secure London, York, Bristol and Coventry.

The towns paid heavily for their immunity from sack. In 1460 Coventry waged forty soldiers for Henry VI and Hull thirteen, and Norwich raised 200 marks to pay for its contingent. In response to a Yorkist summons to combat the northern army (January 1461), Norwich supplied a company of 120 soldiers paid up for six weeks' service at sixpence a day. In the early 1460s Coventry and Hull were making heavier contributions than hitherto to the costs of warfare, to sustain Edward's northern campaigns; Leicester and Nottingham also gave him substantial help. Bristol contributed a loan of £200, and £1,000 worth of military and naval aid, mainly for his campaigns. Leicester spent £180 on succouring the Bosworth casualties.

Those experiences help to explain sour memories of the wars. There is also evidence of their encouragement of disorders. Why did the wars come to an end? Peers may have become more wary of pursuing their ambitions by such hazardous means. Kings may have become more aware of the need not to give occasion for popular or foreign support to potential rebels, and to use their favour and patronage to build up an affinity of supporters who would feel it in their interest rather than to their loss to give speedy military aid. 'Yelverton and Jeney [two Norfolk gentlemen] are like for to be greatly punished, for because they came not hither to the king,' wrote John Paston the younger from Newcastle in 1462. In 1464 there was talk in Norfolk of the appointment of 'a commission to enquire why they of this country that were sent for came not more hastily up after they were sent for. It is reported that the King is greatly displeased therewith'. In February 1470 a commission of array to Coventry charged all those who received a daily wage of 12*d* or more from the king or queen to serve in person or send a substitute. In August Sir John Paston reported that Edward had sent 'for his feed men' to suppress revolt. It was such who flocked to his standard when he advanced south from Yorkshire in 1471. In 1485 the royal retainers, in the king's 'battle' stood by Richard III. Henry VII understood the need to cultivate an affinity in the regions prepared to fight for him. Probably in 1489 Oxford wrote to Sir John Paston

I desire and pray you that ye will in all goodly haste, upon the sight hereof, prepare yourself to be in a readiness with as many persons as ye here before granted to do the King service in my company defensibly arrayed and thereupon so to resort unto me in all goodly haste possible upon a day's warning, horsed and harnessed, to be at the King's wages.

In that year Henry VII wrote to the Yorkshire landowner Sir Robert Plumpton, thanking him for helping to suppress local disturbances and promising 'to remember you in time to come in any thing that may be to your preferment and advancement', with an expectation of local office, 'praying you that if there shall happen any indisposition of our said people, ye will, as ye have begun, endeavour you from time to time for the speedy repressing thereof'. In 1491 Henry wrote thanking Plumpton for similar services, requiring that 'by as wise wages as ye can, ye put yourself in a surety of your menial servants and tenants, and to know assuredly how many of them will take your part in serving us', the number being certified to the earl of Surrey, Vice-Warden of the East and Middle Marches. A statute of 1504, amplifying one of 1496, laid down that all holders of royal grants, offices or fees were obliged to attend the king when he was going to war, on pain of forfeiting their grants. They were to receive the kings' wages during their journeys between home and the royal assembly, and for the duration of their service.

Henry VII: the unknown usurper (1485–1509)

The new king assumed the Crown by virtue of his descent from John of Gaunt. Considerable force was probably given to his claim in the eyes of contemporaries by the manner in which he had attained the Crown: the death of an English king in battle, unprecedented since 1066, bore the marks of divine judgment.

One of Henry's principal political needs was to define a satisfactory relationship between himself and the small group of lay magnates, some of them as nearly related to past English kings as himself, to whose local influence the Crown traditionally turned for judicial, political and military support. After Bosworth Henry took measures to neutralise one potential rallying point for noble dissidents. He dispatched Sir Robert Willoughby to Yorkshire to secure Clarence's son Edward, aged fifteen, heir to the earldom of Warwick, whom many were to regard as the rightful king. In January 1486 Henry demonstrated the firmness of his intent to placate partisans of the House of York by marrying Edward IV's eldest daughter Elizabeth. The birth of sons who survived infancy in September 1486 (Arthur) and 1491 (Henry) gave some assurance for the future of the dynasty.

Moreover, the Yorkist higher nobility presented no united threat to the new king. Always riven by enmities, they had been further divided, and indeed to some extent demoralised and undermined in influence, by the intrigues surrounding Gloucester's attainment of the protectorship and usurpation. Richard had destroyed the predominance at Court of Elizabeth Wydeville's kinsmen. The survivors gravitated to Henry's allegiance. Richard had executed two influential Yorkist nobles: Hastings and Buckingham. Their young sons were to remain loyal to Henry. Another influential Yorkist, John Howard, duke of Norfolk, had been killed at Bosworth. Henry restored his attainted son Thomas to the earldom of Surrey in 1489. His clemency may have been prompted by the influence Howard could wield in East Anglia, counterbalancing the suspect De la Pole interest, as well as by Howard's military talents. Like Edward IV in the first years of his reign, Henry was willing to favour any noble prepared to give him service. It had been difficult for Edward to end the Wars of the Roses in 1461, for he was dependent on a nobility rendered uncertain in loyalties, polarised in struggles for local influence and security. But the political disarray of the higher nobility in 1485 was a recent development: on the whole, nobles seem to have been anxious to reconstitute the polity of the early 1480s, in which the Crown regulated their influence and enmities, rather than revert to the expenses, discomforts and uncertainties of regulation by dynastic strife.

Henry was not well known in English governing circles. William Berkeley, earl of Nottingham and possibly Henry Percy, earl of Northumberland had known him as a child, but the one peer who showed some inclination to support him in arms in August 1485, his stepfather Stanley, had never met him. Stanley (d.1504) was rewarded with the earldom of Derby (October 1485). A nice calculator of odds, he remained loyal to Henry. But his brother Sir William, who had intervened on Henry's side at Bosworth and been appointed Chamberlain of the Household and Chief Justice of north Wales, was attempting to contact the Yorkist impostor Perkin Warbeck in 1493, and was executed for treason in 1495. There were other treacheries. Dorset, Elizabeth Wydeville's son by her first husband, had been suspected of wavering in his support of Henry in exile, and was later to fall under suspicion of plotting with Warbeck. John de la Pole, earl of Lincoln, the cautious Suffolk's eldest son, received Henry's favour in 1485, despite his recent enjoyment of Richard's. But in 1487 Lincoln was to raise rebellion.

On the other hand, Henry forged noble ties which held. His uncle Jasper earl of Pembroke (created duke of Bedford, October 1485) and John de Vere, earl of Oxford, had been Lancastrian exiles. Oxford, as the correspondence with him in the *Paston Letters* indicates, acted as royal deputy in Norfolk. Bedford, recipient of the Welsh Marcher lordships of Pembroke, Glamorgan, Newport, Abergavenny, Haverfordwest and Cilgerran, and Chief Justice of south Wales (in the principality as distinct from the private Marcher jurisdictions) promoted Henry's interests in the region till his death in 1495. As the duke died childless, his lordships reverted to the king as nephew and heir. Besides the Tudor family's properties, Henry held twenty-two Mortimer Marcher lordships: fifty of a total of *c*.136 such lordships were in his hands at various periods. In 1495 Sir William Stanley forfeited Holt, Chirk, and Yale and Bromfield. When William Herbert, earl of Huntingdon, died childless in 1491, his lordships reverted to the Crown, which held Buckingham's until he came of age in 1491. Henry's powers of patronage in Wales outstripped those of any noble. None tried to use influence there as a basis for revolt, as had happened in recent reigns. The king's service was the main attraction. Notable among those who rose in it in the principality and Marches were Sir Rhys ap Thomas, and Henry's illegitimate Beaufort kinsman Sir Charles Somerset, created Lord Herbert by 1504. Following precedents set by Edward IV, Henry used the administrative council set up for his eldest son's Welsh principality as an instrument to enforce royal justice in the areas of jurisdiction remaining in private hands. In 1493 Prince Arthur was granted twenty lordships, castles and manors in the Marches, and was licensed to appoint justices of oyer and terminer in Shropshire, Herefordshire, Gloucestershire, Worcestershire, in the adjacent Marches and in the principality.

In the West Country Henry seems to have intended to revive the traditional focus for Lancastrian loyalties by creating a Cornish supporter, Sir Edward Courtenay (collateral descendant of the former comital house), earl of Devon. In 1495 his son and heir William was married to the king's sister-in-law Catherine of York. Devon was unable to check the Cornish rising in 1497, though he held Exeter against Perkin Warbeck later in the year. His son was imprisoned from 1503 until the end of the reign under suspicion of aiding the Yorkist claimant, Edmund de la Pole, earl of Suffolk.

As a ruler Henry does not seem to have had a general policy of building up noble influence or of undermining it. The loyalties of many magnates were not wholly to be relied on. But circumstances often put them at a disadvantage: Nevilles, Percies, Staffords, Courtenays and Howards for various reasons found themselves dependent on Henry's favour to preserve or consolidate their properties and influence. Some of the greatest inheritances were in the Crown's hands for all or part of the reign. Henry felt sufficiently confident in his power, especially from 1502 onwards, to treat a substantial number of peers with great harshness, obliging them to produce bonds for large sums as fines for contravening statutes, or as surety for good behaviour. In 1507 George Neville, lord Abergavenny, was fined the astronomical sum of £70,650 in the court of King's Bench for unlawfully retaining 471 men below the rank of knight or esquire. The king remitted this to the still crippling sum of £5,000, to be paid in ten annual instalments. Henry VIII cancelled the whole debt in the year of his accession.

Besides his few committed noble supporters, at his accession Henry already had the support of a nucleus of former royal officials and prominent gentry who were to promote his rule ably, mostly men who had fallen foul of Richard III. Eminent among them was the veteran royal councillor John Morton, bishop of Ely (*c*.1420–1500), who had fled to Flanders after Buckingham's revolt. Appointed Chancellor in March 1486, he was translated to the see of Canterbury the following October and received the cardinalate in 1493. Other Tudor adherents who rose in Henry's royal service were Reginald Bray, who achieved prominence as a councillor and expert in estate and financial administration, the Kentish landowner Sir Richard Guildford (Master of the Ordnance and a Chamberlain of the Exchequer) and the leading Somerset knight Giles Daubeney, created a peer March 1486 (Chamberlain of the Household 1495–1508). Daubeney, always highly regarded by Henry, was one of his best military men.

It was crucial for the success of Henry's early rule that he should supplement the support of committed adherents by winning over royal officials, peers and retained gentry on whose expertise and control Edward had based his rule in the 1470s and 1480s. Twenty-nine of Henry's councillors had served Yorkist kings in the same capacity. The career of John lord Dinham (d.1501) may serve as an example of Henry's ability to win over influential Yorkists. Dinham, head of a leading Devon family, had emerged as a supporter of York in 1459, and was created a peer in 1467. He was appointed steward of the forfeited estates of the earldom of Devon in 1469, and, despite his acceptance of Henry VI's Readeption, was in 1475 appointed councillor and played an important part in the administration of the duchy of Cornwall. Henry appointed him Treasurer of the Exchequer in July 1486.

It was the expertise of former Yorkist officials of the Household and their local subordinates that enabled Henry, eventually on a greater scale than Edward IV, to accumulate large monetary reserves (see pp. 108 ff). Such wealth attracted the loyal service of Yorkist peers and gentry. The munificence of Henry's Court, the opulence of his clothes, jewels and banquets and of his building works were intended to advertise his power to reward in peace and war. Their characteristic styles, often reminiscent of those of Edward IV's Court, emphasised tradition and stability. Like Henry IV after 1399 (but unlike Edward in 1461), Henry was able to retain vital elements in the personnel and structure of the previous regime. His achievements were in part attributable to his remarkable personality.

Aged twenty-eight in 1485, Henry had no experience of government. He soon acquired an administrative and financial grasp unequalled by any other English ruler dealt with in this book. An indefatigable worker, his attention to detail did not obscure his larger aims. His early years of intrigue and misfortune had taught him to understand men, especially, perhaps, through observation of the political wrestling of the Tudors and Herberts, families newly risen from the Welsh gentry and competing for influence in Wales. But the strenuous burden of kingship may in the long run have warped Henry's judgment. From *c*.1500 a group of his councillors known as the 'Council Learned' harshly pursued the collection of royal debts and the fining of those who infringed or evaded statutes. Those who exported wool without licence, who concealed land liable to royal wardship, committed offences in office or failed to take up the burden of knighthood, were less likely than hitherto to escape without detection (cf. p. 126). Soon after Henry's death one of his former councillors, Edmund Dudley, in *The Tree of Commonwealth*, obliquely condemned the king's rapacity and its consequences: 'Peradventure of that appetite [insatiable covetousness] have there been some other of late time, and were in manner without fault, saving only that. But how such a king shall have the loving hearts of his subjects, late experience may plainly show it.' This was the bitter fruit of Henry's unrelaxing, eternally vigilant attitudes.

The rebellions and plots in Henry's reign show how slight the hold of the Tudor monarchy had originally been and, in some circles, continued to be. Henry had set an example for little-known claimants and rebels to challenge the rule of a rich and powerful king. In meeting the challenge he was assisted by the failure of opponents to articulate grievances with a wide geographical and social appeal, a result partly of the sectional and regional emphasis of rebels and the fragmented state of Yorkist loyalties. In April 1486 Humphrey and Thomas Stafford, brothers who had fled into sanctuary at Colchester, after fighting for Richard at Bosworth, escaped and tried to raise their Worcestershire retainers and tenants in support of Warwick's claim. Francis viscount Lovell, a favourite of Richard III, gathered supporters in arms at his late master's castle of Middleham in Wensleydale, appealing to former Neville servants and other Yorkshiremen who had enjoyed Richard's patronage. What made this revolt dangerous was that Henry, with an inadequately armed retinue, had arrived in York, whose government had been hostile to his usurpation, and, even more, that he was dependent on the support of the earl of Northumberland, equivocal in 1485, but since restored to the Wardenships which he coveted. The earl could have destroyed Henry, just as he could have destroyed Edward, when precariously placed in Yorkshire in 1471. Instead Northumberland proceeded energetically in co-operation with the royal retinue against Lovell.

The 1486 rebellion collapsed speedily in face of Henry's retaliatory measures. It had been a hasty, ill-co-ordinated rising. A much more dangerous movement arose in 1487. Lambert Simnel, son of an Oxford joiner, was trained to pose as Warwick. Irish nobles were prepared to accept the imposture and assisted at the coronation of 'Edward VI' in Dublin (May 1487). The claimant was joined by Lovell and Lincoln, aided by a force of hired German mercenaries shipped from Flanders. The rebels landed at Furness (Lancs) in June, but largely failed in their attempts to raise support there and in Yorkshire. Henry confronted them at Stoke with a large army, whose first 'battle' alone was able to annihilate the ill-matched force of undisciplined Irish and tenacious mercenaries. Lincoln was killed in the fighting. Apart from him the De la Poles were not involved. In the early 1490s the threat to Henry's rule was not to originate with them, but with an imposture supported abroad particularly by Edward IV's sister Margaret, dowager duchess of Burgundy. Perkin Warbeck first appeared pretending to be Richard duke of York, Edward's younger son, at Cork in October 1491, and kept up the pretence till his capture in 1497. The reappearance of Richard of York, widely thought to have been murdered by Richard III, shows how hard it was for Henry's opponents to find a plausible candidate, since Warwick was locked up in the Tower and the De la Poles, not notable for their dynamism, and chastened perhaps by Lincoln's fate, did not commit themselves yet to pursuit of their claim. Warbeck's attempts to win Kentishmen and Cornishmen to his side failed; the only significant support he received was in Ireland and Scotland.

But in 1497, while the pretender was still at large in Scotland, there occurred a dangerous popular rebellion in Cornwall, provoked by subsidy collection for the Scots war. It was led by Thomas Flamank, lawyer of Bodmin, and a blacksmith, Michael Joseph. Joined by a minor Yorkist peer, James Touchet, lord Audley, they marched in June across southern England, through Wells, Salisbury and Winchester. According to an indictment found by a grand jury in Kent in 1506 against Lord Abergavenny (a peer who had enjoyed Yorkist favour), in June 1497 he had been at Ewelme (Oxon) with soldiers arrayed to oppose the rebels nearby at Wallingford (Berks). Ewelme was the home of Edmund de la Pole, earl of Suffolk, who had succeeded his father in 1493 and been compelled by Henry to accept demotion from a dukedom. The king sent a messenger to Abergavenny and Suffolk at Ewelme, ordering them to take their men to Staines and hold the bridge over the Thames there. He found them in bed together: on his entry Abergavenny hid under the bedclothes. When the messenger had gone, Suffolk asked 'Why shrinkest thou and hidest thyself so? Art thou afeard?' Abergavenny replied 'Nay, but I would not that he saw me here, if a man will do aught what will ye do, now is time.' Suffolk seems to have regarded this as an incitement to treason. Saying enigmatically 'A wilt thou so', he got out of bed, took his companion's boots and prepared to ride.

Since Suffolk was a pretender to the throne in 1506, this merry tale may have been devised to associate Abergavenny with treason. If there is any truth in it, it shows how elements of the nobility in 1497 were not firmly wedded to Tudor rule, but prepared to use commons agitation for dynastic change, as had happened earlier in the Wars of the Roses.

Had the Cornish rebels scored a success against Henry's forces, ambitious and discontented nobles might have been emboldened to rebel against him. But he held London and bridges on the Thames approaches to it securely. The rebels turned in an arc south of the city through Surrey. Henry kept his forces back till they had reached Blackheath, the normal encampment for Kentish rebels attacking London. But there was no response in Kent to the rebel appeals. Henry may have anticipated this, or may have had to await the arrival of Lord Daubeney's army, recalled from its progress towards Scotland, and of the supplementary levies summoned. Henry rode with the army against the rebels. The first 'battle' under Daubeney sufficed to break the Cornishmen, who were encircled by forces Henry had dispatched beforehand to outflank them. He had won convincingly against the most formidable popular challenge to his rule, helped by the fact that he had a paid-up royal army actually in the field, and possibly by the comparative remoteness of Cornwall and tenuousness of ties between its people and those of south-east England.

Henry was still not safe from dynastic conspiracies, but their projectors seem to have become convinced that substantial foreign backing provided the essential ground of success. In 1501 Suffolk and his brother Richard fled to Maximilian's court to get aid for a conspiracy. The earl's standing may have slipped even further because of his imprisonment for homicide in 1499, and Warwick's execution that year may have persuaded him and his brother that their family's claim to the Crown was more plausible. The De la Poles' flight, and Prince Arthur's death in April 1502 prolonged dynastic insecurity. But, whatever murmurs there may have been against the harsh fiscal policies of Henry's final years, no one had the nerve to challenge a formidable ruler whom God had so long sustained. Till his death Henry kept his characteristically vigorous control: his heirs, unlike Henry IV's, did not form a centre of undermining intrigue. The ways in which Henry VII imposed his rule by shrewdly exploiting and developing the methods of his Yorkist predecessors have been subjected to considerable scholarly scrutiny. Nevertheless, it is still mystifying that, after four consecutive kings had lost their thrones as a result of dynastic plotting, this little-known usurper did not succumb too. Instead he went so far as to display tyrannical tendencies, as his councillor Dudley hinted, when arguing the necessity for the Crown to temper justice with mercy after his death: 'And I suppose there is no Christian king hath need of this more than our own prince and sovereign lord, considering the great number of penal statutes and laws made in his realm for the hard and strait punishment of his subjects.'

Henry's rule arose out of a brief period of political uncertainties and scandals, in which the prestige of the Crown had been besmirched. A humanist historian whom he patronised, Polydore Vergil, prefigured his achievement in describing the literal raising of the crown from the mire at Bosworth: 'The soldiers cried, God save King Henry, God save

King Henry! and with heart and hand uttered all the show of joy that might be; which when Thomas Stanley did see, he set anon King Richard's crown, which was found among the spoil in the field, upon his head.'

Henry's style of ruling conspicuously combined magnificence and decorousness. He was the first English king who had an official panegyrist, the blind friar Bernard André of Toulouse, who celebrated his descent, virtues and achievements in verse and prose. Henry and his queen, Elizabeth of York, were not touched by scandal: they were notably pious, like their contemporaries Ferdinand and Isabella, the Catholic Kings of Spain[7]. Unlike her mother, Elizabeth did not promote controversial political ambitions. Neither king nor queen became identified with the interests of a 'Court nobility' or faction, as, to some extent, had Henry VI, Edward IV, and their wives. Henry rewarded his servants well, but, where the rivalries of subjects were concerned, seems to have exhibited to an unusual degree that much-praised but elusive regal virtue – 'indifference'. No group of royal servants were able to monopolise avenues of patronage in the interests of a provincial dominance. The men with the king's ear were the bureaucrats, ambitious and grasping like their predecessors, but favoured insofar as they used in the king's service the zealous, business-like qualities he too possessed.

The reign of Henry VIII (1509–47)

Henry VIII, born in 1491, had many advantages when he inherited the throne in April 1509. He was healthy and vigorous, intelligent and well-educated. He was to be the first king of England to write a book – a theological treatise, the *Assertio Septem Sacramentorum*, published in 1521 to rebut Martin Luther's *De Captivitate Babylonica* (1520). Pope Leo X, on receiving a presentation copy, exclaimed diplomatically, but perhaps with feeling, that it was a marvel that a king should have written thus. Henry was also an accomplished musician: some of the pieces he composed are still heard.

In 1509 Henry was a youth of eighteen, whose commanding physical presence, respect for conventional virtues, delight in popular pastimes and friendly charm made a powerful impression. Like the youthful Edward V, so tearfully remembered by his contemporaries, Henry won hearts. He had a better hereditary claim to the Crown than any of his nobles. His lack of experience of government was, in the circumstances, no handicap. His father had sheltered him from political and administrative toils such as he had endured. The young Henry VIII displayed what was to be a habitual impatience with the tedious aspects of business. Yet he had an intuitive grasp of his interests. No English king was to be better served, or more relentless in discarding those no longer of service.

On his accession Henry was shrewd enough to appreciate the need to retain the personnel and maintain the momentum of his father's system of government. He was not irked when grey-haired councillors proffered untoward advice – he simply ignored it. Brought up among noble kinsfolk, he saw the desirability of appeasing magnates, by cancelling fines and bonds forced on them by his father, and by executing two of the latter's devoted servants – a sharp exposition of his wilfulness. Had he been intent on exercising it by exploiting his prerogatives instead of pursuing youthful pleasures, he might have soon provoked revolt. But like the young Edward III, Henry shared the tastes of young nobles – their love of hunting, jousting, feasting and amorous entertainment. His armours on display in the Tower of London bear witness to some of his enthusiasms. The display of his Court was greater even than his father's. The tradition of holding masques was sustained with more elaboration. At the May festival at Greenwich in 1515, Robin Hood and his Merry Men invited Henry and his queen, Catherine of Aragon, to attend a banquet with their courtiers, which was held in bowers full of singing birds. Robin served venison to the tune of organ, lute and flute. As the Court returned to the palace, it was met by Lady May and Dame Flora in a pageant cart, attended by pasteboard giants. According to a Venetian account, these entertainments were witnessed by over 25,000 spectators. They were presumably dazzled by the monarch's splendid appearance, unlike the Londoners who looked askance in 1470 at the bedraggled Henry VI. The hero of the masque, a mythical robber and deerstealer who gained royal approval, was a popular symbol of sympathy between ruler and commons. In former times kings would on occasion have been likely to encounter in that vicinity not pasteboard giants, but rebellious commons like those of 1483 who, according to the duke of Norfolk, were 'up in the weald, and say that they will come and rob the city [London]'.

It was to be years before Henry's concern with the health of his soul, the future of his dynasty, and the recalcitrance of his subjects dulled his juvenile delight in masques. In 1522 Cardinal Wolsey gave an entertainment for the imperial ambassadors. Ladies personifying the qualities of *amour courtois* appeared in a mock castle, penned in by its vices, enthusiastically symbolised by the children of the chapel royal. A masked company came to the rescue, pelting the custodians with dates, oranges and other fruit. The children retaliated with rosewater and sweets; three even threw their hats. But they were overborne, the ladies danced with their rescuers, who unmasked, revealing their leader (personifying Ardent Desire) as the king. Henry was then aged thirty-one.

Such a king and such a Court were irresistible magnets for peers and gentlemen. Henry was more generous than his father in bestowing titles, and was prepared to favour most of his Yorkist kinsfolk. Though Suffolk, a prisoner in the Tower since 1506, was executed in 1513, lest he should prove a focus for opposition during the king's absence in

France, the attainted William Courtenay was pardoned in 1509 and restored to the earldom of Devon in 1511. His son Henry (born in 1498), the king's cousin and childhood companion, was created marquess of Exeter in 1525. Another royal kinsman, Buckingham's younger brother Henry Stafford (*c*.1479–1523) was created earl of Wiltshire in 1510. Margaret Pole, Warwick's sister, was restored to the Neville earldom of Salisbury in 1513. Happy to honour 'old nobility', Henry had no objection to creating new. An early example of giddy social progress in his reign was Charles Brandon (born *c*.1484), whose father Sir William had fought for Henry VII at Bosworth, and who had been educated in the Household. Esquire for the body in 1509, Brandon was created Viscount Lisle in 1513, duke of Suffolk in 1514.

During the first twenty years of Henry's reign, there were domestic tensions, but arguably since Edward III's reign there had been no comparable length of time during which political stability remained so undisturbed. There were, indeed, growing economic and religious causes for agitation, but these were not to become the main stuff of politics till the 1530s. In many respects the two parts of the reign exhibit a startling lack of continuity. It is not just that in the 1530s new faces replace familiar ones. Older men, such as Thomas Howard, duke of Norfolk, Suffolk, and Henry himself, don new masks for a new sort of drama, in which the objectives and principles of government are in a state of flux, political stability can no longer be to the same extent assumed, and uncertainty about the future preoccupies Henry and his politically aware subjects.

Yet there is a vital connection between the two parts of Henry's rule. The daring innovations of his later years could not have been attempted but for the legacy of two decades of comparative tranquillity. Henry had been on the throne when men attaining their majorities in the early 1530s were born. They had grown up when political interest had mostly centred on the king's ambitious wars and diplomacy, and when, due to his maintenance of the renovated machinery of government, there was not such pressure on him as there had been on Edward IV and so many of his predecessors, to provide 'good rule'. Henry VIII was able to shrug off the burdens of government as much as had Henry VI. They came to rest on the broad shoulders of Thomas Wolsey, born *c*.1475, son of an Ipswich burgess, king's almoner in 1509, bishop of Tournai 1513, bishop of Lincoln and archbishop of York 1514, cardinal 1515 and legate *a latere* 1518, abbot of St Albans 1521, and Chancellor from 1515 to 1529.

Wolsey achieved a domination over government unique in a period when there was an adult king capable of ruling. But he was entirely the king's servant, whose ascendancy depended on his continued ability to cajole and please Henry. Wolsey had to guard against intrigues of nobles often in closer personal contact with the king than himself. He stood alone: his humble origins and priestly order were hindrances in building up an 'interest'. The cardinal was the whipping-boy for men's discontents. When, on 1 May 1517 ('Evil May Day'), rioting Londoners sacked aliens' houses, they uttered threats against his life: an armed guard stayed in his town house, York Place. Dukes as well as apprentices resented his ascendancy. Edward Stafford, duke of Buckingham, who had frequently adorned Henry's Court, made his resentment plain. His sense of hierarchical propriety was outraged when Wolsey washed his hands in water that the king had just used. The duke picked up the basin and emptied it at Wolsey's feet. The latter swore to 'sit upon [his] skirts'. Yet it was usual for English kings to have eminent servants of humble origin. Wolsey irritated exceptionally because he combined commanding influence with ostentation and, on occasion, a failure to show the deference which those of noble birth considered their due. Buckingham's discontent with the cardinal seems to have increased his tendency to speculate injudiciously about his own nearness in blood to the Crown. When a former surveyor of his estates, Charles Knyvet, reported such remarks, Wolsey saw a means of discrediting noble threats. Depositions of ducal servants revealed more indiscretions. In May 1521 Buckingham was convicted of treason and executed[8].

In 1523 Wolsey was the object of gentlemanly and bourgeois discontent. He attempted to browbeat the Commons in parliament into granting the unprecedented sum of £800,000 to finance the king's wars. Eventually they granted over £150,000, phased over four years. Discontent spread to popular levels: widespread resistance to collection of forced loans in the spring of 1525 led to their abandonment (cf. pp. 111–12). Thus Wolsey, humane, civilised, zealous in his master's service, earned widespread abuse because his master, not for the last time, asked him to do the impossible. Henry's resentment at Wolsey's tediously lengthening failure to resolve his increasingly urgent personal problem led to the cardinal's fall in 1529. The failure necessitated resort to policies which required widespread public support: Wolsey was useful only as a scapegoat.

Henry's problem was the queen, Catherine of Aragon. He had married her in June 1509, by virtue of a dispensation granted by Pope Julius II in 1503, necessitated by her previous marriage to Henry's brother Arthur (d.1502). By 1525 the devout and scholarly queen, popular in noble circles, was almost beyond child-bearing age. She had borne six infants, five of whom were stillborn or died soon after birth. Princess Mary (born 1516) alone survived: until Henry and Catherine produced a healthy son, an increasingly unlikely contingency, the succession was not assured. Buckingham's speculations may have been an unpleasant indication to Henry of a trend in noble tabletalk. The uncertainty was an incentive for pretenders: abroad Richard de la Pole maintained his claim till his death in 1525.

A new factor relating to Henry's marital and dynastic problem was that by 1525–6 he had begun to experience an unusual degree of amorous attraction to a Court lady, Anne, younger daughter of Sir

Thomas Boleyn. Though unchaste (he had had an affair with Anne's elder sister), Henry did not have the bad name for sexual immorality deservedly gained by his grandfather Edward IV. In the early years of marriage, Henry had been devoted to Catherine, a devotion now rekindled for Anne, who shared his love of music and dancing, and added to her charms by a resolute display of virtue. The king's dynastic problem and personal feelings combined to produce his conviction that he was not married in the sight of God. His intellectual interests inclined him to elaborate the matter in theological terms. He argued with a display of scriptural erudition that a union between a man and his brother's wife was categorically forbidden, and that the dispensation was invalid.

Wolsey began divorce proceedings in his legatine court in May 1527, publicly citing Henry to answer the charge of cohabiting unlawfully for eighteen years. But the cardinal's powers were insufficient for him to pronounce the marriage null. For over two years he vainly plied his diplomatic skill at the *curia* to gain a favourable trial. His lack of success threatened political ruin. Anne Boleyn, a personal enemy, became the protégée of a powerful faction determined to displace Wolsey's influence, headed by the dukes of Norfolk (her uncle) and Suffolk. The adjournment *sine die* of the legatine court by Wolsey's fellow judge, Cardinal Campeggio, bishop of Salisbury, was the last straw. The next month (August 1529) Wolsey was barred from access to the presence and to foreign policy papers. He was soon to be deprived of the Chancery and convicted in the King's Bench of having exercised legatine authority contrary to the Statutes of Praemunire (see p. 337). His benefices were forfeited, but he was allowed to keep and reside in his metropolitan see of York. However, his opponents feared his continued ambition and Henry's sympathy for him and respect for his ability. In November 1530 Wolsey was arrested on a charge of treason, but died at Leicester Abbey on his way to the Tower.

The divorce suit and Wolsey's fall ended the long period of comparative political tranquillity. Henry was never again able to stand for so long aloof from the business of government. Court and Council were to be cockpits for more intense factional manoeuvring, reflecting the degree of favour enjoyed by Henry's current queen, and the noble and episcopal interests she promoted. High politics began to reverberate with the kind of tensions (complicated by the religious issues) which had slackened since 1485. As noble and provincial nodes of discontent and apprehension at the Crown's revolutionary religious policies flared, Henry was involved in disarming dissent, winning supporters, and enhancing their local authority in place of those plucked down. A measure of his ultimate success in increasing rather than undermining the Crown's authority by these novel courses was the loyalty shown to his vulnerable children, and the inclination of families he had put in the saddle to articulate their rivalries at Court rather than, as during the decline of Lancastrian rule, in the localities. Yet Henry could not foresee that royal authority would survive the storms he attempted to conjure and ride – hence his hesitations, inconsistencies, persecutions and brutalities.

Wolsey's successor as Chancellor was Henry's illustrious friend and servant, the humanist Thomas More. His elevation illustrated the politic care Henry was to take in the latter part of his reign not to tie his Crown to the interests of one faction. At a time when Boleyns were in the ascendant at Court, and when anticlericals were looking boldly for royal support, More was conspicuously not a promoter of the divorce, and he was singular in being a common lawyer prepared to rush fervently into print in defence of the Church. His tenure as Chancellor may have reassured those who feared change.

The pattern for the councillors in whom Henry was to confide in the 1530s was not More, but another lawyer, Thomas Cromwell (born *c*.1485), also not a Boleyn protégé, but a former servant of Wolsey. This outstandingly able and original administrator, of humble Putney origins, was appointed councillor in 1531, and received high office as Secretary in 1534 and Keeper of the Privy Seal in 1536. Cromwell was to be in the 1530s Henry's principal agent in drafting and promoting legislation which gave the Crown control of ecclesiastical jurisdiction, and in devising and overseeing means of its enforcement. The impression has sometimes been given that this spectacular advance of royal prerogative was easily accomplished, on the grounds that the papacy was little regarded in England, and that the Crown already had *de facto* control of the Church. Yet it is clear that, especially in the early years of the 'Reformation Parliament' (1529–36)[9], Henry had to feel his way in the face of widespread indifference and suspicion, wary of opponents. The clergy assembled concurrently in the convocation of Canterbury had no enthusiasm for the divorce or its promotion by an assault on papal powers. Prelates and friends of the queen were active in parliament. The strong body of opinion whose support Henry and Cromwell had to mobilise in the Commons was virulently anticlerical, but not especially concerned about the divorce or papacy.

Since Henry's accession, there had been a resurgence of anticlericalism. The spread of humanist ideals and, more specifically, Lutheran and Lollard ideology, had worked to discredit the clergy. Campaigns by vigorous bishops to root out heretics had irritated secular opinion. London burgesses seem particularly to have resented the exaction of ecclesiastical dues and the punishments of Church courts. Their antagonisms were stiffened by opinion in the fraternities of common lawyers residing in and around the Inns of Court, hostile to the legal immunities and privileges of clerks. When parliament assembled in November 1529, the Commons displayed their strongly anticlerical temper. In the 'Supplication against the Ordinaries', they complained of the alien, uncontrolled operations of canon law, and prayed for remedies against the vexatious proceedings of ecclesiastical courts. Henry, not for the first time, showed sympathy with criticisms of the Church. But reform was a lower priority for him than destruction of opposition to the divorce. The Commons agitation gave him an opportunity to discipline convocation. In 1530 a number of prominent clergy (some of them the queen's supporters) were indicted by writ of *praemunire* for abetting Wolsey's exercise of legatine authority. Then the whole clergy of both provinces was indicted by the same process for exercising their spiritual jurisdiction. In January 1531 convocation submitted, after much wriggling, to Henry's terms for the pardon of the clergy: the payment of huge fines and a heavily qualified recognition of him as 'supreme head of the English Church'.

In 1532, when Cromwell was growing influential in royal counsels, decisive steps were taken to bring the Church formally under royal legislative control and to threaten the pope explicitly with loss of jurisdiction. In March the Commons once more petitioned concerning the laity's grievances against spiritual courts. Henry used this secular mandate in a bitter struggle to coerce convocation into surrendering its legislative independence of the Crown. On 15 May, in the 'Submission of the Clergy', convocation consented that it should promulgate canons in future only with royal assent and licence, that existing canons should be scrutinised by a royal commission, and that only those were to be continued which had been adjudged worthy by king and commissioners. The day after this revolutionary surrender Sir Thomas More resigned the Chancellorship. Perhaps others did not see the submission (embodied in a statute) as so decisive, but subject to future compromise with the recalcitrant papacy. Parliament had modified Henry's attempt to coerce Clement VII by abolishing annates (see p. 336): according to the Annates Act (March 1532), its operation would be enforced only on issue of royal letters patent. Henry, concerned to establish the legitimacy of his acts, was still prepared to seek papal sanction. In August the aged Archbishop Warham died. Henry's candidate for Canterbury was a Boleyn protégé, Thomas Cranmer, a diplomatic and determined scholar who had imbibed reforming ideals at Cambridge. He was consecrated archbishop in March 1533, after Henry had secured bulls of provision from Clement.

Assured of a subordinated convocation and willing archbishop, Henry had married Anne, probably in January 1533. In March the Act in Restraints of Appeals was passed, laying down that various spiritual disputes, including causes of matrimony and divorces, were to be determined only by a hierarchy of English ecclesiastical courts. This opened the way for consideration of the king's suit by convocation, which early in April pronounced in Henry's favour, with few dissentients. Cranmer formally declared his marriage to Catherine null, and his marriage to Anne valid at Dunstable Priory in May, and on 1 June Anne was crowned queen. To guarantee the validity of convocation's and the archbishop's pronouncements it was necessary to repudiate papal authority completely. In March 1534 parliament abolished annates and all other payments to the Roman Court: henceforth their equivalent went to the Crown. The Succession Act ratified the marriage of Henry and Anne, and settled the Crown on their or his future male issue, and, in default, on their daughter Princess Elizabeth, born in September 1533. The Act of Supremacy (November 1534) defined the ecclesiastical authority enjoyed by the Supreme Head, and the Treasons Act imposed an oath of obedience to the king and his heirs, with a renunciation of the authority of foreign potentates (see p. 71).

It is possible to find precedents for some of Henry's ecclesiastical policies, and for some of the political and constitutional methods which he used to promote them. Indeed, the king and his councillors were aware of precedents, as their use of the Statute of Praemunire shows, and were anxious to present their policies as based on sound historical traditions. Nevertheless, these policies were revolutionary. National politics was customarily regulated by a deep rooted adhesion to the traditional privileges of governing groups. Yet in a few years Henry utterly destroyed the basis of the Church's privileges – the recognition of its theoretical independence by the secular power. How did he manage this shift in his conservative-minded realm? Some of the factors that helped have been mentioned. There were twenty years of successful rule behind him. There was the wave of anticlericalism. There was his enhancement of the scope of parliamentary legislation over the clergy, gratifying to the laity. There was his failure to diminish substantially the powers exercised by the secular clergy, to their relief.

But the testing-time of the Henrician Reformation had yet to come. It was not sufficient to manipulate opinion in parliament and convocation. Change had to be enforced by the Crown throughout the realm, a novel exercise of royal power likely to provoke rumour and resistance. Henry had entrusted himself to councillors, above all Cromwell (whom he commissioned in January 1535 to exercise his authority over the Church as 'vicegerent in spirituals') and Cranmer, who would not flinch from enforcing the new order, but were determined to develop it dynamically in the royal and, when possible, the reformed interest. The executions in 1535 of recalcitrant Carthusians, Bishop Fisher of Rochester and Sir Thomas More, condemned under the terms of the 1534 Treasons Act, have been seen as ushering in a period of monstrous royal brutalities, in which, for the rest of his life, Henry spilled the blood of the nobility, and of Catholics and Protestants. This harshness was not simply a reflection of public callousness bred by the Wars of the Roses, but of justified fear that reactionary or anarchical elements might overwhelm a monarchy which was trying to impose a new, disturbing authority.

The discontent of those who opposed the changes, and speculation about further ones heightened by the activities of various novel kinds of royal inquisitors into ecclesiastical affairs, produced in the late 1530s what had traditionally beeen known as a 'time of rumour' (such as in 1381, the early 1400s or 1450), when people became disturbed about political developments, expressing their feelings in wild, dangerous talk and prophecies. In February 1537 a rumour arose in Buckinghamshire that Aylesbury Church should be pulled down and its jewels confiscated. Spreading on market day, it had originated in the common bakehouse. In the same year Robert Dalyvell was telling his Hertfordshire neighbours how he had heard it prophesied in Scotland that the king of Scots should rule England before three years were out. Those 'railing Scots' had shown him a book of Merlin's sayings to prove their point. In the summer of 1538 there was a widespread rumour in East Anglia that the king would take all cattle left unmarked after midsummer. In 1542 it was made a felony to erect tales and prophecies of a political nature upon talk of heraldic devices and similar things.

Thus we are once more in a period when there was widespread mistrust of the ruler, likely to produce disorder and rebellion. Mid-Tudor instability was not just the product of Henrician momentum to change society. It was compounded by economic tensions (see pp. 19 ff). John Griston, planning his popular assembly at Swaffham in 1540, was not alone in his sentiments: 'You know how all the gentlemen in manner be gone forth, and you know how little favour they bear us poor men. . . . For it were a good turn if there were as many gentlemen in Norfolk as there be white bulls.'

Henry's comparative sense of security was probably shattered by the events of 1536–7, when he was confronted by a series of risings north of the Trent in protest against the innovating royal policies – protests which probably evoked in some aspects considerable sympathy in southern society. A sentiment uttered by one of the risers, Thomas Molton, would probably have been echoed up and down the realm: 'There is one of the King's Council, one of so low in birth, that the world shall never be quiet and rest for so long as he [Cromwell] doth continue.'

The risings started early in October 1536 at Louth in Lincolnshire. Whereas the commons of the county had risen in 1470 as a result of gentlemanly incitement, in 1536 the secular clergy played on their fears of taxation, and of a prospective dissolution of parishes and confiscation of their treasures similar to the recent experiences of the ex-religious. Since June commissions had been active in Lincolnshire dissolving monasteries, enquiring as to the fitness of seculars, and assessing and collecting subsidy. Benefice-holders were apprehensive that the operations of the Royal Supremacy might result in their heavy taxation and even deprivation.

The Lincolnshire gentry might well have dispersed these assemblies by promises to seek redress, or even by force. But some families had particular grievances against the Court. The one notable royal servant in residence, Lord Hussey, was out of royal favour, unsympathetic to the Boleyns and religious innovation. So some gentlemen remained passive, others, well-established scions as well as pushing *parvenus*, patronised the commons, organising them and drafting their petitions.

The gentry emphasised their own grievances; for example, about the recent Statute of Uses, which prevented the device of inheritances by will and the evasion of 'prerogative' wardship (cf. p. 126).

But Henry was unimpressed by the Lincoln petition. The shire community was somewhat introverted, disinclined to broaden its appeal by involving neighbouring shires. Royal forces, respectively commanded by the earl of Shrewsbury and duke of Suffolk, though stretched, held Nottingham and Stamford. Henry's answer reached Lincoln on 10 October: he threatened extreme punishment if the assemblies did not disperse. The gentry did not relish being branded rebels: they decided to sue out pardons, and the commons, deprived of leadership, sullenly went home.

The one general effect of this county rising was to spark off what developed into more formidable movements further north, principally in Yorkshire. There were assemblies of commons across the Humber. Their leadership was assumed by the remarkable Robert Aske, a lawyer. He drafted a petition on behalf of the men of East Riding on 15 October, requesting the restoration of suppressed religious houses, for economic as well as spiritual reasons[10], the abolition of the Statute of Uses, the abatement of the subsidy on sheep and cattle, on account of economic decline, and the dismissal of unworthy councillors. Recently promoted bishops were stigmatised as defective in faith.

These articles illustrate some of the secular as well as spiritual grievances and fears in northern society. Generally the North was the poorest part of the realm. Pressure of population on means of subsistence may have aggravated hardships caused by landlords' raising of entry fines and rackrenting, and by benefice-holders' exaction of tithes. The novelties imposed by a remote, unsympathetic and grasping southern Court threatened to make things worse. The leaders of northern society had failed to represent local interests effectively to the king, 'whereby', Aske was to tell them, 'all dangers might have been avoided'. Now revenue from the suppressed abbeys and from benefices was being sucked southwards. The region would be so impoverished, Aske predicted, that it 'should either patyssh[11] with the Scots, or of very poverty enforced to make commotions or rebellions'. Aske's contemptuous reference to 'commotions or rebellions' reflects the distinction which he tried to maintain between them and the movement he led. Armed assemblies petitioning on behalf of the grievances of the 'commonwealth' had frequently been treated as treasonable by the Crown; for example, the Yorkshire assembly of 1405 led by Archbishop Scrope (cf. p. 207). The oath devised by Aske at York on 17 October, to which adherents subscribed, disclaimed treasonable connotations and affirmed traditional northern piety by its emphasis on the primacy of religious over secular aims, and repudiation of partial ones. Aske projected the movement as a 'Pilgrimage of Grace', an act of faith and supplication, using a familiar model of disciplined conduct. The Pilgrims may have lacked the ferocity and acquisitiveness for which northern armies had acquired a name in the Wars of the Roses, but their positive qualities made them disarming.

During the week when the men of East Riding assembled, there were spontaneous risings in the North Riding, the bishopric of Durham, and Northumberland. News of the capture of York probably stimulated remoter activity. The Cumberland men marched on Carlisle, the Westmorland men on Lancaster. The magnates of the North, bred to rule it on behalf of the Tudors, found themselves embarrassingly unable to restrain their kinsfolk, neighbours and dependents. The king's kinsman and boyhood companion Henry lord Clifford (created earl of Cumberland in 1525) was penned in Skipton Castle by the resentful men of Craven, some of them victims of his sharp estate management. His son and brother kept Carlisle. The earl of Northumberland (appointed Warden of the East and Middle Marches in 1527, and a member of the Council of the North in 1533) retired to bed. Prodigal and prone to favourites, the earl had probably alienated kinsfolk and dependants by willing his inheritance to the king, cutting out his brothers' succession rights.

Hope of effective resistance in south Yorkshire depended on Lord Darcy, an experienced if aged commander. He held Pontefract Castle, a key base for any royal force approaching from the south. But on 19 October he surrendered to the Pilgrims, and with some of his gentlemanly companions was persuaded by Aske to join them. The royal commander, Norfolk, exclaimed to the Council in a letter, 'Fye! Fye! upon the Lord Darcy, the most arrant traitor that ever was living'. The duke had good reason to be annoyed, and to parade his hatred of treason to the Council, for the comparative weakness of the king's forces made it necessary for him to enter into delicate negotiations with the Pilgrims, whose representatives he met on Doncaster bridge on 27 October. He promised that two gentlemen could carry their petitions to the king under safe-conduct. Norfolk, the man on the spot, continued to prevail over Henry's desire to threaten the Pilgrims with the pains of treason, as he had the Lincolnshire men. At Doncaster on 6 December the duke received a detailed list of petitions, amounting to a request that Henry should put the clock back to 1529. Norfolk offered pardons, and consideration of the Pilgrims' proposals in a parliament. The leaders then disbanded their forces, though many Pilgrims distrusted royal intentions. On 16 January 1537 Sir Francis Bigod tried to rouse the gentry to arms in the East Riding, but to no avail. Some commons supported him, and Cumberland men in February again vainly attempted to take Carlisle. These insignificant risings gave an excuse for the arrest and execution of leading former Pilgrims. Aske, Darcy and Northumberland's brother Sir Thomas Percy were among those who died.

The Pilgrimage of Grace was the crisis of Henry's reign. It showed that there were elements able to challenge dangerously the new royal policies and choice of councillors. Henceforth overseas opponents of Tudor religion were heartened by the prospect of stirring domestic dissidence. But the revolt had remained regional, an expression of characteristic northern sentiments, despite the appeal its aims had to religious conservatives elsewhere. What now gave the governing groups in different provinces some sense of national unity was a tradition of loyalty, not opposition, to the Crown.

The involvement of so many leaders of northern society in the Pilgrimage of Grace provided an opportunity to bring the region into firmer control. Henry never had any intention of making concessions. A seasoned politician and diplomat, he was adept at baiting the dangerous shoals of men by an appearance of sympathy or flexibility. But his new ecclesiastical polity was not for him just an expedient to regulate royal matrimony, or enhance royal power over subjects. It was not to be modified by their fancies. The Supreme Head had embarked on a lifelong search, clouded by a buzz of advice, for what he could accept as ideal norms of worship and religious conduct, ensuring virtue and godly obedience. Henry in his later years was obsessed by the need to secure obedience – rightly so, for he had donned a mantle of authority none of his most imperially-minded predecessors aspired to; he claimed to regulate and judge men's spiritual beliefs.

But he could not control his wife. Anne Boleyn's imperiousness, thrilling to Henry as a lover, soon irritated him as a husband. He had been sorely disappointed when she bore a daughter; after January 1536, when she miscarried (and Catherine of Aragon died) he was completely estranged. In May 1537 Anne was executed for treason, shortly after her alleged accomplices in adulteries and plots (including her brother Rochford) suffered likewise. Cranmer and fellow commissioners had found that the marriage of Henry and Anne was never legal, because of his prior adultery with her sister. On the day Anne died Cranmer issued a dispensation for Henry to marry his kinswoman Jane Seymour. The dynasty was strengthened by the birth of a son, Edward, in October 1537; the mother died twelve days later.

Councillors who had promoted Anne's marriage, notably Norfolk, Suffolk, Cranmer and Cromwell, survived her demise. The king needed their support and expertise to maintain and enforce his religious policy, especially in recalcitrant localities. Norfolk, for instance, replaced the discredited Northumberland in the East and Middle Wardenships. In May 1537 the earl consented to immediate royal possession of his estates in return for a pension, and in June opportunely died. The Percy lands gave the Crown a firmer basis on which to build patronage of northern gentry at the expense of local noble families which had traditionally wielded royal influence.

In 1538 the Council struck against nobles of Yorkist blood who were potential leaders of religious reaction in southern society. The marquess of Exeter was charged with treason, as were kinsfolk of Reginald Pole, papal commissioner to rally princes for Henry's deposition.

Exeter and Pole's brother Montague were executed: Pole's mother, the countess of Salisbury, was attainted in 1539 and executed in 1541. Royal authority in the West Country was strengthened by the annexation of thirteen manors, forfeited by the late marquess, to the duchy of Cornwall, and by the appointment of a Council of the West to determine transgressions, including treasons, breaches of the peace and unlawful retaining. Its president, Sir John Russell, Controller of the Household, was created a baron in 1539 and granted twenty-six Devon manors, many of them former estates of Tavistock Abbey.

Russell's elevation and endowment illustrate the rise in the last decade or so of the reign of a powerful 'Court nobility', on whom the king relied to implement his will. In Henry's later years there were fine opportunities for gain in royal service. His wars with France and Scotland broadened avenues of military and naval employment. The heavy costs of warfare, raised by inflation, necessitated a drastic increase from 1542 in the rate of sale by the Crown of former monastic lands, which its leading servants were well placed to bargain for. Examples of the 'Court nobility' were Prince Edward's uncle Edward Seymour, created earl of Hertford (1537), William Parr, created earl of Essex in 1543 soon after his sister Catherine married the king, and Thomas Wriothesley, Secretary 1540–4, who received a barony when appointed Chancellor (1544), and built up a Hampshire interest with former estates of Quarr, Titchfield and Beaulieu Abbeys. In the middle decades of the century Court rivalries, the maintenance of the Henrician religious settlement and, on occasion, the succession to the throne were to turn on the ambitions and alliances of such men.

The last years of Henry's reign witnessed no fundamental changes in his religious policy. Hints of shifts in his attitude towards traditional practices and Protestant agitation reflected his uncertainties and the hopes and apprehensions of those trying to win his approval and favour. The religious issue was entangled with rivalry among his episcopal and secular councillors for the ear of the rapidly ageing king, gross, physically infirm, frequently pained by his diseased leg. Their knives were whetted (as was the querulous Henry's) by speculation about the anticipated minority of his son.

In 1540 councillors who resented Cromwell's ascendancy, especially Norfolk and Bishop Gardiner, rather mysteriously engineered his downfall. He was convicted of treason on a variety of mainly trumpery charges and executed in July, the month in which convocation annulled the king's marriage to Anne of Cleves, and Norfolk's vivacious niece Catherine Howard became queen. Norfolk's influence was shaken but not destroyed when Catherine was convicted of adulteries, and executed for treason in February 1542. There were, indeed, a number of influential councillors out of sympathy with the duke and other religiously conservative councillors: besides Cranmer, whose transparent honesty and manifest respect for the Royal Head often gave him a disconcerting influence on Henry, they included Hertford, Essex, John

Dudley, Viscount Lisle, and Sir William Paget. In 1545 the religious conservatives seem to have just failed to get the radically-minded queen arrested – Catherine Parr, Henry's most scholarly consort since his first. But Protestant influences at Court were checked. In December 1546 Norfolk and his son Surrey were arrested. The latter, courtly poet and feckless soldier, was executed for his incredibly silly flaunting of royal descent and predictions about his family's power in Edward's minority. Within weeks of the arrests the king had fallen gravely ill. The old duke was saved from execution by his death.

The reigns of Edward VI and Mary: the testing of the Henrician polity (1547–58)

The decade or so after Henry's death was fraught with trouble for the Crown. He left his son heavily in debt, challenging neighbouring princes and exercising novel spiritual powers dubious to many. Edward was surrounded by a tense, ambitious 'new nobility'. They lacked the authority or will to resist strong current European influences, mainly destabilising ones: the great inflation, a new intensification of the Habsburg-Valois conflict, the hardening of religious battle lines. The period after Henry's affirmation of the realm's status as an 'empire' free of foreign jurisdictions was one in which many leaders of English opinion looked eagerly abroad for help and guidance in altering established religion. It was a period of plots, rebellions and rumours of dissidence. Experience of its religious and political upheavals was to be profoundly felt at various levels of society. Yet social peace, and the fabric of royal authority, survived remarkably intact.

At his accession Edward was aged nine. Henry's will of December 1546, which the 1544 Succession Act made statutorily binding, appointed sixteen executors, with twelve assistants, who were as councillors to exercise collective executive power until Edward was eighteen. His uncle Hertford had little difficulty in persuading fellow councillors that he should receive formal primacy. Four days after Henry's death they chose him as protector: he was elevated as duke of Somerset, and other councillors were rewarded[12]. In March the provisions of Henry's will were illegally breached, though this treasonable conduct was retrospectively sanctioned by statute. Five executors signed letters patent conferring on Somerset the right to exercise executive powers, with the obligation to consult merely an indefinite number of councillors, until the king was eighteen.

Like all but the most wilful and courageous of Henry's servants, Somerset had schooled himself to circumspection. He was reputed an honourable, brave and intelligent soldier. As protector he showed an iron determination to maintain the personal authority of monarchy, imposing his own, often unpopular, opinions in policy-making, and paying regard to his particular clients. Some reflections his fellow councillor Sir William Paget wrote to Somerset after nearly two years of his rule provide a significant assessment of the inevitable crisis of authority after Henry's death and of Somerset's response to it:

And the first degree is to look backward whether at your first setting forward you took not a wrong way, as (saving your favour) I think you did, for you have cared to content all men (which is impossible and especially being subjects in such a subjection as they were left) and be loth or rather to offend any. . . . Then [*i.e. under Henry*] *all things were too straight* [*i.e. strict*] *and now they are too loose; then was it dangerous to do or speak though the measuring were not evil, and now every man hath liberty to do or speak at liberty . . .*

Paget may have been referring to the protector's repeal of restrictive ecclesiastical legislation: the 1401 heresy statute, the Six Articles Act, all restrictions on printing, reading or expounding Scriptures. The protector had encouraged religious radicals by abolishing the Mass and chantries, to the annoyance of conservatives. He had gratified moralising writers and preachers, and encouraged popular agitation against oppressive landlords by appointing a commission to enquire into infringements of anti-enclosure legislation[13].

Paget's perceptive analysis exemplifies the bureaucratic tendency to reduce complex problems to a seemingly manageable issue. Somerset's rule was indeed to collapse, as Paget foresaw it might, because he had tried to 'content all men'. But Somerset had shown a sensitive appreciation of the fundamental threats to the Henrician polity posed by religious tensions and economic malaise. If he had attempted to impose rigid orthodoxy and obedience, more bitter defiances and lasting conflicts might have ensued.

The experience of Somerset's government soon cooled his fellow councillors' ardour for the protectorship. Paget begged him to show more graciousness: . . . 'Think, Sir, that you supply the place of a king and to every wise man every letter, every word, every countenance of yours, is enough to cause the dull horse to enter the fire, and the quick horse to be to busy.' Another councillor, Sir Thomas Smith, denounced to the duchess of Somerset innovators with access to her husband: 'They come to kneel upon your grace's carpets and devise commonwealths as they like, and are angry that other men be not so hasty to run straight as their brains crave.'

In 1549 formidable popular risings broke out. Feeling had run high in the West Country for some time about the likelihood of radical liturgical change. In June bands of peasants, with some priestly but no gentlefolk's encouragement, congregated in arms at Crediton. They demanded a return to the Catholic practices enforced at Henry's death and a moratorium on religious change till the king was of age. Some of them were animated about grasping gentry who had profited from the Reformation. They encamped at Clyst St Mary near Exeter, blocking the road to London. Local gentry, unable to pacify them, took refuge behind the city walls.

By July Norfolk rioting against landlords had escalated into an assembly on Mousehold Heath, outside Norwich. Men flocked there from a majority of Norfolk hundreds. Better disciplined than the local rebels in 1381, they were impressively led by Robert Ket, tanner and tenant farmer from Wymondham. He promoted the dissemination of propaganda, and negotiation with the Crown on petitions. Ket's rebellion posed a more formidable threat than that in the West Country. He had gained control of one of the wealthiest, most populous parts of the realm, where currents of opinion were well attuned to those nearer the capital. The Norfolk men approved the protector's religious radicalism. Their grievances were directed against the economic and tenurial policies of landlords, in a shire where there was fierce competition for profitable arable and pasture. They wanted a moderate pegging of land prices and entry fines, recognition of common grazing rights and safeguard of freehold tenure.

Confronted by the most serious challenges to royal authority since 1536, the protector temporised, vainly hoping that persuasion and the offer of pardons would dissolve the demonstrations. Lord Russell remained immobile, unable to attempt the relief of Exeter, as few western shire levies came to his support. Northampton, rashly attacking Ket, was defeated. By August the royal armies were strong enough to tackle the rebels. Warwick recaptured Norwich, forced the rebels to withdraw, and pursued and slaughtered the remnant[14]. Russell relieved Exeter and went on to rout the western rebels at Sampford Courtenay.

Like the 1381 risings, those of 1549 were caused partly by hostile commons' reactions to landlords' exploitive policies in a period of economic change. But in 1549 local disturbances failed to coagulate into a general rising to the extent they had in 1381. Economic grievances may have been more localised in 1549. The Reformation may have accentuated cultural differences between some local communities. Those with tenurial grievances did not perceive Crown and landlords as allied. The recent commissions into depredations of arable inclined the aggrieved not to strike in the most deadly fashion, at the central governors. The Norfolk leaders, instead of marching on London, preferred to exchange civilities with the Council. Memories of 1497 may have deterred the west countrymen from venturing east. Such circumspect, even timorous provincial manoeuvring was in keeping with the commons' lack of rebellious ideology, far removed from revolutionary trends abroad in 1381.

The rebels' lack of ideological and physical aggressiveness was no comfort for Norfolk gentlemen 'fain to spoil themselves of their apparel and lie and keep in woods and lone places where no resort was'. Mr Wharton, pricked with weapons all the way from the rebels' 'tree of Reformation' into Norwich, would hardly have been consoled to read in Berners's translation of Froissart that Sir Robert Salle had been cut to pieces by the rebels there in 1381. The risings horrified the governors of society. Their success in avoiding political division and breakdown in the next decade or so, compared with the ruling elites of France and Scotland, though affected by similar factional and religious tensions, may have stemmed in part from memories of a seemingly dire challenge they had faced in common. As Paget wrote to Somerset in July 1549: 'The foot taketh upon him the part of the head, and commons is become a king, appointing conditions and laws to the governors.'

His conclusion was ominous for the protector: 'I know in this matter of the commons every man of the council hath misliked your proceedings, and wished it otherwise.' Even before the royal armies were dismissed, councillors were bestirring themselves against Somerset, led by Warwick, who allied with some rusticated landowners too, such as the Catholic earl of Arundel. When in mid-September king, protector and a few councillors went to Hampton Court, Warwick's adherents gathered in London. By early October Somerset was alerted: he dispatched proclamations ordering shire levies to come to the king's protection, the city of London to give support, and Russell and Herbert to rally with the western army. He withdrew with the king to the greater security of Windsor Castle. But no one wanted to fight for the duke. As a result of negotiations between the divided councillors, Somerset agreed to surrender on promise of keeping his life and duchy. He and his coterie were sent to the Tower, where he signed a confession and was eventually released under surety. In the November parliament the protectorship was abolished.

For the rest of the reign the Council exercised authority. Edward was gradually allowed to familiarise himself with the business of kingship. His personal initiatives were exercised mainly in favour of Warwick, who gained a personal ascendancy over the pious, precociously educated and reserved boy. Warwick's influence was paramount in the Household: his clients and well-willers filled its ministerial offices and the honorific Chamber posts which brought them into Edward's company.

John Dudley, earl of Warwick, was highly regarded in governing circles in the autumn of 1549, as the man who had done most to suppress both rebellion and protectorship. His appointment as Warden General of the North (April 1550), the grant to him of extensive estates in Northumberland, Yorkshire and Worcestershire, and his creation as duke of Northumberland (October 1551) were, in contemporary eyes, justified rewards for his services to the Crown. Northumberland was undoubtedly greedy for power and wealth, and in order to maintain his hold on them, was prepared to misappropriate royal revenue and eventually to tamper treasonably with the statutorily established succession. He was no more sinister or reprehensible than the run of Henry's noble executors. His problem was how to maintain an ascendancy won by suppressing quasiregal rule by a subject. In fact he retained a crucial, and unchallenged, control of royal patronage. But he remained nervously preoccupied with devices to win friends and anticipate suspected opponents. His oddest move was an attempt to win the support of the chastened Somerset, pardoned in February 1550, restored to the Council in April, and allied to the Dudleys in June by the marriage of his daughter Anne to Warwick's son Lord Lisle. The earl soon ceased believing that Somerset would be content to play second fiddle. The latter was arrested in September 1551 and executed on conviction of conspiracy in January 1552.

In February 1553 the king developed what was to be a fatal illness, probably acute pulmonary tuberculosis. His imminent demise threatened the Council's interests and policies, for the statutory heir, the king's sister Mary, was stubbornly Catholic and Habsburg. Edward, consumed by the danger his elder sister presented to religious reform, assented to a 'devise for the succession', excluding his sisters' legal rights in favour of the eldest son either of Jane Grey or her sisters, daughters of the duke of Suffolk, and granddaughters of Henry VIII's sister Mary. In May Jane married Northumberland's son Guildford. The weakening king altered the 'devise' to allow Jane to succeed, and a large number of notables were reluctantly persuaded to subscribe to these illegal and, indeed, flagrantly treasonable proceedings. Edward died on 6 July, and three days later Jane was proclaimed in London. Northumberland failed to secure Mary, who rallied loyalties in strongly Protestant Norfolk. Once Northumberland set off in pursuit, his fellow councillors in London went over to Mary (19 July): she triumphantly entered the capital on 3 August. The episode revealed the strength of opinion in favour of the duly constituted Tudor succession – a contrast with the apparent indifference to the success of various claimants which had sometimes appeared in the later fifteenth century.

The new queen, whose fervent Catholic beliefs had made her politically isolated, perforce relied on the existing political establishment, shorn of its more recalcitrant elements[15]. The working core of her council consisted of Edwardian bureaucrats: other councillors were backwoods Catholic gentry, such as staffed her Household, and some conservative ghosts from the Henrician past, notably Norfolk, and Bishops Gardiner (Chancellor) and Tunstall. Her rule was characterised by bickering in Council, sometimes spilling into public debate in parliament, over her plans to enlarge the powers enjoyed by her foreign husband Philip, to commit English support to his foreign policies, to secure as full a Catholic restoration as possible, and a succession which would guarantee its continuance. Mary failed to create a substantial 'interest' in the governing classes wholeheartedly committed to her policies: perhaps, given a few more years, she would have succeeded in doing so. But those classes remained true to Tudor principles of obedience and loyalty (cf. pp. 375–7, 413–14).

This was demonstrated by the 1554 risings, inspired by dislike of her intended marriage to a foreigner, her cousin Charles V's son Philip. Among the principal plotters were Suffolk, Edward Courtenay, a young descendant of Edward IV whom Mary had restored to the earldom of Devon, the Herefordshire landowner Sir James Croft, the Devon landowner Sir Peter Carew, Sir Thomas Wyatt of Allington Castle, and the French ambassador Antoine de Noialles. The plotters aimed to depose Mary and replace her with Elizabeth, married to Devon. The risings, planned for March, were carried out precipitately because of fears of betrayal; Devon had backed out. The rebels proclaimed themselves loyal subjects anxious to prevent the Spanish marriage. Suffolk's efforts to raise the east Midlands were unavailing. The Council commissioned his Leicestershire rival, the earl of Huntingdon, to move against him. Sir Thomas Denys, sheriff of Devon and Cornwall, resolved the doubts of the gentry by garrisoning Exeter against Carew, for whom the commons, mindful of his part in suppressing the 1549 rebellion, would not stir. Croft never stirred.

But in Kent in January Wyatt raised a notable challenge to Mary's rule. A considerable number of gentlemen, tenants and townsmen, mostly from central and west Kent, joined him in arms at Maidstone and Rochester. Two leading Kent landowners, Lords Abergavenny and Cobham, were unable to rally enough levies to challenge his main army. The Council rashly dispatched an inadequate force under the veteran Norfolk. He tried to drive Wyatt out of Rochester, but the London 'whitecoats', arrayed by the aldermen, deserted. By early February Wyatt's men were snug in Southwark. Unable to force London Bridge, they moved upstream to cross at Kingston for an assault on the city. Pembroke, the royal commander, perhaps fearing a repetition of the Rochester débâcle, failed to intercept. With St Paul's spire beckoning them on, the rebels marched from Temple Bar up Fleet Street to assault Ludgate. But the Londoners manned their defences. The Kentishmen (as at Smithfield in 1381) speedily disintegrated into a rabble, surrounded by the royal forces[16].

After the crisis Mary determinedly pressed ahead with plans for her marriage and the reconciliation with Rome. The rebellion had salutarily demonstrated what was by now the traditional reluctance of most nobles and leading gentry to get mixed up with such affairs. Yet it had also demonstrated the continued existence of a lively, volatile, less inhibited opinion among lesser property-holders about national affairs, dangerous when stirred. The spirit of Jack Cade was not dead among Kentish smallholders. Mary seems to have digested the point that secure rule depended on tempering her unpopular policies so as not to alienate the active support of the governing elites.

Elizabethan settlement (1558–87)

Elizabeth's accession, like her sister's, was popularly acclaimed. She aroused enthusiasm as her father's designated heir, a healthy and gracious young woman, victim of her sister's unpopular policies, no lover of the papacy. Confronting her were sullen Marian supporters, hostile bishops, powerful nobles, unsympathetic or overbearing foreign powers. Elizabeth, until perhaps the last decade or so of her reign, proved unable to provide the sense of security craved by her subjects. Her great achievement was to preserve her Crown and its rights, by playing the political game astutely, at times recklessly. The fact that her realm did not sink, like neighbouring principalities, into confessional and factious strife partly reflects her skill – and luck.

The queen's two most pressing domestic problems were to frame and enforce a generally acceptable Protestant settlement (see pp. 377 ff), and to attach to her personal service a nobility divided by the tensions and intrigues of the minority and her sister's rule. There was the danger, which materialised in France in the 1560s, that struggles between noble factions at Court would threaten stability and royal power. The strength of factions derived from their preoccupation, not just with the traditional aspirations of clientage, but with questions agitating the governing elites about the related issues of religion, foreign alliances, the queen's marriage and the succession. For instance, the queen had to treat with wary respect the views of the young duke of Norfolk and his cousin the earl of Sussex, not only because of the predominant Howard territorial influence in Norfolk, but because these lords spoke for many not in their 'lordship' who were suspicious of religious radicalism and wished for a Habsburg alliance.

One of Elizabeth's most consistently influential councillors was the scholarly, sententious Protestant, Sir William Cecil, appointed principal Secretary three days after her accession[17]. Cecil, grandson of a Welsh yeoman of Henry VII's guard who attained the mayoralty of Stamford, had been educated at St John's College, Cambridge, and Grays Inn. He joined the protector's service, and was Secretary 1550–53. Cecil tended to press on Elizabeth the need for more vigorous action against French power, while generally lacking enthusiasm for the Habsburgs. But his influence seemed vitally threatened by the rise in favour of the queen's Master of the Horse, Robert Dudley. Indeed, the latter's growing intimacy with Elizabeth, provoking outraged noble reactions, posed a new threat to the precarious stability of her rule. Dudley wanted to marry the queen, and to that end was prepared to promote or oppose papal, Habsburg, Valois or Protestant interests in the early 1560s. Cecil allied with Norfolk and Sussex against him. But tensions ebbed, and alignments sagged, as it became apparent that despite Dudley's promotion as privy councillor in 1562, and creation as earl of Leicester in 1564, the queen did not intend to marry him.

This limitation on Dudley's favour sprang from her characteristic awareness of the need to content all men by contenting none too fully. Nevertheless, factiousness received an impetus she found hard to contain as a result of Mary queen of Scots' flight to England in 1568. The presence in the realm of the Catholic candidate for the succession excited northern conservatives. Speculation acquired a dangerous 'Court' dimension as its leading denizens devised how her candidacy might be turned to their advantage. Nobles, including Leicester, anxious to 'dish' Cecil, supported the marriage of Mary to the Protestant Norfolk. The duke's feeble attempts to force Elizabeth's hand resulted in his arrest and that of his allies Arundel and Pembroke (October 1569). The earls of Northumberland and Westmorland, who had indulged in more dangerous plotting, reluctantly took to arms, rallying supporters in the bishopric of Durham, first at Brancepeth, then at Durham Cathedral, where they restored the Mass. Advancing to Bramham Moor, they menaced Sussex, lord president of the Council of the North, in York. But few outside the bishopric rallied to the rebels: it was a bad winter. Their local influence, and that of other northern baronial families, had waned, and they had not compensated by careful preparation. At the end of November the earls retreated northwards, pausing to capture Hartlepool and Barnard Castle, and in December fled across the Border. Lord Dacre belatedly tried to raise the West March. In February 1570 his sizeable army, partly composed of Scots 'surnames' was defeated by Hunsdon[18].

The 1569–70 events gave a new stability to Elizabeth's rule. The attempt by a formidable cabal to afforce her policy had collapsed. The alternative of noble rebellion had held no appeal. As a result, the Elizabethan establishment was tilted more rigidly in political attitudes: pro-Catholic, pro-Marian, pro-Spanish sentiments had become associated with treason. Elizabeth may not have entirely relished the ascendancy of one policy, diminishing her freedom of manoeuvre. In the summer of 1570 Norfolk was released: perhaps she foresaw a useful 'conservative' role for him. But the duke proved incapable of digesting his humiliation. He became involved in treasonable Marian plotting, and was duly executed in 1572.

Thus 'conservative' faction was further discredited. In the 1570s and 1580s rivalry for influence in Court and Council reflected the governing class's increasing sense that it was beleaguered by the danger of foreign and domestic subversion. Council and parliament in the 1580s were preoccupied with ways of bringing recusants to conformity and destroying the growing influence of priestly missions from abroad (see pp. 381 ff). Persecutions spelled a danger for Mary which she does not seem to have appreciated: extremists were bound to plot in her favour. Her incrimination in a plot in 1586 enabled Elizabeth's councillors to force the latter's hand to do what most gentlefolk had been clamouring for her to do for several years – sign the warrant for Mary's execution (February 1587).

Though the succession to the throne was to remain uncertain till James I's accession in 1603, the execution of Mary proved to be a political landmark. It practically ended a period, starting in the 1450s, in which rival claims to the throne or its succession had recurrently been a principal matter of political concern and cause of instability. In the later fifteenth century, from 1461 onwards, the example of successful usurpations, and the weak authority of recently installed dynasties combined to inspire the throws of royal kinsmen at the Crown. Henry VIII's lack of a surviving legitimate son till 1537 probably encouraged speculation about the succession. A sense of dynastic insecurity may well have been a principal motivation in his first two annulments of marriage. Henry's statutorily secured devices for the succession were certainly to win lasting respect. But the intensification of faction and religious division under his weak successors from 1553 encouraged tendencies to intrigue and plot for rival claims to Crown or succession.

The dynastic insecurities of the period, unparalleled in length and recurrence, were an important factor in inducing notable changes of emphasis in the aims and methods of royal government. Yorkist and Tudor rulers did not set out to undermine the power of the higher nobility or the privileges of property-holders. They strenuously upheld the authority of the common law, parliaments and county magistracies. What was novel was the degree of awareness among rulers and their ministers that royal judicial and financial institutions needed to be improved and adapted, if their authority was to be stabilised. The necessity of controlling society firmly was even more apparent after Henry VIII's death had opened the way to sharper religious divisions.

Yorkists and Tudors had, for the most part, uneasy heads. They could not always rely as implicitly on the dynastic loyalty of the magnates as most of their predecessors had. Nobles were prone to the blot of ambition. But there were lay experts in estate and financial administration and common lawyers available to staff a revitalised central government. Because they looked for rewards in landed estate and titles of nobility, and not in canonries and bishoprics, they were ideal agents to spread their ethic of service and loyalty to the Crown among landowners, to cuff their fellow magistrates into doing their duty and neighbours into religious obedience. The 'new monarchy' was new in resting on a specially close relationship, social as well as bureaucratic, between central government and the leading knights and gentlemen of the shire communities. Elizabeth's reign was to be a turning-point in that relationship, for in her later years it was to show signs of deep strain.

Notes

1. Alice duchess of Suffolk (d.1477), whose fine effigy can be seen in Ewelme parish church (Oxon). The effigies of her son Duke John and his wife Elizabeth of York are at Wingfield (Suffolk).
2. She was ransomed to Louis XI in 1476.
3. Richard, striking furiously on all sides, overthrew Sir John Cheyney (d.1509), a man of exceptional strength, whose alabaster effigy, wearing Henry's Lancastrian livery collar of SS, can be seen in Salisbury Cathedral.
4. I owe thanks for this translation from Spanish to Dr A. I. K. MacKay.
5. 'Curtinek nob. anglus ex regia Albae Rosae britannorum familia', *De Natione Anglica et Scota iuristarum universitatis patavinae*, ed. A. Andrich and B. Brugi (Padua 1892), p. 131. I owe this reference to Professor Denys Hay.
6. There is a splendid stained glass portrait in East Harling church (Norfolk) of Sir Robert Wingfield (d.1480), Controller of Edward IV's Household. He wears a collar of alternating suns and white roses, with a pendant lion of March.
7. According to Abbot Huby of Fountains, Henry expressed amazement to him at the absence of *conversi* in English Cistercian houses, and an interest in endowing six or eight places for them, in order to encourage monastic vows – '. . . ut horum exemplo alii devoti laici ad fervorem religionis excitati religionis habitum assumere nullatenus erubescerent' (Huby to abbot of Cîteaux, 21 August 1497, *Letters from the English Abbots to the Chapter at Cîteaux 1442—1521*, ed. C. H. Talbot, Camden 4th ser., vol. 4, 1967, p. 208). I owe this reference to Mr L. G. D. Baker of the University of Edinburgh.
8. At Thornbury, not far from Bristol, are the impressive remnants of the great house which Buckingham built but did not live to complete: it has been described as the last medieval castle built in England.
9. The term 'Reformation Parliament' seems to be a twentieth-century one.
10. The North had a large number of religious houses. Sixteen of fifty-five houses suppressed were restored there during the risings.
11. The word may derive from the French *appati* or *pati*, used in France during the Hundred Years War to describe an agreement by inhabitants to pay soldiers for immunity from plunder. Aske's probable use of the term, and the fears he raised by it of Scots 'ransoming' of the North (more characteristic of the fourteenth century) illustrate the traditionalism of the region.
12. William Parr, earl of Essex, became marquess of Northampton; Viscount Lisle, earl of Warwick; Sir Thomas Wriothesley, earl of Southampton.
13. For the economic background, see pp. 19 ff.
14. The fugitive Ket was captured, condemned for treason in London in November, and hanged at Norwich Castle in December.
15. Northumberland was executed, Northampton condemned but reprieved, Suffolk and others heavily fined; twelve councillors were reappointed, sixteen were not.
16. Suffolk and Wyatt were executed, as were the duke's daughter Jane Grey and her husband Guildford Dudley, prisoners in the Tower. Princess Elizabeth narrowly escaped implication.
17. He was appointed Master of the Court of Wards and Liveries in 1561, was created Lord Burghley in 1571, and appointed Lord Treasurer in 1572.
18. Northumberland was handed over by the Scots and executed in 1572, Dacre died in exile in 1573, Westmorland in 1601.

Chapter 8

The Church, devotion and reform

Some structural elements

The medieval Church in England has left many memorials. Its buildings survive in remarkable profusion, neither destroyed nor so drastically altered as many churches have been by waves of political, ideological and cultural change in some other parts of western Europe. Though infused in the sixteenth century by revisionist Wycliffite and Protestant ideals, much of its organisation and many of its traditions were never radically transformed, as some continental Churches' were by Calvinism or the Counter-Reformation. Why, when such revolutionary changes in belief were effected in the sixteenth-century English Church, did so much survive unaltered, to the scandal and despair of radical reformers? A crucial factor was the tenacity of close historic relationships between Crown and Church. A moulding influence on concepts of the Church, stemming in part from the value placed on these relationships, was the zeal of some reformers to trace and maintain continuities within the Church. For instance, Matthew Parker, Elizabeth's first archbishop of Canterbury, characteristically sponsored the publication in 1572 of a closely documented study of the evolution of his office, whose objective, he explained to Sir William Cecil, was 'to note at what time Augustine, my first predecessor, came into this land, what religion he brought in with him, and how it continued, how it was fortified and increased . . . until the days of King Henry VIIIth, when the religion began to grow better, and more agreeable to the Gospel.'

Medieval England had over 9,000 parishes and seventeen bishoprics. Exceptionally for a principality of its size and fame, it had only two archiepiscopal sees, Canterbury and York. This division stemmed from the scheme Pope Gregory the Great outlined to Augustine in 601, based probably on information available in Rome about the lapsed imperial administration of Britannia. Augustine was to remove his cathedral from Canterbury to London, which was to have twelve subordinate bishoprics, as was York, which was to be subject to him, but not to his successors. In fact the scheme was considerably modified by the political geography of Anglo-Saxon England. The transfer from Canterbury was not achieved, the province of York was not founded till 735, and by our period contained only two other bishoprics, Durham and Carlisle (besides claims to jurisdiction over some Scottish ones). In the late eleventh century Norman kings supported Canterbury's claim to jurisdiction over both provinces, though the papacy eventually judged against it in the following century. York emerged as independent, with its distinct provincial assemblies of clergy (convocations) and jurisdiction directly subject to the papacy. But the archbishops of Canterbury customarily came to be appointed to a papal legateship (*legatus natus*) by virtue of their office, giving them an appellate jurisdiction over York.

Canterbury therefore remained pre-eminent. The papacy normally accorded it a privileged jurisdiction appropriate to its striking historical traditions, its association with the most revered English saint, Thomas Becket, and its provincial control over most of the populous and wealthy regions of England and of all Wales. But its archbishops were expccted to exercise their pre-eminence, not so much by intervening in the diocesan affairs of bishops as in a mediatory political role. St Thomas of Canterbury represented in the eyes of the English Church (and, indeed, of English people in general) the tradition of defending rights and privileges against arbitrary Crown action. Ecclesiastics looked to the archbishop to uphold their interests at Court and in Council. The need for him to make a firm stand was reflected on by the chronicler Adam Usk:

In this year [1400] my lord of Canterbury [Thomas Arundel], calling together his clergy, mournfully laid before them how temporal powers fear not to violate the liberties of the church of England, and specially in seizing, imprisoning and in judging bishops, without distinction, just as they would laymen. 'True! my lord,' I said, 'in turning over the corpus of the law and the chronicles more cruelty is found to have been inflicted on prelates in England than in all Christendom.'

This 'cruelty' was inspired by the Church's envied concentration of wealth as well as its irritating jurisdictional privileges. What kept envy at bay? In the 1410 parliament Archbishop Arundel was to be confronted by schemes mooted in the Commons to tap clerical wealth. The revenues of bishops, abbots and priors, it was believed, would maintain fifteen earls, 1,500 knights, 6,200 squires and 100 almshouses, besides providing the king an annual subsidy of more than £20,000 (enough to sustain ten earls). According to the valuations of ecclesiastical incomes calculated for Henry VIII in 1535 (the *Valor Ecclesiasticus*), the seventeen English bishops had a combined annual revenue of over £26,600. The structure of the English Church placed a great deal of wealth in very few hands. This concentration made the Church a potentially valuable instrument of royal policy. The archbishops of Canterbury and their episcopal colleagues inclined to safeguard the Church's privileges by docility to the Crown, leaving rebels to cite the intransigent traditions of St Thomas. Gregory the Great's structure was surviving in time-honoured form by virtue of *raison d'état*.

Relations with the papacy

The exercise of papal authority in later medieval England was in some respects feeble in practice, in others vigorous. Papal decrees condemning heresies and denouncing abuses were dutifully promulgated in provincial and diocesan councils, their texts appearing in the many surviving bishops' registers. The papacy of the period, enmeshed in troubles, took little initiative to persuade kings and bishops to reform the English Church. Popes feared that if they embarked on a universal attempt to reform, their *curia* would be the first target for embittered reformers' zeal. One spiritual matter to which, with traditional sensitivity, the papacy reacted vigorously in condemnation, was heresy (see p. 368). What most impressed popes about the English Church was its wealth. They were preoccupied with ensuring their rights to a share of its patronage and profits as a means of alleviating the financial obligations of the *curia* and of bestowing benefices on worthy clerks who petitioned for papal bounty.

There were certain historic financial claims which the papacy tried to exercise in England. There was the ancient annual tax known as Peter's Pence, which in practice brought in a very small sum. There was the tribute claimed for the feudal overlordship of the kingdom which King John had granted to Innocent III and his successors, an overlordship which parliament repudiated in 1366. Visiting papal commissioners could claim sums for their expenses known as procurations. About twenty monasteries and other corporate religious bodies paid an annual tax (*census*) for their privileges. At the end of the thirteenth century, Boniface VIII had asserted the papacy's sole right to tax the clergy at will, but this had been opposed by Edward I. In the fourteenth century a papacy politically weakened by the clergy's tendency to seek royal protection from its exactions, by its removal from the prestigious centre of Rome to obscure Avignon, and eventually by schism, could only raise subsidies (in the form of income taxes on benefices) with royal consent. Their value to the papacy declined, as the Crown now insisted on taking the lion's share of them itself.

The popes resident at Avignon (1309–76), receiving little income from their Italian lordships and intent on their reconquest, strengthened other methods of tapping clerical wealth – by reservation and provision. John XXII (1316–34) reserved categories of benefices to be filled by papal provision instead of local election or appointment. Those provided ('provisors') were liable to pay a heavy tax for the privilege on their first year's income ('services' or 'annates' according to the nature of the benefice), besides heavy administrative fees. The staples of provision were bishoprics and secular canonries. Canons formed corporate bodies (chapters) responsible for administration and the maintenance of divine offices in some cathedrals[1], and some other exceptionally well-endowed collegiate churches. Canonries were well suited to provision. Most had lucrative prebends – income from land or a parochial benefice, part of the capitular endowment. Some were attached to archdeaconries and deaneries, jurisdictional subdivisions of the diocese. A canonry did not in itself involve pastoral duties ('the cure of souls'), and therefore could be filled without scandal by a cardinal or other papal official resident at Avignon, who appointed a local deputy. Moreover, canons were usually elected by chapters or appointed by bishops, whose rights of patronage the papacy was less chary of abrogating than those of the king and lay nobles.

Nevertheless, shrewd exploitation of provision provoked howls of indignation from local gentlefolk, intensely resentful that clerical wealth should be siphoned off to the ill-reputed court in what the Commons called in 1376 'the sinful city of Avignon'. For instance, for two-thirds of the period 1300–70 the archdeaconries of Oxford, Buckingham and Leicester (Lincoln chapter) were held by alien provisors. Kings, nobles and gentry hoped to use personal influence to get their kinsmen and leading servants elected or appointed to such lucrative benefices rather than the pope's. Provision introduced, alongside characteristic regional patterns of patronage linking 'Court' and 'Country', a context in which the elites were used to operating, a competing curial patronage system which was alien, where few but the most influential Englishmen could play the game with confident or familiar ease.

In 1351, after several years of parliamentary agitation, there was enacted on a Commons petition the first Statute of Provisors. This forbade the introduction of bulls of provision into the realm on pain of forfeiture and imprisonment. In 1353, also on a Commons petition, parliament passed the first Statute of Praemunire, which forbade suit out of the realm, at the *curia*, of cases cognisable in the king's courts. This was intended to keep from papal judgment disputes over benefices involving royal rights to patronage, and was to be supplemented by the 'great Statute of Praemunire' (1393), which prescribed outlawry and forfeiture for parties and their abettors suing at the papal court in such cases.

The papacy was eager to procure the repeal of this hostile legislation, not least because it enshrined the dangerous principle that a secular assembly might limit papal jurisdiction. In fact there was a basis for negotiation with the Crown, which was not irrevocably wedded to the principle, but determined to use the statutes and much emphasised indignation of its subjects as a means of pressure on the papacy. In 1376 and 1398 formal accords with the papacy delimiting provision were reached by Edward III and Richard II, but never ratified by their successors. In practice the Crown continued to make informal compromises. Kings did not use the statutes to exclude provisors, but to force them to seek royal licence before attempting to implement bulls of provision. In fact there was a steady decline in the number of Englishmen provided to canonries, and after 1400 the provision of aliens was rare. If the pope was prepared to appoint royal candidates, kings were ready to exploit the principle of provision. In the fourteenth century it became common (and in the fifteenth century, normal) for the Crown to procure the election of its candidates to bishoprics, then to allow the papacy (to its considerable financial advantage) to quash the election and provide the royal nominee.

The system of provision, though it gave some aspiring English clerics an alternative ladder of promotion, is unlikely to have satisfied the successful. For after paying escalating costs to present their petition at the *curia*, promote favourable consideration, and expedite the verification of their credentials and issue of bulls through a complexity of chancery offices, they had the prospect of losing some or all of their first year's revenue. Moreover, canon law impelled numerous clerical and lay litigants to engage in similarly expensive and tedious process at the *curia*. The auditors of the court of the Rota (or, less frequently, judge-delegates in England) heard appeals from decisions of lower ecclesiastical courts. The apostolic penitentiary dealt with requests for dispensations: for the illegitimate to function as priests, for the infirm to hear Mass in their homes, for kinsfolk within the forbidden degree to marry. There were other kinds of benefits which might be procured from the papacy. The right to sell indulgences for a specific purpose (for example, in order to repair a chapel or bridge) was a boon to poor communities. All sorts of ecclesiastical corporations coveted papal privileges which guaranteed and enhanced their liberties, and were quick to appeal against infringements. St Albans Abbey, like other ancient Benedictine abbeys, jealously prized the bulls which freed it from episcopal jurisdiction. But another characteristic of the papal court may have annoyed all but wealthy and influential litigants and petitioners. There were very few Englishmen employed in the *curia*: it was not so easy to seek out one's 'countrymen' to promote one's business as in the king's court. Had there not been so few resident English cardinals, the papal bureaucracy might have had a larger sympathetic element. The predominance of French, Italian and German curialists probably enhanced English impressions that the papacy was an alien institution.

So papal judicial as well as fiscal activity inflamed anti-papal sentiment. Moreover, the location as well as the self-interested efficiency of the Avignon papacy exacerbated feeling. Conviction grew during the early decades of the Hundred Years War that the Avignon popes and cardinals (the majority of whom were French) were Valois in sympathies. Papal mulcting of the English Church was seen as providing funds for the enemies of the realm. When the schism between recently elected rival popes was considered in the 1378 parliament, there seems to have been no hesitation in rejecting the 'French' cardinal, Robert of Geneva, who returned to Avignon to rule the Church as Clement VII, and in recognising the Neapolitan Urban VI, who managed to keep control of Rome. 'Our Urban' (d.1389) enjoyed fleeting popularity in

England. Reversing traditional papal policies of attempting to mediate between French and English kings, he was willing to sanction English attacks on the schismatic French and their allies by issuing crusading bulls. But his successor, Boniface IX, was not liked. Dependent on the English Church as his main source of revenue, he frantically tried to increase profits by provisions and the raising of clerical subsidies. This provoked heated protests by Richard II, supported by the community of the realm, and the enactment of the 1393 Statute of Praemunire. The burden of sustaining the Roman papacy, combined with growing enthusiasm for the crusade at Court in the 1390s, prompted Richard's support for the 'way of cession' (*via cessionis*) – a scheme that the French and English Crowns should put pressure on their respective popes to resign as a means of ending the Great Schism. The French Crown failed to put sufficient pressure on the anti-pope 'Benedict XIII', and there seems to have been a surprising lack of enthusiasm in England to abandon Boniface. When in 1398 Charles VI withdrew his obedience from Benedict, Richard did not follow suit. His interest in gaining Boniface's support for his 'tyranny' upset a hopeful move to end the schism. But English ecclesiastics were to play a distinguished part in the conciliar movement, whose principal aim was to reunite Christian society. Robert Hallum, bishop of Salisbury, led the realm's delegations to the general councils of Pisa (1409) and Constance (1414–18). At Pisa the English withdrew their obedience from Gregory XII, and at Constance endorsed the repudiation of rival popes, and participated in the election of Martin V (1417), who was to reunite most Catholic allegiances.

The formidable Martin V showed considerable interest in the affairs of the English Church. In particular, he tried in 1426 to persuade Henry Chichele, archbishop of Canterbury, and other bishops, to procure the repeal of the fourteenth-century legislation delimiting the exercise of papal jurisdiction. Martin denounced the Statute of Provisors to the duke of Bedford, since 'it produces, now that the schism is over, a kind of separation between England and the rest of the Church'. But even when an infant, Henry VI, ruled, the papacy was unable to wipe out this traditional, ingrained 'kind of separation', which Martin presciently deplored. He and his successors inclined to rebuild their wealth and authority on another basis: the revindication and exploitation of their territorial rights in Italy. As the papacy grew rapidly in significance as an Italian power in the later fifteenth and early sixteenth centuries, political alignments rather than the vexed question of jurisdictional bounds became the determining factors in its relations with the Crown. Tudor interest in a potentially valuable ally and lack of concern over native grievances against it are reflected in the numerous royal licences for provision of curial officials to prebends, and, indeed, without precedent in our period, of Italians to bishoprics. This cordiality was diplomatic, and hardly calculated to alter that scorn for papal authority which had become a traditional English attitude.

There were the Londoners who had said in 1468 that 'the pope's curse was not worth a fly'. In 1472 Pietro Aliprando reported to the duke of Milan that the English were in the morning 'as devout as angels but after dinner they are like devils, seeking to throw the pope's messengers into the sea'.

Nevertheless, there may have been also a residue of traditional respect for the papacy. The London citizen who reported the contemptuous attitude of some of his fellows in 1468 professed shock at it. Many individuals who encountered papal glory did so, not as resentful petitioners but as pilgrims to Rome, most of them probably less sensitive about its contrast with apostolic poverty than was Martin Luther. Since the Anglo-Saxon period Rome had been a magnet for English pilgrims. They had a hostel there, the recipient of benefactions from well-to-do visitors. For those who never went to be awed by the relics of apostles and martyrs, the distant pope may have seemed to bear little but a formal relationship to the Christ elevated in the priest's hands, and bloodily carved above the chancel screen of their parish church. Yet those who were shocked by the desire of Muslims and Lollards to trample on His image may have respected the papacy as the enemy of such heretics.

The episcopate

Monastic reform encouraged and sponsored by the papacy in the early Middle Ages had led to numerous exemptions from episcopal jurisdiction. Regular Orders, such as those of Cluny, Cîteaux, Prémontré, the crusading Knights of St John, the Franciscan, Dominican and Carmelite friars, possessed self-contained, international systems of discipline, subordinated only to the papacy[2]. Many of the 'independent' monasteries founded before the post-Conquest development of monastic Orders in England had also received papal privileges of exemption. The Benedictines were subject to visitors appointed in the triennial chapter of their provincial *confrères*[3]. There were areas which were jurisdictional 'liberties', where an archdeacon, a cathedral chapter or body of vicars-choral (the chapter's deputies for the performance of services) had a special right to exercise the powers of visitation and correction normally pertaining to bishops.

This proliferation of exemptions and liberties not only undermined the effectiveness of episcopal jurisdiction, but encouraged unfortunate ecclesiastical habits: preoccupation with disputing and defending the bounds of privilege by litigation, polemic, resort to lay patronage, and even violence. The much fissured Church lacked the united ability or will to organise itself to effect reform. It was vulnerable to exploitation by the laity: the most effective unifying force in the Church was the supreme lay power, the Crown.

Royal authority over the Church derived from the strict and (in later eyes) uncanonical control which Anglo-Saxon kings had exercised over the appointment of bishops and abbots, reinforced after the Norman Conquest by the feudal relationship between the Crown and ecclesiastical tenants-in-chief. The Norman and Angevin kings, confronted by the increasingly confident insistence of the *curia* and of reforming clerics that priestly offices were part of a divine, not a lay hierarchy, struggled with some success to maintain that bishops and many abbots were feudal officials, subject to royal appointment, and owing primary allegiance as barons of the Crown. By our period, bishops had come to accept the dual nature of their office, the due they owed to Caesar as well as to God. Kings continued to enjoy possession of episcopal properties during vacancies – the equivalent of lay wardship, known as 'regalian right'. But they had come to recognise that they ought not to engineer the prolongation of vacancies for their profit. In the early twelfth century, the Crown had grudgingly modified the royal role in the selection and investiture of ecclesiastical tenants-in-chief. The Church was allowed its 'freedom' – freedom for chapters to elect bishops, abbots and priors, and for the papacy to adjudicate disputed elections. However, a chapter could not elect until the reception of a writ giving the king's permission, and the elect could not be consecrated until he had performed homage and received the temporalities from the Crown. But, as we have seen, in our period it had become customary for the papacy to provide royal nominees, overriding capitular rights, though king's men were not always appointed. Thomas Gascoigne, chancellor of the University of Oxford in the 1440s, stated the custom of his day, somewhat crudely and polemically: 'There are three things today that make a bishop in England, the will of the king, the will of the pope or of the court of Rome, and the money paid in large quantities to that court.'

These methods of selection produced elements of uniformity in the careers and preoccupations of most bishops. The majority were university-trained secular clerks who had gone to the top in royal service. Monks and friars, whose Order and background might inhibit their administrative efficiency, were not often appointed. A few regulars who had impressed the king as royal chaplains received poorer sees. From the later fourteenth century onwards (a period when noble incomes came under particular strain), there was an influx of royal kinsmen from magnate families into the richer sees. Examples are the earl of Arundel's younger son Thomas Arundel (bishop of Ely 1373, archbishop of York 1388, archbishop of Canterbury 1396), the earl of Devon's younger son William Courtenay (Hereford 1369, London 1371, Canterbury 1381), and John of Gaunt's son Henry Beaufort (Lincoln 1396, Winchester 1404). But most bishops had worked their way up from lower social origins, by expertise as advisers in civil or canon law to the Crown, as specialists in Chancery, Exchequer and Household administration, or as diplomats. William of Wykeham (Winchester 1367) had gained Edward III's favour particularly as surveyor of building works at Windsor Castle in the 1350s. He was not the only bishop of humble family status; others included Henry Chichele (Canterbury 1414) and two outstanding early Tudor archbishops, Wolsey and Cranmer.

Which loyalty did such men put first? A chaplain of Henry VII's leading councillor, Richard Fox (Exeter 1487, Bath and Wells 1492, Durham 1494, Winchester 1501[4]) allegedly had no doubts about his master. According to Roper's life of Thomas More, the chaplain said: 'My master . . . to serve the king's turn, will not stick to agree to his own father's death.' Fox himself, writing in 1517 to his protégé Wolsey, confessed: 'I have been almost by the space of thirty years so negligent that, of four several cathedral churches that I have successively had, there be two, scilicet Exeter and Wells, that I never see and innumerable souls whereof I never see the bodies.' Wolsey himself visited his see of York for the first time for his enthronement in 1530, thirteen years after provision.

It was a reflection of episcopal involvement in royal government that bishops carried on building work at their residences in and near London. Wolsey's palatial works at York Place (later Whitehall Palace) and Hampton Court were famous in their day. The chapel of the bishops of Ely's London house still stands, as do fragments of the bishops of Winchester's hall. The archbishops of Canterbury's house, Lambeth Palace, is the one remaining building which gives a good impression of a fifteenth-century nobleman's London residence. In their great houses bishops tended to live surrounded by an elaborate household organisation, with a large lay staff, as befitted barons and eminent royal servants. On a summer afternoon at Lambeth in 1413, Archbishop Arundel's hall, according to Margery Kempe, was thronged with many of his 'clerks and other reckless men, both squires and yeomen, who swore many great oaths and spoke many reckless words'. Bishop Beckington's jester is sculpted on his tomb at Wells. Most bishops who earned contemporary fame or notoriety did so because of their secular responsibilities. On their account Archbishop Sudbury, and Bishops Moleyns of Chichester and Ayscough of Salisbury, were lynched respectively in 1381, 1449 and 1450. The mobs who killed them showed no respect for the holy office. Despenser of Norwich got a reputation in 1381 as a soldier. Scrope of York (d.1405) alone attracted a cult to his tomb – but his martyrdom had been in a dubious political cause. However, the remoteness of bishops from their spiritual charge varied considerably. Baronial interest, if no other, was an incentive for them to reside in the diocese some of the time – the prudent noble anxious to safeguard his propertied interests did not neglect personal supervision. The remains of considerable building works testify to such episcopal sojournings, as for example at Knole (Canterbury), Farnham (Winchester) and Buckden (Lincoln). Even when resident, their high status, erudition and secular preoccupations may have combined with the complex structure of diocesan administration to make them remote from the majority of their flock. But this, surprisingly, is not the impression given in the reminiscences of Margery Kempe, who (due, indeed, partly, to some persistence and notoriety) became personally acquainted with several bishops (see pp. 361 ff).

A bishop's duties were to ordain priests, consecrate churches, institute to benefices, and preach to the faithful. He had a responsibility for the maintenance by clergy and people of the Christian way of life. The methods by which these duties were fulfilled had been elaborated by canon law and administrative practice. There were episcopal courts to deal with offenders. Bishops were formally obliged to carry out a spiritual tour of inspection, a visitation, every third year. They had to summon synods of the clergy and people.

Some episcopal functions could be performed more or less adequately by absentees. Bishop Arundel held ordinations and heard suits in London at Ely Place. In practice many functions normally devolved (as in much secular administration) on deputies. Bishops alone could perform some spiritual tasks: ordination, confirmation, benediction of newly elected heads of religious houses, consecration of sacred sites, and their rededication after pollution by violence. Titular bishops nominally holding sees in Islamic lands (*in partibus infidelium*), and holders of remote Irish sees, often friars, were appointed to fulfil such functions. But the important men outside the bishop's household in his administration of the diocese were his vicar-general and official principal, both often prebendaries, where the cathedral was not monastic. They received commissions granting the routine exercise of certain episcopal powers for an indeterminate period, automatically terminated by the commissioning bishop's death, besides *ad hoc* commissions. The vicar-general dealt with a mass of business. He instituted clerks to benefices, received their oaths of obedience and enquired into irregularities in the performance of offices. He was responsible for producing those summoned to the bishop's courts and enforcing penances decreed there. He sequestrated vacant benefices and had their revenues collected. He proved wills and appointed their administrators. He summoned and supervised diocesan synods, at which the bishop's mandates and injunctions, correcting and instructing, were published.

In the fifteenth century it was usual to unite the offices of vicar-general and official principal. The latter presided over the consistory court, which heard cases on delation by episcopal officers, deans, parish priests and parishioners, cases between parties, and appeals from judgments in archdeacons' courts. Cases were frequently heard concerning matrimonial offences, defamation, tithes, perjury and usury. The bishops did not stand completely aloof from their justice. They had advisers on canon law among their household clerks (e.g. the chancellor) to whom they committed cases reserved by mandate, or consulted when giving personal audience.

There were also subordinate officials responsible for ecclesiastical discipline within regional subdivisions of the diocese: archdeacons, who had prebends and frequently more than one parochial cure annexed to their office, and rural deans selected from the resident parochial clergy. The archdeacon was obliged to hold annual visitations and a consistory court (modelled on the bishop's) to deal with delinquencies. He also received episcopal commissions, for example, to cite offenders before courts, pronounce sentences of excommunication, supervise the collection of cathedral fabric funds and make specific enquiries. Archdeacons sometimes summoned chapters of clergy and laity to provide information and check on abuses. But generally archdeaconries were sinecures, coveted by clerics in royal and higher ecclesiastical administration for their lucrative procurations. In practice the work was done by the archdeacon's official, assisted by the rural deans responsible in subdivisions of the archdeaconries.

Officials of the Church courts had a grubby reputation. Chaucer's portrait of the archdeacon's summoner bitingly elaborates his blackmailing activities. One of Langland's figures declaims: 'Bring together all the deans, sub-deans, archdeacons, bishops' officers, and registrars, and have them saddled with silver bribes, so they'll condone our sins – adultery, divorce, and private usury – and let them carry the bishops about on their visitations.'

Such literary images are important reflections of current opinions, but they do not tell the whole truth. They must be weighed against the official documentary evidence for the exercise of episcopal jurisdiction. For instance, in 1380 Bishop Arundel of Ely heard a case within his diocese at Chatteris. Richard Fisher had been cited before him for having 'treated his wife very badly, greatly injuring her by breaking her leg, and causing her other great injuries'. He confessed, and swore that 'henceforth he would treat her with marital affection, and would see that she had medicine to heal her, as far as possible'. He was enjoined to go round Chatteris Church as a penitent before the procession on three successive Sundays, to pay 20*s* to the fabric fund of Ely Cathedral within a year, and to do penance there on the feast of St Etheldreda. Thus the aristocratic bishop tried to remedy villagers' marital problems. Church courts undoubtedly helped to regulate social friction, and provided a tribunal for complaints against clerical conduct, though allowing opportunities for extortion and malicious accusation.

Much of the routine of diocesan administration seems to have functioned with reasonable efficiency in the absence of bishops, and without the necessity of their detailed supervision when present in their dioceses. This organisational smoothness was a tragedy for the Church. Officials lacked the weight of a bishop's authority needed to deal with abuses by the powerful, such as religious houses' neglect of their appropriated parish churches. Moreover a bishop should have been a father to his flock, leading them by personal example, exhortation and correction. Such disparate figures as Wulfstan of Worcester in the eleventh century, Robert Grosseteste in the thirteenth and Hugh Latimer of Worcester in the sixteenth were inspired by this hallowed ideal. It was not dead in the later Middle Ages. Langland nobly expressed it: incidents show that Thomas Arundel and other bishops were aware of it. But contemporary pressures moulded their activities to another current concept of office. Wide-ranging governmental functions were regarded as more pressing for bishops than the personal discharge of pastoral responsibilities. The typical bishop was a courtly, politic, well-educated administrator who presided distantly over diocesan affairs, and counselled kings and fellow magnates, maintaining the Church's interests against the more than occasional impudence of laymen, entertaining and building finely, and looking kindly on the privileges and petitions of his flock, clergy and laity.

The bishops were, on the whole, remarkably distinguished and conscientious, the antitheses of the vicious caricatures of satirists and heretics. But, because of the factors discussed, their qualities shine forth more clearly in personal benefactions than in discharge of their historic functions. For instance, Edward III's servant Bishop Wykeham laid down the principal models for fifteenth-century educational foundations: his colleges at Oxford and Winchester. He endowed New College in 1379 with seventy scholars, an unprecedented number, and complemented this in 1382 with his grammar school at Winchester, larger than any previous English school. Arundel's concern as archbishop of Canterbury for the spiritual welfare of the literate laity is reflected by his interest in a translation of a famous Italian Franciscan work of *c.*1290–1300, *Meditationes Vitae Christi.* Nicholas Love, prior of Mountgrace Charterhouse, produced his English version, *The Mirror of the Blessed Life of Jesu Christ*, shortly before 1410. It was submitted for Arundel's approval: he authorised its issue 'to the edification of the faithful and the confutation of heretics or Lollards'[5].

Bishop Fox (d.1528), so maligned by his chaplain, and so worthless a pastor on his own admission, was a benefactor of Magdalen College, Oxford, founder of Corpus Christi College there, and of grammar schools at Taunton and Grantham, and instrumental in the foundation of St John's College, Cambridge. His building modifications can still be seen in Winchester Cathedral. But, apart from such colleges and fabric works, perhaps the most striking architectural remains of episcopal benefaction are the residences of the vicars choral at Wells. Bishop Ralph of Shrewsbury commenced *c.*1354 the buildings of a street of two parallel rows of adjoining houses for fifty vicars. This was made into a quadrangle by the erection of a refectory at one end, and a chapel, paid for by Bishop Bubwith (d.1424) at the other. Bishop Beckington (d.1465), a distinguished diplomat and minister in Henry VI's service, provided a gateway to the close and an enclosed passageway bridging a lane direct from the cathedral to the vicars' refectory, so that they could go to and from the performance of the liturgies without straying in town. His executors repaired many of the houses and built a chamber over the vicars' chapel to house their library.

One of the most penetrating series of comments on a medieval English bishop is to be found in Sir Thomas More's *Utopia*. He illustrates, in a highly complimentary way, the grave, lively tabletalk encouraged by John Morton, cardinal-archbishop of Canterbury (d.1500), in whose household he had stayed as a boy. This is how he describes Morton:

He was a person that one respected just as much for his wisdom and moral character as for his great eminence. . . . He had the sort of face that inspires reverence rather than fear. He was quite easy to get on with, though always serious and dignified. Admittedly he was rather inclined to be rude to people who asked him for jobs, but he meant no harm by it. He only did it to test their intelligence and presence of mind, for he found these qualities very congenial, so long as they were used with discretion, and considered them most valuable in public life. He was a polished and effective speaker, with a thorough knowledge of the law. He also had a quite remarkable intellect and a phenomenal memory – two natural gifts which he'd further developed by training and practice.

Apparently the king [Henry VII] *had great confidence in his judgement, and at the time of my visit the whole country seemed to depend on him. This was hardly surprising, since he'd been rushed straight from the university to court, when he was not much more than a boy, and had spent the rest of his life in public service, learning wisdom the hard way, by having to cope with a long series of crises.*

Thomas More, eager seeker after piety, recalling his master with affectionate respect, praised him only for intellectual, moral and administrative attainments. Whereas Henry VI's chaplain had felt moved by his lord's austerity amid worldly distractions to write in praise of his religious virtues, no bishop's chaplain did for his master.

Chantries, parishes, and the secular clergy

'It was never merry in England while we had cardinals among us', remarked the duke of Suffolk, on hearing of Cardinal Wolsey's dismissal from the Chancellorship in 1529. There was widespread anticlericalism at all levels of later medieval English society, which Henry VIII was able to exploit against the papacy, the monasteries, and obdurate clergymen. But layfolk needed a variety of services from the Church which, however anticlerical or irreligious they were, they regarded as necessities of life and death. Over past centuries the Church had been granted vast amounts of property, plate and precious cloth by men and women desperate to gain spiritual merit by good works, and to pay for Masses to be offered for the repose of their souls after death, and on the anniversary of their decease. Urgency of desire to have body and soul enfolded within the Church's protection speedily after the point of death is reflected in the will of Henry lord FitzHugh (1424):

My body to be buried in our Lady Kirk, within the abbey of Jervaulx, and I desire that it be carried there with all possible haste after my death and buried by daylight if it does not arrive too late, but if it does, then I will that it be interred the same night; also I will that one thousand masses be said for my soul with all speed.

Many heirs must have been mortified by the size of bequests which their fearful parents and ancestors had piously made. The religious houses alone possessed on the eve of the Dissolution about a half of the Church's wealth, the bulk of it acquired by the mid-thirteenth century. At times of general financial stress caused by high taxation or economic recession, some medieval landowners made pointed remarks about the clergy's duty to relieve the burdens of the laity. Indignation was stoked up by the sermons of some fourteenth-century friars, who questioned the theological basis of ecclesiastical accumulation of wealth and castigated the covetousness of rich clergy. Gentlefolk had not forgotten that their predecessors had endowed monasteries, and displayed a residual proprietorial sense by using them as 'hotels' on their travels, and procuring from them pensions and lodgings for retired servants.

Yet men of widely differing status, however bitterly they resented ecclesiastical wealth, privileges, immunities from secular judicial process, exercise of judicial powers and derelictions of duty, grudgingly allowed the Church its rights. The heir accepted his parents' alienation of manors. The likes of John Ravynis of Monkton in Thanet, convicted in 1468 of shaving beards on Sundays, particularly during service time, accepted that they were liable to punishment if they tried to earn their bread honestly on the Sabbath. They accepted because they believed in the priests' unique mediative power between God and the laity and feared its withdrawal by excommunication[6]. The priest had the power to administer to them the Body of Christ, to absolve sins, dispense from the canons, and assist the release of souls from the agonies that they must all endure. God and Satan were manifest in the world. Hardheaded fifteenth-century London merchants, laboriously composing their prosaic, often parochially minded and anticlerical annals, noted unusual phenomena and occurrences, aware that they must have portentous significance in the mysterious unfolding of a divinely ordained historical process. Yet such Londoners' worldly display impressed foreigners. The English were reputed for their stolid enjoyment of sensual pleasures. But since doubt was intellectually and emotionally difficult, sensualists were as eager for the Church's spiritual benefactions as were ascetics. Though grants of land to monasteries had fallen to a trickle, and few houses were founded, they still received gifts for fabric or furnishing, for the privileges of burial and celebration of soul-masses. The sinner tried to ensure the purification of his soul, and mimed its anticipated transformation, by having the corrupt body placed in hallowed surroundings, perhaps the conventual Lady Chapel, while nearby, now blessed, might be former worldly toys, silverware and cloth-of-gold, amid which the sinner had disported in giddy youth. Nobles placed over their tombs realistic effigies of themselves attired in worldly hierarchic splendour, surrounded by carved religious and secular symbols whose exquisite detail and bright hues reminded men of the magnificence of the deceased's households. But tomb sculptures were not the vulgar celebration of past wealth and power which they later became. They were intended as images of the serene perfection of the heavenly host, within which the soul (like the corrupt body) would be transfigured.

Representations of the deceased, often engraved on brass or carved in alabaster, had a spiritual function. They were intended to recall obligations to celebrate anniversaries with services: the inscription at the foot of the brass or surrounding the effigy recorded the correct date for the celebration of the 'obit' (Latin *obitus*, death). The fascinating detail and individual idiosyncrasies of tomb sculpture arrested the attention of passers-by, emphasising the merit and plight of the soul, occasionally by the representation of a pitiful corpse. The testament of Isabel countess of Warwick (1439) prescribes her abasement, willing that 'my Image to be made all naked . . . my hair cast backwards'. Increasing literacy was an incentive to combine representation with inscription: the casual visitor was now more likely to understand information provided[7]. The injunction on the brass of John lord Cobham (d.1354) places an obligation on the visitor by parodying the conventions of hospitality in the baronial hall: 'You who pass round this place pray for the soul of the courteous host, called John de Cobham. May God grant him entire pardon.' Over a century later Sir Thomas Malory has one of his chivalrous heroes pronounce an affecting last will: ' "Now", said Balin, "when we are buried in one tomb, and the mention made over us how two brethren slew each other, there will never good knight nor good man see our tomb, but they will pray for our souls." '

Increasing lay literacy in the period, since much of it was directed to mastering liturgies and psalms, and reflecting on moralising commentaries and saints' lives, produced a wider and more sophisticated awareness of religious needs. 'I have heard', says one of Langland's characters, 'great men at their meals talking about Christ and his divine powers as if they were clerics.' Equally among the illiterate, religious sensibility was probably enhanced from the second half of the fourteenth century onwards by the recurrence of epidemics of pestilence. Horrifying features of the Black Death were its complete unpredictability and the speed with which many victims succumbed. Medieval terror sprung not so much from the sense of human tragedy (as ours might), as from the threat to souls unprepared for death. The Scots countess of March wrote to Henry IV in 1404: 'Now the pestilence is so severe and cruel where we are that I am very much afraid lest I should die in the great debt which I have incurred.'

Characteristic attitudes to religion in the period lie behind the proliferation of chantries in England from the thirteenth century onwards. A chantry was the provision of an endowment, temporary or perpetual, for daily or weekly Masses and other services for a private intention, usually the repose of the souls of the donor and others he named in his foundation charter. Some founders granted endowments to monasteries, and to the chapters of secular cathedrals and collegiate churches, imposing an obligation, often to be fulfilled by a particular monk or vicar choral, to say Masses. But since a priest was not supposed to say more than one Mass a day, it became increasingly the custom to provide an endowment for a priest whose sole duties would be concerned with the chantry. Perpetual endowments were often entrusted to 'undying' corporations: the mayor and corporation of a town, the dean and chapter of a cathedral, a monastery, a craft gild, the rector and parishioners of a church. They would be obliged to hire a succession of chantry priests and supervise their fulfilment of the terms of appointment. Another popular way of founding a perpetual chantry was to create a benefice with episcopal sanction. According to the terms of the founder's charter, its patronage would belong to him and his heirs or to a religious corporation, and the terms of service would be subject, like a parochial benefice, to episcopal jurisdiction. The chantry priest would have security of tenure and full control of the endowed property, including his house.

Chantry masses were celebrated in extraparochial chapels, at existing side altars in parish churches, or in specially built chapels between their bays, often at a little altar at the end of the founder's tomb, sometimes (as consecration crosses testify) on top of the tomb. Cathedrals and town churches often contained large numbers of chantries, some stately enclosed chapels, others (including temporary ones) occupying the side altars at different times, not always the same altar. At York in 1461 there were twenty-four priests responsible for different chantries in the minster. Warwick the Kingmaker and his brother George Neville, bishop of Exeter, then received Edward IV's licence to alienate properties to endow a college where the chantry priests would live under the discipline of a common rule. Their quadrangular building, St William's College, is now the meeting place of the Convocation of the Province of York.

Kings and magnates sometimes afforded to provide for their souls and those of their kinsfolk and friends by founding and endowing colleges of priests, living together according to constitutions enforced by the diocesan. Their dwellings adjoined a parish church whose advowson was sometimes appropriated to the college by the founder's gift, and which was often rebuilt at his expense to accommodate the chantry priests in the choir. An example is Fotheringhay College, whose foundation was implemented in 1411–12 by Edward duke of York, Richard II's politically slippery cousin, who had composed in English a treatise on hunting, *The Master of Game*, dedicated to the future Henry V, in whose service he was to die at Agincourt in 1415. The college was dedicated to the Blessed Virgin and All Saints. According to York's statutes, there were to be a master, twelve fellows, eight clerks and thirteen choristers. They were to pray in the parish church for the good estate and souls of the king and queen (Henry IV and Joan of Navarre), the prince of Wales, the duke of York, and all faithful souls. In the will made shortly before his death, Edward, 'of all sinners the most wicked', ordered his burial in the collegiate church, and bequeathed in perpetuity to its master and his companions many of the furnishings and jewels kept in the ducal chapel. The college buildings have disappeared; of the rebuilt church the fine nave survives, constructed according to the terms of a contract made by Edward's nephew, Richard duke of York, in 1434. Collegiate and other chantry priests sometimes had the duty of supervising and teaching in an attached school. There was often a subordinate almshouse, whose inhabitants were bedesmen obliged to pray for the founder. Poor Yorkist tenants were housed at Fotheringhay.

Edward of York's provision of Masses for the faithful living and departed, and of lodging and meat for feeble dependants, shows that, characteristically of a college founder, he acknowledged social responsibilities. Nobles were doubtless aware of the kind of moral sentiments which were to be graphically illustrated in a literary and artistic theme particularly popular in the next generation: the *danse macabre*, in which Death led off every man without discrimination of rank. In 1430 the dance was painted in the new cloister at St Paul's, with John Lydgate's sententious explanatory verses. Yet noble and bourgeois, by chantry foundations, maintained a sort of distinction of rank beyond the grave, pouring out wealth for their souls' ease, as poor sinners could not do. Thus they attempted to identify the spiritual nobility, extolled by preachers, with the nobility of blood and wealth, just as they were trying to reinforce the latter's material ascendancy, by limiting the right to don rich clothes, to give liveries, sit as a knight of the shire or participate in gild elections and governance. Luxurious chantries were not just the product of better religious education and greater fear of sudden death. Like the newly ostentatious and extravagant noble way of life, their origins lay too in elitist reactions to intellectual challenges and social threats. Service to chantries must have sucked in a large amount of clerical talent. The chantry priest, particularly when serving the less rigidly regulated temporary chantry, had fewer and less onerous duties than the parish priest. At the dissolution in 1547, there were ninety collegiate chantries and 2,374 chantries and other institutions (religious gilds and free chapels) with chantries attached.

The movement of lay devotion in the later Middle Ages placed another burden of exploitation by the rich on the Church, which mostly distracted from the discharge of pastoral responsibilities. By this period the parish priest had a well-defined office. He was canonically obliged to celebrate the liturgical offices daily, administer communion at least three times a year to the parishioner, confess him or her at least once, and preach four times. He was to instruct, reconcile, perform works of mercy, and discharge his responsibilities for the fabric and possessions of the church. He was not to wear unsuitable clothes, frequent inns or brothels, or associate with suspect females. The priest responsible for the discharge of the cure was granted its benefice in return. He, the rector, occupied the rectory and its appurtenant property: farm land (glebe), and tenements. He received an annual tithe, the value of one-tenth of the parishioners' incomes. He was paid special fees for conducting some services, such as Requiem Masses, and customary dues such as the mortuary (a tax on the goods of the deceased parishioner) and burial fees.

Benefices varied considerably in income, according to the size and prosperity of the parish, and the extent of the propertied endowments. According to the *Valor Ecclesiasticus* (1535), 87 per cent of the 397 livings in the diocese of Coventry and Lichfield were worth less than £20 p.a., 10 per cent less than £5. Many rectors, especially those with lucrative parishes, drew the income without performing the cure. The accumulation of parochial benefices for profit (pluralism) had intensified the abuse of non-residence. But from the mid-thirteenth century onwards, pluralism had declined. John XXII, in his decree *Execrabilis* (1317), forbade anyone, except cardinals and kings' sons, to hold more than two benefices, one of them with cure of souls, on pain of forfeiture. English bishops did grant dispensations to hold benefices in plurality, but rarely permitted the tenure of more than one parochial cure at a time.

Non-residence was rooted in the situation that the right of presentation to benefices (advowson) was the private, heritable possession of hundreds of individuals and corporate religious bodies: the king, magnates, gentlefolk, collegiate chapters and monasteries. They regarded advowson as a source of income for their servants. In surveys of lords' estates drawn up by their officials, benefices and their incomes were tabulated along with manors and rents. Sir John Fastolf's secretary, William Worcester, reveals in a letter of 1454 how his master regarded benefices: 'I have five shillings yearly, all costs borne, to help pay for bonnets that I lose. I told my master so this week, and he told me yesterday he wished me to have been a priest, so I had been disposed to have got me a living by reason of a benefice.' The separation of benefice from cure was so normal that it could be earnestly defended by clerics: it was a means of paying for ecclesiastical administration and higher education. Roger Otery, a clerk in the bishop of Hereford's household, wrote in 1366:

Both he who resides and he who does not reside are understood to serve the altar, so long as they live a good life and expend well the income they derive. And I say also that by the custom of the English Church it was and is the used and approved custom, from time out of mind, and tolerated by the Roman Church, that the bishops and other patrons of the said realm of England can provide their well-deserving clerks with benefices, especially sinecures, up to any number, without any contradiction or offence to the Holy See.

One means by which 'well-deserving clerks' were provided was by the permanent appropriation of a benefice to an office or institution: to a particular prebendal stall in a cathedral or collegiate church, for example, or to the vicars choral who observed the canonical hours there. The desire of gentlefolk and burgesses to succour their souls by the foundation of perpetual Masses produced a massive transfer of advowsons to monasteries and colleges. In Yorkshire, in 1535, 392 out of 622 parish churches were appropriated. In a great majority of these appropriations, vicarages had been ordained. Vicars received an agreed proportion of the incomes from benefices. Sometimes they had a house, and parts of the glebe and tithes; often, a rather low pension from the impropriator. At Fryston, acquired from a lay benefactor by the vicars choral of York in 1332 in return for obligations to maintain chantries, the perpetual vicarage instituted the following year seems to have been well endowed. The vicar (to be presented by the archbishops and, *sede vacante*, the chapter) was to have a third of the rectory house to live in, including the hall with a chamber behind the hall-seat, and another chamber. In the undercroft he was allotted a granary, kitchen, bakehouse and brewhouse: he was also to have a courtyard and garden, 18 acres of land in Fryston and 14 acres in Wheeldale, with meadows, tithes of lambs, cows, calves, pigs, fowl, geese, ducks, doves, mills, hemp, linen, herbs and leeks, $5\frac{1}{2}$ marks at the four terms of the year, oblations, lenten tithes, altarage, and tithes of corn. The vicar was obliged to provide a chaplain at his own expense to celebrate Mass three times a week in the chapel of Wheeldale and to pay for the chantry at Fryston. To what extent impropriators made certain that vicars performed their responsibilities, and fulfilled their own to the maintenance of the church fabric, is not clear. They are suspected of widespread negligence. An example of a church magnificently rebuilt by the impropriator is Adderbury, whose patronage belonged to New College, Oxford.

The stranger visiting a rural parish would have been as likely as not to find that the resident parish priest was not a propertied rector or vicar, but a salaried chaplain (sometimes termed a curate) employed by one or the other often at an annual wage less than a quarter of the income from the benefice. It is difficult to be sure how well these poor parish priests and resident rectors of poor parishes, and ill-paid vicars, performed their office. They were butts for the strictures of often unsympathetic superiors. Living in the village community, they were a prey to temptations and a target for malicious denunciation. Their alleged shortcomings and misdeeds make painful reading in the records of diocesan courts.

Clerical mortality during the Black Death may have produced a crisis in the recruitment of parish priests. Langland reflected on the greater financial attractions of performing soul-masses in London: 'Then I heard parish priests complaining to the bishop that since the Plague their parishes were too poor to live in; so they asked permission to live in London, where they could traffic in masses, and chime their voices to the sweet jingling of silver.' The increase of soul-masses was driving up the wages demanded for serving perpetual chantries as well as cures. In his will of 1368 Gervase de Wylleford, a rector, endowed two chaplaincies for his soul at 6 marks p.a. each, a rate one mark higher than the statutory one. Gervase made the proviso: 'And if perchance these chaplains are not able to take such a sum for their salary without offence to the king and his statute then I will that they receive for their salary whatever will be allowed and ordained.' In a constitution ordained in the Convocation of Canterbury at Gloucester in 1378, Archbishop Sudbury, with some literary huffing at the cupidity of clerical wage-earners, fixed the maximum annual wage for chantry priests at 7 marks (£4 13*s* 4*d*), and for curates at 8 marks (£5 6*s* 8*d*). It is unlikely that parochial chaplaincies became sufficiently lucrative in that or the following century to attract graduates or former university students. Wages were often so low for curates that they probably tended to move to other parishes in a manner unsettling for parochial life. At present it is hard to substantiate any but a few generalisations about parish priests. Unlike many of their superiors, whose property-holding and administrative activities have left a documentary residuum, they remain a faceless clerical proletariat. An exception, who left his impression in literary sources, is John Ball, a leader of the commons in 1381 (cf. p. 179), whose Christian conviction and indignant hatred of his superiors may be an idiosyncratic reflection of current or traditional attitudes among such chaplains.

There is not much evidence of systematic efforts by those superiors to educate curates and monitor their performance of office. Candidates for ordination to the full priestly order and for first institution to a benefice were examined for suitability by a bishop or his commissary. The ordinand had to show moral stability, ability to read Latin, means of livelihood, and to be (unless dispensed) at least twenty-five years of age. It is not clear that such examinations (and similar ones before institution) were customarily more than perfunctory. Certainly there were no ecclesiastical endowments specifically provided to train priests beforehand.

However, it is dangerous, when looking at a society in which social pressures were much less fully reflected in official acts and proceedings than in ours, to assume that documentary silence is conclusive. Concern among some higher clergy for the education of priests appears in their composition of manuals to instruct them simply in the requisite duties and conduct. In a period when laymen were becoming more literate, there may have been greater expectations that clergy should be. The increasing number of elementary and grammar schools provided greater opportunities for learning Latin. Curates who were considered inadequate or pernicious by the neighbourhood could be denounced to diocesan courts or visitors. Robert Becket, curate in the diocese of Lincoln, was accused *c*.1500 by parishioners before the bishop's chancellor of attempting to rape a village wife. Laying a noble (worth 6*s* 8*d*) on her bed, he seized her, declaring 'he must needs have his pleasure of her'. She put up a struggle in which a jug was knocked over: Becket sent her away to procure another woman for him. He subsequently extorted 20*d* from the goodwife's husband as a bribe, not to cite her for adultery! The churchwardens remonstrated with Becket about his conduct: village girls mocked him. The chancellor treated the distraught curate kindly – it had been testified that in other respects he was dutiful.

This case and others strongly suggest the pressure of opinion of parochial communities on the conduct of parish priests. They were expected to perform a reconciliatory role in village society. However, in respect of doctrine, ritual and morals, their *mores* may have derived from the beliefs and habits of peasant communities rather than from liturgies and manuals. For they often seem to have condoned their parishioners' appropriation of saints' days and consecrated ground for communal carousing and licentiousness. Instead of inculcating a Christian ethic and worship based firmly on reasoned beliefs, and on the authoritative precepts of the Church, they may have tended to confuse its values with those of a rural magical system which invested material objects with numinous properties. William Inold, vicar of Rye, was accused in 1538 of having 'as a witch' given a child three drinks from the chalice 'for the chine cough'. Richard Lawson, parish priest of Windsor, was accused in the same year of having used a piece of wick to measure the church and churchyard, and then having made it into a wax candle called a 'tryndell', the light of which, he told his parishioners, would 'mitigate and assuage the plague, the high indignation and displeasure of God'.

Such deficiencies may have been encouraged by indifference among impropriators and benefice-holders, and among gentlefolk tending to withdraw socially into the privacy of their chambers in emparked manor houses. They frequently received licences to build private chapels and possess portable altars, where their domestic chaplains ministered, often, probably, according to the more literate modes of devotion becoming popular in the elites (see pp. 356 ff). Nevertheless, it would perhaps be mistaken to assume that the rich were uniformly indifferent to the conduct of curates. A much emphasised duty of lordship, reflected in remarks in private correspondence as well as in homiletic literature, was the obligation to ensure the decorous and virtuous conduct of one's servants. Elites which set such store by a precise and impressive performance of public rituals, secular as well as religious, may have been concerned about liturgical authenticity and quality in the churches where their chantries were housed, and which they had often finely adorned.

Concern of rectors and vicars for their churches is shown by frequent bequests of service books and treatises to them, for example, of two graduals[8] by John Oudeby (d.1414) to Flamstead Church, where he was rector and where his brass can be seen. Gentlemen contributed to the fabric funds and donated furnishings to help secure well-maintained chantries in parish churches. Sir William Bruges, by his will of 1449, lavished presents on the place of his intended burial, St George's, Stamford. A collection of rich plate, much of it from his chapel at Kentish Town, was to be placed in the safeguard of the parishioners and kept in their treasury. Parochial communities were responsible for the upkeep of their church's nave and the provision of its instruments of worship. Their lively activities are witnessed by the large number of naves enlarged or rebuilt in this period, and by the insertion of larger windows, all in the popular, standardised style which has been labelled 'English Perpendicular'. By the fourteenth century the office of churchwarden had evolved. Two were elected annually, one by the parishioners, the other by the incumbent. They received contributions or rates, determined by vestry associations, for church repairs or the provision of ornaments. They managed bequests such as Bruges's and organised brewing for church ales, parochial fêtes which were to arouse the prim ire of later generations of Puritans.

The activities of churchwardens, and the adornment and rebuilding of parish churches, were probably stimulated by the discharge of parochial liabilities by rising rural elites of yeomen and entrepreneurs – well-to-do tenant farmers, clothiers and craftsmen. Better educated, with a firmer grasp of the doctrines and narratives underlying images painted on the glass, stone and woodwork of their churches, they may have been an important formative influence on the conduct and outlook of parish priests. Nevertheless, it is likely that the latter's calibre was generally higher in the larger towns and more prosperous lowland regions. Lucrative job prospects and pickings may have attracted the better-educated into urban curacies. Burgesses whose gilds often centred their ceremonial activities on a parish church, may have pushed up clerical standards. Margery Kempe's autobiography (cf. pp. 361 ff) shows the impressive grasp of religion which could be gained by the illiterate daughter of a leading burgess in a Norfolk port. She derived immense devotional stimulus from the liturgy and sermons, and gives glimpses of how the life of parochial communities centred on town churches, interest focusing on solemn feast-day processions and visiting preachers, and opinions dividing about her eccentric devotional behaviour and visions. Her book provides a unique personal testimony about the rich variety of religious experience in early fifteenth-century England. Our awareness of intellectually divergent devotional trends in the period raises the question of how parish priests responded to the demand for different kinds of religious experience. Our comparative ignorance about them makes it difficult to be certain whether they were moulding parochial opinion to a sharper, better defined image of Christ, or clung to the magic of their rites and to bucolic pleasures.

Devotional trends

The organisational deficiencies of the later medieval Church are more apparent than its virtues: contemporary literary invectives and judicial accusations have left a strong impression of shortcomings and backslidings. Such evidence is not very enlightening about the characteristics of religious feeling and observance, and must be balanced by the evidence of devotional literature. This suggests that the nature of religious perception in the governing elites was undergoing profound changes, which were eventually to make them receptive to doctrinal change and ecclesiastical reform. The characteristic secular culture had been one whose concepts were founded on those oral traditions and visual images which the literate clergy had sanctioned. But the spread of literacy among well-to-do layfolk was to stimulate the evolution of a secular elite whose perception of a numinous pattern in the world sprung not from coincidental associations of ideas and things, but from the logic of word patterns, particularly from constructions based on the Word of God, the Bible.

By the fourteenth century it was customary to instruct noble boys (and probably girls) in Latin grammar, as well as in the vernacular. Thomas lord Berkeley (d.1361) considered that his guests would be capable of reading French, for he had verses from the Revelation of St John the Divine translated into it by his chaplain, John Trevisa, and painted on the roof timbers of his chapel in Berkeley Castle, where they can still be seen. At the age of five, in 1360, Edward III's youngest son, Thomas (the future duke of Gloucester), had an instructor in grammar. The earl of Suffolk, in his will of 1415, left his son a 'little primer' (elementary prayer book). The use of sacred and related texts in education quickened noble religious sensibilities. From the fourteenth century onwards there survive in profusion not only the heavy, magnificent service books laid open for use in the chapels of noble households, but books of the canonical hours, psalters (psalm collections), breviaries, and collections of tracts and sermons compiled for the individual use of the master or mistress, to be held and read during services or in the privacy of chambers. A few nobles even essayed devout composition. Sir John Clanvow (d.1391), one of Richard II's

Chamber knights accused by Walsingham of heresy, wrote a homiletic treatise in English.

The literary taste of many devout layfolk (as well as devout monks and secular clerks) was drawn to the collection of some remarkable devotional treatises written in English in the fourteenth century. The authors were contemplatives, writing principally to instruct others who had withdrawn from the active life, on how, through disciplined meditation, to free themselves from the fog of sin and see with what Richard Rolle calls 'the inward eye', the love that Christ has for them. Rolle (d.1349), a Yorkshire hermit, was one of the most popular authors. His *Incendium Amoris* (Fire of Love) reveals him as an intensely human figure, a passionate man not just explaining analytically how he has schooled his desires to a love of Christ, but lyrically extolling the sense of union with the beloved which the contemplative can achieve with Him. Rolle describes the attainment of this state of harmony in terms of intense physical and mental sensations: 'A conscious and incredibly sweet warmth kindled me, and I knew the infusion and understanding of heavenly, spiritual sounds, sounds which pertain to the song of eternal praise, and to the sweetness of unheard melody.'

The Cloud of Unknowing (*c*.1370) is a slighter work by an unknown author. He is concerned to contrast the virtues of the contemplative and active lives, to define those human cravings which hinder the soul's perception of Christ, and show how they can be dispersed. In a remarkable passage, he distinguishes spiritual vision from the pious fraud of belief in physical relevations. There were some who

if they read, or heard it read or spoken about, that men should lift up their hearts unto God, at once they are star-gazing as if they wanted to get past the moon, and listening to hear an angel sing out of heaven. In their mental fantasies they penetrate to the planets, and make a hole in the firmament, and look through! They make a God to their liking, and give him rich clothes, and set him on a throne.

The author's sharp, satirical contrast between magical religion and cerebral spirituality briefly reveals the gulf between the religious rationale of the literate and of the masses, which was eventually to destroy the doctrinal unity of the medieval Church.

A rival to Rolle's works in popularity was the *Scale of Perfection*[9], by Walter Hilton (d.1396), Augustinian canon regular at Thurgarton. Addressing an enclosed anchoress, he gives an admirably clear exposition of how the reader can progressively understand and master the root of self-love in the soul, so that it can experience the burning love of Christ, attaining the state of withdrawal from worldly preoccupations in which 'you seem to see our Lord Jesus in your soul in bodily form as He lived upon earth. You see Him taken by the Jews and bound as a thief, beaten and despised, scourged and condemned to death.' Such vivid imaginative perceptions are characteristic of the contemplatives. Rolle felt the sensation of heat; the author of the *Cloud*'s temporal preoccupations are felt as a deadening lump: the vision of aspects of the Passion are common. Yet these are controlled imaginings. The sensations are only seen as valuable and valid in that they are intense realisations of spiritual truths, and it is these truths which the authors are above all anxious to embrace and communicate.

Such themes are also displayed in the *Revelations of Divine Love* by Julian (*c*.1342–*c*.1416), a woman of intellectual power, vivid visual imagination and great sweetness of character, who became famous as an anchoress in a cell attached to a Norwich church. In an age whose preachers were second to none in gloomy anticipation, Julian's serene optimism, her faith in God's purpose and reassurance of His mercy, shine forth. There is an immediacy about her spiritual visions of and communings with Christ, sometimes arresting in its precision and excitement: 'And He showed me more, a little thing, the size of a hazel-nut, on the palm of my hand, round like a ball. I looked at it thoughtfully and wondered, "What is this?" And the answer came, "It is all that is made".' Even more startling is Julian's vision of Christ on the Cross, which has a contemporary visual counterpart, expressing some of the same emotions, in the retable presented to Norwich Cathedral (*c.*1380) by Bishop Despenser and local knights, showing the Passion, Raising from the Dead, and Ascension. Julian, intent on experiencing the pain Christ suffered, minutely anatomises the changing physical effects of His wounds. It is a *tour de force* of realism which parallels the best in Flemish Passion painting of the fifteenth century. In Julian's descriptions, as in such painting, emotion is controlled and informed: the analysis is precise, and leads logically to an appreciation of spiritual truths.

The contemplatives wrote with their fellow solitaries first in mind, men and women living in cells in their regular communities, or in remote hermitages. The finest collections of contemplative literature were probably in the monastic libraries of the few Orders which especially stressed meditative discipline and study, such as the libraries of the London Charterhouse founded in 1347 by the professional soldier Sir Walter Manny, and the Bridgettine house founded by Henry V on the banks of the Thames at Syon. But the contemplatives also had a wide appeal to those engaged in the 'active' life, such as ecclesiastical administrators who were *jurisperiti*, servants of kings and nobles, pluralists and absentees, respect for whose burden of authority was insistently enjoined by the authors. Lay gentlefolk were attracted to collect and study their works too. In fact the ideals of the contemplatives challenged those prevalent in the active life, which prescribed, for noble clerks and laymen, attention to a variety of business skills and a hierarchical display of splendour. But the devout man, according to Rolle,

takes no more pleasure in sitting next to a king than to a pauper, because he is considering, not the riches and dignities of men generally, but the life and merits of each one singly. He does not regard it as important that he should glitter with gold or be attended by a huge retinue, or go about in episcopal purple, or wear a mitre.

Henry VI and Thomas More were two laymen who tried to combine the contemplative and active lives. Henry's private appearance showed a humility which seemed to betray the ideals of hierarchy: 'It is well known that from his youth up he always wore round-toed shoes and boots like a farmer's. He also customarily wore a long gown with a rolled hood like a townsman.' Henry thus abased himself to the level of a peasant or bourgeois, in the spirit preached by Rolle. Nevertheless, he preserved the public image of kingship. In 1445 he received French envoys 'dressed in a long robe of cloth of gold, trimmed with marten and sable'. In an illustration to the book of poems and romances presented by the earl of Shrewsbury to his queen, Margaret of Anjou in that year, Henry sits enthroned at Court, wearing a blue, ermine-trimmed robe over gold and purple vestments. Thomas More too tried to combine the two sets of values, active and contemplative: 'And albeit outwardly he appeared honourable like one of his calling, yet inwardly he no such vanities esteeming, secretly next his body wore a shirt of hair.'

Some of the prelates absorbed in worldly avocations have left memorials hinting at an inner spiritual awareness. For instance, in Canterbury Cathedral, the effigy of Archbisop Chichele displays his mitre and ceremonial robes in a way Rolle might have despised, between pillars adorned with richly canopied figures of saints, and beneath a frieze of angels holding heraldic shields. The rich colour-scheme – reds, blues and greens dominated by gilding – has been protected and maintained by the fellows of his Oxford foundation, All Souls. But beneath Chichele's honourable image, proclaiming the dignity of his office, is one of a naked, rotting corpse, dissolving into dust but for hope of the Resurrection. The contrast provided a forceful sermon for pilgrims, still perhaps full of the worldly delights of their journey, processing to St Thomas. There are about twenty such corpse images, under conventional effigies, of fifteenth-century prelates. The ugliness of physical decay had become a popular moralising theme in the later fourteenth century. Thomas Wimbledon dwelt on it with particular impact in the famous sermon he preached at Paul's Cross in 1387, and Archbishop Arundel, in his will of 1414, ordered a lowly burial for his 'foetid and putrid cadaver'. The theme is relevant to the contemplatives' attempts to subordinate those material desires, that self-love centred in the body, which obscured the rays of spiritual vision.

Contemplative writings had a particular appeal to the ecclesiastical establishment because they proposed a rational means of salvation by interior reformation, without threatening the doctrine or organisation of the Church. Prelates could heartily approve the contemplatives' fierce rejection of heresy or criticism of the active life as distractions from the soul's search for God. They could draw personal consolation and inspiration from the contemplatives' assurance that spiritual attainments could be grasped, not by a withdrawal from the world to a life of corporate monastic worship, but by learning techniques for mental isolation.

The contemplative, like the credulous worshipper of saintly cults, reverenced the images abounding in later medieval churches. Julian's visions reflect the crucifixions carved over chancel screens and painted on their panels. But such images, abundant and lovingly carved, only *seem* to indicate cultural strength and unity in the Church, for they were being used in two divergent ways. On the one hand there was the mass of illiterate people who confused spiritual virtues with physical talismans. Erasmus was to pour scorn on their magical beliefs: 'I laugh at the folly of my companion who chose rather to venture his salvation upon a skin of parchment than upon the amendment of his life.' Such traditional attitudes were to be tenacious, not only among the illiterate, as the fame of Elizabeth Barton, 'the nun of Kent' in the 1520s and 1530s shows. A servant in the household of Archbishop Warham's steward at Aldington, in 1525 she gained a local reputation as a visionary, and after an impressive public seizure was restored to normality while kneeling before an image of Our Lady, in the chapel of Court-le-Street. After she was placed in the convent of St Sepulchre's, Canterbury, her revelations acquired a dangerous political edge, discrediting Henry VIII's divorce policies. In July 1533 she and her spiritual directors were arrested, and her books and writings were examined. John Halcote, abbot of Hyde, preached at Paul's Cross in November, attempting to expose her as a pious fraud. For instance, he said that a letter to Elizabeth from St Mary Magdalene, kept as a solemn relic in Canterbury, was a forgery, and that a monk of St Augustine's had confessed 'the limning of these golden words, Jhesus Maria, which be written about the letter'. The nun and her accomplices were to be attainted and executed at Tyburn in 1534.

In simple souls inclined to nervous disorders, like Elizabeth Barton or, in an earlier generation, Margery Kempe, the visions of contemplatives may have enhanced belief in the physical properties of saints and helped to induce ecstatic trances. But one of the principal objectives of the contemplative writers had been to guard against such dangerous effusions by providing a sensible methodology. They used the cult images as a starting-point for an essentially literate analysis of their souls' relationship with the creator. Their self-reliant rationalism has more akin to the thought processes of Erasmus than to the vapourings of these two tiresome, unfortunate women. At the level of the well-educated, the popularity of contemplative writers is a token of devotional sophistication which, though drawing inspiration from the forms of traditional rituals and cults, used them in a radically different way.

The religious life of Margery Kempe

Margery Brunham was born *c*.1373 and married *c*.1394 John Kempe, recently admitted burgess of Lynn. In the 1430s she dictated to amanuenses an autobiography concerned with her religious experiences, including her visions and the tribulations she endured as a result of her public manifestations of devotion. Margery's impassioned words graphically convey the development of her sense of sin, and of her conviction that God had shown her especial grace: 'This little treatise shall treat somewhat in part of His [Christ's] wonderful works, how mercifully, how benignly and how charitably He moved and stirred a sinful caitiff unto His love.' She was careful to make the point that she had some kind of ecclesiastical sanction for writing about spiritual matters, an eccentric female occupation. 'Worthy and worshipful clerks' had averred that 'this creature [*Margery*] was inspired with the Holy Ghost, and bade her that she should have them written down and make a book of her feelings and revelations'.

According to her account, as a young woman she had been wilful and high-spirited, proud of her lineage, vain and pretty, strongly attracted physically to her husband and tempted to commit adultery. She casually mentions having had fourteen children. But she experienced a breakdown which necessitated her being placed for some time under restraint:

Anon, for the dread she had of damnation on the one side, and his [*her confessor's*] *sharp reproving of her on the other side, this creature went out of her mind and was wondrously vexed and laboured with spirits for half a year, eight weeks and odd days. . . . And in this time, she saw, as she thought, devils . . . sometimes ramping at her, sometimes threatening her, pulling her and hauling her . . .*

A few years later, after she had resumed her imperious and ostentatious worldly life, Margery experienced conversion. She started to do harsh penance for her sins, developed an interior spiritual life of dialogue with Christ, and desired ardently to lead a celibate life. After narrowly escaping from a fall of masonry in church she persuaded her husband John to accompany her on a summer tour of Yorkshire shrines. When they were going from York to St John's tomb at Bridlington 'in right hot weather', she carrying a bottle of beer and John a cake in his bosom, his desire was met with fervent revulsion, and he at length agreed to let her live in chastity. They went on pilgrimage to Canterbury, where Margery provoked popular disturbance by the sort of display which was to bring her notoriety. She would interrupt liturgies and sermons by weeping and 'roaring' with intensity of emotion, and compounded these irritating habits by reproving swearing, and telling moral tales, especially aimed at wicked, presumptuous priests. All this was not just irritating, it was in the highest degree imprudent at a time when people were alarmed about the spread of Wycliffite heresies, whose adherents often made critical remarks like some of hers. In Canterbury Cathedral, after her sobbing had angered pilgrims, her readiness to cite Scripture to the monks who then questioned her intensified hostile reactions:

Then she went out of the monastery, they following and crying upon her: 'Thou shalt be burnt, false Lollard. Here is a cartful of thorns ready for thee, and a tun [*barrel*] *to burn thee with. And the creature stood outside the gates of Canterbury . . . many people wondering at her. Then said the people: 'Take and burn her*[10].

Uplifted by this experience of the sort of revilement Christ had suffered, she determined at His bidding to wear white raiment, and to go on pilgrimage to Rome, Jerusalem and Compostella. First she sought audience with Philip Repingdon, bishop of Lincoln, who in his Oxford youth had been a distinguished and enthusiastic disciple of Wycliffe. Margery wished him to receive her oath of chastity, to bestow on her its symbols, a ring and cloak, and to license her white raiment. When he arrived, having heard that she had been waiting three weeks, he immediately summoned her 'and said he had long desired to speak with her, and he was right glad of her coming'. She requested a private interview, told him about her meditations, and received his assent to her requests. The bishop invited her to dinner, feeding the poor before he ate, at which sight 'this creature was stirred to high devotion'. But his clerks asked Margery 'hard questions', and after dinner Repingdon told her in his chamber that his counsel would not allow him to profess her in such singular clothing. But Christ boosted her morale, telling her, 'Daughter, say to the bishop that he dreadeth more the shames of the world than the perfect love of God'. Repingdon took this divine reproof in good part, directed Margery to petition Archbishop Arundel of Canterbury, and gave her 26*s* 8*d* to buy clothing and pray for him. In his garden at Lambeth the archbishop proved sympathetic, finding no fault in her revelations and granting without fees her petitions to choose her confessor and receive communion every Sunday. He listened with restraint to her strictures on his servants: 'Full benignly and meekly he suffered her to speak her intent, and gave her a fair answer, she supposing it [the conduct of his household] would then be better. And so their dalliance contined till stars appeared in the firmament. Then she took her leave and her husband also.'

In 1414 Margery left her long-suffering husband to go on pilgrimage to the Holy Land, sailing in a party of pilgrims from Yarmouth to Zierikzee, then travelling to Constance. There her companions (including her maidservant) abandoned her, infuriated 'because she wept so much and spoke always of the love and goodness of Our Lord, as much at the table as in other places'. She was lucky to find an aged Devonian willing to guide her over the Alps, despite his fear of being robbed of his jacket. She met up safely with her former companions at

Bologna, who grudgingly received her on condition that she made merry at table. At Venice they displayed an unaccustomed readiness to embark in whichever ship she favoured, but on their return there from Jerusalem (where she acquired a staff made from Moses's rod) abandoned her again with alacrity. In 1415, after a penurious stay in Rome, she made her way to Middelburg and took ship to Yarmouth.

Her thirst for pilgrimages was not completely slaked. She arrived *c*.1417 at Bristol, to seek a passage to the shrine of St James at Compostella in Castile. Her odd behaviour in church produced the usual mixed reactions. Summoned to appear before the bishop of Worcester (Thomas Peverel?), she was shocked by the attire of his men in the hall, 'all slashed and pointed in their clothes'. But the bishop proved kind, hailing her familiarly as John Brunham's daughter from Lynn, requesting her to eat with him, and asking for her prayers. Her embarkation for Spain was fraught with her fellow pilgrims' misgivings: 'It was told to her that, if they had any tempest, they would cast her into the sea, for they said it would be because of her.' Fortunately, the voyages were calm, but Margery brought trouble on herself on the way back to Lynn. In a church in Leicester, which had been the first urban centre of Lollardy, she was inwardly stirred by the sight of a crucifix: 'Then the fire of love kindled so eagerly in her that . . . it caused her to break out with a loud voice and cry marvellously, and weep and sob so hideously that many a man and woman wondered on her therefor.' Her conduct was reported to the mayor, who, acting according to his obligation under a statute of 1414 to arrest suspected heretics, had her detained. There the steward of Leicester sought to discover whether she understood Latin (which she did not) and then, she says, tried to seduce her. An ecclesiastical commission, headed by the abbot of Leicester, pronounced her orthodox and treated her kindly, but the mayor remained suspicious: 'I will know why thou goest in white clothes, for I trow [believe] thou art come hither to have away our wives from us, and lead them with thee.'

Her alarming experiences in Leicester did not deter Margery completely from her wanderings: she returned to York, to make her devotions at the tomb of St William in the Minster. After ignoring a warning against prolonging her stay from a friendly cleric, she was examined by clerics and brought before the archbishop of York[11] at Cawood, accused of heresy by his officials. After his questions they said

'We know well that she can say the articles of the Faith, but we will not suffer her to dwell amongst us, for the people have great faith in her dalliance, and peradventure she might pervert some of them.' Then the archbishop said to her, 'I am evil informed of thee. I hear it said that thou art a right wicked woman.' And she answered back, 'I also hear it said that ye are a wicked man.' . . . Then, anon, the archbishop said, 'Where shall I get a man who might lead this woman away from me?'

Immediately there started up many young men and every one of them said, 'My lord, I will go with her.' The archbishop answered, 'Ye be too young. I will not have you.' Then a good man of the archbishop's household asked his lord what he would give him if he should lead her. The archbishop proffered him five shillings, and the man asked a noble [6s 8d]. *The archbishop answering said, 'I will not spend so much on her body.' 'Yes, good sir,' said the creature* [*Margery*], *'Our Lord shall reward you right well in return.' Then the archbishop said to the man, 'See, here is five shillings, and lead her fast out of this country.'*

The long-suffering prelate was not yet to be rid of her, for on her way through Holderness, a lordship of Henry VI's uncle Bedford, she was arrested by ducal yeomen and escorted back to archiepiscopal custody, on the way reviled, as a result of her reputation as a Lollard, by women who ran out of their houses shaking distaffs.

For most of the rest of her life, Margery seems to have remained in Lynn. She was penitently concerned to attend to the physical needs of her husband (died *c.*1430), who was senile and incontinent. She was also concerned about her son, 'a tall young man' apprenticed to a burgess of Lynn, in whose service he went overseas. This son took after his mother when young by wearing vain clothes and talking of dalliance. Despite her lengthy exhortations, he fell into the sin of lechery. 'Soon afterwards, his colour changed, his face waxed full of weals and blubbers as if he were a leper.' Consequently his master discharged him. The young man repented his mode of life, went on business to Danzig, married and resided there, and returned to Lynn a changed man. After his death Margery made a hazardous journey with his widow to Danzig.

The autobiography gives unique insights into social mentality. It echoes the gossip and backbiting of the bourgeoisie of an important Norfolk port, and gives glimpses of its physical environment. There was its boisterous, changeable weather, as when one day in 1421 the inhabitants rushed in panic to find the Guildhall on fire, with sparks in the bright and clear air threatening the nearby church of St Margaret. The agitated Margery looked up at sparks drifting into the choir: three 'worshipful' men with snow on their clothes came in to reassure her: 'Margery, God hath wrought great grace for us, and sent us a fair snow to quench the fire with.' There were the warehouses stored with stockfish (dried cod and herring), which rats attacked, and the servants boiling the stockfish for the table:

Christ to Margery: *'Thou shalt be eaten and gnawed by the people of the world as any rat gnaweth stockfish.'*

'Daughter, thou art obedient to My will, and cleavest as sore to Me as the skin of a stockfish cleaveth to a man's hand when it is seethed.'

But Margery feared the treacherous North Sea: her spiritual imagery draws on domestic and rural sights and sounds. Christ appears to her on the Cross 'fuller of wounds than ever was a dove-house of holes' and the Holy Ghost sounds like a bellows, a dove, a robin.

Margery makes clear that she had, though married, independent status and wealth in Lynn society. She put down her husband's complaint of her pride by reminding him that her father had been mayor of the town and alderman of its Trinity Gild. 'And therefore she would keep the worship of her kindred whatever any man said.' This she did by buying fine attire. She invested in setting up brewing and milling businesses, perhaps because John was not making enough money to maintain their household in the desired style – on one occasion he requested her to settle his debts. But her businesses failed, and by the time she returned from Middelburg she had fallen into debt, evoking condemnation from Lynn folk who remembered her past extravagance. Much of the animus against her may have arisen from her failure in her secular roles, the mismanagement of her inheritance and neglect of housekeeping.

Margery's inability to settle down to and cope successfully with the roles demanded of her by a censorious, parochial society may have induced her extreme and nervous reactions. The transcending world of spiritual experience offered an escape route, even if it was one which involved her in an agonising psychological struggle, one whose completeness was sometimes threatened, as by her sexual fantasies. In her new spiritual life, the drama of rejection could be constantly re-enacted, but now with a firm inner conviction of being justified. Assurance could be sought throughout the realm from the holy and the exalted. In the alleged conversational fragments she reproduces she appears as addressing bishops on equal terms, an egalitarianism surely springing from her spiritual convictions rather than her pride in lineage. A factor encouraging social mixture and geographical mobility was the interest, which seized all ranks, in discovering spiritual manifestations. There was the friar whom Margery heard preaching in St James's chapel-yard at Lynn: 'Some men, if they thought he would preach in the country, they would go with him or else follow him from town to town, such great delight had they to hear him.' Margery implied that she was a phenomenon of widespread interest. An English priest she met in Rome had heard of her before setting out. An English anchorite despaired of her on hearing reports from abroad. At Leicester a man of Boston said she was reputed holy in his town.

A religious activity promoting geographical mobility and social mixing was the pilgrimage. Her evidence confirms the complaints of moralists about the worldly spirit in which pilgrims often travelled. Indeed, there are hints that the company in which she set out for Jerusalem were shocked at her attempts to upset this atmosphere. For the pilgrimage was one undertaking in which large numbers of men and women could to some extent excitingly liberate themselves from the narrowly domiciled, hierarchically regulated lives most of them led. These circumstances made it essential for companies of pilgrims to abide by their own internal rules, which Margery persistently broke. She had freed herself from parochial and hierarchical restrictions by entering a universal spiritual world, one in which her public effusions were appreciated by Italians and Palestinians, but regarded as bad form by her reticent, ceremonious compatriots.

Most of our knowledge of attempts by the laity to combine the active and contemplative life comes from noble examples: Margery is an important exception. She was unerringly orthodox in belief and deferred to the directions of bishops and confessors. She felt fulfilled within the Church, receiving inspiration from sermons, the celebration of feasts, shrines, images, devout communings with often concerned and long-suffering priests and friars, who earned her respect and admiration. It is a tribute to the instruction imparted by the urban clergy that Margery, who had no Latin, gained an excellent grasp of the Gospels and tenets of the Faith. One great source of inspiration was mystical writing: she consulted Julian at Norwich, and naïvely rivalled St Bridget of Sweden in intimacy with Christ. Despite her spiritual afflictions, Margery's religious experience was a joyful one. She was not obsessed with fear of death and torments to her soul: her references to pestilence are casual.

Though Margery, in common with Lollards, reproved swearing, and behaved in a conspicuously puritanical way, she could not identify with a heresy which rejected her cults of the Passion, the Virgin and saints, and which repudiated the priestly authority which, despite her pertness, she reverenced. But her ostentatious devoutness caused many to suspect her of heresy. Her book suggests that lesser officials and sections of the populace were quick to react to such suspicions, and that some of the bishops treated importunate denunciations with tolerant scepticism. She gives the impression that different sorts of officials were working with remarkable efficiency to enforce legislation against heresy. The impression may derive from the forceful reactions which her singularity provoked, touching raw nerves of the elites. Here was a woman who stepped out of accustomed roles, threatening to become a source of subversive authority, especially among her sex, in a society in which the late fourteenth-century ideological and physical threats to the established order were well remembered.

Margery was accepted by many clerics and laymen as a shining example of orthodox devotion. Nevertheless, in her impassioned ramblings, her attempts at self-analysis, one can discern a stage in the evolution of attitudes which were basic to those who challenged the authority and doctrines of the Church in the later Middle Ages and the sixteenth century. Margery's inner spiritual perception became so brightly illuminated that the promptings she received from her 'voices' were more real and urgent than those of ecclesiastics. They induced her to ask the latter to approve her singular mode of life and comforted her after rejection. When a confessor refused her requests, Margery obeyed, but remained convinced that he was wrong. She resolved incipient conflicts according to her psychological needs, representing rejection and revilement as a continuous expiation, a minor *via dolorosa* whose every burden became glorious. The more intellectually robust were to take the even more lonely path of challenging orthodoxy. Margery's incoherent descriptions of her dilemmas are not to be dismissed as the half-baked imitations of a quirky and pretentious woman. Her book is an important document illustrating part of the nature of the spiritual crisis which was to engulf western Christendom. The tortuousness of her individual solution shows why others turned to more radical divisive ones.

John Wycliffe and Lollardy

John Wycliffe (*c*.1330–84) was a junior fellow of Merton College, Oxford, in 1356. By 1372 he had incepted doctor of divinity, and in the 1370s he crowned his reputation as a philosopher, becoming the leading Oxford theological authority. Archbishop Arundel, later a bitter opponent of his beliefs, is alleged to have remarked in 1407 that 'Wycliffe . . . was a great clerk and many men held him a perfect liver'. In his prolific lectures and treatises, Wycliffe raised uncomfortable fundamental questions about the nature of the Church and the significance of Christian worship. His determination to relate his theological questions to the moral, political and social problems agitating sections of the governing groups stimulated academic adulation and, outside Oxford, a *frisson* of interest among devout and anticlerical courtiers and royal councillors. Probably shortly after receiving his doctorate, Wycliffe was retained by the Crown. He was to enjoy the patronage and protection of Joan, widow of Edward prince of Wales (d.1376), and of the prince's brother John of Gaunt, who may have instigated his anticlerical sermons in London in the autumn of 1376, designed to turn opinion against Bishop Wykeham (see p. 174).

Wycliffe's noble patrons were apparently slow to grasp the fundamental subversiveness of his arguments. This may have been partly because of the technical form in which some of them were couched, partly because monastic accusations against him could be attributed to malice, and partly because it seems to have been only during the last few years of his life (1381–4), when he was living in rustication, that he elaborated some of his heresies. Because his treatises were based partly on lectures, and are not always precisely datable, it has been difficult for scholars to establish the exact sequence by which the controversial don evolved into the heresiach with a renovating vision of the Christian message. Among his most important works, written in the 1370s, were *On Divine Dominion* and *On Civil Dominion*. These were followed by *On the Eucharist* and a trilogy, *On Simony*, *On Apostasy* and *On Blasphemy*.

Wycliffe stressed God's absolute knowledge and power: He alone could confer the grace necessary for salvation. The Church was not a hierarchy in which laity was subordinate to clergy, nor was it the community of all true believers: 'The holy catholic church, i.e. the universal church, is the body of all the predestined, past, present and future.' Prayers for souls were useless, and the authority of popes and priests, who might not be among the elect, was not divinely conferred but the result of historical accident. The only certain source of authority was the revealed Word of God, the Bible, on the study of which, guided by the precepts of the fathers and the godly, the laity should wholly base their beliefs and conduct. Priests were no more spiritual mediators between God and mankind than they were doctrinal ones. The consecrated elements were not miraculously transformed by a priestly operation, but gained a spiritual as well as a material dimension, dependent on the recipient's state of grace. Clerical functions could be performed by laymen in that state. The most important ones were to preach, to expound Christ's precepts, and to set an example of copying them by living frugally. Secular rulers had a duty to ensure that the Christian people were well taught and led, stripping the clergy of their fraudulently acquired corrosive wealth.

The elaboration of these views was to provoke violent clerical reactions, gradually all but submerging rapturous academic discipleship. Since there was no papal inquisition in England, action to suppress Wycliffe's views depended on the initiative and vigour of particular critics and ecclesiastical authorities. As a result of lobbying at the *curia* by his old Benedictine opponents, Gregory XI promulgated in 1377 bulls condemning nineteen of his propositions as heretical. His teaching on dominion and grace, and questioning of papal and episcopal jurisdiction were singled out. But the papal impulse against Wycliffe soon faded as a result of the Great Schism, and the English bishops, hampered by the favour Wycliffe enjoyed at Court, and by Archbishop Sudbury's nerveless leadership, remained dumb dogs. Not until 1382 did Wycliffe's Oxford opponents receive firm backing from the hierarchy. William Courtenay then succeeded as archbishop of Canterbury: an old opponent of Gaunt and Wycliffe, he was not the man to be deterred from doing his duty. Moreover, the Peasants' Revolt is likely to have produced a climate of opinion more favourable to the suppression of subversive opinion. Monastic writers may not have been alone in placing the blame for the rising partly on incitement by Wycliffite preachers. In fact the first indisputable evidence for adhesion to Wycliffe's views at a popular level dates from 1382. His adherents soon became known as 'Lollards'. The word may derive from the Dutch *lollaerd* – mumbler of prayers. Hostile writers punned on the English 'loller', loafer, and the Latin *lolia*, tares.

In May 1382, at a synod held in the London Blackfriars, Courtenay procured the condemnation of ten of Wycliffe's propositions as heretical and of fourteen as erroneous. In June, by royal letters patent, the archbishop and his suffragans were licensed to arrest and imprison heretics without invoking the secular power. He proceeded to prosecute in support of the Oxford opponents of the Wycliffites. In November convocation met at Oxford and set up a committee to investigate the teaching of all senior members of the university. Academic Wycliffites were thus compelled to recant, though their master, probably by grace of his secular patrons, was unmolested in his retirement at Lutterworth, where he plied his pen busily and unrepentantly till his death.

Some of his views continued to have sympathisers at the Courts of Richard II and Henry IV: discussion of them was not entirely snuffed out in academic circles. At a synod held at Oxford in 1407, Archbishop Arundel presented thirteen constitutions for approval. They condemned unlicensed preaching, false doctrines on the sacraments, the reading or teaching of Wycliffe's works (except those approved by a committee to be set up to examine them), and unauthorised translations of the Bible. Masters of Oxford halls and colleges were to hold regular inquiries into the opinions of their residents. Such measures, among other factors, stifled the vigour of Lollardy as an academic and gentlemanly heresy, but were less effective at a popular level. There are, however, doubts about the nature of the connections between popular heresy and Wycliffe, about the extent to which it was organised as a separate church with clearly defined, uniform beliefs and practices, and to which its scattered cells retained into the early sixteenth century continuity and conformity of worship.

There are a number of reasons for these doubts. Wycliffe was a theologian writing primarily to convince fellow scholars, not a popular proselytiser. His works, which the authorities were to destroy diligently, were not widely known among Lollards. The texts of some of them survive only because Czech followers of Hus journeyed to England to make copies. Archiepiscopal persecution prevented the development of a Wycliffite school of writers at Oxford. The Lollard sect was to be composed mainly of men and women whose lack of literary education, and need to labour at a craft or in farming, deprived them of the ability or leisure to develop speculative pursuits. The persecutions endured by Lollards disinclined them, when able, to commit to paper more than the bare pastoral necessities: possession of MSS by artisans was to be regarded as suspicious. Much of the evidence for the continued existence of Lollardy comes from records of the examination and condemnation of suspects in diocesan archives[12], from cryptic royal administrative orders and the hearsay of chroniclers.

Margery Kempe's book illustrates how inaccurate informed as well as popular opinion could be about the identity of Lollards. Though in the 1380s and 1390s there had been 'hooded knights' in the Household notorious for remaining covered in the presence of the Host, it is unlikely that in later decades the majority of Lollards would have behaved with Margery's reckless ostentation. 'Lollard' had become a term of vague popular abuse covering a multitude of sins and some uncongenial virtues. Suspected Lollards were often skilful at concealing their opinions, habits and connections from examining officials. The latter, through zeal and exasperation, were often careless in distinguishing whether offences stemmed from sheer hatred of clergy, ignorance and obtuse contempt for canonical requirements or genuine sectarian beliefs. The nature of Lollardy can be only dimly perceived, hidden through the dark glass of its adherents' concealments and the distorting lens of hostile reports.

Wycliffe seems to have hoped that his reformation would be effected with what turned out to be the ephemeral support of nobility and Crown. He may not have realised that the brash confidence displayed by prosperous craftsmen and labourers and the solid introversion characteristic of burgeoning weaving communities would provide fruitful soil for his message. Though the essence of his writings was theological, from them could be distilled a plain man's brand of Christianity whose appeal was to last into the 1530s, when it merged with continental streams of reform. The distillation was accomplished by a shadowy, mainly anonymous group of his disciples. They made two translations of the Bible from Latin to English. The first (in which Wycliffe's Oxford adherent Nicholas Hereford had a hand) was highly literal, intended presumably to be used alongside the Vulgate text. The second, completed in 1396, was more free-ranging. This, the 'Lollard Bible' was widely read in the fifteenth and early sixteenth centuries: over 235 MSS survive, the great majority shorn of the original distinctively Lollard preface. Attempts were also made to supply manuals of instruction: there are many copies of one sermon cycle written mostly by scribes from the East Midlands.

Early evidence for the effects of Wycliffite popular preaching and pastoral work was the existence of Lollard communities in Leicester in 1382 and Northampton in 1389. Heresy soon became well-established in the Midlands (e.g. in Coventry), in Bristol and the adjacent regions to the north, bordering the Welsh Marches, and in London. The example of John Walcote shows how heresy spread, socially and geographically. A shepherd of Hasleton, he was prosecuted in the diocese of Worcester in 1425. He admitted that he had been reputed a heretic for over ten years, not only at Hasleton, but in London, Bristol, Northampton and elsewhere. He had known many leading Lollards, including William Swinderby (a prominent early preacher at Leicester and elsewhere), John Purvey (Wycliffe's secretary at Lutterworth) and Sir John Oldcastle (see pp. 214–15). Walcote was accused of having said that the Cross and images of the Virgin and saints should not be venerated, and that he would burn them to keep himself warm; that it was better to give alms to the poor than to go on pilgrimage to Canterbury, Walsingham and other shrines. He denied that prayers to saints were efficacious, but apparently accepted the validity of transubstantiation and the priestly office.

A reflection of clerical and royal nervousness at the widespread diffusion of Lollardy and the ineffectiveness of diocesan administrations in dealing with it was the passing of the statute *De Heretico Comburendo* in 1401. This obliged sheriffs and their fellow justices not only to assist bishops' officers in hunting down and arresting suspects, but to search them out on their own initiative. The statute introduced into England the death penalty for relapsed heretics, to be carried out by royal officers in a peculiarly horrible manner. But Lollards were reluctant to relinquish the political aspirations which had been excited by Wycliffe and his disciples. Since the Crown, especially after the accession of the implacably orthodox Henry V, had turned against them, they turned against the Crown. In 1414 there was the Lollard Revolt (see p. 215). The débâcle revealed how far 'respectable' support had ebbed: by associating Lollardy so clearly with treason, it intensified the drain. The last notable attempt at religious rebellion (anticlerical rather than heretical in tone) was in 1431, when a popular assembly at East Hendred attempted to march on Abingdon Abbey. It was feebly supported and easily suppressed. The political failure of Lollardy, its enforced retreat into secretiveness and purely religious activity, enabled it to survive and eventually flourish as a popular religion. Lollardy had shaken off what had turned out to be a disastrous incubus of political aspirations originating in a particular climate of opinion in Richard II's reign. In the later fifteenth and the sixteenth century, Lollards were to gain confidence and to proselytise as a result of new waves of anticlericalism and of new intellectual movements in the governing groups which were sympathetic to some of their aims. From the 1480s onwards, there was a steady rise in the volume of processes against suspects.

Why did Wycliffe fail to found a courtly rather than a popular reformation? One reason may have been that his views had appealed in ruling circles in the last decades of the fourteenth century, when they had been experiencing a crisis of confidence, but that the appeal declined as the crisis resolved itself. There were no interests in England which had a strong permanent motivation to reform the Church. The Crown already had fairly effective means of putting pressure on papacy and clergy: once the Great Schism had broken out, they were more at a disadvantage. The secular nobility did not need a devout cause in whose name they could curb royal power. Nor were they strongly inclined to destroy clerical wealth, since they already exploited it in many ways, and the cessation of war in 1389 temporarily eased their tax burdens.

Moreover, Wycliffe's theology probably never did have as much appeal in gentle circles as his pleas for an austere practice of the Christian life and his condemnations of clerical vice. Many devout laymen (and, perhaps especially, devout laywomen) were probably repelled by his rejection of cults which provided starting-points for their experience of union with Christ. By the 1400s, after the Peasants' Revolt, the excesses of some heretics and the recurring political uncertainty, the elite was more interested in stability than change. Wycliffe's reformation became an anachronism, the projection of a period of ephemeral restlessness. Nevertheless, his was one of the most influential English minds of the fourteenth century. His tortuous intellectual reconstruction of the Church and Christian life transcended the circumstances of his time, inspiring continental reformers, as well as a budding native sect.

The Reformation

In the 1520s the presses spread the trenchant and absorbing views of Martin Luther and other reformers through Germany and western Christendom with unprecedented speed. Luther evolved an intense personal belief that salvation could not be achieved through men's puny works, but solely through the merits poured out by Christ on those who blindly surrendered their lives to His mercies. God alone, not saints, popes or priests, could freely bestow grace. The papacy, the Orders, the secular clergy, were corrupt and in many respects fraudulent, mulcting and misleading layfolk who sinned in ignorance of Christ's Word, revealed by Scriptures, the sacraments of baptism and eucharist, and honest preaching.

Some of the devout and scholarly in England were eager to plumb this purifying German whirlpool. Their generation was already stirred by the revitalising ways of appreciating Scripture propounded by the 'religious humanists', notably Colet and Erasmus. They sought a new understanding of its precepts by studying the Bible's original language within its historic social and intellectual context, stripping away the traditional accretions of the Latin Vulgate. A circle of devout, reform-minded scholars at Cambridge in the 1520s was influenced by Lutheran doctrines. Luther's insistence on the importance of Scripture and his criticisms of clerical abuses were in general more readily absorbed in England than his theology. For Lollardy, indigenous and easily understood, continued to attract the incorrigibly dissident. Moreover, its liveliness prolonged the traditional revulsion to heresy as treasonable. Before Henry VIII's quarrel with the papacy, English heretics could not hope for the protection of royal kinsfolk, as they could in France under Francis I. If the Tudors had remained fervently Catholic, they would have had to come to terms with a powerful secular impulse to reform and modify the privileges of the Church, an impulse with heretical components. But they would have stood a good chance of maintaining a Catholic polity, by using traditional royal control of the Church to keep the clergy in line, and mobilising that great amorphous body of conservative religious sentiment which was in fact often to exasperate and alarm them.

Henry VIII's personal and political preoccupations were chiefly responsible for putting the Church's authority on a new, highly individual and relatively unstable basis. To some modern eyes it may seem frivolous that a king's original motive for the piecemeal abrogation of papal powers and eventual substitution of a dubious Royal Supremacy (1532–4) had been to procure the annulment of his marriage, and legal union with the undistinguished lady whom he had wooed like a lovesick squire half his age. His passion was indeed a subject for ribald and contemptuous comment – ominously, even among some of his humbler subjects. A king's sexual life was a matter of concern to his lieges: the prosperity of the realm depended on divine approval of his unions (cf. pp. 62, 295). Papal prevarication for nearly three years over a royal divorce suit was a vicious, unwarranted blow to a dynasty that deserved well of the papacy. The king's conscience about intimate sins was bared for prolonged public scrutiny and gossip. Once admitted, his doubts could not be retracted without loss of prestige, and without leaving a permanent query over the succession. Henry unwittingly entered a trap from which he was to find that schism was the only escape route (see pp. 314 ff).

For the rest of his life the Supreme Head was often to display horror at what he defined as heresy, and a reverence for Catholic practices shared by the majority of his subjects. The Act of Six Articles (1539) affirmed transubstantiation, the sufficiency of communion in one kind, the prohibition of marriage by priests, the inviolability of vows of chastity, the validity of private Masses, and expediency of auricular confession. The Act, and the harsh punishments it prescribed for the propagation of contrary opinions, delighted conservative-minded councillors. They were concerned to prevent heretically inclined colleagues and clerics from exploiting the Royal Supremacy as a means of undermining Catholic beliefs. Conservative bishops continued to persecute Lollards, Lutherans and 'sacramentary' heretics, often with the encouragement of king or councillor.

Their alarm was justified. Schism could not but stimulate heresy. To justify the Royal Supremacy to scholars and gentlefolk, and to implant it in the hearts of ignorant, suspicious countryfolk and their likeminded parish priests, Henry relied heavily on religious radicals' sermons, pamphlets, treatises, plays and enforcement of discipline. Hesitantly and suspiciously he patronised theologians less gripped by his 'Caesaropapism' than by the opportunities it gave them to inculcate new views about old truths, which were being constantly thrown up in an enthralling, fast-moving continental debate among Protestants. Henry unwittingly inaugurated a period in which men with revolutionary views about religious beliefs – and, eventually, church government – had access to the antechambers of power.

Henry's dependence on men basically opposed to his Catholicism was enhanced by the surprisingly dynamic view he took of the Royal Supremacy. For him it was no cynical device to enhance royal power and secure the future of the dynasty, but a weighty personal responsibility to define and maintain orthodoxy, and to correct the clergy and educate the people. This royal interest was indeed fitful, constrained by political considerations and, especially in Henry's last years, fear of encouraging religious radicals. Nevertheless, Henrician reforms gave a powerful impetus to the spread of the Erasmian principle that the Christian life should be modelled on knowledge of the Gospel, rather than patterned by traditional rituals. A royal injunction of 1536 ordained that every parson was to provide volumes of the Bible, both in Latin and English, and place them in the choir of the parish church for every man to read. A 1538 injunction condemned pilgrimages as 'superstitious practices'. Cults were attacked by the physical destruction of shrines. In 1539 the first officially approved translation of the Bible into English was published[13].

As was frequently to be the case with measures of religious reform throughout the century, it is unlikely that such re-education was generally effective, owing to the shortage of well-qualified clergy as well as the tenacity of ancient beliefs. But one successful achievement of the Henrician Reformation was the dissolution of the monasteries (1536–40), motivated partly by a desire to increase Crown wealth and lands. As vicar-general Cromwell organised a general visitation of monasteries: in their reports his visitors emphasised the shortcomings and abuses they had found. A bill for the suppression of all those with a clear income of less than £200 p.a., on the grounds of their denizens' 'manifest sin, vicious, carnal and abominable living', easily passed both Houses of parliament (February 1536). Provision was allowed for monks to transfer to other houses, and many houses liable to dissolution were exempted. There was little resistance, except by those who participated in the restorations insisted on by the northern rebels. Thereafter the Crown pursued a piecemeal but seemingly inexorable process of suppression: by the time of the final Act of Dissolution (1539), the bulk of remaining houses, and the friaries, had negotiated their dissolutions with royal commissioners. The ancient principles as well as the current practices of monasticism were out of tune with popular social and religious ideals: it was an age of Livian rather than Benedictine virtue. Positive revulsion as well as normal lack of zeal seems to have been widely present within the Orders. Some ex-religious became notable Protestant ministers. Probably the majority of former monks were granted life pensions. But since they were reduced in value by administrative fees, by liability to assessment for clerical subsidy, and inflation, and were often in arrears, they tended not to provide adequate livelihoods. Many ex-religious consequently made new careers as secular priests.

Ardently conservative landowners were as eager to profit from the downfall of the monks as their radical neighbours: the Dissolution was the achievement of the Henrician Reformation that had lasting general approval. But the religious policies pursued by Edward VI's councillors were to be sharply divisive. There was a grain of truth in the Marian condemnation of Edwardian ecclesiastical legislation as devised by 'a few of singularity', promoting 'amongst us in very short time numbers of divers and strange opinions and diversities of sects' [14]. Inspired by a curious mixture of zeal and self-interest, Edward's Council embarked on reforms embodying the controversial, hitherto heretical doctrines of continental Protestants, yet did not feel strong enough to enforce them by harsh statutory punishments. The 1547 parliament repealed the Act of Six Articles, authorised communion in both kinds, and dissolved colleges, free chapels, chantries and religious gilds ministering to 'blindness and ignorance'. The chantry surveys showed that over the two previous decades many lay patrons had 'resumed' endowments – an indication, as was the acquiescence in their dissolution, of declining attachment to an important aspect of Catholic practice[15]. In 1549 priests were given statutory permission to marry, and parliament sanctioned a Book of Common Prayer, of moderately Protestant character, to replace the hallowed Latin liturgy. The version approved in 1552 gave communion a markedly commemorative instead of a sacrificial character.

Edwardian government used the Church more overtly, and, to some, blatantly, as a limb of secular authority, treating the bishops as royal appointees and divesting some of them, as well as the chantries, of their estates. Concurrently, leaning heavily on the theological advice of Cranmer and distinguished foreign scholars, the Council procured the establishment of an advanced form of Protestant belief as the state religion. But at Edward's death in 1553, this was too recent and tenuous an achievement to have created a coherent, powerful 'Protestant interest' dedicated to fighting for its maintenance. Conversely, it had not generated a strong Catholic 'backlash' for Mary to exploit. Her first parliament only went as far as destroying the Edwardian settlement. Divine service and administration of the sacraments were officially restored to their state at Henry's death. Parliament's ability to influence the operation of the Royal Supremacy, when a weakly-placed ruler was attempting alterations, was demonstrated by its refusal in 1554 to revive anti-heresy laws and the Six Articles Act. Pope Julius III's reluctant concession of *de facto* recognition to lay tenure of former religious lands, not the sole force of the queen's will, secured parliamentary consent later in the year to a restoration of Catholic obedience. Parliament declared the realm's repentance for its schism and supplicated for absolution, for the reception of papal authority, the repeal of anti-papal legislation and the abolition of the Royal Supremacy. The papal legate, Cardinal Reginald Pole, absolved the nation's collective sin (November 1554). Parliamentary humility could not disguise the fact that the estates had bargained stiffly over religious matters which the queen's father would have regarded as his concern.

The revival of the anti-heresy laws gave the settlement teeth. The first executions took place early in 1555. Queen and Privy Council urged bishops, their commissaries, archdeacons, and justices of the peace to secure conformity. Mary even appointed commissions of clerics and laymen on her own authority to deal with this and other ecclesiastical matters, exercising powers supposedly given up with the Supremacy. The task of uprooting Protestantism was facilitated by the imprisonment of some of its leaders, such as Cranmer, Latimer and Ridley (who were executed for their heresies), and the exodus abroad of others. Gentlefolk tended to conform, at least in public. When they did not or maintained private Protestant worship, the silence of magisterial neighbours and deficiencies of diocesan administration often shielded them. Persecution fell heavily on the less well protected, lower down the social scale. Sixty per cent of convicted heretics in the diocese of London whose occupation is known were artisans and craftsmen; 113 were condemned in the diocese's courts and burnt – more than a third of all those who died in the Marian persecutions. The proportion may have been high because the diocese was heavily populated, Protestantism had taken deep root there, and Bishop Bonner and his archdeacons were under the watchful eyes of the Privy Council. The persecution helped to ensure general conformity. But it revealed that in some regions Protestantism had taken a tenacious hold at the lower as well as upper levels of society. The hold may have been strengthened by the making of so many notable and admirable martyrs, who gave their lives purely for religion's sake, without political taint.

Their sufferings (and those of Lollards and other anti-Catholic martyrs) were to be immortalised by John Foxe in a book which proved so popular that it was commonly referred to as *The Book of Martyrs*, rather than by the author's compendious title[16]. Foxe has helped to create the impression that the Marian restoration of Catholicism was negative, not creative. Mary's personal preoccupation with restoring the religion of her youth reinforces the impression[17]. Re-evaluation of Pole's policy as archbishop of Canterbury has led to a greater understanding of positive Catholic aims. His lack of encouragement for a campaign of popular anti-Protestant polemic, and his lack of enthusiasm for the introduction of Jesuits probably stemmed from a desire to stifle that popular debate about sacred truths which Henry had loosed. As a humanist who considered that society should be moulded by elitist excellence, Pole may have considered it imperative to re-educate the leaders of society in Catholic truths, raising the standards of the clergy and providing peers and gentry with gentle instruction and examples of well ordered worship. Catholics considered that it was men of high rank who, through their corrupt self-seeking, had been largely responsible for the recent sectarian excesses.

Values which Pole and his friends hoped to inculcate may be reflected in the biography of Sir Thomas More which Nicholas Harpsfield, archdeacon of Canterbury, was writing towards the end of Mary's reign[18]. As a layman, humanist, lawyer and leading royal servant, More was the one opponent of the Henrician Supremacy whose example might still command general respect. The superb anecdotage available about him provided material for a model of Catholic piety befitting nobleman and bureaucrat, far removed from the conduct exhibited by some of Edward's councillors. Indeed, the attempt to confine discussion of faith and conduct to the gentlefolk, and to teach the commons merely to learn religious obedience, may have had a considerable appeal to the governing groups of the 1550s, who in 1549 had experienced how dangerous the dissemination of reformist opinions among the populace could be.

Since the efforts in Edward's and Mary's reign to alter the established orthodoxy drastically were cut short, they had the effect of making enforcement of a uniform religious belief even more difficult than it had become under Henry. By recalling to conservative gentlefolk their obligations to the Universal Church, Mary laid the foundation for an eventually lively Elizabethan Catholicism. But by driving fervent Protestants into exile, she also unwittingly helped to create Elizabethan Puritanism. Determined to enforce religious change despite a weak political base, Edwardian and Marian governments stressed parliamentary as well as royal authority in ecclesiastical matters. Elizabeth's policy initially followed the same trend. The Act of Supremacy (April 1559) conferred on the Crown 'by authority of this present Parliament' perpetual powers of visitation and correction over the ecclesiastical estate – a somewhat narrowly defined prerogative. In deference to contemporary opinion about female inferiority, the queen was not entitled Supreme Head in the Act, but 'supreme governor of this realm . . . as well in all spiritual and ecclesiastical things or causes as temporal'.

The Act abolished papal jurisdiction, repealing the Marian statutes which had recognised it, and reviving Henrician anti-papal legislation. An Act of Uniformity prescribed the 1552 Book of Common Prayer, but, to the dismay of many Marian exiles, insisted on the more 'backward' use of ornaments and ceremonies in the 1549 version. Yet the optimistic boldness of the settlement generally reflected their pressure, effective since Elizabeth was highly dependent on them to implement a settlement reflecting her deep anti-Catholic convictions. As refugees in Germany and Switzerland, English Protestants had been exposed to the full blast of rising Calvinism. Controversies over aspects of it in the English congregation at Frankfurt foreshadowed contentions in the Elizabethan Church. Some at Frankfurt wished to adhere to the 1552 Prayer Book, others agitated for the new discipline. In the *Institutes of Christian Religion*[19], Calvin had developed the themes of the majesty and inscrutability of God on an impressive

Scriptural basis. Faith in Christ was the mark of those elected to salvation. Faith was nurtured above all by the Word of God, and commemorated by frequent celebration of the Lord's Supper, in which Christ was spiritually but not corporeally present. Secular government, Calvin believed, had been ordained by God, and the civil magistrates had a duty to maintain the Christian life. But Church government should be based, in line with early Christian principles, on the authority of presbyteries, with a ministry of pastors, teachers, deacons and colleges of elders, exercised particularly in synods, occasions for exhortation, brotherly admonition and excommunication.

Elizabeth never had the least sympathy with Calvinist schemes for ecclesiastical reorganisation, which threatened her prerogative. She remained in many ways a religious conservative, believing in a form of Real Presence, and reverencing the priestly office. But since the Marian bishops were singularly defiant, accepting deprivation rather than subscribing the Oath of Supremacy, she had to fill twenty-five bishoprics, mainly with former exiles. Many of them, and the ministers they promoted, were inclined to Calvinist beliefs, at least puritanically abhorring prescribed ceremonies, vestments, and parts of the liturgy as remnants of popery. Her first archbishop, Matthew Parker (not a former exile) wrote shortly before his death in 1575 to Burghley: 'Does your lordship think that I care either for cap, tippet or surplice, or wafer-bread, or any such? But the laws so established, I esteem them.'

Consciousness of the magnitude of the task of conversion, as well as reverence for royal authority, probably induced many Protestants to tolerate and uphold distasteful prescriptions. For they were aware of being a handful of enlightened ministers in the 'superstitious' gloom. Catholic practices remained widespread. In 1569 the vicar of Findon (also the schoolmaster) was not alone among the Sussex parish priests in teaching Catholic beliefs. In 1628 Sir Benjamin Rudyerd described Wales and the North as scarcely Christian in belief: 'The prayers of the common people are more like spells and charms than devotions.'

Elizabethan efforts to spread a 'popular reformation' were handicapped by defects in the Church's organisation and personnel, some of ancient provenance, others the result of recent religious and social changes. In the 1560s there was a shortage of well-qualified clerics. There had been a falling-off in recruitment since the 1540s, due to the decline in the prestige of the priestly office, and of incomes from benefices whose tithes were commuted, as a result of inflation. Lay impropriators who held rectories formerly appropriated to religious houses often failed to make sufficient financial provision for vicars. Edward Dering, preaching before the queen in 1570, declared benefices to be 'defiled with impropriations, some with sequestrations, some loaden with pensions, some robbed of their commodities'[20]. Consequently pluralism and non-residence remained rife, and the few well-qualified ministers, the graduates, were often among the pluralists and non-residents.

Many Elizabethan bishops and archdeacons diligently held visitations to detect clerical unorthodoxy and unworthiness. But since common law protected benefices as freeholds, it was extremely difficult for diocesan authorities to effect deprivations unless an incumbent went out of his way to flaunt defiance of statutory or canonical requirements. With the protection of patrons and connivance or indifference of parishioners, parsons might neglect their ministry or continue Catholic practices. If a parson was deprived there was small chance that a bishop would be able to prevent a patron exercising his freehold right of advowson to appoint a successor of like persuasion. Churchwardens who tried to do their duty by detecting and punishing recusants (those who failed to attend parochial services), and parsons who made presentments of them at visitations, might risk the wrath of the local Catholic squire. Diocesan courts proved ineffective. Much of their time was consumed by private suits (e.g. about tithe and probate) brought at the instance of litigious gentlefolk. Their penances and sentences of excommunication had little effect on the conduct of gentlemen and those they protected.

The problems of enforcement facing ecclesiastical authorities led many ministers of Calvinist persuasion, besides sympathisers with traditional religious practices, to flout legal prescription. In 1564 the queen ordered the bishops to enforce the wearing of vestments on nonconforming Puritans, and in 1565, in conference with Parker, the bishops drafted the *Book of Advertisements*, which expounded correct liturgical observances. A number of incumbents who refused to conform were deprived of their livings, including Thomas Sampson, the dean of Christ Church, Oxford, and leading Marian exile. But the earl of Huntingdon appointed Sampson as master of Wyggeston Hospital in Leicester, an office he was to hold for life. The earl's action illustrates the difficulty of containing Puritan nonconformity. Peers, privy councillors, Household officials, influential gentry and merchants were among the patrons of 'godly ministers'. They were to include the queen's favourite Leicester, used by God 'many times as a notable instrument for the good both of the Church and commonwealth'[21]. Such pious patrons regarded advowson as a means to institute instruction of the Word, rather than to provide rewards for their servants. Some happily saw their ministers not only preaching and providing living examples of the Word, but breaking the law by ministering the service facing the people, wearing plain 'Geneva gowns', and substituting communion tables for altars.

By the 1570s the universities, particularly Cambridge, were turning out a new wave of Calvinist ministers, whose impatience with the slow progress of reformation made them more inclined to attack ecclesiastical institutions than many of the older generation of former exiles had been. Some of these radicals mobilised their sympathisers in the Commons to agitate for presbyterian instead of episcopal Church government (1569–72). But the queen's adamant opposition stopped the movement. She was also intensely suspicious of the reforming activities of zealous ministers. Some bishops in the southern province welcomed and helped to organise regular 'exercises'. At these, two or three clerics would expound Holy Writ before their assembled colleagues and layfolk, and, after the latter's departure, the clerics would examine each other's scriptural knowledge. The queen suspected such 'prophesyings' as Trojan horses of presbyterianism, and in 1577 ordered their suppression. But in the 1580s radical ministers went further, holding unlicensed assemblies which assumed more deliberately presbyterian forms. One or more parishes acquired a regular synod ('classis'), where the authority of the Prayer Book was discarded in favour of the scheme of Walter Travers's *Book of Discipline*, and the authority of bishop and archdeacon replaced by that of pastor and elders.

But by the early 1590s the 'classical' movement had declined under the pressure of persecution. The queen found an effective opponent of it in John Whitgift, appointed archbishop of Canterbury in 1583. He supplemented episcopal authority in his province by summoning presbyterian ministers into its Court of High Commission. Composed of ecclesiastics, this sat in London, exercising a statutory jurisdiction under royal commission in spiritual causes. The court had met more regularly since *c.*1580, attracting a press of private litigants, who considered it more effective than diocesan courts. Many Puritans, forced by the High Commission's procedure to take a prior oath to answer unspecified charges truthfully, were trapped by their replies to the court's interrogatories, and had to retract their errors or lose their benefices.

Not all classes were suppressed, not all presbyterians deprived. Some ejected ministers found influential employment as private chaplains or as lecturers appointed to expound the Scriptures by pious urban corporations. But the decline of the classical movement exposed the limitations of religious radicalism. Some adherents showed more interest in setting up sectarian congregations of perfect believers than in attempting a general reform of the Church. Others, including many gentlemanly patrons, were not prepared to sustain opposition to the royal will. A series of scurrilous attacks on bishops by a prudently anonymous pamphleteer, 'Martin Marprelate' (1589) shocked many Puritans. Sir Francis Hastings wrote to his brother Sir Edward '. . . let us all be warned by other perils to keep ourselves every way from consenting to Martin's course . . . for I am verily persuaded he hath no warrant out of God's book for the manner of his dealing'. Many gentlemen probably looked askance at the threat to their advowsons contained in the presbyterian *Second Admonition to Parliament* (1572), which gave the regional synod, the 'conference', responsibility for filling the parochial ministry. Others jibbed at brotherly admonitions descending on them from the pulpit, such as the 'godly, learned and painful preacher, Master Eusebius Pagit' gave to Sir Richard

Grenville, according to Hastings. The latter enlightened Grenville as to the spirit in which such criticisms should be received: 'The man whom the Lord hath throughly seasoned with humility, he falleth flat before the sceptre of the word, and yieldeth to be censured by it, as a means to reform him.'

By the 1590s new generations of graduates were becoming influential among the clergy, many of whom, although Calvinist in theology, were less critical of the established Church, more respectable since its longer establishment. Its doctrine was better propagated and enforced, as a result of bishops' fears of Catholicism, the Crown's attempts to mobilise courts and magistrates against Catholics and Puritans, and the more abundant supply of well trained Protestant ministers. The Church's relative strength at James I's accession helps to explain his confident, pragmatic dealings with Puritans. Their Millenary Petition (1603), requesting a conference to discuss reforms, showed their continued strength, and ability to organise politically. But their petitions, and delegates at the Hampton Court Conference (1604) displayed a spirit according with the reform articles rejected in convocation in 1563 rather than with the radical anti-episcopal movement of the 1580s. A Calvinist by upbringing, James I was more sympathetic than his predecessor to complaints about the need for a better-qualified ministry, about pluralism, non-residence, and 'superstitious' ceremonies. James did not regard the Prayer Book as sacrosanct. If he did not use his authority to force the bishops to effect changes urged by Puritans, he also did not use it extremely to enforce uniformity.

James showed a pragmatic spirit towards Catholics as well, alleviating their drastic persecution whilst continuing to restrict their influence. The character of English Catholicism had altered fundamentally since the 1560s. At his accession the Catholics were a well-defined minority sect: their religion was maintained clandestinely in noblemen's and gentlemen's households by missionaries trained abroad, who were liable, like many of their protectors, to ferocious statutory penalties. From the 1580s onwards recusants had been more persistently pushed out of public office, fined and coerced.

Catholicism had declined as a popular religion in the 1560s. The Marian restoration had not lasted long enough to produce sufficient recruits to the priesthood. Protestant graduates gradually had some impact on popular beliefs, and prosecutions for recusancy were probably more effective against common folk than gentry. The attempt to revive Catholicism in the 1570s, coinciding with an intensification of antagonisms between the Crown and foreign Catholic powers, was viewed by government as a deadly political threat. In 1570 Pius V posed a dilemma of religious and political allegiances to recusants and to the many Catholic 'schismatics' who conformed occasionally. His bull declared the queen to be a heretic, deprived her of her pretended title to the Crown, and absolved her subjects from their oaths of obedience. From 1574 onwards English seminarists were landing clandestinely and residing in Catholic landowners' households, instructing their inhabitants more precisely in their religious duties, and dissuading them from occasional conformity. They used these households as a network of bases from which to carry out conversions.

Government measures intensified against recusants and missionaries in the 1580s. An Act of 1581 made it treason to withdraw the queen's subjects from their allegiance, or from the established Church to the Roman religion. Recusancy became an indictable offence, punishable in quarter sessions by the prohibitive fine of £20 a month, instead of the old one of 12*d* a week. Failure to pay fines due twice yearly made the defaulters liable to have their goods and two-thirds of their lands forfeited. The exemption of peers was to facilitate their continued recusancy. In 1585 conviction of being a Jesuit or seminary priest was in itself constituted as treason, and the provision of aid or comfort to such, a capital felony. In 1593 convicted recusants were forbidden to move without licence more than five miles from their domicile: those unable to pay their fines were made liable to deportation.

In the 1580s persistent recusants were subject to all sorts of harassment: the levy of ruinous fines, sequestration of property, imprisonment, confinement to the houses of Protestants, double assessments on the subsidy roll. Yet diocesan authorities and justices of the peace were not always effective and zealous in prosecution. Their efforts were supplemented by summonses to the Court of High Commission and by commissions to lord-lieutenants and selected gentlemen, empowered to discover and summon suspected recusants and priests, and to judge their offences. Catholicism was reduced to a minor 'country house' sect, whose adherents maintained a distinctive and to some extent isolated piety, linked to the continental Counter-Reformation rather than the mainstream of English experience. The intensity of persecution lessened in the 1590s and 1600s, as the threat of Catholic invasion receded, and it became clear that most recusants were anxious to maintain a distinction between their religious and secular allegiances. Under James the Crown was safely able to relax its campaign against hardened Catholic families, though maintaining its vigilance against proselytising seminarists.

The Reformation was the crowning achievement of the medieval Church. The theology, erudition and idealism of Reform owed its particular development and appeal to trends in scholarship and devoutness which had become widespread among educated clergy and laity by the early sixteenth century. The dissemination and enforcement of reformed orthodoxy was heavily dependent on the workings of medieval forms of ecclesiastical administration.

Though the organisation of the medieval Church and many aspects of its clergy's traditional ways of behaviour survived the English Reformation unchanged, the Church's place in society had fundamentally shifted. Much of the wealth and political influence possessed by the clerical estate was prised from it in the sixteenth century. By the end of the century, many clerics as well as educated layfolk had come to regard the existing episcopal authority as an unnatural usurpation, since they found no warrant for it in Scripture. Lay supporters of episcopacy tended to value it mainly as a limb of royal authority over the Church. But the new authority of the Royal Supremacy, which in some respects appears a logical development of the informal control which the Crown had exercised over the medieval Church, had itself come under attack from Catholics and Puritans. Particularly in the decade or so after Henry VIII's death, the Crown's ecclesiastical tergiversations destroyed the almost universal acceptance of one 'natural order' in the Church. Men's minds were busily set to framing a new order agreeable to their particular concept of God's will. Consequently the extension of royal prerogative by the Supremacy had to be vigilantly maintained, and produced a new sphere of tension between Crown and subjects.

As a result of the Reformation, the respect accorded to traditional authorities in ecclesiastical affairs became less assured, more a matter for theological debate and polemical argument. Clerical authority, besides being formally subordinated to Crown and parliament, and exposed to anticlerical assaults, could no longer be grounded on its role in the traditional religious order. Popular religion had been based on sensual rather than intellectual perceptions, on the unhesitating acceptance of myths rather than the critical appreciation of textual precepts. Propitiatory ceremonies were performed to avert the perennial disasters threatening corn, kine and souls. The priest, able to perform the miraculous intercessory rite of the Mass, was the chief purveyor of a magic which reformers tried to stamp out as 'superstition'. In place of numinous priestly authority, they expounded the exalted nature of the trust to guide and instruct the Christian people which God had confided to sovereigns and their deputies, or to ministers. They often justified this authority by scriptural citation. Examination of the Word now provided the theoretical basis of religion, which, as Parker informed Cecil, had to be 'agreeable to the Gospel'. This was, indeed, a potentially radical principle, which might be used to loosen the roots of institutions.

As often happens when an elite rejects the traditional justification for an institution, the realities of power and self-interest as well as the force of ideals determined the amalgam of tradition and principle on which the revised institution was based. Puritans' attempts to reform Church government on first principles signally failed. Their vigour in proselytising the 'superstitious' may indeed have helped to thwart their more ambitious aims, by adding to the unreformed Church's 'credibility'. Sovereigns threw the weight of their authority against Puritan reforming attempts. They no longer saw advantage to the Crown in encouraging ecclesiastical change. Elizabeth propped up a Church which for long lacked sufficient conviction to justify its prescriptions, or dynamism to uphold them, without considerable royal prompting and assistance. Under the early Stuarts some Erastian Churchmen were to develop ideological bases strong and broad enough to provide an alternative to the Calvinist or Catholic doctrines, to which the religious-minded had become accustomed to turn for spiritual inspiration. This was the eventual fruit – one causing bitter divisions – of Elizabeth's remarkable achievement in sustaining an ecclesiastical polity cobbled together from worn institutions and clashing traditions, to fit the circumstances of 1559.

The staying-power, the laxities and divisions of the Elizabethan and Jacobean Churches, cannot be related solely to the effects of royal policy. They reflect a shift in influence over ecclesiastical affairs from prelates and sovereigns to lay landowners. As a result of the Reformation, the latter gained many of the former estates of religious houses, a larger share of advowsons, impropriations, and leases of episcopal and capitular lands. As peers and members of parliament they legislated concerning the Church, as lord-lieutenants, special commissioners and justices of the peace, they helped to enforce the legislation, as patrons of livings they rode their religious and ecclesiastical hobby-horses. The degree of respect and support which the ecclesiastical hierarchy received had become highly dependent on the individual opinions of the local governors of society, conscious of their rights as magistrates, lay patrons and impropriators. While numbers of them flouted orthodoxy or worked diligently to overthrow the hierarchy, the majority were probably suspicious of reform, determined to maintain things as they were rather than allow a revival of clerical pretensions. The Reformation had largely succeeded in transforming intellectual attitudes to religious belief and practice, but had largely failed to create a dynamic and complementary transformation of ecclesiastical institutions.

Notes

1. Cathedrals served by secular chapters were Chichester, Exeter, Hereford, Lichfield, Lincoln, London, Salisbury, Wells and York. Those with monastic chapters were Canterbury, Carlisle, Durham, Ely, Norwich, Rochester, Winchester and Worcester.
2. For indications of the critical effects of the Schism on the Cistercian houses in England, cut off from constitutional government by French mother-houses recognising the Avignon papacy, see Rose Graham, 'The Great Schism and the English monasteries of the Cistercian Order', *English Hist. Rev*., xliv (1929). I owe this reference to Mr L. G. D. Baker.
3. Benedictine cells were subject to the mother-house (e.g. Wymondham and Tynemouth to St Albans). In 1530 there were at least 825 religious houses in England and Wales: 502 monasteries, 136 nunneries, 187 friaries. Altogether they then housed about 7,500 men and 1,800 women.
4. His career illustrates another frequently used method of papal appointment – translation from one bishopric to another.
5. Cf. the note in a copy made for Edmund Grey, earl of Kent, 1416–90 (National

Library of Scotland MS. 18. 1. 7, f. 161). The *Mirror* was one of the most popular devotional treatises of the fifteenth century: some fifty MSS survive and it was printed by Caxton in 1486, Wynkyn de Worde 1494, Pynson 1494 and 1506, and Worde four more times in the first thirty years of the sixteenth century.

6. A popular motif on priests' brasses in the fifteenth and early sixteenth centuries is the chalice, sometimes with the Host either held in the priest's hands or as the solitary motif.
7. The first surviving inscription in English on a brass, at Brightwell Baldwin in Oxfordshire, dates from *c*.1370. Most fifteenth-century inscriptions on brasses are in English.
8. Collections of the antiphons sung at Mass between the Epistle and Gospel.
9. Printed by Wynkyn de Worde in 1494 at the request of Henry VII's mother, Lady Margaret Beaufort. He brought out new editions in 1519, 1525 and 1533: Julian Notary printed it in 1507.
10. For Lollardy, see pp. 368 ff. The statute providing for the burning of relapsed heretics had been passed in 1401.
11. Either Henry Bowet (d.1423) or John Kemp, who succeeded in 1426.
12. Bishops' registers did not record cases systematically: act books of episcopal courts of audience, which were not so carefully preserved, record other cases.
13. A translation of the New Testament by William Tyndale had been published at Worms in 1525–6. Using his work, Miles Coverdale published a complete translation of the Bible in 1535, and carried out a revision for the approved 1539 version.
14. From the 1553 Act repealing certain Edwardian statutes.
15. Collegiate churches received the status of parish churches. An Act of 1545 had enabled the Crown to dissolve chantries, but did not denounce their doctrinal basis.
16. The first edition was entitled *Actes and Monuments of these latter and perilous dayes, touching matters of the church* (1563). An expanded version in three volumes was published in 1570, and there were two more editions in Elizabeth's reign (1583,1598).
17. The queen was particularly interested in promoting the revival of former religious communities. Only six were restored, including Westminster Abbey.
18. I owe thanks to Ms Penelope Winder for information about this text.
19. First edition 1535, definitive edition 1559.
20. In 1603 the bishops estimated that 3,849 out of 9,284 livings were impropriated.
21. The Puritan Sir Francis Hastings to Leicester's stepson the earl of Essex in 1588, commenting on Leicester's death.

Chapter 9

England's changing role in Christendom, 1453–1585

Traditional relationships with neighbouring principalities

In the mid-fifteenth century the diplomacy of the English Crown was traditionally concerned above all with France, Scotland and the Low Countries. Relations with the papacy, in important respects different by nature, were also of special concern and historical complexity. In the period under review attitudes to all these powers were to undergo customary ebbs and flows, but were besides to be fundamentally altered. The loss of Normandy in 1451 and of Gascony in 1452 stiffened the publicly expressed resolve of English rulers to reassert their rights in France, and their secret communications and negotiations to support discontented French princes, opponents of the 'new monarchy' whose 'tyranny' was to be delineated by Thomas Basin, bishop of Lisieux, a former councillor of Charles VII, and by Philippe de Commynes, a former councillor of Louis XI. But the failure of the English Crown to match the growth in authority and wealth of the French monarchy probably made the loss of possessions in France irreversible. Henry VII, who had learned more about the Valois monarchy than most other English kings, may have been aware of this shift in the balance of power between the two Crowns, but it is not likely to have been clear to most politically aware Englishmen. Henry VIII was to bring the claim to the French Crown more persistently and elaborately into his diplomacy than any of his predecessors since Henry V. As late as 1597 John Chamberlain wrote of speculation that the force intended for the 'Islands Voyage' was destined for an invasion of France, 'which troubles our discourses how or where it shall be employed: the common sort talk of Calais'.

The gradual recession of English hopes to revive dominion in France facilitated improved Anglo-French relations, though the enmity of powers with such long-standing traditions of conflict, and present ability to threaten one another's shores remained lively. In 1492 Charles VIII of France and Henry VII concluded the treaty of Étaples, the first real peace treaty between the two Crowns since 1360. Henry's successors found it comparatively easy to conclude their brief French wars with peace treaties, whereas his predecessors, trapped in a skein of issues stretching back to the Treaty of Paris (1259) had managed in the previous century only to implement truces.

During the period covered by this chapter, the English Crown succeeded remarkably well in safeguarding the northern counties from large-scale Scottish incursions, though not without the need for strenuous diplomatic and, on occasion, military activity, and for the maintenance of expensive garrisons and defence works in the Marches, even in time of truce. At Berwick, ramparts and bastions built in the most up-to-date style in the first years of Elizabeth's reign testify to the watchful concern of a normally parsimonious government. In 1568 the governor of the town, Henry Carey, lord Hunsdon, wrote urging the queen to complete the defences. Then 'no sudden approach of the French need be feared', he argued, displaying the typical apprehension of Elizabethan men of affairs that a foreign power would use politically divided Scotland as a base from which to threaten English security. Garrisons and bastions were also necessary to constrict the cattle-raiding depredations of 'reivers'. The lawless activities of English uplanders (particularly those of Redesdale and Tyndale) and of their Scots counterparts (e.g. from Liddesdale) exacerbated relations between the two Crowns (cf. pp. 141 ff).

At the start of our period English dynastic strife had enabled the Scots, soon after the death of the able James II, to demolish two frontier fortresses garrisoned by the English, Roxburgh and Wark (1460), and to recover Berwick by treaty with the adherents of Henry VI (1461). But these successes were exceptional: the comparative military weakness of the Scottish Crown, and the recurrent minorities which undermined the authority of Stewart sovereigns, normally put them at a disadvantage in relations with England. James IV (1488–1513) was to be the most threatening. After his reign a principal concern of the Tudors (reflected in Hunsdon's remark) was to prevent French domination of Scotland. This led, after the death of James V (1542), to Henry VIII's ill-judged attempts to secure the marriage of the infant Mary queen of Scots for his son and heir Prince Edward. The 'English' party among the Scottish lay magnates which, like his recent forbears, Henry had cultivated, proved to be, not uncharacteristically, a straw rope. Consequently there ensued outbursts of war, to the detriment of the Scots. But the spread of Protestantism among the lairds and burgesses of lowland Scotland generated a new current in Anglo-Scottish relations. The 'reformed' in Scotland, like their English brethren, were obsessed by the threat to 'true religion' and their lives from popish reaction. Fear of the machinations of 'Antichrist' gave influential groups of Scotsmen and Englishmen a basis of common political interest. In Scotland the influence of the 'reformed' party was to weaken the traditional French alliance.

The principalities of the Low Countries continued to play a vital part in English calculations, partly because their markets were the main outlets for the increasing number of 'broadcloths' exported by English 'merchant venturers' (see pp. 29 ff), and partly because their rulers, the Valois and their successors the Habsburg dukes of Burgundy, were the French Crown's most formidable opponents. Like the kings of England, they had claims to lands in France – principally to the duchy of Burgundy and towns in Artois and Picardy. The wealth which was to accrue in the early sixteenth century to the Habsburgs from their many territorial acquisitions, especially from Castile and its American possessions, and from the commercial rise of Antwerp, made Tudor rulers and councillors anxious to secure their protection for the realm and favour for its trade. But Henry VIII's repudiation of papal supremacy over the Church in 1534 was to sour relations with the staunchly Catholic Habsburg family. However, it needed additional stresses before the traditional Habsburg-Tudor connection finally dissolved in the 1570s. The main precipitant was Philip II of Spain's autocratic rule in the Low Countries and the strife this provoked. Violent persecution of Protestants, and tyrannical coercion of nobles and burgesses in a region so close to English shores and intimately known by many Englishmen, provoked fears and resentments which, coagulating with other grievances against the Spanish Crown, coaxed Elizabeth into war with Philip. Another consequence of the civil strife in the Low Countries (a consequence which led to further oceanic friction with Spanish overseas interests) was that English merchants were forced to sail further afield to find new 'vents' for cloth and other commodities, producing radical shifts in the pattern of English trade routes.

Centuries of negotiation over control of the English Church, and of compromises which in practice led to a sharing of responsibility in the matter, had brought the Crown into a more settled and active diplomatic relationship with the papacy than with any other power. Before Henry VIII's reign, the only permanent diplomatic representation of the English Crown was to be found in Rome at the papal *curia*. The new factor in Anglo-papal relations in the later fifteenth century was the evolution of the papacy, after the Great Schism had been ended in 1418, as a leading territorial power in Italy. The first two Tudors considered it as a valuable ally with whom to oppose French expansion there. Consequently they and their councillors took more interest in the politics of the *curia* and of papal elections than had their predecessors. Political rather than theological considerations were to lead to Pope Clement VII's prevarications over Henry VIII's suit for nullification of his supposed marriage to Catherine of Aragon, aunt of the Habsburg Emperor Charles V, whose influence dominated Italy after 1527. The débâcle of English influence at the *curia* represented by the failure of the suit produced a conclusive breakdown in Anglo-papal relations. After 1534 Henry occasionally put out indirect, discreet feelers for reconciliation, but only as a means of delaying the feared preaching of a crusade against him. Even during Mary's brief restoration of papal supremacy over England, relations between the Roman and English Courts never became more than formally cordial.

Pius V's bull excommunicating and deposing Elizabeth (1570) hardened the developing Protestant conviction in England that the papacy was dedicated to the subversion of all Protestant government, and that it could not, like some other Catholic powers, be treated as politically flexible. Partly as a consequence of this attitude, the English Crown was unable to play the supporting role in Italian affairs to which it had aspired in the later fifteenth and early sixteenth centuries. But the Jesuits who began to land clandestinely in England in the early 1580s, however dedicated the majority were to eschew political controversy, gave the papacy an unprecedented influence in parts of English landed society. Catholics, including many converts, were brought more firmly and directly within papal allegiance and ecclesiastical discipline. Under the Stuart dynasty, this paradoxical byproduct of the Royal Supremacy over the English Church led to backstairs negotiations between Crown and papacy. In the 1630s a papal agent was to be secretly accredited to Charles I's Court.

Thus there were in the period fundamental changes in English relations with principal neighbours. Those with the two traditional enemies, the Crowns of France and Scotland, haltingly improved, whereas two traditionally friendly powers, the papacy and the dynasty ruling the Low Countries, after drawing closer, at length became deadly opponents, the objects of godly Englishmen's execration. Another important development was the decisive eclipse of English sovereigns' wealth and authority by that of close continental neighbours. But the successes of Edward IV and Henry VII in upholding influence and prestige abroad may have helped to give Henry VIII the temerity to challenge the Valois, the papacy and the Habsburgs. More showily and ambitiously than any of his predecessors, Henry aspired to dominate, as ally or arbitrator, the diplomacy of western Christendom. As a young man he toyed with the traditional medieval ideals of leading a crusade to repulse the Ottoman Turks, then threatening the Christian powers in the Mediterranean and in central Europe, and of being elected king of the Romans, to bestride the Christian Empire. In the 1530s, more practically but still ambitiously, he was to implement and develop a concept half-formed in the minds of some Englishmen – the concept that England was by itself an 'empire', not subordinate to other jurisdictions in Christendom. In 1513 one writer, relating the visit of Sigismund king of the Romans to England in 1416, described how his jurisdiction had been symbolically repudiated before he set foot on English soil. 'And this was thus devised for saving of the King's Imperial Majesty, which is an Emperor within his Realm.' The independence, the self-sufficiency of England, as asserted by Henry, was to become one of the germinal ideas influencing the behaviour of generations of Englishmen. The concept, under the pressure of intellectual, military and economic conflict with the continental defenders of Catholicism, was to blossom into insular and oceanic attitudes, into a characteristic deprecation of the European nature and links of English civilisation, informing education, literature, habits of mind and the formulation of foreign policy during the following three centuries.

The causes of change in English foreign relationships in the second half of the fifteenth century were partly domestic and partly external. From the accession of Edward IV in 1461 until that of Henry VIII in 1509, English rulers experienced an unusual degree of dynastic insecurity. They feared that the intrigues of fugitive claimants to the throne, if tolerated and indeed subsidised by foreign rulers, would lead to their own overthrow, as indeed happened to Edward IV in 1470, Henry VI in 1471 and Richard III in 1485. Henry VIII, more secure in his early years, had little to fear from Richard de la Pole, recognised as 'Richard IV' by Louis XII and Francis I of France. This obscure exile existed in reduced circumstances at Strasbourg, befriended by Henry's spies. Nevertheless, more ridiculous and implausible figures had challenged Henry VII's rule within the realm. A principal object of the foreign policy of Edward IV and Richard III, as well as Henry VII, had been to neutralise the threat of claimants, principally by treaties of amity and mutual defence, and by marriage alliances with neighbouring dynasties. The fears about the loyalty of subjects which underlay this concern inclined Edward and Henry VII to caution in foreign relations, to a willingness to establish good relations, and even to compromise with enemies, which contrasted with the oft-recalled traditions of venturesome and scornful belligerence attributed to Edward III and Henry V.

The principal external cause of change was the growing financial and military strength of the French Crown from the 1440s onwards. Charles VII and Louis XI had considerable success in asserting their sovereignty over princes and lords on whose allegiance, alliance or neutrality the English Crown had frequently relied. The dukes of Brittany retained a precarious freedom of action, but the Gascon lords, such as the counts of Armagnac, were thoroughly subordinated, and after the death of Charles the Bold, duke of Burgundy, in 1477, Louis XI seized all his heir Mary's French possessions except Flanders. The early Tudors, confronted like Edward III in the 1330s with a powerful French monarchy, were thrown back on his somewhat barren expedient of alliances within the Holy Roman Empire, and on equally unproductive Spanish ones. What saved England from any serious French attempt at invasion until 1545 was the decline of French royal interest in the affairs of northern Europe. Charles VIII, Louis XII and Francis I were able to indulge their Italian ambitions, as previous French princes had aspired to do, because of the comparative absence of domestic and external threats. From 1477 onwards, the Burgundian line had its hands full trying to master the Low Countries and later the Spanish and Italian inheritances, and could not devote attention to its claims in France and the claims of its frequent ally, England. The military potential of the English Crown had failed to keep pace with that of continental neighbours, and English kings were frequently preoccupied with their domestic insecurity. The French Crown had an array of weapons to deflect amateurish English incursions, such as stirring the Scots, subsidising rebels, buying off English allies, and offering indemnities, annuities and marriages to English kings.

Practically freed from Burgundian and English threats, Charles VIII from the mid-1490s and his successors in the early sixteenth century pursued their claims to the kingdom of Naples, the duchy of Milan and the overlordship of Genoa. For centuries control of Italy, with its imperial and papal associations, had seemed to medieval rulers the key to wealth, prestige and leadership in Christendom. Such control was to elude the Valois as it had eluded past German emperors and kings. Then in the 1510s and 1520s the Habsburg Emperor Charles V succeeded to many principalities in different parts of Christendom. He became ruler of most of the Low Countries, of Spain and Naples, and of the Habsburg inheritances in central Europe. The emperor posed the first formidable challenge to the French Crown since the death of Charles the Bold. The rivalry of Habsburg and Valois, especially for control of Italy, dominated European diplomacy for much of the sixteenth century. This provided a measure of security for the English Crown, since the resources of both powers were too stretched against one another for either to concentrate for long on peripheral English affairs. The fact that England was peripheral was due to its weakness rather than to its geographical position. Henry VIII was unable, even when using all the strength he could muster, to influence decisively the outcome of the Habsburg–Valois conflict, or benefit from it territorially. After his death in 1547 English rulers and councillors, lacking his determination and flamboyance, showed themselves well aware of comparative English weakness. They were perforce less hidebound by traditional claims and alignments, more clear-sightedly preoccupied with winning a measure of security from external threats, considering that the Crown needed to be a satellite of one of the two 'great powers', as it was too vulnerable to stand on its own, yet strong enough to preserve some freedom of action from a protector.

The foreign relations of usurping kings (1461–1509)

After his seizure of the Crown in 1461 Edward IV's main aims in foreign policy were to secure recognition of his title and the expulsion of Lancastrian fugitives from neighbouring principalities. The ruling dynasties of France, Castile, Aragon, Scotland and Burgundy all had ties of kinship or marriage with Henry VI. Henry IV of Castile had particular reason to suspect Edward, as the latter (unlike the Lancastrians) maintained a claim to the Castilian throne. Charles VII of France (d.1463) and his son Louis XI (d.1483) had reason to suspect his intentions too. Edward was Norman by birth and his father had twice been royal lieutenant in France, and a sympathiser with English landowners who had lost estates in Normandy and Maine. As Charles VII's reply to James II's proposals for attacking England (1457) shows, French councillors were sensitive to the potential English threat: 'The English, having held the said country [Normandy] for the space of twenty-two years or more, know the landing places and all the condition of the country quite as well as those persons do who reside therein . . . only six hours of a favourable wind suffice to pass from England into the said country of Normandy.' In Guienne 'the people of the district are at heart entirely inclined to the English party'.

In June 1462 Charles VII permitted his fugitive kinswoman, Henry VI's queen, Margaret of Anjou, to reside in France and provided her with funds to recruit a force which sailed to Scotland and on to Northumberland. Its objective was to rally the support of the Scots, and of adherents of northern English lords disgruntled at the regional dominance of the earl of Warwick and his brothers. But, sailing late in the year, the fleet was partly wrecked off the Northumbrian coast. In November, at Edinburgh, Henry VI made an indenture promising to grant George Douglas, earl of Angus, in return for aid in recovering his realm, a duchy with estates in the north of England worth 2,000 marks p.a. Angus would be permitted to hold the duchy by deputy even when fighting with the king of Scots against England. But Scots support was insufficient to consolidate Lancastrian gains in Northumberland. Angus died soon after the agreement. In 1463 Henry VI and James III failed in an attempt on Norham Castle. Charles VII of France's successor Louis, who as dauphin had favoured the Yorkists, was loath to commit himself decisively to support the Lancastrians and Stewarts. He had diplomatic problems enough – with Aragon, Brittany and with Burgundy's son, Charles count of Charolais. Louis found an ally for his pacific intentions in the aged Duke Philip of Burgundy, who was anxious to promote a crusade against the Ottoman Turks. The duke negotiated an Anglo-French truce at St Omer in October 1463. Without the prospect of French help, James III's councillors abandoned the Lancastrian cause the following year. Since 1462 Edward IV had retaliated effectively by threatening to intervene in Scottish affairs. John of the Isles, earl of Ross, and his kinsman Donald Balloch, had undertaken to enter Edward's allegiance and to aid him militarily in Scotland and Ireland, receiving pensions, as did James, the forfeited earl of Douglas and his brother John lord Balvenie, fugitives in England since 1455. In June 1464 an Anglo-Scottish truce was concluded, to last fifteen years. Edward was prepared to settle without recovering Berwick or Roxburgh, showing himself more accommodating to the Scots than any English ruler since 1328.

His early caution in foreign affairs, dictated by his realisation of the precariousness of his rule, is reflected too in his first hesitant reactions to the resurgence of Franco-Burgundian conflict, muted by Philip of Burgundy's policy since the peace of Arras (1435). In 1465 the duke of Brittany and Duke Philip's son Charolais were prominent in a princely coalition, the 'league of the public weal', which aimed to take over Louis's government. Edward was courted by both parties. The earl of

Warwick, on whose family the House of York depended for its control of the northern parts, persistently advocated an alliance with the king of France, and opposed any undertakings inimical to the truces. The earl appears to have been dazzled by the French Crown's unrivalled powers of patronage and flattered by Louis's show of personal confidence. He may have feared that French hostility would encourage Percy adherents and the Scots to challenge the Nevilles' precarious northern hegemony. Once Charolais, after the death of his father in 1467, had full control of the great Burgundian inheritance, Edward, despite Warwick's feverish diplomacy, moved speedily towards an alliance with him, agreeing to Duke Charles's proposal that he should marry Edward's sister Margaret, and in 1468 formally allying with him and Francis, duke of Brittany. The marriage, celebrated at Damme, near Bruges (July 1468), helped to revive Anglo-Burgundian cordiality and to promote the influence of the Burgundian style of elaborate courtliness. John Paston the younger, present at the wedding festivities, wrote to his mother that 'there were never English men had so good cheer out of England that ever I heard of', and 'as for the Duke's court, as of lords, ladies and gentlewomen, knights, squires and gentlemen, I heard never of none like it, save King Arthur's court'.

Warwick's subsequent attempts to control Edward prevented the latter from exploiting his anti-French alliances – alliances which, indeed, contributed to his loss of the throne. In 1470 Warwick and his son-in-law, Edward's brother Clarence, fled to France and were there skilfully reconciled by Louis XI's mediation to Margaret of Anjou and her son Edward prince of Wales. Louis provided the aid which enabled Warwick to place Henry VI once more on the throne. But Charles of Burgundy allowed the fugitive Edward IV to reside in Holland and, as the threat of Anglo-French attack grew in 1471, to promote his claim to the Crown. In March 1471 Edward sailed from Flushing in the *Antonie* of Veere, his hired German ships (from towns of the Hanseatic League) being paid for with a Burgundian subsidy. His triumphant restoration reduced the revived Lancastrian interest to a few exiles, notably Henry VI's half-brother Jasper Tudor, earl of Pembroke, and his young nephew Henry Tudor (the future Henry VII) in Brittany.

Louis XI now had no counterweight against the alliance of Edward with Burgundy and Brittany. Anglo-Burgundian cordiality was to reach a pitch not attained since Bedford's time. Burgundian lords were welcome at the English court. Louis *seigneur* de la Gruthuyse, who had been attentive to the exiled Edward, was in 1472 created earl of Winchester. In 1474 Duke Charles agreed to aid Edward's intended campaign to recover his rights in France, a realm now 'oppressed by tyranny'. In return Edward as king of France would free the duke of Burgundy and his successors from feudal allegiance, dismantling the unity of the realm so tenaciously maintained by the Valois. Edward took precautions against Scottish intervention by betrothing his youngest daughter Cecily to James III's son and heir James duke of

Rothesay (the future James IV). Since Louis XI showed no inclination to make concessions to English pretensions, Edward landed at Calais in July 1475 and assembled a large, well-equipped army in the March. But his plans soon went awry. Duke Charles, whose forces were disarrayed by their losses in Lorraine, joined him with only a small retinue. The English failed to secure an intended base for operations: Louis de Luxembourg, count of St Pol, renegued on his promise to hand over St Quentin. Edward advanced cautiously through Picardy with his swarm of archers, carting his great guns. Ahead were well defended towns and a large French army, but no sign of Burgundian or Breton reinforcements. Louis seized the opportunity to open negotiations. Envoys met at Lihons-en-Santerre near Amiens. The English claimed the French Crown or, at least, Normandy and Guienne. But there was soon agreement to relegate differences to arbitrators. In effect, the English settled for an indemnity, an annual pension for Edward, and a truce of seven years. Edward and Louis, in their projected 'true, sincere and perfect friendship', were not to succour one another's rebels, but to harbour and support each other, if 'either of the princes be driven out of his lands and dominions . . . by the guile, cunning, and diobedience of a subject or subjects of either of them'. It was agreed that Louis's son and heir Charles should marry Edward's eldest daughter Elizabeth (who, in fact, just over ten years later, married Henry VII).

Under truce, parties of English soldiers were entertained free within the city walls of Amiens, which was soon awash with noisy, drunken Englishmen. Louis's councillor Philippe de Commynes recalled how he entered one tavern 'where a hundred and eleven bills had been run up although it was not nine in the morning. The house was full, some were singing, some were sleeping and were just plain drunk.' In August Louis XI and Edward IV met at Picquigny to swear to the truce in conditions of elaborate security. With a few companions they conversed at the middle of a specially constructed bridge over the Somme, divided by trelliswork 'such as lions' cages are made from'. Nevertheless, according to Commynes, who took part in the meeting, the two kings got on well. Louis, aware of Edward's amorous inclinations, jokingly offered him some entertainment with the ladies of Paris, and promised that his companion the cardinal of Bourbon would shrive him of any resulting sins. Edward's eager response disconcerted him: he told Commynes afterwards that 'he [Edward] could meet some artful female in Paris who knew how to speak such fine words that she would make him eager to return'.

Edward publicly declared that the truce had been made 'Consideryng the Povertie of his Armye, the nygh approchyng of Wynter, and smale Assistence of his Allies'. Some of his leading councillors and retinue captains, such as Lords Hastings and Howard, were reconciled to the truce by Louis's grant to them (as to their master) of lavish annuities. Many of those who had paid subsidy for the campaign, or had set their hearts on the gains and chivalrous contests of war, were less pleased. The most illustrious critic of the truce was the king's younger brother, Richard duke of Gloucester. Commynes considered the truce a prime example of his king's astuteness, recounting French attempts to stifle their mirthful contempt for the foolishness of the sententious and superstitious English. But Commynes was writing with the benefit of hindsight. Less than two years later Charles of Burgundy died in battle with the Swiss at Nancy (January 1477). His heir was a daughter of seventeen, Mary. Louis XI's forces gained control of the duchy of Burgundy and the Somme towns, and threatened Flanders. Mary retained with difficulty her possessions in the Empire: the county of Burgundy (Franche-Comté) and the Netherlandish territories, notably Brabant, Holland and Zealand.

Edward could not have foreseen in 1475, any more than Louis, the disaster which was to cripple the embryonic Burgundian state. Edward's decision to make a truce was realistic. It did not preclude future alliances with Burgundy and Brittany against the French Crown. But in 1475 (like Henry VII in France in 1492) he had no effective allies. An attempt to carry on the war would have further taxed English resources: no more than Henry in a similar situation could he risk domestic unpopularity. Moreover, Edward benefited financially from the invasion. Without risking defeat he made the Valois pay dearly. Arguably it was more sensible, if less prestigious, to receive by the hands of Valois officials the income of French estates, avoiding the burdensome problems entailed in actually ruling them, of which the expense of maintaining the Calais garrisons was a reminder.

Edward's subsequent reluctance to endanger the truce with France by helping to prop up the remnants of the Burgundian inheritance was a more questionable policy. Mary of Burgundy married the gallant but impecunious young knight, Maximilian archduke of Austria (son and heir of the Habsburg Emperor Frederick III), who struggled to uphold his wife's titles in the Low Countries. Edward refrained from aiding him against his Flemish opponents and their royal French patron, though a number of English soldiers entered his service. The king listened to Louis's proposals for a partition of Mary's inheritance, and vainly negotiated for a fulfilment of the marriage contract between the dauphin and Princess Elizabeth. Louis was so anxious to keep the English preoccupied that he incited James III to countenance a breach of the Anglo-Scottish truce. In 1480 Edward was planning a retaliatory invasion of Scotland, which materialised in 1482 under the command of his brother Gloucester, lieutenant in the North. The intervention was supported by Scottish exiles at the English Court, notably the long deprived earl of Douglas and a more recent arrival, James III's brother Alexander duke of Albany. In May 1482 Albany was recognised by Edward as king of Scots, and in return promised to perform homage to him and to cede Berwick, Lochmaben, Liddesdale, Eskdale and Annandale. Apart from the recovery of Berwick, this policy was a reversal of the usual English one pursued since the later fourteenth century of not trying to alter radically the frontier line. One motive may have been the desire of the king and his brother to improve security on the West and Middle Marches by gaining forward bases and the allegiance of particularly troublesome Borderers. The concern of both Crowns over their 'reiving' may have been one reason for growing diplomatic preoccupation with the 'debatable land', a wild tract of country between the Esk and Sark where sovereignty was disputed.

Gloucester, supported and supplied by an impressive navy commanded by John lord Howard, crossed the Tweed into the Merse with the earl of Northumberland. The duke divided his army, one force aiding the siege of Berwick, the other under his leadership advancing on Edinburgh. He was able to mount this ambitious strategy because the Scots nobles summoned for aid by James III had turned their forces against the royal favourites. Their *coup* enabled Albany to gain restoration and eventual recognition as lieutenant-general of the realm, but not his brother's kingship. Gloucester could not attempt to implement to the full Edward's treaty with Albany and contented himself with negotiating the surrender of Berwick and a truce. Like Warwick, whose northern influence he had inherited, the duke was probably primarily concerned to secure an understanding with the Scottish Crown which would guarantee the old frontier.

Edward does not seem to have been pleased by this abandonment of his more grandiose Scottish schemes, which he was to attempt to revive in 1483. Moreover, it now became clear that his continental policy was in ruins. Mary of Burgundy died in 1482, leaving an infant son Philip as heir. The Flemish estates had him in ward, and, together with the nobles and burgesses of Brabant, refused to recognise Maximilian as regent for his son. Maximilian's position was so precarious in the Low Countries that in 1482 he made peace with Louis: by the Treaty of Arras he abandoned the claim to the Burgundian lands seized by the French Crown, recognised French sovereignty over part of Flanders (*Flandre gallicante*), and promised to marry his daughter to the Dauphin Charles. Edward was humiliated by this treaty: Louis had spurned the pledge to marry the dauphin to his daughter, and refused to allow him to be a party to the agreement.

One result of deteriorating Anglo-French relations was that the sailors of southern England and Normandy were emboldened to attack each other's shipping. The political uncertainty in England after Edward's death in 1483 led to an increase of indiscriminate English naval attacks against foreigners. Richard III, installed as ruler in July, was made well aware of the damage this threatened to foreign relations. A letter in the infant Duke Philip's name outlined the complaints of his Flemish subjects: English sailors had been throwing them overboard and the herring fishers had heard them boasting that worse would follow. The instructions drafted in July for Richard's ambassador to Francis duke of Brittany admitted that upon Edward IV's 'hasty departing . . . out of this world, divers folks of simple disposition, peradventure supposing that the peace had been expired by the death of the said king' fell to plundering at sea. A diet (congress) of English and Breton commissioners was proposed to adjudicate claims for redress. A similar proposal was contained in the instructions for Richard's envoy to the Catholic Kings of Spain, Ferdinand and Isabella.

Richard was not only anxious to establish good relations with his brother's allies, Brittany and Spain: he was, for the time being, friendly towards France. John lord Dinham, the lieutenant at Calais, was instructed to negotiate with his neighbouring French counterpart about infractions of the truce, and in August Richard wrote to Louis XI protesting his determination to keep the truce and his desire for friendship, and requesting assurance that English merchants could resume sailing to Bordeaux with surety against molestation. Other rulers failed in their attempts to tempt Richard to break the truce and prepare to invade France. Queen Isabella's envoy Sasiola arrived at Warwick Castle, where the Court was installed, and expressed her willingness to assist Richard if he wished to recover his rights in France. By word of mouth, Sasiola outlined her grievances against Louis XI and said that she would be prepared to grant Richard 1,000 or more spears and 3,000 footmen for war against France. The duke of Brittany was also considering the chance of getting Richard's alliance against Louis. Since he controlled Henry Tudor, a possible claimant to the English throne, he thought he could put pressure on Richard: his envoy was to say to Richard that the duke had resisted Louis's demands to hand over Henry to him, but that the next time he asked, compliance might be necessary, unless Richard was prepared to send specified military aid to Brittany.

Changes in the diplomatic scene may have encouraged hopes that Richard could be converted into a 'hawk'. At the end of August 1483 Louis XI died: there was speculation whether Maximilian, consolidating his authority in the Low Countries, would break the peace he had made with the French Crown and its satellite, Flanders. From Calais, Lord Dinham addressed the Chancellor, Bishop Russell of Lincoln, eagerly anticipating that Richard would now want to ally with Burgundy and Brittany to attack the French Crown, inherited by a minor, Charles VIII. He wrote: 'I have much ado to keep men still in peace here, for they would fain be in hand with the Frenchmen; howbeit I trust that matter shall not be attempted till the king's pleasure be known therein, or unto the time occasion be given them by land as it is daily seen by water.' Maximilian's capture of Utrecht, he said, was 'thought a great thing here' and the pro-French party in Flanders was quaking: 'There is great rumour in the duke's [lands] of that they will set upon Picardy to get it again to enlarge their frontiers, which I pray God may soon take effect.'

The immediate steps which Dinham advised were that Richard should ordain a navy to patrol the straits of Dover, 'to show himself as a king to rule and keep his streams', and that strict measures should be taken to ensure that those sailing from English ports did not rob the ships of Maximilian's and the duke of Brittany's subjects. However, Dinham turned out to be over-optimistic about Maximilian's prospects. There is no evidence that Richard and his Council were as euphoric. Royal letters despatched to the Castilian court in September confirmed the cautious reactions to Isabella's proposals already contained in the instructions of an English embassy. The duke of Brittany's actions show that he despaired of English aid, though it may have been the unusual policy on which he now embarked which eventually led to deepening hostility between the French and English Courts.

When the duke of Buckingham rebelled in October 1483, Duke Francis of Brittany financed and equipped an expedition to aid Henry Tudor in gaining the throne. Henry, rightly judging when he reached the south-west coast of England that his chances of success were slender, returned to Brittany without having made landfall. The upshot was that Richard became involved in war with Brittany: there were seizures in the ports and attacks at sea, and on Christmas Day 1483, in Rennes Cathedral, English exiles swore to support Henry's claim to the throne.

From about this time the regency council of Charles VIII, controlled by his forceful elder sister, Anne of Beaujeu, showed hostility to Richard. Henry Tudor, after the failure of his attempt, was allowed to land in Normandy and travel back through the province to Brittany. In January 1484, in a session of the Estates General meeting at Tours, Guillaume de Rochefort, chancellor of France, denounced the king of England as a tyrant who had murdered his nephews, Edward IV's sons. In February the duke of Bourbon, urging the Estates not to neglect defences, alleged that Picardy was open to attack by Maximilian, that the Spanish kings had designs on the frontier provinces, and that Richard was preparing to invade France. Nevertheless, in March Richard empowered Thomas Langton, bishop of St Davids, to conclude a truce with Charles VIII and make arrangements for a diet. But it may be that the French regency, fearing that the Crown's traditional adversaries were likely to take advantage of the minority by concluding an alliance, preferred to exploit the unusual state of Anglo-Breton hostility by taking Duke Francis's part against Richard. In April a French embassy made proposals at the ducal court in response to Francis's requests for military aid. Maximilian seems to have been worried by diplomatic alignments so inconducive to an alliance of England, Burgundy and Brittany. Before June 1484 he dispatched a secretary to Richard to offer his mediation with Brittany. Richard brushed off the proposal by making the prior stipulation that Francis should hand over English exiles, or put them where they would be harmless. However, a rupture in Franco-Breton relations promoted

Richard's objectives. Charles's councillors had encouraged a plot by Breton nobles to oust the duke's influential treasurer, Pierre Landois. But the plot misfired and in May the nobles fled to France, to appeal for the Crown's aid. The ducal government hastened to come to terms with the English. In June an Anglo-Breton truce was proclaimed and the English Crown ordered 1,000 archers to prepare to go to the defence of the duchy. In return Richard must surely have insisted on measures against Henry Tudor. Though the truce was implemented, nothing apparently came of any other Anglo-Breton plans. But in the autumn Henry nearly fell into Richard's clutches. Duke Francis, whose recurrent ill-health was once cause of the erratic course of Breton foreign policy, fell sick. Landois agreed to hand Henry over to the English. Hearing about his impending fate, Henry with great coolness and presence of mind escaped into Anjou: in October 1484 the councillors of his kinsman Charles VIII ordered that he should be given honourable reception.

In fact, Henry's sudden appearance may have been an embarrassment to the French councillors, since they had been trying to restore better relations with Richard: in September he had granted safe-conducts for a French embassy. The regency has need to appease Richard, for its princely opponents, notably Louis duke of Orleans, were intriguing determinedly to overthrow it, in conjunction with Francis and Maximilian. In October Charles VIII was committed to war with the latter in Flanders and in December referred to reports that Maximilian's men were saying that, once their master had subdued the Flemings, with English aid he would recover Burgundian lordships in France. The duke's hope of doing so, and fears that Richard might yet succumb to French blandishments, are reflected in his instructions drafted probably early in 1485 for an embassy to the English Court. His envoys were to ask for precise military aid for his coming campaign against the Flemings, and in return were to specify the help he would give for the recovery of English claims in France. Richard was to be urged not to make a truce with the French Crown, disgracing himself in the eyes of his subjects as Edward IV had done. Never, Maximilian argued, had the time been so ripe for an English invasion of France, whose government was weakened by princely divisions, and in no position to threaten Richard. In conclusion he suggested steps for his mediation to make a peace and defensive alliance between England and Brittany.

It is likely that Richard temporised over these proposals. From April 1485 the truce was renewed with Brittany, but peace was not made. Nor did Maximilian secure English support against the Flemings – probably for the reason which he anticipated, that it might damage English commerce with Flanders. But by June 1485 the Flemish opposition was crumbling fast. The conjunction was forming which French councillors had long striven to prevent: there was a Burgundian ruler able and eager to invade France to reclaim the lost inheritance, and an English king stubbornly unwilling to renew the truce. Though Richard had pursued a cautious foreign policy in the first months of his reign, and had made strenuous diplomatic efforts to secure or neutralise Henry Tudor when he was in Brittany in 1484, it seems that once Maximilian started to emerge as a strong ruler in the Low Countries, he was unwilling to reject, as Edward IV had done after 1475, the possibility of an Anglo-Burgundian alliance. Therefore, apparently, Charles VIII's government at last supplied Henry Tudor with the means to invade England.

Henry set sail from Harfleur in July 1485 with a force of French and Scots mercenaries and English exiles. According to a report made to the Catholic Kings of Spain in March 1486 by their retired councillor, Mosén Diego de Valera, the French king supplied him with 2,000 soldiers paid for four months under the command of Philibert de Chandeé, a loan of 50,000 crowns, and a fleet commanded by 'Colon', who can be identified as the nephew of Guillaume de Casenove, the vice-admiral of France. This was the necessary basis for Henry's successful invasion. During the battle of Bosworth, according to Valera, Richard was advised and supported by one 'Salaçar', of Spanish origin, who can be identified as 'Salazar the little', one of Maximilian's best captains in the Low Countries in the 1480s. The foundation of the Tudor dynasty, like the Readeption of Henry VI in 1470, and the restoration of Edward IV in 1471, had, besides the domestic context, a crucial background of Valois-Burgundian rivalry. Indeed, the contemporary Burgundian chronicler Jean Molinet saw the battle of Bosworth partly as a conflict between a native force and an invading French one: he alleged that Henry's victory was due to the fighting qualities of his French soldiers.

Henry VII needed to safeguard against a repetition of this sequence. Little known, except at the French court, where, as a prince of Valois descent who had experienced misfortune, he was regarded with sympathy and pity, he aimed to win the goodwill and respect of foreign princes, so drawing the stings of plots hatched by foreign exiles against his novel rule. He faced the implacable hostility of Edward IV's sister Margaret (d.1503), widow of Charles the Bold of Burgundy, powerful because of her possession of dower lands in the Low Countries. She aided the rising of John de la Pole, earl of Lincoln in 1487, and in the 1490s was to countenance (as did her kinsman Maximilian) the deceptions of the Frenchman Perkin Warbeck, son of a citizen of Tournai, who intrigued and fought for recognition as her deceased nephew, Richard duke of York (see p. 309).

This centre of hostility to Henry's rule in the Low Countries might have inclined him to cultivate further the friendship of his kinsman and protector Charles VIII, which he was anxious to keep at the start of his reign. But growing French pressure on Dukes Francis and Maximilian was to drive Henry reluctantly but more decisively than his Yorkist predecessors in the 1480s into alliance against the French Crown. In

1487, after the failure of his plots against Charles VIII's government, Duke Francis was exposed to French pressure to marry his daughter and heir Anne to Charles. No English king could accept with equanimity the absorption of Brittany as a French royal appanage. But Henry could not bring himself to accede to Francis's request for military aid, and refused to license an expedition under Sir Edward Wydeville's command. Nevertheless, some Englishmen, as in the 1340s, were eager to establish themselves in Brittany, as a letter written by William Paston to his brother Sir John (13 May 1488) reveals:

Those that resorted thither [*to Southampton*], *to have gone over with him* [*Wydeville*] *tarried there still in hope that they should have been licensed to have gone over; and when they saw no likelihood that they should have licence, there was 200 of them that got into a Breton ship, the which was late come over with salt, and bade the master set them on land in Brittany. And they had not sailed past six leagues but they aspied a Frenchman, and the Frenchman made over to them; and they fared as though they would not have meddled with them, and all the English men went under the hatches, so that they showed no more than those that came to Southampton with the ship, to cause the Frenchman to be the more gladder to meddle with them; and so the Frenchman boarded them, and then they that were under the hatches came up, and so took the Frenchman, and carried the men, ship, and all into Brittany.*

But these aspiring mercenaries were soon routed, when the ducal army covering the approach from Fougères to Rennes was defeated at St Aubin-du-Cormier (July 1488). Duke Francis had to submit: he died within weeks. Henry now came to the aid of the young Duchess Anne with an alacrity which Edward IV had failed to display when Mary of Burgundy had been left fatherless in 1477. He concerted alliances with Maximilian, intended as Anne's bridegroom, and with the Catholic Kings of Spain, with whom he had taken care to cultivate good relations from the early months of his reign. The Anglo-Spanish alliance of 1489 included a project of marriage between their daughter Catherine and Henry's son Arthur, born in 1486. In April 1489 an English army had landed in Brittany under the terms of the recent alliance with the duchess. Henry wrote jubilantly to his friend the earl of Oxford, describing the consternation which its advances had caused French garrisons. He continued:

Our said cousin, the Duchess, is in her city of Rennes; and our right trusty knight and counsellor, Sir Richard Edgecombe, there also, having chief rule about her; and the Marshal of Brittany makes ready to join with them in all haste with a good band of men. Many noblemen of that country repair to our said army to take their part.

Henry's high hopes of success were soon to be dashed. The Duchess Anne's adherents proved incapable of uniting to offer effective opposition to the French. Henry's strenuous attempt to reconstitute the old alliance of England, Burgundy and Brittany had been a signal failure. Neither Anne nor Maximilian had sufficient authority in their provinces to make it effective, and the Catholic Kings were too wary to become deeply involved.

In October 1492, some time after Anne's marriage to Charles VIII, Henry with Maximilian's encouragement led an army of 26,000 across to Calais and down the coast to besiege Boulogne. It was one of the most imposing expeditions which an English king had led to claim his rights in France. But it was late in the year for campaigning, the English had no effective allies, and Henry was exposing his person (and perhaps the March of Calais) to the full weight of French attack. As he had shown by his bold march across the Midlands in 1485, and by his rash progress to the North in 1486, Henry was prepared to gamble on occasion. In 1492 his calculations proved correct. Charles VIII was eager to buy the English off, being anxious to stake his claim to the kingdom of Naples and use it as a base for a crusade against the Ottoman Turks. Though, by his interventions in Brittany and Picardy, Henry VII had displayed a belligerence worthy of Edward III, Tudor and Valois interests led to the extremely rapid conclusion of the peace of Étaples (November 1492), the first effective and lasting peace between the realms in the later Middle Ages, which simply set aside for the time being the ancient issues of the English Crown's claims in France.

For the next ten years, due to Henry's care not to become closely involved in the conflicts caused by the Italian ambitions of Charles VIII (d.1498), and of his successor Louis XII, he had little to fear from the leading continental princes. The Valois courted his alliance or neutrality, and the Catholic Kings, disturbed by French threats to Aragonese interests, committed themselves in 1497 to fulfil a marriage contract between their daughter Catherine and Prince Arthur: the bride arrived in England in 1501. The one recurring source of princely hostility was to be James IV, the vigorous young man who succeeded his father James III as king of Scots in 1488. Though the truces were renewed, Henry failed to establish with James IV the amicable relations he had with his father, possibly because of the youth's suspicion of Henry's contacts among the Scottish nobles, and the intensity of his desire to recover Berwick. In 1491 Archibald Douglas, earl of Angus, under attack from his king, had agreed, in case his lands in Scotland could not be held with English help, to hand over to Henry the formidable castle of The Hermitage, which would have given the English an advanced western base, and a means to control the reivers of Liddesdale. In September 1496, James briefly supported an invasion of Northumberland by Perkin Warbeck (see p. 309) and in 1497 raided there in person, besieging Norham Castle[1]. The defences held firm.

Though Henry had no personal ties in the North, he was well served there. Some noble families in the Marches may have had lingering

Lancastrian sentiments. The earl of Westmorland (d.1499) remained characteristically unrebellious. The earl of Northumberland, ambitious but politic, served Henry well till his death in 1489, after which the Percy interest was eclipsed for a decade, as the earl's son did not come of age until 1499. The northern estates on which Warwick the Kingmaker and Gloucester had based their regional influence remained in the king's hands, for the prospective heir, Clarence's young son, Edward earl of Warwick, was imprisoned in the Tower until his execution in 1499. From 1489 onwards Henry appointed a Vice-Warden of the East and Middle Marches lacking local roots and entirely subservient to the royal will – the able soldier Thomas Howard, earl of Surrey, who after his punishment for fighting against Henry at Bosworth was eager to gain royal favour.

In September 1497 a truce with James was concluded at Ayton with the aid of Spanish mediation. In January 1502 Henry secured a remarkable diplomatic success by concluding an Anglo-Scottish peace, as novel an achievement as his peace with France. By its terms his daughter Margaret was to marry James, a condition fulfilled at Holyrood Abbey in August 1503. James granted to his bride as dower Ettrick Forest and Newark Castle, the earldom of March and the lordships of Dunbar and Cockburnspath, among other lordships – perhaps as a means of promoting amicable relationships in the Anglo-Scottish Borders.

But a succession of deaths sorely shook Henry's peace of mind and threatened his dynastic security. Prince Arthur died in April 1502, his mother Elizabeth of York in February 1503, and Isabella of Castile in November 1504. Isabella's death dislocated some of the characteristic alignments in European diplomacy. Control of Castile was now disputed between her husband, Ferdinand of Aragon (who sought the patronage of his former opponent Louis XII of France) and the ruler of the Low Countries, Philip the Fair, duke of Burgundy, son of the Emperor Maximilian, and husband of Isabella's daughter and heir Joanna. In 1506 Henry formally recognised Philip's rule in Castile. But soon afterwards Philip died, leaving a son aged six (the future Emperor Charles V) as his heir. In December 1507 a treaty of alliance between Henry and Charles (whose guardian was his grandfather Maximilian) arranged for a marriage between Charles and Henry's daughter Mary. Henry showed himself more appreciative than had Edward IV to the need to uphold the House of Burgundy. His ability to protect its interests was never fully put to the test, because Ferdinand was too weak to control Castile, and Louis XII was primarily interested in pursuing his claim to the duchy of Milan.

Henry VII had a weak hand in foreign policy, but he played it resolutely, achieving realistic settlements with France and Scotland. He was to remain for much of his reign more exposed to dynastic plotting than Edward IV had been after 1471. There was the fear that heavy war taxation might provoke popular unrest, which during the

Wars of the Roses had sometimes coalesced with noble rebellion. The danger had been appreciated by an anonymous councillor of Edward IV (the second continuator of the Crowland Abbey Chronicle). Commenting on Edward's 1475 expedition to France, he wrote that the king,

seeing that things had now come to such a pass, that from thenceforth he could not dare, in his emergencies, to ask for the assistance of the English people, and finding that (a thing which really was the case) it was through want of money that the French expedition had, in such a short time, come to nothing . . . he turned all his thoughts to the question how he might in future collect an amount of treasure worthy of his royal station.

In April 1489 there was a rising in Yorkshire in protest against the collection of subsidy granted for the war in Brittany, and in 1497 Cornishmen revolted over payment for the expedition against the Scots.

The mainstay of Henry's predecessors against the French Crown, the ability of its leading vassals to pursue independent foreign policies, crumbled completely in his early years. Like his granddaughter Queen Elizabeth, Henry recognized his handicaps. When the security and peace of the realm were at stake, in the years 1489–92, he showed himself prepared to risk war, as she was to do in Scotland in the 1560s and against Spain in the 1580s, despite dynastic and other domestic weaknesses. Henry's good fortune, which he sedulously cultivated, was that no continental power perceived a lasting need to threaten his rule: the foreign subsidising of rebellion in England, a feature which had helped to keep the Wars of the Roses going since the 1460s, waned. A testimony to Henry's success in foreign relations is the fact that he could afford to neglect the fleet of royal ships maintained by Edward IV and Richard III. Whereas Edward had fifteen or sixteen ships by 1481, Henry had only five by the end of his reign.

War and diplomacy under Henry VIII (1509–47)

The young Henry soon showed that he would not let his mettle be bridled by his father's cares. One of his burning ambitions seems to have been to assert the ancient royal claims in France, without much consideration – unlike those of his councillors who approved of his father's caution – of the availability of resources and allies, or of the dangers inherent in provoking the Valois. Though a large range of foreign ambitions was to animate Henry, French ones remained especially cherished, apparent in the joy with which, middle-aged and in poor health, he once more jogged in arms over the plains of Picardy in 1544. Henry's revival of warlike, aggressive ambitions is not altogether surprising. His father had not renounced his claims in

France, though he had felt it inexpedient to pursue them. Young nobles, eager to display chivalrous valour, were the king's companions. The rise of humanism was acquainting them with Roman moralists' praise of the military as well as civil virtue of antique heroes, and stimulating an interest in past English captains and campaigns. Gentlemen were conscious that their recent ancestors had performed great feats in France and that, as John Leland was to record in his notebooks, the fine mansions they built had sometimes been paid for with the gains of war. In 1513 an anonymous author dedicated to the king a life of the warlike Henry V in English, based chiefly on Tito Livio's near-contemporary humanist panegyric (see p. 216), and on anecdotes preserved in the household of the Butler earls of Ormonde. He purposed to give Henry an example of honour, fame and victory, displayed in the life 'of that puissant prince King Henry V, your ancestor'. In 1523 and 1525 the London printer Richard Pynson published the first volumes of an English translation of Froissart's *Chronicles*, undertaken at Henry's suggestion by the courtier and descendant of Edward III, John Bourchier, lord Berners.

But Henry's renewal of the French wars cannot be viewed exclusively as a bookish and artificial revival of ancient valour. For men were not so conscious as we are that political conditions had irrevocably changed since the days of Edward III and Henry V. Contemporary princes, including the Habsburg claimants to the duchy of Burgundy, might prove as eager allies against the French Crown as French dukes and counts had done in the past. The military methods described by Froissart were still recognisable. English armies continued to be partially recruited, as they had been in the fourteenth and fifteenth centuries, by county commissions of array and by indentures of contract made with native nobles and wealthy gentlemen. The ordinances of war printed by Pynson for the Crown in 1513, laying down the code of discipline to be observed by the army in France, were closely based on Henry V's military ordinances. Retinues still contained a high proportion of longbowmen: the traditional weapon's virtues, despite the increasing effectiveness of handguns, were long to be extolled in royal proclamations and by literary tacticians. Nevertheless, Henry VIII's armies differed radically in their balance of arms and in their tactics from those of the Hundred Years War, though some differences were probably foreshadowed in campaigns of the Wars of the Roses. Henry's knights fought as skirmishing and pursuing cavalry, no longer dismounting to merge in the mass of infantry with archers and billmen. The noble Englishman once more stood out on the field as a superior chivalrous being – and as a good a target for gunners. The importance of artillery in the field had been enthusiastically appreciated in England from the 1450s onwards. Since then guns had become more manouevrable and effective. Infantry remained the most important arm on the battlefield, but indispensable adjuncts to the billmen on continental expeditions were provided now by arquebussiers and artillerymen (often, like companies of pikemen, foreign mercenaries), besides native archers.

In 1510 Henry renewed the peace of Étaples with the well-placed Louis XII, but the following year he joined the Holy League formed by Pope Julius II with the aim of ejecting the French from Milan (November 1511). The English roles were to check French naval activity in the Channel, and to send a force to Castile to co-operate with Ferdinand of Aragon in the conquest of Aquitaine. Henry made a more ambitious commitment than his recent predecessors, whose expeditions against France had been based principally on military alliances with rulers of the Low Countries, and on the use of Channel ports. The upshot taught Henry their good sense. The unprofessional army which landed at San Sebastian in Castile (June 1512), commanded by Thomas Grey, marquess of Dorset, succumbed to the enervating effects of the summer heat and local wine. Dorset failed to agree on a plan of campaign with King Ferdinand. Ravaged by dysentery, prone to mutiny and plunder, the English ignominiously embarked for home without having struck a significant blow, or having received their sovereign's licence to return. The Archduchess Margaret of Savoy, regent in the Low Countries for her nephew Charles duke of Burgundy, commented justly that Englishmen had 'so long abstained from war, they lack experience from disuse, and, as it is reported, they now be almost weary of it'.

Henry was prepared to drop recriminations and learn from mistakes. In April 1513 a new alliance against Louis XII was sworn with Pope Leo X, the Emperor Maximilain, Margaret of Savoy and Ferdinand. Henry's ambitious councillor, Thomas Wolsey, worked indefatigably to organise the pay, transport and supply of an impressive army which, under the king's command, assembled in the March of Calais during June 1513. The inexpert English retinues, organised and commanded, in the traditional manner, by leading nobles such as the duke of Buckingham and the earl of Northumberland, were stiffened by 14,000 German and Swiss professionals. On this occasion no reliance was placed on Maximilian's habitually facile promises of military aid: true to Burgundian tradition he was to add little but his flattering presence to Henry's army. Owing to the absence of the main French forces in Italy, and Henry's good sense in never straying far from friendly territory in the March of Calais and the Low Countries, he retrieved his military prestige. Ill-fortified Thérouanne in Artois surrendered in August, after an imprudent relieving force had been routed in an exhilarating cavalry skirmish, the 'Battle of the Spurs'. The wealthy city of Tournai, a French enclave in a sea of Habsburg territory, surrendered in September, after being briefly subjected to the honour of a royal siege.

This ostentatious continental success was to have less lasting significance than the achievement earlier in the month of Henry's lieutenant-general in the north of England, the earl of Surrey, against the Scots. After his accession Henry had renewed the peace with his brother-in-law James IV. But relations between the sovereigns were never cordial. James may have resented and feared the ambitious pride of his vigorous young kinsman. Breaches of the peace led to royal recriminations. In July 1512 James concluded an alliance with Louis XII, and the following year crossed the Tweed with a fine army, rapidly reducing some of the castles of the Eastern March, including Norham, with his impressive artillery train. Surrey was able to intercept the Scots not far south of the Border. At Flodden field (9 September 1513) the earl, perhaps with a confidence bred of deep knowledge of James's weaknesses as a commander, boldly handled his forces so as to exploit their tactical advantages. The accurate English artillery fire goaded the Scots from a strong defensive position, enabling the English billmen to break up the Scottish infantry with their unwieldy pikes. James IV perished in the fray, leaving an infant son, James V, as king of Scots.

Flodden gave some security to the north of England, but Henry's advanced positions on the continent remained precarious. Due to his military isolation, to the great cost of the 1513 expedition, and the heavy expense of garrisoning Tournai, whose inhabitants were restive under alien rule, it was impossible for him to mount the expedition he had planned in order to consolidate and augment his acquisitions. Prompted by Wolsey, Henry negotiated with Louis: in August 1514 peace was concluded on the basis of *de facto* recognition of the existing territorial position. The French king accepted Henry's sister Mary in marriage. But within months Louis died (1 January 1515), and was succeeded by his young cousin Francis I, anxious, despite his renewal of the Anglo-French peace (April 1515), to recover Thérouanne and Tournai. To distract the English, he despatched to Scotland his courtier John Stewart, duke of Albany, to claim the regency during the minority of James V. He also set about undoing the achievement of the Holy League by restoring French rule in the duchy of Milan – an objective attained as a result of his famous victory over the highly reputed Swiss mercenaries at Marignano (September 1515).

Wolsey devised diplomatic missions to tie up the French in Italy. At Zürich, Richard Pace negotiated the hire of 12,000 Swiss to attack Milan for the sum of 20,000 crowns. But Henry's ambitious plans to invade France in 1516 had to be abandoned: his ally Maximilian and his Swiss proved ineffective against the French defences in Lombardy. Another ally, Ferdinand of Aragon, died in 1516. His grandson Charles of Burgundy, ruler of the Low Countries, was intent on securing his claims to the Spanish kingdoms and unwilling to challenge the French in Milan. Other rulers, notably Maximilian, only toyed with Henry's schemes for a new anti-French league. Wolsey, taking advantage of Leo X's attempts to promote a general peace in Christendom, was once again able to give Henry's belligerent policies a more pacific, realistic turn by negotiating peace with Francis. Henry was now prepared to give up his prize, Tournai, as alarms about French intentions of attacking it faced him with the great expense of completing his new citadel there. By the peace treaty of October 1518, preliminary agreement was reached that the city should be surrendered for an indemnity of 600,000 crowns, and that Henry's daughter Mary should be betrothed to the dauphin of France. Francis undertook to keep Albany in France and the parties professed their willingness to undertake a crusade against the Turks.

Over the next few years Wolsey was able to prolong his master's fitful interest in the attainment of peace in Christendom. Wolsey tried to gain international prestige for himself by attempting to mediate between Francis I and his emergent rival, the Netherlandish and Spanish ruler Charles of Habsburg, who in June 1519, when aged nineteen, was elected king of the Romans in succession to his grandfather Maximilian, beating the rival candidatures of Francis and Henry. In May 1520 Henry entertained his kinsman Charles at Canterbury, and the following month splendidly advertised his pacific intent by meeting Francis at a luxurious encampment between Guines and Ardres, on the frontier of the March of Calais. The congress was called 'the Field of Cloth of Gold' by contemporaries, dazzled by the size and magnificence of the royal retinues, the marquees and their furnishings and of the prefabricated palace, which Henry erected near Guines Castle, as spectacular to contemporaries as the Crystal Palace of the 1851 Great Exhibition.

But this display of largesse and courtesy failed to produce a lasting atmosphere of cordiality between the two courts. Unlike Richard II's meeting with Charles VI of France near Calais in 1397, it had been preceded by several years of belligerence rather than friendly social contact. Henry was not sufficiently powerful nor trusted to prevent a Valois–Habsburg confrontation. His interest in Wolsey's manifestly failing policy, which in any case was not to the taste of bellicose nobles and courtiers, waned. Queen Catherine's nephew, the Emperor Charles V, appeared temptingly capable of aiding the English Crown's ancient claims in France. In 1521 Henry became secretly committed to war with France, if peace efforts failed. At Bruges, Charles V reached agreement with Wolsey to marry Princess Mary. He granted the cardinal a substitute for his French pension and promised to support his candidature at the next papal election. In 1522 the emperor, being entertained at Windsor, concerted plans for a joint assault on Francis I. The duke of Norfolk's son Thomas Howard, earl of Surrey advanced from Calais with a force which assisted at the unsuccessful imperial siege of Hesdin. In 1523 Henry's boon companion and brother-in-law the duke of Suffolk advanced from Calais and pillaged the Seine valley. In 1524 Surrey crossed the border into Scotland to challenge the francophile Albany, once more regent. But in the end Henry had even less to show for the ambitious projects of 1523–5 than for his war of 1511–14. His comparative lack of financial resources, and the need to divert some to check the Scots prevented the exploitation of favourable strategic opportunities in northern France.

Charles V, showing his mettle in international affairs, shrugged off Henry's ambitions. After the imperial forces had defeated and captured Francis I at the battle of Pavia (February 1525), he ignored Henry's appeals, giving neither military nor diplomatic support to his grandiose proposals for a partition of France. Wolsey's feverish efforts to raise large taxes – necessary if an English army was to achieve anything on its own – provoked bitter opposition when collection was attempted in the localities. Henry's moment of greatest opportunity in France slipped past, because his ally did not wish to aggrandise him, his own resources were no longer sufficient, and his subjects, despite their fondness for recalling past victories over the French, were unwilling to open their purses for long to pay for new ones. Henry VIII took years to learn painfully the kind of lessons about Anglo-French conflict which Richard II had known before he came of age, Henry V had recognised soon after his shattering successes, and which were axiomatic to the policies of Edward IV and Henry VII. But Tudor statesmen digested the lessons of 1525. It marks another stage in the termination of the Hundred Years War, the last occasion on which an English prince seriously put forward a scheme for the domination of France.

In the wake of these disappointments, Wolsey negotiated a peace treaty with Francis I (August 1525), which stipulated that Henry was to receive a French pension of 100,000 crowns for life. In April 1527 Henry allied with him in order to check the growth of imperial power in Italy. The capture of Rome by Charles V's army in May further threatened papal independence. Henry and Wolsey rightly feared that Pope Clement VII would consequently delay proceedings in the king's suit for the nullification of his marriage to the emperor's aunt, Catherine of Aragon. In January 1528 Henry declared war on Charles V: he was prepared to subsidise a French expedition to recover Milan and 'rescue' Clement. A war against the traditional ally was unpopular in England, especially as it disrupted trade with the principal English markets in the Low Countries and Spain. In June 1528 there was an Anglo-imperial armistice. French failure in Italy undermined Wolsey's hopes for anti-imperial alliances and the success of the royal suit. By the spring of 1529 Clement had resigned himself to the prospect of imperial hegemony in Italy. 'I have quite made up my mind to become an imperialist and to live and die as such,' he remarked. In August peace was concluded between Charles V and Francis I by the treaty of Cambrai. In October Wolsey was dismissed from the Chancellorship (cf. p. 315).

During the next few years Henry's marital and religious policies were to produce novel and lasting changes in England's relationship with the rest of Christendom. The statutes of 1532–3 threatening the *curia's* jurisdiction over England provoked the unenthusiastic excommunication of Henry (July 1533). The retaliatory declaration of Royal

Supremacy (1534) marked Henry's definitive move to schism. The hitherto ostentatiously orthodox king stood in danger of having a crusade preached against him, like the despised Hussites of Bohemia and Lutherans of Germany. It was not in Henry's interest when Charles V and Francis I concluded a truce of ten years in 1538. Papal hopes rose: Pope Paul III issued a bull, prepared three years previously, deposing Henry and absolving his subjects from allegiance. Henry listlessly followed the counsel of Thomas Cromwell in seeking, without much response, the alliance of German Protestant princes opposed to Charles V, and of Christian III of Denmark. With extreme reluctance, sacrificing his sombre state of widowerhood, the king took a bride – Anne, the gauche sister of William, duke of Cleves, Juliers and Berg and of Gelderland – in order to gain a minor but strategically placed anti-imperial, anti-papal ally (January 1540).

The necessity for Cromwell's 'Protestant' diplomacy declined, as relations between French and imperialists characteristically worsened. Charles V was too politic and immersed in international problems to have opposed his heretic kinsman fanatically. His able ambassador at the English Court, Eustace Chapuys, had kept open avenues of communication, and one pathetic obstacle to better relations had disappeared when the unhappy, discarded Queen Catherine died in January 1536. By 1543 the English and imperialists were committed to a joint campaign against France.

In the early 1540s Henry seems to have regained some of the youthful zest for ambitious foreign aims, which the failures and hazards of the two previous decades had impaired. To secure the Border he pressed for a conference at York with his nephew James V, a Catholic prince married to a French princess, Mary daughter of Claude duke of Guise. Henry hoped to persuade his nephew to turn against the papacy and the French, but in September 1541 James humiliated him by failing to come to York, though Henry for the first time in his reign had progressed that far north. Henry determined on negotiation backed by coercion. A skirmish in the West March at Solway Moss (November 1542) resulted in the capture of Scots nobles. Within weeks of hearing the bad tidings, James V died, aged thirty, leaving a newborn daughter Mary as queen of Scots. Henry planned to exploit this favourable turn by releasing the Scottish nobles, when they had given assurance to promote the repudiation of papal authority in Scotland, Mary's marriage to his son and heir Edward, and the acknowledgement of the English Crown's ancient claim to suzerainty.

This immoderate reversion to the antiquated precedents of 'forward' policies in Scotland was to revive once familiar frustrations for English councillors and miseries for Lowland Scots. The factions on whom Henry relied to maintain the marriage treaty of July 1543 failed to prevent its repudiation by the Scottish parliament. In May 1544 the earl of Hertford landed at Leith with an expedition which burnt and pillaged Edinburgh and the Lothians, as Henry's memorial of vengeance to Scottish perfidy, but also with the more practical motive of denying a base to French forces. In the summer and autumn the Wardens kept up raiding pressure in the Borders, especially effective from their eastern bases at Berwick, Norham and Wark. Lairds and 'surnames' in Merse and Teviotdale gave assurances: Coldingham was garrisoned and, on the West March, a badly needed forward base was occupied at Langholm. These achievements were endangered when in February 1545 one of their chief architects, Sir Ralph Eure, Warden of the Middle March, was defeated and killed at Ancrum Moor, when challenging the power of the earl of Angus and Walter Scott, laird of Buccleuch. In September Hertford led an expedition to reassert English influence, taking Kelso Abbey by assault and burning corn along the Tweed and its tributaries.

The English ascendancy in the frontier war rested on a narrow balance of military superiority. Henry as well as his lieutenants and wardens recognised the need for planting garrisons on Scottish soil, to maintain both that superiority and an influence over Scottish government. But he wanted quick and cheap results, for his eyes were fixed on France. Consequently his Scottish ambitions floundered, though the local commanders energetically kept up the frontier offensive.

In 1543 Charles V and Henry had planned a joint invasion of France. Their forces were to converge on Paris. In July 1544 Henry landed at Calais to join his army, sluggishly led by the dukes of Norfolk and Suffolk. Henry had sensibly abandoned the plan to co-operate with the fickle emperor, sending part of his army in his father's footsteps to besiege Boulogne (another part besieging Montreuil). But the son was more interested in the triumph of gaining the port, promoting his dominance in the Narrow Seas. In September the garrison capitulated to him, and the emperor made a separate peace with Francis I. For the first time Henry faced the French without allies. They planned to attack southern England in the summer of 1545. As in 1386 a large invasion force was assembled, this time at the new base of Le Havre in Normandy. It faced some formidable defences. During the insecure years since the break with the papacy Henry had augmented his ships: he possessed about forty, forming the nucleus of the fleet. Large sums had been spent on strengthening and building fortifications, particularly to defend the southern coasts (1538–41). New forts, some designed by a Moravian engineer, Stefan van Haschenperg, mounted and were intended to withstand artillery[2]. In July 1545, when an invasion fleet of more than 200 ships sailed off Hampshire into the Solent, it faced well prepared defences. Some French forces landed on the Isle of Wight. Henry came to join his army, and watched as his warships in Portsmouth harbour, commanded by John Dudley, lord Lisle, weighed anchor to challenge the French. This was when one of his most famous ships, the *Mary Rose*, sank with great loss of life. But the French withdrew, having failed to worst English naval and military power, or to isolate the besieged English garrison in Boulogne. In June

1546 peace was made. Henry undertook the eventual surrender of Boulogne in return for a large indemnity.

Henry's last French war, with no Wolsey to organise it, had been wastefully conducted. The inflation of the 1540s multiplied costs and induced a sober readiness to make peace. But Henry had dissipated much of the Crown's recently acquired land to pay for war, selling many of the former monastic estates. Plans to use some of the acquired wealth for educational endowments were mostly shelved. Henry the heroic general and chivalrous knight had triumphed over Henry the scholar and patron of humanism – and also, to some extent, over the augmentor of Crown lands, who had spectacularly if tardily emulated Edward IV's and Henry VII's attempts to enable the king to live of his own.

Henry VIII, by repudiating papal allegiance, took a step which was eventually to influence profoundly the conceptual framework and the aims of English foreign policy. He is one of the individuals who had the most dynamic influence on the history of English diplomatic relations. Yet this was the incidental product of expediency rather than ambition. Henry's abiding aims and methods were profoundly traditional. His interest in transoceanic exploration was perfunctory and occasional, conditioned by the need not to offend the Habsburgs. His success in pursuing old-fashioned territorial gains was small. Foreign observers sometimes found him ridiculous, and their low estimates have been echoed by some continental historians. Yet it was not just sycophancy that led his councillors to have a profound respect for the mature Henry's judgment in foreign affairs. Perhaps his greatest achievement in this sphere, within the contemporary context, was to give his subjects the conviction that no other king since Henry V had been so respected and feared abroad.

Shrinking ambitions and growing insecurity (1547–85)

In the first year of Edward VI's reign his uncle, the Protector Somerset, who had acquired a military reputation campaigning in Henry's last years, with his fellow councillors vigorously pursued some of their late master's foreign aims, however much in other respects they may have brushed aside his dying wishes. The vulnerable defences of Boulogne were strengthened at great cost, and in September 1547 Somerset led an army across the eastern Scottish border, intent on preventing the consolidation of French influence in Scotland, and proclaiming his intention of procuring Queen Mary's marriage to Edward. Within a few days he won what was to be the last of those shattering and somewhat barren Tudor victories over the Scots. The earl of Angus's army, covering Edinburgh on the coast at Musselburgh and along the River Esk, was in a strong tactical position. But with inadequate flank protection, the central mass of Scots pikemen moved from their defences to attack the English, who pounded them from all sides. When the Scots broke, the slaughter was immense, for they lacked cavalry to cover the retreat. As a consequence of the victory of Pinkie Cleugh, the English were able to establish garrisons controlling the eastern Scottish coast as far north as Arbroath. In 1548 Haddington was made the principal base for controlling Lothian, being stuffed with soldiers.

But this precarious high point of military success was too costly to maintain. The Scottish regent, James V's determined widow Mary of Guise, procured French help. In June 1548 a French force landed at Leith to protect the capital. Under their protection the Estates met defiantly in Haddington Abbey to ratify the marriage treaty between the dauphin and their queen, and a future Franco-Scottish union of Crowns. The queen was dispatched to France. The English had to defend Haddington resolutely: they evacuated it in October 1549. The protector's Scottish policy was ruined by domestic discord, and by the French king Henry II, whose forces had invested Boulogne in August. The Council, prompted by Warwick, approved negotiations with the French, which began in January 1550. By the terms of the treaty made in March, Boulogne was to be immediately surrendered in return for an indemnity.

The treaty marked the start of a decade in which English rulers showed anxiety to retreat from dangerously bold Henrician foreign aims. The weakness of Edward's government was not as inimical to the realm as might have been the case, since Henry II and Charles V were locked in a struggle in which England was a lesser stake. Northumberland, offensive to Charles because of the harshness shown to this cousin Mary Tudor, sought French protection. By the treaty of Angers (July 1551), Edward resigned his claim to the marriage of Mary queen of Scots, and was betrothed to Henry II's daughter Elizabeth.

Edward VI's successor, his sister Mary, had grown to rely on the distant protection of her Habsburg kinsmen. A policy of alliance with them was acceptable to many of her subjects. To nobles and councillors it appeared comfortably traditional. Merchants trading with Antwerp and Spain welcomed it: some hoped it might procure a direct share in the American trade. But the novel succession of a female raised the problem of her marriage. There was disquiet at the prospect of a foreign king. In the 1460s Sir John Fortescue had asserted that no one ought to rule who had been born out of the realm. Henry VIII's wars and anti-papal propaganda had stoked up patriotic anti-alien feelings. They had been expressed in Edward Hall's polished and influential vernacular account of recent English history, published by Richard Grafton in 1548. In 1544 the antiquary John Leland had published his *Assertio inclytissimi Arturii Regis*, violently attacking the Italian Polydore Vergil for his presumption in querying the achievements, indeed the existence of King Arthur.

Most of Mary's councillors opposed the project of a match with

Charles V's son Philip. Bishop Gardiner, her ageing, sick Chancellor promoted the suit of the earl of Devon. But by the end of October Mary had promised Charles's ambassador Simon Renard that she would marry Philip. In January 1554 the marriage treaty was publicly proclaimed. Philip was to assist the queen in governing and adhere to the laws and customs of the realm. Offices were to be filled by Englishmen, even some in his household. He was not to involve England in his present war with France, nor remove the queen, her jewels, ships and guns from the realm. If she died childless, his rights as king consort were to be abrogated. Opposition to the rule of an unknown, foreign, Catholic prince was compromised by Wyatt's rebellion (see p. 329).

After Gardiner had married Philip and Mary in Winchester Cathedral, the king stayed in the realm for just over a year (July 1554–September 1555). Fears that royal patronage might be diverted to grasping aliens proved unfounded. In political, religious and personal matters Philip behaved with politic sense. His Spaniards were obliged to respect the natives, even to the extent of sampling beer. Philip's interest in English affairs, where he was so constricted, understandably waned, especially when the queen failed to produce the heir which would guarantee his continued rule. In 1555 more promising fields of activity opened for him, when his father resigned to him the rule of the Spanish kingdoms and the Low Countries. When hostilities broke out between Spain and France in 1557, Philip revisited the touchy English, to persuade his loving queen to browbeat her subjects into entering the war fully in his support. As parliament (January–March 1558), as had become usual since Henry's death, was too critical of royal policies and distrustful of the stability of authority to grant large subsidies for overseas expeditions, English help was not worth much. In July 1557 7,000 soldiers commanded by William Herbert, earl of Pembroke crossed to assist against the French at St Quentin. Checked in the Low Countries, the French prepared a stroke against Calais. In a brilliant winter campaign (January 1558), the duke of Guise rapidly over-ran the March. A few months later the French threatened to take the Channel Islands too by their seizure of Alderney. Mary died in November 1558, without having been able to take effective measures for the recapture of Calais. Its loss, shameful to gentlemen nurtured on traditions of valour in the French wars, may have further helped undermine sentiments in favour of Tudor–Habsburg alliance.

Despite the brevity of Mary's reign and the feebleness of her role in international affairs, it was perhaps a highly influential period in the hardening of commonly expressed views about foreign relations. Hostility to the Habsburgs for the first time became a popular cry. The experience of religious persecution, hitherto an aspect of episcopal discipline and royal prerogative, became associated with allegiance to an alien king and pope.

In Elizabeth's reign uncertainty over foreign and domestic threats, over the succession and the prolonged, intensifying Catholic reactions against militant Protestantism produced new pressures on the making of foreign policy. There developed competing groups comprising nobles, councillors, members of parliament, clerics and pamphleteers eager to persuade the sovereign to conform to increasingly doctrinaire views of international affairs. As Catholic and Protestant factions polarised in neighbouring realms, the predominantly Protestant English governing elites became more sensitive to a conjunction of foreign and domestic threats. With 'hard-line' views in the ascendant in the 1570s and 1580s, royal freedom of manoeuvre in foreign affairs became more difficult to maintain.

Policy in the first decade of the reign was characterised by dissent between those who felt it necessary, in view of the realm's weakness and the expansionist tendencies of the French Crown, to cultivate or appease the Habsburgs, and those who, viewing Philip II as the protagonist of the papal Antichrist and persecutor of the godly reformed, wished to break with him and other Catholic rulers, encouraging and sustaining their rebellious subjects. Both policies were advocated by powerful conciliar and noble factions. The situation encouraged Elizabeth's preference for diplomatic manoeuvring rather than positive commitment. Nevertheless, she eventually embarked on dangerous military ventures, promoting Protestantism by intervention without royal allies in both Scotland and France. Neither episode, surprisingly, ended in disaster nor in a financially crippling prolonged commitment – as a result of domestic developments in those countries, her servants' diplomatic skills, and her own flexible ability to distinguish and abandon inessential aims.

From the first Elizabeth showed a politic willingness to maintain good relations with Philip II, which he reciprocated, despite their mutually hostile memories of her sister's reign, and distaste for each other's religious inclinations. His ambassador, the count of Feria brought his proposal of marriage, which was received in the same cool, polite spirit as it was given. In April 1559 both powers made peace with France. A face-saving formula covered English acceptance of the loss of Calais. Philip married a Valois princess, a *rapprochement* which did nothing to ease English fear of France. Neither did the death of the belligerent Henry II, mortally wounded in July at the tilt. For his son Francis II was married to Mary queen of Scots, who ostentatiously maintained a claim to the English throne. In the eyes of the Roman Catholic Church, she was a legitimate descendant of Henry VII, whereas Elizabeth was an illegitimate one. The English Crown, which had so long exploited claims to sovereignty in neighbouring principalities, was now confronted by a formidably backed ruler who could plausibly mete out to it the same baleful treatment.

But Mary's interests in Scotland had stood in jeopardy since May 1559, when a revolt, headed by lords favouring Protestants, broke out there against her mother's francophile regency. If the prospective Franco-Scottish 'dual monarchy' was to be sundered, English support for the rebels was necessary. Subsidies alone proved insufficient. Sir William Winter was instructed to prepare a fleet which could be used to blockade the French in Leith. Plans were laid for a reluctant Thomas Howard, duke of Norfolk, to lead an army of 6,000 to Berwick. Only after discordant conciliar debates were the interventionists, notably the Secretary Sir William Cecil, able to persuade their colleagues to approve invasion plans. But the queen hesitated. Winter alone was authorised to attack: in January 1560 he raided the Forth estuary, capturing supplies intended for the French force threatening the rebels at St Andrews. It was not enough. Next month, at Berwick, the Protestant leaders agreed that Elizabeth should take Scotland under her protection, to preserve its liberties, and in March an English army under Lord Grey of Wilton trod the familiar paths across the Border. The queen committed her insecure, financially weak Crown to another confrontation with the Franco-Scottish alliance, necessarily in a more sensibly modest spirit than English interventions of the 1540s. But all did not go well. In May the English were badly repulsed in an assault on the French entrenchments at Leith. But the death of the regent Mary of Guise left her supporters in political disarray. In July 1560 Cecil negotiated the Treaty of Edinburgh. The Scots queen was to recognise Elizabeth's English title. Most of the foreign soldiers were to be withdrawn from Scotland, and its parliament was to submit a list from which councillors would be chosen. The possibility that the agreement would be reversed was lessened by the death of Francis II in December and the succession of his brother Charles IX, a minor. But Mary continued to look to French rather than English support to consolidate her rule in Scotland, after she landed at Leith in August 1561. Her reliance on it was to be undermined by the outbreak and recurrence of Protestant rebellion in France.

Elizabeth surmounted the threat of a confrontation with the Franco-Scottish alliance at the start of her reign, not so much because of a somewhat unconvincing military intervention, but because problems of royal authority, fusing with interconfessional tensions, deprived the ancient adversaries of their customary effectiveness. One result of the war was the establishment of lasting (if frequently frayed) bonds with sections of the Scottish governing class. But relations with the Scots queen remained tricky. Mary angled for public recognition in England as heir presumptive, with an established reversion after Elizabeth's descendants. But Elizabeth refused to commit herself. In 1561 Mary's secretary Maitland reported that she had said to him: 'I know the inconstancy of the people of England, how they ever mislike the present government and have their eyes fixed upon that person that is next to succeed . . . I have good experience of myself in my sister's time, how desirous men were that I should be in place and earnest to set me up.'

The growing tendency of factions to organise on a religious basis made it inevitable that, whatever attitude Elizabeth took up over the succession, she would be under strong pressure to modify it from councillors, parliaments and agitators at large. Her judgment that it was less dangerous not to commit herself was probably correct. If Mary had been her publicly acknowledged heir, English Catholics might have been encouraged in flouting the established ecclesiastical order and, if harshly disciplined, to rebel. If Elizabeth had tried to secure Mary's recognition in parliament, she might have encountered adamant opposition from her Protestant supporters, and the organisation of a powerful faction in support of a native candidate. Such possibilities made it easier for her to endure speculation and even intrigue among her councillors and nobles over the succession, and impudent pressure on her, especially from parliaments, to alleviate the problem by marriage. She was able to avoid commitments on both issues because there was no obvious candidate for either the succession or for her hand who could attract the support of a predominant following.

The foreign bridegroom most persistently canvassed between 1560 and 1567 was Philip's cousin Charles archduke of Austria. His Catholicism marred the attraction of his alliance as a means of cementing Habsburg friendship, in case of a resurgence of Franco-Scottish hostility. Charles's cause was canvassed by the duke of Norfolk and some of his kinsmen, not least in order to counter Northumberland's son Robert lord Dudley. By 1560 he was so high in royal favour that soberminded councillors such as Cecil feared the queen would arouse a political storm by marrying this upstart son and grandson of traitors, whose wife died that year in suspiciously mysterious circumstances.

In 1562 plans were afoot for a meeting at York between Elizabeth and Mary which might have put their relations on a stabler basis. But, to the relief of fervent Protestants, the conference did not materialise. Both queens hoped for gains from the victory of the opposing sides in the French civil war which broke out in 1562. Elizabeth acted with an adventurous temerity more characteristic of her father, prompted by Dudley rather than Cecil. In October she allied with the Protestant rebel prince of Condé, garrisoning Le Havre under the command of Dudley's elder brother Ambrose earl of Warwick, in the expectation of exchanging it for Calais. But in March 1563 the Huguenots made peace with Charles IX, and in July the English attempt to retain Le Havre singlehanded collapsed after the garrison was ravaged by plague. Peace was made with France in April 1564: French domestic absorption precluded more adverse consequences from this striking demonstration of English military weakness and diplomatic isolation. In the next few years French internal tensions induced Mary to seek Spanish or English protection, though she remained too unaccommodating for Elizabeth. In 1564 the latter rather oddly proposed Dudley as Mary's husband, a socially demeaning marriage but one which might have secured her the right to the succession, as wife to an impeccably Protestant English magnate. Instead in 1565 she married her kinsman Henry Stewart, lord Darnley, a step which could not but arouse suspicions in Elizabeth's and Protestant Englishmen's minds, since Darnley was a Catholic of Tudor descent.

Mary's marital problems – her estrangement from and the assassination of Darnley, her marriage to the Protestant Bothwell (1567) – were speedily to ruin her standing in international and Scottish affairs. Her nobles rebelled and proclaimed her infant son as James VI. Elizabeth, shocked by Mary's reckless conduct, but consumed with royal rage at theirs, was assiduously courted by both parties. In May 1568 Mary fled to England, landing at Workington in Cumberland. Henceforth, until her execution in 1587, Mary was a force in English domestic politics. For nine years the two queens had zestfully played diplomatic chess. Their failure to make concessions was to place them, in a new age of more deadly national and religious confrontation, in a mutually less flexible and more dangerous relationship.

The tensions between England and Spain which occasionally tautened in the 1560s and 1570s were eventually to snap in the outbreak of a war, instigated by Elizabeth, which was only ended in 1604, by James I. It would be hard to find a previous war undertaken with so much reluctance by one English monarch and abandoned with such alacrity by another. It was one of the longest continuous wars the English had fought in recent generations, paralleled only by the conflict of 1420–44 with Valois France. That war had been about the maintenance of the English Crown's claims to exercise sovereignty in France. In contrast to traditional English interventions on the continent, motivated by the desire for conquest and gains of war, the war with Spain was not primarily concerned with territorial claims. Philip II was to deny Elizabeth's sovereignty in England, and she flouted his in the Low Countries and Americas. But the basic issue of the war for the English Crown was the threat to the Elizabethan settlement arising from the lengthy struggle between Philip and his subjects in the Low Countries. In the early 1580s that struggle entered a critical phase: a concentration of Philip's vast resources on the problem threatened to destroy the existing political and religious balance in north-west Europe, for decades unstable, replacing it by a Spanish, Roman Catholic hegemony.

In this international crisis, the ability of the English Crown to maintain its diplomatic independence and its form of polity, so suspect since the 1550s, but never strongly challenged, was at last placed at stake. The interminable, expensive, debilitating war may seem to have been barren of achievement. Spanish military and naval power was not destroyed, nor the Spanish grip on the Low Countries and Americas prised loose. But the English Crown demonstrated an unexpectedly formidable ability to safeguard the realm from invasion and internal subversion, and to distract, hamper and weaken a much stronger opponent by the skilful deployment of subsidies, warships and soldiers. Though James I, a foreigner and an unusually fervent peacelover, was disinclined to put matters to the test again, the wár had given those who tried to influence foreign policy in the early seventeenth century a new sense of confidence. Dispirited by the political intrigues of her later years, Elizabeth compared herself to Richard II, but to the rulers of Oliver Cromwell's Commonwealth she was a Henry V.

For two decades prior to the outbreak of the war, events had hardened mutual suspicion and hostility. In the 1560s the Courts of Westminster and Madrid regarded each other with cordial dislike. Elizabeth and Philip both had councillors eager to promote hostilities, but awareness of their own weaknesses magnified in each cautious monarch's eyes the ability of the other to do damage, and made them draw back from the brink. Elizabeth was exasperated by Philip's failure to commit himself to a fully conciliatory policy in the Low Countries, or to discountenance plots against her rule by his servants, and English and Irish Catholics in his dominions. But she was well aware of her weaknesses. The unstable French Crown could not be relied on to oppose the Spaniards effectively in the Low Countries, or to limit its own ambitions there. Though Mary queen of Scots was in honourable English custody from 1568, and Elizabeth an arbiter of the fate of her Crown and the Scottish factions, there was little joy for the English in the rule of a weakened Protestant nobility, tainted by rebellion, and threatened by a Marian party which remained a military force in Scotland till 1571. Perhaps most dangerous of all, Mary's presence in England was an irresistible incentive for malcontents – Catholic northerners, nobles who resented the dominance at Court of Leicester or Cecil and disliked anti-Spanish policies, exiles and papalist fanatics (see p. 331). There was no satisfactory solution for Elizabeth's Marian problem. Had she succeeded in restoring the queen of Scots, as she tried to do in 1570, she might have provided a future rod to her back. Had she received her at Court as queen, she would have instantly created a rival sun in her own realm, at least as dangerous as she herself had been in her sister's reign.

Philip had plenty of reasons for his exasperation with Elizabeth. He abhorred her religion and her aid to rebels against royal and papal authority in Scotland and France. He was indignant that the ruling groups of southern England, whom he had tried vainly to appease when he was their king, showed contempt for his authority by harbouring his rebels in their ports and trading illegally with his settlers in America. But he feared that if he went to war with England, the rebels in the Low Countries would be emboldened and that English sailors would effectively cut his vital sea communications with Flanders. So, though Elizabeth provided him with a clear *casus belli*, an unmistakable pointer to the hostile drift of her policy in 1568, he failed to take advantage of her diplomatic weakness and domestic crises in the next few years.

In 1568 five Spanish ships sought refuge from bad weather and the threat of Low Countries privateers at Plymouth and Southampton. They were transporting £85,000 worth of bullion to pay the arrears of Alva's army in the Netherlands. Technically, the bullion still belonged to Genoese bankers who had loaned it to the Spanish Crown. The queen renegotiated the loan with them – she had possession, and her credit was much better than Philip's. There followed Anglo-Spanish trade embargoes and seizures of shipping, which further demonstrated her power to inhibit Alva. Yet he and his master did nothing more: they had their hands full elsewhere. They gave no more but fair words to the noble English plotters preparing to move in favour of Mary. The one serious revolt against Elizabeth's rule collapsed by February 1570 without having received any Spanish help (see p. 331). Spaniards, including the ambassador Mendoza, were certainly implicated in Norfolk's Marian plotting in 1571. That muddled business, efficiently exposed by Elizabethan intelligence services, was no great threat, though it increased anti-Spanish feeling.

But as Burghley perceived when he opened negotiations with Alva in March 1572, the logic of the situation, of comparative Spanish passivity and English success, pointed to *rapprochement*. The Marians had suffered crushing reverses in England and Scotland: the treaty of Blois (April), promising Anglo-French amity, was another blow to them and another reason for Philip to court the queen. Unfortunately, unforeseen events were to make the possibility remote. In March the queen had ordered Philip's privateering Netherlandish rebels to leave her ports. As no one anticipated, least of all these 'Sea Beggars', they ignited a new revolt in the Low Countries. Their accidental capture of Brill in April led during the next three months to the fall of almost all Holland and Zealand. Despite the queen's abhorrence of rebellion, she could not strengthen Philip's military power and affront English Protestant opinion by coming to terms with him at the expense of the Dutch. Moreover, Protestant opinion was further hardened against Catholic rulers by the infamous massacre on St Bartholomew's Day (24 August 1572), when, in order to maintain her influence over her son Charles IX's court, Catherine de Medicis countenanced the slaughter of Protestants in Paris and elsewhere.

Such coups and plots against co-religionists further hardened reciprocal English and Spanish convictions, growing over decades, that they were faced by an international conspiracy whose chief protagonists were at heart uncompromising. As Philip was now obliged by lack of resources to rely on negotiation, rather than force, to restore his rule in the Low Countries, he needed English neutrality. But he was too suspicious of the queen and her councillors to believe that he could seriously seek her support to uphold his rule. Elizabeth, who wanted Philip to settle with his rebels, deflating French ambitions, likewise feared his good faith. The defiant Protestant rebels, led by William prince of Orange, had high-placed English friends who encouraged their resistance and advocated support for them. Leicester, flexible in his attitude to Philip in the early 1560s, was now an anti-Spanish ally in Council of Sir Francis Walsingham, the zealous Protestant who became Secretary of State in December 1573.

In the early 1580s the diplomatic and military stalemate ended: the balance of power seemed to be turning decisively in Spanish favour. Consequently, Elizabeth at last gave way to Protestant arguments, allying with the Netherlands rebels. During the 1570s Spanish and Catholic activities had appeared to maintain their menace. In 1574 the first priests landed clandestinely, to spearhead organised efforts to strengthen Catholic loyalties. Unprecedently, colleges were founded abroad to educate English exiles and fugitives in religious practices proscribed by statute[3]. In 1579, with Spanish connivance, a papal army (albeit not of formidable size) landed in Ireland. Philip's governor in the Low Countries, the Italian prince, Alessandro Farnese of Parma, reasserted sovereignty over the Union of Catholic provinces. But the turning-point was an upswing in Spanish oceanic resources. From *c.*1580 the output of the South American silver mines rose significantly. That year Philip successfully asserted his claim to the Portuguese succession, gaining control of the other great colonial empire and its fleet.

Elizabeth's reaction was to look more favourably on French schemes for intervention in the Low Countries. In the years 1580–83 she pinned her hopes on the questionable military and political abilities of her ill-visaged, charming suitor Anjou, brother and heir of Henry III (who had succeeded their brother Charles IX in 1574). On nearly all sides anti-Spanish, Protestant causes seemed to be faltering, adding awe-inspiring conviction to the arguments of godly fanatics carrying on the tradition of gloomy prophecy about the papal Antichrist. Only in Scotland were such machinations, encouraged by Mary, checked: in 1582 Protestant lords decisively asserted control over James VI, strengthening Elizabeth's ability to intervene in continental affairs. Elsewhere all was black. In 1583 the Spaniards at last secured the Azores, a strategically important Portuguese base, and in 1584 Anjou died, having failed abysmally to halt Parma's conquests in the Netherlands.

Philip's naval and military successes were matched by a decisive diplomatic one, triggered by Anjou's death. This had made the Protestant Henry of Navarre heir to the French Crown. The Catholic League, headed by the Guise family, were ready to become 'Spanish' to prevent this. In December 1584 they accepted Philip's subsidy, in March 1585 they rebelled, and in June they forced their terms on Henry III. Correspondingly, Philip's attitude towards the meddling English and their queen had hardened. In May 1585 he seized their ships in his ports. He may have realised that his policy entailed war, however repugnant to it Elizabeth had shown herself for years. No English monarch could contemplate the French Crown being in any alien's pocket but his or her own. In June a Dutch embassy offered Elizabeth their sovereignty, which, true to her monarchical principles, she refused: the door to Anglo-Spanish agreement was to be slammed but not walled up. In August 1585, by treaty, the Crown agreed to subsidise a force under an English commander in the Low Countries for as long as the war lasted. The English were to garrison Flushing and Brill as securities for repayment. The queen authorised Sir Francis Drake, most renowned of pirates, to attack Spanish ports and possessions, in reprisal for the seizures of English ships. At last the challenge to the universal power of Spain and Catholicism urged by doctrinaire politicians seemed to be at hand. The queen, more likely, hoped that the war would be brief, and that it would restore, with more guarantees of security, the *status quo* which had been breaking down since her youth. Neither sort of expectation was to be substantially realised.

Decisions about relations with foreign powers remained to the end of our period a jealous preserve of royal prerogative. The sovereign could declare war and make peace, truces and alliances in his name and on his initiative. The content of diplomatic exchanges was a matter of private royal intent; diplomatic records were normally kept secret. Yorkist and Tudor rulers were active in overseeing the drafting of instructions for envoys and letters to foreign princes, and in reading reports and examining envoys. The characteristic insecurity of their rule gave them zest for these traditional kingly preoccupations. Reflecting this interest, the Council seems to have spent a lot of time debating foreign affairs, in order to proffer advice to the ruler. Any royal minister might be entrusted, as adviser or envoy, with foreign business, including members of the Household who were not councillors. Wolsey and Cromwell stand out as ministers who received an informal delegation to conduct foreign policy.

In practice contingencies imposed some limitations on royal freedom of action. A wise ruler took notice of the caveats of his experts, the Secretaries who drafted his correspondence, and the experienced envoys who carried on the substance of negotiations with foreign powers. He ignored at his peril the drift of debates and recommendations in Council. For its members' viewpoints often reflected caucuses of opinion among royal servants, nobles, gentry and merchants. The English Crown remained peculiarly dependent on the support of the 'community of the realm' in implementing its foreign policies. Its armies were raised and officered by nobles and gentry. Its expeditions were paid for partly by taxes subscribed specifically for the particular objective by the community. Therefore sovereigns were often obliged to bring their foreign policies into more general debate, justifying them in proclamations, and seeking parliamentary approval for them.

The Crown's tendency to involve the political community in the approval and implementation of foreign policies provided incentives and opportunities for the public expression and stirring of discontents. Magnates sometimes inclined to view foreign relations as a means of bolstering fortunes, through the command of expeditions, the grant of pensions by foreign princes and the support of their influence at the English Court. Warwick in the 1460s, like Gloucester in the 1390s, opposed the Court partly because his foreign ambitions were being thwarted by royal policy. Leicester in the 1560s was discreetly conducting his own private 'foreign policy'. He had a better grasp than Warwick the Kingmaker of the limitations imposed by the need not to offend his sovereign. He was to show more ability in exploiting the historic tendency of the broad ranks of the governing elites, stimulated by the royal need to involve them, to express lively opinions about the conduct of foreign affairs.

Among the traditional popular attitudes which royal policy-makers had to take into account were a preference for peace, hatred and contempt for French and Scots, and belief that the Crown should be capable of crushing them in short and relatively inexpensive campaigns. Non-co-operation, riot and revolt could be provoked by reverses and large financial demands. In 1449–50 widespread indignation at the defeats in France had fuelled the attacks on Henry VI's ministers (see p. 111). In 1489, 1497 and 1525 royal demands for war taxation provoked serious local disturbances (see p. 111).

There were some strong regional and sectional currents of opinion. The inhabitants of the northern counties had a deeply ingrained fear of Scottish raids. Failure to provide adequately for defence was liable to provoke disaffection in a region difficult to control from Westminster. But much nearer at hand there were southern coastal communities vulnerable to attack, whose insecurity was likely to provoke hostile reactions to the Crown in a politically sensitive region. Hence Henry VIII's big investment in coastal defences. London merchants traditionally led the clamour that the seas should be well guarded against foreign pirates and rivals, that trade with the Low Countries should be conducted on favourable terms, and that the Crown should back native venturers against their German and Italian rivals. Yorkist and Tudor government was perhaps especially aware of the advantages accruing from fostering the interests of native 'venturers', since more efficiently collected and assigned customs revenues were a prop for its reorganised finances (see pp. 110–11). But rulers did not base foreign policy on trading interests, as the author of *The Libel of English Policy* had advocated in the 1430s (see p. 49). Historians have sometimes evinced disappointment that the first two Tudor rulers showed little interest in founding the British Empire. Despite the examples set by their Portuguese and Spanish kinsmen, they were lukewarm in backing Bristol's Transatlantic projects. In the 1530s and '40s, when Frenchmen were active in undermining the Iberian colonial monopolies, the English were remarkable for their absence. But this did not necessarily imply royal neglect of overseas trading interests, rather a care to protect them. Throughout the first half of the sixteenth century there was usually a remarkable coincidence between dynastic policies and the major English trading interests. Both pointed to Habsburg alliances, the economic disadvantages of whose rupture were appreciated by Tudor councillors.

Considering the sense of involvement in foreign policy which had developed in the 'community of the realm', their appreciation that they could gain or suffer by its conduct, and conviction that they had a duty to promote the common weal against the malicious aims felt to be characteristic of aliens, it is surprising that rulers retained relative freedom of action. The youthful Henry VIII made war and peace according to his impulsive reactions to Wolsey's letters and to dispatches from abroad, read perhaps in a few available moments after a day's hunting. One reason for this freedom may have been that the options which English rulers normally pondered were influenced heavily by traditional ideals and factors. They were profoundly conventional men who inherited and were content with existing methods and criteria for the conduct of foreign policy. They were skilful as well as lucky. No English ruler was killed or captured by a foreign foe. Though Henry VIII and Somerset tried hard to, none created an 'interest' abroad (as Edward I had done in Scotland, and Edward III and Henry V in France), which it was difficult for their successors to relinquish, without suffering loss of dignity and provoking angry domestic reactions.

But in the sixteenth century there were radical changes in relations with other powers, eventually threatening rulers with the imposition of new domestic constraints on their conduct of foreign policy. Though Henry VIII aspired to a traditional aggressive imperialism, Tudor Englishmen feared that their security was threatened by foreign military power and internal subversion, particularly after the Reformation. Famous Tudor victories – Flodden and the defeat of the Spanish Armada – were, unlike Crécy or Agincourt, essentially defensive (as was, arguably, Pinkie). Tudor military power, though it revived significantly under Henry VIII and Elizabeth, was dwarfed by that of the Valois and Habsburgs. The 'imperial' claims of the English Crown were turned to defend the assertion of sovereign independence in religious as well as secular affairs. In the latter half of the sixteenth century, the concurrent and inter-reacting growth of international religious subversion, and of the rise of the Spanish Empire as the principal European power, acted as powerful magnets imposing new universal patterns on the politics of the European governing elites. Keenly Protestant Englishmen felt desperately menaced: some advocated a complete identification of English and international Protestant interests. Powerful, ideologically motivated caucuses, well placed in Court and country, put pressure on Elizabeth and James I to modify their policies, creating lasting traditions of an 'opposition' in foreign policy, articulated especially through parliaments.

Changes in diplomatic technique and the development of printed propaganda made such caucuses better informed about foreign affairs and better able to influence them by personal interventions and by spreading information. The first resident English ambassadors accredited to foreign courts appeared in Henry VIII's reign. A network of permanent diplomatic representation had developed among Italian powers in the fifteenth century, spreading in its last decades to northern Europe, as its princes became increasingly involved in Italian affairs. The first power to be permanently represented at the English Court was Venice, from 1496 onwards. Already there may have been a tendency for ambassadors to reside for long periods. Roger Machado, member of a traditional *ad hoc* delegation embarking for Spain in 1489, recorded that in their company was a Spanish embassy which had been in England for about a year. Sixteenth-century residents had to provide regular news dispatches for sovereigns, secretaries of state and councillors, to communicate with the court to which they were accredited, and to distribute pensions, to intrigue, and recruit agents. They often had little standing at their own court and were regarded by their hosts as spies and subverters. The urgency produced by growing international tensions greatly increased their value to the Crown. They could provide crucially up-to-date information and work against the policy of hostile foreign factions (as foreign ambassadors likewise did in England). But a politically motivated ambassador such as Sir Nicholas Throckmorton, Elizabeth's in France, could be a boon to those trying to put pressure on royal policy – for he favoured the Protestant interest by providing information to like-minded councillors, and a channel for communication between them and their French co-religionists.

Notes

1. Mons Meg, the great gun which can be seen at Edinburgh Castle, was trundled out from there for this campaign, but its carriage collapsed on the way.
2. Among the notable remains of these are the castles at Deal and Walmer (Kent), Camber (Sussex), St Mawes and Pendennis (Cornwall).
3. The foundations were Douai in 1568, Rome 1579, Valladolid 1589, Seville 1592.

Chapter 10

Continuity and change: the late Elizabethan and early Stuart polity

The institutions of government, and the constitutional conflicts about their functions and relationships in the early seventeenth century, were to some extent moulded by the modifications achieved and issues raised in the period between the depositions of Edward II and Richard II. In 1600 Court, Council, Lords, Commons, judges and local magistrates were in many respects functioning in ways which had emerged or were emergent in 1400. By then kings had recognised various specific limitations on their prerogative. These had been conceded, and continued to be observed, not so much as a result of pressure from ephemeral baronial coalitions, as in deference to the petitions of lively 'shire communities', conjoined habitually as part of the 'community of the realm' in parliaments.

The man of 1400, transported two centuries onwards, would have discovered a world in which many institutional as well as physical features were at first glance, if often misleadingly, familiar. He might have recognised the names or functions (and sometimes both) of numerous offices at Court, in Chancery and Exchequer, King's Bench and Common Pleas, and in the administration of dioceses, shires, towns and villages. He might have met men claiming political privilege and social deference on account of familiar titles of peerage, gentility, civic office and gild mastership. A tiny minority of lords, gentlemen and merchants still owned most property and wealth. Under their rule, the mass of the population was still organised into categories of tenants, rural labourers, apprentices, artisans and servants.

Yet evidence of change was widespread. Jacobean London was fast becoming 'the great wen', unrivalled in size and wealth or in importance as a centre of internal and international trade, of governmental activity and cultural influence. Hundreds of villages existing before the plague pandemic, particularly in the Midlands, had disappeared in the fifteenth century. Woodland and arable had become widely depleted in favour of pasture. William Harrison wrote in *The Description of England* (1587):

Where in times past many large and wealthy occupiers were dwelling within the compass of some one park, and thereby great plenty of corn and cattle seen and to be had among them . . . now there is almost nothing kept but a sort of wild and savage beasts, cherished for pleasure and delight. . . . if the old records of every manor be sought and search made to find what tenements are fallen either down or into the lord's hands, or brought and united together by other men, it will soon appear that in some one manor seventeen, eighteen, or twenty houses are shrunk.

But the England of his period was possibly as populous as, and certainly wealthier than, at any previous time. Prosperity was more widely diffused, geographically and socially. Hitherto remote, isolated communities were flourishing on handicraft production, particularly the woollen industry, and on mineral exploitation. They were being connected up in a national economy manipulated by new as well as old sorts of entrepreneurs, catering for larger markets at home and abroad.

A probable result of institutional as well as economic changes, some of them in process in the fifteenth century, was that the 'middling' ranks of society, principally the gentry, had by the late Elizabethan period gained in wealth and power relative to the Crown and other 'estates'. Sheepmasters, graziers, clothiers, financiers and merchants often tried to ascend from their yeoman or bourgeois status by investing recently accumulated profits in land, augmenting the number and wealth of gentlemanly and squirearchical families.

The Crown's foreign and domestic policies, particularly under the Yorkists and Tudors, concurrently provided opportunities for similar augmentation. The revivals by Henry VII's successors of belligerence abroad necessitated, after inflation started to bite hard into income, the sale of many Crown lands, on whose accumulation royal finances had become heavily dependent in the later fifteenth century. Many purchasers were of middling rank. They were also provided with gainful opportunities by the Crown's need to enhance its authority against the forces of regional particularism, which were expressed in factious disorder, dynastic rebellion, and resistance to religious uniformity. There was an expansion of offices in central government, and reliance to staff them on laymen trained as accountants and common lawyers, rather than on clerics. In the shires the governmental responsibilities of 'magisterial' gentry were greatly extended. The visitor from 1400 might well have been surprised by Thomas Wilson's statement (1600) that 'no man, not the greatest in the land . . . [has] more authority than the meanest but as he deriveth it from the Prince by commission'. The remark reflects a tendency to identify public wholly with princely authority, rather than with a plurality of jurisdictions. In the past, peers, prelates and gentlemen had exercised more vitally an ingrained authority in their individual capacities as lords of franchises, hundreds and manors, as heads of kin, familial patrons of servants and retainers, protectors of tenants and 'well-willers'. Kings had relied on landowners' authority for the fulfilment of commissions, trusting them to use it in the Crown's interest, on account of their royal familial bonds. As Sir John Fortescue wrote: 'to him [the king] be cousins the most and greatest lords of the realm'. But from the 1460s royal cousinhood was undermined as an instrument of government, by dynastic strife and suspicions, and the many consequent noble forfeitures, which shook families' 'natural' authority.

In the sixteenth century changing economic and social conditions made it more difficult for restored and newly raised noble families to revive their old authority to the full. Inflation increased the costs of maintaining a great household, and of building up a network of patronage. But attempts to raise rents snapped good relations with tenants. Neighbouring gentlefolk often came to differ in religion from their 'natural' lords. They were acquiring the habit of fighting out their enmities over property and precedence in judicial arenas renovated or newly erected by the Crown, such as Chancery, the conciliar courts or the High Commission. Consequently they relied less on the local great household as a resort for arbitration and settlement, or for maintenance in chicanery or violence. They were less interested in sending sons to be educated for courtly and military service there, and to forge familial bonds with nobles. Instead gentlemen increasingly attended at the universities and Inns of Court. There they acquired the bureaucratic and cultural skills necessary for appointment to the lucrative range of offices at Court and in central royal administration, and for patronage by sovereigns and their attendant lords and privy councillors. The decline of the Arthurian cycle's popularity was not just the result of scholarly doubt and new fashions in antique heroes. The world of the Arthurian fellowship was losing its relevance in landed society.

In the sixteenth century authority came to emanate principally through the Privy Council and Secretaries of State. They developed more formal, businesslike and active relations with peers commissioned as lord-lieutenants, and with them and leading gentry commissioned jointly as justices of the peace. The magisterial gentry's many-sided responsibilities powerfully stimulated their conception of themselves as a sort of 'county government' (in deferential partnership with peers), naturally entitled to receive commissions entrusting local authority. Their sense of pride and right is reflected in their patronage of the new *genre* of county histories[1].

The gentry were among those who gained in the sixteenth century at the clerical estate's expense. Everywhere after the Reformation the ruin or conversion to secular use of former religious buildings testified to the destruction of much of the clergy's traditional wealth and power. Lay landowners benefited as possessors of former monastic and collegiate lands, and as impropriators. The general decline in awe for ecclesiastical authority, and the frequent somersaults in official orthodoxy (a notable characteristic of the English Reformation) made the Crown partially dependent on the civil magistrates for the enforcement of religious uniformity.

In the early seventeenth century the symbolism of majesty, the congeries of central royal offices, and hierarchy of social ranks and parliamentary 'estates' still formally existed in much of the pattern set by 1400. But functions of royal administration, and royal relationships with the landed community were fundamentally altered. In 1600 Thomas Wilson wrote that the kingdom was 'an absolute Imperial Monarchy held neither of Pope, Emperor nor any but God alone'. This 'imperial' power had flowed into every corner of the realm, largely submerging the old 'natural' bonds of clerical and noble authority with which it had previously intermixed. But it was an imperial power wielded largely by groups of landed and urban magistrates. There was a new institutional equation, in which a gentry 'estate' was a leading factor.

The gentleman of 1600 had much in common, in his dynastic and landholding concerns, with his predecessor of 1400. But his intellectual processes and political attitudes were in some respects markedly different. Though both believed in the divinely ordained hierarchies of Creation, the gentleman of 1400 (unless he was one of a handful of 'gentle' Lollards) accepted the existing plurality of authorities, of which the Crown was one, as natural and basically unchanging. Plague, popular revolt and the deposition of kings had certainly sharpened his awareness of changes taking place in society. But these were seen as expressions of mutability, the mysterious workings of the divine will in history. They did not stimulate a diversity of views about the way society should be organised. The gentleman of 1600, tending to be more literate and widely read, and more secular in education, had a sharp sense of the crucial nature of recent changes, and a more analytical appreciation of the power of human forces to remould society. He was aware of discontinuities with the past, particularly in religion and economic organisation. Sixteenth-century men were familiar with the statutory plucking-down of ancient beliefs and institutions, and erection of new-fangled ones. James I was to attempt to abolish even England[2]. Interests and institutions were defended or attacked with reference to biblical interpretations, the construction of ideal commonwealths, and antiquarian researches. The scholarly buttressing of viewpoints encouraged intransigent rather than flexible habits of mind. Individual judgment and conviction had gained respectability as guiding-lights. When two Catholic gentlemen from Sussex refused in 1569 to subscribe to the Oath of Supremacy, the commission of peace wrote in mitigation to the Privy Council that they had refused 'with such humbleness as it seemed to us not to be of stubbornness, but as they said their consciences [were] not yet satisfied.' In 1605 forty-five Northamptonshire gentlemen petitioned the Crown against the deprivation of nonconforming Puritan ministers. The Privy Council, considering the petition to be 'mutinous, seditious, malicious, factious, tending to rebellion' summoned its author, Sir Francis Hastings. He stoutly declared: 'If the ministers did refuse the ceremonies upon a humour and disposition to disobey and not upon conscience, none should be more opposite to them than myself. But seeing it is through the tenderness of their conscience, let not me lay a blot upon them . . . for that myself have some experience of the tenderness of conscience.' The monarchy had become heavily dependent for the exercise of its extended authority on a civil magistracy likely to be touchy, obstinate and pedantic in defence of its convictions, quick to recall limits to royal prerogative and to exalt its own rights.

Moreover, some of the traditional respect accorded to sovereigns had declined. 'Superstitious' royal ceremonies, like the anointing at the coronation, and the 'royal miracle' (healing scrofula) were less regarded. James I, despite his insistence that he was a god among men, displayed considerable embarrassment at the latter ceremony, and had the inscription on the gold coin hung around the necks of sufferers altered to express disbelief in the miracle. Ritual had lost its charisma, at least, for the educated:

And what art thou, thou idol ceremony? . . .
What is thy soul, O adoration?
Art thou aught else but place, degree and form,
Creating awe and fear in other men?
(Henry V, iv, I.)

Henry VIII's Supremacy, establishing a unique spiritual pinnacle for the monarch, had its authority eroded by the tendency of subjects to regard it as a device to subordinate the clergy, by minor and female successions, and by the spread of Calvinist beliefs. Elizabeth tried to lift her prestige by encouraging an increasingly artificial Court cult of chivalry centring on her person, and by making tart definitions of prerogative. James's awareness of the need to gain respect for majesty inspired his stream of elaborate and learned aphorisms, in print and in speeches to parliament, exaggeratedly exalting the powers divinely bestowed on him.

The need was increased because the success of the Tudors in creating an 'absolute Imperial' authority, and in defending it against foreign and domestic threats, had by his reign made the exercise of some personal functions of monarchy less needful in some men's eyes. Old and new external threats, which the community expected sovereigns to oppose with a display of military ability, had dramatically declined. The Welsh, more assimilated to English society, and, by the statutes of 1536–42, fully integrated into the English system of government, no longer menaced neighbouring shires. The last Anglo-French issue of ancient contention was effectively resolved by the loss of Calais in 1558. James VI of Scotland's improved relations with Elizabeth in the 1590s lessened the need to guard against the use of his realm as a base for invasion, and his succession to the English throne ended such fears. As he declared to parliament in 1604, the island 'is now become like a little world within itself, being intrenched and fortified round about with a natural and yet admirable strong pond or ditch'. His succession facilitated the pacification of the Anglo-Scottish Marches, which he renamed 'the Middle Shires', boasting (with some exaggeration) in 1607 that they 'are now become the navel or umbilic of both kingdoms, planted and peopled with civility and riches. Their churches begin to be planted, their doors stand now open, they fear neither robbery nor spoiling'.

The peace with Spain in 1604 ended long hostilities, in which more powerful adversaries had proved themselves incapable of implementing their threats against the realm. The queen's navy had shown itself a new force giving protection against seaborne invasion. The tradition of sovereigns' military leadership, echoed by the queen at Tilbury in 1588, when she visited the army assembled to oppose the Spaniards, and in Shakespeare's *Henry V*, was discarded by James I. Until the resurgence of European warfare in the 1620s, fears that the realm was threatened by Spain subsided. James's diplomacy, much denigrated by his more belligerent and anti-papist subjects, had been until then a major factor in sustaining Protestant interests, as well as Anglo-Spanish amity. He was the first king of England in our period to boast of his pacifism: 'I know not by what fortune the dicton of *Pacificus* was added to my title at my coming to England. . . . But I am not ashamed of this addition'.

Personal rule was less needful for domestic order as well as defence. The 1569 rebellions showed that even in the far north magnates had difficulty in mobilising their traditional clients in arms against the Crown. The rebellious schemes floated by the earl of Essex, his friends the earl of Southampton and Lord Mountjoy, and his harebrained military men in 1599–1600 were the wild projects of a Court 'affinity' and its hangers-on, stoked up by Essex's desperate ambition to win undisputed favour with the queen. His London revolt in 1601 was a ludicrous affair, shunned by the inhabitants among whom he had such popularity.

Nevertheless, in Elizabeth's reign there had been widespread and prolonged fears that her rule would be challenged by dynastic-cum-religious dissidence. They failed to materialise. The horror of the Gunpowder Plot (1605) momentarily revived fears of Catholic treason. But as James declared with some justice to parliament, the plot was the work of a few fanatics, not of the English Catholics as a whole. Though he was to remain fearful of such attempts, avowed as well as secret Catholics, members of the Howards' and Buckingham's affinities, received favour at his Court.

The decline of the medieval bases of landowning authority lessened individual agitation for royal intervention in local politics, of the sort with which the Pastons had bombarded Edward IV (see pp. 283–5). Though maintenance in the localities was still common, its intensity seems to have declined. Opponents were more inclined to let fly with Westminster subpoenas than rural *vi et armis*. The lessening need for a variety of customary royal initiatives made men more impatient with exercises of prerogative which they found irksome. From the 1590s the Crown's financial expedients began to provoke more vociferous and persistent lines of attack in the Commons: expedients were denounced as unconstitutional as well as oppressive. The war with Spain, more prolonged than any since the Hundred Years War, had increased tensions. Once again the community was called on by the Crown to provide huge, repeated war subsidies. Royal measures to organise and finance county defences were on occasion criticised by local magistrates as infringements of their authority. The peace did not solve the problems of financing central government. James failed to stop its expenses and the number of its officers from increasing. They could no longer be rewarded with benefices, nor with profits from the many Crown lands sold off. Inflation had depleted the value of official salaries. Competition for the rewards of royal patronage became fiercer.

The agitation of suitors was now centred more exclusively on the Court. So was the indignation of mulcted landowners: in James's reign the term 'the Country' was first used to describe caucuses of critics in the Commons. Faction at Court had intensified in the 1590s, polarising as a result of Essex's attempts to oust the Cecils from favour. Some Jacobean factions did not hesitate to stir criticism in the Commons, in order to discredit rivals at Court – the Howards set a notable example of this in 1614.

Rapacious exploitation of the Crown's and community's resources by Court factions was not new. It had provoked the Commons agitations in 1376 and 1449. The 'shire communities' had attained a strong sense of their mutual rights in relation to the Crown's, particularly in the fourteenth century. They had procured royal recognition of limitations on prerogative, and even promoted Household purges and reforms. The Tudors skilfully exploited social and political circumstances, largely replacing the authority of a plurality of 'estates' by that of the 'state'. But their achievement had limitations. Royal government became heavily dependent on the co-operation of magisterial gentry. They retained medieval sensibilities about the rights of 'shire communities'. But the iconoclastic advances of state authority had contributed to the lessening among them of medieval reverence for customary institutions, and of reliance on the sovereign's personal initiatives and interventions for defence and justice. Late Elizabethan and Jacobean tensions over the Crown's fiscal expedients and over Court patronage quickly touched off fundamental issues about how authority in the state should be divided between reconstucted monarchy and landed community.

The governors of society in 1600 were acquiring the habit of tracing with antiquarian zeal the supposed origins of the functions of institutions, the privileges of ranks and the descents of families. At a time of unresolved religious and constitutional confrontations, they were eager to demonstrate the credential of historical continuity. They had a pedantic fascination with survivals and relics from a moribund world of baronial dynasties and feudal tenures, clerical pretensions and religious fraternities, seasonal rituals and ceremonies. Their keen historical awareness derived from the continued vitality of so many features of government and rank flourishing in 1400, and the dying out, much of it recent, of some medieval institutions, and ingrained habits and values. By 1600 the ordering of society was more completely justified by the literate logic of didactic constructions, producing a plurality of often conflicting arguments. The medieval consensus, which had produced a general acceptance of many fundamental features of society, sanctioned by the magic of communal rituals and ceremonies, had been irrevocably fractured.

Notes

1. The first one published was William Lambarde's *Perambulation of Kent* (1576).
2. He could not get agreement in parliament to his various proposals promoting an Anglo-Scottish union. In 1604 he assumed by proclamation the title, 'King of Great Britain'.

Bibliography

General

Baker, D., ed., *Portraits and Documents. The Later Middle Ages 1216–1485*, Hutchinson, 1968.

Chrimes, S. B., *Lancastrians, Yorkists and Henry VII*, Macmillan, 1964.

Chrimes, S. B., **Ross, C. D.**, and **Griffiths, R. A.**, ed., *Fifteenth-century England 1399–1509*, Manchester U.P., 1972.

Du Boulay, F. R. H., *An Age of Ambition. English Society in the Late Middle Ages*, Nelson, 1970.

Elton, G. R., *England under the Tudors*, Methuen, 1971.

Holmes, G. A., *The Late Middle Ages, 1275–1485*, Nelson, 1963.

Jacob, E. F., *The Fifteenth Century 1399–1485*, Oxford U.P., 1961.

Keen, M. H., *England in the Later Middle Ages. A Political History*, Methuen, 1973.

Lander, J. R., *Conflict and Stability in Fifteenth-century England*, Hutchinson, 1969.

Loades, D. M., *Politics and the Nation, 1450–1660*, Fontana Collins, 1974.

McKisack, M., *The Fourteenth Century 1307–1399*, O.U.P., 1959.

Myers, A. R., ed., *English Historical Documents*, vol. 4, 1327–1485, Eyre and Spottiswoode, 1969.

Russell, C., *The Crisis of Parliaments. English History 1509–1660*, O.U.P., 1971.

Wilkinson, B., *The Later Middle Ages in England*, Longman, 1969.

Williams, C. H., ed., *English Historical Documents*, vol. 5, 1485–1558, Eyre and Spottiswoode, 1967.

Chapter 1

Brie, F. W. D., ed., *The Brut, or the Chronicle of England*, Early English Text Soc., 2 vols, 1906–8.

Dobson, R. B., and **Taylor, J.**, 'The medieval origins of the Robin Hood legend: a reassessment', *Northern Hist.*, 7 (1972).

Letts, M., ed., *The Travels of Leo of Rozmital*, Hakluyt Soc., Cambridge U.P., 1957.

Loomis, L. R., 'Nationality at the Council of Constance', *American Hist. Rev.*, 44 (1939).

Polydore Vergil's English History from an Early Translation, ed. H. Ellis, Camden Soc., 1846.

Sneyd, C. A., ed., *A Relation, or rather a True Account, of the Island of England . . . about the year 1500*, Camden Soc., 1847.

Chapter 2

Some general aspects and problems

Bean, J. M. W., 'Plague, population and economic decline in the later Middle Ages', *Econ. Hist. Rev.*, 2nd ser., 15 (1962–3).

Beier, A. L., 'Vagrants and the social order in Elizabethan England', *Past and Present*, 64 (1974).

Blanchard, I., 'Population change, enclosure, and the early Tudor economy', *Econ. Hist. Rev.*, 2nd ser., 23 (1970).

Bowsky, W. M., ed., *The Black Death. A Turning Point in History?*, Holt, Rinehart and Winston, New York, 1971.

Carus-Wilson, E. M., ed., *Essays in Economic History*, 2 vols, Edward Arnold, 1954.

Cooper, J. P., 'The social distribution of land and men in England, 1436–1700', *Econ. Hist. Rev.*, 2nd ser., 20 (1967).

Cornwall, J., 'English population in the early sixteenth century', *Econ. Hist. Rev.*, 2nd ser., 23 (1970).

Drummond, J. C., and **Wilbraham, A.**, *The Englishman's Food. A History of Five Centuries of English Diet*, revised D. Hollingsworth, Cape, 1958.

Hollingsworth, T. H., *Historical Demography*, Hodder and Stoughton, 1969.

Hoskins, W. G., *The Age of Plunder. King Henry's England 1500–1547*, Longman, 1976.

Jones, W. R. D., *The Tudor Commonwealth 1529–1559*, Athlone Press, 1970.

Morris, C., 'The plague in Britain', *Historical Journal*, 14 (1971).

Outhwaite, R. B., *Inflation in Tudor and Early Stuart England*, Econ. Hist. Soc., Macmillan, 1969.

Phelps Brown, E. H., and **Hopkins, Sheila V.**, 'Seven centuries of the price of consumables, compared with builders' wage-rates', *Economica* (1956).

Postan, M. M., *The Medieval Economy and Society*, Penguin Books, 1975.

Pound, J., *Poverty and Vagrancy in Tudor England*, Longman, 1971.

Ramsey, P., *Tudor Economic Problems*, Gollancz, 1965.

Ramsey, P., ed., *The Price Revolution in Sixteenth-Century England*, Methuen, 1971.

Schofield, R. S., 'The geographical distribution of wealth in England, 1334–1649', *Econ. Hist. Rev.*, 2nd ser., 18 (1965).

Tawney, R. H., and **Power, E.**, ed., *Tudor Economic Documents*, Longmans, 3 vols, 1924.

Thomas, K., 'Work and leisure in pre-industrial society', *Past and Present*, 29 (1964).

Agrarian economy and peasant society

Ault, W. O., *Open-Field Farming in Medieval England. A Study of Village By-Laws*, Allen and Unwin, 1972.

Bean, J. M. W., *The Estates of the Percy Family 1416–1537*, O.U.P., 1958.

Bennett, H. S., *Life on the English Manor*, C.U.P., 1937.

Beresford, M. W., *The Lost Villages of England*, Lutterworth Press, 1954.

Beresford, M. W., and **Hurst, J. G.**, ed., *Deserted Medieval Villages*, Lutterworth, 1973.

Campbell, M., *The English Yeoman under Elizabeth and the Early Stuarts*, Yale U.P., 1942.

Davenport, F. G., *The Economic Development of a Norfolk Manor*, Cambridge, 1906.

Davies, C. S. L., 'Peasant revolt in France and England: a comparison', *Agric. Hist. Rev.*, 21 (1973).

Davies, R. R., 'Baronial accounts, incomes, and arrears in the later Middle Ages', *Econ. Hist. Rev.*, 2nd ser., 21 (1968).

Du Boulay, F. R. H., 'A rentier economy in the later Middle Ages: the Archbishopric of Canterbury', *Econ. Hist. Rev.*, 2nd ser., 16 (1963–4).

Du Boulay, F. R. H., 'Who were farming the English demesnes at the end of the Middle Ages?', *Econ. Hist. Rev.*, 2nd ser., 17 (1964–5).

Du Boulay, F. R. H., *The Lordship of Canterbury*, Nelson, 1966.

Dyer, C. C., 'A redistribution of incomes in fifteenth-century England?', *Past and Present*, 39 (1968).

Faith, R. J., 'Peasant families and inheritance customs in medieval England', *Agric. Hist. Rev.*, 14 (1966).

Hallam, H. E., 'Population density in medieval Fenland', *Econ. Hist. Rev.*, 2nd ser., 14 (1961–2).

Harvey, B., 'Work and *festa ferianda* in medieval England', *Jnl Ecclesiastical Hist.*, 23 (1972).

Hatcher, J., *Rural Economy and Society in the Duchy of Cornwall 1300–1500*, C.U.P., 1970.

Hilton, R. H., *The Economic Development of some Leicestershire Estates in the 14th and 15th Centuries*, O.U.P., 1947.

Hilton, R. H., *The Decline of Serfdom in Medieval England*, Econ. Hist. Soc., Macmillan, 1969.

Hilton, R. H., *The English Peasantry in the Later Middle Ages*, O.U.P., 1975.

Hilton, R. H., ed., *Peasants, Knights and Heretics*, C.U.P., 1976.

Hodgett, G. A. J., *Agrarian England in the Later Middle Ages*, Historical Association, 1966.

Holmes, G. A., *The Estates of the Higher Nobility in XIVth Century England*, C.U.P., 1957.

Hoskins, W. G., *The Midland Peasant*, Macmillan, 1957.

Jack, I. R., ed., *The Grey of Ruthin Valor*, Sydney U.P., 1965.

Kerridge, E., *The Agricultural Revolution*, Allen and Unwin, 1967.

Kerridge, E., *Agrarian Problems in the Sixteenth Century and After*, Allen and Unwin, 1969.

Laslett, P., *The World we have lost*, Methuen, 1965.

Laslett, P., and **Wall, R.**, ed., *Household and Family in Past Time*, C.U.P., 1972.

Orwin, C. S. and **C. S.**, *The Open Fields*, O.U.P., 1967 edn.

Raftis, J. A., *Tenure and Mobility. Studies in the Social History of the Mediaeval English Village*, Pontifical Institute of Mediaeval Studies, Toronto, 1964.

Spufford, M., *Contrasting Communities. English Villagers in the Sixteenth and Seventeenth Centuries*, C.U.P., 1974.

Tawney, R. H., *The Agrarian Problem in the Sixteenth Century*, Longmans, 1912.

Thirsk, J., *English Peasant Farming. The Agrarian History of Lincolnshire from Tudor to Recent Times*, Routledge, 1957.

Thirsk, J., ed., *The Agrarian History of England and Wales*, vol. 4, C.U.P., 1967.

Thirsk, J., *Tudor Enclosures*, Hist. Assoc., 1970 reprint.

Wood, M., *The English Mediaeval House*, Dent, 1965.

Trade and industry

Bowden, P. J., *The Wool Trade in Tudor and Stuart England*, Macmillan, 1962.

Carus-Wilson, E. M., *Medieval Merchant Venturers*, Methuen, 1967 edn.

Carus-Wilson, E. M., and **Coleman, O.**, *England's Export Trade, 1275–1547*, O.U.P., 1963.

Davies, R., *English Overseas Trade 1500–1700*, Econ. Hist. Soc., Macmillan, 1973.

Holmes, G. A., 'The "Libel of English Policy" ', *English Hist. Rev.*, 76 (1961).

Nef, J. U., *The Rise of the British Coal Industry*, 2 vols, Routledge, 1932.

Nef, J. U., *Industry and Government in France and England, 1540–1640*, O.U.P., 1940.

Postan, M. M., *Medieval Trade and Finance*, C.U.P., 1975.

Power, E., *The Wool Trade in Medieval English History*, O.U.P., 1941.

Power, E., and **Postan, M. M.**, ed., *Studies in English Trade in the Fifteenth Century*, Routledge, 1933.

Ruddock, A. A., *Italian Merchants and Shipping in Southampton, 1270–1600*, Southampton Record Soc., 1951

Scammell, G. V., 'English merchant shipping at the end of the Middle Ages: some East Coast evidence', *Econ. Hist. Rev.*, 2nd ser., 13 (1960–1).

Warner, G., ed., *The Libelle of Englyshe Polycye. A poem on the use of Sea-Power, 1436*, O.U.P., 1926; also printed in *Political Poems and Songs*, vol. 2, ed. T. Wright, Rolls ser., 1861; modern version in *Complaint and Reform in England 1436–1714*, ed. W. H. Dunham and S. Pargellis, O.U.P., 1938.

Willan, T. S., *Studies in Elizabethan Foreign Trade*, Manchester U.P., 1959.
Winchester, B., *Tudor Family Portrait*, Jonathan Cape, 1955.

Urban government and society

Baker, T., *Medieval London*, Cassell, 1970.
Bartlett, J. N., 'The expansion and decline of York in the later Middle Ages', *Econ. Hist. Rev.*, 2nd ser., 12 (1959–60).
Bird, R., *The Turbulent London of Richard II*, Longmans, 1949.
Clark, P., and **Slack, P.**, ed., *Crisis and Order in English Towns 1500–1700*, Routledge, 1972.
Clark, P., and **Slack, P.**, *English Towns in Transition 1500–1700*, O.U.P., 1976.
Cornwall, J., 'English country towns in the fifteen-twenties', *Econ. Hist. Rev.*, 2nd ser., 15 (1962–3).
Dyer, A. D., *The City of Worcester in the Sixteenth Century*, Leicester U.P., 1973.
Everitt, A., ed., *Perspectives in English Urban History*, Macmillan, 1973.
Gillett, E., *A History of Grimsby*, O.U.P., 1970.
Hill, J. W. F., *Tudor and Stuart Lincoln*, C.U.P., 1956.
Hoskins, W. G., *Provincial England*, Macmillan, 1963.
Jordan, W. K., *The Charities of London 1480–1660*, Allen and Unwin, 1960.
MacCaffrey, W. T., *Exeter 1540–1640*, Harvard U.P., 1976 edn.
Painter, G. D., *William Caxton*, Chatto and Windus, 1976.
Platt, C., *The English Medieval Town*, Secker and Warburg, 1976.
Reddaway, T. F., 'The livery companies of Tudor London', *History*, 51 (1966).
Spencer, B., *Chaucer's London*, London Museum, 1972.
Thrupp, S. L., *The Merchant Class of Mediaeval London 1300–1500*, Michigan U.P., 1948.
Williams, G. A., *Medieval London. From Commune to Capital*, Athlone Press, 1970 edn.

Chapter 3

General

Allen, J. W., *A History of Political Thought in the Sixteenth Century*, Methuen, 1928.
Chrimes, S. B., *English Constitutional Ideas in the XV Century*, C.U.P., 1936.
Chrimes, S. B., and **Brown, A. L.**, ed., *Select Documents of English Constitutional History 1307–1485*, Adam and Charles Black, 1961.
Crow, M. M., and **Olson, C. C.**, *Chaucer Life-Records*, O.U.P., 1966.
Elton, G. R., *The Tudor Revolution in Government*, C.U.P., 1953.
Elton, G. R., *The Tudor Constitution*, C.U.P., 1962.
Elton, G. R., *Studies in Tudor and Stuart Politics and Government*, 2 vols., C.U.P., 1974.
Hurstfield, J., *Freedom, Corruption and Government in Elizabethan England*, Cape, 1973.
Kenyon, J. P., *The Stuart Constitution, 1603–1688*, C.U.P., 1966.
Morris, G. C., *Political Thought in England. Tyndale to Hooker*, O.U.P., 1953.
Slavin, A. J., ed., *Tudor Men and Institutions*, Louisiana State U.P., 1972.
Smith, A. G. R., *The Government of Elizabethan England*, Arnold, 1967.
Tanner, J. R., *Constitutional Documents of the Reign of James I*, C.U.P., 1952 reprint.
Tout, T. F., *Chapters in the Administrative History of Mediaeval England*, 6 vols, Manchester U.P., 1920–33.
Wilkinson, B., *Constitutional History of Medieval England 1216–1399*, vols 2–3, Longmans, 1952–8.
Wilkinson, B., *Constitutional History of England in the Fifteenth Century (1399–1485)*, Longmans, 1964.
Willard, J. F., **Morris, W. A.**, **Strayer, J. R.**, and **Dunham, W. H.**, ed., *The English Government at Work, 1327–1336*, 3 vols, Mediaeval Academy of America, 1940–50.

Crown, community and parliament

Bellamy, J. G., *The Law of Treason in England in the Later Middle Ages*, C.U.P., 1970.
Brown, A. L., 'The commons and the council in the reign of Henry IV', *English Hist. Rev.*, 79 (1964).
Dunham, W. H., ed., *The Fane Fragment of the 1461 Lords' Journal*, Yale U.P., 1935.
Elton, G. R., 'Tudor government: the points of contact: 1. Parliament', *Trans. Royal Hist. Soc.*, 5th ser., 24 (1974).
Elton, G. R., 'The early journals of the house of lords', *English Hist. Rev.*, 89 (1974).
Fortescue, Sir John, *The Governance of England*, ed. C. Plummer, Oxford, 1885; modern version in *Complaint and Reform in England*, ed. Dunham and Pargellis.
Harding, A., 'Plaints and Bills in the history of English law, mainly in the period 1250–1350', in *Legal History Studies 1972*, ed. D. Jenkins, Wales U.P., 1975.
Harriss, G. L., *King, Parliament, and Public Finance in Medieval England to 1369*, O.U.P., 1975.
Hinton, R. W. K., 'English constitutional theories from Sir John Fortescue to Sir John Eliot', *English Hist. Rev.*, 75 (1960).
McFarlane, K. B., 'Parliament and "bastard feudalism" ', *Trans. Royal Hist. Soc.*, 4th ser., 26 (1944).
McKisack, M., *The Parliamentary Representation of the English Boroughs during the Middle Ages*, O.U.P., 1932.
Moir, T. L., *The Addled Parliament of 1614*, O.U.P., 1958.
Neale, J. E., *The Elizabethan House of Commons*, Cape, 1949.
Neale, J. E., *Elizabeth I and her Parliaments,* 2 vols, Cape, 1953–7.
Notestein, W., *The House of Commons 1604–1610*, Yale U.P., 1971.
Powell, J. Enoch, and **Wallis, K.,** *The House of Lords in the Middle Ages*, Weidenfeld and Nicolson, 1968.
Roskell, J. S., *The Commons in the Parliament of 1422*, Manchester U.P., 1954.
Roskell, J. S., 'The problem of the attendance of the Lords in medieval parliaments', *Bull. Inst. Hist. Res.*, 29 (1956).
Roskell, J. S., *The Commons and their Speakers in English Parliaments 1376–1523*, Manchester U.P., 1965.
Ruigh, R. E., *The Parliament of 1624*, O.U.P., 1971.
Russell, C., 'Parliamentary history in perspective, 1604–1629', *History*, 61 (1976).
Sayles, G. O., *The King's Parliament of England*, Arnold, 1975.
Schramm, P. E., *A History of the English Coronation*, trans. L. G. Wickham Legg, O.U.P., 1937.
Willson, D. H., *The Privy Councillors in the House of Commons 1604–1629*, Minneapolis U.P., 1940.

Central offices and law courts

Aylmer, G. E., *The King's Servants. The Civil Service of Charles I, 1625–42*, Routledge, 1961.
Brown, A. L., 'The authorization of letters under the Great Seal', *Bull. Inst. Hist. Res.*, 37 (1964).
Brown, A. L., 'The King's councillors in fifteenth-century England', *Trans. Royal Hist. Soc.*, 5th ser., 19 (1969).
Brown, A. L., *The Early History of the Clerkship of the Council*, Univ. of Glasgow, 1969.
Brown, R. Allen, Colvin, H. M., and **Taylor, A. J.,** ed., *The History of the King's Works. The Middle Ages*, 2 vols, H.M.S.O., 1963.
Elton, G. R., 'Tudor government: the points of contact. 11. The Council', *Trans. Royal Hist. Soc.*, 5th ser., 25 (1975).
Fortescue, Sir John, *De Laudibus Legum Angliae*, ed. S. B. Chrimes, C.U.P., 1942.
Harding, A., *A Social History of English Law*, Penguin, 1966.
Harding, A., *The Law Courts of Medieval England*, Allen and Unwin, 1973.
Hastings, M., *The Court of Common Pleas in Fifteenth Century England*, Cornell U.P., 1947.

Hill, M. C., *The King's Messengers 1199–1377*, Arnold, 1961.
Hoak, D. E., *The King's Council in the Reign of Edward VI*, C.U.P., 1976.
Ives, E. W., 'The common lawyers in pre-reformation England', *Trans. Royal Hist. Soc.*, 5th ser., 18 (1968).
Jones, W. J., *The Elizabethan Court of Chancery*, O.U.P., 1967.
Kirby, J. L., 'Councils and councillors of Henry IV, 1399–1413', *Trans. Royal Hist. Soc.*, 5th ser., 14. (1964).
Lander, J. R., 'The Yorkist Council and administration', *English Hist. Rev.*, 73 (1958).
Lander, J. R., 'Council, administration and councillors, 1461 to 1485', *Bull. Inst. Hist. Res.*, 32 (1959).
MacCaffrey, W. T., 'Place and patronage in Elizabethan politics', in *Elizabethan Government and Society. Essays presented to Sir John Neale*, ed. S. T. Bindoff, J. Hurstfield and C. H. Williams, Athlone Press, 1964 reprint.
Morgan, D. A. L., 'The King's affinity in the polity of Yorkist England', *Trans. Royal Hist. Soc.*, 5th ser., 23 (1973).
Myers, A. R., *The Household of Edward IV*, Manchester U.P., 1959.
Otway-Ruthven, J., *The King's Secretary and the Signet Office in the XV Century*, C.U.P., 1939.
Pronay, N., 'The Chancellor, the Chancery, and the Council at the end of the fifteenth century', in *British Government and Administration. Studies presented to S. B. Chrimes*, ed. H. Hearder and H. R. Loyn, Wales U.P., 1974.
Pulman, M. B., *The Elizabethan Privy Council in the Fifteen-Seventies*, California U.P., 1971.
Ullmann, W., ed., *Liber Regie Capelle*, Henry Bradshaw Soc., 1961.
Virgoe, R., 'The composition of the King's Council, 1437–61', *Bull, Inst. Hist. Res.*, 43 (1970).
Wilkinson, B., *The Chancery under Edward III*, Manchester U.P., 1929.

Finances and financial administration

Bell, H. E., *An Introduction to the History and Records of the Court of Wards and Liveries*, C.U.P., 1953.
Gras, N. S. B., *The Early English Customs System*, Harvard U.P., 1918.
Harriss, G. L., 'Aids, loans and benevolences', *Historical Journal*, 6 (1963).
Harriss, G. L., *King, Parliament, and Public Finance in Medieval England to 1369*, O.U.P., 1975.
Hurstfield, J., *The Queen's Wards*, Longmans, 1958.
McFarlane, K. B., 'Loans to the Lancastrian Kings: the problem of inducement', *Cambridge Hist. Jnl*, 9 (1947).
Prestwich, M., *Cranfield: Business and Politics under the Early Stuarts*, O.U.P., 1966.
Richardson, W. C., *Tudor Chamber Administration 1485–1547*, Louisiana State U.P., 1952.
Wolffe, B. P., *The Crown Lands 1461–1536*, Allen and Unwin, 1970.
Wolffe, B. P., *The Royal Demesne in English History*, Allen and Unwin, 1971.

Chapter 4

General

Davis, N., ed., *The Paston Letters. A Selection in Modern Spelling*, O.U.P., 1963.
Davis, N., ed., *Paston Letters and Papers of the Fifteenth Century*, vol. 1, O.U.P., 1971.
Gairdner, J., ed., *The Paston Letters 1422–1509*, 4 vols, John Grant, 1910.
Kingsford, C. L., ed., *The Stonor Letters and Papers 1290–1483*, 2 vols, Camden ser., 1919.

Royal rights and local administration

Bean, J. M. W., *The Decline of English Feudalism 1215–1540*, Manchester U.P., 1968.

Beard, C. A., *The Office of Justice of the Peace in England in its Origins and Development*, Columbia U.P., 1904.
Bell, H. E., *An Introduction to the History and Records of the Court of Wards and Liveries.*
Harding, A., *The Law Courts of Medieval England*, Allen and Unwin, 1973.
Hunnisett, R. F., *The Medieval Coroner*, C.U.P., 1961.
Hurstfield, J., *The Queen's Wards*, Longmans, 1958.
Smith, A. Hassell, *County and Court: Government and Politics in Norfolk, 1558–1603*, O.U.P., 1974.
Somerville, R., *History of the Duchy of Lancaster*, vol. 1, 1265–1603, Chancellor and Council of the Duchy of Lancaster, 1953.
Thomson, G. Scott, *Lords Lieutenants in the Sixteenth Century*, Longmans, 1923.
Willard, J. F., Morris, W. A., and **Dunham, W. H.,** ed., *The English Government at Work, 1327–1336*, vol. 3.
Williams, P., *The Council in the Marches of Wales under Elizabeth,* Wales U.P., 1958.

Landowning society: general

Bellamy, J. G., 'The Coterel gang: an anatomy of a band of fourteenth-century criminals', *English Hist. Rev.*, 79 (1964).
Cliffe, J. T., *The Yorkshire Gentry from the Reformation to the Civil War*, Athlone Press, 1969.
Denholm-Young, N., *Seignorial Administration in England*, O.U.P., 1937.
Dunham, W. H., *Lord Hastings' Indentured Retainers, 1461–83,* Trans. Connecticut Academy of Arts and Sciences, 1955.
Eliot, Sir Thomas, *The Book Named The Governor*, ed. S. E. Lehmberg, Dent, 1962.
Ferguson, A. B., *The Indian Summer of English Chivalry*, Duke U.P., 1960.
Hexter, J. H., 'The education of the aristocracy in the Renaissance', *Reappraisals in History*, Longman, 1961.
Holmes, G. A., *The Estates of the Higher Nobility in XIVth Century England*, C.U.P., 1957.
Keen, M., 'Brotherhood in arms', *History*, 47 (1962).
Laslett, P., *The World we have lost*, Methuen, 1965.
McFarlane, K. B., 'Parliament and "bastard feudalism" ', *Trans. Royal Hist. Soc.*, 4th ser., 26 (1944).
McFarlane, K. B., *The Nobility of Later Medieval England*, O.U.P., 1973.
McFarlane, K. B., 'Bastard feudalism', *Bull. Inst. Hist. Res.*, 20 (1947).
Mathew, G., *The Court of Richard II*, John Murray, 1968.
Orme, N., *English Schools in the Middle Ages*, Methuen, 1973.
Rosenthal, J. T., *Nobles and the Noble Life 1295–1500*, Allen and Unwin, 1976.
Russell, John, *The Book of Nurture*, ed. (with *The Babees Book*) F. J. Furnivall, Early English Text Soc., 1868.
Simpson, A., *The Wealth of the Gentry, 1540–1640*, Chicago U.P., 1961.
Stone, L., *The Crisis of the Aristocracy 1558–1641*, O.U.P., 1965.
Stones, E. L. G., 'The Folvilles of Ashby-Folville, Leicestershire and their associates in crime', *Trans. Royal Hist. Soc.*, 5th ser., 7 (1957).
Zeeveld, W. Gordon, 'The pilgrims and social equality', *Foundations of Tudor Policy,* Methuen, 1969.

Landowning society in the Anglo-Scottish Borders and the problems of government in the north of England

Beckingsale, B. W., 'The characteristics of the Tudor north', *Northern Hist.,* 4 (1969).
Brooks, F. W., *The Council of the North*, Hist. Assoc., 1966 edn.
Bush, M. L., 'The problem of the far north; a study of the crisis of 1537 and its consequences', *Northern Hist.*, 6 (1971).
Carey, Robert, *Memoirs*, ed. F. H. Mares, O.U.P., 1972.

Fraser, G. M., *The Steel Bonnets, The Story of the Anglo-Scottish Reivers*, Barrie and Jenkins, 1971.

Hay, D., 'England, Scotland and Europe: the problem of the frontier', *Trans. Royal Hist. Soc.*, 5th ser., 25 (1975).

James, M. E., *Change and Continuity in the Tudor North. The Rise of Thomas First Lord Wharton*, St. Anthony's Press, York, 1965.

James, M. E., *A Tudor Magnate and the Tudor State: Henry Fifth Earl of Northumberland*, St. Anthony's Press, York, 1966.

James, M. E., 'The First Earl of Cumberland (1493–1542) and the decline of northern feudalism', *Northern Hist.*, 1 (1966).

James, M. E., 'The concept of order and the northern rising 1569', *Past and Present*, 60 (1973).

James, M. E., *Family, Lineage and Civil Society . . . in the Durham Region, 1500–1640*, O.U.P., 1974.

Miller, E., *War in the North*, Univ. of Hull, 1960.

Rae, T. I., *The Administration of the Scottish Frontier 1513: 1603*, Edinburgh U.P., 1966.

Ramm, H. G., McDowall, R. W., and **Mercer, E.,** *Shielings and Bastles*, H.M.S.O., 1970.

Reed, J., *The Border Ballads*, Athlone Press, 1973.

Reid, R. R., *The King's Council in the North*, Longmans, 1921.

Smith, R. B., *Land and Politics in the England of Henry VIII: the West Riding of Yorkshire, 1530–1546*, O.U.P., 1970.

Storey, R. L., 'The wardens of the Marches of England towards Scotland 1377–1485', *English Hist. Rev.*, 72 (1957).

Storey, R. L., *Thomas Langley and the Bishopric of Durham 1406–1437*, S.P.C.K., 1961.

Tough, D. L. W., *The Last Years of a Frontier*, O.U.P., 1928.

Tuck, J. A., 'Richard II and the border magnates', *Northern Hist.*, 3 (1968).

Tuck, J. A., 'Northumbrian society in the fourteenth century', *Northern Hist.*, 6 (1971).

Chapter 5

To 1399

Armitage-Smith, S., *John of Gaunt*, Constable, 1904.

Barron, C., 'The tyranny of Richard II', *Bull. Inst. Hist. Res.*, 41 (1968).

Campbell, J., 'England, Scotland and the Hundred Years War', in *Europe in the Late Middle Ages*, ed. B. Smalley, J. Hale and J. R. L. Highfield, Faber, 1965.

Clarke, M. V., *Fourteenth Century Studies*, ed. L. S. Sutherland and M. McKisack, O.U.P., 1937.

Dobson, R. B., ed., *The Peasants Revolt of 1381*, Macmillan, 1970.

Du Boulay, F. R. H., and **Barron, C. M.,** ed., *The Reign of Richard II. Essays in Honour of May McKisack*, Athlone Press, 1971.

Galbraith, V. H., ed., *The Anonimalle Chronicle 1333 to 1381*, Manchester U.P., 1970 reprint.

Goodman, A., *The Loyal Conspiracy. The Lords Appellant under Richard II*, Routledge, 1971.

Gray, Sir Thomas, *Scalacronica*, trans. H. Maxwell, James Maclehose, Glasgow, 1907.

Harriss, G. L., *King, Parliament, and Public Finance in Medieval England to 1369*, O.U.P., 1975.

Hilton, R., *Bond Men Made Free. Medieval Peasant Movements and the English Rising of 1381*, Temple Smith, 1973.

Holmes, G., *The Good Parliament*, O.U.P., 1975.

Mollat, M., and **Wolff, P.,** *The Popular Revolutions of the Late Middle Ages*, Allen and Unwin, 1973.

Nicholson, R., *Edward III and the Scots. The Formative Years of a Military Career 1327–1335*, O.U.P., 1965.
Nicholson, R., *Scotland. The Later Middle Ages*, Oliver and Boyd, 1974.
Palmer, J. J. N., 'The Parliament of 1385 and the constitutional crisis of 1386', *Speculum*, 46 (1971).
Reville, A., *Le soulèvement des travailleurs d'Angleterre en 1381*, L'École des Chartes, Paris, 1898.
Tuck, J. A., 'Richard II and the border magnates', *Northern Hist.*, 3 (1968).
Tuck, J. A., *Richard II and the English Nobility*, Arnold, 1973.

From 1399

Bean, J. M. W., 'Henry IV and the Percies', *History*, 44 (1959).
Blacman, John, *Henry the Sixth*, ed. M. R. James, Cambridge, 1919.
Brown, A. L., 'The commons and the council in the reign of Henry IV', *English Hist. Rev.*, 79 (1964).
Chronicon Adae de Usk 1377–1421, trans. E. M. Thompson, Henry Frowde, London, 1904.
Davies, R. R., 'Owain Glyn Dŵr and the Welsh squirearchy', *Trans. Honourable Soc. of Cymmrodorion* (1969).
Harriss, G. L., 'Cardinal Beaufort – patriot or usurer?', *Trans. Royal Hist. Soc.*, 5th ser., 20 (1970).
Jack, R. Ian, 'Owain Glyn Dŵr and the Lordship of Ruthin', *Welsh Hist. Rev.*, 2 (1964–5).
Kingsford, C. L., ed., *Chronicles of London*, Oxford, 1905.
Kingsford, C. L., ed., *The First English Life of King Henry the Fifth*, Oxford, 1911.
Kingsford, C. L., *English Historical Literature in the Fifteenth Century*, Oxford, 1913.
Kingsford, C. L., *Prejudice and Promise in XVth Century England*, Oxford, 1925.
Kirby, J. L., *Henry IV of England*, Constable, 1970.
Lloyd, J. E., *Owen Glendower*, O.U.P., 1931.
McFarlane, K. B., 'At the death-bed of Cardinal Beaufort', in *Studies in Medieval History presented to Frederick Maurice Powicke*, ed. R. W. Hunt, W. A. Pantin and R. W. Southern, O.U.P., 1948.
McFarlane, K. B., *Lancastrian Kings and Lollard Knights*, O.U.P., 1972.
Political Poems and Songs, vol. 2., T. Wright ed., Rolls ser., 1861.
Rogers, A., 'Henry IV, the Commons and taxation', *Medieval Studies*, 31 (1969).
Vickers, K. H., *Humphrey Duke of Gloucester*, Constable, 1907.
Wolffe, B. P., 'Acts of resumption in the Lancastrian parliaments 1399–1456', *English Hist. Rev.*, 73 (1958).
Wolffe, B. P., *The Royal Demesne in English History*, Allen and Unwin, 1971.

Chapter 6

General

Fowler, K., *The Age of Plantagenet and Valois*, Elek, 1967.
Fowler, K., ed., *The Hundred Years War*, Macmillan, 1971.
Perroy, E., *The Hundred Years War*, trans. D. C. Douglas, Eyre and Spottiswoode, 1951.

The war in the fourteenth century

Cuttino, G. P., *English Diplomatic Administration 1259–1339*, O.U.P., 1971 edn.
Fowler, K., *The King's Lieutenant. Henry of Grosmont, First Duke of Lancaster 1310–1361*, Elek, 1969.
Froissart, Jean, *Chronicles*, selected and trans. G. Brereton, Penguin, 1968.
Hewitt, H. J., *The Black Prince's Expedition of 1355–1357*, Manchester U.P., 1958.

Jones, M., *Ducal Brittany 1364–1399*, O.U.P., 1970.
Le Patourel, J., 'Edward III and the kingdom of France', *History*, 43, 1958.
Le Patourel, J., 'The treaty of Brétigny', *Trans. Royal Hist. Soc.*, 5th ser., 10 (1960).
Palmer, J. J. N., *England, France and Christendom, 1377–99*, Routledge, 1972.
Russell, P. E., *The English Intervention in Spain and Portugal in the Time of Edward III and Richard II*, O.U.P., 1955.
Sherborne, J. W., 'The battle of La Rochelle and the war at sea, 1372–5', *Bull. Inst. Hist. Res.*, 42 (1969).

The war in the fifteenth century

Allmand, C. T., 'The Anglo-French negotiations, 1439', *Bull. Inst. Hist. Res.*, 40 (1967).
Allmand, C. T., *Henry V*, Hist. Assoc., 1968.
Allmand, C. T., ed., 'Documents relating to the Anglo-French negotiations of 1439', *Camden Miscellany XXIV*, Royal Hist. Soc., 1972.
Dickinson, J. G., *The Congress of Arras 1435*, O.U.P., 1955.
Newhall, R. A., *The English Conquest of Normandy 1416–1424*, Yale U.P., 1924.
Richmond, C. F., 'The keeping of the seas during the Hundred Years' War: 1420–1440', *History*, 49 (1964).
Richmond, C. F., 'English naval power in the fifteenth century', *History*, 52 (1967).
Rowe, B. J., 'Discipline in the Norman garrisons under Bedford' and 'The Estates of Normandy under the duke of Bedford, 1422–35', *English Hist. Rev.*, 46 (1931).
Taylor, F., and **Roskell, J. S.**, ed. and trans., *Gesta Henrici Quinti: the Deeds of Henry V*, O.U.P., 1975.
Vale, M. G. A., *English Gascony, 1399–1453*, O.U.P., 1970.
Williams, E. Carleton, *My Lord of Bedford 1389–1435*, Longmans, 1963.

Military organisation and consequences of war

Allmand, C. T., 'The Lancastrian land settlement in Normandy, 1417–50', *Econ. Hist. Rev.*, 2nd ser., 21 (1968).
Allmand, C. T., ed., *Society at War*, Oliver and Boyd, 1973.
Barnie, J., *War in Medieval Society. Social Values and the Hundred Years War 1337–99*, Weidenfeld and Nicolson, 1974.
Hay, D., 'The division of the spoils of war in fourteenth-century England', *Trans. Royal Hist. Soc.*, 5th ser., 4 (1954).
Hewitt, H. J., *The Organization of War under Edward III, 1338—62*, Manchester U.P., 1966.
Keen, M. H., *The Laws of War in the Late Middle Ages*, Routledge, 1965.
Lewis, N. B., 'The organisation of indentured retinues in fourteenth-century England', *Trans. Royal Hist. Soc.*, 4th ser., 27 (1945).
Lewis, P., 'War propaganda and historiography in fifteenth-century France and England', *Trans. Royal Hist. Soc.*, 5th ser., 15 (1965).
McFarlane, K. B., 'The investment of Sir John Fastolf's profits of war', *Trans. Royal Hist. Soc.*, 5th ser., 7 (1957).
McFarlane, K. B., 'England and the Hundred Years War', *Past and Present*, 22 (1962).
McFarlane, K. B., 'A business partnership in war and administration, 1421–45', *English Hist. Rev.*, 78 (1963).
Newhall, R. A., *Muster and Review*, Harvard U.P., 1940.
Postan, M. M., 'The costs of the Hundred Years' War', *Past and Present*, 27 (1964).
Powicke, M.R., *Military Obligation in Medieval England*, Oxford U.P., 1962.
Sherborne, J. W., 'Indentured retinues and English expeditions to France, 1369–1380', *English Hist. Rev.*, 79 (1964).
Sherborne, J. W., 'The Hundred Years' War. The English navy, shipping and manpower, 1369–1389', *Past and Present*, 37 (1967).
Upton, Nicholas, *De Studio Militari*, selected by F. P. Barnard from trans. by John Blount, O.U.P., 1931.

Chapter 7

The Wars of the Roses

Armstrong, C. A. J., 'Politics and the battle of St. Albans, 1455', *Bull. Inst. Hist. Res.*, 33 (1960).

Griffiths, R. A., 'Local rivalries and national politics: the Percies, the Nevilles, and the Duke of Exeter, 1452–1455', *Speculum*, 43 (1968).

Griffiths, R. A., 'Duke Richard of York's intentions in 1450 and the origins of the Wars of the Roses', *Jnl Medieval Studies*, 1 (1975).

Harriss, G. L., 'The struggle for Calais; an aspect of the rivalry between Lancaster and York', *English Hist. Rev.*, 75 (1960).

Haward, W. I., 'Economic aspects of the Wars of the Roses in East Anglia', *English Hist. Rev.*, 41 (1926).

Historie of the Arrivall of Edward IV, ed. J. Bruce, Camden Soc., 1838.

Lander, J. R., *The Wars of the Roses*, Secker and Warburg, 1965.

Lander, J. R., *Crown and Nobility 1450–1509*, Arnold, 1976.

Lyle, H. M., *The Rebellion of Jack Cade, 1450*, Hist. Assoc., 1950.

McFarlane, K. B., 'The Wars of the Roses', *Proc. British Academy*, 50 (1964).

Ross, C., *The Wars of the Roses*, Thames and Hudson, 1976.

Stapleton, T., ed., *Plumpton Correspondence,* Camden Soc., 1839.

Storey, R. L., *The End of the House of Lancaster*, Barrie and Rockliff, 1966.

The Great Chronicle of London, ed. A. H. Thomas and I. D. Thornley, Corporation of the City of London, 1938.

Thomson, J. A. F., 'The Courtenay family in the Yorkist period', *Bull. Inst. Hist. Res.*, 45 (1972).

The Yorkists and Henry VII

Chrimes, S. B., *Henry VII*, Eyre Methuen, 1972.

Hanham, A., *Richard III and His Early Historians, 1484–1535*, O.U.P., 1975.

Hay, D., *Polydore Vergil: Renaissance Historian and Man of Letters*, O.U.P., 1952.

Kingsford, C. L., *English Historical Literature in the Fifteenth Century*, Oxford, 1913.

Lander, J. R., *Crown and Nobility.*

Lockyer, R., *Henry VII*, Longmans, 1968.

Mancini, Dominic, *The Usurpation of Richard III*, ed. and trans. C. A. J. Armstrong, O.U.P., 1969 edn.

More, Sir Thomas, *The History of King Richard III*, ed. R. S. Sylvester (*Complete Works*, vol. 2, Yale U.P., 1963).

Morgan, D. A. L., 'The King's affinity in the polity of Yorkist England', *Trans. Royal Hist. Soc.*, 5th ser., 23 (1973).

Polydore Vergil, *The 'Anglica Historia' of Polydore Vergil, 1485–1537*, ed. and trans. D. Hay, Camden ser., 1950.

Polydore Vergil, *Three Books of Polydore Vergil's English History*, trans. H. Ellis, Camden Soc., 1844.

Ross, C., *Edward IV*, Eyre Methuen, 1974.

Scofield, C. L., *The Life and Reign of Edward the Fourth*, 2 vols, Longmans, 1923.

Storey, R. L., *The Reign of Henry VII*, Blandford, 1968.

The reign of Henry VIII

Anglo, S., *Spectacle Pageantry, and Early Tudor Policy,* O.U.P., 1969.

Bush, M. L., 'The Tudors and the Royal Race', *History*, 55 (1970).

Cavendish, George, *The Life and Death of Cardinal Wolsey*, ed. R. S. Sylvester, Early English Text Soc., 1959.

Davies, C. S. L., 'The pilgrimage of grace reconsidered', *Past and Present*, 41 (1968).

Davies, C. S. L., 'A new life of Henry VIII', *History*, 54 (1969).

Dodds, M. H., and **R.**, *The Pilgrimage of Grace, 1536–1537, and the Exeter Conspiracy, 1538,* 2 vols, Cambridge, 1915.
Elton, G. R., *Policy and Police: Enforcement of the Reformation in the Age of Thomas Cromwell*, C.U.P., 1972.
Elton, G. R., *Reform and Renewal: Thomas Cromwell and the Common Weal*, C.U.P., 1973.
Elton, G. R., *Henry VIII*, Hist. Assoc., 1974 reprint.
Fletcher, A., *Tudor Rebellions,* Longman, 1968.
James. M. E., *A Tudor Magnate and the Tudor State.*
James, M. E., 'Obedience and dissent in Henrician England: the Lincolnshire rebellion 1536', *Past and Present*, 48 (1970).
Lehmberg, S. E., *The Reformation Parliament 1529–1536*, C.U.P., 1970.
Scarisbrick, J. J., *Henry VIII*, Eyre and Spottiswoode, 1968.
Slavin, A. J., ed., *Tudor Men and Institutions*, Louisiana State U.P., 1972.
Smith, R. B., *Land and Politics in the England of Henry VIII: the West Riding of Yorkshire, 1530–1546*, O.U.P., 1970.
Zeeveld, W. Gordon, *Foundations of Tudor Policy*, Methuen, 1969.

Reigns of Henry VIII's children

Beckingsale, B. W., *Burghley Tudor Statesman 1520–1598*, Macmillan, 1967.
Bindoff, S. T., *Ket's Rebellion, 1549*, Hist. Assoc., 1968 reprint.
Bindoff, S. T., **Hurstfield, J.**, and **Williams, C. H.**, ed., *Elizabethan Government and Society. Essays presented to Sir John Neal*, Athlone Press, 1964 reprint.
Bush, M. L., *The Government Policy of Protector Somerset*, Arnold, 1975.
Emmison, F. G., *Tudor Secretary. Sir William Petre at Court and Home*, Longmans, 1961.
Handover, P. M., *The Second Cecil. The Rise to Power, 1563–1604, of Sir Robert Cecil, later first Earl of Salisbury*, Eyre and Spottiswoode, 1959.
Harbison, E. Harris, *Rival Ambassadors at the Court of Queen Mary*, Princeton U.P., 1940.
Hurstfield, J., *Freedom, Corruption and Government in Elizabethan England*, Cape, 1973.
Jones, W. R. D., *The Tudor Commonwealth 1529–1559*, Athlone Press, 1970.
Jordan, W. K., *Edward VI: the Young King*, Allen and Unwin, 1968.
Jordan, W. K., *Edward VI: the Threshold of Power*, Allen and Unwin, 1970
Levine, M., *The Early Elizabethan Succession Question 1558–1568*, Stanford U.P., 1966.
Levine, M., *Tudor Dynastic Problems 1460–1571*, Allen and Unwin, 1973.
Loades, D. M., *Two Tudor Conspiracies,* C.U.P., 1965.
MacCaffrey, W., *The Shaping of the Elizabethan Regime*, Cape, 1969.
Neale, J. E., *Queen Elizabeth*, Cape, 1934.
Neale, J. E., *Elizabeth I and her Parliament*, 2 vols, Cape, 1953–7.
Neale, J. E., *Essay in Elizabethan History*, Cape, 1958.
Read, Conyers, *Mr. Secretary Cecil and Queen Elizabeth*, Cape, 1955.
Read, Conyers, *Lord Burghley and Queen Elizabeth*, Cape, 1960.
Rowse, A. L., *Tudor Cornwall*, Cape, 1951.
Rowse, A. L., *The Expansion of Elizabethan England*, Macmillan, 1955.
Williams, N., *Thomas Howard Fourth Duke of Norfolk*, Barrie and Rockliff, 1964.
Williams, N., *Elizabeth Queen of England*, Weidenfeld and Nicolson, 1967.

Chapter 8

General

Cross, C., *Church and People 1450–1660*, Fontana Collins, 1976.
Dickens, A. G., *The English Reformation*, Batsford, 1964.
Hay, D., 'The Church of England in the later Middle Ages', *History*, 53 (1968).
Pantin, W. A., *The English Church in the Fourteenth Century*, C.U.P., 1955.

Thompson, A. Hamilton, *The English Clergy and their Organization in the Later Middle Ages*, O.U.P., 1947.

Ecclesiastical institutions and their roles in society

Aston, M., *Thomas Arundel. A Study of Church Life in the Reign of Richard II*, O.U.P., 1967.

Bossy, J., 'Blood and baptism: kinship, community and christianity in western Europe from the fourteenth to the seventeenth centuries', *Studies in Church History*, vol. 10, ed. D. Baker, Eccles. Hist. Soc., 1973.

Bowker, M., *The Secular Clergy in the Diocese of Lincoln 1495–1520*, C.U.P., 1968.

Cook, G. H., *Mediaeval Chantries and Chantry Chapels*, Phoenix House, 1947.

Dobson, R. B., *Durham Cathedral Priory 1400–1450*, C.U.P., 1973.

Dunning, R. W., 'Rural Deans of England in the fifteenth century', *Bull. Inst. Hist. Res.*, 40 (1967).

Hair, P., ed., *Before the Bawdy Courts*, Elek, 1972.

Harrison, F., *Life in a Medieval College*, Murray, 1952.

Heath, P., *The English Parish Clergy on the Eve of the Reformation*, Routledge, 1969.

Jacob, E. F., *Essays in the Conciliar Epoch*, Manchester U.P., 1963.

Knowles, D., *The Religious Orders in England*, vols 2–3, C.U.P., 1955–9.

Knowles, D., and **Hadcock, R. N.,** *Medieval Religious Houses. England and Wales*, Longman, 1971 edn.

Lawrence, C. H., ed., *The English Church and the Papacy in the Middle Ages*, Burns and Oates, 1965.

Lunt, W. E., *Financial Relations of the Papacy with England 1327–1534*, Mediaeval Academy of America, 1962.

McHardy, A. K., 'The alien priories and the expulsion of aliens from England in 1378', *Studies in Church History*, vol. 12, ed. D. Baker, Eccles. Hist. Soc., 1975.

Mason, E., 'The role of the English parishioner, 1100–1500', *Jnl Eccles. Hist.*, 27 (1976).

Owen, D., *Church and Society in Medieval Lincolnshire*, Lincs. Local Hist. Soc., 1971.

Owst, G. R., *Literature and Pulpit in Medieval England*, O.U.P., 1961 edn.

Perroy, E., *L'Angleterre et le grand schisme d'occident*, J. Monnier, Paris, 1933.

Scammell, J., 'The rural chapter in England from the eleventh to the fourteenth century', *English Hist. Rev.*, 86 (1971).

Scarisbrick, J., 'Clerical Taxation in England, 1485–1547', *Jnl Eccles. Hist.*, 12 (1961).

Storey, R. L., *Thomas Langley and the Bishopric of Durham, 1406–1437*, S.P.C.K., 1966.

Storey, R. L., *Diocesan Administration in the Fifteenth Century*, St. Anthony's Press, York, 1959.

Wilkie, W. E., *The Cardinal Protectors of England*, C.U.P., 1974.

Wood-Legh, K., *Perpetual Chantries in Britain*, C.U.P., 1965.

Devotional trends

Blacman, John, *Henry the Sixth*, ed. M. R. James, Cambridge, 1919.

Boase, T. S. R., *Death in the Middle Ages*, Thames and Hudson, 1972.

Butler-Bowdon, W., selected and trans., *The Book of Margery Kempe*, Jonathan Cape, London, 1936.

Evans, J., *English Art, 1307–1461*, O.U.P., 1949.

Hilton, Walter, *The Ladder of Perfection*, trans. L. Sherley-Price, Penguin, 1957.

Julian of Norwich, *Revelations of Divine Love*, trans. C. Wolters, Penguin, 1966.

Knowles, D., *The English Mystics*, Burns Oates and Washbourne, 1927.

Knox, R., and **Leslie, S.,** selected and trans., *The miracles of King Henry VI*, C.U.P., 1923.

Lovatt, R., 'The *Imitation of Christ* in late medieval England', *Trans. Royal Hist. Soc.*, 5th ser., 18 (1968).

Orme, N., *English Schoold in the Middle Ages*, Methuen, 1973.

Pantin, W. A., 'Instructions for a devout and literate layman', in *Medieval Learning and Literature. Essays presented to Richard William Hunt*, ed. J. J. G. Alexander and M. T. Gibson, O.U.P., 1976.

Rolle, Richard, *The Fire of Love*, trans. C. Wolters, Penguin, 1972.

The Cloud of Unknowing, trans. C. Wolters, Penguin, 1961.

Vale, M. G. A., *Piety, Charity and Literacy among the Yorkshire Gentry, 1370–1480*, St. Anthony's Press, York, 1976.

Lollardy and the Reformation

Alexander, G., 'Bonner and the Marian persecution', *History*, 60 (1975).

Aston, M., 'Lollardy and sedition, 1381–1431', *Past and Present*, 17 (1960).

Bossy, J., 'The character of Elizabethan Catholicism', *Past and Present*, 21 (1962).

Bossy, J., *The English Catholic Community 1570–1850*, Darton, Longman and Todd, 1976.

Collinson, P., *The Elizabethan Puritan Movement*, Cape, 1967.

Cross, C., *The Puritan Earl*, Macmillan, 1966.

Cross, C., *The Royal Supremacy in the Elizabethan Church*, Allen and Unwin, 1969.

Darby, H. S., *Hugh Latimer*, Epworth Press, 1953.

Deanesly, M., *The Lollard Bible*, C.U.P., 1920.

Dickens, A. G., *Lollards and Protestants in the Diocese of York 1509–1558*, O.U.P., 1959.

Dickens, A. G., *Thomas Cromwell and the English Reformation*, English Universities Press, 1959.

Haller, W., *The Rise of Puritanism*, Harper, New York, 1938.

Hembry, P. M., *The Bishops of Bath and Wells, 1540–1640*, Athlone Press, 1967.

Hill, C., *Economic Problems of the Church from Archbishop Whitgift to the Long Parliament*, O.U.P., 1956.

Hill, C., *Society and Puritanism in Pre-Revolutionary England*, Secker and Warburg, 1964.

Knappen, M. M., *Tudor Puritanism*, Chicago U.P., 1939.

Leff, G., *Heresy in the Later Middle Ages*, 2 vols, Manchester U.P., 1967.

Loades, D. M., 'The enforcement of reaction, 1553–1558', *Jnl Eccles. Hist.*, 16 (1965).

Loades, D. M., *The Oxford Martyrs*, Batsford, 1970.

Macfarlane, A., *Witchcraft in Tudor and Stuart England*, Routledge, 1970.

McFarlane, K. B., *John Wycliffe and the Beginnings of English Nonconformity*, English Univ. Press, 1952.

McFarlane, K. B., *Lancastrian Kings and Lollard Knights*, O.U.P., 1972.

McGrath, P. V., *Papists and Puritans under Elizabeth I*, Blanford, 1967.

Manning, R. B., *Religion and Society in Elizabethan Sussex*, Leicester U.P., 1969.

Marchant, R. A., *The Puritans and the Church Courts in the Diocese of York, 1560–1642*, C.U.P., 1960.

Marchant, R. A., *The Church under the Law: Justice, Administration and Discipline in the Diocese of York, 1560–1640*, C.U.P., 1969.

Oxley, J. E., *The Reformation in Essex*, Manchester U.P., 1965.

Palliser, D. M., *The Reformation in York, 1534–1553*, St. Anthony's Press, York, 1971.

Pogson, R. H., 'Reginald Pole and the priorities of government in Mary Tudor's Church', *Hist. Jnl*, 18 (1975).

Porter, H. C., ed., *Puritanism in Tudor England*, Macmillan, 1970.

Ridley, J., *Thomas Cranmer*, O.U.P., 1962.

Seaver, P. S., *The Puritan Lectureships*, Stanford U.P., 1970.

Thomas, K., *Religion and the Decline of Magic*, Weidenfeld and Nicolson, 1971.

Thomson, J. A. F., *The Later Lollards 1414–1520*, O.U.P., 1965.

Usher, R. G., ed., *The Presbyterian Movement in the Reign of Queen Elizabeth as Illustrated by the Minute Book of the Dedham Classis 1582–1589*, Camden ser., 1905.

Woodward, G. W. O., *The Dissolution of the Monasteries*, Blandford, 1966.

Youings, J., *The Dissolution of the Monasteries*, Allen and Unwin, 1971.

Chapter 9

Bush, M. L., *The Government Policy of Protector Somerset*, Arnold, 1975.
Chrimes, S. B., *Henry VII*, Eyre Methuen, 1972.
Commynes, Philippe de, *Memoirs. The Reign of Louis XI 1461–83*, trans. M. Jones, Penguin, 1972.
Cruickshank, C. G., *Army Royal. Henry VIII's Invasion of France, 1513,* O.U.P., 1969.
Cruickshank, C. G., *The English Occupation of Tournai, 1513–1519*, O.U.P., 1971.
Donaldson, G., *Scotland. James V to James VII*, Oliver and Boyd, 1965.
Goodman, A., and **MacKay, A.,** 'A Castilian report on English affairs, 1486', *English Hist. Rev.*, 88 (1973).
Harbison, E. Harris, *Rival Ambassadors at the Court of Queen Mary*, Princeton U.P., 1940.
Jordan, W. K., *Edward VI: the Young King*, Allen and Unwin, 1968.
Jordan, W. K., *Edward VI: the Threshold of Power*, Allen and Unwin, 1970.
Lockyer, R., *Henry VII*, Longmans, 1968.
MacCaffrey, W., *The Shaping of the Elizabethan Regime*, Cape, 1969.
Mattingly, G., *Rennaissance Diplomacy,* Cape, 1955.
Nicholson, R., *Scotland. The Later Middle Ages*, Oliver and Boyd, 1974.
Read, Conyers, *Mr. Secretary Walsingham and the Policy of Queen Elizabeth*, 3 vols, O.U.P., 1925.
Read, Conyers, *Mr. Secretary Cecil and Queen Elizabeth*, Cape, 1955.
Read, Conyers, *Lord Burghley and Queen Elizabeth*, Cape, 1960.
Ross, C., *Edward IV,* Eyre Methuen, 1974.
Russell, J. G., *The Field of Cloth of Gold*, Routledge, 1969.
Scarisbrick, J. J., *Henry VIII,* Eyre and Spottiswoode, 1968.
Scofield, C. L., *The Life and Reign of Edward the Fourth*, 2 vols, Longmans, 1923.
Wernham, R. B., *Before the Armada. The Growth of English Foreign Policy 1485–1588*, Cape, 1966.

Chapter 10

Fox, L., ed., *English Historical Scholarship in the Sixteenth and Seventeenth Centuries*, O.U.P., 1956.
Harrison, William, *The Description of England*, ed. G. Edelen, Cornell U.P., 1968.
Houston, S. J., *James I,* Longman, 1973.
McKisack, M., *Medieval History in the Tudor Age*, O.U.P., 1971.
Notestein, W., *The English People on the Eve of Colonization 1603–1630*, Harper, N.Y., 1954.
Southern, R. W., 'Aspects of the European tradition of historical writing: 4. The sense of the past', *Trans. Royal Hist. Soc.*, 5th ser., 23 (1973).
Stone, L., *The Crisis of the Aristocracy 1558–1641*, O.U.P., 1965.
Stone, L., ed., *Social Change and Revolution in England, 1540–1640*, Longmans, 1965.
Stone, L., *The causes of the English Revolution 1529–1642*, Routledge, 1972.
Willson, D. H., *King James VI and I*, Cape, 1956.
Wilson, Thomas, 'The State of England *Anno Dom. 1600*', ed. F. J. Fisher, *Camden Miscellany XVI*, Royal Hist. Soc., 1936.

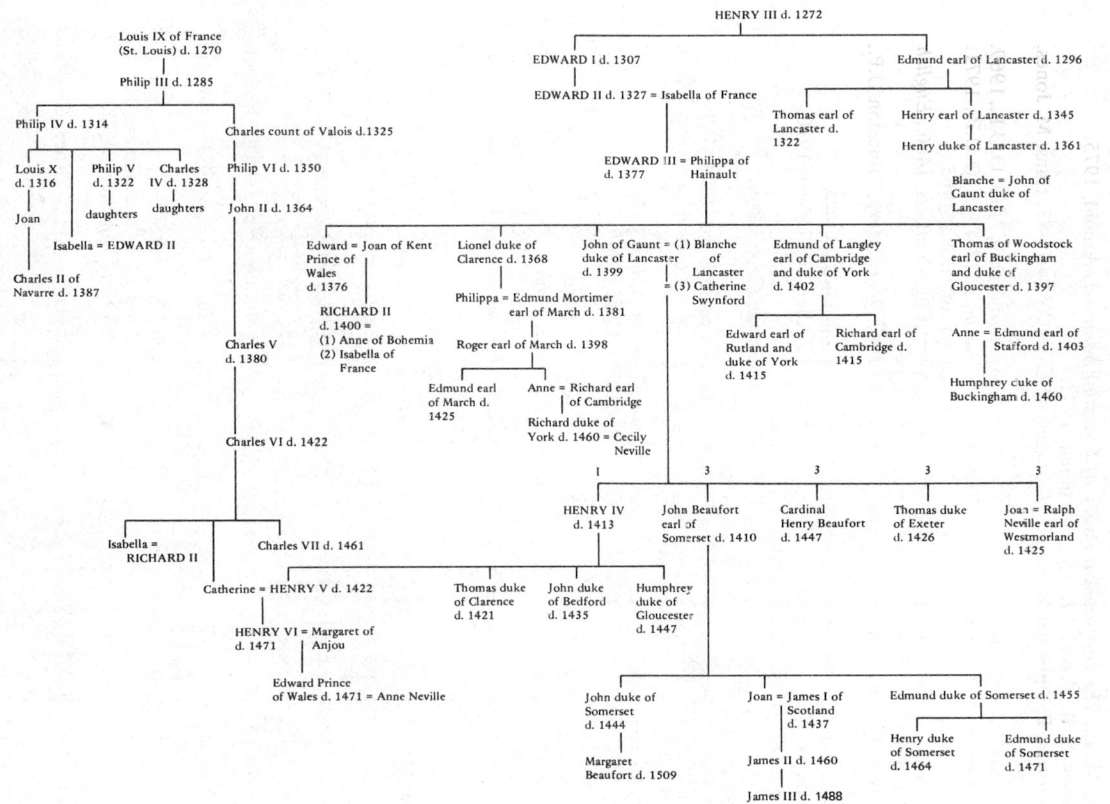

Fig. 8 The royal descent, Henry III to Henry VI.

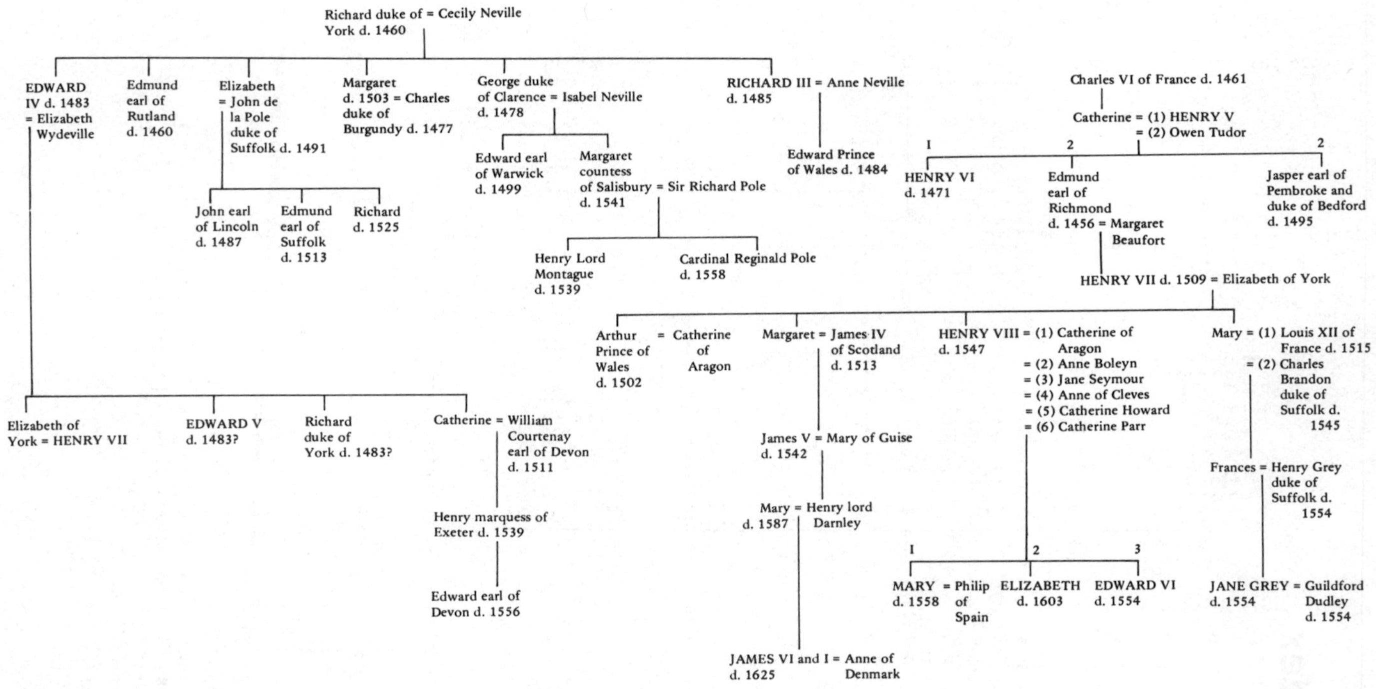

Fig. 9 The royal descent, Edward IV to James I.

Index

LIFE'S TOO SHORT!

Also by Abraham J. Twerski, M.D.

When Do the Good Things Start?

Waking Up Just in Time

I'd Like to Call for Help, But I Don't Know the Number

I Didn't Ask to Be in This Family

Seek Sobriety, Find Serenity

LIFE'S TOO SHORT!

Pull the Plug on Self-Defeating Behavior and Turn on the Power of Self-Esteem

Abraham J. Twerski, M.D.

ST. MARTIN'S PRESS NEW YORK

Design by Sara Stemen

ISBN 0-312-11846-5

First Edition: April 1995

10 9 8 7 6 5 4 3 2 1

Books are available in quantity for promotional or premium use. Write to Director of Special Sales, St. Martin's Press, 175 Fifth Avenue, New York, N.Y. 10010, for information on discounts and terms, or call toll-free (800) 221-7945. In New York, call (212) 674-5151 (ext. 645).

CONTENTS

INTRODUCTION

In 1965 I became director of psychiatry of a major psychiatric hospital, which served as the primary emergency receiving center for a population of three million and as the admitting service for two major state hospitals, in addition to having a population of three hundred psychiatric patients of its own. The barrage of calls and demands on my energies, both during the day and throughout the night, finally exceeded my saturation point. I had to get away.

In making vacation plans, I sought only one thing: peace and silence. I did not want to go sight-seeing or to be entertained at Disneyland. All I wanted was to be beyond the reach of a telephone and to be left alone.

When someone suggested Hot Springs, Arkansas, this seemed to fit the bill. During the off-season (Hot Springs is a horse-racing town), the community is very quiet. Furthermore, the hot mineral baths might provide relief for my chronic backache.

I checked into a hotel, and the following morning I entered the spa, where I was led into a small cubicle and immersed in a whirlpool bath. This was paradise! Not only was I comforted by the warm, swirling waters, but I was also beyond anyone's reach. The emergency room, social workers, police, nurses, doctors, lawyers, and patients and their families could not reach me. I just relaxed in what was heaven on earth. After six or seven minutes, I emerged from the bath and remarked to the attendant how wonderful this experience had been—just what I needed. The attendant politely told me that I had to return to the bath; the treatment began with soaking twenty-five minutes in the mineral water. I got back in the water, but after five more minutes I again emerged and told the attendant that it was enough. He instructed me that if I did not stay for the full twenty-five minutes I could not continue with the next phase of the treatment. What had begun as heaven was now purgatory. I watched the second hand on the clock move slowly. Each minute seemed an hour, and the final ten minutes of the bath were an eternity, barely tolerable.

Later that day I reflected on what had been a rude awakening. I had been able to take *three years* of a harassing schedule in stride but could not take paradise for more than *seven minutes!*

A bit of analysis led me to conclude that many people are probably not capable of enjoying true relaxation. We are quite adept at enjoying diversion, such as watching television, going to a ball game, reading a book, doing handwork, or chasing a golf ball. All such activities are diversionary because they divert our attention and focus it on whatever we happen to be doing.

What had happened to me in that cubicle was that I had

been deprived of all diversions. There was no one to talk to, nothing to look at, nothing to read, and nothing to listen to. I had been left alone, in the immediate company of my-self. All there was in that cubicle was me. I was alone with me. I concluded that my intolerance of relaxation came from my being unable to stand my own company. *I didn't like myself.*

At the ripe old age of thirty-eight, having been a practicing psychiatrist for five years, I began to question why I did not like myself. Eventually I discovered that my image of myself was incorrect. My self-image was quite unlikable. I felt I was a phony. My rabbinical beard and garb portrayed a spiritual person, but I felt I did not measure up to spirituality. I was greedy, envious, selfish, and resentful. I acted as though I were humble, when in fact I was proud and vain. My humility was but a facade for my arrogance. I pretended to be erudite, but my ignorance was overwhelming. I could successfully relate to people only as long as I managed to maintain this facade, but I was always apprehensive that some astute person would see through it to the "real me."

Had anyone told me that I did not know my real self, I would have disputed it. Who else could know me as well as I did? But after a fair amount of self-searching with a bit of help, I discovered that this was indeed the case.

Since then I have been engaged in getting to know myself better, and it has been most rewarding. As you will see, people who have a negative self-image are apt to do many things that are counterproductive, and I was no exception.

I was a "people pleaser," constantly doing things for

others, because I desperately wanted everyone to like me. I felt I had to buy friendship and affection. I never refused a request, regardless of how unreasonable it was, because I could not risk offending or alienating anyone. I pretended I was glad to do the favor, but inside I resented people for imposing on me.

On many occasions I was grossly underpaid for my services, but I acted overjoyed and enthusiastically thanked people for what they had given me. On the other hand, on several occasions when people gave me larger amounts of money in appreciation of something I had done, I refused to accept the bonus in order to impress them.

When others received honors that I felt I deserved, I was magnanimous, pretending to be happy for the recipient of the award, whereas inside I seethed with rage. These were only some of the mechanisms I used to persuade others that I was not the person I felt myself to be.

I feel much different about myself now. When someone asks me to do something, I am free to refuse if I feel it is an unrealistic imposition, and when I do things for others, it is with sincere goodwill. I charge what I feel is a fair fee for my services and do not have to fear that people will accuse me of avarice.

I have proof that my efforts at self-awareness have been successful. I have returned to Hot Springs several times since, and I can fully enjoy twenty-five minutes of relaxation in the whirlpool!

If we have a negative self-image, we may interpret many things as if they are related to us, whereas in reality they have nothing to do with us.

Peanuts® by Charles M. Schulz. Reprinted by permission of United Feature Syndicate, Inc.

The bird sat on Charlie Brown's shoe for a moment, then flew off as birds do. The bird's flight has no connection at all to Charlie Brown, but given that Charlie feels he is unlikable, he interprets the departure as a rejection.

This negative attitude tends to drain people of their energies and may result in self-defeating behavior. In the pages ahead, I investigate this phenomenon and suggest some ways it can be overcome.

But first, why the cartoons? There is truth in the adage that one picture is worth a thousand words. Not only does an illustration convey a message, but it can do so more emphatically. In the cartoon, we can actually feel Charlie Brown's distress and loneliness.

We can see ourselves in a cartoon and identify with the

characters, whereas we might not apply the written word to ourselves. There is often an inherent resistance to recognizing certain behavioral traits in ourselves, and a cartoon may be a vehicle that can help us bypass or break through this resistance.

I have found cartoons to be a potent vehicle in psychotherapy, and I have utilized the brilliant intuitive insights of Charles Schulz in my three books, *When Do the Good Things Start?*, *Waking Up Just in Time*, and *I Didn't Ask to Be in This Family.*

This is a self-help book, and the cartoons are included for their educational value, but there is certainly no harm if they elicit a chuckle. In fact, if we can laugh at ourselves a bit, this is a major achievement. Overcoming self-destructive behavior is important business, but we may be able to handle the challenge better if we stop taking ourselves too seriously.

Part I

Defeating the Self-Image Delusion

ONE

You're Better Than You Think

A young woman was admitted for treatment because of her heroin addiction. All her veins had become obstructed from injecting herself with narcotics, which resulted in multiple abscesses. This otherwise attractive woman was a pathetic sight because of the many lesions.

In the admission interview she told me that she was a nurse and had easy access to drugs. She had used sedatives for insomnia and Percocet for menstrual cramps. These were taken on her own, not prescribed by a physician. She became addicted to both medications, and when she feared that the hospital would note that drugs were missing, she began using street drugs, eventually gravitating toward heroin. The narcotic habit resulted in her being unable to work, and after using up all her savings, she sold everything, including herself, for money to buy drugs.

I noted that she was wearing a locket, which she said was gold, and asked her why she had not sold it for heroin. She said that it was her mother's and that she would never part with it. I asked her to show it to me. After she handed it to me, I picked up a sharp instrument and acted as if I were about to scratch the locket.

"What are you doing?" she asked with a tone of panic.

"Just scratching this a little bit," I said.

"Why do you want to do that?"

"Oh, it's just something I like to do."

"But that's mine!"

"I know. I will give it back to you."

"But I don't want it all scratched up. It's beautiful, and it's valuable to me."

"You mean that when something has beauty and value, you do not allow it to be marred and ruined?" I asked. Then, taking her hands and showing her the bruises and abscesses, I said, "Do you see what this says? These self-inflicted wounds are a loud statement that says 'I am not beautiful. I have no value.' "

People who do not have a sense of self-worth are prone to do destructive things to themselves or inadvertently allow themselves to be injured. Overcoming self-defeating behavior requires self-esteem.

Drug and alcohol abuse are only two of many ways to be self-destructive. The ways we may injure ourselves are legion: dropping out of school, having an unplanned pregnancy, allowing our weight to get out of control, and entering unhealthy relationships are just a few. Most of us are not totally unaware of the destructive nature of our behavior. If we do things that are injurious to ourselves, it is most often not due to ignorance but to an attitude of "I don't really care. It doesn't make that much difference." Even if we protest that we *do* care, on a subconscious level we really do not.

Protecting something valuable is a natural reaction. When we are dressed in fine clothes, we take much more care to avoid soiling them than if we are casually dressed. The proud owner of a new automobile will wash and wax it and avoid pulling up against hedges that might scratch the glossy surface. When we neglect ourselves, it is not that we have lost this natural reaction. As the young woman's concern for the gold locket indicates, she did not consider herself to be of much value or of any beauty.

For more than twenty years, my psychiatric practice has been devoted primarily to problems of substance abuse. I have never encountered a patient who did not have a negative self-image *prior to the use of alcohol or drugs.* Although the consequences of addiction certainly intensify low self-esteem, unwarranted feelings of shame precede the substance abuse in every case.

Many of the examples I cite are cases of alcohol or drug addiction, since these are the ones I see most frequently. But the self-image problem that prevails in this condition is equally present in other self-destructive behavior. Furthermore, just as alcohol or drug addiction is nondiscriminating—it affects both men and women, young and old, rich and poor, learned or illiterate—so are many other varieties of self-destructive behavior. Without exception, the feelings of shame that characterize people with alcohol and drug addictions are a result of a distorted self-perception.

The man in the cartoon on the next page is fortunate; he is aware that the image he sees is a distortion. Think of how someone would feel if he looked into the trick mirror and believed the distorted image to be a replica.

Many problems that bring a person to a psychotherapist's office are the result of this kind of self-devaluation. Sustained recovery from any self-destructive lifestyle requires a change of attitude, one that promotes a positive rather than a negative self-image.

"THANK GOODNESS THIS IS A TRICK MIRROR!"

Learning the truth about oneself and uncovering the beautiful self that exists underneath unhealthful behavior can eliminate shame and a negative self-concept.

Life is too short not to live it as the real you. Putting up a facade is a waste of energy that can leave you drained. Discovery of the "real you" eliminates any necessity for masquerading. It is never too late to make this discovery and live a happier and more constructive life.

TWO

Why You Feel So Bad When You Should Feel Good

Many people may say, "I don't have a distorted self-image. I know myself thoroughly and accurately, and I know for a fact that I am inadequate."

Very capable and gifted people who have come to think of themselves as inadequate may not budge from their belief even in the face of undeniable evidence to the contrary. One woman, a highly skilled physician who had graduated from college summa cum laude and had won the coveted Phi Beta Kappa Award for scholastic excellence, had intense feelings of inadequacy. When I pointed out to her that she could not possibly deny her intellectual superiority, her response was "When they told me I had won the Phi Beta Kappa Award, I knew they had made a mistake."

Again and again I encounter highly accomplished people with profound feelings of inferiority who harbor a negative self-concept.

Where does this negative attitude toward oneself come from, and why is it so prevalent? We might assume that children who grew up under conditions of poverty and emotional deprivation or abuse would develop negative self-concepts. This is often the case. But we find the same feelings of inadequacy and inferiority in people who grew up in stable and comfortable environments with apparently loving and caring parents.

We can only hypothesize why this occurs. A child's only support are his parents, who care for him and serve as a bridge between his needs and his world. The noted psychiatrist Silvano Arieti says that the child must preserve his trust in his parents at all costs. If he sees them as unreliable, the anxiety of being adrift in the world without adequate support is virtually incompatible with sanity. The child must therefore see his parents or other adult caregivers as wise, just, and trustworthy.

Rose Is Rose® by Pat Brady. Reprinted by permission of United Feature Syndicate, Inc.

If parents punish a child, and the child does not fully understand why he is being punished, the child cannot afford to think, "My parents don't know what they are doing." This thought is too threatening. The child instead concludes, "My parents are right. I deserve this punishment because *I am bad.*" If the child cannot attribute the punishment to anything he did to warrant it, he concludes, "I am bad. Even if I don't do things that are wrong, I am just bad." The child may develop feelings of shame, guilt, and inferiority, even though he may not have any idea why he should feel this way.

"Life's so unfair! I got spanked first thing when I was born, and I hadn't done anything bad yet!"

Beattie Blvd.™ by Bruce Beattie. Reprinted by permission of Newspaper Enterprise Association, Inc.

Similarly, when things happen that really are irrational, the child may not conclude, "The world is crazy," but rather, "I do not have the capacity to understand," and come to have no confidence in his ability to understand or to make judgments. When feelings like this develop early in life, they may haunt a person well into adult life.

Sometimes a sibling who is younger or has special needs may receive extra attention from the parents. A child may not be able to understand the situation and may conclude: "My parents like my brother/sister more than me. I am not likable."

Various circumstances prevalent in today's society may aggravate the feelings of inadequacy. Years ago, people grew up and lived in the town where their parents and grandparents lived, sometimes even in the same house. Today, multiple generations living in the same community are a rarity. It is interesting to see the trend toward finding one's roots, which seems to indicate that having identifiable and respectable roots gives a person a positive feeling.

Eek & Meek® by Howie Schneider. Reprinted by permission of Newspaper Enterprise Association, Inc.

Roots that are as impersonal as the big bang theory do not contribute much to one's self-esteem.

Also, in today's mobile society, many children attend schools in several different communities before they enter high school, as a result of their parents' changing jobs. Being an outsider and having to work one's way into the existing clique is an ordeal. When this challenge must be repeated several times in a young person's life, it may have a significant impact on his self-concept.

Once a child develops a negative self-image, he is likely to act on that assumption and reinforce his condition. For example, thinking that he is inadequate, he will not try to achieve, because he believes he will fail. Many children do poorly in mathematics because they approach the subject with a preconviction that they are "too dumb" for math. They indeed fail as a result of not trying, and their poor grades confirm that they are "dumb."

These self-fulfilling prophecies may influence many aspects of our behavior, so that by the time we are adults the conviction of inadequacy has been reinforced many times over. A person who develops feelings of inferiority is likely to feel inferior about feeling inferior, and this can develop into a very severe vicious cycle.

"This inferiority complex I've got . . . I assume it's not a very good one, is it?"

Cartoon by Bill Hoest. Copyright Wm. Hoest Enterprises, Inc. Reprinted with permission.

There are many things that people assume to be true that are not at all accurate. Indeed, people who have delusions of inferiority are more convinced of their beliefs than are people who have a correct perception. If a paranoid person believes that the FBI is spying on and persecuting him, no amount of logical argument will dissuade him. His psychotic convictions are as unyielding as the Rock of Gibraltar. A conviction about oneself may contradict the facts, but the person who has come to think of himself as inferior is as unimpressed by facts as is the psychotic paranoid.

Failure to recognize one's personality strengths is somewhat similar to being ignorant of one's assets. Imagine that you are heir to a fortune but do not learn of the bequest. You may be struggling for subsistence when you could be living in luxury.

Everyone encounters difficulties in life. But the person who is out of touch with the reality of his character assets may not be able to utilize these abilities and adjust satisfactorily to the situation.

A patient assumed his position on the psychiatrist's couch, and the doctor said, "Tell me what your problem is."

The patient began, "I have a sixty-four-room mansion located on four hundred acres of beautiful countryside. I have a housekeeper, cook, and chauffeur. My children attend the finest schools. I own three luxury automobiles—"

At this point the doctor interrupted. "I asked you to tell me your problem."

The patient responded, "I'm about to get to that. You see, I make only $150 a week."

Just as a person who has delusions of great wealth runs

into trouble by spending lavishly, so does a person who is intellectually gifted but fails to use these skills.

But what if a person *is* inadequate? After all, some people actually are deficient in various desirable traits. In these cases there is no distortion of the self-perception. But these people usually make a relatively satisfactory adjustment to the reality of their lives. They are not likely to have the various self-destructive behaviors that characterize people with *unwarranted* feelings of shame.

Think of it this way. Suppose you have a small automobile with a four-cylinder engine that is capable of generating sixty horsepower. It doesn't burn up the road, but it gets you where you want to go fairly smoothly. Now suppose you have a car with a powerful V-8 engine that can generate three hundred horsepower, but two of the eight cylinders are not functioning. It still generates more than two hundred horsepower, but it does not give you a smooth ride. Why? Because smooth performance requires all eight cylinders to be functioning.

As with engines, so with people. A person with lesser endowment may make a satisfactory adjustment to his limited capacities, while a person of much greater capacities who thinks he is defective may make a less satisfactory adaptation to life.

Let me cite an incident in my own childhood that illustrates the ability to adjust to inadequacies.

As a child, I was an avid baseball fan. This was not an unusual phenomenon in the era of Lou Gehrig, Joe DiMaggio, Ted Williams, Bob Feller, and other giants of baseball fame. I had a burning desire to play baseball, but I was hampered by two real problems: I couldn't hit and I couldn't catch. I was clearly a liability on any team, and consequently I was never chosen to play.

Hoping to buy a position on the team, I came to the playground and gave all the kids caramels. They gladly took the candy, but I still was not chosen to play.

In desperation, I resorted to another maneuver. Not far from the playground there was a sporting goods store that displayed a bat in the window. This was no ordinary bat. It was a shiny brown Louisville Slugger with a royal blue felt handle and with Lou Gehrig's signature etched into it. Before and after school the kids would push their noses against the windowpane, trying to get as close a look as possible at the dream bat.

This bat was indeed only a dream. It sold for $1.25 at a time when the average family lived comfortably on $30 a week and when $18.75 could buy a suit with two pairs of pants. No child could think of spending $1.25. However, I saw it as my only hope of getting to play baseball.

I had a bank that held the nickels, dimes, and quarters that I received from members of my father's congregation as Hanukkah favors. I was not supposed to touch this money, but it was a matter of life and death. I pried the bank open, took out $1.25, and purchased the bat.

The kids at the playground were in disbelief. "Lookit! The kid! He's got the bat! Hey, kid, can we use the bat?"

"Only if I play," I said.

The two team captains chose their sides, and after everyone had been chosen, I remained with the coveted bat.

"Well, someone's gotta take him. It's his bat."

"We don't want him. You take him."

"Why should we take him? We got Eddie, and he stinks!"

The bickering went back and forth until one captain came up with a Solomonic solution. "Okay, we take him, but his outs don't count."

After several days, the folly of going through the motions of striking out was evident, and I withdrew from the game, letting the kids use my bat anyway. From then on I spent recess studying.

This was hardly an ego-edifying experience, but I look back on it with amusement. It registers no discomfort whatsoever. Although it was unpleasant at the time, I do not associate any feelings of humiliation with it.

Why? Because the defects involved were real. I couldn't hit or catch a ball. I was not athletic. So what? I had other areas of potential excellence, such as scholastic abilities, and I developed them instead. We can compensate in various ways for an actual limitation. It is only the misperception of fantasized defects that gives rise to psychological problems.

Let us now look at some of the things that happen when people have imaginary defects. They may try to cover up these defects, which often results in awkward behavior. Since these kinds of "cover-ups" are common, we may be able to identify our own use of such techniques by observing them in others. If we can understand that the defects we are trying to conceal are imaginary, we may be able to dispense with these maneuvers and make much more satisfactory adjustments to various life situations.

Part II

Understanding the Problems of Low Self-Esteem

THREE

Fear of Rejection

Ralph had accumulated a string of unsuccessful romantic relationships. He dated frequently but was never able to develop an ongoing relationship. The young women he met showed some initial interest in him, but without exception they subsequently turned him away. Ralph had resigned himself to this situation.

Ralph's best friend was in the Navy and was given an assignment that would take him out to sea for at least six months. He therefore asked Ralph to take out his girlfriend and show her a good time once in a while. Ralph did so, and she fell in love with him.

What happened is easily explained. Ralph had a very poor self-image. He was convinced that no woman would be interested in him if she saw the "real" Ralph, so he tried to impress his dates by putting on a facade that was artificial and awkward and resulted in the reverse of what he hoped. When he was entertaining his buddy's girlfriend, he was not trying to impress her and was relaxed and natural. This gave her the opportunity to see the *real* Ralph, with whom she fell in love.

Arlo & Janis by Jimmy Johnson. Reprinted by permission of Newspaper Enterprise Association, Inc.

Yes, we often expect people to act "natural" when photographing them, and it seems to escape us that posing is not natural. Ralph's posing in order to impress women was about as natural as Joey posing for his father. Little wonder that his dates found him unattractive. When he stopped his posing, his natural, pleasant personality came through.

The terms *self-image* and *self-perception* convey a concrete idea. If we perceive an object, we assume it is there just as we see it. We do not think, "Perhaps that object is really not there, and I am just hallucinating." When we see an image, we assume it to be real. Our perceptions tell us what reality is, and we act according to our perceptions.

We naturally assume that what we perceive to be reality is also what others perceive as reality. If I see a bus coming down the street, I naturally assume that everyone else sees a bus coming down the street.

This is also true of a self-image or a self-perception. If I see myself in a certain way, that is reality. I do not go around thinking that my perception may be distorted. If my self-image is one of inadequacy and inferiority, then I am certain that other people perceive me as such.

If my self-image is negative, and I am convinced that others see me negatively, this poses a serious problem for me. Why would anyone deserve my companionship? Since it is obvious to me that no one would wish to be in my presence, any effort that I make to associate with people will inevitably result in their rejecting me. Since rejection is extremely painful, I must avoid it at all costs. Clearly the most effective method of avoiding rejection is to avoid associating with people. I become a "loner." I prefer to be by myself.

Most loners say that they prefer to be alone because they are private people and don't like others intruding on their privacy. Do not believe this; they are lying either to you or to themselves. Loners crave companionship as much as everyone else does, but their fear of rejection outweighs their desire for companionship.

Not all people with a negative self-image are loners. Some may think, "Of course, if anyone got to know me, he would reject me. But I am clever enough to put on a facade so that people will not get to know the true me." These people can be very entertaining socially. They feel safe in public because they can act in a way that prevents others from getting to see the "true self."

The telltale feature of this latter type is that they may feel threatened by intimacy. It is one thing to put on an act for a few hours in a superficial relationship where we may feel safe in being able to conceal the "true self." It is another thing to be exposed day after day to the same person in an intimate relationship. "Oh, no! I can't continually put on an act! Sooner or later she will see through the facade and then leave me for sure."

Many couples have a wonderful courtship, but the relationship turns sour soon after marriage. Other couples have a grand time dating, but as soon as there is any talk about commitment, one or both partners terminate the relationship. The reason in both cases is the same: Intimacy may constitute a threat of exposure, and exposure, they feel, is certain to result in rejection. To avoid rejection, avoid intimate relationships.

There is another mechanism that dooms relationships, and that is precipitation of rejection.

Bob was a handsome, personable, straight-A student whose self-image was the opposite of his actual self. He perceived himself as homely, dull, and unintelligent. When he met Carol, a charming student nurse, he thought he didn't stand the slightest chance. He was flabbergasted when she agreed to go out with him. He was even more surprised when she continued to date him.

Bob could not understand why a young woman as lovely as Carol gave him the time of day. He concluded that the reason Carol accepted his requests for dates was that she was very sensitive and did not want to hurt his feelings. He knew that this could not be a lasting relationship. Obviously, Carol was not going to make a long-term commitment out of pity for him. He therefore knew that it was inevitable that she would terminate the relationship. Whenever he picked up the phone to call her, he was overcome with intense anxiety. This is the time she is going to say it. "Bob," she will say, "it's hard for me to say this to you. I don't want to hurt your feelings. You're really a swell person, but I just can't see you anymore." He knew that she was going to say it, just as he knew that the sun was going to rise in the east.

When Carol did not reject him and agreed to go out with him, Bob was overjoyed. But when he called her the next time, the anxiety over the anticipated rejection recurred even more intensely. The suspense over the rejection that he was certain was forthcoming became so unbearable that he sent her father a telegram: "Congratulations. In seven months you'll be a grandfather." Carol told him never to call her again.

Bob tormented himself for having precipitated this rejection, but it is clear why he did so. Painful as it was, the rejection was a finality. Living with the suspense and anticipation of its imminent occurrence was intolerable. Getting the rejection over with was the lesser of two evils.

A variation of this theme occurred with Frank and Lois, who had been happily married for seventeen years. Frank was a building contractor, and they were financially comfortable. When their youngest child began attending school all day, Lois sought something productive to do with her time, and after completing courses received her realtor's license. After she made several sales, Frank underwent a radical personality change. He became irascible, screaming at her when she left the house to show a home to prospective buyers. "A married woman should not be going out alone at night!" "On weekends a mother should be home with her children." Lois did not know what to make of this Jekyll and Hyde transformation and convinced Frank to see a psychiatrist.

The dynamics of this case were easily detected. Frank's self-image was profoundly negative, and he could not believe that Lois truly loved him. He felt that the only bond in their marriage was that he provided her with economic security. If she were to become economically self-sufficient, there would be no reason for her to stay with him. He saw her newly acquired earning capacity as undermining the marriage, and he fought it aggressively, almost succeeding in ruining their marriage with his erratic behavior. Eventually, with counseling, Frank was able to accept that Lois's love for him was genuine.

These are only a few of the ways a negative self-image can lead to self-defeating behavior in relationships.

FOUR

Demanding Recognition

The feeling of being insignificant can be so devastating that some people take radical measures to make certain that their existence is recognized. If we think back to grade school, we can remember the class clown who called attention to himself by overt misbehavior. His being singled out by the teacher and being sent to the principal's office was a desperate attempt to be noticed. Such maneuvers are by no means restricted to young people.

If we feel distressed because of a negative self-image and think that other people do not appreciate us, we may seek recognition in an effort to convince ourselves as well as everyone else that we are respectable people and are not as bad as we are afraid we may be. We may push for recognition in different ways. For example, David always insists that the banquet committee seat him at a conspicuous place just in front of the speakers' table. He doesn't realize that he is forcing himself on others. Even if they cater to his whims, this does not endear him to them. To the contrary, such techniques make him less desirable company, and he may precipitate the very thing he is trying to avoid.

When inviting people to a family celebration, the host may say, "I better get Aunt Vera's invitation out first. If we somehow forget her, or if she thinks anyone else was invited before her, we'll never hear the end of it." Aunt Vera demands recognition "or else," which is hardly likely to elicit much affection.

There is nothing wrong with wishing to be recognized, but when we feel good about ourselves we assume that our presence is noticed at least by some people. If we feel inferior, we may feel that our presence is not noted at all, or if it is, it is not noted adequately by a sufficient number of people.

Following a public lecture, there is often a question-and-answer period. Many people ask pertinent questions of the speaker, but every so often someone delivers a speech. There is little doubt that this person wants to make everyone in the audience aware that he is there and has something to say, even though it may have nothing to do with the subject of the lecture. The folly of such a maneuver is that the inappropriateness of this person's comments may cause people in the audience to feel that he is a fool. This is an example of how some maneuvers to escape the negative self-image feelings backfire. This person, who desperately seeks to impress others, actually causes them to think poorly of him.

Demanding recognition in order to overcome feelings of shame and inferiority is as futile as trying to fill a bottomless pit. Just as the drug addict may require ever-increasing doses of narcotics to get high, the person who seeks recognition is likely to be chronically dissatisfied and constantly demand greater recognition.

"Guess what, Roger! I'm going to be on the 11-o'clock news!"

Cartoon by Bill Hoest. Copyright Wm. Hoest Enterprises, Inc. Reprinted with permission.

These desperate attempts not only are ineffective in bringing about the desired results but destructive; they produce a lowering of self-esteem, which in turn provokes the person to even more radical measures.

FIVE

Co-Dependence

The term *co-dependence* initially came into use in reference to a family member—usually a spouse—of an alcoholic or other chemically dependent person. The addict was the "dependent" person, being literally dependent on a chemical, and the co-dependent was the "significant other," who was often an "enabler," catering to the addict's needs and whims. A typical description of the dependent/co-dependent relationship is that the dependent person plays a tune and the co-dependent answers to it. It is said that the co-dependent sometimes is sicker than the dependent person.

Recently, co-dependency has been applied to relationships other than addiction in which one person plays a tune and the other dances to it; the latter is not doing what he or she really wants to do but what another expects. The "dancers" may lose control of their own lives and destiny because their behavior is being dictated by someone else.

If we have good self-esteem, we are unlikely to be manipulated. Others may try to change our personality,

"I KNOW THERE'S SOMETHING EMOTIONALLY WRONG WITH MY HUSBAND. HE SPENDS HIS ENTIRE DAY AT THE BAR."

but we can stand our own ground. Of course, standing one's own ground may not always be commendable; sometimes a personality could benefit from constructive changes.

But if we lack a firm sense of self, we are vulnerable to allowing others to define who we are. We may take on a chameleon-type existence, being one thing for our spouse, another for our employer, another for our minister, another for friend A, another for friend B, and so on.

"Stop trying to change me."

Cartoon by Bill Hoest. Copyright Wm. Hoest Enterprises, Inc. Reprinted with permission.

Yes, people with "soft tops" are likely to be convertibles.

Willy 'N Ethel by Joe Martin. Reprinted with special permission of North American Syndicate.

Here's a broader definition of co-dependency:

Co-dependency is the denial or repression of the real self. It is based on the wrong belief that love, acceptance, security, success, closeness, and sal-

> vation are *all* dependent upon one's ability to do "the right thing." In the process, the co-dependent denies who [he/she] really is.*

This definition can apply not only to family members of chemically dependent people, but also to the alcoholic or addict. It is an adaptation that is often found in people who grew up with an alcoholic parent or a parent who was dysfunctional in other ways. Since dysfunction of various kinds is widespread, it should come as no surprise that many people have developed co-dependency traits.

Patricia is the second child in a family. Her father had hoped for a boy and grudgingly accepted his fate when the first child was a girl. When Patricia was born, the second disappointment was a bit too much. When Patricia soon discovered that she was supposed to have been a boy, she felt that in order to get her father's love, which she fervently desired, she had to *be* a boy. She developed tomboyish behavior, hoping to satisfy her father. Unfortunately, her best efforts fell short of the mark, because to Patricia's father, a tomboyish girl was still a girl.

When Patricia was eight, the blessed event occurred—a son was born. Still vying for her father's affection, Patricia doted on her brother, hoping to forestall her father's transferring all his love to the real boy in the family. She continued to be the tomboy, especially since Chris was still an infant. When Chris was not quite three, their mother came down with multiple sclerosis, and Patricia, rather than the older sister, took on the obligation of being the mother in the family. Patricia thus played the role of boy, nursemaid

*Robert C. Subby, *Lost in the Shuffle* (Deerfield Beach, Calif.: Health Communications, 1987).

to Chris, nurse to her mother, and surrogate wife—all in order to merit the affection and attention of her father. She never gave any thought to what she wanted to be herself.

Patricia's older sister married, Chris joined the Army at eighteen, and then her mother died. Patricia fell in love. The young man was accepted in law school, and it was the natural thing for Patricia to help support him through his training. After all, she was Patricia the caregiver, who cared for people to earn their affection. Her first child was born before Bob completed law school, and it was not too much for her to care for the child and continue to work. She had been well prepared to sacrifice her own needs in order to care for others.

After the second child was born, Patricia began feeling tired. She was often completely drained by the end of the day. Bob was putting in long hours at the office, and Patricia was alone and lonely. She had given to everybody, but no one was giving to her. She had no one, not even herself, because there had never been a "self." She sensed her neediness and felt guilty about it, because she was not supposed to be a needy person. To the contrary, she was supposed to provide for the needs of others, because that is what would make her likable. Having needs of her own would mean making demands on others, and people might become alienated if she wanted them to give to her instead of her giving to them. Besides, who was there that could give to her? Dad was six hundred miles away and had remarried. The children were little and needed care. Bob was hardly ever home. Like an empty bank account, Patricia was emotionally depleted.

At some point Patricia found that taking a drink assuaged her loneliness and alleviated her guilt. Alcohol made life more tolerable.

There is no need to go on with the details of Patricia's story, which developed into a textbook case of alcoholism. She made the circuit of doctors and psychiatrists, becoming addicted to pills, attempting suicide, and ultimately losing Bob and the custody of her two children.

The entire tragic tale can be traced back to a single factor: Patricia had never had a self and had never considered what she really wanted to do with her life. She was a co-dependent, convinced that the only way to be loved was to be of service to others. Her identity was totally dependent on what others thought of her, rather than on what she thought of herself.

Not all co-dependence takes as tragic a course as Patricia's, but the principle in her story can be applied more generally. People who lack an internal identity and fashion themselves according to what they think others want them to be in order to find favor with them invariably make wrong choices, detracting from their self-fulfillment and happiness.

Developing a sense of self does not mean being selfish. There are, of course, times when putting one's own needs first is inconsiderate and selfish, but if we understand what a sense of self and identity is all about, we can see that this is not the kind of selfishness that is morally reprehensible.

When flying in a plane, the flight attendant announces, "In the event of the loss of cabin pressure, oxygen masks will appear before you. If you are traveling with a child, put your own mask on first and then assist the child with his." Can you expect a devoted mother to be so selfish as to put her interests before that of her child? But there is a valid reason for these instructions. Once the mother is receiving oxygen, she can make certain the child gets his, and both will be safe. If she attempts to help the child first, she may become confused due to oxygen deprivation and unable to put the child's mask on properly. Neither she nor the child will get oxygen. *The mother must assure her own well-being in order to help the child.*

This is the principle of developing a sense of self and an identity. Patricia's adaptation to what she thought her father wanted her to be and then being a caregiver ultimately resulted in her two children having an unhappy mother, then an exhausted mother, then an alcoholic mother, and finally no mother at all. The two human beings she had brought into the world and for whom she had prime responsibility did not get proper parenting because of Patricia's desire to be everything to everybody. There is nothing noble or praiseworthy about this kind of self-sacrifice.

There is little that Patricia could have done about herself as a child. Ideally, parents love their children unconditionally and children feel this and are secure in their parents' love for them. But the ideal is not often achieved. Patricia may have been reading her father correctly, and when she was a child, her reaction was completely understandable. If her mother had detected what was happening, she might have been able to help Patricia or avail her of competent counseling. But there were no gross signs of trouble for her mother to identify. Everybody seemed fairly happy, so why assume otherwise?

Although Patricia showed no overt signs of unhappiness until relatively late, there was still time for appropriate therapy. If her early recourse to alcohol had been picked up as an act of desperation and the proper treatment sought, Patricia could have been helped to stop trying to buy love and affection. She could have been helped to a sense of self-esteem, to believe that she was a good person who deserved to be loved and who would be loved even if she did not efface herself in order to provide for others. At this point, Bob could have been brought in as an ally, and he could have helped her realize she was indeed lovable. With proper group support, sharing her feelings and discovering that she was not alone in how she felt about herself, Patricia could have relinquished her desperate efforts to buy the affection that she could really get for free. She could have discovered that she did not have to be the super person she thought she must be, but simply be a good, adequate wife and mother, who deserved to receive and to be cared for just as much as she was expected to give and care for others.

It is never too late to acquire a sense of self. If you recognize that you grew up in a dysfunctional family, be aware that you are at high risk for being co-dependent. You would do well to familiarize yourself with the symptoms of co-dependency. You would also be wise to seek out support groups that are sensitive to these problems, such as Adult Children of Alcoholics, Co-dependents Anonymous, or Families Anonymous. Even if you do not have any disabling symptoms, you might nevertheless consider an evaluation by a competent psychologist, just as you undergo a routine medical checkup even when you feel well.

The conditions that can result in co-dependence are ubiquitous and legion. The misery that co-dependence can cause for you and for others, especially your children, is often avoidable. You don't need to be this way. Life's too short.

SIX

Hypersensitivity

People with a negative self-image may be exquisitely sensitive. Things that do not affect anyone else may elicit a marked reaction. It's much like someone who has a severe sunburn: A light touch causes her to wince with pain. The sunburned person knows that her skin is unusually sensitive and does not impart hostile intent to the person who touched her. But people with a negative self-image may not be aware that they are abnormally sensitive. When someone says or does something that causes them emotional pain, they are likely to conclude that the other person intentionally insulted or provoked them.

A man comes home from work, enters the house, and says, "Hello, everybody. I'm home!" The wife and children are in the den, watching an interesting television program. They respond with "Hi, honey" and "Hi, Daddy." A person with a positive self-image who knows that his wife and children love him will hang up his coat, go into the den, and embrace his family. Someone who is overly sensitive will say, "Hi, honey? Is that the kind of appreciation I get for working all day to feed and clothe my family? The damn television program is more important than coming out to welcome me. What an ungrateful bunch!" From that point on, the evening is apt to go downhill. Little love can be generated in either direction when someone is bristling with resentment.

The wife and children may have been very happy to have the husband and father home. They may fully appreciate his efforts on their behalf. The fact that they did not leave the television set at a high point in the program and run out to greet him is in no way an indication of their lack of love or admiration. However, because he seriously doubts that he deserves being loved, he interprets their failure to greet him as a confirmation of his feelings about himself.

Constructive criticism can result in improving ourselves. Whether it is an instructor who corrects our work or a friend who makes a legitimate observation about something we say or do, we can learn to avoid mistakes and to do things in a better way.

People with a negative self-image, however, may be so sensitive that they react adversely to constructive criticism. Believing that they are inadequate and fearing that others will detect their inadequacies, they may take a critical remark as evidence that their inadequacies have been exposed. They may respond to a critical remark as though it were an insult, and this reaction may be detrimental to others as well as to themselves.

How intensely a negative self-image can affect our response to criticism is demonstrated by a personal experience. Many years ago, while I was still in the throes of my own negative self-image, I was invited to deliver several lectures at a continuing education course for alcoholism and drug counselors. More than one hundred therapists had enrolled for the course, and the month afterward I received a packet with their evaluations of my lectures. As I paged through, my ego soared. Everyone was saying very flattering things about my presentation. Then I came to one review that was very critical. I was devastated! For two weeks I was depressed, until it dawned on me that 109 to 1 is an excellent score. Clearly the 109 favorable evaluations were correct. However, my initial response was to remember that Lincoln had said that you can fool only some of the people. I thought that I had succeeded in fooling 109 of the attendees, but this one person saw through my act and knew the truth about me. Feeling negative about myself resulted in my interpreting a 109 to 1 vote in favor of the single dissenting opinion!

How we feel about ourselves can also determine how we react to criticism and insults. These are never pleasant, but we can react along a spectrum from indifference to violence.

A young woman completed her treatment for alcoholism but returned home to a very difficult marriage. I followed her progress in recovery, and she was doing extremely well. About a year later I received a phone call from her. She was sobbing. Eventually she was able to tell me that she could no longer take her husband's verbal abuse. He constantly accused her of being a failure as a wife and mother.

After she calmed down a bit, I asked her to listen very carefully to what I had to say. "I think that the scar on the right side of your face is repulsive," I said.

After a moment of silence she said, "Pardon me?" I repeated my unkind remark, and she said, "I don't understand."

"What is there not to understand? I spoke plain English."

"But I don't have a scar on my face."

"Then what did you think when I told you how ugly it was?"

"I didn't understand what you were talking about."

"You see," I pointed out, "when I say something derogatory to you and you know it is not true, you don't react with hysterical sobbing. Instead you say, 'I don't know what you are talking about.'

"When your husband insulted you and you knew he was wrong, your reaction should have been 'You must be hallucinating. I am an excellent wife and mother.' You might not have been happy about what he said, but you did not have to react so intensely.

"I suspect that your reaction was due to your thinking that he might be right. Even though it is early in your recovery, you are functioning extremely well. We never deny our dereliction during the active addiction, but that is now a thing of the past and we should be focusing on the positive aspects of recovery. A positive attitude toward yourself would have made your husband's comments merely irritating, not demolishing."

None of us likes being the target of derogatory remarks, but how we react to them may depend to a great extent on how we think of ourselves.

It has been said that no one can put me down except myself. When we feel good about ourselves, uncomplimentary remarks and even frank insults may not exactly roll like water off a duck's back, but they can be much more easily dismissed and certainly need not make us feel worse about ourselves.

SEVEN

Narcissism

Lloyd requested a psychiatric consultation. His problem? He had had a relationship with a woman whom he claimed he loved very much but to whom he had been both verbally and physically abusive. She finally terminated the relationship and refused to see him. He now recognizes how wrong he was and deeply regrets his behavior. He will never act this way again. He wants her to know this so that she will consider renewing their relationship, but she won't talk with him. He hoped that I would call her and, as a psychiatrist, tell her that I have determined that he is sincere in his remorse and that she should give him another chance.

I told Lloyd I would do no such thing. He cried, pleading that he be given the chance to prove himself and insisting that this was the most important thing in his life. He continued to call me several times a day, and when I refused to vouch for him, he drove to the woman's home and accosted her as she left for work. She promptly called the police. He then slashed her tires and made threatening phone calls, harassing the woman whom he claimed to "love" so deeply.

Psychologists use the term *narcissism* to describe a person who is extremely self-centered and self-adoring. The term comes from the Greek myth of Narcissus, a handsome young man who fell in love with his own reflection. In reality, narcissists do not love themselves at all. They are indeed self-centered and demand that everyone else adore and respect them, but this is precisely because they do *not* love themselves. Narcissistic people have extremely poor self-images, and they are scared that they cannot be loved or appreciated. They are so terrified that they may forcefully demand to be loved and respected because they doubt that it can happen spontaneously. Narcissism is thus an extreme form of hypersensitivity.

Lloyd is a narcissist. If he genuinely cared for the woman, he would not have harassed her. But Lloyd cared primarily for himself. He perceived her rejection as a blow to his fragile ego. Lloyd's case is typical. The behavior of narcissists is invariably self-defeating, since their need to possess and dominate frightens people away.

Being rejected in a romantic relationship is always unpleasant. But if we have a positive self-image we are likely to react more realistically. After the wound heals, we can conclude, "I guess we were not meant for each other," and go on to develop other relationships. The narcissist, however, has serious doubts about his or her lovability and reacts to rejection as if this were a life-threatening event.

There are other areas of exquisite sensitivity that may

elicit a severe reaction from a narcissist. Lloyd's related to his doubts of lovability. People who have serious doubts about their competence may react somewhat similarly when they feel that their abilities are being questioned.

As another example, let us look at two women who became physicians. A developed a negative self-image early in life, although she is very talented. The discomfort of feeling inadequate caused her to seek ways to escape this distress, and noting that doctors are highly respected, she chose a career in medicine. The M.D. after her name would be prestigious, and the gratitude from patients would help her overcome her feelings of inferiority.

Feelings of inferiority that have no basis in reality cannot be corrected by such maneuvers. If your television set is broken, a repairman can restore it to proper function. If it is not broken, but you just don't happen to like the picture, nothing the repairman can do will satisfy you. Replacing tubes and other parts that are in fact not defective will accomplish nothing.

Some people do have actual defects, for which they can compensate in reality. A person who has lost his vision may develop a very keen sense of touch or hearing, which can help compensate for the absence of sight. But he cannot compensate for a deficit that exists only in his imagination.

A's negative self-image is a delusion. She is oblivious to her many positive assets, and no amount of compensation will eliminate this misconception. Seeing the M.D. after her name may temporarily soothe her, but feelings of inferiority will continue to haunt her. When a grateful patient thanks her for her help, it is like aspirin for a chronic headache, relieving the distress for only a brief period of time. A is in constant need of reassurance.

B, on the other hand, is no more gifted than A, but she grew up with a positive self-concept. She knows she is bright, and she considers herself a likable person. B, too, chose a medical career, but not for A's reasons. B thought she would enjoy the practice of medicine. She wishes to help people and feels good when she does so. But she is not dependent on their gratitude for a sense of well-being.

Let us now take a patient into these two doctors' offices and see how their self-image influences the way they relate to the patient.

John Doe consults Dr. B because of abdominal distress. Dr. B takes a careful history, performs a physical examination, and does several blood tests. On the basis of these, she assures John that there is nothing seriously wrong with him and suggests an appropriate diet to eliminate the abdominal discomfort.

Two weeks later John returns, complaining that the pain has worsened. Dr. B decides to do a complete workup and has John undergo upper and lower gastrointestinal X rays, kidney studies, and a sonogram. After these are completed she shares with John the good news that there is no sign of any tumor, ulcer, gallstones, or kidney stones. The pain, Dr. B explains, is due to a spastic condition of the intestines, which should be relieved by antacids and antispasmodic medication, which she prescribes.

Two weeks later John again appears in Dr. B's office, doubled up with pain, complaining that the medication has not helped and that he hasn't slept a single night in the past two weeks.

Dr. B feels bad that she has not been able to help John but does not feel threatened by John's failure to recover. Dr. B knows that she is a competent physician and genuinely wants to help John, so she tells him, "This stumps me, John. I can't put my finger on the reason for your pain. Let me refer you to a gastroenterologist."

Now let's see what happens if John consults Dr. A instead. The first two visits go exactly as they do with Dr. B. However, when John returns for the third visit with a persistent complaint of pain, Dr. A does not respond the way Dr. B does.

Remember, Dr. A needs her patients to tell her how wonderful they feel and what a great doctor she is. John's persistent complaints of pain are a threat to Dr. A's ego, so she interprets these complaints as a reflection on her adequacy, as though John has said, "What kind of doctor are you, anyway, that you are not helping me?" The nagging feelings of inadequacy that have plagued Dr. A since childhood are reinforced by John's failure to improve.

Dr. A is likely to respond in one of three ways:

"Hmm," Dr. A says pensively. "This is more serious than I thought, John. There must be something that is not showing up on the X ray. I believe we should do an exploratory laparotomy to get at the source of the trouble."

There are certainly cases where exploratory surgery is necessary, but this is not one of them. Dr. A hasn't the foggiest notion what she is looking for. She is essentially going on a fishing expedition in John's abdomen, and is doing so because she cannot admit that she doesn't know what the problem is. She cannot refer John to a gastroenterologist because admitting that others may know something she doesn't is an affront to her fragile ego. In order to assuage her own ego pain, she subjects John to surgery.

An alternative response may be:

"Look here, John. The tests we have done are absolutely thorough. There is simply nothing that could be causing your pain. It is psychosomatic pain, all in your head. You need psychiatric help, and I am going to refer you to a psychiatrist."

In this response, Dr. A thinks—mistakenly—that John is accusing her of not being a good doctor. "Well," Dr. A thinks, "I'll tell you something. You're crazy. Your opinion doesn't count for anything. You need your head examined!"

Here is another possible response:

"I'm sorry that the cause of your pain isn't showing up, John. I am going to give you something to help you feel better. Here is a prescription for pain medication, which you take every four hours. I will also give you something to help you sleep at night."

John begins taking the medication as prescribed. But, as is common, several weeks or months later, his body becomes accustomed to the medications and they no longer have an effect. John increases the doses and eventually develops a serious addiction to pain pills and sedatives.

Any of Dr. A's responses are detrimental to John. Dr. A is primarily concerned with protecting her fragile self-image, and all three diagnoses are directed more toward her own needs than John's.

Whether it is doctor-patient, teacher-student, counselor-client, or any type of service delivery, results are likely to be unfavorable when the person delivering the service is motivated more by his or her own needs than by those of the recipient of the service.

Narcissists believe that they are never wrong. They seem to know everything better than anyone else. There is no point in arguing with narcissists because even if they are convinced that they are wrong, which is unlikely, it is impossible for them to admit it. They will maintain their position with rational or irrational reasons, or sometimes with no reason at all.

Charles Schulz, the author of the *Peanuts* comic strip, shows us two varieties of people with a negative self-image. The first is Charlie Brown, a pathetic character who fails at everything because he believes he is going to fail and is convinced that he can never do anything right. The second type is Lucy, who is a narcissist and considers herself God's gift to the world. Lucy is domineering, opinionated, and always right.

Peanuts® by Charles M. Schulz. Reprinted by permission of United Feature Syndicate, Inc.

Lucy is infatuated with Schroeder, who ignores her. Lucy nags Schroeder, demanding affection from him, but everything she does only annoys him.

The tragedy with narcissism is that it is self-defeating. Love cannot be given on demand. In fact, the more a person demands to be loved, the less he or she will be loved. Some narcissists are very sensitive and can detect that they are not being loved, and this drives them into a frenzy where they demand it even more. It is obvious that this sets up a vicious cycle that frequently results in emotional and/or physical abuse.

Peanuts® by Charles M. Schulz. Reprinted by permission of United Feature Syndicate, Inc.

Schulz cleverly demonstrates that Lucy's apparent self-adoration is really a desperate attempt to escape the torment of her feeling so poorly about herself.

Lucy is the flip side of Charlie Brown. Her grandiosity is a desperate defense against her negative self-image. When Schroeder says something complimentary toward her, she no longer needs her defensiveness, and her underlying feelings emerge.

EIGHT

Fear of Happiness and Fear of Failure

Brenda was very anxious, obsessed with a fear that her baby would suffer crib death. "I get up several times during the night to check on her and see if she is breathing. I just dread going over to the crib." Brenda's emotional condition was getting progressively worse by sleep deprivation. It was a vicious cycle.

Brenda had no immediate contact with a case of crib death; her only exposure to it was on television or in magazines. Why, then, was she so anxious? "Because the child is so beautiful, and I know I don't deserve having such a beautiful child."

It is hard to believe that there are people who dread enjoying life. Some people have a sense of foreboding. They are afraid that if they enjoy things, something terrible will happen. Consequently, they consciously or unconsciously torment themselves or deprive themselves of pleasure.

They may feel so undeserving of good fortune that they anticipate misery. Sometimes this is tied to a religious belief in a punitive god who is going to punish them for being bad. Those who think they are bad expect to be punished. Sometimes they do not have a concept of a loving god, or if they do, they may think of themselves as so unworthy that even God could not love them.

Jim had a repetitive problem with alcoholism, and he relapsed after each course of treatment. During one course of treatment it appeared that Jim had turned the corner. There was a marked change in his attitude, and the staff was optimistic that he was sincere about his recovery. Sure enough, several months later Jim was still sober and regularly attended AA meetings. I met him when he was ten months sober and made a note on my calendar to congratulate him on his first year of recovery.

Four days prior to his anniversary, Jim was admitted for detoxification after days of heavy drinking. His appearance was dreadful. He wept, "You've got to believe me, Doc. I didn't enjoy drinking.

"I was approaching a full year of sobriety. I haven't been sober for a single month since age eleven. It was too good to be true. I received a promotion at work, and for the first time I could remember, my wife told me she loved me. I knew it couldn't last and that something terrible was going to happen. Every time the phone rang, I just knew it was to tell me that my little girl had been hit by a car. I couldn't take the suspense. I had to get it over with."

People sabotage themselves in many ways. They climb a ladder, only to topple it as they near the top. We say they are afraid of success. Why would anyone fear success? Because when you don't feel you deserve it, success can produce a great deal of tension.

Medications that are very helpful may have negative side effects. To a person who has a negative self-image, things that should bring about happiness may also have "side ef-

Peanuts® by Charles M. Schulz. Reprinted by permission of United Feature Syndicate, Inc.

fects," and the person may actually do something to precipitate distress.

We can thus see how a negative self-image may lead to a great variety of self-defeating behaviors and that both to function optimally and to enjoy life, a correction of the self-image is essential.

Ernie graduated from accounting school with good grades. Full of enthusiasm, he dressed up in his three-piece suit and took his new briefcase to his first job interview. Although he felt that the session went well, the interviewer told him that they were really looking for someone with a master's degree in business administration.

Ernie returned home not only disappointed but virtually shattered. The following day he did not get out of bed until noon, and that pattern continued. He avoided job interviews, giving various excuses why he could not make them. When his parents prodded him about looking for a job, Ernie began complaining of sundry aches and pains. He made the round of doctors, who could not find any reason for his complaints.

No one likes to fail. However, since we have no assurance of how anything will turn out, we do things with full awareness that we may fail. As painful as failures may be, they should not be devastating. If we do fail, we lick our wounds, learn what we can from the experience, and go on living and trying again.

This may not be true for someone with a negative self-image. Like Charlie Brown, if one is absolutely convinced of failure, there is no purpose in trying.

People who perceive a failure as a total devastation don't try anything because the risk of failure is too great. They just drift along, being carried wherever the tide takes them. Although doing nothing results in the greatest failure of all, it is easier for them to accept passive failure than active failure. Furthermore, they can come up with a myriad of rationalizations about why they did not try. They may fantasize that if it had not been for circumstances beyond their control, they would have tried and succeeded.

Those who are unable to retreat into passivity must find other ways to avoid failure. A common mechanism is *perfectionism.* Perfectionists think of all possible causes of failure and then take the necessary steps to prevent them. This is usually impossible to accomplish, and furthermore, the enormous energy spent in closing every gap may leave a person without enough strength to get anything done.

There is no precise line separating appropriate caution from pathologic perfectionism. And there are indeed some situations that require greater caution than normal. Yet there are degrees of perfectionism that are clearly abnormal.

I worked with a nurse who was deathly afraid of making a medication error. She went through a ritual of checking and rechecking medications to the point where medications that were to be dispensed at 7:00 A.M. were not dispensed until after 8:00. After giving a patient the medication, she asked that it be given back to her so that she could make certain it was the right one. She eventually stopped patients from swallowing the medication after it was in their mouths, in order to retrieve it and recheck it. At this point she was dismissed. Her perfectionism resulted in the ultimate failure: the loss of her job.

"Reasonable" perfectionism is just that: perfection

guided by reason. When perfectionism is not guided by reason but is subject to emotion, it may know no bounds, particularly when the dominant emotion is fear of making a mistake. What is "just a mistake" to many people and accepted as one of the unavoidable components of life can be a devastating experience to a person with a negative self-image. A mistake can be a confirmation of feelings of unworth. Living can become a terrifying experience.

I was once riding in a car with a friend, and we were listening to a tape of a recovering alcoholic who described his earlier years as "feeling like I was walking through a minefield, where the next step might blow me to bits." My friend brought the car to a screeching halt and broke out in a cold sweat. "I never thought anyone else felt like that," he said.

Many people feel that way. Their negative self-concept leads them to believe that they are going to fail, and a failure is indeed confirmation of their worst fears about themselves. These fears may generate intense anticipatory anxiety, which may then be the cause of failure. I refer to this as the "William Tell Phenomenon."

According to the legend, William Tell was an excellent archer who was ordered to shoot at an apple perched on his son's head, and indeed succeeded. If any archer other than Tell had been told to aim at an ordinary bull's-eye, he might well hit it. But he might not. In any event, his hand would be steady, since there would be nothing at stake to generate anxiety. The worst that could happen would be to miss the bull's-eye. However, if like Tell he had to shoot an apple off his child's head, the dread of missing the apple and harming the child would be so devastating that he could not possibly hold the bow steady, and any chance of shooting accurately would be doomed.

A disproportionate fear of failing may generate so much anxiety that success is impossible. This is why people with scant self-confidence may fail at challenges that are well within their range.

NINE

Compartmentalization

Some people have a negative self-image that is global: They think negatively of themselves in every way. Others have a partial distortion of their self-perception: They recognize some of the positives about themselves but negatively distort other aspects of their personality.

Dr. Brown spent most of his waking hours in either the hospital or the office, weekends included. He began his hospital rounds early in the morning, went to the office in the afternoon, and returned to the hospital until late at night. He was a teacher par excellence, greatly admired by the house staff, students, and nurses, and his patients virtually adored him. Some of the nurses commented that the reason he spent all his time in the hospital was to avoid his home. They assumed that his wife must be a shrew.

One day I received a call from Dr. Brown, who asked me to see his wife about her depression. I was rather surprised to meet a woman who was the epitome of kindness and gentleness, nothing like what the nurses had pictured. In relating the factors she felt had contributed to her depression, she said, "You know my husband, how dedicated he is to medicine. Well, I'm an insecure person, and I always needed a shoulder to rest my head on, but he was never there for me. Our children grew up without a father. Oh, yes, if they were sick he took excellent care of them, but he was their doctor rather than a father."

I subsequently interviewed her husband, whom I knew to be not only a first-rate physician but also a wonderful person. It came to light that he thought poorly of himself as a person. His negative self-concept did not extend to his profession, but as a human being, he felt he was inadequate.

"He doesn't know his name, just that he's a Doctor."

Dr. Brown was comfortable at the hospital and at the office because he felt adequate as a doctor. At home he had to function as a person providing emotional support for his wife and guidance for the children. Because he felt inadequate in this latter role, he avoided it.

If, on a stifling hot summer day, we have access to two

rooms, one of which is air-conditioned, we will certainly choose the more comfortable room. It is a law of nature that living things gravitate to the most comfortable surroundings.

For Dr. Brown the hospital and office were comfortable. Home was uncomfortable, not because his family was too demanding or inconsiderate, but because he felt he lacked what the family needed.

Like many other people who spend excessive hours at the office, Dr. Brown was able to deceive himself that his professional responsibilities demanded these hours. This was not true for him, and it is not true for many others who do not spend enough time with their families.

There are probably more "compartmentalized" people than we imagine. Ask a person who he is, and he is likely to tell you what he *does*. Not too many people respond with "I am a gentle, soft-spoken person. I enjoy reading, and I am a nature lover." Many more people say that they are an accountant or legal secretary or computer analyst. Their identity is essentially tied to what they do. Their sense of self is very limited.

A dancer sought psychiatric consultation for depression. In describing the pervasive feelings of dejection that had plagued her since childhood, she noticeably brightened when she talked about performing. "That's when the true me comes out." Since she performed only several hours a week, her "true self" appeared for only a small fraction of her life. For the greater part of the week she was morose. She had no knowledge of her true self, only a mistaken concept from which she escaped when she performed skillfully. She was a classic example of "look at what I *do,* not at what I *am.*"

A schoolteacher whose marriage had deteriorated because of his emotional abusiveness refused to accept my suggestion that his behavior was related to his low self-esteem. It was clear that he sought to reinforce his sagging self-concept by exercising his authority as master of the house. "I do not have poor self-esteem," he said. "I am an excellent teacher, and I have been selected several times by the students in the school as the best teacher on the staff. Parents are invariably thrilled when they find out their children are in my class." Like the doctor and the dancer, his identity was as a teacher, not as a person. Since he could not do any teaching with his wife, he felt bankrupt in her presence. Although his behavior at school was exemplary, his behavior at home was intolerable. As a good teacher, he would listen, teach, and relate with a feeling of self-confidence. As a husband, he felt unworthy and reacted defensively by adopting an overbearing attitude.

A positive self-image allows us to be good spouses and parents. A negative self-image deprives us of the love we can both give and receive.

TEN

Depression

People with feelings of inferiority are likely to feel depressed. To alleviate this depression, they must correct their self-image. It is important, however, that the type of self-image distortion be identified, because it is possible that it is a *consequence* of depression rather than a cause, and that treatment with medication may be necessary along with psychotherapy.

We now know that there are a variety of chemical changes that can produce depression. A number of medications, both prescribed and over the counter, can cause depression. Among these are decongestants, frequently used for relief of sinus conditions, hay fever, or the common cold; some appetite suppressants; and some antihistamines, especially if taken more often than recommended. It is also possible for internal bodily changes such as hepatitis, infectious mononucleosis, or any severe viral illness, a surgical procedure, or the hormonal changes of the premenstrual, postpartum, or menopausal phases to result in depression. Sleep disturbance can result in depression, and it is possible for depression to be of genetic origin. A grief reaction following a personal loss can progress into a clinical depression, but it is important to be aware that severe depression can be based solely on a biochemical change.

The symptoms of severe depression may include loss of sleep, loss of appetite, loss of interest in things, loss of sex drive, crying, inability to concentrate, despair, and death wishes. These feelings are generally accompanied by *intense feelings of worthlessness and inadequacy,* the feelings comprising low self-esteem.

It is important to recognize that in this situation, the feelings of worthlessness and inferiority may be secondary to a depression of biochemical origin. When the depression is relieved with proper treatment, the feelings of worthlessness may disappear. A person who had a very positive self-image may develop a severely negative self-image due to a clinical depression. When the depression is appropriately treated, the positive self-image returns.

One of the distinguishing features between depression due to a negative self-image and clinical depression is that the latter almost invariably has an onset. The person "felt fine until about eight months ago." When depression stems from feelings of inferiority, it has generally been a part of that individual's personality for as long as anyone can remember. The problem is that during clinical depression, a person may be looking at life through smoked glass. He sees the past, present, and future as all being bleak. He may very well say, "I felt this way about myself since I can remember," which may not be true. Family members may be able to provide more accurate information about when the negative feelings occurred.

We do not yet have a laboratory test that can diagnose clinical depression. When in doubt, it may be wise to get treatment for the clinical depression, and then one can direct attention to the feelings of inferiority from a negative self-image. Trying to deal with a negative self-image in the presence of an untreated clinical depression can result in the development of many misleading misconceptions.

People suffering with depression may develop feelings of hopelessness, and if they do not see any light at the end of the tunnel, they may attempt suicide. If they can be helped to an awareness that their perception of reality is not accurate, and be given hope that things can turn out much better than they expect, this tragedy can be averted.

Paul is an attorney who was thirty-six years old when he consulted me for treatment of his depression. He admitted that he had been seriously contemplating suicide.

After listening to his description of how everything in life had gone wrong for him, I asked Paul whether he had ever made a concerted effort at getting to know himself, or whether he had just taken himself for granted without any self-examination. When he stated that he had never really done any serious introspection, I pointed out to him that in all likelihood he lacked true self-awareness. I reminded Paul that just a few weeks earlier there had been an account in the news of a man who went berserk and killed several people at random in a busy shopping center.

"What do you think about a person like that?" I asked.

"He must be insane," Paul said. "Why would anyone kill people he doesn't even know?"

I then pointed out to Paul that inasmuch as he lacked self-awareness, he was in fact a stranger to himself, and although he felt depressed, this did not give him an excuse to kill a stranger. To do so would be as irrational as the person who went berserk in the shopping center. I told Paul that regardless of how depressed he felt, the idea of suicide would have to be delayed until he had a valid self-awareness. Once the latter was achieved, we could then discuss the entire issue of suicide. Paul actually smiled at the idea.

Paul entered group therapy directed at self-awareness and self-esteem enhancement. Two years later I received a letter from him stating that he had come to know himself much better and that suicide was absolutely the last thing he would consider. "I like this guy too much to think of killing him."

Estelle was depressed following the birth of her third child. Her second child, who was at that time seven, had a serious hearing deficit, and Estelle was determined to mainstream the child rather than have him in special education classes. She devoted a great deal of attention to this child, but now she had a baby to attend to as well. When she entered treatment she appeared physically exhausted. She considered herself an inadequate mother because she was unable to respond to all the needs of her children.

Estelle required some medication for the depression, and she also entered into a therapy group. Here she was helped to see that she was dealing very adequately with some major challenges of parenting. The group encouraged her to try and get additional help so that she could devote her attention to her children without overtaxing her capacities. As her depression lifted and her self-esteem improved, Estelle functioned very well and did succeed in mainstreaming her child in school.

We all have off days, and there are many circumstances in life that can cause us to feel depressed. However, when symptoms of depression persist or become disabling, we need to seek competent treatment.

ELEVEN

Anxiety

Anxiety is another condition that can be caused by either psychological or biochemical factors. Appropriate medication is often necessary for biochemical anxiety.

A word of caution is necessary here. There are many antianxiety medications. However, like alcohol, these medications relieve anxiety by depressing the brain so that the person is less sensitive. The problem with these medications is that their effect lasts for only several hours. Many people become immune to them. They then take increasing doses to eliminate the anxiety, and since most of these medications are potentially addictive, they may develop severe addictions. When this happens, the person has a complicated problem: addiction on top of chronic anxiety.

Anxiety is a feeling very similar to fear. However, in fear there is a threatening situation. A person concerned about a medical condition may feel threatened by an undesirable diagnosis. In anxiety there are no apparent threats. Common feelings of anxiety include a sensation of impending doom and/or palpitation, shortness of breath, chest pain, and dizziness. These symptoms may occur in varying degrees of intensity. Such sensations may result from physical causes, such as certain medications, especially decongestants and caffeine, low blood sugar, or thyroid disease. Very severe and sudden anxiety attacks are called panic attacks, and it is believed that some of these are caused by a biochemical imbalance similar to that which may cause depression. Anxiety may also exist in a chronic, low-key form.

The psychological causes of anxiety are not always evident. Some psychologists postulate that there may be an unconscious threat; the person is afraid of something but is not aware of what it is. Sometimes there are no physical sensations; the person feels haunted, like something terrible is going to happen. Not knowing what it is, he or she has no way of controlling or avoiding it.

A negative self-image is often a component of anxiety. A person who is secure and self-confident is not likely to feel overwhelmed by the challenges in life. But a person with feelings of inadequacy is understandably more vulnerable to anxiety. Recall the man who described himself as feeling as though he were walking through a minefield. Although with each step he realized that he had thus far been safe, this did not diminish his fear that the next step would result in an explosion. In addition to increased fear, a person with the negative self-image may also be reluctant to seek outside help, seeing this as an admission of weakness.

Barbara is an attorney who consulted a psychiatrist because of severe panic attacks. In the absence of any threatening circumstances, Barbara would develop heart palpitation, tightness of the chest, shortness of breath, and dizziness. Her doctor prescribed a medication that significantly reduced the frequency and severity of the attacks, but Barbara was left with a pervasive feeling of anxiety. She was afraid to drive, so her husband drove her to and from work. She felt fairly secure at home or in the office, but other situations intensified her anxiety, and she essentially avoided all other activities, remaining in the security of home or office.

Barbara was offered a promotion at work, but this would entail periodic trips out of town, which she could not consider because of her anxiety. She therefore consulted a psychologist for behavior modification treatment. The psychologist correctly concluded that Barbara's anxiety was related to feelings of inadequacy, although her academic and work careers had attested to her competence. In addition to practicing behavior modification techniques, Barbara entered group therapy.

Barbara's low self-esteem was intensified by her inability to function away from the security of the home or office. Her anxiety, which was partially due to feelings of inadequacy, thus intensified her feelings of inadequacy, resulting in a vicious cycle.

The group therapy helped Barbara gain a better sense of herself, and with the encouragment and support of the group she began venturing out of her home and office. Each successful trip improved her self-esteem, and the negative vicious cycle was replaced by a positive, self-reinforcing pattern. Barbara eventually accepted the promotion, and she is able to travel without fear or anxiety.

Bob is a successful financial adviser who stuttered as a child. He eventually overcame the problem, but he still avoids speaking before groups, since this reactivates his stutter. Bob's firm began giving seminars on financial planning, and Bob's job assignment now required speaking in front of rather large groups. Bob tried to prevent his anxiety from provoking the stutter by taking tranquilizers, but these made him drowsy and interfered with his presentation.

Bob was a child of an abusive, alcoholic father, and his early life was replete with trauma. The psychologist he consulted decided not to dwell on the origins of the anxiety but rather on the consequences of the traumatic childhood—his consequent low self-esteem. Bob had come to anticipate failure, and each time he had to speak before a group he was apprehensive that he would blurt out something stupid and be sharply criticized for it.

Group therapy was selected as the most effective treatment method. As Bob came to a better self-awareness, his anticipation of failure decreased, and he was eventually able to speak successfully in front of large groups. Interestingly, this had a ripple effect: His business activities, social activities, and even family situation improved greatly.

No one knows what the future holds. Life is full of surprises, some pleasant, others unpleasant. The more adequate we feel, the less threatening the unknown stresses become. I have noted that people with negative self-images may have greater expectations of unpleasant things happening to them. They have a twofold problem: expecting trouble and not feeling competent to cope with it. As the next chapter shows, this may contribute to the development of alcoholism or other addictions.

TWELVE

Alcoholism and Other Chemical Addictions

Addiction to alcohol or to other mood-altering chemicals can take various shapes and forms, and we still aren't sure why some people develop addictions and others do not. There is undoubtedly a genetic vulnerability in some people, but genetics alone does not account for these conditions.

There are obviously some psychological factors involved in addiction, and one of them is negative self-image. I'm not referring to the feelings of inferiority that result from being addicted to alcohol and/or drugs, although there are an abundance of these. Virtually all addicted people had a negative self-image *prior* to becoming involved with alcohol or other drugs. Here's a typical account given by a surgeon, now more than thirty years sober. "I did not take my first drink until I was seventeen, and I did not start my heavy drinking until I was twenty-six. But I can clearly remember when I was nine years old, feeling that I was different from all the other kids and that they were better than I was." These feelings of inadequacy and inferiority preceded his drinking by many years. I have yet to meet an alcoholic or drug-addicted person who had a positive self-image prior to becoming addicted.

In Chapter 1, I noted one reason why a negative self-image is conducive to addiction: The natural resistance to ruining an item of value is absent in a person who does not see himself or herself as valuable. A second important factor is a person's feelings about his or her competence to cope with challenges.

There are only two possible ways of dealing with any challenge in life: coping or escaping. There is no third option. Ignoring a problem is simply a passive way of escaping.

In some situations the correct action is to escape. If your automobile is stalled on the railroad tracks and you see a train approaching at 120 miles per hour, this is not the time or place to cope. Escape is appropriate because the challenge is overwhelming. A 180-pound person is no match for a 60-ton diesel.

We can break reactions down into a simple formula: If the challenge is much greater than you, escape. If you are greater than the challenge, cope. If you appear to be about equal, or if the challenge appears to be only a bit greater, enlist some outside help.

Although this formula seems elementary, many people choose not to cope with life's challenges. Why? The decision whether to cope or escape ultimately depends on how we size up ourselves in comparison to the challenge. In the case of the diesel engine, we decide to escape because the challenge is too great. In cases where the challenge is in reality not overwhelming, we may feel overwhelmed if we see ourselves as not having the capacity to cope. Depending on how inadequate we feel, we may escape from many challenges that are perfectly within our capacity.

Of the many methods of escape, one of the most common is to numb one's feelings with chemicals. Many people use alcohol or other chemicals to try to render themselves oblivious to their problems. Of course, reality problems that are ignored rarely evaporate. To the contrary, they usually get worse, making escapist tactics even more likely in the future.

It is unfortunate that there is a cultural ethos that encourages pathological escapism. The media bombard us with the idea that we should use chemicals to escape from problems. A commercial recommends that if you feel tense after a day's work, you should take an over-the-counter tranquilizer. But feeling tense after a harrowing day at work is a perfectly normal response that does not require any medication. A number of years ago, the manufacturer of a tranquilizer ran a commercial in which a woman discovered that her sink drain was clogged on the day she was to serve a special dinner for her husband's boss. In desperation she turned to her friend for help. Instead of suggesting calling a plumber, the friend recommended taking this tranquilizer to allay her anxiety. This is the message of addiction.

In one of my lectures at our rehabilitation center, I used this commercial as an illustration. Several months later I received a letter from a woman who had undergone treatment at our center for a combined alcohol and tranquilizer addiction. She wrote that she wanted to demonstrate her new efficiency in recovery and invited sixteen people to a New Year's dinner. On New Year's Day she discovered that her sink drain was clogged, and her husband could not get it unclogged. Since it was New Year's Day, getting a plumber was impossible.

"My husband looked at me with grave concern. In my

drinking days, a much lesser stress would have sent me to the bottle. But I remembered your lecture, and I just burst into laughter.

"We used the sink in the powder room to wash vegetables and prepare the food, and after dinner the guests helped me carry the dishes down to the laundry tub in the basement and even volunteered to wash them. We had a great time. I can only think of the disaster that would have resulted if this had happened before I was in recovery."

Using medication to relieve average workday tension is never advisable. This tension is best dealt with by jogging, listening to music, handiwork, reading a book, relaxation exercises, and so on. Escaping from tension by depressing the alertness of the brain with alcohol or other chemicals is counterproductive and may lead to addiction. Medications should be reserved for illnesses, and even then used carefully to avoid addiction. Certainly where there is no illness, there is no need for medication.

The idea behind these commercials is an insult to our intelligence. We are capable of coping with clogged-up drains, work tension, and many other problems. We are capable of surviving the normal tensions of life and dissipating them with healthful measures. To tell us to use chemicals for relief is demeaning. Unfortunately, people with negative self-images are highly susceptible to the seduction of these messages.

In recovering from addiction, you learn more about yourself and discover coping capabilities of which you were unaware. This is one of the excellent steps advocated by the twelve-step fellowships such as Alcoholics Anonymous and Narcotics Anonymous. The fourth and fifth steps require making a thorough, painstaking inventory of yourself and sharing it with another person. Repeating this process helps eliminate many negative misconceptions. Accepting guidance from a sponsor provides an objective perspective, which further helps correct the distorted perspective, and in this way you gradually overcome your negative attitude toward yourself. A similar program of self-awareness is very helpful in correcting an erroneous self-concept and can serve as a preventative measure to avoid development of addictions that are the result of escapist maneuvers.

THIRTEEN

Eating Disorders

Eating disorders, particularly compulsive eating and bulimia, have some resemblance to alcoholism and drug addiction. Eating should provide the body with necessary nutrition, and hunger is the body's way of notifying us that we need food. When the body's nutritive needs are satisfied, hunger should disappear. Craving for food after the body's needs have been met is not healthy hunger but a result of something gone awry in the body.

Imagine coming home, turning on the light switch, and discovering that instead of the lights going on, the garbage disposal was activated. Clearly there has been a cross-up in the wiring, so you call an electrician to untangle the system.

Hunger should be activated only by the body's nutritional needs. When something else activates hunger, this indicates of a cross-up in the body's wiring. Food is supplying something other than nutrition. It's like activating the garbage disposal when you want the lights on.

A cross-up is likely to occur when the system is in some type of distress: depression, anger, anxiety, loneliness, envy, or other unpleasant emotions. Somehow, the signals got mixed up and the body is calling for food to relieve the discomfort. Food then becomes a kind of drug, much like alcohol. It makes no difference what type of food it is; it doesn't have to be sugary or starchy. *Food that is not for nutritive purposes is a drug.* Virtually everything that has been said about alcohol or other mind-altering chemicals can be said about nonnutritive food intake.

As with chemical dependency, low self-esteem is found in virtually every person with an eating disorder. For the person with an eating disorder, the relationship with food becomes a substitute for relationships with people. The reason for turning to food instead of cultivating relationships is often due to a feeling of low self-worth, so the person may despair of having a meaningful relationship. "Why should anyone like someone like me?"

To people with low self-esteem, relationships are unreliable. "If the person I like ever gets to know me, he won't like me anymore." Food becomes a substitute for relationships because it is totally reliable. Food never rejects you.

As I mentioned earlier, people with low self-esteem are reluctant to acknowledge their neediness and their dependence on others. By turning to food instead of to other people, they maintain denial of their neediness.

As with alcohol, escaping into eating often leads to a vicious cycle. The low self-worth that initiates the eating disorder becomes aggravated as you lose control over food and either binge or gain too much weight. The guilty feelings generated by overindulgence make you feel even worse about yourself, causing further escape into food.

Food can become a tranquilizer in a variety of ways. It is possible that in some people there are physiological reasons. We know that the brain produces chemicals known as endorphins, which give a person a pleasurable sensation.

There is reason to believe that in some people food intake stimulates endorphin production, and it has been postulated that in anorexia, loss of weight does the same thing. Some anorexics have described a rush with weight loss that is similar to what a drug addicts describe as a chemical high.

For some people, food became a manifestation of love early in life. Parents who lacked self-esteem may have felt that they were not giving their children enough. As one young mother said, "I give myself totally to my children, but so what? They still have nothing." In such instances it is not unusual for parents to try to compensate by giving the children food, which then becomes symbolic of parental love. This impression is carried into later life. If you do not feel deserving of love from any other source, you may turn to food.

Earlier I explained how people with low self-esteem may have a fear of success. This is also a frequent occurrence in eating disorders and may explain the yo-yo phenomenon of weight loss and gain. To some people, maintaining the weight loss is an intolerable success!

Eating disorders are self-defeating. They may drain your energies so much that little strength remains for advancement. They are often aesthetically disfiguring, and they certainly are physically unhealthful.

Part III

Turning on the Power of Self-Esteem

FOURTEEN

Self-Assessment and Support: The Road to Recovery

I have described the problems that are caused by low self-esteem. Now what is the solution? How do we develop a positive self-image? It is by no means simple, but it can be accomplished.

The first step is accepting the possibility that our self-concept is invalid. Otherwise there is no possibility of any change. We have no motivation to make a self-assessment if we already know ourselves. Furthermore, why would we bother to search through a pile of rubble if we are convinced it contains nothing of value? We must have reason to believe that there is something of value to be found in order to make the effort.

It is not easy to shed convictions about one's self-image. If it is correct that the negative self-image begins in childhood, then a person who begins a self-assessment in middle age must be ready to let go of ideas that he or she has harbored for forty or more years. There is great resistance in relinquishing ideas that have been deeply entrenched for so long.

The second step is to make lifestyle changes that promote

a more positive self-image, and there may be fierce resistance to this. We are creatures of habit, and most of us are reluctant to change established patterns.

When lecturing on this theme, I often ask the audience to fold their arms across their chest and note whether they habitually cross the left arm over the right or vice versa. I then suggest they do it the opposite way and report how they feel. People invariably report an awkwardness in folding their arms in the opposite way, and they cannot maintain that position for an extended period of time without discomfort. If altering a simple posture is fraught with discomfort, imagine how distressful it is to alter significant behaviors. The tendency to return to a familiar, well-established pattern because it is more comfortable often inhibits the drive to develop an altered self-image.

The third step is to be extremely patient. A self-image that has prevailed for the greater part of our life is not going to be replaced quickly. Changes in self-concept are gradual and come in small increments. Relapses into the old self-concept are frequent. It may take years before there are substantive changes in self-image.

If these three conditions are satisfied, we can begin a self-assessment. Doing this alone may be of limited value. We have been looking at ourselves through distorting lenses and are not likely to see anything different if we look again. Nevertheless, some progress may be made, and there is no harm in trying to do it on our own.

Let's begin with the premise of this book, "I am better than I think I am." A sculptor finished a masterpiece, and when an observer marveled at his artistry, he said, "It really wasn't that great an accomplishment. I saw the statue inside the slab of marble, and all I had to do was chip away the pieces so that it could be visible to everyone." Knowing that there is a great deal of good inside ourselves makes the job simpler.

Now let's look at what gives a person value. Our feeling good about ourselves is related to our unique human aspects, our character and personality. Some of the unique human character traits are love, honesty, courage, humility, generosity, and empathy. It is safe to assume that we all possess these, and if they have not been manifest in our lives, it is because they have been concealed. Like the sculpture, we need to expose them.

One major difference between people and animals is that we can make intelligent choices based on concepts of right and wrong, good and bad, rather than having our behavior determined by whatever it is the body craves. To the degree that we make intelligent choices and exercise our unique human traits, we gain pride and self-esteem.

Keep in mind that making intelligent choices may not initially give us as comfortable a lifestyle as that of following our urges and drives. In other words, gaining self-esteem may require sacrificing some of the things we are attracted to. But it is a price well worth paying.

Self-esteem requires trust in ourselves. Co-dependent people do not trust their own impressions and judgments and continually look for cues in how other people react to them. Are they smiling and appear to be approving, or does a frown indicate disapproval?

It is wise to seek advice from others. When we talk about a problem, we often discover facets of which we had been unaware. Our own clear understanding and the perspective of an objective person can help us make better judgments, but this is different from being dependent on other people for every choice or decision. Although we should be flexible, we should begin making our own decisions and trusting our own opinions. If we make mistakes, these can be positive learning experiences, not devastating failures.

We all make mistakes. Some are costly, and we have every reason to regret them. But the function of regret should be to alert us not to repeat these mistakes, rather than self-condemnation. We learn many important things in life by experience. The proverb "Experience is a hard teacher, but fools will learn no other way" is wrong. Fools are those who fail to learn from experience. If you have made a mistake, even a serious one, and you have learned not to repeat it, then you are wise.

Obtaining a positive self-image means dispensing with the old one. It is easy to act out of habit; thinking how we are going to act takes effort. It is clear, however, that development of a new self-image requires a break with the past. It is only natural to follow the path of least resistance and revert to old, well-established patterns. So we must remain on guard and keep our wits about us, welcoming opportunities for constructive change.

Trusting ourselves allows us to be assertive, not necessarily aggressive, but appropriately assertive. Assertiveness gradually replaces pathological withdrawal and allows us to advance. Such progress reinforces self-trust, putting into motion a positive self-reinforcing cycle.

A young woman consulted me at the urging of a friend who had told her, "Cathy, you are letting life pass you by. You've got to see someone for help."

Cathy was thirty-eight, a charming woman who held a clerical position in a university. She had had this job for eleven years and had consistently assumed more responsibilities. She recognized that she was doing the work of three people. However, she had never asked for a promotion.

Cathy's social life was nil. Her only relationship was

with a married man who saw her at his whim. Although he said that he loved her, there was no indication that he intended to make their relationship permanent. She was frustrated playing second fiddle to the wife whom he said he did not love, but she did not assert herself to establish her position as the woman he truly loved. It was clear that Cathy held on to this relationship because she felt unlovable, and it was too risky to jeopardize a relationship with the one person who said he loved her. If she made him choose between his wife and her, she was certain he would reject her and then she would be totally alone, without hope of finding anyone else.

After eleven years, Cathy did not have any friends from work. Her office was at the far end of a long corridor, in a rather forsaken cul-de-sac where there was no traffic. No one came without some very specific business. Cathy had never made an effort to have her office moved to a more congenial spot.

Cathy brought her lunch from home and ate in her office. When I asked her why she didn't eat in the university cafeteria or in any of the restaurants near the campus, she replied, "Everybody has their own friends at their tables, and nobody wants a stranger imposing upon them."

Cathy could not see that she had effectively isolated herself from people and that her loneliness was largely self-inflicted. The therapeutic breakthrough occurred when I had to cancel an appointment with her, and I couldn't find her phone number. The directory assistance operator told me that Cathy's number was unlisted.

At the next appointment I asked Cathy why she needed an unlisted number. Her rationalizations were very poor, and I was able to show her how far her efforts at isolating herself had gone. Having an unlisted phone number kept her from being contacted by anyone, and like any other defense mechanism, it also permitted her to fantasize, "If people were able to contact me they certainly would. The reason they aren't is only because my number is unlisted." But Cathy was really convinced that her phone would not ring. A silent phone with a listed number would confirm her fear that she was undesirable company. By having her number unlisted, she did not have to deal with this stress.

I outlined several steps Cathy was to take. (1) She would have her phone number listed in the directory. (2) She would no longer eat lunch in her office but go to the cafeteria and approach a table where there was an empty seat and ask, "May I join you?" (3) She would try to relocate her office to an area that was less isolated. (4) She would approach her boss with the well-documented evidence that the work she was doing justified a promotion and possibly a secretary to assist her. (5) She would let her gentleman friend know that she did not plan to continue being his plaything. She did not wish to break up his marriage, but she was looking for a serious, long-term commitment. If this was not his intention, she did not wish their relationship to continue.

Cathy didn't have to make all these changes at once. First she listed her phone number, which was not much of a problem. She had difficulty approaching a table of strangers in the cafeteria, but finally she did ask and was pleasantly surprised when the people welcomed her. She continued to feel awkward approaching, but she persevered and eventually struck up conversations and made friends with many people.

Cathy's request for a promotion was granted without any hassle, and shortly after that she had her office moved.

She began to attend more university functions and eventually began to date other men. Then she terminated the relationship with the married man.

All of these changes came about gradually and were very painstaking, extending over two years. There were numerous rationalizations that Cathy presented to avoid challenging her symptoms, and various other types of resistances.

It is a good idea to write down things we don't like about ourselves. No change is possible until we identify what it is that we wish to change. Once we identify a behavior or feeling, we can begin by making a change "just for today." As Lao-tzu wisely noted two thousand years ago, "A journey of a thousand miles must begin with a single step."

For example, perhaps you don't like your passivity and your failure to stand up for your rights or assert your opinion. Decide that for the next twenty-four hours you will be on the alert to practice self-assertion. You may find that at work someone takes something of yours without asking, because this is how you have trained him. Today you will say, "Pardon me, Bill, but I may have to use this now. If you need it, please ask for it." Or if your husband leaves the table without removing the dishes, you say, "Honey, it's your turn to do the dishes tonight." Such remarks coming from you may elicit a quizzical reaction. You have to do this only today. Tomorrow you will consider tomorrow's tactics.

The "Serenity Prayer," written by the theologian Reinhold Niebuhr and adopted by AA, has two components: accepting things we cannot change and changing things we can. We must accept the past; it cannot be changed. But acceptance does not mean approval. I can accept that I have been a certain way, but I need not approve of this and I can muster the courage to change.

Change need not be radical. In fact, radical changes are rarely helpful. We must accommodate to changes and give others the opportunity to accommodate. Changes should preferably be in small increments.

Nathaniel Branden, a pioneer in self-esteem psychology, recommends completing sentences such as, What I like most about myself is . . . What I like least about myself is . . . I would like to be . . . I am happiest when . . . , and to review these sentences, making gradual changes to eliminate negative qualities and to implement positive traits. This can be a beginning of building self-esteem.

There is no denying that past events have an impact on how we perceive and value ourselves, but it is important to realize that nothing is cast in stone. With a bit of determination and effort, we can make changes.

Frequently we are unaware of unwarranted feelings of inadequacy that obstruct our progress or interfere with relationships. I have used the psychological insights of cartoonist Charles Schulz, who so clearly illustrates Charlie Brown's resignation to failure, Lucy's defense of belittling everyone, and Snoopy's flight into fantasy, in my previous books *When Do the Good Things Start?* and *Waking Up Just in Time*. It may be helpful to amuse yourself by reading these strips, and while smiling at these lovable characters jot down the traits you can identify in yourself.

Identifying our negative self-image symptoms and confronting them is only a small step. The problem is that without urging and support, we are likely to revert to our previous behavior, justifying it by rationalizations.

This is why it is generally necessary to have the help of an outside observer, preferably a counselor or therapist who is qualified to detect distortions in self-perception.

Not all psychotherapists are well suited to address a negative self-image problem. Some who are deeply rooted in psychodynamic theories may not have the proper approach for correcting a negative self-image.

I discovered this myself early in my psychiatric career. In medical school, we spent the first year studying anatomy, biochemistry, physiology, and human tissues. That marked our last contact with anything normal. The remainder of our education was focused on pathology: tumors, disease-causing bacteria and viruses, trauma, and abnormalities in physiology. Our thinking became pathology-oriented, and whenever we were confronted with a person with symptoms, our thoughts took the direction of looking for what was wrong with the person.

When I became a psychiatrist, I continued to look for what had gone wrong with my patients. The psychodynamic theories I was taught reinforced this approach. I searched through my patients' experiences, all the way back to their early childhoods, to find the source of the pathology. The idea was that if the patient realized the source of the symptoms and this could be extirpated, the symptoms would disappear.

The theory sounds logical, but I was disappointed in the results. Patients often said, "I understand everything thoroughly, Doctor, but I don't feel any better."

I then came to a realization that I later found was encapsulated by Charles Schulz in four simple frames.

People are composed of thoughts and feelings, which is the "inner self," and also of actions and behavior, which can be considered the "outer self." Others cannot know what goes on inside us, because our thoughts and feelings are private. What people see is our actions and behavior. Furthermore, even though we know at least some of our own thoughts and feelings, we are probably more affected by what we do than by what we think.

Peanuts® by Charles M. Schulz. Reprinted by permission of United Feature Syndicate, Inc.

In this comic strip, Schulz is telling us that changing our thoughts and feelings may have little impact on our behavior. Sally's "outer obnoxiousness" really indicates that she never had any true "inner peace." Behaving with courtesy and consideration to others is more likely to result in inner peace than inner peace resulting in more pleasant behavior. Modern psychologists, many of whom belong to one of the behaviorist schools, therefore advocate changing behavior first, working from the outside in.

As I became involved in the treatment of alcoholism, I noted the striking difference in approach between traditional psychotherapists who treated alcoholics and the Alcoholics Anonymous program. The psychotherapists focused on searching for the reason why a person drank and most often ended up with a person who had a good understanding why he or she was still getting drunk. Alcoholic Anonymous focused on the disturbed behavior: "Don't pick up the first drink, and get yourself to meetings," and these results were much more impressive.

"Oh, no! Not another self-esteem problem!"

How would the above patient be approached? A traditional psychodynamic psychotherapist would continue to work with the patient "lying under the couch" (not to be taken literally) in the hope that the patient would eventually develop sufficient self-esteem to be able to lie *on* the couch. A much more effective approach is to have the patient lie on the couch and stipulate that unless the patient does so, the therapist will not treat him. Either the patient is allowed to continue his destructive behavior until the magical insight eliminates it, or he can be helped to challenge the symptom and allow the dynamics to be worked out afterward.

The best way to treat a negative self-image is first to alter the behavior that is a manifestation of the distorted self-concept: The loner should begin mixing with people; the people-pleaser should learn how to say no when it is appropriate; the anxiety-ridden person should be encouraged to proceed even in situations that are stressful; the passive person should be helped to become more assertive. All the behaviors that the therapist has identified as being products of the negative self-image must be changed. The role of the therapist is to give the client the necessary support to make these difficult and anxiety-provoking changes and encourage him or her to do so.

Group therapy has advantages over one-to-one therapy in self-image problems. In spite of the ubiquity of the negative self-image, many people think that no one else feels as they do. The awareness that we are not alone is in itself uplifting. Also, knowing other admirable people who have unwarranted feelings of inadequacy may help us realize that we too may be oblivious to our own assets. Finally, the support in making difficult behavioral changes, sharing these experiences, and encouraging others to be assertive and act positively is of inestimable value.

A combination of group therapy and individual therapy may be particularly effective in ridding oneself of unwarranted feelings of shame. For example, a woman who harbors intense feelings of shame and resentment because of being sexually molested as a child may not be able to talk about it in a group. Yet simply relating the incident and even discussing her feelings with the therapist may not alleviate these painful emotions. A therapist utilizing the Gestalt technique might suggest that she pretend that the person who assaulted her is sitting in the other chair and encourage her to express her feelings toward that person. Or the therapist may suggest that she visualize herself as a little girl and express her feelings toward the child, as well as speak for the child. These techniques mobilize much more emotion and can be more effective than simply talking about the experience.

In group therapy, a number of people meet with a therapist. The therapist has generally interviewed participants and identified the particular problems that need correction. The group has a great deal of freedom in discussing various issues, although the therapist may set limitations on which issues will be dealt with in the group. The therapist is likely to offer interpretations of what is happening in the group process, and with professional help, very profound emotional issues may be analyzed.

Self-help groups are a bit different. People get together to exchange life experiences and what they have learned from them.

A group consists of preferably between six and ten people who wish to focus on self-realization and self-actualization. The sine qua non for such a group is a pledge of confidentiality and secrecy, so that members feel free to discuss important emotional issues. The group may choose any of the books on self-esteem as a text, and members take turns reading paragraphs aloud. After each paragraph, members are encouraged to discuss their own experiences. The first few sessions are apt to be rather sterile, since people have not yet gained a sufficient trust in one another to feel free to talk about intimate issues. As sessions continue, there is a gradual thawing, and soon any one sentence of the book may stimulate a meaningful discussion, with free exchanges of ideas and feelings. It is not necessary to have a professional psychologist involved regularly, but it is advisable to have a competent group therapist sit in at an occasional meeting to observe and recommend how the group can maximize its efficiency. Spouses or other close relatives should not be in the same group, since this may result in a reluctance to discuss feelings that concern them. Close friends are also apt to have feelings that they might conceal from each other but would reveal to strangers. They too should not be in the same group.

How do such groups begin? In community lectures on the subject of self-esteem I have suggested that notices be placed in schools, churches, synagogues, and workplaces, inviting people to join in planning a self-fulfillment group. An announcement might read as follows:

BE ALL THAT YOU CAN BE
ANYONE INTERESTED IN SELF-FULFILLMENT?
SOME OF US ARE!
YOU MAY JOIN IN PLANNING A SELF-ENHANCEMENT
GROUP BY CALLING
JANE SMITH AT 444-1111
OR BILL SMITH AT 111-4444

You might also place notices on supermarket bulletin boards or in community newspapers. However, ads may attract curiosity seekers rather than people sincerely interested in self-help.

Responses to the notices may vary greatly. You may get many responses or few expressions of interest. Patience and perseverance are necessary when beginning. Keep in mind that Alcoholics Anonymous, which now numbers millions of people across the world, began with only two individuals who sought to help each other.

Just as individual and group therapy can complement each other, therapy groups and self-help groups can be mutually beneficial.

Some significant emotional changes may occur in self-help groups, but these occur spontaneously from the exchanges within the group rather than from issues analyzed professionally. For example, people who attend AA meetings may indeed have profound behavioral changes as they abstain from alcohol and begin to alter their addictive behavior. They may become less selfish, more considerate, more truthful, less cantankerous, and more forgiving as they examine their own behavior. However, these changes come about as gradual and spontaneous consequences of achieving sobriety, rather than from being analyzed and interpreted.

FIFTEEN

How It Worked for Barbara

It is extremely difficult to convey in writing how a group session works, whether it is a self-help or a therapy group. Many of the important transactions are nonverbal: gestures, facial expressions, other body language, vocal intonations, and so forth. Also, the changes generally occur gradually and extend over a long period of time. Reading an account of an effective group experience can result in the misconception that dramatic changes occur rapidly. Nothing could be farther from the truth.

Keep these two important points in mind when you read the case histories here. I will try to depict what happened to several people in groups. Remember that each example represents many sessions.

Barbara, twenty-nine, came to the group because she said she had a dilemma and needed advice, not therapy. Barbara enjoyed her work as a flight attendant, as well as a good salary. She lived with her widowed mother, her father having died at age fifty-two of a heart attack.

Barbara reported that her mother used to have an occasional drink, but after her father died, her mother's drinking increased. A year ago, when Barbara's younger brother went off to college, her mother's drinking increased to the point where she frequently became forgetful and occasionally stuporous. Barbara's flight schedule kept her away from home many days of the week. When Barbara began talking to her mother about the excessive drinking, she replied that she drank because she was lonely. She told Barbara that if she would quit her job with the airline, she would not drink so much. Barbara did not want to quit her job, but she felt guilty pursuing her own needs at the expense of neglecting her mother.

Two other people in the group were involved with conflicts over caregiving, and although their cases were different from Barbara's, there were enough similarities that they could provide support for her. Eventually it turned out that both these group members had feelings of unworthiness, and their caretaking bolstered their self-esteem.

Barbara had never thought of herself as having low self-esteem or that her concern for her mother was anything but the normal concern of a child for a parent. When her mother's drinking became symptomatic, Barbara had consulted an alcoholism specialist who told her that she was in no way responsible for her mother's drinking and not to allow her mother to convince her otherwise. She was told that quitting her job would not help her mother's alcohol problem. Nevertheless, Barbara continued to be in conflict, so she came to therapy. The group helped her realize that her inability to accept the recommendation of the professional indicated that there were other factors in her indecision.

After a number of sessions Barbara revealed for the first time that she had an older brother who had been a hellraiser since childhood. Both parents had been preoccupied with trying to control his behavior. In order to gain attention from her parents, Barbara became the "perfect child," trying to be different from her brother in every way. She made good grades at school, was helpful with the housework, prepared meals, and helped care for her younger brother. She had never realized that she harbored resentments against her parents for not showing enough appreciation for what she was doing, instead giving all the attention to the renegade brother, who eventually became addicted to drugs and drifted away.

Over a period of time Barbara was helped to see that her mother's loneliness was her mother's problem, and that as a healthy woman of fifty-six, she could do a lot to make her life interesting and enjoyable. Her mother did indeed need companionship, but as long as Barbara was available, her mother had no reason to look elsewhere. In other words, Barbara was not doing her mother a favor by staying with her. Her mother needed help to overcome her drinking problem and to establish herself in a relationship and perhaps a job. It became evident that Barbara wanted to stay with her mother to satisfy her own need to be loved. Since childhood she had been trying to earn her parents' love.

During the many sessions, Barbara was helped to see that she had many admirable qualities. The other group members genuinely cared for Barbara, and she was able to see that she could be liked by others even though she was not doing things for them. Barbara thus became aware that she was a person who deserved to be admired and loved in her own right. As she began to feel better about herself, she was able to see how her self-image had suffered in her childhood and how that had affected all other aspects of her life. She was having trouble developing meaningful relationships, and she had not taken advantage of promotional opportunities at work.

Eventually Barbara was able to extricate herself from the mother-job conflict. Together with her younger brother they had a therapeutic confrontation that resulted in her mother entering an alcoholism treatment program. Barbara's mother is now six years sober and has remarried. Barbara recently married and is working in a supervisory position with the airline.

Barbara's course in group therapy took about eighteen months with a group that met twice weekly. Although the presenting problem was indeed satisfactorily resolved, a number of other problems turned up, some of which she could not identify in herself but could easily see in other group members. The group helped her identify these problems in herself, too. As her self-image improved, she was able to overcome them as well.

SIXTEEN

How It Worked for Betty

At a public lecture, I spoke about the role of low self-esteem in eating disorders. I suggested that in addition to whatever therapy people were involved in, they should form small self-help groups to deal with problems of self-esteem. Following the lecture, eight people joined together to form a group. Three were anorexic-bulimics, three were compulsive overeaters, and two were family members of anorexic-bulimics (a husband and a mother). The family members were not related to others in the group.

Betty was the mother of a nineteen-year-old anorexic-bulimic. Her daughter was attending an out-of-town college and had refused treatment, so Betty joined the group to learn how to deal with her daughter. The group took a popular book on eating disorders as their text.

Betty was forty-five, and she had divorced her husband after fifteen years of emotional and physical abuse. Her daughter, Veronica, was the oldest of three children, with two younger brothers. Betty had recognized that her husband was abusive when she was pregnant with Veronica, but she did not turn to her parents for help because they had disapproved of the marriage and she wanted to show them that they were wrong. After the two boys were born, she began to see that she could not change her husband. She still wanted to turn to her parents for help, but she knew that they would tell her to leave her husband. She wanted to keep the marriage going for the children's sake; she was not going to allow them to suffer the problems of a broken home.

Things continued to deteriorate, and Betty got divorced when Veronica was eleven. Veronica did not react adversely to the divorce. She was a chubby child, but this did not appear to bother her. She did well in school and had friends. Veronica's eating disorder became apparent at age sixteen, when she took diet pills and starved herself to lose weight, but also had periodic binging. This continued until she left for college, and Betty was concerned that this erratic eating pattern would result in her flunking out.

After the first few sessions, someone in the group overheard Betty telling one of the bulimic young women that she would be happy to help her and to feel free to call her any time of the day or night, especially if she had the urge to binge. At the next session, the woman who had overheard the conversation raised the question of whether it was advisable for Betty to try to help this bulimic young woman. Her relationship with her own daughter had not helped the bulimia. Betty felt that she was being accused of having caused her daughter's bulimia and that the group assumed that she would exert a pathological effect on this woman. The group asked Betty why she had offered to make herself available any time of the day or night and wondered whether this wasn't putting herself out too much. Betty responded that when someone needed help immediately it would be a mistake to make her wait.

As far as Betty was concerned, the group emphasis gradually turned away from her daughter's bulimia to her own self-effacing behavior. Betty tended to apologize for things that did not require an apology. When anyone in the group said something critical of her, Betty would pout but would not defend her opinion.

At one point Betty shared that she was in a relationship with an abusive man. The group asked why she was allowing this relationship to continue, in light of her experience with her husband. Betty tried to justify the relationship, but the group was not convinced.

Eventually Betty let it be known that none of her three children really respected her and that they took advantage of her. She constantly did things for them but never demanded anything in return. The group pointed out that she had made a doormat of herself in her marriage, in her current relationship, and with her children.

The group helped Betty recognize that her behavior was caused by a poor self-image and showed her that they did not see her the way she saw herself. Betty presented very little information about her own personality development, and the group did not press her on it. Instead, she was encouraged to stand her ground with the man she was seeing and with her children.

The focus had shifted radically from what Betty could do for her daughter to what she could do for herself. In regard to her daughter, Betty came to realize that she was not responsible for Veronica's eating disorder and that she would accept help in time. Once Betty's self-image improved, she no longer needed to be the controlling mother and was able to accept that she was powerless over her daughter.

Don't assume that the group was preoccupied with Betty and her problems. (For demonstration purposes I focused on her.) As Betty made these favorable changes, so did other group members. The group was mutually supportive and shared in everyone's progress. When Betty stood her ground and refused to accept abuse from her gentleman friend, the group took pride in her achievement, just as Betty felt elated by the progress other group members made with their problems.

Again, this account is oversimplified. These weekly sessions went on for several years; it was a slow process. None of the changes occurred dramatically, and at times the group considered disbanding because they felt they were not accomplishing anything. On several occasions a professional group therapist was asked to evaluate the group and point them in a proper direction. After three years, the members concurred that they had achieved their goals, and the group dissolved, planning to meet every three months for old times' sake. There was general agreement that everyone had come to a more realistic and more positive self-awareness and that they were much more capable of coping with their respective problems. Those members who had been in larger groups, such as Overeaters Anonymous or Weight Watchers, felt that the small-group experience had not only enhanced their eating disorder recovery but had salutary effects in other aspects of their lives.

When one behavior change occurs, it can affect the entire personality. Personality is analogous to the decor of a room. If you buy a new chair, it may clash with the carpet, which now must be replaced. The old wallpaper now does not match the rugs, so that must be replaced. This necessitates new draperies that will blend with the wallpaper. By the time the changes have been completed, the room has a totally new look, which began with only a new chair.

Much the same happens with an alteration in personality. Change in any one character trait may throw the entire system out of harmony, and other traits may have to be altered. In this way, a totally new personality may eventually result.

A word of caution is necessary here. Although improvement in self-esteem is salutary, it may cause a disharmony in a relationship. For example, John and Mary seem to have a satisfactory marriage. A problem in Mary's life caused her to seek psychotherapy, and a negative self-image was diagnosed. Perhaps one of the manifestations of Mary's negative self-image was a passivity due to a lack of trust in her decision-making capabilities. As a consequence of this, Mary was very comfortable having her husband assume all the responsibilities of making decisions and perhaps controlling the family finances as well. John, on the other hand, likes to be in a controlling position, and Mary's passivity was exactly what he needed in a wife. If Mary's self-image changes so that she becomes more assertive and now wishes to participate in the decision making or have a say in the family finances, John may be displeased with the new development in her personality.

In other words, a relationship may begin with a nonverbalized understanding of the terms of the relationship. If either partner now significantly changes those terms, the basis for the relationship may disintegrate and an incompatibility develop.

This is why when someone has a problem with addiction, family members are also strongly urged to become involved in self-help groups. Otherwise, the recovering person may progress in personality development while the nonaddict spouse and/or children remain static. Similarly, it may be necessary for family members to make appropriate adjustments in themselves, and possibly even become involved in psychotherapy, when a close family member undergoes a self-image change.

SEVENTEEN

How It Worked for Linda

Linda sought treatment for alcohol and tranquilizer dependency at age thirty-four. Her use of alcohol began at age fifteen. Linda was very thin, probably anorexic, and her grandfather had suggested that she could gain weight by drinking beer because it is high in calories. Linda discovered that beer opened a new world for her. She had been very shy and self-conscious, avoiding relationships with boys and even with most girls. She did not think she could be liked.

Linda's father was a bookkeeper and her mother was a schoolteacher. She recalls them being very mechanical, providing a comfortable home but being emotionally detached. She had a twin brother who was very bright. Linda felt far inferior to him.

Once beer entered her system, Linda became a different person. She felt witty and sociable. She could relate well to boys, but she needed the alcohol to give her courage and bolster her personality. Although her reliance on beer kept increasing, it did not cause her any overt problems. She drank her way through college, where she majored in interior decorating. Upon graduation she got a job as a clothes buyer for a department store and occasionally did some furniture buying.

A few years later she fell in love with Alvin, an English instructor. Linda's parents did not approve of Alvin, but she married him anyway. Linda earned more than Alvin, who began relying on her income rather than his own. He became a substitute teacher and stayed home much of the time, claiming he was doing essential reading for his job, although he certainly did not advance himself in his profession. Alvin was markedly unhelpful in caring for the two children who were born in the first years of the marriage. He was constantly critical of Linda, who continued to work while trying to care for the children.

The quantity of alcohol Linda needed to keep her functioning could no longer be met by beer, and she switched to spirits. She found herself tremulous in the morning before her first drink but was concerned that the odor of whiskey would be detected at work. She obtained a prescription for Valium to get her through the day, turning to alcohol after work. She began to have memory lapses, which caused many problems at work and resulted in her losing her job. Soon after, Alvin sued for divorce and custody of the children, and Linda made a suicide attempt. When her alcohol and tranquilizer addictions were identified, she was referred to our rehabilitation center for treatment.

Linda's sense of unworthiness was understandable but unrealistic. She had considered herself inadequate even when she was supporting the family and running the household. Ridding herself of the unwarranted feelings of shame would be a major focus for her recovery. By realizing that her life had become unmanageable, she relinquished the illusion of needing to be a superperson and a supermom. She realized that it was okay to be just Linda, a human being who sometimes needed help.

Initially Linda was urged just to attend AA meetings and stay sober; psychodynamic insights could wait. She was fortunate in finding a sponsor with many years of sobriety who took a sincere interest in Linda and made herself available day and night for any of her problems.

After six months of sobriety, Linda found a part-time job as an interior decorator. She was able to get visitation rights to her children, who were happy to have their mother again. After the first year of sobriety, her sponsor suggested that she begin working on the fourth step, which was doing an inventory of her life.

Linda began to realize that she had suffered from unwarranted feelings of shame since childhood. She recalled how she had withdrawn from her friends and had isolated herself for no valid reasons. She now discovered that people enjoyed her company and that they actually sought her friendship.

One of the men she met in the recovery program became interested in Linda, who was thrilled to find that she could attract a man. Linda's sponsor was adamant that she not become sexually involved, pointing out that she was vulnerable to being sexually exploited because she was so starved for affection. Linda did avoid sexual entanglement and was pleasantly surprised to find that her friend was interested in her companionship even in the absence of sex.

Linda's employer was pleased with her work, and she began to work full time. She eventually did the fifth of the twelve steps in the AA program, sharing her history with an empathic priest who was able to help her see some of her self-image distortions.

After three years of sobriety, Linda was asked to become

a sponsor. Linda discovered in the woman she sponsored many of the self-image distortions and defense mechanisms that had been her own, and in helping her overcome these she was able to correct her own misperceptions. Linda was also able to see how her attraction to Alvin had been based on her erroneous self-concept. Her unwarranted feelings of shame and inadequacy had resulted in her becoming a doormat and tolerating his abuse.

As Linda progressed in her sobriety, her relationship with her children improved. They eventually expressed a desire to be with her rather than with their father, and Linda gladly assumed custody.

Linda excelled as an interior decorator and her boss offered her a partnership in the firm. Today Linda is nine years sober and has a very active social and business life, in addition to being the mother of two teenagers, hardly a small feat.

At a recent meeting, I asked Linda why she had not considered marriage. She laughed and said, "You've done too good a job on me. I now like myself so much that I don't think anyone else is good enough for me."

"You've restored my ego to the point where I now feel the need of a more prominent doctor"

EIGHTEEN

How It Worked for Adrienne, Ronald, and Amy

Group therapy can be exciting. When a group of people get together with a sincere desire to improve their lives and overcome their emotional difficulties, anything can happen—and often does. Sometimes the group experience is intense and dramatic, as in the case of Adrienne.

Fifteen-year-old Adrienne had been referred to treatment by the juvenile detention center after she had been arrested for drinking and possession of marijuana.

In addition to marijuana and alcohol, Adrienne and her friends had used LSD, Percoset, Valium, and a variety of other substances that they got from their parents' medicine cabinets or on the street.

I asked Adrienne if she had ever worked in the kitchen and what she did with scraps of leftover food or peelings and the like. She said that she threw them in the garbage, of course. "Why don't you find someplace else to put them?" I asked. Adrienne responded that that was an absurd question, because there was no other place to throw garbage.

"Just look at this list of garbage you have used," I said.

"If you know garbage belongs in a garbage can, how come you put this in yourself?"

"I wanted to get high. All the kids were doing it."

"It is not quite true that all the kids were doing it. Some kids were doing it and some kids weren't, and you chose to associate with those who did. My guess is that you thought of yourself as being some kind of garbage can, and that's why you put this garbage in yourself."

Adrienne's eyes became a bit misty. "I never thought I was any good," she said.

Adrienne's mother was sixteen when Adrienne was born. Another child was born two years later. When Adrienne was four, her alcoholic father disappeared. Her mother was overwhelmed with the care of two children without financial or emotional support and had them placed in foster homes.

Adrienne began acting out against authority at an early age, and she did poorly in school. She was more than her foster parents could manage, and it was evident to Adrienne that they were not thrilled to have her. To Adrienne the world was a hostile place, where you get what you fight for, and the weaker ones lose out.

Adrienne appeared to be a very sweet, lovable, and sensitive young woman who was full of anger at being dealt a raw deal. Her defiance against authority and refusal to comply with rules became apparent in the therapy group. The therapist tried desperately to reach her and invested much time and effort in individual sessions, making only a slight dent in her armor. It seemed as though Adrienne was trying to get herself kicked out, perhaps because she had come to expect rejection as normal in life.

During the third week of therapy, Adrienne announced that she was leaving treatment. The therapist told her that she would be returned to the juvenile detention center if she left against the staff's advice. Adrienne did not care; she would leave anyway. The group tried to convince her how foolish this would be, but she would not budge.

At this point the therapist broke down crying and left the room. After several minutes the therapist returned, still tearful, accompanied by a staff member. She said that she was going to quit because she could not tolerate investing so much of herself in another person and seeing her self-destruct. "I put everything I had into Adrienne because I feel for her and know that she can make it. My father abandoned us when we were little, and I know what she feels like, but that's no reason to destroy herself."

Adrienne got up and sat near the therapist, putting her arms around her, and both cried together. The role reversal was striking. Several of the group cried along with them. The first one to speak was Adrienne, who said, "I'm sorry to hurt you, and I appreciate your caring, but my mind is made up. I'm going to leave and take my chances." The group tried to persuade Adrienne to stay, but to no avail. There was much shouting at her, but she just shouted back.

The following morning Adrienne requested a session with the staff supervisor and confided that she had been taken by surprise. She couldn't remember anyone ever caring for her before. "I was an imposition on everybody. I was a piece of crap that no one could get rid of. Yesterday was the first time in my life somebody really cared about what was going to happen to me. I don't know how to handle that yet. I'm so confused. I want to stay just a few days more to figure things out."

This incident was not planned or orchestrated; it was a spontaneous occurrence in an empathic setting. These are the kinds of things that can occur in such an environment.

Adrienne's story does have a happy ending. She completed residential treatment, and arrangements were made with an appropriate foster family, who was supportive during the next two years of outpatient treatment. She graduated from high school with good grades and went to community college. She is considering a course in counseling, hoping to put her personal experience to work.

Ronald is a young man of eighteen who had a group experience of another kind. Prior to admission to our facility he had been living on the street. His self-concept can be summed up by two statements in his self-evaluation sheet. In response to what he thinks of himself, he wrote, "A worthless piece of shit," and in response to a question about what he feels most positive about, he wrote, "I can beat up my older brother."

In a group discussion, Ronald said that he began using alcohol and drugs when he was eleven. His only drug-free period lasted for eight months when he lived with his grandmother who was disabled by a stroke. He had cooked, kept house, done the shopping, and looked after her until she died. The therapist asked why he had not listed this as one of his accomplishments, but Ronald dismissed the question as insignificant.

One of the group members picked up on this point and said that it was too important to dismiss. It was obvious that when Ronald was doing something worthwhile, he was able to abstain from drugs. With the help of the therapist, the group focused on Ronald's inability to accept his achievements, particularly the caring aspect of his personality. This served as a wedge to pry open the tight seal of self-denigration. This single item helped Ronald realize that he had been unable to accept anything positive about himself and served as the seedling of self-esteem that was expanded in therapy.

Amy, age sixteen, also presented a thoroughly worthless image of herself. She said that she had abandoned herself to a life of drugs and prostitution and didn't really care what happened to her.

One of the group shrewdly commented, "If you don't care at all about yourself, why are you wearing braces? Obviously, you do care about yourself, at least about your appearance."

Amy denied this and said that the aunt she lived with had a daughter about her age who had braces. Her uncle and aunt felt that if they did not provide Amy with equal treatment, they would be showing favoritism. "They don't care about how I look either. It's just that my aunt feels guilty about my being an orphan, and she does things for me for the sake of my mother."

The group did not accept this. "Wearing braces is no fun, and if you didn't want them you could have said no. The fact that you are wearing them shows that you do care about yourself. All the stuff you are giving us about not giving a damn about yourself is just a big lie."

Amy's facade of self-abandonment was gently and successfully dismantled by the group. She was eventually helped to see that she cared very much about herself but had despaired of anyone else caring for her.

Although insights such as these can be brought out in individual therapy, the variety of experiences and the impact that peers can exert greatly increase the efficacy of treatment in a group. It matters little what the presenting symptom is. The underlying factor of a negative self-image invariably emerges and can be more easily corrected in a group setting.

Part IV

Dealing with Problems Along the Way

NINETEEN

Relapse versus Growth

Recovery from a negative self-image is gradual. As is the case with any extended recovery process, the course is not a steadily smooth uphill slope. One does eventually reach the top, but rarely without sustaining some slips on the way.

Slips that occur after a person has begun to improve may be more painful than the original chronic depressive state. It's like falling off a ladder. If you are standing on the first rung, the fall probably won't cause any injury. The higher you have climbed on the ladder, the more severe the fall. Similarly, someone who has felt more or less unhappy day after day may actually have become accustomed to that state of existence. If the person begins to feel much better and then has a recurrence of even a brief depression, this is felt much more keenly.

Even after reaching an essentially stable stage, there is always the possibility of relapse. To understand why this happens, try a simple exercise. Take a piece of thick cardboard and fold one corner. Now straighten out the fold. Where the cardboard was folded, there is a crease. This crease will remain regardless of how much you flatten the fold. If you try to bend the cardboard at any other place, you will encounter some resistance, but at the crease, the slightest pressure makes the cardboard bend.

A person who recovers from a negative self-image may be left with a "crease." Anything that occurs, even years later, that constitutes a threat to the ego is likely to resurrect all the feelings of inadequacy that he or she had already overcome. Some or all of the symptoms that accompanied the negative self-image may emerge again. People who have recovered from alcoholism or another chemical dependency are vulnerable to relapse into chemical use at this time. Awareness of this possibility may help prevent a panic reaction or chemical use in the event of a relapse.

Subsequent challenges to the ego are highly probable. If we continue to function at a fixed low level of performance we do not arouse any expectations from anyone. We, our families, and our employers won't expect more of us than our routine performance. As we gain self-confidence, our performance level is likely to increase, and as a consequence we may be given additional assignments. Our employers may assign us to new duties, our families may expect more, and we ourselves may accept new challenges. Just as the cardboard yields with even minimal pressure, any new expectation of us may constitute a stress, which can reawaken the feelings of inadequacy that had been lying dormant.

Earlier I reported the case of a physician who had achieved outstanding scholastic honors yet had a very poor self-image. Her alcoholism had resulted in her dismissal as medical director of a health facility.

Early in her recovery she took a part-time job with relatively minimal responsibilities. After several weeks, she encountered some very severe stresses. I suggested that she discuss this with her AA sponsor. Several weeks later she again reported being in a crisis, and I gave her the same advice. I inquired how the previous crisis had been resolved, and she stated that it had been trivial, but this time she was really in a severe crisis.

These calls recurred every few weeks with an identical pattern. What had been a major crisis several weeks earlier had been easily resolved, but this time it was major.

In a therapeutic interview I pointed out this pattern to the physician. As she performed successfully at work, new demands were constantly being made of her. No one asks someone who is functioning poorly to do more, but people who perform well are very likely to be asked to increase their functioning. Each new demand resurrected her self-doubts and constituted a crisis. With the help of her sponsor, each hurdle was overcome, allowing her to function at a higher level, which then led to increased expectations of her, resulting in a very positive but stressful cycle.

The same stresses that may trigger a relapse may also be stimuli for growth. I once came across a fascinating description of how lobsters grow. The lobster, encased in a hard, unyielding shell, grows until the shell becomes restrictive and stifling. It then retreats to a sheltered place, sheds its shell, and gradually forms a new one. This process is repeated numerous times until the lobster reaches its maximum size. Each time the lobster sheds its shell, even in the safety of its retreat, it is at the mercy of sudden currents of water or predatory fish. The outer shell is its protective armor, and when it temporarily loses this defense it become vulnerable. Yet in order to grow, the lobster must take such risks.

I have often told lobster lovers that they should be grateful that lobsters do not have recourse to doctors. If they did, then at the first sign of discomfort, the lobster would get a prescription for a tranquilizer. Instead of shedding its shell and growing, it would eliminate its discomfort with medication and would remain in its tiny original shell until it died.

When you feel emotionally uncomfortable, think of this as a possible signal that you are ready for a growth spurt. You may indeed get relief from a chemical, but it will stifle further growth. If you present your problem to a counselor, therapist, sponsor, or someone who can help put things in their proper perspective, a relapse can be averted and actual growth may occur. People who maintain contact with a self-help group have an accessible resource that can prevent a psychological relapse from escalating into a full-blown negative self-image problem again, or into recourse to chemical use.

TWENTY

Resistance to Self-Awareness

Many people with a negative self-image exhibit a reluctance to discover their true selves. They are convinced that a self-discovery will reveal only the negative aspects of their personality. Confronting these goblins is indeed frightening.

We all have things in the past of which we are not proud. But these should not deter us from self-discovery. We should talk about them, learn from them, and then discard them.

Sometimes resistance to self-exploration does not come from fear of discovering character defects. The people I mentioned earlier who have a fear of happiness are reluctant to discover their virtues and personality assets.

To understand why someone wouldn't want to discover her assets, consider Pat. This twenty-three-year-old woman was admitted to treatment for a drinking problem. At the admission interview, she asked whether she could undergo psychological testing.

"Why do you want psychological tests?" I asked.

"I'm afraid I might have brain damage from drinking," she said.

I assured her that she did not have any brain damage and that there was no need for psychological tests. However, the following day she inquired whether she might have a brain-wave test, and I again assured her that there was no need. The next day she requested a CT scan of the brain.

"I have already told you that you do not have brain damage," I said.

"But how can you be sure? You don't know how much I drank."

Pat's inability to accept reassurance puzzled me, but after a lengthy interview the mystery was solved. She *wanted* to have brain damage! Then she could say to her family, "Leave me alone. I am not capable of achieving sobriety. Recovery from alcoholism is difficult enough for normal people, but I am brain damaged and cannot be expected to overcome my addiction." Similarly, if they wanted her to become gainfully employed, she could say, "Me? Hold a job? You must be kidding. I can't take on any responsibility. I'm brain damaged." If she was urged to go to school, she would say, "Me? College? Impossible. I'm brain damaged." As tragic as brain damage is, it would have been the perfect out, exempting her from any efforts to remain sober and improve her life.

Variations of this attitude can be discovered in many people. There is a strange kind of comfort in resigning ourselves to a state of inadequacy. We are then exempt from trying.

Again, participants in a group effort can diminish this resistance in two ways. First, it's likely that a person harboring such resistance will observe it in another person and can then be helped to discover it in himself or herself. Second, the encouragement and support of the group can help overcome the anxiety resulting from the implied need to perform at a higher level and assume greater responsibilities.

Ethan complained in his therapy group that his work performance had recently deteriorated, and he attributed this to anxiety he felt over an impending promotion. He was about to be elevated to a supervisory position, and he questioned his capacity to give direction to others. His worries about disappointing everyone and failing in this new position were interfering with his concentration. One group member suggested that perhaps his diminished performance was his way of persuading his superiors that he was not as capable as they thought he was and that they should retract the promotion.

Another group member was a retired executive who offered to provide Ethan with some guidance in a supervisory role. In fact, this person was bored in his retirement and welcomed the opportunity to share his experience with Ethan. Ethan did accept the promotion and performed very well in his new position. The therapist then raised the question of whether there might not be other instances in which Ethan performed inadequately in order to avoid being asked to take on greater responsibilities. It emerged that this had indeed been a pervasive trait in Ethan's life, which had affected his domestic and social, as well as occupational, life.

Pinpointing this single self-defeating tactic helped Ethan investigate other ways he was avoiding responsibilities that would promote positive feelings about himself.

TWENTY-ONE

Getting in Touch with Feelings

A true awareness of the self, the whole self, requires an awareness of all our feelings. Frequently, we disown some feelings because we consider them improper, because we are afraid we cannot control them, or because they are simply too painful. There may be considerable resistance to acknowledging these feelings, and as long as we continue to disown them, we cannot arrive at a valid self-awareness.

It is easy to understand why some feelings are disowned. What is harder to understand is why it is difficult to acknowledge perfectly normal, positive, and even salutary feelings. I gained some insight into this phenomenon as a result of two events that followed in close succession, one at home and the other at work.

One day my wife pointed out to me that the faucet on the laundry tub was leaking. When I tried to turn the valve to cut off the water flow to the faucet, I was unable to do so and had to call a plumber. The plumber was no more successful at this than I was, and he explained that the valve was frozen in its position and had probably not been touched since the house had been built seventy years earlier. The only way to fix the faucet was to turn off the main valve that controlled water flow to the entire house.

After thc water was shut off and the faucet dismantled, the plumber confronted me with the sad findings that the entire interior of the faucet was eroded, and the unit had to be replaced. After the work was finished and the main water valve was turned on, I discovered that every time I turned on any faucet in the house there was an initial explosive discharge of rusty water, which gradually became a smooth, clear flow.

The following day I saw a young man in consultation. After two weeks of intensive group therapy, Joshua appeared to be detached from all feelings, showing no emotion whatever. During the interview it emerged that when he was ten, his father died suddenly, and he recalled looking at himself at the mirror and saying, "You are not going to cry," and indeed he did not.

It became evident that at age ten Joshua had tried to shield himself from feeling grief, but because he was unable to find a way to turn off this specific feeling, he turned off the "main valve," as it were, shutting off *all* feelings. Not only did he not experience the pain of grief, but he had rendered himself insensitive to all emotions, sad as well as happy. Since age ten he had felt no anger, no pride, no love, no joy.

The problem he now confronted was that in order to experience feelings, *any* feelings, he had to open the "main valve." Having been without feelings of any kind for so long, he saw this as threatening. He felt that emotions of any kind would overwhelm him, much as the opening of any faucet after the main valve was turned on was followed by an explosive discharge. He therefore was frightened of joy and pride as well as shame and sadness.

Once Joshua understood this, he allowed himself to relax his guard a bit. His group provided the support necessary to carry him through the initial experience of feeling emotions once again. It is much easier to understand why someone would wish to avoid painful feelings, and indeed it is quite common to utilize one or more psychological defense mechanisms to protect us from emotional distress. There are times, however, especially in therapy, when we should recognize the experience of emotional distress as a positive, growth phenomenon.

At our rehabilitation center one day, a young man asked to speak to me privately, then threw his arms around my neck and began crying bitterly. "You've got to help me, Doc," he sobbed. "I can't take it. I can't take the pain." He told me he had entered our facility the day before. Paul was twenty-three and had been using drugs since he was fourteen.

"From the time that you began using until now, what was your longest period of abstinence?" I asked.

"I haven't had any," Paul answered.

I then told him about a young woman who had been involved in a serious automobile accident, sustaining multiple fractures. She had no sensation or motion in her right arm. The neurosurgeon performed a nerve repair but explained to her that there was no guarantee that feeling would recur. It would be perhaps three to four months before the success of the operation could be determined.

After three months had passed, she dropped a lit cigarette she was holding in her left hand, and it fell on her right hand, causing her to feel pain. She promptly jumped up in joy and ran around the room happily screaming, "I'm hurting! I felt pain!"

For this woman, the pain was an indication that the surgery had been successful. The distress of the burn paled in significance to the tidings it bore, that she would have the use of her right hand again.

I then pointed out to Paul that for nine years he had essentially anesthetized his brain with chemicals and had felt no sensations whatever, neither joy nor sadness. Paralyzing the brain with drugs had arrested his personality development. Now that the drugs were out of his system, his capacity to feel was returning, and this meant that he would be able to grow and mature. Although I empathized with his suffering, I stressed that the positive aspect of being able to feel again should outweigh his pain. "What you ought to do," I said, "is to go into the lobby and shout for joy, 'I'm depressed! I'm depressed!' just as the woman danced for joy to feel pain. You are regaining the function of your mind, and that should be a euphoric experience, in spite of the distress."

Chemicals are not the only method people use to avoid feelings. Our unconscious mind may shield us from distress, and it may take considerable effort to overcome these natural protective maneuvers. However, no true self-awareness can be achieved as long as we alienate a part of the self from the whole.

TWENTY-TWO

Anger and Hostility

From the writings of Sigmund Freud, it is apparent that in his days repressed sexuality was a major psychological problem. In these days there is very little about sexuality that is repressed. Instead, the prime emotional culprit today is probably repressed anger.

Many of us have difficulty with anger. We are taught in early life that feeling angry is wrong. As children we are scolded when we express anger. Some of us fear that expressing anger will prevent people from loving us. In whatever way it comes about, there is a widespread impression that it is bad to express anger or to be hateful. Consequently, people who do harbor such feelings are apt to think of themselves as bad or unworthy, and this contributes to feelings of shame that may have their onset very early in life.

Let me define my terms. Anger is a feeling that is aroused when we are provoked, either physically or by being denied something we desire and believe is rightfully ours, or by an insult to our pride. The feeling that results from such provocation is beyond our control. In other words, we cannot choose not to be angry when provoked. The most we can do is to repress the anger, which may occur if we are convinced that feeling angry is wrong or a threat to our likability. Repressed anger is pushed into the unconscious portion of the mind where it is beyond reach and cannot be properly dissipated. It slowly festers and exerts damaging effects on other feelings and behavior.

If anger is what we feel when we are provoked, and we realize that we have no voluntary control over this emotional response, then we can avoid thinking of ourselves as bad for allowing such feelings to occur. Anger is not a matter of choice. Furthermore, such anger will occur even if the person who provokes us is someone we love, including parents, spouse, children, friends, or God. To sum it up: It is not wrong or sinful to feel anger.

What we do with the feeling of anger is something altogether different, because we have choices on how to manage the feeling. Repressing anger can result in emotional upset, and some psychologists advocate discharging the anger by screaming or hitting a punching bag. There is not a shred of evidence that this diminishes anger; to the contrary, it may intensify anger.

One of the most important things to know about anger is that although we may be unable to prevent it, we are capable of controlling its expression. Many people fear that they will not be able to control their anger and will lose the affection of loved ones who are the targets of their anger. This is like having a minefield within oneself and being under the constant tension of "what will happen if I explode." We should develop confidence in our ability to control our behavior and realize that although we may have no control over some *feelings,* we have a great deal of control over our *actions.*

If the fear of anger is eliminated, we can begin safely to dissipate it, not by kicking the cat or hitting the wall, but by simple reflection. First, were we correct in assessing the provocation? Sometimes the provocation is unintentional—someone steps on our toes in the theater or even accidentally spills coffee on us. There is a momentary flash of anger, which soon passes after the person says "I'm sorry." We have all been perpetrators of such accidents, and because we can easily understand that there was no malice, our anger quickly dissolves. But note: Even in such common situations, anger does occur, because it is an involuntary reflex response. It is brief because we can easily empathize and dismiss it. This is the prototype of a reasonable response to anger: Feel it and then dismiss it.

This is not as easily achieved when the injury or insult is more severe and where there was indeed malice. The feeling of anger is more intense, and there is invariably an impulse to retaliate. Even if we try to comply with a spiritual requirement to forgive, the anger remains.

In working with alcoholics, I have witnessed a useful technique. A recovering corporate attorney found himself suddenly unemployed as a result of company downsizing. Not having been in private practice and not having saved any money during his years of active drinking, he was in dire straits. He was then approached by a group of investors who wished to develop a chain of retail outlets, and they made him president of the new venture. Once he had opened three stores for them, they voted to oust him, and it was evident that they had simply exploited him. I met him shortly after his ouster and he said, "I am very bitter about this, but I will go to an AA meeting tonight and drop off my resentments there. You see, if I hang on to them, I will drink again, and that is something I refuse to do."

This man realized the destructiveness of harboring resentments. In his situation the danger was clear: relapse into drinking. The awareness of this danger led him to seek ways to dispose of his resentments. Hanging on to them would not achieve anything for him and could seriously aggravate his plight.

People who are not concerned about a relapse into drinking may not be aware that there are other harmful effects in harboring resentments. The internal rage may cause or contribute to depression or to many psychosomatic conditions such as migraine, high blood pressure, or ulcers. Simply for survival purposes, we must find a way to dissipate anger.

How does involvement in AA or other self-help group relieve resentments? You ventilate your feelings to sympathetic ears. Others may respond with similar experiences of their own, and sincere empathy can provide much relief. Some may point out that what they had seen as unqualified disasters subsequently turned out to be blessings in disguise. Sometimes an objective observer may point out that your interpretation of the incident was mistaken, and you can achieve a perspective that significantly mitigates the episode. Finally, you can be helped to realize that we do foolish things that harm others and later regret them. Perhaps those who harmed us regretted their actions.

The attorney did indeed benefit from AA meetings. He is now the chief executive officer of a billion-dollar corporation and in a much stronger position than had he continued with the retail outlet venture. He now looks at that unpleasant episode as a blessing in disguise.

Since anger and hostility are intimately associated with early feelings of shame, their continued existence, even if justified, is likely to rekindle or perpetuate feelings of shame. We do not have to be motivated to achieve sainthood in order to rid ourselves of anger. It is simply in the best interest of our physical and emotional health.

TWENTY-THREE

Shame versus Guilt

Shame and guilt are both unpleasant emotions. They are often used interchangeably, and a person may say "I feel guilty for what I've done" and "I'm ashamed of what I did," referring to the same act. Actually these two easily confused feelings are different, and it is helpful to distinguish between them.

According to current psychological thinking, guilt comes from doing something wrong, violating a moral or ethical principle. When such a violation occurs, guilt is a healthy feeling. It stimulates us to rectify the wrong by making restitution, by apologizing, or by religious expiation, whichever is appropriate. The discomfort of guilt also serves a preventative purpose. It can discourage us from wrongdoing because of the knowledge that afterward we will feel guilty.

There is also an unhealthy type of guilt, which occurs when we feel guilty for something that was not a violation of a moral or ethical principle. Pathologic guilt may occur when we only fantasize a misdeed. We may also feel guilty for harboring an improper thought, even though we aren't

"Thank goodness for guilt!"

Grin & Bear It by Wagner. Reprinted with special permission of North American Syndicate.

able to control the thought. In such cases, making amends or expiating is of no value because there is no realistic basis for guilt. This type of guilt requires psychological treatment.

I recall Sally, whose father died of a heart attack when she was twelve. She came into treatment at age thirty-eight, consumed with guilt because she felt she was responsible for her father's death. She confessed this "sin" numerous times, and finally a priest recommended psychiatric counseling. He understood that she was not confessing a real sin and that her feeling guilty for her father's death was inappropriate. This is an example of unhealthy guilt.

However, whether the guilt is healthy or unhealthy, both are related to an act, real or fantasized. Guilt is thus the feeling accompanying "I made a mistake."

Shame is of a different character and may have nothing to do with a real or fantasized act. Shame is a feeling of "I am no good." If an automobile that was functioning perfectly could think and feel, and had the feeling of "I am a lemon," that would be equivalent to shame. In such a case, there is no way to fix the car, since there is nothing wrong with it. If guilt can be summed up as "I *made* a mistake," shame is the feeling "I *am* a mistake," when there is no justification in reality for such a feeling.

Shame is a deeper, more painful, and more pervasive feeling than guilt. Whereas we can relieve guilt through amends or expiation, there is no similar action that can remove the feeling of shame. Thus, shame may result in despair.

Humans are complex organisms. Our bodies are kept healthy by a host of automatic defensive and internal control mechanisms that operate beyond our awareness. The immune system, the white blood cells, the hormone levels, and sundry other systems respond to changes in the environment to protect and preserve us.

This is also true of the psychological system. The unconscious mind utilizes a number of mechanisms to protect our ego.

As I have noted, the feeling of shame is essentially hopeless. If I am essentially bad, regardless of my behavior I am doomed. If my very essence is unlikable, then I will never be likable, because my essence cannot change. I am therefore doomed to a life of loneliness and rejection.

This feeling is so intolerable that the unconscious mind sets into operation one of its ingenious mechanisms to help us feel better. If the unconscious could speak aloud, we would hear it say, "I can help you get rid of this torment of feeling doomed to eternal unlikability. Here's what you do: Provoke people to dislike you. Be rude and obnoxious. Then when people don't like you, you can attribute it to your behavior rather than to your essence. You will have the comfort of thinking, 'I really am basically a likable person, and people would like me and will like me when I stop my obnoxious behavior.' But if you don't behave obnoxiously, you will have to attribute your being disliked to your very essence, and that is an unbearable pain, because there is no relief."

Harry Stack Sullivan, one of America's greatest psychiatrists, said, "It is easier for a person to feel rejected for what one *does* than for what one *is.*" This was echoed by a recovering alcoholic and drug addict, who by age thirty-two had spent more than half his life in reformatories, prisons, and mental hospitals. In a talk he gave at an AA meeting, he mused, "Why did I drink and use drugs? I don't know." Then he paused and said, "Yeah, I do know why. I wanted people to hate me because I was a drunk and a junkie, not because I was Richie."

This is a keen insight. Richie was convinced that people would dislike him, and he had felt this way since childhood. To think he was despised because he was Richie was intolerable because he had no way of being anyone but Richie. If, however, he could attribute people's despising him to his obnoxious behavior, this was much less painful. He could console himself with the thought that he could become likable if he just stopped provoking people. In this way, he would not have to think himself doomed to loneliness.

Nancy by Jerry Scott. Reprinted by permission of United Feature Syndicate, Inc.

This defense mechanism is widespread. Because it rests on a false assumption, it is both tragic and destructive. Richie was in fact a likable person. People who are likable, and who could enjoy companionship and intimacy, may resign themselves to a life of solitude. Richie suffered from delusions of inadequacy, unworthiness, and unlikability—in a word, shame. What the unconscious does in some cases is to convert shame to guilt. Unfortunately, as long as this unwarranted shame persists, its conversion to guilt continues, and the provocative behavior persists.

Unless the underlying shame is eliminated, it is impossible to eliminate destructive behavior. This may be one of the factors in recidivism, where people repeat antisocial acts and are not deterred by the prospects of imprisonment. They are convinced that they will be ostracized regardless of what they do, and their antisocial behavior makes the inevitable ostracism more tolerable. Richie and many others like him can attest to this. Richie's change of behavior followed a therapeutic breakthrough in which he was able, perhaps for the first time in his life, to feel that he was likable.

As I mentioned, people who suffer from shame may have difficulty accepting good things and often anticipate distress. The woman in Chapter 1 is an example of this. Because of the abscesses that resulted from her heavy drug use, she had to be hospitalized for two weeks and then returned for rehabilitation. Two weeks into the latter, I met her in the lobby and was impressed by her physical improvement. She had been free of drugs for four weeks, was receiving proper nutrition, and her infections had cleared up. I remarked to her, "You're really looking good."

I was stunned when my innocent remark evoked a response of expletives. The following day she apologized:

"I'm sorry for what I said yesterday. You said something positive to me, and I just don't know how to handle that."

People who are shame-ridden may actually feel more comfortable when they are treated poorly, since this is familiar to them. Salutary treatment may constitute a challenge they do not know how to manage. In this way shame may be self-perpetuating, since their behavior is likely to elicit reactions that confirm their low self-worth.

TWENTY-FOUR

Learning Our Limitations

Healthy self-esteem is the result of valid self-assessment, neither underestimating nor overestimating oneself. Indeed, overestimation that is manifested as grandiosity is invariably a defense against feelings of unworthiness. People who feel adequate and worthy do not need to boast about their importance, and they do not need the accolades of others to give them a feeling of worth.

Realizing our limitations is no reason for feeling inadequate. Adequacy depends on what we are supposed to do. The fact that a harmonica cannot produce the music of an accordion does not detract from its excellence as a harmonica. We need to be aware of our limitations, but this should not cause us to feel deficient. People with low self-esteem often see normal limitations as defects and try to be superhuman.

Eek & Meek® by Howie Schneider. Reprinted by permission of Newspaper Enterprise Association, Inc.

Meek is right. Our limitations are a fact of life. Others recognize them in us. Why should we deny them?

A classic example of denying limitations is the alcoholic. Alcoholism deprives a person of self-control. There is increasing evidence that this loss of control is biochemical and has nothing to do with willpower. People who are strong in every other personality trait may lack control in regard to alcohol. This lack of control is a natural limitation, similar to the lack of control of the hay fever sufferer who inhales pollen. However, alcoholics classically refuse to accept their natural limitations and deny that they have a disease. They consider control of alcohol to be totally volitional and view the absence of control as a defect. They cannot admit to having such a defect.

We are not omnipotent. An accurate assessment of human capabilities reveals many limitations. If we think we should not have certain limitations, we may consider ourselves deficient, and this may result in feelings of shame. Insisting that we should be what we cannot be constitutes false pride, which is often a defensive response to shame.

False pride is frequently evident in regard to accepting help. Because of normal limitations and frailties, we are often in need of help. Some people reject help, seeing its acceptance as an indication of weakness. Indeed, they may see dependence of any kind as a weakness and exhibit independence even to their own detriment. It is not unusual to see a person like this who has suffered a heart attack disconnect the intravenous tubes and monitors in the intensive care unit and leave the hospital against medical advice. Some people engage in dangerous, reckless behavior, as though they were not subject to human vulnerabilities.

On the other hand, awareness of our true potential should result in both true pride and humility: pride in our capacity for excellence, and humility in the realization that given our enormous capacities, we have hardly scratched the surface in terms of achievement. True pride and humility both militate against self-destructive behavior of any kind. We realize that we are too valuable to damage and that self-destructive behavior will diminish our capacity to achieve.

A thorough self-analysis should result in awareness of our capacity to achieve, which should stimulate us to greater performance and acceptance of our limitations.

People can be motivated to perform by two forces, one healthy and the other unhealthy. To the casual observer, both may seem to be doing the same thing, but they are as different as night is from day. There is a distinction between high achievers and overachievers.

High achievers are gifted and know that they have something to offer. They have positive feelings about themselves and enjoy sharing themselves with others. The more they give, the more they are stimulated to give. As a result, they may never reach an end point because they are always stimulated to do more. However, the need to do more does not detract from the satisfaction of what has already been done.

The prototype for the high achiever is a nursing mother. She may be uncomfortable when her breasts are engorged with milk and feel great relief when her infant nurses. However, in several hours her milk supply is replenished, and she again experiences discomfort until the baby again nurses. The repeated discomfort does not diminish the feeling of satisfaction of having fed the baby earlier.

We can probably all recall having instructors who enjoyed teaching and who were stimulated when students challenged them to produce more. We may have observed artists who love to perform and cheerfully respond to requests for encores and enjoy giving them perhaps even more than the audience enjoys listening to them.

High achievers may never be able to sit back and do nothing for long periods of time. Yet they can relax at intervals, having enjoyed their past performances.

Overachievers may be equally gifted, but they operate out of shame. A gnawing sensation that they are somehow not good drives them to vindicate themselves by performance. They may indeed achieve great things, but even realization of the achievements does not give them lasting relief. The reason for this is that we can never successfully compensate for a deficiency that does not in fact exist. Real deficiencies can be compensated for, as when a blind person develops an acute sense of touch or hearing. But if a person who is very attractive has the delusion that he is homely, nothing that he does will eliminate that feeling of homeliness. Overachievers, by definition, desperately try to gain a feeling of worth to assuage the pain of feeling unworthy. Since their feelings are unwarranted, nothing they do is likely to eliminate the feeling of shame. Overachievers may have a momentary feeling of worth when their achievements are publicly acknowledged, but within seconds the feeling of being not good enough overtakes them.

Like high achievers, overachievers always do more and

more but, in sharp contrast to high achievers, are never satisfied. They cannot relax because they are shame-conscious. Consequently, they may eschew relaxation and constantly push themselves. As we have seen, shame-oriented people may not accept realistic limitations, and overachievers may overexert themselves. Overachievers are therefore more vulnerable to diseases of stress such as high blood pressure, heart attacks, ulcers, and migraines.

I was asked to see a patient in consultation because of a recurrent bleeding peptic ulcer. Tom was in his forties, a very ambitious man who had become wealthy as a result of his business endeavors. He was constantly on the go, and in addition to his many business commitments was in the forefront of community activities. He had received wide acclaim for his contributions.

"If you walk into my living room," Tom said, "you will see a wall full of plaques and tributes. They mean nothing to me." Although he had done much good, which he should have enjoyed, his motivation was to prove himself, something he could never successfully accomplish.

Overcoming a negative self-concept allows overachievers to become high achievers. The goal of changing the self-concept to a positive one is not to convert an ambitious person into a beachcomber, but to allow the person to perform at the same high level without jeopardizing his or her physical and emotional health.

Just as it is appropriate to tell an alcoholic or drug addict, "You're too good to do this to yourself," it is appropriate to say this to an overachiever. An awareness of one's positivity will allow a person to achieve without inflicting damage on himself or herself.

TWENTY-FIVE

Setting Priorities

We must decide on the role or roles we desire for ourselves. Too often we drift through life rather than steer a course. Defining a role at least enables us to steer. Drifting may result in letting others define our role.

What is it that I wish to be? If I wish to have several roles, is this realistic, or must I relinquish one or more? If I desire to maintain several roles, which takes priority?

A woman may decide that she wishes to be a wife, mother, daughter, professional person, and active community member. Looking back on her pattern of functioning, she may find that the demands of all these roles have on occasion caused conflict. When a particular function could not be fulfilled, she may have considered herself to have failed in that role. Reevaluating herself in the light of realistic goals will allow her to set priorities and to realize that making a choice between conflicting demands on her time and energies does not constitute dereliction.

Clear definition and prioritization can result in a more efficient modus operandi. For example, it may be possible to maintain multiple roles if we delegate certain functions.

We must decide which functions we wish to delegate and which we wish to fulfill personally. Then delegation can be accomplished without inappropriate guilt.

Some working people feel guilty that they put their small children in day care or that an older child is a latchkey child, coming home from school to an empty home. They may feel that they are derelict in proper parenting. This is a typical area of parent-career conflict and may cause emotional distress.

Resolution of the conflict does not mean abandoning either role. Choosing a proper day-care program and spending quality time with children may permit very wholesome parenting. If the career absorbs so much time and energy that it encroaches on adequate relationships with the children, we can delegate some career responsibilities or even cut back. When done with proper planning and consistency, neither function need suffer. Problems arise when we move helter-skelter, investing more time at home one week, perhaps driven by guilt, and more time at the office the next week, being spurred on by ambition or professional demands. This inconsistency can result in confusion and a great deal of emotional turmoil.

Ventilating these conflicts in a group and receiving objective input may allow a parent to arrive at a plan for living, as well as to make midcourse changes when they are called for. A child's illness or any other crisis at home may cause chaos in a person who is drifting, but can be managed much more efficiently if one is steering.

Ellen came to one session of her self-help group very upset. She had advanced to a supervisory position in her company and was under particular stress because labor problems at the firm had resulted in a much greater workload for her. Several weeks earlier her father had suffered a stroke and was now to be discharged from the hospital. He could have been admitted to a rehabilitation institute, but her mother insisted on his receiving physical therapy at home. Ellen did not think this was right, because the quality of treatment at home was not as good as that at a facility. Her mother was strong-willed, adamant that only she could care properly for her husband. Ellen realized that her mother was being unrealistic and that caring for her father would require more time and energy than her mother could possibly provide, so she decided to quit her job or at least ask for a leave of absence in order to assist in her father's care.

The group explained to Ellen not only that she would be making an unwise move for herself, but that by complying with her mother's wishes she would be an accomplice to her father not receiving the best possible treatment. They suggested having the doctor and perhaps the minister impress upon her mother the importance of providing the best treatment available, something her home could not offer. They pointed out that if Ellen was firm in telling her mother that she would not interrupt her work for an inappropriate demand, her mother would be more apt to listen to reason. Ellen received a great deal of support from the group, and with the help of the doctor, minister, and social worker, she was able to convince her mother to allow treatment at the rehabilitation institute.

At the next session, Ellen was commended for doing the right thing. She then began to ventilate guilty feelings about her decision, since her mother was critical of the care her father was receiving, insisting that she could care better for him at home. It then emerged that Ellen had assumed the caregiving, co-dependent role all the way back to her childhood. Her self-worth was contingent on what she could do for others, and she felt that doing anything for herself was wrong and selfish. Although this was a pattern that had permeated her entire adult life, it had not become apparent until the crisis with her father. The group continued to support Ellen and urged her to see a therapist for resolution of her co-dependency. With professional help and the group's support, Ellen was able to continue her career while providing realistic and appropriate help to her parents.

Stella was a secretary for a small law firm. When the firm merged with another, she was promoted to office manager, to supervise the clerical staff and coordinate intraoffice activities. As the firm continued to grow, the demands on Stella became excessive and unreasonable, and she began to experience burnout.

Stella attended meetings of Adult Children of Alcoholics, and in a discussion meeting she presented her dilemma. She said that instead of hiring additional clerical staff, her employers were piling the work on her. She was spending many evenings and weekends at the office. When asked why she did not simply tell her employers that she was overworked, Stella admitted that it was virtually impossible for her to refuse any request. The group readily identified with Stella, since many children of alcoholic parents suffer from the "can't say no" syndrome. Self-effacement and people-pleasing are frequent characteristics of children of alcoholics.

One of the group suggested that perhaps they should practice saying no and proposed a psychodrama where one member would make a request, and each member had to refuse the request as tactfully as possible.

For example, one member said that she had to leave town for a week and asked that someone take care of her dog so that she could save the expense of a kennel. Each member had to say no politely and give a plausible reason. This was an enjoyable game, and members began to give each other scores on their tactfulness in refusal. One member could not think of any plausible reason and gave some absurd reason that provoked laughter. The group realized that this strategy had successfully defused the issue and that practice saying no within the protective confines of the group would make it easier to apply the same technique in real life.

It became apparent that Stella's difficulty in refusing an improper demand was by no means restricted to the office. She exhibited the same trait with her husband, children, and friends. Furthermore, other members of the group shared this trait with her. They therefore decided that they were going to stop their people-pleasing maneuvers and report back to the group each time they succeeded in doing so.

Eventually one of the group shrewdly observed that this change in their behavior was not all that radical. They had merely switched to pleasing the group by reporting how they were able to avoid pleasing others. The group concluded that although this was true, the strategy had yielded dividends. They were now able to refuse unreasonable requests. Stella, for example, had worked up the courage to tell her employers that she was frazzled by the workload and that they needed two more secretaries. She was pleasantly surprised that they readily implemented her suggestion. This had a ripple effect on her behavior with her family and friends, and Stella gained self-esteem and self-assertion.

The group came to realize that it had become a kind of "self." In other words, people-pleasers find it difficult to deny requests in order to please themselves, because satisfying themselves is fraught with feelings of guilt. Whereas satisfying the individual self aroused guilt, sharing the experience with the group lessened the torment of guilt. This feeling of safety within the group could eventually be transferred to an individual experience, so that they could avoid people-pleasing even in the absence of group approval. The legitimacy of refusing unreasonable requests had become internalized.

This insight and technique might have been achieved through individual therapy, but the group technique enhanced and facilitated the process. People who have attended self-help groups attest not only that they have been able to discontinue various ineffective behaviors, but also that their sense of self-esteem has significantly increased.

Part V

Understanding Self-Esteem

TWENTY-SIX

Components of Self-Esteem

Positive self-esteem is composed of competence and worth. Unwarranted feelings of incompetence can be eliminated through self-analysis and by participating in a therapeutic or self-help group. Once we discover the positive aspects of our personality, we develop much more confidence in our ability to cope with stress.

Feelings of competence and adequacy are not the only determinant of self-esteem. Suppose you had suffered a stroke, which affected your speech and walking. Are you entitled to self-esteem? If the only criterion for self-esteem is competence, then you would have no claim to self-esteem. Surely this is not so. There must be another factor. And that is worth. Human life may be thought of as having an intrinsic value apart from what we can or cannot do. This value is independent of intelligence, skills, or our contributions to society.

What is the source of this value? We can easily see how value can be based on productivity, since a productive person contributes and enriches society. If we do not consider productivity, on what basis can we consider human life per se valuable?

One major source of value for human life may be found in religious teachings. The words of Moses are an excellent example: "See I have set before you this day life and good, death and evil" (Deuteronomy 30:15). In most religions, life is equated with good, not only productive life, but life per se, whether the person is a surgeon who performs life-saving procedures or a drifter who is a social parasite. From society's perspective, the surgeon has great value and the drifter does not. From the perspective that life per se is valuable, the enormous difference between the two is insignificant. Even without a religious basis, however, human life can be considered to have an intrinsic value.

These are not philosophical concepts that are relegated to ivory-tower thinkers. These ideas can have practical application in our decision making.

For example, lives can be saved by organ transplant surgery. A person whose liver is failing and whose body is otherwise sound may have many years of life if the liver can be replaced. However, donor organs are scarce. At any one time there are a number of candidates for a liver transplant, and an available donor organ may be compatible with several potential recipients. On what basis do we decide whose life to save? Age? Marital status? Occupation? IQ? Other criteria?

Most ethicists state that there is no way of prioritizing, and organs can be allocated only on a first come, first serve basis. It is generally accepted that social value should not enter into the decision-making process. One person's life is equal to another's. There is a concept of worth that is inherent in human life. This worth is the redeeming feature of self-esteem, especially when the criteria of social value are absent. Conviction about the value of human life per se should enhance the self-esteem of the frail, the elderly, and all who realize that at any moment we may be struck by a condition that can deprive us of our functional capacity.

TWENTY-SEVEN

What Is Humanity? What Is Spirituality?

Assuming that there is an intrinsic value to human life, we may ask, How do we define human life?

I do not intend to discuss issues such as the irreversibly comatose patient or the patient who has suffered advanced brain deterioration, as with Alzheimer's disease. This is a category all its own. What I am discussing is the feeling of self-esteem, which does not apply to people who are in a state of global unawareness.

Science has classified humans as *Homo sapiens,* sharing membership in a group that is comprised of apes, chimpanzees, baboons, orangutans, and the like. The uniqueness that sets us apart from other hominoids is *sapiens,* or intellect.

There are many features over and above pure intellect that characterize us and distinguish us from other forms of life. We have the capacity to learn from the past, contemplate the purpose of our existence, bring about self-improvement, think about the consequences of our actions, delay gratification, and make moral choices.

All these uniquely human characteristics comprise the

spirit and distinguish humans from animals. When we exercise these capacities we are being spiritual. Note that this definition does not involve any religious orientation. An atheist will concur that humans possess these features and hence have a spirit and can be spiritual.

It follows, then, that the quality of our humanity is commensurate with our spirituality. The more we exercise our uniquely human capacities, the more excellent human beings we are. The less we exercise these characteristics, the more we approach similarity to other living things and the less we resemble the ideal human being.

A feeling of worth is within everyone's reach. People who exercise their unique human capacities to the utmost should feel very worthy as human beings, regardless of their level of education, economic status, or occupation. People who are derelict in exercising these traits, and who may feel less worthy as human beings, can gain self-esteem simply by sincerely resolving to maximize their spirituality.

The ability to maximize these human traits may vary greatly with the circumstances of one's life. If I am suffering from a severe disease, I may not be able to do much, if anything, in the way of self-improvement. But all that is necessary for a legitimate sense of worth is that I do whatever I can do at any given time.

A young woman was stricken with a particularly virulent type of multiple sclerosis. She lost her sight and then became bedridden, unable to take care of her personal needs. She required total care and could not contribute to her family in any way. This woman was nevertheless entitled to self-esteem because she accepted her suffering with faith and serenity; she was a spiritual human being. Spiritual in what way? In the acceptance of her suffering. Because it was all she could do, this was all that was expected of her.

If I have failed to maximize my spirituality, recognizing that I have been in error and resolving to correct my lifestyle is a redeeming feature. A resolve for self-improvement enhances the quality of my humanness and worth. Even serious past mistakes need not consume me with guilt or detract from my newly acquired feeling of worth.

A young woman who was working on the fourth of the twelve steps in her Alcoholics Anonymous program, making a moral inventory, had written a long list of things she had done wrong during her active addiction. I asked her whether she would now repeat such behavior, and she vehemently insisted that she would never do such things again. "If so," I said, "then all these things you have listed as negatives are learning experiences, and all learning experiences must be considered positive and listed in the positive column of the inventory ledger rather than in the negative." This is an example of the component of spirituality, learning from one's past.

Spirituality is a growth process, not a thing. Since we are always capable of self-improvement, there is never an end point to spiritual growth. The theologian Baal Shem Tov, the founder of Hasidism, was once consulted by a student who complained of severe frustration. It appeared to the student that the harder he strove to achieve a closeness to God, the more distant he was from his goal.

The teacher responded with the following example: Suppose a father wishes to teach his child how to walk. He waits until the child is capable of standing upright and then places himself very close to the child, perhaps a foot away, holds out his hands, and beckons the child to come. The child, wishing to reach the father and seeing the supportive hands so close to him, has the courage to take the first tiny step. If the father was to embrace the child at this point, the skill in walking would not be achieved. Instead, the father immediately jumps back a bit, perhaps two feet away, and again beckons to the child. The child, having successfully taken the first step and seeing the father still very near to him, ventures another step or two. Again the father retreats and continues doing so until the child learns how to walk independently.

If we were able to read the child's mind, we would undoubtedly find him frustrated. Although he continues making efforts to reach the father, it appears that the harder he tries, the more distant he is from his father. What is happening here is that there are two divergent goals. The goal of the child is to reach the father; however, the goal of the father is to teach the child how to walk independently. The father could embrace the child at any point and thereby satisfy the child's quest, but that would abort the learning

Arlo & Janis by Jimmy Johnson. Reprinted by permission of Newspaper Enterprise Association, Inc.

process. The only way the father can reach his goal is to retreat and to stimulate the child to walk.

Spirituality is a constant growth process. Once we feel we have finally achieved spirituality, we have probably lost it. If we constantly strive toward self-mastery, self-improvement, and establishing higher goals for ourselves, even sometimes with frustration, we're on the right track.

Of course, an individual can establish goals in life that do not contribute to a feeling of worth. Popping every kernel of popcorn does not get a person closer to spirituality.

A man once came to a psychiatrist's office but denied having any problems at all. "Then why have you come?" the psychiatrist asked.

"My family made me come," the man said. "They think that there is something wrong with me."

"What does your family think is wrong with you?"

"They think that I am crazy because I love pancakes."

"That's absurd. There is nothing wrong with loving pancakes. I love pancakes myself."

The man's eyes brightened. "You do! Then you must come to my home, because I have crates of them in the attic."

If I prepare several pancakes for breakfast, and perhaps a few extra to put into the freezer for later, no one will take issue with my behavior. As long as pancakes are used as food, they have a positive function. But if I accumulate so many pancakes that they no longer serve as a food item, but are assumed to have an intrinsic value, I am obviously suffering from a serious mental distortion.

We have no difficulty judging the pancake collector as mentally ill. But what about a multibillionaire who continues to work to increase his immense fortune? Money is a means for acquiring the necessities and luxuries of life. Saving money for a rainy day is equally understandable. But if I were to accumulate so much money that I could not exhaust it in many lifetimes and still continued to strive to increase my wealth, I would not appear very different from the pancake collector.

As rational human beings, and particularly as spiritual people, we should have goals that can withstand critical evaluation. There may not be universal agreement on what is a proper goal in life, but at the very least, we should be examining our lives as to whether we have goals and whether the goals are indeed appropriate.

During active drinking or drug use, people cannot see themselves as spiritual beings. In moments of clarity they may realize that they are really operating at a subhuman level, and this contributes very little to self-esteem. As sobriety progresses and they become aware of an ability to master the impulse to drink and many other destructive drives, they begin to appreciate themselves as spiritual human beings, a discovery that significantly promotes self-esteem. They become aware that whereas frustration and contentment are mutually exclusive, frustration and happiness are compatible. We can actually be happy while also being frustrated if we are aware that frustration often accompanies an active growth process. There is joy in constantly undergoing a process of self-improvement.

TWENTY-EIGHT

Helping Our Children Develop Self-Esteem

In all my public lectures I emphasize the crucial role of self-esteem and of achieving a valid self-concept. Invariably, someone in the audience asks, "What can we do as parents to make sure our children have self-esteem?" My answer is "Self-concepts are contagious. Parents who have feelings of security and self-confidence are likely to pass these on to their children. Parents who have negative self-concepts pass those on to their children. The most effective way to instill self-esteem in one's children is for the parents to develop it themselves."

Parents who spend time with their children convey the message "You are important to me," and that is a major component of healthy self-esteem. Parents who lack self-esteem, however, avoid close relationships with their children. These parents may explain, "I have to be out there earning money to give my children what they need. If I do not put away money for their summer camp/braces/college education, I will be depriving them of a vital need." While I do not minimize the importance of these things, I must emphasize that if they are achieved at the expense of adequate parent-child relationships, the price is too high. A healthy self-esteem that comes out of a parent-child relationship exceeds even a college education.

Merely spending time with children is not enough. We must behave in ways that encourage our children's self-esteem. For example, a child must learn good from bad and right from wrong, and we must provide the necessary discipline. It is extremely important to do so in a manner that does not generate shame.

Proper parenting consists of adopting principles that promote self-esteem. Bear in mind that a child's feelings of self begin to develop in infancy, when he or she is a tiny creature living in a world populated by giants. We must remember this and try to make our children feel secure in surroundings that can overwhelm them with anxiety. Parents are the child's primary resource in a world that may appear very threatening. Bringing a child into the world carries with it an obligation of providing emotional as well as physical nurturing. Starting the child off with self-esteem is particularly crucial, because negative feelings are self-reinforcing and self-perpetuating. A child who believes that he or she will fail is likely to do so, and this failure further lowers his self-esteem, thus making the next challenge an even greater threat and minimizing chances of success.

Children need to know that they are loved, and parental love should be unconditional. Even when children misbehave, even when a grown-up son or daughter acts in such a manner that parents must sever the relationship, parental love should never disappear. I was quite young when I studied the Scriptures and read about the rebellion of Absalom against his father, King David. Absalom was merciless in pursuit of his father, yet when David ordered his generals to quell the rebellion, he instructed them to "spare the child." When David learned that Absalom had been killed in battle, he grieved for him and wept bitterly. "My son, my son. Would that I had died instead of you" (Samuel II 18:33). Parents have the capacity to love a child even when the child is a mortal enemy.

Loving a child does not mean being tolerant of the child's misbehavior. Quite the contrary. We must express our disapproval of destructive behavior in whatever way is necessary—but without making our love for the child contingent on anything. Loving parents act in the interest of the child when the child lacks the capacity to do so. A good analogy is when parents have their infant child immunized. After the first immunization the child may retain a vivid memory of the pain inflicted by the doctor in the white coat, and on subsequent visits to the doctor's office begin to cry at the sight of the white coat and even try to claw and bite the parent who restrains him. The infant may seem to hate the parent who has colluded with the doctor, but the parent nevertheless acts in the child's behalf to prevent serious diseases later in life. The same love and consideration must accompany all parental behavior that is in the child's welfare. If it is necesary to evict a grown-up son or daughter who persists in intolerable destructive behavior, it must be done with the same love that characterized restraining the child for the painful immunization.

Things that appear trivial to adults may be of great importance to children. If we dismiss these things, a child may get to feel that she is unimportant, a fundamental component of low self-esteem. When a child cries over a lost toy or a playmate who was mean, we sometimes dismiss this as "you shouldn't cry over something so silly." This is a devaluation of what is important to the child and a message that her feelings don't count.

Young children see their parents as omniscient and omnipotent. They need to be carefully weaned from this attitude. If a child thinks that his parents are infallible and that he is the only one who makes mistakes, it can depress his self-esteem. If a child learns that parents, too, can make mistakes, he is less likely to condemn himself for his errors. We should admit when we are wrong and should apologize for our mistakes. Parents who insist that a child apologize but never set an example may cause the child to consider himself the only defective person in the family.

Promises to a child should never be broken. In order for a child to develop a sense of responsibility and trustworthiness, she must have a role model for trust. There may be ways to justify "white lies" with other adults, but there is no justification for lying to children. To a child, a lie is a lie regardless of its character.

Obviously, parents must make many decisions for their children, who lack the maturity and wisdom to decide for themselves. However, whenever a child can be permitted to decide things for himself, we should encourage it. Not allowing the child to exercise his immature capacities to make decisions has the same result as not allowing him to exercise his muscles: Neither will develop. A child who is not given the opportunity to think and to act for himself may begin to think of himself as a nonentity, or as a mere appendage of his parents.

A young child accompanied her parents to a restaurant for dinner. After the waitress took the parents' orders, she turned to the child and asked her what she desired. The child responded, "Two hot dogs and a Coke." The mother smiled knowingly at the waitress and said, "You can bring her roast beef with potatoes and vegetables." Shortly afterward the waitress returned with two hot dogs and a Coke.

The mother was amazed, but the child's eyes lit up brightly and she grinned from ear to ear. "Look, Ma!" she said. "She thinks I'm real!"

From a purely scientific aspect, the mother's concept of proper nutrition was correct, but from the point of view of allowing the child to be a "self," she was in error. This is an example of how devoted, caring parents may inadvertently undermine a child's self-esteem.

Right along with acknowledging mistakes and apologizing, parents should share some of their own childhood mistakes and experiences. The goal in rearing a child is for him to become a decent and wholesome human being, not a robot or an angel. As role models, we should demonstrate that we are humans too.

Suppose my daughter gets a detention for passing notes in class. Her feelings may be a combination of humiliation, guilt, anger, and defiance. If I say, "That reminds me of when I had to stay after school and write one hundred times 'I will not pass notes in class,' and then I had to get Grandma to sign the paper," my daughter may ask, "You did? What did Grandma do to you?" "Nothing. She just said that it better never happen again, and I never did it again." Sharing this experience with a child is likely to diminish her shame and anger and actually increase her respect for authority. It allows her to identify with me and realize that when people make mistakes and learn not to repeat them, they grow up to be respectable people. Don't be surprised if the child wants to know more about the event. "Tell me again about how you were made to stay after school. Didn't Grandma scream at you? What kind of notes did you write? Did you hate the teacher?" These and similar questions indicate the child's need to vindicate herself by identifying with you. The violation of rules is not being condoned, but neither is the child being condemned.

Children need strokes and acknowledgments of their achievements. Nothing promotes trying to succeed as success. Displaying a test paper with a good grade or a child's artwork on the refrigerator door is encouraging to the child. We must look for the positives and acknowledge them.

At the same time, we should be truthful. False compliments are of no value. Children are not stupid, and if they feel that our commendation is only empty words, they will not be stimulated to receive more insincere praise.

When my seven-year-old grandson came home from his fourth violin lesson, he asked, "Do you want to hear me play?" and proudly extracted the bow from the case. Although the melody was grossly off tune, I was about to say, "That was beautiful. I'm really proud of you." I caught myself, because it was not beautiful, and to say so would have been a lie. Instead I said, "I know that tune. Let's have a concert. You play and I'll sing it." We did so, and the child beamed with pride. I had acknowledged his playing a melody that I could recognize, and I had not lied to him.

The occurrence of an emotion is neither good nor bad. Like the law of gravity, it is simply there. What we do with a particular emotion is a matter of morals and ethics and can be good or bad, but the pure emotion itself is a neutral phenomenon.

We should be keenly aware of this, because children are full of raw emotion. They must learn how to deal constructively with emotions. Improper management of emotions can be harmful, but children should not be condemned for having emotions. Children have no control over having an emotion, and condemning them for the emotion is likely to make them feel that they are bad. This is how children develop unhealthy feelings of shame.

Children may experience intense anger, hate, and envy. If we acknowledge these feelings nonjudgmentally and the child feels comfortable sharing these feelings, then even a very young child can be taught how to deal with them. But if we categorically condemn all such feelings, the child will be threatened by their exposure and will conceal them and won't have the opportunity to learn how to manage them. She may even repress them, and they will fester in her unconscious and may become the source of various personality disorders and neurotic symptoms.

Children are very sensitive. Insults or unkind words have a much greater impact on a child than on an adult. If we injure a sapling, the resulting distortion of growth is apt to be of much greater magnitude than a similar injury to a fully grown tree.

Never embarrass a child. If there were ten commandments of child rearing, this would be the first. When a child needs to be punished, do this without humiliating him in front of friends or even siblings. It's best to take him into another room where the discipline can be carried out. If he is humiliated in the presence of friends or siblings, the pain and anger at being embarrassed may turn into defiance and negate the desired effects of the discipline.

Promoting self-esteem by proper parenting is not a simple task, and there is not too much latitude for error. If our expectations are beyond the child's capacities, she may develop feelings of failure. The child won't conclude, "My parents' expectations of me are unjustified," but rather, "There must be something wrong with me that I can't do what I'm supposed to." On the other hand, if we do too much for the child and do not allow her to grow, she may develop unwarranted feelings of helplessness. Either extreme may result in feelings of inferiority, so we should thoughtfully consider our expectations, being alert and sensitive to our children's reactions to these expectations.

It is important to be as open as possible with children. Keeping secrets is fraught with dangers. First, many secrets are not well kept, and when the child discovers that something has been kept from him he may lose trust in us. He may join the charade and act as if he does not know, which ends up with everyone walking on eggs. Second, a well-kept secret may result in the child's fantasizing, and the fantasy may be much worse than the reality. That Uncle Moe was arrested for embezzlement may be very embarrassing to the family, but it is much worse if the child is allowed to fantasize why Uncle Moe no longer is at Sunday supper. The child may overhear bits and pieces about Uncle Moe, and having been exposed to all kinds of lurid tales on television, may fantasize that Uncle Moe is the serial killer or child molester who has eluded the police. Finally, a child is apt to sense that something is being concealed. When children are taken into our confidence, this enhances their esteem, whereas keeping them in the dark is apt to depress self-esteem.

Let's return to the first point in this chapter. Parents may underestimate their role as models for their children. Screaming "Stop shouting" is worthless because children will emulate the act rather than accept the verbal message. If we wallow in feelings of shame and inferiority, it will not result in our children developing a positive self-image. We can learn to grow in self-awareness and self-confidence with our children. If we avoid self-destructive behavior because it is beneath our dignity, our children will be more apt to develop similar guidelines, internalizing our behavior.

What about pushing our children to achieve? Our society is highly competitive, and there are advantages to high achievement. Should we encourage our children to achieve excellence? Are we putting them at risk of disappointment if they fail to meet that goal?

Failures are a natural part of life, not disasters. A baseball player who has a batting average of .400 can command a salary of millions of dollars a year, yet he misses hitting safely six out of ten times. Great athletes have made fumbles or struck out with the bases loaded. The prospect of failure is not a devastating threat if what is riding on it is the reality of that particular event: the ball game, the exam, the job. If a particular challenge is overemphasized, it may be invested with a greater amount of anxiety than is warranted.

Wilbur was nineteen when he came for a psychiatric consultation because he was failing in college, even though he had been a straight-A student in high school. Wilbur came from a family of coal miners. He was the first of the entire family to go to college, and his father continually boasted that his son was unique and would finally bring respectability to the family. His father took great pride in Wilbur's excellence in high school and was certain that Wilbur would perform similarly in college. He often let Wilbur know that he was gladly making many sacrifices for his college tuition and that it all was worth it because of the honor Wilbur would bring to him with his stellar academic achievement.

Wilbur reported that he studied hard and absorbed the material, but when he sat down for an exam his mind went blank. He had failed several exams, and these failures had been devastating to his self-confidence.

Far too much was riding on the exams. It was not his own academic performance that was at stake but the entire family honor and the vindication of his family's respectability. His anxiety was paralytic, causing Wilbur's mind to go blank.

But even the overemphasis on success as in Wilbur's case does not compare to the fear of loss of love. Children who feel that parental love is contingent on their successful performance are at great risk of failure.

Verbal reassurances have their limitations; nonverbal communication can be much more convincing. If children feel sincere in their parents' love for them, and that this love will not be affected by their success or failure, they are free to operate without paralyzing anxiety. It is not enough to tell children that they are loved regardless of their performance. They must feel this.

At an Al-Anon meeting, Nora narrated the ordeal of dealing with her husband's alcoholism for many years and the many blessings they enjoyed in his years of sobriety. The one major disappointment in her life had been that she could not bear a child. In her younger years she had never been denied anything she wanted, and she had great difficulty accepting her infertility. Nevertheless, they made peace with their fate and adopted two children.

Imagine her euphoria when, at age forty-two, she became pregnant. There was no question in her mind that this was direct divine intervention. This child was going to be a Rhodes scholar.

"I thought that during my years of recovery in Al-Anon all my anger and resentment had gone forever, but it suddenly returned in a massive proportion when I held my dream baby in my arms for the first time. He had Down syndrome.

" 'God, why did You do this to me? I had resigned myself to being biologically barren and adopting my two children. Why did You tease me? You are cruel and unfair.' I knew these were not nice thoughts, but I could not help them.

"Every night my husband and I prayed over the crib. 'God, You have been so kind to us. You have performed so many miracles in our lives. Now we ask You for just one more miracle. Please change him.'

"Then, after many nights of prayer, the miracle occurred. God answered our prayers, and He changed *us*.

"If that little child did not come into the world for any other purpose than what I am about to tell you, it was all worth it. When I sit in the rocking chair and cuddle him in my arms, and I look at his pudgy little hands that have only the one crease, and at his funny-looking eyes, and I realize how much I love this child with all his defects, then I know for certain that God can love me even with all my defects."

This is what is meant by unconditional love, but I am not quite sure whether Nora had the sequence of events in their proper order. She said that when she realized how much she loved the child in spite of his imperfections, then she knew that she was lovable in spite of her imperfections. I suspect it was the other way around. Nora's years of recovery in Al-Anon had brought her to a realization that she was lovable, and she had developed a healthy self-esteem. Of course it would have been a thrill to have a child who was a Rhodes scholar, but she did not need her child's performance to vindicate her. In this way, she was much different from Wilbur's father. The fact that her child would never perform brilliantly could be dealt with objectively.

Her pride and honor were not at stake, and she could love her child unconditionally.

Parental love is biological, and unconditional parental love is the natural state of a parent-child relationship. If parental love becomes conditional, it is because of the parents' low self-esteem and their need to be vindicated by their children's performance. This is why I said earlier that self-esteem is contagious and that parents who feel good about themselves are likely to pass these feelings on to their children. They can allow their children to be "selves" rather than extensions of the parents.

TWENTY-NINE

It's Never Too Late

A person may come to a self-awareness and achieve a positive self-esteem at any age. It is never too late.

During my first year of psychiatric training I was asked to see a woman in emergency consultation. The reason for the urgency never was clear to me, but I was fascinated by the story she told me in the first hour.

Isabelle was sixty-one at the time and had been abstinent from alcohol for five years. She was one of three daughters of an Episcopalian priest who enjoyed an excellent reputation in the community. Late in her adolescence, Isabelle was introduced to alcohol, and she drank alcoholically right from the start. She married at twenty, and at twenty-two had a son. When she was twenty-four her husband told her that she would have to choose between alcohol and the marriage. "I could not fool myself. I knew that I could not give up the bottle and that I was not being an adequate wife or mother. I did not contest my husband's divorce suit."

Now that she was unattached, she supported herself as an escort to some of the social elite. She was able to live quite comfortably, and there was never a dearth of alcohol.

After several years, the alcohol began to affect Isabelle's behavior so much that her clientele no longer desired her company. She then began catering to a lower social strata, and within a relatively short time was prostituting in a flea-bag hotel. Her family was outraged by her behavior and disowned her.

Isabelle's heavy drinking resulted in numerous hospitalizations for detoxification. Medical records of several hospitals revealed that over a twenty-two-year period she had had more than one hundred hospital admissions. Every time she was taken to Alcoholics Anonymous meetings but promptly returned to drinking after discharge.

At age fifty-six she did a strange thing. She contacted a lawyer and arranged to have the court commit her to a state mental hospital for one year. After discharge from the hospital, she obtained a job as housekeeper for a respected physician who was a widower and an alcoholic. Several times a year the doctor had to appear at governmental functions or foundation meetings, and then Isabelle would detox him and get him into respectable shape.

From a distant cousin, Isabelle learned that her son was living in New England and had two children. She wrote to her son, asking permission to visit her only living relatives, and the response was "Please stay away. We told the children you had died."

Isabelle told me all this during the first interview, and I was so fascinated by her account that I failed to ask her why she had requested a psychiatric consultation and particularly what the urgency was. As a fledgling psychiatrist, I knew that change does not occur without motivation, and there certainly had to be a very intense motivation to cause a person to place herself in a state mental hospital under court commitment for a whole year. Because of my curiosity, I suggested that Isabelle return for a subsequent appointment, and my search for the motivation continued in our weekly sessions for thirteen years. The interviews were terminated when at age seventy-four she died peacefully in her sleep.

Since Isabelle never revealed to me the secret of her motivation, which she perhaps was unaware of herself, I was left to my own devices to figure it out. My conclusion was as follows.

Every so often, a new volcano appears. Deep at the core of the earth, there is a pool of molten rock under exceedingly great pressure. Over hundreds of years, this molten lava threads its way through cracks and crevices in the earth's crust until it finally breaks through the surface and erupts. Prior to the moment of eruption, the presence of molten lava was unknown to anyone who observed Earth's surface at that spot.

I believe that at the core of every human being there is a nucleus of pride, dignity, and self-respect. Many factors may combine to conceal these feelings from one's awareness. However, like the molten lava, these feelings may slowly work their way to the surface, seeking expression. At some point in a person's life, there is a breakthrough, and the individual has at least a momentary awareness of his or her dignity and self-esteem. This realization may result in the thought, "My behavior has been beneath my dignity. I am too good a person to be acting this way." Perhaps this is what the twelve-step program refers to as a "spiritual awakening."

Occasionally when my alarm clock goes off I turn off the bell in order to sleep just a few moments more, only to wake up several hours later. Once when I had to make an early morning flight, I placed the alarm clock on the other side of the room. I knew that by the time I had walked across the room to turn it off, I would remain awake.

I believe that Isabelle's placing herself in the state mental hospital was a similar tactic. In those days there were no rehabilitation centers, and she knew no other way to avoid regressing into the behavior pattern that she now felt was beneath her dignity. This was indeed an act of desperation. Having come to a momentary realization of who she really was, she could not allow herself to be dragged into behavior that was unbecoming of her pride.

Isabelle made this radical change at age fifty-six, and the last seventeen years of her life were exemplary. She assisted countless people in recovery from alcoholism and served as a living example that "it is never too late."

THIRTY

Doing Good and Feeling Good

Everyone wants to feel good, both in terms of being free of discomforts and having positive pleasurable sensations. Some people use destructive methods to avoid discomfort and obtain pleasure—alcohol, mood-altering chemicals, compulsive gambling, eating disorders, indiscriminate sexual activity, and so on.

A common denominator to all of these destructive methods is that the sensation of relief or euphoria they provide is transient, which drives the individual to repeat the behavior in order to achieve the desired sensation.

In contrast to the ephemeral nature of destructive behaviors, the pleasurable sensation that results from having helped another human being is usually long-lasting. Thinking about a meal that I enjoyed last week may do nothing for me today, whereas the awareness that I helped someone in a difficult life situation several years ago still provides me with a sense of pride and achievement.

The experience of helping someone does not provide the momentary thrill of a drug or drink, but the durability of the good feeling more than compensates for the lack of the intense high.

One of the reasons why doing good for others can provide such a meaningful and sustained pleasurable sensation is that we identify with other people. When we help others, we attest to the value, dignity, and respectability of the person whom we consider deserving of help. This is of even greater impact when we are nondiscriminating in our will-

Peanuts® by Charles M. Schulz. Reprinted by permission of United Feature Syndicate, Inc.

ingness to help others. The message it imparts is not that a particular individual is worthy, dignified, and valuable, but that all humans are worthy, dignified, and valuable. Helping another person is thus a confirmation of our own dignity, value, and respectability. In other words, helping others enhances our self-esteem.

Not only does the benevolent act give us a feeling of pride, it also attests to our own value as caring human beings.

We have come to know Charlie Brown as having devastatingly low self-esteem. But look what happens to Charlie Brown when he has an opportunity to help another person.

Peanuts® by Charles M. Schulz. Reprinted by permission of United Feature Syndicate, Inc.

BIBLIOGRAPHY

Andrews, Louis M. *I Deserve Respect.* Minnesota: Hazelden, 1993.

Bernie, Patricia, and Louis Savary. *Building Self-Esteem in Children.* New York: Continuum, 1981.

Branden, Nathaniel. *Breaking Free.* New York: Bantam Books, 1989.

———. *The Disowned Self.* New York: Bantam Books, 1976.

———. *The Psychology of Self-Esteem.* New York: Bantam Books, 1973.

Bryant, Robert G. *Stop Improving Yourself and Start Living.* San Rafael, Calif.: New World Library, 1991.

Buxbaum, Edith. *Your Child Makes Sense.* New York: International Universities Press, 1949.

Chess, Stella. *Your Child Is a Person.* New York: Viking, 1965.

Cudney, Milton R., and Robert E. Hardy. *Self-Defeating Behaviors.* New York: Harper, 1991.

Dunbar, Flanders. *Your Preteenager's Mind and Body.* New York: Hawthorne Books, 1962.

Dunbar, Flanders. *Your Teenager's Mind and Body.* New York: Hawthorne Books, 1962.

Elkins, Dov P., ed. *Glad to Be Me.* Englewood Cliffs, N.J.: Prentice Hall, 1976.

English, O. Spurgeon. *Fathers Are Parents Too.* New York: Putnam, 1951.

Fraiberg, Selma H. *The Magic Years.* New York: Scribner, 1959.

Ginott, Haim G. *Between Parent and Child.* New York: Macmillan, 1965.

———. *Between Parent and Teenager.* New York: Macmillan, 1969.

———. *Between Teacher and Child.* New York: Macmillan, 1972.

Harris, Sydney. *The Authentic Person.* Allen, Tex.: Argus Communications, 1972.

Hegarty, Carol, and Earnie Larsen. *Believing in Myself.* New York: Prentice Hall/Parkside, 1991.

Hendricks, Gay. *Learning to Love Yourself.* New York: Simon & Schuster, 1982.

Hillman, Caroline. *Recovery of Your Self-Esteem.* New York: Simon & Schuster, 1992.

Josselyn, Irene M. *The Happy Child.* New York: Random House, 1955.

Jourard, Sidney. *The Transparent Self.* New York: Van Nostrand, 1964.

Kalellis, Peter M. *A New Self-Image.* Allen, Tex.: Argus Communications, 1982.

Larsen, Tony, *Trust Yourself.* San Luis Obispo, Calif.: Impact Publishers, 1979.

Rapoport, Rhona, Robert Rapoport, and Ziona Stelitz. *Father, Mother, and Society.* New York: Basic Books, 1977.

Robinson, Brian. *Heal Your Self-Esteem.* Delray Beach, Fla.: Health Communications, 1991.

Rogers, Carl R. *On Becoming a Person.* Boston: Houghton Mifflin, 1961.

Steinem, Gloria. *Revolution From Within.* Boston: Little, Brown, 1992.

Wheelis, Allen. *How People Change.* New York: Harper Perennial, 1976.